B
DOUGLASS

McFeely, William S.

Frederick Douglass.

$24.95

DATE			

© THE BAKER & TAYLOR CO.

Frederick Douglass

Books by William S. McFeely

FREDERICK DOUGLASS

GRANT: A BIOGRAPHY

YANKEE STEPFATHER: GENERAL O. O. HOWARD
AND THE FREEDMEN

Frederick Douglass

William S. McFeely

W · W · NORTON & COMPANY

New York   London

Lines from Ovid, *Metamorphoses,* translated by Rolfe Humphries
(copyright 1955), are reprinted by permission of the publisher, Indiana
University Press.

———————

The text of this book is composed in 12/13 CRT Bembo,
with display type set in Typositor Lucian.
Composition and manufacturing by the Haddon Craftsmen, Inc.
Book and ornament design by Margaret M. Wagner
First Edition

Library of Congress Cataloging in Publication Data
McFeely, William S.
Frederick Douglass/by William S. McFeely.
p.   cm.
Includes bibliographical references.
1. Douglass, Frederick, 1818–1895.   2. Abolitionists—United
States—Biography.   3. Afro-Americans—Biography.   4. Slavery—United
States—Antislavery movements.   I. Title.
E449.D75M374 1991
973.7'092—dc20
ISBN 0–393–02823–2   89–36517

W. W. Norton & Company, Inc.
500 Fifth Avenue, New York, N.Y. 10110
W. W. Norton & Company Ltd.
10 Coptic Street, London WC1A 1PU

1 2 3 4 5 6 7 8 9 0

For Mary, again,
and for Matthew, Eric, and Samuel

Contents

Illustrations

NEW BEDFORD, 1840s. Whaling Museum, New Bedford, Mass.

MAIN STREET, NANTUCKET. From the collection of the Nantucket Historical Society, Nantucket, Mass.

BIG SHOP, NANTUCKET. From the collection of the Nantucket Historical Society, Nantucket, Mass.

AFRICAN BAPTIST CHURCH, NANTUCKET. From the collection of the Nantucket Historical Society, Nantucket, Mass.

SUSAN B. ANTHONY. Elizabeth Cady Stanton, Susan B. Anthony, et al., editors, *The History of Woman Suffrage.* 6 vols. (Rochester and New York, 1889–1922).

LUCRETIA COFFIN MOTT. Elizabeth Cady Stanton, Susan B. Anthony, et al., editors, *The History of Woman Suffrage.* 6 vols. (Rochester and New York, 1889–1922).

ANNA DICKINSON. Elizabeth Cady Stanton, Susan B. Anthony, et al., editors, *The History of Woman Suffrage.* 6 vols. (Rochester and New York, 1889–1922).

MARIA WESTON CHAPMAN. Boston Public Library.

SOJOURNER TRUTH. National Portrait Gallery, Smithsonian Institution.

WILLIAM LLOYD GARRISON. National Portrait Gallery, Smithsonian Institution.

WENDELL PHILLIPS. National Portrait Gallery, Smithsonian Institution.

HARRIET TUBMAN. J. B. Leib Photo Company.

ABBY KELLEY FOSTER. American Antiquarian Society, Worcester, Mass.

"THE FUGITIVE'S SONG." American Antiquarian Society, Worcester, Mass.

ROCHESTER. University of Rochester Library, Rochester, N.Y.

NOTE FROM DOUGLASS. University of Rochester Library, Rochester, N.Y.

NOTE FROM DOUGLASS. University of Rochester Library, Rochester, N.Y.

AMY POST. University of Rochester Library, Rochester, N.Y.

ANTISLAVERY MEETING. J. Paul Getty Museum, Los Angeles, Calif.

FREDERICK DOUGLASS. American Antiquarian Society, Worcester, Mass.

THE FOLLOWING PHOTOGRAPHS APPEAR BETWEEN PAGES 274 AND 275.

FREDERICK DOUGLASS. National Park Service, Frederick Douglass National Historic Site.

ROSETTA DOUGLASS. Anacostia Neighborhood Museum, Smithsonian Institution.

ANNA MURRAY DOUGLASS. Courtesy of Prints and Photographs Collection, Moorland-Spingarn Research Center, Howard University.

LEWIS HENRY DOUGLASS. Courtesy of Prints and Photographs Collection, Moorland-Spingarn Research Center, Howard University.

Frederick Douglass

1
Tuckahoe

THE TUCKAHOE is a quiet creek. Frederick Douglass, when he was a child, lived on its low banks. When he was a man, he walked boldly and talked clearly in a world noisy with hatred, but the country he first knew was tranquil. The Eastern Shore, the long peninsula that puts its back to the Atlantic and faces the great, broad Chesapeake Bay, is gentle. Wrested ruthlessly from the Indians in the seventeenth century, it had long been cleared and farmed when Frederick was born in February 1818. Streams, shaded with trees, divided the fields and flowed to join slow, meandering rivers that, in turn, met tidal waters reaching deep into easy terrain. Frederick's first home was a solitary cabin in the woods bordering a brook that separated the farther fields of two farms owned by the man who owned him. But the boy knew nothing of being owned as he sunk his toes in the clay bottoms of the shallow pools over which skater bugs glided.

Rabbits and deer invaded the fields from the woods, and turtles sunned on logs in the Tuckahoe, into which the brook fed. The birds, in rich confusion, made the sounds of morning; one of the great sights came at migrating time, when ducks in flocks settled on the marsh-bounded water below the mill dam. This was Frederick's outdoors home; when he went indoors, his shelter was a cabin built with timbers cut from the woods, sheathed with the slabs of bark left when they were squared, and caulked and floored with clay from the brook. There was no being alone here; a rough-runged ladder led to a rail-bottomed loft that provided added sleeping quarters for his family of cousins and an infant uncle in this house of his grandparents, Betsy and Isaac Bailey.

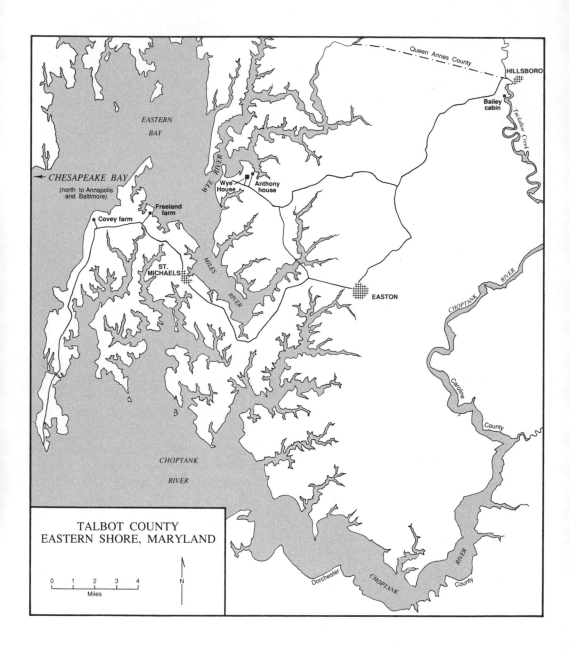

Queen Annes County

HILLSBORO

Bailey cabin

Tuckahoe Creek

EASTERN
BAY

CHESAPEAKE BAY
← (north to Annapolis
and Baltimore)

WYE RIVER

Wye
House

Anthony
house

Freeland
farm

Covey farm

MILES

ST.
MICHAELS

RIVER

EASTON

CHOPTANK

RIVER

Caroline

County

B

CHOPTANK
RIVER

CHOPTANK

RIVER

County

Dorchester

TALBOT COUNTY
EASTERN SHORE, MARYLAND

0   1   2   3   4
Miles

N

Betsy Bailey, a tall, strong, copper-dark woman, was the granddaughter of the first of her name of whom there is a record—in 1701—in this north corner of Talbot County, Maryland. She was born in 1772 and bore her first child in 1790 and her last, at age forty-eight, in 1820. Two years earlier, her second daughter, Harriet, gave birth to Frederick Augustus Bailey. The baby's great-great-grandfather Baly, or his forebears, like many other Talbot County slaves, may have been imported into the British West Indies before being sold to Maryland tobacco planters.

Nothing of Africa was left in the given names—Harriet, Henry, Susan—repeated in affirmation of a sense of family continuity generation after generation, but "Bailey" may have had an African source. In the nineteenth century, on Sapelo Island, Georgia (where Baileys still reside), there was a Fulfulde-speaking slave from Timbo, Futa Jallon, in the Guinea highlands, who could write Arabic and who was the father of twelve sons. His name was Belali Mohomet. "Belali," spelled in various ways, is a common Muslim name; indeed, Billal was the name of a black slave who was a muezzin, a caller to prayer, much admired by the prophet Muhammad: "Verily, as I . . . was mounting the stairs of God, I heard your footsteps before me." "Belali" slides easily into the English "Bailey," a common African American surname along the Atlantic coast. The records of Talbot County list no white Baileys from which the slave Baileys might have taken their name, and an African origin, on the order of "Belali," is conceivable. Baly had been owned by Richard Skinner, a prosperous tobacco planter on the Miles River neck; Baly's granddaughter Betsy was the most valuable asset that Skinner's granddaughter Ann Catherine Skinner brought to her marriage to Aaron Anthony.

American slavery was often homemade, rather than cut from a standard pattern, and it is striking how many different forms of the slave experience Frederick Douglass, as Frederick Bailey came to call himself, touched in his relatively few years as a slave. Because Betsy was a slave, her children and their children were slaves, but she lived with Isaac, a free man with the same surname as hers. If they were related, it is not known how. Isaac worked as a sawyer, while Betsy lived according to her own rules. In her cabin, Frederick could scarcely have experienced the formalities of American chattel slavery. His education in its disciplines, both subtle and brutal, came later, beginning when he was brought as a child to Wye House, the great self-sufficient plantation of Edward Lloyd. When, at twenty, he escaped slavery, it was from a city in which slaves engaged in urban commerce, hiring themselves out as artisans or day laborers. Between the years on the plantation and those in the city, with their different and contradictory ways of life, he worked, more typically, as a field hand alongside two or three other slaves, raising cash crops for struggling farmers. But that was all long after he had left his grand-mother's cabin.

His earliest memory was of swinging on a rung of the ladder to the loft. As he put his early sensations together into a narrative, he recalled (moving backwards in time) mimicking farm animals, splashing into the creek without having to take off any clothes (because all he had on was a shirt), and being fed "corn-meal mush" with an oyster shell for a spoon. Douglass made the events of his childhood, like almost all the experiences of his early life that he described in his three autobiographies, into parables of slavery. Ostensibly telling how the slave child escaped "many troubles which befall and vex his white brother," such as being "chided for handling his little knife and fork improperly," he made it clear that the slave child was deprived of all implements of gentility. But in this instance, as in too few others, private and sensuous recollections break through the moral he sought to point. "His days, when the weather ... [was] warm," he wrote (and we confidently believe him), were "spent in the pure, open air, and in the bright sunshine," running "wild."

Betsy, his grandmother, was the central presence in his early life. He reported no memory of his mother from the period before he was six years old. Both the records (which he never saw) and his family's tradi-tional history, as he understood it, leave no doubt that Harriet Bailey was his mother. But he had no recollection of seeing her during his years in Betsy's cabin, even though she appears to have been nearby, working in Aaron Anthony's fields or hired out to work on a neighboring farm. He could only recall her from the "four or five" visits she later made, at night, when he was living twelve miles away on the Lloyd plantation. She may not even have walked there specifically to see him.

As if to insist that she was real, Douglass wrote that her "personal appearance and bearing are ineffaceably stamped upon my memory." She was, he said, "tall, and finely proportioned; of deep black, glossy com-plexion; had regular features, and, among other slaves, was remarkably sedate in her manners." He chose to see her as grander than her peers. Years after she died, reading James Cowles Prichard's *Natural History of Man,* he came across a picture of an Egyptian pharaoh with a striking likeness to her. This handsome portrait became his image of Harriet Bailey—of his mother. It was a heroic and androgynous way for her to be remembered, but the image does nothing to dispel the mystery of this dimly known tragic figure.

Douglass wrote chillingly, "I cannot say I was very deeply attached to my mother." He placed the blame squarely on slavery: "The slave-mother can be spared long enough from the field to endure all the bitterness of a mother's anguish, when it adds another name to a master's ledger, but *not* long enough to receive the joyous reward afforded by the intelligent smiles of her child." A look at the roster of Betsy's descendants in the estate inventory of her master in large part confirms this contention. But nothing prevented slaves, living close by, from visiting. To be sure, even frequent visits would have been a poor substitute for the constancy of a daily life together, but Harriet did not make them at all. Perhaps Frederick knew she could have done so; his insistence that his smile would have been intelligent conveys not only his sense of his own superiority but also a suggestion that, whatever the reason, his mother had not appreciated him as she should have.

There is no question about the importance that he gave in retrospect to the absence of a strong relationship to his mother. His coolness toward her was not, he thought, the natural feeling he should have had: "I never think of this terrible interference of slavery with my infantile affections, and its diverting them from their natural course, without feelings to which I can give no adequate expression." In the first of his autobiographies, telling of his mother's death, which occurred when he was about seven—Harriet Bailey has been denied even a firm death date—he wrote, "I received the tidings of her death with much the same emotions I should have probably felt at the death of a stranger."

This stark account was softened with sentimentality in his later versions. In the second, he wrote, "Death soon ended the little communication that had existed between us; and with it, I believe, a life—judging from her weary, sad, downcast countenance and mute demeanor—full of heartfelt sorrow." In his final telling, he omitted the reference to her "downcast countenance and mute demeanor," and instead credited "the natural genius of my sable, unprotected, and uncultivated mother," who he was told could read, with somehow instilling in him his "love of letters."

The differences between these three accounts illustrate as sharply as anything could the difficulty of knowing Frederick Bailey. Most of what we can learn about him is what Frederick Douglass chose to tell us in his three unidentical autobiographies. *Narrative of the Life of Frederick Douglass* (1845) is the brief, pungent declaration of freedom of a runaway slave writing a powerful antislavery tract. In *My Bondage and My Freedom* (1855) a mature writer gives deeper reflections on slavery. By then, Douglass could pause longer over the story of his life as a slave, but voids in it suggest that there were unbearable memories that had to be omitted. *Life and Times of Frederick Douglass* (1881, revised 1892) is the memoir of a famous man relishing his honors while smarting from those denied him. Like *Bondage,* it brings his story forward to the time of its writing, but the slavery days are still there, as if to remind an America eager to forget that slavery cannot be purged from the national memory.

Throughout his life, Frederick Douglass was obsessed with an eagerness to know about his origins—to know who he was. Dickson Preston, a meticulous and sympathetic historian, has brought together an astonishingly rich cluster of facts confirming Douglass's account of his early life, firmly establishing the family lineage, and determining from an inventory of his master's slaves the time of Frederick's birth—February 1818 (a year later than the date that Douglass himself calculated). But Preston's diligent scholarship has not revealed the fact Douglass most wanted to know—who his father was.

"My father was a white man. He was admitted to be such by all I ever heard speak of my parentage," he wrote in *Narrative of the Life of Frederick Douglass*. Doubtless he remembered such talk from Betsy's cabin, as people accounted for his difference in color from his brothers and sisters. This talk would have led to his first consciousness of what is termed racial difference; he would have looked at his body and learned that he was "yellow"—had a muted, dull complexion lighter than that of his "quite dark" grandparents and, he would observe later, that of his still "darker" mother. He also heard talk of a legendary and perfectly plausible Indian ancestor; something in the bone structure and the set of the eyes suggested this, not only in Frederick but in his mother and grandmother. He was probably still too young, in Betsy's cabin, to articulate any queries about his paternity although it is more than likely that he had already heard it "whispered," even if he had not understood what he heard, "that my master was my father."

Douglass wrote later of his boyhood in Betsy's cabin as "spirited, joyous, uproarious, and happy," but drew a picture of the surrounding area that does not just reflect what he saw as a child. His description of the "worn-out, sandy, desert-like appearance of its soil," the "general dilapidation of its farms," and the "ague and fever" that rose from the Tuckahoe is more a metaphor for the barrenness of slavery than the recollection of a six-year-old. It does, however, return attention from the idyllic to the realities of carving out a living in this remote country. As a free black woodcutter in a rural area of a slave state, Isaac Bailey was on the margin of the economy; he and Betsy and the family in their charge probably lived in extreme poverty. His security was even more precarious than that of his kin who were slaves; he had no master to fall back on when he was injured, as a worker with saws and axes was apt to be, fell ill, or simply got old. Betsy, living for so long as the wife of a free man, may have been in similar danger. There are conflicting stories about whether her master felt any obligation to care for her when she was old and widowed. She did stay on in her cabin.

If the small house was indeed in the woods, as Douglass remembered it, the problem of providing food was immediate; you cannot grow vegetables under trees. The Baileys were allowed the use of some arable land—perhaps they had cleared it themselves—but even so, their future as an independent black family was not assured. Contrary to myth, country people do not have some intuitive knowledge of how to make the earth bloom; even with a good plot of ground, families may fail to produce a crop adequate for survival.

In this realm Betsy became legendary. Intelligent and physically powerful, she had made herself an expert in fishing and farming. The nets she wove were in "great demand" in the nearby towns of Hillsboro and Denton, and she also put them to good use herself. Douglass remembered her being "in the water half the day" gathering in the abundant shad and herring. When spring came, she not only planted her own sweet potatoes but was called on to help others in the neighborhood get theirs into the ground properly. At harvest time, her fork went into the ground so deftly that none of the crop was pierced and lost, and she had the foresight to put aside sound seed potatoes for planting the next season. As Douglass noted, her "good luck" was, in fact, her "exceeding care" in every step in the achievement of sufficient and nutritious food.

Douglass's stress on the impressive competence of his grandmother in what might have been thought of as masculine functions, his ascription both to her and to his mother of a bearing that would have fit men of dignity and accomplishment, is significant. There is no similar description of his grandfather or of any other man he knew while a slave. For the rest of his life Douglass looked to women as confidants, companions, and sources of strength. They rather than men could be comprehended and counted on to be able.

They could also be the source of immense anguish. If Betsy was allowed extraordinary liberty to run her own life and to make her own living, she paid a great price for this freedom. She apparently was required to care for all of the infants in the Bailey family, so that their mothers— her daughters—could work. They labored on the Tuckahoe farms in which her master, Aaron Anthony, had invested, or were hired out by him to work in the fields of others.

Anthony was an absentee master; he lived a dozen miles away at Wye House, the estate just in from the Chesapeake Bay that he managed for the Lloyd family. What provision, if any, he made for the care of the children he owned is unknown; perhaps Betsy bought her independence by agreeing to rear her grandchildren without any assistance, such as rations of corn. Their care must have been taxing, and before they were old enough to help her with a hoe or the nets, they were summoned to

Wye House by Anthony. There they lived in "Captain Anthony's" house or in quarters adjacent to it. Frederick's older brother and sisters, Perry, Sarah, and Eliza, and his cousin Tom had already made this move.

On a summer day in August 1824, when Frederick was six, he and his grandmother left the cabin, walked up to the crossroads, and turned southwest. The walk was long, much longer he soon learned than the one in the other direction, to Hillsboro, probably the only town he had been to. For much of the trip his powerful grandmother must have had to carry the tall, heavy child. It may well be a mark of the austerity of Anthony's Tuckahoe farms, that there was no horse the resourceful Betsy could commandeer for the day. Turning at one crossroads town, they walked between great fields, blanketed in heat, to reach another, and soaked in perspiration kept resolutely on through the Lloyds' "Long Woods." Finally, having walked twelve miles, they came to Wye House. A generous lawn's-width short of the long, straight drive leading under great trees to the main house was a parallel road that led to the slave quarters. They took it; through the trees between the narrow roads, Frederick could catch sight of the great house, and as the two of them came past, they reached their master's small, neat cottage and the quarters where their relatives lived. Looking off the other way across Long Green, they saw the broad stretch of the Wye River.

Suddenly, the long, hot trek was over. Curious children came out to look over the newcomer, and followed him and their grandmother into the kitchen, where the two got desperately needed drinks of water. Cautiously, Frederick agreed to go back into the yard with them, but he did not join in as they ran "laughing and yelling around me." Their exuberance would have been more intimidating if he had not known that his grandmother was back in the house. But soon she was not. Taking what she saw as the least tormenting way to accomplish the parting she was resigned to, Betsy quietly left to walk the long miles back to Tuckahoe. When one of the children, with "roguish glee" shrieked at him, "Fed, Fed! grandmammy gone!" he fled back to the kitchen to find her.

But she *was* gone. He rushed out to the road; she was not in sight, and he could not run down its emptiness alone. He threw himself on the ground, and crying, pummeled the dry dust. When his older brother, Perry, tried to console him with a peach, he threw it away. He was carried in to bed and cried himself to sleep. And he never fully trusted anyone again.

2

Wye House

And here Clymene's son
Came climbing, up the stairway to the palace,
Entered the palace which might be his father's,
Turned toward the face that might have been his father's,
And stopped, far off; he could not bear that radiance.

—*Ovid, "The Story of Phaethon,"*
translated by Rolfe Humphries

WITH THE RESILIENCE and wonder of a bright child, Frederick explored the world he had entered. At its center was a place so grand as to have been unimaginable back on the Tuckahoe, and despite warnings from Aunt Katy, the slave who had charge of him, he would not stay away. Wye House, its white assuredness reaching out to wide, green lawns, faced the drive in from the Easton road and looked out privately, at the back, on the quiet splendor of a beautiful garden and an orangery. The curious boy could sneak up and, from behind a thick-trunked shade tree, watch people laughing and talking as they strolled in from the fine sloop *Sally Lloyd,* just arrived from Annapolis, or stepped down from a carriage from Easton and entered Edward Lloyd's house.

He could see Colonel Lloyd too. Often busy and brusque, but sometimes stopping to notice and smile at a slave child, this man who ruled with unbridled authority over the domain in which Frederick Bailey now lived was the most compelling figure the boy had ever encountered. If Frederick Douglass, writing a book about slavery years later, had sought to construct an archetypical master of a great plantation, he might have taken as his model a grandee in New Orleans with a larger bank account, a delta planter who owned more slaves, a South Carolinian with a more flamboyant house, a Virginian with a more celebrated name, but none of these creations would have stood taller than the tidewater aristocrat of Wye House. In all the South there were not a hundred men who could rival Edward Lloyd of Maryland, and he would have deferred to none of them. Douglass did not have to imagine such a man when he wrote; he knew him.

Edward Lloyd, though not Frederick's owner, was exactly the master Douglass's white antislavery readers wanted the pleasure of meeting—and rejecting. He was privileged in ways they were not, and that privilege derived from the relentless exploitation of slaves. A former governor of Maryland and United States senator, this Democrat advocated universal suffrage; his deep appreciation of American freedom was grounded in a slave-labor system that had nurtured his own abundance of liberties. Northern opponents of slavery could see in Lloyd and his plantation the insidious best of the slave system.

"Immense wealth and its lavish expenditures filled the Great House with all that could please the eye or tempt the taste," Douglass recalled over half a century later. "Fish, flesh, and fowl were here in profusion . . . wild goose, partridges, quails, pheasants, pigeons. . . . The teeming riches of the Chesapeake Bay, its rock perch, drums, crocus, trout, oysters, crabs and terrapin. . . . The dairy, too . . . poured its rich donations of fragrant cheese, golden butter, and delicious cream. . . . The fertile garden . . . was not behind in its contribution [of] tender asparagus, . . . crispy lettuce, . . . delicate cauliflower, eggplants, beets, lettuce, parsnips, peas, and French beans. . . . [There were also] figs, raisins, almonds, and grapes from Spain, wines and brandies from France, teas of various flavor from China, and rich aromatic coffee from Java." For Frederick, Wye House was both the palace of his imagining and the emblem of slavery's evil. "The table of this house groaned under . . . blood-bought luxuries. . . . Behind the tall-backed . . . chairs, stood the servants. . . . They resembled the field hands in nothing except their color, and in this they held the advantage of a velvet-like glossiness. . . . The delicately-formed colored maid rustled in the scarcely-worn silk of her young mistress. . . . Viewed from Col. Lloyd's table, who could have said that his slaves were not well clad and well cared for? Who would have said they did not glory in being the slaves of such a master?"

Frederick Douglass saw Lloyd as a symbol of the slave system, but there is also a far more personal reason why he lingered long and lovingly over the shadow thrown on his childhood by this man. During Douglass's lifetime of imagining (and attaining) a world of grace and elegance, Wye House was the lodestar, and in the richest of dreams, Edward Lloyd would have been the father for whom he was ever searching. Fifty-five years after Frederick Bailey left the Lloyd place, a famous Frederick Douglass came back to Wye House and raising his glass to his hosts, Lloyd's great-grandsons, "he trusted that God, in his providence, would pour out the horn of plenty to the latest generation." Douglass's eye was on the young Lloyds as he spoke, but he may have had his own grandchildren in mind; they could have had a common forebear.

While a young child, at a time when the science of genetics was still a nicely distant discipline, Frederick had heard things "whispered" (and perhaps some unfunny jokes) about a white father. When he first wrote about himself, in his late twenties, he said unequivocally that his father was white, that this fact was "admitted to . . . by all," and that he had heard hints "that my master was my father." This was precisely what an antislavery audience expected to hear, and taken literally, it pointed to Aaron Anthony, Frederick's and his mother's actual master, as the most obvious object of any speculation. A plausible possibility, too, was the "Mr. Stewart" to whom Anthony had hired out Harriet Bailey.

But when Douglass spoke of his master in *Narrative of the Life of Frederick Douglass,* he was usually referring to Thomas Auld, his owner at the time he escaped. Auld, who was twenty when Douglass was conceived, learned to build and sail boats in the nearest boat-building town, St. Michaels, a short sail across the Miles River and up the Wye River to Wye House. There is no record of when Auld first came to Wye House with the sloop *Sally Lloyd,* which was built in St. Michaels. It is possible that as he crested into manhood and became the captain of the Lloyds' fine boat—one of those on which the plantation depended for social and commercial contact with the world—he may have been attracted to the handsome Harriet Bailey, even as he thought to court Lucretia Anthony, the daughter of Wye House's manager. And, with both Harriet and Betsy absent from Wye House, it is equally possible that in all the years of Frederick Bailey's and Thomas Auld's complex relationship, neither of them knew for certain who Frederick's father was.

Ten years after he spoke of his master as his father, Douglass wrote, "I say nothing of *father* for he is shrouded in a mystery I have never been able to penetrate." But he went on to repeat the whisper about his master. In his final telling of his story, more than a quarter of a century later still, he omitted any link to his owner and said simply, "Of my father I know nothing." He craved that knowledge, but may have been wary of achieving it, lest the man prove to have been Aaron Anthony or someone even less glamorous or compelling.

Douglass never explicitly said whom he most suspected to have been his father, but late in life he was still intrigued by the story of a slave son of Edward Lloyd's who was bitterly resented by a half brother whom he clearly resembled. Occasionally, in an exuberant moment in an emotional antislavery lecture, Frederick Douglass would make Edward Lloyd into his master, and hence his father. As Oscar Wilde, for one, was aware, the imaginings of foundlings know no bounds; those of mulatto slave children, with a myriad of conflicting clues to ponder, could be rich indeed—isn't that leap of hair straight up from a wide forehead in the Wye House portrait mine as well?

We do not know where Harriet Bailey was or whom she was with at the moment of Frederick's conception, and it is unlikely that her son ever figured it out either. She was only infrequently at Wye House, but once there, the handsome woman could have caught the lustful eye of Edward Lloyd, of one of Lloyd's two adult sons, or even of one of their grand guests. There is no reason to think that she did indeed attract Lloyd; there was every reason for her brilliant son, with his fertile mind constantly fashioning himself, to imagine such an occurrence.

The Lloyds had been on the Eastern Shore as long as the Baileys, perhaps longer. They were Welsh Protestants who, taking advantage of Maryland's act of religious toleration, had been planters since the middle of the seventeenth century. Five generations of the family lay buried in the graveyard close to the "Captain's house," Aaron Anthony's dwelling built of brick from the Lloyds' demolished house of 1660, Edward Lloyd, master of Wye House, built in the 1780s, was one of the country's most expansive hosts. He was also the owner of an enormous agricultural enterprise. On his thirteen farms, covering approximately ten thousand acres, his 550 slaves raised sufficient wheat to make him one of the largest producers of grain in the country. (And more than enough to give pause to those who contend that slavery could never have taken hold in the wheat country of the West.)

Cotton was the crop that Douglass's readers, hazy about what was where in the South, expected planters and slaves to be raising, and here, of course, he disappointed them. Even tobacco, a proper slave crop, on which the Lloyd fortune had been based, was being abandoned; the last runty planting went into the ground the first spring Frederick lived at Wye House. But except for producing the inappropriately progressive wheat crop, the Lloyds' place was a classic of American plantations—a magnificent anachronism, bringing the eighteenth century intact into the nineteenth. It was in no way the yeoman's typical raw farm. It was a complex economic entity. Lloyd took direct responsibility for its management, assisted by Aaron Anthony, hired to be his chief lieutenant; next in command were overseers for each of the farms. Tools and supplies came from the shops of wheelwrights, carpenters, and netmakers clustered on

Long Green, at the homeplace, in which almost every implement needed for farming and for maintaining the elaborate life of the estate could be made or repaired. The plantation was self-sufficient; only the luxuries—and they were many—had to be imported.

Each overseer had to produce a crop on his particular farm, and he was given considerable autonomy in the discipline of the slaves, whose job it was to get that crop in. The overseer also had to keep the slaves busy, with no time to be restless, during the considerable stretches of the year when a wheat crop needs little labor. Douglass vividly remembered, from a story told him when he was a child, just how far the overseers' authority extended. One of them, Austin Gore, was whipping a slave, Denby, and the man broke from the agony and splashed into a stream, until the water was over his tortured back. Gore called to him, three times, to come back; Denby did not move. The overseer raised his gun, and red rings spread out over the water.

Gore was promoted—transferred to the homeplace—rather than penalized, but he was criticized all the same. He defended his action on the grounds that whatever Denby's unspecified transgression, an example had to be set, but the shooting broke the code with which Lloyd maintained discipline on his farms. The most immediate and brutal permissible punishment was whipping, which Denby had known to the point of revolt. Neither the possibility that reports of such punishment were exaggerated nor the recognition that accounts of floggings were one of the most sought-after forms of nineteenth-century pornography (disguised in the plain wrapper of a call to virtuous antislavery action) disposes of the fact that whippings inflicted on slaves prolonged pain, sometimes with permanent disabling aftereffects.

The code also demanded the avoidance of leniency. Neither the overseer nor, certainly, the master was to do anything to ameliorate the harshness of a slave's life. Such actions would only lead to expectations of greater liberty. The Lloyds allowed no manumissions, no hope of freedom to disrupt the basic order of the world the slaves were ordained to inhabit. And food and clothing were kept sparse; as wage earners too were taught, those who have little work to survive.

Proper Marylanders were given to understand that the Lloyds did not sell their slaves. And indeed, the substantial rise in the number of Lloyd slaves over the decades, braked only by massive sales south after this Edward Lloyd's time, is impressive evidence not only of great natural increase but of the fact that prior to the 1850s, these people were seldom sold. But seldom is not never, and the possibility of being sold was an effective disciplinary tool. To be permitted to stay at home, avoiding both separation from one's family and an unknown fate, was the carrot; the

Gore shooting Denby. From *Life and Times,* 1881.

threat of sale, the much-feared stick. Frederick was haunted by the departure of a headstrong cousin, sold by her—and his—master, Aaron Anthony, for her rebelliousness, and lost into Alabama, and there are records of similar sales of Lloyd slaves.

Frederick Douglass was too young when he lived at Wye House to generalize as he would later about the nature of the slave system, but he was precisely the right age for individual acts of physical brutality to become indelibly recorded in his memory. Although he asserted in his formal discussion that more "slaves are whipped for oversleeping than any other fault," none of the whippings he described, and few recalled by former slaves interviewed in the 1930s, have any direct relation to getting work done. The lash was used primarily not to increase production, but rather to express the intense emotions—anger, frustration, jealousy—of some of the white partners in the quadrille of slavery.

Early one morning, hearing screams, Frederick sneaked into the kitchen and saw his young aunt Hester, her "wrists . . . firmly tied, and the twisted rope . . . fastened to a strong staple in a heavy wooden joist above, near the fireplace. Here she stood, on a bench, her arms tightly drawn over her breast. Her back and shoulders were bare to the waist. Behind her stood old master, with cowskin in hand, preparing his barbarous work with all manner of harsh, coarse, and tantalizing epithets. The screams of his victim were most piercing. He was cruelly deliberate, and protracted the torture, as one who was delighted with the scene. Again and again he drew the hateful whip. . . ." Hester loved Ned Roberts, a handsome slave of the Lloyds', and Anthony hated her for it.

Remembering Wye House, Douglass in *My Bondage and My Freedom* wrote one of the great accounts in our literature of the ordinariness of both the cruelties of slavery and its stifling boredom. But his boyhood observations of the sufferings common to most slaves were made at exactly the time when he was coming to perceive his own life as extraordinary. There are no pictures of him as a child or an adolescent; the photographs of him as a young man suggest that he may have been a strikingly beautiful child, but the 180 other slaves living on the homeplace—the attractive servants in the great house among them—must have had a good many children, so Frederick cannot have been alone in being appealing.

His physical appearance, then, did not make him unique; his extraordinary mental capacity, early in evidence, did. The first manifestation of intellectual prowess was his skill at mimicry, which stayed with him for the rest of his life and was the mainstay of a not very nimble sense of humor. Mimicry, like "rhythm in their bones," is one of the stereotypic talents assigned to Africans by racist thinking, but stereotypes deserve scrutiny rather than embarrassed dismissal. Copying sounds, a fundamental mode of learning, was one of the very few available to the slave. It is not surprising that Frederick was adroit at imitating both the farm animals in the barn and the social animals in the house, nor that many observers noted similar abilities in slaves across the South. Frederick used his skill as a base for what became a beautifully structured intellect; others were denied the chance to achieve that progression. Many people, blocked as Douglass was not, mocked those who held them in slavery by imitating them with a pungent wit that often, in hints, got back to their victims in ways that made them both wary and uncomfortable.

Fortunately, science has not yet imposed on us an explanation of the source of fine minds. Curiosity is still free to roam, and in the case of Frederick Douglass, whether we look to genes, to environment, or to good luck, we find Betsy Bailey. This extraordinary woman was unlettered, but evidently possessed a mind capable of making finely logical connections. She was an ideal respondent to all of the "why" questions her intensely curious grandson must have fired at her. Douglass proudly claimed that his mother was literate. If this was so, Harriet Bailey's intellectual achievement, like Frederick's, probably owed much to the encouragement of Betsy, who could so intelligently read a river or the furrow of a field.

Twelve miles away from Betsy's cabin, in the Anthony house, Frederick's brightness caught the attention of two other women—Aunt Katy, the cook in charge of the children, and Lucretia Anthony Auld, Anthony's daughter. Their responses could not have been more opposite. For her part, Aunt Katy stood in the long tradition, both fictional and all too real, of cooks who tyrannized the families they defiantly served. A member of the other of the two slave families owned by Aaron Anthony, she was only a distant relative of Frederick's; the title "Aunt" was one of respect. Or dread.

Women and men who presided over critical plantation enterprises, like the laundry sheds, carpentry shops, and harness rooms, were called "Aunt" and "Uncle" often by their owners and always by the younger slaves, who cherished an African tradition of grave decorum and deference to those older, wiser, and in greater authority than they. Katy's particular authority, if limited, was great. As Douglass put it, "What he [Anthony] was to Col. Lloyd, he made Aunt Katy to him." She ruled Anthony's household with an iron hand. "Ambitious, ill-tempered and cruel," she was responsible not only for her own children, but for the young Baileys in the Anthony household. To preserve the importance of her small domain, she did not permit them to stray from it and associate with the Lloyd slaves. Her white people, intimidated as well, felt the power of her will all the more because of the Anthony family's anomalous position. Anthony and his three grown children, two sons and a daughter, had no social interchange with the great house, and none of the overseer families easily exchanged visits with the Anthonys. As a result, they lived an oddly isolated life near the center of the complex system of farms that he managed. And they lived in a house that Aunt Katy ran.

Frederick slept on the floor of a closet in her kitchen and ate, with an oyster shell or a piece of shingle, from a wooden trough. "Like so many pigs," the children would "devour the mush. . . . He that ate fastest got most." But if Frederick pushed his way in too aggressively, Katy would whip him or send him away from the food. When Frederick, at six, moved into the plantation manager's house, Aaron Anthony, fifty-seven, had been a widower for eight years and, as Dickson Preston has shrewdly deduced, was probably undergoing not only physical disintegration but diminishment of his mental powers as well. He was scarcely the person who, orphaned at age two—he was another fatherless child—had, as a young man, gotten a job on a Lloyd boat and earned the title, "Captain." Anthony had courted a planter's daughter, Ann Catherine Skinner, married her when she was pregnant, and soon after became the manager of the Lloyd estate, a post he held for a quarter of a century.

When Anthony, the viceroy, rode out each day to administer the Lloyd realm, he left his house in hands even more imperious than his own. Aunt Katy "had a strong hold upon 'old master,' " Douglass recalled; "she was a first rate cook, and very industrious." She was also dangerous. On one of her rare visits, Harriet Bailey discovered that her son had gone a full day without food; asked why, Frederick replied that Aunt Katy had said she "meant to starve the life out of me." With "fiery indignation," Harriet ordered Katy never to do this again, and right there in the tyrant's own kitchen, she made her son a sugar cake. At last, he was "somebody's child"; sitting on his mother's knee eating the cake, he was "a king upon his throne." But "my triumph was short. I dropped off to sleep, and woke in the morning only to find my mother gone." It was the last time he saw her.

His mother's intercession did not endear him to Aunt Katy, and neither did the interventions of the woman who was nominally her mistress. Lucretia Auld, young and still childless, was allowed by Katy little to do in her father's house. Finding Frederick an engaging companion, she made something of a pet of him, and when she too discovered him to be hungry, she got food to the child, thereby increasing Katy's ire. Katy had in some way twisted her resentment of a cheating world into an almost pathological need to abuse Frederick. She wanted no one in her charge to outstrip her own children or herself in importance in the household;

The last time Frederick saw his mother. From *Life and Times,* 1881.

it was as if by withholding food she was starving a rival into puniness and insignificance.

The person for Lucretia to turn to in seeking help for the boy should have been her father, his owner, but such a request would have been at once appropriate and awkward. She must have known that Frederick was rumored to be Anthony's son, so she would have been interceding for a child who could have been her brother, but whose possible kinship would never have been discussed openly within the family. Whatever were her entreaties, they failed. Anthony did not prevent Katy from harassing the boy.

Despite Katy's tyranny, Frederick went off on adventures of his own. Katy ordered him to stay away from the Lloyd slaves, who, being from the great house, may well have regarded her with less respect than she thought her due; Frederick disobeyed. The garden was enticing and the orangery was full of exotic trees bearing strange fruits, but the house itself, back across the garden and the graveyard, was more compelling still. In time, he did gain entry. And he was not smuggled into the kitchen by a Lloyd slave for a backstairs peek; instead, Daniel Lloyd, a son of the house, took him inside and into the front rooms. One of the wonders of the world of American slavery is that before puberty, the children of the slaves and those of the masters were often allowed to play together. In the grander establishments, a white family might arrange for a young slave child to be simultaneously an always available playmate and a step-and-fetch-it servant.

Daniel, laden with privilege, may have been almost as lonely amidst the crowd of people at the great house as Frederick was. Far younger than his siblings, he had no peers. The nearest neighbors of the Lloyds' rank, if any there were, were miles away. The boy surely could not play with the children of the overseers. The only appropriate companion, paradoxically, was a slave, who could present no threat of encroachment on Lloyd superiority since his position was unequivocally fixed. Although Daniel was five years older than Frederick, the two boys probably achieved their friendship on their own. For Aaron Anthony to have suggested Frederick as a friend for Daniel would have been outside the limits of his relationship with Edward Lloyd. Lucretia, although living only yards away, probably never exchanged more than a nod with any of the women of the Lloyd house. Had the Lloyds been seeking a slave child for their son, they would have looked to the children of their own house slaves. Instead, it was Frederick who played with Daniel.

We know that Daniel went shooting, while Frederick (and presumably a good dog) retrieved the birds. The boys' intimacy must have extended far below such hunting-print surfaces, but nothing is harder than friendship to write about. In his writings, Douglass never more than hinted at the meaning of his short, close association with Daniel Lloyd. And like Benjamin Franklin before him, as a writer of moral tales Douglass never allowed himself to report an encounter in which he saw no value. But his books are full of hints of the rich lore banked during his days with Daniel Lloyd.

First in worth was the voice he chose. With a child's exuberance, Frederick already could use the local tongue to gain the attention and admiration (and sometimes the resentment) of anyone he met. But he was coming to know that he would want to talk to a world beyond Talbot County, with a tone and a diction other than those of the county and the slave. And the manner of speech most readily available for the taking was that of Massachusetts.

The Lloyds had hired a tutor, Joel Page, of Greenfield, Massachusetts, to educate Daniel. The young gentleman had to be taught to read and write, to calculate, and—though speech was little discussed, lest it be thought not a natural skill—to speak in a cultured way. A Lloyd could not sound like the county, like a slave. Page, a lonely, middle-aged bachelor in an anomalous social situation, coped with the phenomenon of slavery by studiously avoiding the slaves. Sitting alone in the garden, he rebuffed even Frederick, who, undeterred, imitated the patterns of speech Page was teaching Daniel, and those he heard from other "cultured" white people.

Frederick had chosen to sound like the people of the great house. He chose as well to know about them. He missed nothing as he and Daniel roamed the house, when they were not banished from the scene because of the Lloyd's almost ceaseless entertaining. And he pressed Daniel relentlessly for details: Who was coming on the *Sally Lloyd* for the week? Who was sleeping in what room? What were the big, square silver dishes used for? What did people say at the table? What was a governor? a senator?

He was ceaselessly curious about this world from which he was excluded. For the rest of his life he resolutely resisted this exclusion, but he seems to have taken it as a challenge rather than something to resent without hope of overcoming. Had the Lloyd place stood on the other side of the Chesapeake, it could have been "the plantation that supported and endured that smooth white house and that smooth white brass-decorated door and the very broadcloth and linen and silk stockings the monkey nigger stood in to tell him to go around to the back. . . ." Faulkner's Thomas Sutpen turned away from that door full of fury and a passion for revenge, determined—in the greatest of Southern novels, *Absalom, Absalom!*—to create a new world for himself.

Frederick Bailey had a not altogether different quarrel with that closed door. He would, in time, turn away from it and toward the realities of nineteenth-century America in order to create a new life for himself. Unlike Thomas Sutpen, Frederick seems to have had no sense that he should scratch and gouge his way past insulting social degradation. He simply knew that he belonged inside the great house; at age seven, he was ready to move in. There was only the fundamentally silly problem that, by accident, he was a slave. As he faced the door, he had his young back turned on slavery and other slaves. His was a precarious loneliness. But even a lonely seven-year-old can hope for the best. All that he thought he needed to be welcome inside that front door was for the accident of slavery to go away.

To someone eager to apologize for slavery, a proper, happy ending to Frederick's story would have been for him to open the door for himself. In this version, Lloyd would purchase him and make him Daniel's man-servant, or place him on the crew of the *Sally Lloyd* or in some other favored task. Then the handsome, well-informed, well-spoken young man, by virtue of his abilities, would rise to be, perhaps, the butler in livery—the monkey nigger—orchestrating the social world of Wye House. (Such an outcome would also, of course, have meant the end of the Frederick Douglass story before it ever began.)

None of this happened, for Lucretia and Thomas Auld had a different idea about what to do with the boy. Indeed, the two Aulds, soon joined by Thomas's brother and his wife, entered Frederick's life in a way that was to have immense ramifications not only for him but also for the abolitionist movement and for the nation's concept of what slavery was like. If Harriet Beecher Stowe made Simon Legree, as an overseer, the unvarnished villain of American slavery, Douglass's vilification of the Aulds in lectures and in his books turned these sometimes troubled people, caught powerless in a confusing world, into embodiments of the evil master and mistress. And yet his attacks on them only partially disguise his complex and ambiguous relationship to all four.

Douglass accused the Aulds of cruelties and presented their behavior as evidence with which to indict the whole slave system, but his attacks do not fully hide the fact that these were four perplexed and limited people struggling to respond to the needs of an unusual boy who was also a slave. Somehow, that boy had made them feel that he must be specially provided for, but the society in which they lived—in which slavery was so firmly fixed—gave them no satisfactory room in which to do so. Lucretia Anthony Auld had begun the tie to Frederick by noticing him, learning of his persecution by Aunt Katy, and surreptitiously feeding and caring for him. Douglass portrayed her, in his accounts, as the well-meaning but patronizing kind mistress. But in actuality, as he was later to acknowledge, she was more than that. She, or probably more accu-rately, she and her husband, had decided that Frederick had to get away from the Eastern Shore, and they acted on that decision.

In 1826, Aaron Anthony, unwell, was eased out of his position. A new manager was chosen for Wye House, and Anthony moved to one of his Tuckahoe farms, taking his slaves and his family with him. Thomas Auld traded mastery of a fine Chesapeake boat for ownership of a small store, which he and Lucretia ran in the small inland village of Hillsboro, close to the Anthony farm. Aunt Katy was hired out, so Lucretia and Thomas no longer had to worry about her harassment of Frederick, as long as they made sure he was not sent to the same farm as Katy. They could have left the boy with Anthony, to grow up to be a field hand; if concerned about bettering his lot, they could have tried to arrange for him to be purchased by Edward Lloyd, with the hope that he would go into personal service with the family; or, if they wanted to keep a close eye on him, they could have asked Anthony for permission to take Frederick into the store with them. They chose none of these routes.

Instead, Lucretia and Thomas Auld undertook to separate Frederick from an environment that they could see would stunt this remarkable slave child. They arranged for him to go to Baltimore to live with Thomas's brother, Hugh Auld, and his wife, Sophia. In his accounts of the move, Frederick suggested that Sophia Auld's need for help in caring for her two-year-old son provided his opportunity. But if she had needed help with a two-year-old, Lucretia and Thomas would surely have tried to arrange for one of the teen-age girls in the Anthony household to be sent; an eight-year-old boy was almost sure to be at least as much trouble as the child he was supposed to look after. The initiative for Frederick's move, though welcomed in Baltimore, came from the Eastern Shore. This was the first of three crucial occasions on which the Aulds—Lucretia and Thomas, and after her death, Thomas alone—interfered with the normal flow of events in this slave's life. The reason for the move to Baltimore was to give Frederick Bailey a different home, a different life.

All those he knew were scattering. As the boy left Wye House, he realized that his people—his family, despite his misgivings about the lot of them—would be leaving too. Frederick was being sent away from home again. As Lucretia dressed the boy in his first trousers and put him in the care of his engaging, kind, young cousin Tom, a crewman for the Lloyds, she no doubt tried to reassure him that his new mistress, Sophia, was kind and that her home in Baltimore would be comforting. Tom, despite a bad stutter, was a great source of gossip and had never failed to report, after a trip up the bay, that everything else in the world "was nothing to Baltimore." He assured Frederick that all would be well there—or, at least, better.

Looking back, Frederick Douglass remembered the world he was leaving with bitterness: "I looked for *home* elsewhere, and was confident of finding none which I would relish less than the one I was leaving." The great house should have been his, but exploring it as a wondering boy, he had learned that it could not be. He went away from Wye House with a child's dream of new beginnings, and yet, all the promises of what lay ahead in Baltimore must have been distant comfort to the little boy alone on the boat that slipped from the wharf at Long Green—that took him away from all the people he had ever known, and reached down the river into the broad, beautiful bay. It may not have eased his mind that his companions on board were sheep on their way to the slaughterhouse.

3

Fells Point

HE CAME, as a child, from the country to the city, and he never
willingly went back.

After an overnight trip, the sloop docked at Smith's Wharf early on
Sunday morning, and once the sheep had been herded up the hill in the
heat, Tom took Frederick back down to Alice Anna Street and a spare,
narrow house on the corner of an alley. When the door opened, "I saw
what I had never seen before; it was a white face beaming with the most
kindly emotions; it was the face of my new mistress, Sophia Auld."
Suspicious, cautious, yet yearning for steady affection, he "hardly knew
how to behave toward 'Miss Sophia.' " Her sister-in-law, Lucretia, had
also been kind to Frederick, but he had always felt he had to play the
endearing child outside her window in order to gain that kindness. With
Katy's food trough in mind, he wrote, "I had been treated as a *pig* on
the plantation; in this new house, I was treated as a *child.*"

His defenses yielded: "How could I hang down my head . . . when
there was no coldness to repel me, and no hatred to inspire me with fear?"
Sophia took him into the house, and he met her husband, Hugh Auld,
a broad-shouldered shipbuilder, and their two-year-old son, Tommy. The
little one was told that this was "his Freddy": Frederick was to look after
him, a task that, initially, consisted largely of seeing that he did not toddle
into the street crowded with wagons carrying cargoes and fittings for the
ships at the docks close by. The Aulds lived in Fells Point, Baltimore's
busy shipbuilding center on the east side of the harbor. Baltimore was
one of the nation's major ports; from here foodstuffs were shipped to

Europe, and into the port came not only cargo but great numbers of immigrants.

Frederick's new home was inviting, and he welcomed the changes in his life. His tow shirt—in the city, he would have had to learn to be embarrassed when it flew up as he ran—was replaced with pants and a tuck-in shirt; instead of a grain sack to pull around himself on cold nights, there was a "good straw bed, well furnished with covers"; and instead of cornmeal mush or, worse, dry cracked corn, there was bread. But more critical than these dignities and comforts was the "natural and spontaneous" warmth of Sophia Auld, who brought him into a family: "If little Thomas was her son, and her most dearly beloved child, she, for a time at least, made me something like his half-brother in her affections." Frederick "soon learned to regard her as something more akin to a mother, than a slaveholding mistress."

Sophia Keitley came from a poor family near St. Michaels; she is reported to have worked for wages as a weaver before marrying Hugh Auld and moving with him to Baltimore. It is unlikely that she had much education, but as a committed Methodist, she was devoted to her Bible and labored to read from it. As she sat with Tommy on one knee and the book on the other, she drew Frederick to her side, and read—or told—its stories to both boys.

After more than a year in this calm and comforting household, in which he was almost part of the family, the slave boy was wrenched away from Sophia and sent back to the Eastern Shore. Aaron Anthony had died in November 1826; since he had left no will, his property was to be divided equally among his daughter, Lucretia, and his two sons, Andrew, an alcoholic, and Richard, an unsuccessful farmer. Before the settlement could be effected (but after her husband's legal claim to her share was secure) Lucretia died. Her widower, Thomas Auld, was to receive her portion. In October 1827, Hugh Auld was instructed to send Frederick back to the Tuckahoe farm where all of Anthony's slaves, as capital goods, were to be assembled and distributed in the settlement of the estate.

It was a "sad day" as Frederick, in his city clothes, was put aboard a wide, shallow-draft sloop that took him down the bay and then, slowly, up the Choptank River and into the shallow Tuckahoe Creek. He had left, in a sense, a mother and a brother—"We, all three, wept bitterly"— to go back to the place of his earliest recollections. He arrived to find himself in the midst of a cruelly convened family reunion—and in his case, the usual "my, how you've growns" translated into "my, how Freddy has changed." Now, even more than when he had been in Katy's kitchen, this particular Bailey was different. Different and lucky, and once more, his luck held. Despite his city ways, he managed not to provoke Aaron Anthony's drunken son, Andrew, into an attempt to beat him into his place. Instead, Frederick was the observer, forced to see his brother, Perry, thrown on the ground by Andrew and kicked in the head so hard that blood ran from his ear and nose.

This brutality, rather than drawing him closer to his doomed siblings, somehow separated Frederick from them. His older sisters, Sarah and Eliza, who like Perry had been at Wye House with him, as well as his younger sisters, Kitty and Ariana, whom he had last seen when he left their grandmother's cabin, were like strangers to him. Perhaps to ease a sense of guilt, perhaps because he believed it to be true, he later reckoned that because he "had known what it was to be kindly treated," he felt the terror of the distribution more acutely than they did. Douglass did not reckon with the possibility that the others simply had not been able to articulate the terror as he later did. Indeed, he left the impression that those who are hit the hardest do not feel the hurt.

He did see one relative as an exception to this dubious proposition; his grandmother was special. In 1845, when Douglass first wrote, with deep feeling, of her being left behind alone in her cabin to be old, to die, he did not know whether or not she was still alive. (And when he bitterly chastised her master for abandoning her to isolation, he may have been chastising himself for not being there to care for her.) What he did know was how terrible was the sum of her long life. Before she died, in 1849, nine of her children, grandchildren, and great-grandchildren had been sold south and thereby more poignantly lost to her than were those who had died. And back on October 18, 1827, after weeks of frightening uncertainty, she and her children and grandchildren were lined up on Aaron Anthony's farm while two lawyers, coldly conscientious, checked lists of names and assigned valuations, and distributed the people among the three heirs.

At this crucial moment, these slaves were the property of something worse (because unknowable) than a master; they were owned by an estate. From that bleak house, they were to be consigned, according to the laws of inheritance, to fates over which they had not even the slight control that personal relationships made possible.

In this particular settlement, the lawyers did respect family groupings. Betsy and four of her daughter Harriet's children remained on the Tuckahoe, the property of the dreaded Andrew Anthony. Betsy could, at least, stay where she had always lived and cared for some of her grandchildren. In addition, she must have gotten some sour amusement in watching the hapless Richard Anthony pass under the mastery of Aunt Katy and her family. Thomas Auld, merely a son–in–law of the man whose estate was being divided, was granted Frederick's favorite aunt, Milly, and her four children, and, in one of the few breaches of family grouping, Frederick and his sister Eliza.

There was no obvious logic in the assignment of Frederick and Eliza to Thomas Auld; had the lawyers continued to observe family groupings, as they did in other instances, the two would have gone with Betsy to Andrew Anthony. Instead they went to Auld, who, for whatever private reason, almost certainly had asked particularly for Frederick. By so doing, he saw to it that he and not his inept and callous brothers-in-law would own Frederick; and then, to the boy's immense relief, he completed the rescue by sending him back to the mothering home of Sophia Auld in Baltimore. For a second time, Auld had interceded in Frederick's behalf.

For the next five and a half years—for the rest of his childhood— Frederick was the light-colored slave boy living with a family that owned no slaves. Wildly curious, he had to confront what it was to be a person who was called black, though he wasn't, and who was owned, though his owner was far away. He was living in a city, completely removed from his early surroundings—the "home" clung to by slaves who, like his grandmother, found solace in their immediate world and knew no other sanctuary. Save for an occasional report from a slave seaman in from the Eastern Shore—and huge quantities of gossip did cross the bay—he was entirely isolated from all of his blood relatives.

Frederick Bailey was alive and alert, in a household that gave him the security and a neighborhood that gave him the stimulation he needed to expand his wonderfully curious mind. He could run in the streets, watching the older boys while dodging their taunts, and return to a house that was a haven of cheerful affection. Sophia sang hymns as she worked; the two boys tumbled around her, singing snatches of the songs in imitation of her. Frederick began paying strict attention when she read to them from the Bible. In later years, acutely conscious of the process of his education and perceptive in his remembrance of it, Douglass recalled being fascinated by the relationship between the words coming from her mouth and the marks on the pages of the book she held. He was curious about "this *mystery* of reading" and "frankly, asked her to teach me to read." Sophia, drawn to his quick mind, and perhaps intrigued by the thought of testing the educability of an African child, began to do so. Soon he could "read" memorized passages on familiar pages.

Without knowing exactly what she was doing, Sophia Auld began the end of slavery for this particular slave. Perhaps not entirely unwittingly (although she surely would not have thought about her actions in the way scholars of slavery have done since), she was a dangerous subversive. She undercut the fundamental psychological discipline of slavery, and thereby raised the expectations of a slave to a point beyond which bondage was not endurable. In the most comforting of ways, she destroyed the slave boy's comfort.

Proud of her accomplishment, Sophia called on Frederick to show her husband what he had learned. To her dismay and, indelibly, to Douglass's, Hugh Auld was not delighted with the boy's display of intellectual promise. He understood, if his wife did not, just what a dangerous pursuit she had been engaged in, and exploded with what Douglass shrewdly called "the first . . . antislavery lecture to which it had been my lot to listen." As Douglass recalled it, Auld said, " 'If you give a nigger an inch, he will take an ell;' 'he should know nothing but the will of his master, and learn to obey it.' 'Learning would spoil the best nigger in the world;' 'if you teach that nigger . . . how to read the bible, there will be no keeping him;' 'it would forever unfit him for the duties of a slave;' and '. . . learning would do him no good, but probably, a great deal of harm—making him disconsolate and unhappy.' 'If you learn him how to read, he'll want to know how to write; and, this accomplished, he'll be running away with himself.' "

Hugh Auld knew what he was talking about. Looking back, Douglass described this discourse as "oracular"; it accurately predicted his future. But the time was still a long way off when he would seize the chance, in Auld's splendid phrase, for "running away with himself."

When Frederick was nine, and again when he was twelve, Baltimore was the scene of legal actions involving white men who had insulted each other. The disputes were of seemingly small importance. In the first instance, one party was knocked to the ground and the assailant was fined one dollar; in the second, the man who had done the insulting was jailed, but his punishment was not fierce—the prisoner took his meals with his jailer's family. Yet these quarrels reverberated down through our history.

The man knocked to the ground was Benjamin Lundy; the man put in jail was William Lloyd Garrison. The men with whom they had their disputes were slave traders; the subject of the disputes was slavery.

Austin Woolfolk was a prosperous Baltimore merchant whose place of business was on Pratt Street. Like other businessmen then and since, he was eager to be regarded not only as successful but also as benevolent. In his advertisements he stressed his discretion and kindliness. Woolfolk was a slave trader.

The Maryland economy was changing. There were fewer and fewer huge slaveholding enterprises like Wye House. Landowners were looking for nonagricultural sources of income, which, it turned out, were not dependent on slave labor. It was not considered good form for Marylanders of substance to mistreat their people by dividing families, but it was even worse form to slide down the ladder economically. The landowners sold certain assets—slaves—in order to invest in others—mercantile or manufacturing enterprises. The Maryland archives record hundreds of sales of slaves, then in great demand in the cotton belt south and west of Maryland. Frederick's aunt Maryann and his cousin Betty were sold south in 1825, for example. That year, Talbot County slaveowners received $22,702 from sales of their people to Woolfolk alone. They made their sales discreetly, but they made them.

In 1827, Benjamin Lundy was indiscreet. The unembarrassable Quaker, publisher of the *Genius of Universal Emancipation,* which he worked on wherever he happened to be on his peripatetic crusade to end slavery, printed an account of Woolfolk's having cursed one of his wares as the black man stood on the gallows, about to be hanged for participation in an attempted seizure of the *Decatur,* carrying him from Baltimore to Savannah. In his narrative, Lundy called the slave trader a "monster in human shape." The merchant sought out the editor and knocked him to the ground. Picking himself up, Lundy did not strike back, but instead went to the courthouse and sued Woolfolk for assault. After many delays, a judge levied a fine of one dollar, saying Woolfolk had been greatly provoked.

A year later, in Boston, Lundy described the incident, and the ugliness of the slave trade, to a group that included another editor, the conservative young William Lloyd Garrison. Garrison later credited his commitment to the antislavery cause to this meeting with Lundy, in the boarding house at which they were both staying; soon he was attacking slavery in his Vermont newspaper. Impressed by his convert, Lundy *walked* from Baltimore to Bennington in the winter of 1829 to persuade Garrison to join him in Maryland.

The following summer Garrison did come to Baltimore—the city where his mother had lived, briefly, and died. He and Lundy stayed at a boarding house on Market Street run by two Quaker ladies. Garrison soon met Jacob Greener, John Needles, and William Watkins, antislavery leaders in the black community. Immediately, the two editors began to take as their primary target in the *Genius of Universal Emancipation* the locally hated slave trade that resulted in the sale south of slaves who, in Baltimore, held hopes of entering the growing and articulate free black society. Their most sensational attack was on two New Englanders, Francis Todd and Nicholas Brown, the owner and captain, respectively, of a Newburyport ship, the *Francis,* then conveying eighty-five slaves, sold by Woolfolk, from Maryland to a plantation on the Mississippi River south of New Orleans—the site of the most dreaded slave markets.

Todd and Brown sued for libel, and Garrison, as author of the piece (which was no more offensive in its rhetoric—"domestic piracy," "horrible traffic"—than the typical campaign invective of the day) was fined fifty dollars. And when he did not pay the fine, he was sent to jail, and from his cell skillfully assailed slaveholders everywhere. Eager to quell this incipient and effective martyrdom, Garrison's jailers released him after forty-nine days. The publication of his new newspaper, the *Liberator,* followed, beginning on January 1, 1831. In the first issue, announcing as his goal the abolition of slavery, Garrison proclaimed, "I WILL BE HEARD." And he printed his account (along with documents from the case) of this, his first major action directed toward his goal.

Frederick Bailey had been listening to words like "abolition" and "slavery" for a long time. They were in constant, if surreptitious, use in the black community. Frederick knew that he was a slave and would be one all his life. He had learned those facts by talking to people, but he began to know that there were other ways to learn things. He began to read. At first, he had recited words from the Bible as he read along with Sophia. Down at the shipyard he watched as men put boards marked "L.F." on one particular side, his left hand's side, of the front of the craft they were building; boards marked with other letters went consistently to other parts of the ship. When he was about eleven, he began to recognize that letters could be joined to form words, which designated objects and actions. He matched the shipyard letters to those in the front of the *Webster's Spelling Book* that Tommy brought home from school and learned to write from memory all the letters of the alphabet. On Monday afternoons, when Sophia went to her Bible class and left him in charge of the house, he surreptitiously got out Tommy's copybook and began writing the words that he could now spell.

He was curious about his world and curious most of all about what it meant to be a slave in that world. Ever since Wye House, he had known that slavery was something unfair, and that the unfairness was bad and should be ended: "I was eager to hear any one speak of slavery. . . . Every little while, I could hear something about the abolitionists. It was some time before I found what the word meant. It was always used in such connections as to make it an interesting word to me. If a slave ran away and succeeded in getting clear, or if a slave killed his master, set fire to a barn, or did anything very wrong in the mind of a slaveholder, it was spoken of as the fruit of *abolition.* Hearing the word in this connection very often, I set about learning what it meant. The dictionary afforded me little or no help. I found it was "the act of abolishing;" but then I did not know what was to be abolished. Here I was perplexed. I did not dare to ask any one about its meaning, for I was satisfied that it was something they wanted me to know very little about."

One day, probably when he was as old as thirteen, he was reading in a newspaper about petitions in Congress "praying for the abolition of slavery" in the District of Columbia. Suddenly, he knew what the word "abolition" meant, and from that moment on, he "always drew near when that word was spoken, expecting to hear something of importance to myself and fellow-slaves." In 1841, Douglass told an antislavery audience of reading a speech by John Quincy Adams presenting petitions to the House of Representatives for the abolition of slavery in the District of Columbia. He remembered, too, reading the speech aloud to other slave boys; it was something he could talk to them about. And it gave him hope: someone wanted to do something about the situation in which they were caught.

There were also suggestions that he had better not wait for that something to happen: "I went, one day, on the wharf of Mr. Waters; and seeing two Irishmen unloading a large scow of stone, or ballast, I went on board, unasked, and helped them. When we had finished the work, one of the men came to me, aside, and asked me a number of questions, and among them, if I were a slave. I told him 'I was a slave and a slave for life.' The good Irishman gave his shoulders a shrug, and seemed deeply affected by the statement. He said 'it was a pity so fine a little fellow as myself should be a slave for life.' They both had much to say about the matter, and expressed the deepest sympathy with me, and the most decided hatred of slavery. They went so far as to tell me that I ought to run away, and go to the north; that I should find friends there, and that I would be as free as anybody. I, however, pretended not to be interested in what they said, for I feared they might be treacherous. White men have been known to encourage slaves to escape, and then—to get the reward— they have kidnapped them, and returned them to their masters." Frederick Bailey had gained an important idea—for the future.

But boys don't live in the future, and there was a lot of life, rough and immediate, in Fells Point. All too often, the two constables were called to log in another body fished up from under one of the wharves, and the night watchman had to be eluded as he patrolled the docks. Boys trailed along after seamen just come ashore, trying to catch some of their swaggering worldliness. As Frederick grew, he began to do more than just watch. Sixty years later, he wrote to Benjamin Auld, Tommy's younger brother, reminiscing about Sundays spent with the "Point boys" fighting at the old drawbridge with the "Town boys" who had come over to try for their share of the excitement on the docks. He was, he admitted, "sorry to say" that he "was often . . . as bad as the worst."

If there was any democracy in Maryland in the 1830s, it existed down the Fells Point alleys and behind the wall of Durgin and Bailey's shipyard.

There a ragtag band of little boys went about the deadly serious business of playing. No one had yet succeeded in teaching them that color or status had anything to do with who should be hunkering down with whom on curbstones or cellar doors or behind the shipyard. The boys talked about everything and anything, including what they would be when they grew up. Frederick reminded some that while they would be free at twenty-one, when they reached their majority, he would not. They could not see that this made sense, and said so. "I do not remember ever to have met with a *boy,* while I was in slavery, who defended the slave system." Sharing other ideas and curiosities with these boys, Frederick tried, on his own, to replicate the school classes to which they could go, but he could not. His Webster's speller—his only book, probably supplied by one of his fellows—was often out of his pocket as words from the classroom spilled into their talk. One day a scholar read, probably with nicely mocking cadence, from an anthology of oratory that his teacher had assigned. If Frederick laughed, he also listened.

With fifty cents that must have have been the product of passionate hoarding, and with the wonderful nerve—the overcoming of all fear of embarrassment—that a twelve-year-old is capable of, Frederick went into Knight's bookstore, in the neighborhood, and bought his own copy of *The Columbian Orator.* Seldom has a single book more profoundly shaped the life of a writer and orator. As its title suggests, this collection of speeches, published in the first of many editions in 1797, was committed to the proposition that American boys, as the inheritors of a tradition of great oratory, were destined to speak the virtues of the new republic. In the public mind, oratory was not just a demonstration of great learning, though it was sometimes that, nor was it simply entertainment, though it was decidedly that as well, and people listened for hours; oratory was power.

In his brief, forthright introduction, the compiler of *The Columbian Orator,* Caleb Bingham, invoked Cicero to prove the point. Caesar, whose victory at the Battle of Pharsalia had given him "the empire of the world," upon hearing Cicero speak, fell into "such a fit of shivering, that he dropped the papers which he held in his hand." Here was evidence of a force more impressive even than the biblical power of the Word that Frederick had been told about in church. For an eager student, the assignment was clear: "The best judges among the ancients have represented Pronunciation, which they likewise called Action, as the principal part of an orator's province." If he could say words—say them correctly, say them beautifully—Frederick could act; he could matter in the world. Like Cicero, if he could persuade, he could move the universe.

Alone, behind the shipyard wall, Frederick Bailey read aloud. Laboriously, studiously, at first, then fluently, melodically, he recited great speeches. With *The Columbian Orator* in his hand, with the words of the great speakers of the past coming from his mouth, he was rehearsing. He was readying the sounds—and meanings—of words of his own that he would one day speak. He had the whole world before him. He was Cato before the Roman senate, Pitt before Parliament defending American liberty, Sheridan arguing for Catholic emancipation, Washington bidding his officers farewell. These were men whose words surely were actions, and the virtues they extolled had a reach so broad that a Baltimore slave boy could include himself within their range. This reach was not gained with puffs of wind, words so abstract that they had no meaning for Frederick. *The Columbian Orator* was a book of liberties, of men exhorting mankind to a sense of higher callings, and, what was more, it did not ignore that denial of liberty that was slavery.

In one curious piece, "Slave in Barbary," not a speech at all, but a brief play, a polyglot group of captives are to be sold at a slave auction in the domain of "Hamet, Bashaw of Tunis." The bashaw—dressed, in accordance with the eighteenth-century European concept of the exotic, in a great puffed turban and hugely ballooned pants—is, because Moorishly Eastern, a wise tyrant. He presides over the fate of those being sold. One well-born Venetian, pleading with Hamet in an attempt to gain his brother's release, reminds us of the universality of slavery by recalling the open sale of Turks in his native city. Then, much to the consternation of the slave trader, who does not like to see goods taken off the market, he produces sufficient money to buy his brother's freedom. The merchant is cheered when a third brother, Francisco, who has arrived to retrieve the first two, is promptly put up for sale.

As the various captives expostulate with their captors on their coming fate, an Irishman is permitted an elegant speech in which he cites the unnaturalness as well as the unfairness of slavery, while an American slave, Sharp, the property of a captured United States naval officer, Kidnap, is required to speak in dialect: "No, masser planter! [he is addressing Hamet] he [Kidnap] get drunk! he whip me! he knock a me down! he stamp on a me! he will kill a me dead! No! no! let a poor negur live wid a you, masser planter . . . fore I go back America again; fore I live wid a masser Kidnap again." The auctioneer thinks Sharp, well broken in with the whip, should command a fine price, and begins the auction. The sale of Sharp and Kidnap turns out to be an act of poetic justice (if no other kind), for the purchaser decides to put Kidnap under Sharp's "instruction." Hamet has freed neither of them, but in a grandiloquent gesture, he does free the noble Francisco with the ringing declaration: "Let it be remembered, there is no luxury so exquisite as the exercise of humanity, and no post so honourable as his, who defends THE RIGHTS OF MAN."

What the Baltimore boy made of this costume-party piece is anybody's guess; it is less hard to imagine how he responded to "Dialogue between Master and Slave." It, too, deals not with the ending of all of slavery, but with the extrication of one individual from bondage, but in doing so it confronts philosophical problems raised by slavery that have concerned thinkers as far back as Aristotle. In a classically structured exchange—from which Douglass could quote decades later—the Master says that he has been kind and that the slave should be grateful; the Slave replies that kindness is irrelevant—that he wants liberty. The Master then asks, "Suppose I were to restore you to your liberty, would you reckon that a favour?" The Slave answers, "The greatest." "I do it, then," says the Master; "be free." But instead of a hymn of gratitude, the Master—standing for all masters—is treated to a warning: "Now I am indeed your servant, though not your slave. And as the first return I can make for your kindness, I will tell you freely the condition in which you live. You are surrounded by implacable foes, who long for a safe opportunity to revenge upon you and the other planters all the miseries they have endured. The more generous their natures, the more indignant they feel against that cruel injustice which has dragged them hither. . . . You can rely on no kindness on your part, to soften the obduracy of their resentment. . . . Superior force alone can give you security. As soon as that fails, you are at the mercy of the merciless. Such is the social bond between master and slave!"

Nothing of this was lost on the Baltimore slave. Echoes of this valedictory would ring out over Frederick Bailey's master, Thomas Auld, in the days and decades to come. After Lucretia's death, Thomas gave up the store in Hillsboro, broke all save one of his ties to the Anthony family—he remained linked to the Baileys, taking with him Eliza and the others of the family that he had inherited—and went back to his home town of St. Michaels.

There he married again—both well and poorly. Rowena Hambleton was the daughter of a prosperous farmer living five miles west of the little port. She was also an ill-tempered woman; having married a shopkeeper-postmaster, she sought to compensate for her diminished social status by being imperious with her slaves. She was also determined that her husband drive hard bargains in dealing with this property. Frederick's cousin Henny had been painfully crippled by a fall into a fire as a child and her hands were permanently closed. Rowena, resenting both the care of this useless slave and the fact that her brother-in-law and his wife in Baltimore had, *gratis,* the use of a now-strong adolescent male who belonged to

Thomas, insisted that the Hugh Aulds take Henny as well as Frederick. They did, but Sophia soon found Henny to be too much trouble, and persuaded her husband to send her back. Thomas's response to his brother's action was, as Frederick recalled it, "If he cannot keep 'Hen,' he shall not have 'Fred.' "

There may also have been another reason why Frederick was sent to St. Michaels. The year was 1833. Nat Turner and his rebels—Douglass firmly spoke of him as Nathaniel Turner—had been brutally repressed in 1831, but not forgotten. The revolt had taken place not all that far down the Chesapeake Bay, in Virginia. Turner had been a too-bright slave, hired out and not under a master's direct discipline and, what is more, a preacher, self-educated and eloquent. His insurrection failed, but it left young black men like Frederick with new hope, and in great jeopardy.

The free black people of Baltimore, with their proximity to the North and their engagement in the energetic commerce of an active seaport, were, with the possible exception of their counterparts in New Orleans, the most restless black people within the slave states. Frederick was already experiencing this restlessness, both within himself and in the world he was exploring. He had grown physically powerful at an early age, and with that growth came the approach of sexual maturity. Puberty put a gulf between him and his "family." The delicate relationship of boy to mother that he had treasured with Sophia Auld eroded as she sensed a new tension. By his own admission, his surliness contributed to the estrangement as much as did her discomfort. He pulled away too from his "brother" Tommy: "the time had come when his *friend* must become his *slave*. So we were cold, and we parted. It was a sad thing to me, that, loving each other as we had done, we must now take different roads." In sullen, secretive ways Frederick withdrew into his own world.

He spent more and more time with his friends, boys from whom he could learn and whom he could teach. As his voice croaked and descended into the resonance that was to characterize one of the great instruments of the nineteenth century, he put it to dangerous use. Frederick, talking with white boys about the inequity slavery, declaiming about the rights of man and about liberty, quoting a God of Moses and deliverance— Frederick, an outspoken teen-ager surly with white people—was a boy to be wary of, and one who needed to be wary.

Young Frederick Bailey was powerfully drawn to religion. He been moved by the Word as he and Sophia Auld read the Bible, and when he was twelve, having already met some of the free black boys who attended the Bethel chapel of the African Methodist Episcopal Church, he began attending the new Sabbath school for black children at the

Dallas Street Methodist Church. There, for the first time, he saw a black man—"a real black man," Dr. Lewis G. Wells, a local physician and lecturer—read from his own written manuscript. Inspired, Frederick himself began teaching in the Sabbath school when he was only about fourteen. His mistress, Sophia Auld, constantly struggling with the state of her soul, had as her spiritual mentor the Reverend Beverly Waugh, who sought to bring her more firmly into the fold when he preached at the Wilks Street Methodist Church. He even came to the Philpot Street house, to which the family had moved from nearby Alice Anna Street, to press his cause. Frederick heard him at prayer, and if not inspired to look to Waugh for his own spiritual guidance, he was influenced to seek such inspiration.

He found it in the exhortations of three other preachers. The first, identified only as "Mr. Hanson" and not listed as minister in any Baltimore church, was probably an itinerant evangelist; he preached that "all men, great and small, bond and free, were sinners in the sight of God; that they were, by nature, rebels against His government; and that they must repent of their sins." The second, Charles Johnson, was a black caulker and lay preacher in the Bethel chapel; he reached the impressionable boy emotionally "in tones of holy affection." Frederick soon underwent one of the nineteenth century's classic experiences of conversion. The familiar rhetoric describing the torment of doubt, the flash of truth, and then the coming through to faith, belies the intensity of the experience for the person achieving salvation. Long after his faith was gone, Douglass recalled the profound importance to him of this conversion: the boy burned with religion. But it was "Uncle Lawson," or, as Douglass later styled him, "good Father Lawson," who led him in "religiously seeking knowledge."

The "pious Lawson, who was," Douglass later declared, "in all the Christian graces, the very counterpart of 'Uncle Tom,'" was a drayman for a Fells Point ropemaker and lived in Happy Alley, around the corner from the old Alice Anna Street house. Despite Hugh Auld's threats—never carried out—to whip him if he didn't stop wasting time in the alley, Frederick began spending long hours with Lawson, an only partially literate lay preacher. As the boy, the better reader, searched the words of the Bible, Lawson sought their spirit. He saw huge promise in the boy, spoke to him, Douglass said, of "what I ought to be," and predicted that he would do "great work" for the Lord. The fact that Douglass's work turned out to be secular in no way diminishes the shaping power of this wise and kind old man. He gave Frederick a sense of destiny.

In addition to his time with Uncle Lawson, the increasingly strong and remarkable boy was spending more and more time with young men—some free, some not—who talked quietly at work along the docks and in the shipyards, and on into the night, of something better than slavery and prejudice. Quaker abolitionists from Philadelphia, with magnificent confidence in their righteousness, moved among the people of their neighboring city of Baltimore, questioning slavery, as their brother Benjamin Lundy had done. With caution, so did the free black members of Baltimore's Methodist and Baptist churches. Under the cover of debates on colonization, the conservative scheme for ending slavery by sending the blacks back to Africa, there was surreptitious talk of funding manumissions and aiding runaways. The nervous white enemies of this seditious talk were ready to punish severely any black boy who might try to take action about the things he had heard and thought.

Hugh Auld had long had a sense of what he had to deal with in Frederick. He knew where the boy's literacy might lead, but despite his perceptive speech on the subject, he appears to have simply looked the other way when he found Frederick's books in the house or overheard him talk about his reading. Later, in a way that would endear him to self-satisfied reformers, Douglass priggishly dismissed Hugh Auld as gone into "brandy." But brandy would not necessarily have prevented him from being a trenchant observer. And, perhaps, protector.

Hugh's decision to return Frederick to Thomas, then, may have been more than a reaction to the family quarrel. Indeed, he may actually have discussed Frederick's rebelliousness with his brother. By separating the boy from his relatives, the two had unwittingly seen to it that he had no family ties strong enough to keep him from trying to escape from slavery. They must have realized that the bright, big, unsubmissive, unhappy boy was likely to try running away, or might get involved in antislavery or other forbidden activities that could easily lead to a slave's death. The Aulds may have reasoned that the boy becoming a young man would be safer out of Baltimore and back on the Eastern Shore, living like any other ordinary field-hand slave.

When he had just turned fifteen (but thought he was sixteen and seemed larger, older, wiser, than his age) Frederick Bailey was sent from Baltimore, not back home, but to a new place and into what two well-meaning white men may have thought to be the safety of rural slavery. In March 1833, he was told he was going back to Thomas Auld and was put on a boat for the run-down port of St. Michaels.

4

St. Michaels

THE BAY SLOOP *Amanda,* the sweet, briny smell of the oysters she had hauled to the city lingering below her sails, came up to the worn wharves of St. Michaels. While the boat was taking him south, back to the country, Frederick had watched steamers, their stacks letting off the smoke of the furiously burning wood that heated the boilers, head north to the canal through to the Delaware River and Philadelphia. Out on the water, he had begun to think that someday the bay might be the way for him to go north, but now he had come the wrong way.

The new source of power for ships had doomed the building of sailing craft at St. Michaels, and the men of the town had put down their mallets to drag for oysters. The old shipbuilding docks were already out of repair when the tall, strong-featured boy, his body more powerful and his face more severe than could be accounted for by his fifteen years, walked past sheds blackened by the salt air, across a narrow footbridge, and up a short street of unpainted houses to find Thomas Auld.

Frederick had seen Thomas Auld only on the rare trips the shopkeeper made to Baltimore, but he had not forgotten who had sent him back to Baltimore after the distribution of the Anthony slaves. Now, returning to the Eastern Shore in the spring of 1833, the boy hoped to find in Thomas an uncle, an older brother, perhaps even a friend. At the door of the Aulds' St. Michaels house—it was a store and post office as well—Amanda, Thomas and Lucretia's appealing small child, welcomed him warmly, but as he responded, her stepmother immediately instructed him to be respectful. Rebuffed, he looked to Thomas, who saw before him not so much a winning young boy as a compelling adolescent.

Frederick could not read the austerity visible in his owner's face as the two looked sternly at each other.

Frederick loved Thomas, and that love was returned. There is no other way to account for the extraordinary dimensions of their relationship and, paradoxically, no other explanation for the severity with which, later, the former slave spoke of his former master. When, as a renowned antislavery orator, Frederick Douglass issued his absolute condemnation of slavery, he had to repudiate the possibility of such a relationship within its confines. In *My Bondage and My Freedom,* immediately after his description of his St. Michaels reunion with Thomas, he wrote, "Bad as slaveholders are, I have seldom met with one so entirely destitute of every element of character capable of inspiring respect, as was my present master, Capt. Thomas Auld." And then he continued his indictment: "When I lived with him, I thought him incapable of a noble action. The leading trait in his character was intense selfishness."

Thomas Auld had failings, but "selfishness" in its usual meaning was not one of them. Stingy he was; henpecked he was, by a wife whose cruelty to the slaves he tolerated; cold he was, and even brutal. But he was too poor, had acquired too few things, was demanding of too few attentions, gave too much evidence of having cared for others (including Frederick), for "selfishness" to make sense. Frederick Douglass was reaching for a quick, simple indictment, to get himself past the fact that his feelings about his former master were complex. Douglass had had to break with Thomas Auld in order to free himself from slavery, and the only way to cover the pain of that break was to drain Auld of his true personality. In Douglass's book, Master Thomas was simply a character, presented as the quintessential slaveholder.

But in St. Michaels in 1833, Frederick wanted to make something very different of Thomas. He wanted his religious conversion. Once he became the antislavery activist, Douglass was intensely rational, and his outspoken anticlericalism, with its resolute condemnation of the churches for their hypocritical condoning of slavery and racial prejudice, makes it difficult to realize that as a youth he was powerfully, emotionally drawn to religion. His later stern, reasoned criticism of religion was born of the disillusionment he experienced when his religion failed him. But in 1833, Frederick's own conversion still burned within him.

Recalling a rare November shower of meteors, in a passage that suggests a messianic Nat Turner more than the later orator and editor, Douglass described himself as having seen the supernatural in nature: "The air seemed filled with bright, descending messengers from the sky. It was about daybreak when I saw this sublime scene. I was not without the suggestion, at the moment, that it might be the harbinger of the coming of the Son of Man; and, in my then state of mind, I was prepared to hail Him as my friend and deliverer. . . . I was suffering much in my mind. It did seem that every time the young tendrils of my affection became attached, they were rudely broken by some unnatural outside power; and I was beginning to look away to heaven for the rest denied me on earth."

But Frederick was seeking more than rest from religion. In one of the best-written passages of *My Bondage and My Freedom,* Douglass described a week-long camp meeting at Bay Side, three months after he reached St. Michaels. From Baltimore had come two steamboats full of worshippers who stayed in the first row of "stately tents" pitched just behind the half circle of hundreds of seats. Eastern Shore farmers had come as well, to sleep in or under their wagons, which ringed the tents. Around it all, "huge fires were burning . . . , where roasting, and boiling, and frying, were going on, for the benefit of those who were attending to their own spiritual welfare within the circle."

On this particular night Frederick was concerned not with his own spiritual welfare, but with that of another. Thomas Auld had been persuaded to come, and the boy eagerly watched every step on his road to salvation. There were no seats for the blacks; they stood in a fenced-off area behind the altar, from which they were very occasionally addressed over the preachers' left shoulders. Directly in front of the exhorters was a "pen" filled with straw, into which as many as a hundred "mourners" could throw themselves on their knees to experience conversion. "I ventured," Douglass reported, "to take my stand at a sort of half-way place between the blacks and whites, where I could distinctly see the movements of mourners, and especially the progress of Master Thomas." He wanted to catch his eye now, to see his master stripped of mastery, to meet him evenly as one believer beholding another.

Somewhat heretically, young Frederick believed in a doctrine of good works: " 'If he has got religion,' thought I, 'he will emancipate his slaves; and if he should not do as much as this, he will, at any rate, behave toward us more kindly.' " A great deal might be riding on this particular conversion. Frederick watched eagerly, but though he saw that Auld's "face was extremely red, and his hair disheveled, and . . . heard him groan," he grew suspicious when he "saw a stray tear halting on his cheek, as if inquiring 'which way shall I go?' . . . The hesitating behavior of that tear-drop, and its loneliness, distressed me, and cast a doubt upon the whole transaction." Others, however, were convinced; they proclaimed that "Capt. Auld had come through." And he did not disappoint them. From that day on, no one in St. Michaels was more eager than this convert in arranging revivals, in leading his family in prayer, in exhorting his neighbors to worship. But Frederick was profoundly disappointed in

Auld and in the Methodist church. Although one minister, George Cookman, much respected by his black congregants, adhered to the old tenet that slavery was a sin and urged its end, the majority of his fellow clergymen did not, and they saw to it that Cookman was moved out of Talbot County. When one local man heeded Cookman and freed his slaves, Frederick was hopeful, but none of the others, including Thomas Auld, followed his lead.

Thomas did not free him, and nothing in the master's piety translated into generosity. In the summer and fall of 1833, recalling Sundays back in the city—if "I could not go to Baltimore. . . . I could make a little Baltimore here"—Frederick gathered some of the other young men around him for a Sabbath school. The first meeting was so successful that word got around the town. At the second, "we had scarcely got at work—*good work*" of teaching the gospel to the black children of the town, when two teachers in the regulation Methodist Sabbath school, along with Thomas Auld and a number of other members of the church, broke in. Asking Bailey if he "wanted to be another Nat Turner" and die the way he did, they raised stout sticks against the scholars and broke up the school.

Now it was painfully clear to Frederick where his master stood. Publicly, Auld had joined with other men to destroy a devoutly led Methodist Sabbath school. Privately, he had substituted emotional religiosity for the affection he did not dare express for Frederick. The boy had been cheated. This was Thomas's "selfishness"; he would not share his faith with one who desperately needed him to do so. This withholding did mortal damage to Frederick's own faith and to their friendship—and great damage to his trust in friendship itself.

Worse still was Auld's treatment of Frederick's crippled cousin Henny. Her inability to work because of her twisted hands, as well as her bitterness, was a source of constant guilt and frustration for Thomas. When his wife complained, he tied Henny up and whipped her, reciting "with blood-chilling blasphemy" as he did, "That servant which knew his lord's will, and prepared not himself, neither did according to his will, shall be beaten with many stripes." So much, thought Frederick, for the benevolence that flows from Christianity.

It was clear that Thomas was not going to rescue him through either manumission or the creation of some special world within slavery, and Rowena, who was so stingy that her slaves were often desperate with hunger, was determined to make an obedient, profitable slave of Frederick. She succeeded in doing precisely the opposite. Frederick's sister Eliza taught him the time-honored ways of slave rebellion—an instruction forgotten, a tool misplaced, a task half-performed. In exasperation,

Rowena Auld, reminding Frederick of Aunt Katy, tried to starve the two into submission. Their response was to steal; later, in the account he wrote for God- and larceny-fearing Yankees, Douglass sought, without convincing himself, to justify this action. He disliked defying the morality Sophia Auld had taught him, and he was miserable in the world to which she had dismissed him.

The sullen, strong boy was not proving useful in town. In January 1834 he was hired out to Edward Covey, an ambitious man trying to scratch a farm out of land he rented about seven miles from St. Michaels. The land ran from the Bay Side road to a low bluff on one of the most beautiful stretches of the Eastern Shore coast. Covey, a Methodist more pious even than Auld had become, was known for his ability to break the will of those working for him, so that they became industrious, profitable slaves. Frederick Douglass spoke of him as a "nigger-breaker," using the term as if it referred to an established profession, though he was simply describing this particular man's reputation. His famous account of the crucial year with Covey, which he repeated in countless antislavery lectures as well as all three of his autobiographies, would seem to be a tale of a single slave's thwarting of a master seeking to break his will. But it is a story of far more than this.

One cold morning, soon after his arrival, Frederick was sent by Covey into the woods with a team of oxen. The awkward, frightened boy, who had had no experience with draft animals, lost control of the difficult beasts, and there ensued a madcap dash—described with a touch of humor—through fences and into the trees. He almost had his skull crushed, but the only sympathy he received when he returned was to be told to go back to the woods. Covey "then went to a large gum-tree, and with his axe cut three large switches, and, after trimming them up neatly with his pocket-knife, he ordered me to take off my clothes. I made him no answer, but stood with my clothes on. He repeated his order. I still made him no answer, nor did I move to strip myself. Upon this he rushed at me with the fierceness of a tiger, tore off my clothes, and lashed me till he had worn out his switches. . . ." This was as close as a Victorian author could come to speaking about the sadistic abuse of males by males. Covey's savage attack strongly suggests a perversion of homosexual attraction into vicious cruelty.

For six months there were regular beatings and regular labor, plowing and tending the fields. Covey worked along with his slaves, but he was also fond of spying on them, in a way that led Douglass to give up the image of the tiger for that of another creature: "He seldom approached the spot where we were at work openly, if he could do it secretly. He always aimed at taking us by surprise. Such was his cunning, that we used to call him, among ourselves, 'the snake.' " It is not hard to imagine the scornful pleasure the slaves took when, themselves playing the spying games, they caught Covey crawling on his hands and knees in order "to avoid detection" and to "rise nearly in our midst" and hiss out orders to work harder. "His comings were like a thief in the night. . . . He was under every tree, behind every stump, in every bush, and at every window. . . . He would sometimes mount his horse, as if bound to St. Michael's, . . . and in half an hour afterwards you would see him coiled up in the corner of the wood-fence, watching every motion of the slaves." And those glistening black backs bared to the sun were enticing. As if joining them in sexual motion, he sought to make them work and work and work some more. If they faltered, the action was spoiled; if they fell, he was in a rage.

"On one of the hottest days in the month of August, 1834, Bill Smith [another hired slave], William Hughes [Covey's cousin], a slave named Eli, and myself were engaged in fanning wheat." Each had his task, as the wheat was thrown before the fan, and the grain separated from the chaff was neatly leveled and measured into half bushels with a narrow hickory board. Suddenly, Frederick collapsed with sunstroke; the rhythm of the work was broken, and Covey, just as suddenly, was right there. Asked why the fanning had stopped, Bill reported that Frederick was sick. Going over to the shade into which the boy had crawled, Covey looked at him for a considerable moment, asked what was the matter, and when he got only a groaned answer, kicked him and told him to get up. When Frederick tried to do so and fell back, Covey kicked him again and grabbing the slat of hickory, slashed at his head. Blood poured from the cut.

The stinging blow helped clear his head; able to think again, Frederick decided to run away and tell Thomas Auld how he was being treated. As he started through the woods to St. Michaels, Covey followed, but the boy refused to listen to demands that he come back. He did not dare take the road, but pressed through the tangle of briers and brush, his cut bleeding so badly that he was afraid he would die from the loss of blood. His clothes were torn and clotted when he finally got to Thomas's house to ask for help.

Thomas offered none. Douglass's accounts of this conversation do not suggest why he was so hardhearted, nor do they indicate just how devastating was this rebuff. Love turned to hatred that evening. Frederick never forgave Thomas's ridicule of his claim that if he returned to Covey he would be killed, nor did he forgive the grudging permission to stay the night—without supper or breakfast. The next morning, Saturday, Frederick walked back, on the road, and climbed over the fence into

Covey's farm, hoping to hide until Sunday. He stayed first in the hot confines of a field of full-grown corn and then sought the cool of the woods across the St. Michaels road from Covey's place.

There he encountered Sandy Jenkins, perhaps the most perplexing friend of Frederick's long life. A free black man who eked out a bare livelihood as a hired hand, Jenkins was warm, witty, and generous. With his wife, also free, he lived in a cabin in a swamp just inland from the farms where he worked. He had a link to Africa that Douglass was never able to explain convincingly to his Northern antislavery audiences, or to himself: Sandy Jenkins believed in magic. Taking Frederick home with him for the night—he and his wife risked much in harboring a runaway—he gave the confused boy a root to protect him from Covey's blows. Jenkins said it had always worked for him, and the next morning, Sunday, it seemed to work for Frederick too. When, in fear, he went back to the farm, Covey smiled at him and drove off to church—perhaps, in part, to discover in town if Auld was likely to intercede for the boy.

Before dawn on Monday, Frederick was in the barn caring for the horses. When Covey came in, he gave the impression that he would ignore the slave's having run away. But as Frederick sat in the loft, with his legs dangling, Covey suddenly grabbed and tried to tie them. Resisting, the boy braced himself firmly. Covey tugged, and Frederick "gave a sudden spring" and landed on top of the man. "Whence came the daring spirit necessary to grapple with a man who, eight-and-forty hours before, could, with his slightest word have made me tremble like a leaf in a storm, I do not know; at any rate, *I was resolved to fight,* and what was better still, I was actually hard at it. . . . I felt as supple as a cat, and was ready for the snakish creature at every turn." Wrestling furiously, Frederick grabbed Covey by the throat. Totally surprised by the attack and quaking as Frederick's fingernails drew blood, Covey croaked out a call for help to William Hughes, his cousin.

Hughes pulled Frederick's hands away in order to bind them, but Frederick gave a powerful kick and Hughes doubled over in pain. When Covey, frightened, ordered the furiously aroused slave to be still, Frederick thundered that six months of brutality were enough. The two lunged for each other again, and Covey dragged Frederick out into the yard toward a piece of lumber that he could use as a weapon. At this point Covey spotted Bill Smith, who had just returned after spending Sunday night with his wife, and called to him to help subdue Frederick. But Bill, with splendid nonchalance, instead treated Covey to a bit of black America's verbal rebellion. By feigning misunderstanding of his orders, the black man on the street—or the hand in the field—could outwit the white man.

Douglass, looking back, recognized that this was what occurred; there was "something comic" afoot. In response to Covey's order to grab Frederick, Bill, "who knew *precisely* what Covey wished him to do, affected ignorance. . . . 'What shall I do, Mr. Covey,' said Bill. 'Take hold of him—take hold of him!' said Covey. With a toss of his head, peculiar to Bill, he said, 'indeed, Mr. Covey, I want to go to work.' '*This is* your work,' said Covey; 'take hold of him.' Bill replied, with spirit, 'My master hired me here, to work, and *not* to help you whip Frederick.' It was now my turn to speak. 'Bill,' said I, 'don't put your hands on me.' To which he replied, 'MY GOD! Frederick, I ain't goin' to tech ye,' and . . . walked off."

Suddenly another danger loomed. Caroline, a slave owned by Covey, arrived to milk the cows; "she was a powerful woman, and could have mastered me very easily, exhausted as I now was. As soon as she came into the yard, Covey attempted to rally her to his aid. Strangely—and, I may add, fortunately—Caroline was in no humor to take a hand in any such sport. We were all in open rebellion, that morning."

Frederick and Covey fought on in the intimacy of battle—"He held me, and I held him"—and, crucial to an understanding of the outcome, Frederick neither knocked out Covey nor pinned him. Instead, they grappled for what Douglass, no doubt exaggerating but making a telling point, said was "nearly two hours." In impotent rage, Covey struggled against Frederick's remarkably strong arms and firm hands—and struggled too against the mocking grins of Frederick and the other slaves. With as much supple shrewdness as brute strength, these slaves humiliated the snake.

In telling this story, Douglass digressed to employ a now-famous transcendental, feminine image of freedom—"vessels, robed in purest white," riding the "broad bosom" of the Chesapeake, in splendid view from Covey's farm—and, to further delight his antislavery audience, he proclaimed a self-deliverance: "He only can understand the deep satisfaction I experienced, who has himself repelled by force the bloody arm of slavery. . . . It was a glorious resurrection." But when he was right there on the ground wrestling with Covey, he was at one with his fellow black slaves. They, not he alone, bested Covey. Bill and Caroline helped not simply by disobeying Covey's orders to hold Frederick, but by bringing into play the psychological counterattack. Caroline was later whipped for her insolence; Bill was not, because his master forbade it.

More surprisingly, neither was Frederick; for the remaining months of his stay with Covey, he was not struck. Conceivably, Auld had sent word that there were to be no more beatings. Douglass himself attributed his luck to Covey's embarrassment; calling in the constable to whip a slave would have been an admission that he was not the Negro breaker he claimed to be. But it seems at least as likely that Covey's restraint was a direct result of the action of the slaves: one slave had fought back physically—and bravely—but all three had attacked him psychologically, with telling effect.

Stepping outside his story to summarize, Douglass the abolitionist informed "my dear reader, [that] this battle with Mr. Covey . . . was the turning point in my *'life as a slave.'* . . . I was *nothing* before; I WAS A MAN NOW." Now, he told his antislavery audience, he was determined "to be A FREEMAN." This emphasis on his own transformation was in behalf of the cause, as Frederick Douglass understood it in 1845 and 1855, but in isolating himself in order to point the moral, he was forgetting something that had been at the heart of the story that Frederick Bailey— and Bill and Caroline—had worked out together on the Covey farm that August morning.

5

The Freeland Farm

FREDERICK spent Christmas 1834 in St. Michaels with his family—
and with the Aulds. The slaves were relieved of most work during the
week between Christmas and New Year's. It was a time of respite and
celebration—there was good food, there was good music—but Frederick
may well have begun to form his later judgment that "these holidays
. . . [are] among the most effective means, in the hands of the slaveholders,
of keeping down the spirit of insurrection among the slaves." In January,
uncomfortable about having been vulnerable to Christmas cheer and
Christian kindness, he left St. Michaels to begin work on another farm.
Thomas Auld had hired him out to William Freeland—compared to
Covey, a lenient master—for the year 1835.

From the worn old fields of the Freeland farm, Frederick Bailey could
look out across the Chesapeake Bay. Once again, the beautiful expanse
of water seemed to awaken something in him; indeed, here he was to have
perhaps the most intense emotional experience of his life. Living on the
Freeland farm for something over a year, he achieved friendship. "I had
become large and strong," he wrote, "and had begun to take pride in the
fact." And now the seventeen-year-old found himself working with other
young men as restless, as energetic, as he.

John and Henry Harris were brothers owned by the Freelands; the
others, like Frederick, had been hired. Handy Caldwell was a slave living
nearby; Sandy Jenkins was the free black man who had given Frederick
a root to protect him in his struggle with Edward Covey the year before.

The five made a kind of sport of their hard work, competing to see
who could swing the widest scythe or hoist the heaviest heifer, but they

"were too wise to race with each other very long" lest Freeland, whose depleted soil needed a lot of working, learn just how much labor they were capable of. "Such racing, we had the sagacity to see, was not likely to pay. We had our times for measuring each other's strength, but we knew too much to keep up the competition so long as to produce an extraordinary day's work." It was this caution alone that curbed these men "ever so much excited for the race."

And there was excitement of another kind—other "mischief" to be done; "I had not been long at Freeland's before I was up to my old tricks," Frederick recalled. The Harrises were "remarkably bright and intelligent, but neither of them could read," so out came Webster's speller and *The Columbian Orator.* Frederick Bailey, teacher, was back at work that summer—on Sundays, under an oak tree—conducting school. The "contagion spread. I was not long in bringing around me twenty or thirty young men." His pupils were as eager as he: "It was surprising with what ease they provided themselves with spelling books." Perhaps these were the castoffs of their young masters; if not, the owners may have wondered, as their mothers switched them, how they had managed to misplace books they remembered carrying home from school. The black scholars, for their part, struggled almost physically to press each sound from their mouths. And then, as they painstakingly articulated the words and connected one to another in a sentence, concepts like "promise" and "future," like "change" and "escape," came to have meaning.

Douglass later claimed that he and his friends kept the school "as private as possible," but in fact there was little possibility of maintaining privacy. Three strapping young men might have managed, for a time at least, to find a hidden place for study, but not thirty. They were aware that the good people of St. Michaels would have preferred them to get drunk and wrestle away their Sundays instead of engaging in the subversive business of learning, and they cannot have believed that their masters did not know what they were up to. But where they met was a mystery; writing about the school twenty years later, Douglass did not give the name of the free black man who let them meet in his house when cold drove them indoors, lest he be punished.

Frederick's year was going splendidly. Watching the increasing dismay among his white neighbors as he stirred up their workers, he could see his importance to his black brothers growing. He was a leader among a substantial group of his peers, many of them older than he. His self-confidence soared, and even more importantly, he was, he said, bound with "hooks of steel, to my brother slaves," the four with whom he worked: "They were, every one of them, manly, generous and brave, yes; I say they were brave, and I will add, fine looking. It is seldom the lot of mortals to have truer and better friends than were the slaves on this farm." Of the two to whom he was the closest, he wrote, "Toward Henry and John Harris, I felt a friendship as strong as one man can feel for another; for I could have died with and for them."

As the months went on, Frederick "began to disclose" to the Harris brothers "my sentiments and plans; sounding them, the while, on the subject of running away." With passion, he read from the pages of his *Columbian Orator*—"that (to me) gem of a book, . . . with its eloquent orations and spicy dialogues, denouncing oppression and slavery." The Harrises heard him; they began to see that they too must seek a way out of bondage. They started using the dangerous word "escape." There were many arguments about the wisdom of trying to run away, to escape, particularly when they began talking with others about it. Handy Caldwell was apparently no longer working on the Freeland farm by then, but Sandy Jenkins was still there, and they discussed the matter as well with Charles Roberts and Henry Bailey, slaves working on a nearby farm. (One of the most curious aspects of Douglass's telling of this story is the absence of any comment on his kinship to Henry Bailey, Betsy's youngest child and therefore his uncle, though two years his junior. Like Frederick, Henry was owned by Thomas Auld; he was hired out to Rowena's father, William Hambleton.)

The six "revolutionary conspirators" found "our feelings were more alike than our opinions" as, time and time again, they discussed slavery and their escape from it. But their talk drove them relentlessly on, and finally they "were ready to act"; the question now was "*how* the thing is to be done." Frederick was the only one who could have read a map if, as is unlikely, they had obtained one, but even without a map, he knew that up the Chesapeake—northward—was the way to go. He had learned in Baltimore that boats went up the bay, through the canal that crossed to the Delaware River, and on into free territory. He knew about Pennsylvania, where there was no slavery; he knew as well that slaveholding Delaware, sharing the Eastern Shore with Maryland, offered no safe routes of escape. He was aware, too, that somewhere north of all this lay New York City, with its evil reputation for returning runaways. And he had heard of far-off Canada, with its more certain promise of freedom.

Since none of the men could sail, stealing a sailing vessel in St. Michaels was not in the plan; stealing William Hambleton's big oyster-gathering canoe was. The broad bay could be as turbulent as the sea, so to avoid being swamped they would hold close to the shore, and wary of being spied on, make their long, slow way up the Eastern Shore's many-fingered coast. Then, in the vicinity of a town called North Point that Frederick understood to be on the canal, although he had no clear idea of where, they would abandon the canoe and, on foot, slip unseen into Pennsylvania.

The planning—the conspiring—was exhilarating and terrifying. There were "phantoms of trouble. . . . Now, it was starvation, causing us, in a strange and friendless land, to eat our own flesh. Now, we were contending with the waves, (for our journey was in part by water,) and were drowned. Now, we were hunted by dogs, and overtaken and torn to pieces by their merciless fangs. We were stung by scorpions—chased by wild beasts—bitten by snakes; and, worst of all . . . we supposed ourselves . . . overtaken by hired kidnappers." Somehow, Frederick had the nerve to whistle past all these graveyards by quoting a slaveholder's famous declamation: "GIVE ME LIBERTY OR GIVE ME DEATH." He conceded that "it was a *doubtful* liberty, at best, that we sought; and a certain, lingering death in the rice swamps and sugar fields, if we failed." But they were determined not to fail. They were resolute, or, at least, all but one of them were.

"In the progress of our preparations, Sandy, the root man, became troubled," Douglass recalled laconically. Unlike the others, Sandy Jenkins was not "quite free from slave-holding priestcraft." The others were: "It was in vain, that we had been taught from the pulpit in St. Michael's, the duty of obedience to our masters." The plotters would not consider their "hard hands and dark color as God's mark of displeasure;" indeed, "Nature laughed" at such nonsense. And Douglass added, "I had now become altogether too big for my chains."

Sandy Jenkins, however, was not free of the superstitious power of a misread Bible, a well-rubbed root, or a dream. One morning he reported, "I dreamed, last night, that I was roused from sleep, by strange noises, like the voices of a swarm of angry birds that caused a roar as they passed. . . . I saw you, Frederick, in the claws of a huge bird, surrounded by a large number of birds, of all colors and sizes. These were all picking at you, while you, with your arms, seemed to be trying to protect your eyes." Sandy insisted that Frederick take heed—and here, in his account, Douglass rendered Sandy's words in demeaning dialect: "Dare is sumpon in it, shose you born; dare is, indeed, honey."

Heeding his own warning, Sandy dropped out of the conspiracy (it is not clear if he ever intended to leave his wife and accompany the others), but Frederick and his companions would not be dissuaded. On Friday, April 1, 1836, their food and clothes bundled tightly, the band slept what they deeply hoped would be their last night in bondage. Waking to a "tempest and tumult of my brain" that he claimed he could never adequately describe, so intense were his feelings, Frederick realized that the "trial hour had not yet come." It was, he knew, "easy to resolve,

but not so easy to act." And yet, it "was too late to look back." After
Sandy's defection, the five—John and Henry Harris, Henry Bailey,
Charles Roberts, and Frederick Bailey—had declared to one another that
to falter and abandon their plan of escape would be to acknowledge that
they were "fit only to be *slaves.*"

According to plan, Frederick went to work as usual that Saturday
morning. While spreading manure, he felt a "sudden presentiment, which
flashed upon me like lightning in a dark night." Turning instantly to
Sandy Jenkins, working next to him, he said, "Sandy, we are betrayed."
Sandy replied, "Man, dat is strange; but I feel just as you do." Frederick
said no more. When the horn sounded for breakfast—which, in his
anxiety, he could not even think about—he started for the house. As he
came near to it, he looked down the long lane to the gate and saw four
white men on horseback, leading two black men, lashed. Charles Roberts
and Henry Bailey had been dragged over from the Hambleton farm,
down the St. Michaels road. Seeing them, Frederick knew that it was "all
over . . . we are surely betrayed." William Hambleton, who seldom
moved his horse above a walk, galloped up the lane, rolling dust behind
him. Reining his horse—and his anger—he asked, with his usual circum-
spection, where Freeland was. Frederick directed him to the barn.

As Frederick and John Harris stumbled, terrified, into the kitchen,
Mary, the cook, demanded to know what was going on. The two pled
ignorance. Then Freeland rushed into the room and ordered the two male
slaves out into the yard. At the door, Frederick saw that the posse was
"armed to the very teeth"; there was, he concluded, no point in resisting.
He and John had their hands tied behind their backs, but when Henry
Harris came in from the barn and was told to cross his hands for tying,
he, "in a voice so firm and clear, and in a manner so determined, as for
a moment to arrest all proceedings," said, *"No I won't."* Frederick was
as stunned by this courage as were the white men, who pulled out their
pistols and put them against Henry's chest. With great calm, Henry
damned them and dared them to shoot. Then he wrenched the guns from
the "puny hands of his assassins." He soon lost his grip on the guns—
which he did not know how to use—and took on the men hand to hand,
struggling powerfully, one against five. At last, beaten with gunstocks
and wrestled to the ground, he was subdued and bound.

"Henry put me to shame," Frederick wrote later; "he fought, and
fought bravely. . . . [while] John and I . . . made no resistance." Frederick
had not broken free of his loosely knotted bonds to try to help Henry,
but in the confusion caused by the fight, he did manage to toss the pass
he had written for himself into the kitchen fire. And in the aftermath of
Henry's struggle, the posse stupidly forgot to search the others for their

passes, which they had been told Frederick had counterfeited and which would have been firm evidence of an intent to escape. Instead, the slaves were ordered to march into St. Michaels.

As the captives were herded out of the yard, Freeland's mother appeared with biscuits for the Harris brothers. Pointing an aged finger at Frederick, she shrieked, "You devil! you yellow devil! It was you that put it into the heads of Henry and John to run away. But for *you,* you *long legged yellow devil,* Henry and John would never have thought of running away." Frederick fixed her with a stare of fierce, implacable hatred—his silent shout that John and Henry were his friends, not her boys. Screaming in "wrath and terror," she fled back into the house, slamming the door behind her.

On their way into town, Frederick managed to whisper to Henry to eat his pass along with his biscuit; one by one the men destroyed the incriminating papers. "Own [Admit] nothing!" he muttered to them. "Own nothing!" As they walked—on the day before Palm Sunday— "crowds of idle, vulgar people," with "all manner of ribaldry and sport," jeered them. Pointing to Frederick, already identified as the ringleader, they called out that he should be hanged, or burned, or like Nat Turner "have the *'hide'* taken from my back." Frederick loathed the humiliation as much as he feared being killed.

When they reached town, they were interrogated in Thomas Auld's store. Frederick was wryly amused (and pleased) that his master doubted the allegation that the men had engaged in a conspiracy. He probably was also perplexed by the game his master was playing. Auld knew that his hysterical neighbors could easily elevate the escape plot into a slave insurrection, led by his slave. And if they did so, torture and death lay ahead for Frederick. To quiet the rising excitement, Auld acknowledged only a partial belief in Frederick's guilt and insisted that he and the others be given a hearing. As owner of the chief conspirator, Auld had charge of the interrogation.

The young men denied any intention of escaping, each explaining that he had simply been working, in the usual way, that morning. As he answered the questions being hurled at him, Frederick shrewdly figured out that they had but one accuser: "Master Thomas would not tell us *who* his informant was; but we suspected *one* person *only.* Several circumstances seemed to point SANDY out, as our betrayer."

Hitherto, Douglass had indicated his contempt for Sandy's defection only by rendering his speech in dialect, and now, having declared him guilty, he stepped back: "We all loved him too well to think it *possible* that he could have betrayed us. So we rolled the guilt on other [unnamed] shoulders."

The questioning over, Auld contended that only if the slaves had murdered someone would the evidence have justified instant hanging. Instead, they should be sent to jail and tried. The five were dragged behind horses, stumbling, for fifteen miles, to Easton. There the sheriff put Frederick and the two Harrises in one jail cell and Roberts and Bailey in another. At least for the moment, their owners had gotten their valuable property safely away from would-be lynchers. But a new enemy appeared: "A swarm of imps, in human shape—the slave-traders, deputy slave-traders, and agents of slave-traders—that gather in every country town of the state, watching for chances to buy human flesh, (as buzzards to eat carrion,) flocked in upon us, to ascertain if our masters had put us in jail to be sold."

Slave traders kept their eyes on the jails for likely merchandise—Austin Woolfolk maintained a branch of his business in Easton—but how they could actually have gotten their hands on the men in their cells is not clear; nevertheless, Douglass tells us that they did. Perhaps he was stretching the truth, adding excitement for his antislavery audience. He certainly did not neglect the erotic dimension of his story as he described how "they one by one subjected us to an examination, with a view to ascertain our value; feeling our arms and legs, and shaking us by the shoulders to see if we were sound and healthy; impudently asking us, 'how would we like them for masters?' " The five men stood "quite dumb, disdaining to answer them." When Frederick's only response was to show in his face his detestation for "the whisky-bloated gamblers in human flesh," he was detested in return: "One fellow told me, 'if he had me, he would cut the devil out of me pretty quick.' "

At their cell window, Frederick and the Harrises tried, without luck, to get the attention of the black waiters "flitting about in their white jackets" in front of the hotel across the street. The prisoners were hoping that these expert gleaners of gossip might have picked up word of their fate, but they got no help from that quarter. Alone in their surprisingly well fitted out white man's cell, Frederick, John, and Henry were in great suspense: "Every step on the stairway was listened to" with apprehension. They knew a sale south was likely for slaves undisciplined enough to plot an escape. But for the Harrises, Roberts, and even Henry Bailey, old ties held: there was no trial, and Freeland and Hambleton came to take their valuable property home. Mrs. Freeland was to get her boys back; Frederick was to lose his friends forever.

"Noble" was Frederick's word for Henry Harris, the closest friend he was ever to have. Now, "as reluctant to leave the prison with me in it, as he was to be tied and dragged" into it, Henry was taken away by William Freeland. "Not until this final separation," Douglass wrote twenty years later, "had I touched those profounder depths of desolation, which it is the lot of slaves often to reach. I was solitary in the world, and alone within the walls of a stone prison, left to a fate of life-long misery." He was anticipating the "ever dreaded slave life in Georgia, Louisiana and Alabama," from which he could not escape. He was also mourning the loss of friendship and even the loss, in some sense, of his humanity. In his "loneliness," he felt that the "possibility of ever becoming anything but an abject slave, a mere machine in the hands of an owner, had now fled."

Thomas Auld had a problem. His slave was known to be dangerous. Mrs. Freeland regarded him as one who could stir to insurrection slaves she insisted on believing were loyal; Hambleton threatened to shoot the troublemaker if his son-in-law did not get him out of the county. Rowena knew that she and Thomas could get the price of a new house for a slave who had been nothing but trouble since his arrival in St. Michaels. If Frederick were to escape, as he had already tried to do, the money he was worth would go with him. Auld was under severe pressure to sell his slave, but he could not bring himself to do so. Frederick's seaman cousin, Tom, who had an excellent ear for news, reported that Auld "walked the floor nearly all night" before going to the jail to release Frederick.

Whatever the tortured bond between the two, whether kinship or some other equally strong tie, Auld could not doom the boy, now grown to be a man—a person—about whom in his clumsy, tormented way he cared immensely. Telling both his neighbors and Frederick that he was going to sell him to a friend in Alabama, Auld brought his slave home after he had been alone in the jail for a week. Frederick knew that Auld had no friend in Alabama and uneasily sensed that he was wavering. When the two were alone, in what must have been a moment of great intensity, Thomas told him he was sending him back to Baltimore, to Hugh, to learn to be a skilled laborer. With a trade, Frederick could be hired out at a profit, or so Auld must have told his wife. And—as he probably did not tell her—he promised Frederick that if he worked diligently at a trade (and stayed out of trouble) he would set him free when he became twenty-five. As he raised the young man's hopes, Auld must have known that he would now lose Frederick—not into endless labor in a cotton field in the Deep South, but to the risks of Baltimore.

The escape attempt had taught Thomas Auld how likely it was that the resolute, stubborn, strong, and bright young man would either get into fatal trouble in the city or escape into freedom in the North. Either way, he would be lost to him. Quietly, Thomas put Frederick on a boat for Fells Point.

Freedom would come for Frederick Bailey, but not with the purity with which it had been contemplated by the fine-looking band of young black men. Frederick knew he would not wait until the far-off age of twenty-five to test the reliability of Auld's promise; he would free himself somehow. But when that great goal was attained, he would be a debtor. Frederick Bailey owed his chance to seek freedom not to the camaraderie of the brave Henry Harris, but to the largesse of an ambiguous Thomas Auld. For his freedom—for his life—he would for the rest of that life be beholden to a white man whom he had loved and whom he now had to remember to loathe.

6

Baltimore

THE FLAT STREETS behind the Fells Point docks, wedged tightly with three-story brick houses, had changed less than the young man who walked them. Frederick Bailey was trying to regain his bearings. He had loathed field-hand slavery, but leaving it behind, he had also left the closest friends he would ever know. He and they had tried to set themselves free; caught—and spared, to their shame, by their masters—the others had gone back to their bleak fields, perhaps for ever. Alone, Frederick had hung suspended over the void of lynching and the abyss of being sold south, only to be pulled back by the merciful hand of his master, who wrenched repentance from him. Thomas Auld had warned his slave that if he insisted on being free-willed and freewheeling, he would end up dead or sold into alien Southern fields bleaker than any his friends would know. But, Auld told Frederick, if he behaved, some-day, perhaps when he reached twenty-five, he would be set free.

As he wandered through the streets of Baltimore with his master's vague promise of manumission in mind, Frederick Bailey asked himself what being a free black man in that city would mean. He remembered that ten years ago, when he pointed out "anything that struck me as beautiful or powerful," his cousin Tom, who worked on the *Sally Lloyd,* would reply "that he had seen something in Baltimore far surpassing it." To black Marylanders the city was a haven; being there gave Frederick courage. His self-confidence had been born in Betsy Bailey's cabin and restored on the floor of Covey's barn, as he wrestled for his sense of self. It had gathered strength as other men followed him in his escape attempt; it had weakened in the solitude of the Easton jail. He had been frightened, and now he had translated that fear into contempt for his slave condition and perhaps contempt, as well, for others who, like him, were slaves.

Free Baltimore could give him his chance; it was "the very place, of all others, short of a free state, where I most desired to live." Thousands of former slaves and descendants of slaves lived in the city; so did people still owned but permitted to hire themselves out, and therefore able to determine where they would do their own day's work. By following their example, Frederick would make a free man of himself. He would show Thomas Auld; he would allow Hugh Auld to arrange for an apprenticeship, but once he had learned his trade he would elbow past the Auld brothers and set himself up as a mechanic—an artisan—in the energetic port city. Then, proud of more than his physical strength and his ability to attract attention, he would straighten his back and step out of his scruffy country clothes and into the best in the city that he could afford. He would, with dignity, become one of the achingly respectable "free people of color" of Baltimore.

Douglass's autobiographies say little about these free people and their anomalous society. Instead, his books proclaim an undeviating quest for total freedom and describe a life that was a complete repudiation of slavery—the antithesis of the accommodation to slavery that had been made by the dependent free African Americans living precariously within a society committed to slavery's continuance. Frederick Douglass does not tell us that these were precisely the people with whom Frederick Bailey associated between 1836 and 1838 in Baltimore. In those years, he was testing their world.

At first, Frederick again lived with the Hugh Aulds on Philpot Street, but things were not as they had been. He had left as a fifteen-year-old boy; when he came back, at eighteen, he had matured physically, had worked in the fields, had been to jail. Tommy too had changed; he was entering adolescence, and more and more, the focus of his life was outside his home. As impressive as Frederick must still have seemed to him, Tommy appears to have picked up enough street racism to know that he no longer wanted a nigger older brother: "The loving relations between me and Mas' Tommy were broken up. He was no longer dependent on me for protection, but felt himself a *man,* with other and more suitable associates. In childhood, he scarcely considered me inferior to himself— certainly, as good as any other boy with whom he played; but the time had come when his *friend* must become his *slave.*" Sophia too kept her distance from the black man that Frederick now was; only Hugh seems to have been comfortable with the almost-adult who now shared his house. He immediately arranged for Frederick to serve as an apprentice caulker in his own trade, shipbuilding, in William Gardiner's shipyard.

However, Hugh was out of step with the times. There had been little racism in evidence in the shipyards when he had first worked in them. There did not need to be as long as free men and slave men worked together simply getting the job done. The earlier social structure had been secure enough so that workers did not feel pitted against one another; now, with a greater clamor for jobs, the managers had learned that the workers could be kept in line with threats that if they did not work satisfactorily, someone else could easily be hired. By 1836, with more and more black people coming into the city to seek jobs as hired-out slaves or, increasingly, as free men, and with a great many white immigrants from Europe and from rural Maryland competing for those same jobs, the use of racism as a managerial tool was on the rise.

In Andrew Jackson's America, the mechanics—the skilled workers honored by the republic—had great expectations. Unfortunately, they could count on neither the economic system nor their own self-confidence to bring them to their goals without conflict. When the white workers heard "not infrequent murmurs," Douglass recalled, "that educating the slaves as mechanics may . . . give slave-masters power to dispense with the services of the poor white man altogether," they took action—directed not at their employers, but at their fellow workers. They "made a cowardly attack upon the free colored mechanics, saying *they* were eating the bread which should be eaten by American freemen."

Just before Frederick went to work in Gardiner's yard, the white workers had struck, knowing that the shipbuilder had a large, lucrative contract to build, in a hurry, warships for the Mexican government. Previously, black and white workers had labored side by side, but now Gardiner gave in and fired the free black carpenters. In surprising contrast, black ships' caulkers, by being good at their job and by deferring to the white-dominated association of mechanics, managed to monopolize that essential, highly skilled trade until the 1850s and were not forced out of the yards until after the Civil War. In 1836, the seventy-five or so triumphant white carpenters of the Gardiner yard, back at work, expressed their scorn and their guilt by tormenting the only people in their path, the score of young apprentices who were at their beck and call.

" 'Fred., bring that roller here.'—'Fred., go get a fresh can of water.'—'Fred., come help saw off the end of this timber.' " He was being summoned by more than one worker at a time in the time-honored practice of hazing apprentices, but for him the taunts had a special edge: " 'Halloo, nigger! come, turn this grindstone.' . . . 'darkey, . . . why don't you heat up some pitch?' . . . 'D——n you, if you move, I'll knock your brains out!' " The white apprentices were subjected to hazing too, but they had available a convenient target for their resentment; they turned not on their tormentors, but on Frederick: "They began to put on high looks, and to talk maliciously of *'the niggers;'* saying, that 'they would take the country,' that 'they ought to be killed.' " They resented the fact that the carpenters, having driven out the blacks who were in their own line of work, had not forced Gardiner to fire the apprentice black caulker in their midst. Frederick suspected that he had been kept on because, unlike the fired carpenters, he was a slave.

One day, Ned Hays—Douglass never forgot the names of his fellow apprentices—grew so angry with Frederick for bending a bolt that he went after him with an adze, a razor-sharp tool. Frederick countered with a swing of his maul, a heavy wooden hammer, that drove the adze out of Hays's wounded hand. The fight stopped there, for the moment. On another day, Edward North—Douglass in his account of the fight also referred to him as Ned, suggesting that there had been more cordial days—ordered Frederick do so some fetching for him. When he refused, North hit him, and instead of hitting back, Frederick simply picked up the big man—he was the largest of the other apprentices—and threw him from the staging onto thc dock.

Clearly, Frederick had demonstrated that, one at a time, he could handle any of the young men, and relying on the comradeship that they had felt when they began working together, he was for a time able to keep them from combining against him. But Hays's and North's beatings rankled, and some time later these two, along with Bill Stewart and Tom Humphreys, lay in wait. As Fred came alongside the boat where they were working, he saw one of them, holding a brick, standing directly in his path. Instantly, he felt the presence of two others, one on each side. And just as he comprehended what was coming, the fourth attacked from behind, hitting him on the head with a handspike, a heavy metal bar used for easing timbers into place. Stunned, Frederick crashed into a pile of timbers. When he regained consciousness, they were beating him clumsily with their fists. Stretching things a bit, he described the fight: "With a sudden surge, and despite their weight, I rose to my hands and knees," but one of them "planted a blow with his boot in my left eye, which, for a time, seemed to have burst my eyeball." The assailants, seeing his closed eye and the blood streaming from his face as, nevertheless, he rose to his feet, were frightened by what they had done and fled.

Frederick grabbed the handspike and "madly enough, attempted to pursue them." Now, the older carpenters intervened, but they did so to stop his attack, not to protect him. "No one said 'that is enough.' " Rather, they circled him menacingly, and "some cried out, 'kill him—kill him—kill the d——d nigger! knock his brains out—he struck a white person." But no one moved; sullenly they turned away, and Frederick left the yard and struggled to the Aulds' house.

When Sophia saw the bloodied young man, the distance dissolved. She immediately tended his wounds with skill and compassion: "No mother's hand could have been more tender than hers." When Hugh Auld came home, his reaction was one of fury. He cursed the whole lot of those in the shipyard, but—at least as Douglass the antislavery polemicist recalled it twenty years later—he spoiled his splendid outrage by denouncing the assault as an infringement of his "rights of property."

As soon as the pain abated, he took Frederick to the nearby magistrate's office and demanded that a warrant be issued for the arrest of the four assailants. "Mr. Auld, you saw this assault of which you speak?" the magistrate asked. "It was done, sir, in the presence of a ship yard full of hands." "Sir, . . . I am sorry, but I cannot move in this matter except upon the oath of white witnesses." "But, here's the boy; look at his head and face, . . . *they* show *what* has been done."

The magistrate was firm; he "could issue no warrant on my word against white persons; if I had been killed in the presence of a *thousand blacks,* their testimony, combined, would have been insufficient to arrest a single murderer." Hugh Auld's patience with his world gave way; he—and Frederick—left, "disgusted." Douglass drew on this experience to write, in *My Bondage and My Freedom,* one of the most succinct and pungent analyses of the racist component of the capitalistic labor system in our literature: "The slaveholders, with a craftiness peculiar to themselves, by encouraging the enmity of the poor, laboring white man against the blacks, succeeds in making the said white man almost as much a slave as the black slave himself. The difference between the white slave, and the black slave, is this: the latter belongs to *one* slaveholder, and the former belongs to *all* the slaveholders, collectively. The white slave has taken from him, by indirection, what the black slave has taken from him directly, and without ceremony. Both are plundered, and by the same plunderers. The slave is robbed, by his master, of all his earnings, above what is required for his bare physical necessities; and the white man is robbed by the slave system, of the just results of his labor, because he is flung into competition with a class of laborers who work without wages. The competition, and its injurious consequences, will, one day, array the non-slaveholding white people of the slave states, against the slave system, and make them the most effective workers against the great evil. At present, the slaveholders blind them to this competition, by keeping alive their prejudice against the slaves, *as men*—not against them *as slaves.* They appeal to their pride, often denouncing emancipation, as tending to place the white working man, on an equality with negroes, and, by this means, they succeed in drawing off the minds of the poor whites from the real fact, that, by the rich slave-master, they are already regarded as but a single remove from equality with the slave. The impression is cunningly made, that slavery is the only power that can prevent the laboring white man from falling to the level of the slave's poverty and degradation. To make this enmity deep and broad, between the slave and the poor white man, the latter is allowed to abuse and whip the former, without hindrance."

At the time Douglass wrote this, in 1855, he had no idea how effectively the form of social control he described would survive the ending of slavery. When he declared that the competition was made keener by "keeping alive their prejudice against the slaves, *as men*—not against them as *slaves,*" he was discussing what we would call racism; his optimistic faith in what would be accomplished by the passage of time was misplaced.

Hugh Auld took Frederick out of Gardiner's yard after the beating, brought him back into his house—the young man had apparently been boarding out—and got him a different job. Hugh had lost his own modest shipbuilding business while Frederick was on the Eastern Shore; now, working as a foreman at Asa Price's yard, he arranged for Frederick to complete his apprenticeship there; he would then become a journeyman caulker. The arrangement was ideal except for one fact: this young man eagerly learning about the liberties of free men was helping to build at least three ships, the *Delorez,* the *Teayer,* and the *Eagle,* that were headed for the clandestine slave trade.

Swift and fine, ships like these were designed to be fast enough to elude the British naval ships that patrolled the African coast to suppress the trade. After being launched in Baltimore, with American registry, they were sailed to Cuba or Brazil, chartered to citizens of those slave countries, and sailed by their American crews to Liverpool to be fitted, secretly, with chains and other gear for the grim business. Price certainly would not have advertised that his wares were destined for such illegal and ugly usage, but as intelligent and curious a worker as Frederick Bailey could hardly have failed to find out why, for example, tanks in the bilge had to be caulked for the storage of fresh water rather than the sea water usually used for ballast and the storage areas under the deck were so shallow (though wide) that a person could barely squeeze into the space. But Douglass never made mention of the fact that the ships on which he had proudly done work were slavers.

Money has its ways. Asa Price was prospering despite the decline in the shipbuilding trade in general; Frederick Bailey, who had become one of his best workers, earned $1.50 a day as a journeyman at Price's yard or, with Hugh Auld's encouragement at whatever other yard had jobs. Accordingly, a considerable sum, as much as nine dollars, went into Hugh Auld's pocket each week, and Frederick began to think of other uses for this money. With the rising expectations of one who could imagine himself economically independent, the slave became rebellious. Contemplating that "dollar and fifty cents per day," he reflected that "I contracted for it, earned it, collected it; it was paid to me, and it was *rightfully* my own; and yet, upon every returning Saturday night, this money—my own hard earnings, every cent of it—was demanded of me, and taken from me by Master Hugh." And as he counted out the money, Auld "would look me in the face . . . and reproachfully ask me, '*Is that all?*' "

In the early spring of 1838, Thomas Auld was in Baltimore buying goods for his store, and Frederick appealed to him for the right to not only hire himself out but keep some of his pay, in return for providing his own room and board. This system was widely practiced in Baltimore. He would still be an asset owned by his master, but one in danger of getting lost in the underground of the large free black community. By hiring themselves out and taking responsibility for their own keep, slaves obtained release from a master's daily discipline. The arrangement was advantageous to masters because they continued to receive some income, but no longer had to provide shelter and food to slaves who were of little use in a changing rural economy. But these unbound bondspeople were a concern to civil authorities, who were hard put to devise alternative means of social control.

Thomas Auld said no to the proposition. He feared that Frederick, on his own in the city, would get into trouble, and feared too that kidnappers might sell him south if, as seemed likely, he tried to escape to the North. Auld did not want to lose a slave, and he did not want to lose Frederick Bailey. "He recounted, with a good deal of eloquence, the many kind offices he had done me, and exhorted me to be contented and obedient. 'Lay out no plans for the future,' said he. 'If you behave yourself properly, I will take care of you.' Now, kind and considerate as this offer was, it failed to soothe me into repose."

Rebuffed by Thomas, he waited two months, and tried the idea on Hugh. Knowing of Thomas's refusal, Hugh was astonished by Frederick's gall. But he knew, too, that Frederick was wielding real economic leverage. Reluctantly, Hugh Auld agreed to the following terms: "I was to be allowed all my time; to make all bargains for work; to find my own employment, and to collect my own wages; and, in return for this liberty, I was required, or obliged, to pay him three dollars at the end of each week, and to board and clothe myself, and buy my own calking tools." The three dollars was to be paid whether work was available that week or not.

Frederick Bailey, at twenty, was poised precariously over his future. Hugh Auld had "armed my love of liberty with a lash and a driver, far more efficient than any I had before known." He was driven to make money, not only to pay Auld and support himself, but also to reconstruct his life. He had to make enough money to buy a set of free papers (those carried by every free black person), which would allow him to assume another's identity and escape, or the far larger sum, probably at least a thousand dollars, to buy himself, if Thomas Auld would sell. More immediately, he wanted the means of entering into the life of the community that he saw other young men—free black men—engaging in.

He was both exhilarated by the prospect of being responsible for himself and frightened by the very real possibility that the arrangement would not work. In the wake of the severe economic depression of 1837, jobs in the shipyards were hard to come by, harder still to count on. Beginning in May 1838, Frederick Bailey was in an almost feverish quest for money. "In the enjoyment of excellent health," he was "ready to work by night as well as by day."

Douglass never reported what his night work or non-shipyard work may have been. Only the snippets of rumor—none of which fit with his later claim to have always sought total freedom—survive to suggest that he tried being a domestic servant. Later gossip had it that recalling Wye House and how things in a fine house were done, the articulate, handsome, light-skinned young man hired himself out as a butler in the home of John Merryman, a stockbroker, at 48 Calvert Street. One of his tasks was said to have been to conduct a Merryman child to a school described as the E. M. P. Wells School; Mrs. Elizabeth Wells, on Caroline Street, conducted such a school.

Accompanying his charge, Frederick Bailey—the story is that he was using the name "Edward" at the time, as if he did not want to accept this way of life as really his—may have gotten to know the teachers at the school. It was possibly from one of them that he learned to play the violin. (With a mimic's good ear, teaching oneself to fiddle is possible, to play Mozart, improbable.) One person whom we know encouraged him as he became a competent amateur violinist was Anna Murray, a free black woman who was working on Caroline Street. The Douglass's daughter, Rosetta Douglass Sprague, has said that her parents met at the home of a family named Wells, although in her recollections "over a space of fifty years or more" she thought her mother's employer was not

Elizabeth Wells, but Peter Wells, a postman, who lived farther along the same street. What we know with certainty is that Frederick Bailey and Anna Murray met and courted.

Frederick Douglass wrote tantalizingly little about his bride—how they met, what she was like. An unwillingness to reveal the circumstances could account for some of his reticence, but, in addition, two taboos held him back. Nineteenth-century men, living before Freud taught us to leap at every signal, could write with great openness about certain of their emotional relationships. With the words "homosexuality" and "incest" unspoken, such sexual acts, in a sense, did not exist. Douglass could therefore write openly about Henry Harris without betraying even a hint of any sexual activity that might have been a component of that friendship. Similarly, the barricade against thoughts about incest meant that Douglass could speak candidly about the remoteness or closeness of his relationship with his mother, Harriet, or his grandmother, Betsy, or even his "mother," Sophia Auld. On the other hand, so ingrained was the assumption that women were the vessels of male lust that men's affectionate relationships with women other than relatives were not talked about publicly in polite society, except in the most general terms. Any richer discussion would have led immediately to the assumption that the friendship had not been chaste. In the public view, chastity was to yield only to marriage, which was itself characterized by rigid propriety.

The result is that Douglass's books are barren of any hint about the development of his early emotional relationships with women other than relatives, real or surrogate. There must, after all, have been girls playing on the wharves as well as boys, but from his books you would not know it. And when at last a woman does appear, the account is so decorous and restrained that the effect is comical—or would be if its brevity did not so limit our understanding of a relationship of forty-four years, his marriage to Anna Murray. In the autobiographies, she is introduced—and she is the first woman other than a relative or a child that we meet— virtually as an afterthought. It is almost as if Dear Reader is told, Oh, by the way, needing money for a train ticket in order to escape, I borrowed it from a good lady; we were married a few weeks later in New York.

Anna Murray, five years Frederick's senior, was also a child of the Eastern Shore. She was born, probably in 1813, on the far side of Betsy Bailey's Tuckahoe Creek, near the town of Denton, in Caroline County. Not even the indefatigable Dickson Preston could substantiate the facts of her life, which come to us only from her daughter's sketch written after her mother's death. Reportedly, Anna's parents were Mary and Bambarra Murray, who were manumitted just a month before her birth.

Anna was the eighth of twelve children. At seventeen, she was in domestic service in Baltimore with a family named Montell; later she worked for the Wellses for several years. It was in service that she became the adept housekeeper which, proudly, she was to be for the rest of her life.

That Anna Murray and perhaps her mother—there was a Mary Murray running a cookshop on Ruxton Street in 1836—moved from the country to the city is not at all surprising. Between 1790 and 1850, the total population of Caroline County dropped from 7,028 to 6,096 and the number of slaves decreased from 2,057 to 808, while the number of free black people increased from 421 to 2,788. These statistics indicate that the number of black people in the county scarcely grew at all, but Mary and Bambarra Murray, with their twelve children, would have known full well that the population had not been static. Black people were moving to Baltimore.

In Baltimore County, the number of free black people rose during the first half of the nineteenth century by more than 3,000 percent. This increase resulted partly from the freeing of urban slaves, but far more from the migration into the city of freed country people. Slavery was no longer the valued agricultural institution that had once made the Lloyds rich. Anna Murray grew up in a city where by 1850, a decade after she left, nearly 30,000 free people of color lived alongside 175,000 white people; less than 7,000 of their neighbors were still slaves.

The free people of color lived a strange but not poorly defined existence in a world uneasily set apart from both the world of slavery and that of free white people. And yet, as Michael Johnson and James Roark have told us in *Black Masters,* their fine study of Charleston's free people of color, theirs was no island apart. They carefully emulated the mores of a white society that, however uncomfortable it may have been about the institution of slavery, was nevertheless fully committed to maintaining its own dominance as a master class. The free people of color, no matter how hard they might pretend that they did not have to, deferred to this white authority. Their relationship to their fellow blacks who were still slaves was, if anything, more troubling. Brotherly ties of sympathy conflicted with an almost desperate need to distance themselves from those still in the despised condition of bondage. The port of refuge for the free people of color in the cities of the slave South was a construct of bourgeois values, maintained with the starchiest of respectability.

The churches were the bulwark of this society. At the Bethel chapel in Fells Point (where Frederick had been converted) and the other leading black church, the Sharp Street Methodist Church in the city proper, the merits of colonization, the only scheme for ending slavery that was acceptable in a white slave-holding city, were debated much as they were by cautious people repelled by slavery in churches in the North. And like their counterparts in the North, these prudent churchgoers were cautious about too open a discussion of William Lloyd Garrison's writings in the *Liberator* or David Walker's *Appeal,* which condemned colonization and called for the freeing of slaves right then and there.

Although Frederick was a slave, these churches, as well as the rear pews of other Methodist churches, which he sometimes attended, were open to him. But, unable to find satisfaction any longer in the passionate business of faith, he seems to have drawn less sustenance from these institutions than he had when, as a young boy, he was taken to Bethel by neighbors in Happy Alley. Now the neighbors who mattered were a group of free black caulkers in Fells Point, known to him from work, who had banded together in the East Baltimore Mental Improvement Society. In this organization, typical of many formed in black urban communities—North and South—in the effort to achieve both the respectability and the true intellectual challenge denied them by white society, the ambitious young men engaged in formal debates. Frederick found his intellect stretched, and talking with the free caulkers—he was the club's only slave—he could learn what it was like to live as they did or, more cautiously, he could explore the matter of escaping. "I owe much to the society of these young men," he wrote.

Of the institutions that Americans look to for sustenance, the family is assumed to be the strongest, but Frederick, just emerging from his teen years, lived alone. Cut off from all relatives, he was denied whatever strengths the institution held. From his days with Betsy Bailey and Sophia Auld, he knew what it was to be in a family, what he was missing now. By the summer of 1838, he had in mind getting a family of his own. Since he recorded nothing of their courtship, the arrangements Frederick and Anna were making can only be guessed at. The one certainty is that they were contemplating marriage; almost immediately after he went north, she joined him and they were married. But that summer they were not up north yet.

With Anna securely placed as a domestic servant and putting some money aside out of meager wages, and with Frederick pocketing as much as six dollars a week after paying Hugh Auld, the two should have been able to set up a modest but satisfactory household. Frederick would, for a time at least, have remained a slave, but his children, as the offspring of a free woman, would have been free. Nathan Wells, one of the most remarkable leaders of the free black community, was already talking of opening a school for free black children (he did so in 1840), and the Baileys could aspire to send their children there. Articulate and, as was important now that he was an adult, economically independent, Frederick

Bailey, with his bride, could look forward to fitting into respectable black Baltimore very well indeed.

One Saturday late in the summer, Frederick had plans to go with several of his friends to a camp meeting twelve miles outside the city. These events were at least as much social as religious, and he was looking forward to the outing eagerly. That day there was an unexpected delay in the shipyard, and he did not get away in time to pay Auld before joining his friends. Grown cocky, Frederick reasoned that he could pay his master on the morrow. But he had such a good time at the camp meeting that he stayed over for another day. When he returned, two days late, he found a fiercely angry Hugh Auld who ordered him to give up his independent employment and housing and move back where Auld could keep an eye on him—and could once again take all of his earnings.

Frederick Bailey's initial impulse was to "measure strength" with Auld, as he had with Covey, but, coolly, he realized that "resistance to him could not have ended so happily for me." For one thing, Hugh Auld was brawnier than Covey, but that was not the deterrent. Frederick grasped that Auld, with a powerful temper, "was not a man to be safely resisted by a slave," and also that whether he resisted or acquiesced, all would be lost. Physical violence might lead to his being sold south immediately; almost worse, in this passionate moment, was the thought of going back into Auld's household. Being a totally bespoken slave again would mean the end of the liberties he cherished, of the chance to make up his own mind about what to do and when to do it, and the possibility of living with the woman he was going to marry. She would be right there in Baltimore, and they would probably be able to see each other often—but not to live together. No, having reached as far as he had, Bailey had not a moment's thought of going back into the slave situation into which Auld was ordering him. The Auld brothers had lifted the lid on their slave's hopes too widely ever to get it shut again. Now, he—with Anna—would run away.

The escape took three weeks to work out. Once he realized that his "insolent answers" and "sulky deportment" had made Auld suspicious that he "might be cherishing disloyal purposes," Frederick grew shrewd. He got up before dawn, went to Butler's shipyard, where he had worked satisfactorily before, got a job, and at the close of the week presented Auld with a full nine dollars. When this behavior was repeated the second week, Auld rewarded the slave with "TWENTY-FIVE CENTS! and 'bade me make good use of it!' I told him I would, for one of the uses to which I meant to put it, was to pay my fare on the underground railroad."

Partly because he deliberately omitted details that might be helpful to those trying to block escape routes, and partly because such actions carry

an aura of the romantic, the account of the escape from slavery of
Frederick Bailey and the emergence in freedom of Frederick Douglass has
a spontaneous ring. But in fact, the whole undertaking was carefully, if
hastily, planned. Half a century later, Douglass told W. H. Siebert, the
historian of the underground railroad, that he had helped other runaways
plan their escapes long before he worked out his own plan. He was fully
aware of the remarkably active network of antislavery people who helped
move fugitives along well-established routes. The first major free city
north of Baltimore was Philadelphia, and the close ties between the
African Methodist Episcopal churches in the two cities were put to use
in passing the word that a slave was coming and needed shelter or
guidance on the way. One major route went northward through New
Jersey, up the Hudson River to the Mohawk Valley, then westward to
Rochester and across Lake Ontario to Canada. Another, the one Frederick
chose, led across Long Island Sound to New England. Both, unfortunately, involved passing through New York City, known as a fertile
ground for slavecatchers.

In the privacy of the family, it was always said that Anna sold a
featherbed to finance the journey, and having suggested that Frederick
impersonate a sailor, altered his clothing to make it look like a seaman's.
Wisely, he would not try to sneak by looking nondescript and shabby;
he was never good at that. There may have been special urgency during
those tense weeks in September, when hours away from the Aulds' were
hard to find. Anna may have been pregnant. Rosetta, their first child,
whose birthday was said to be June 24, just nine months after her parents'
marriage, was tormented as a young woman with nasty innuendos about
having been conceived out of wedlock—"where was thee born, was thy
father married . . . before he left slavery?" In the 1830s in New Bedford
only a third of the births were publicly recorded, and there is no evidence
to prove or disprove the charge.

Even without such a pressing incentive, these three weeks must have
been a time of compelling tension because the risks that lay ahead were
great. When later Douglass wrote about the experience, he said with
uncharacteristic modesty that there was not "anything very heroic" about
his escape, but it was certainly the result of more than "luck." Significantly, he added that its success was "due to address rather than courage."
Actually, the escape took courage in rich measure—and logistical problems were indeed skillfully addressed. Since all free blacks, when traveling, had to carry proof that they were not slaves, he obtained the papers
of a free seaman. These may have been purchased, but they may, as he
suggested, have been a gift, and if so, a most generous one. A great many
free black people, in a world in which they risked enslavement or

reenslavement, ventured a great deal to assist runaways. Frederick had also obtained the names of white Quakers and fellow blacks who could be trusted to help him on his way once he reached the free states.

On Monday, September 3, 1838, in a red shirt, with a kerchief nonchalantly knotted around his neck, a sailor's flat-topped broad-brimmed hat on his head, and the seaman's papers in his pocket, Frederick Bailey got into a hack driven by his friend Isaac Rolls, a black man. In order to bypass the ticket window—where the papers, which described a man far different in appearance, would be carefully checked—they waited outside the railroad station until just before the train to Wilmington was to pull out. Then the cab raced up to the train and stopped alongside the colored car. (Rolls knew where it would be.) His bag in hand, the seaman jumped aboard just as the train started.

The car was crowded and the train was going fast, "but to my anxious mind, it was moving far too slowly," Douglass recalled. "Minutes were hours, and hours were days." They were nearly to Havre de Grace when the conductor came into the car to take tickets. "The heart of no fox or deer, with hungry hounds . . . in full chase, could have beaten more anxiously or noisily than did mine"; and the runaway could only rely on the "jostle of the train, and the natural haste of the conductor," in a train crowded with passengers. But here was another reason why the disguise had been chosen; he was banking on the "kind feeling which prevailed in Baltimore, and other seaports at the time, towards 'those who go down to the sea in ships.'" The expert mimic had not caulked ships or walked the wharves for nothing: "I knew a ship from stem to stern, and from keelson to cross-trees, and could talk sailor like an 'old salt.'"

As terrified as "a murderer fleeing from justice," Frederick Bailey watched the conductor's gruff encounters with the other black passengers, only to find that he brightened when he turned to the sailor: "I suppose you have your free papers?" The runaway replied boldly, "No, sir; I never carry my free papers to sea with me," and pulled out the seaman's papers. The American eagle at the top of them caught the conductor's eye, rather than the description below, of another man; taking "my fare" (probably cash, or else someone had bought a ticket for him), he commented to Frederick that he was "all right," and "went on about his business."

But the fugitive was not home free yet. At Havre de Grace, he boarded a ferry to cross the Susquehanna River, and on the boat encountered a Baltimore acquaintance, a black deckhand, who insisted on asking about where he was going and why. Frederick ducked out of that conversation as quickly as he could. Then, as he again boarded a northbound train, he looked across at the southbound train waiting a few feet on the next track. A ship's captain who frequented the shipyard where Frederick had worked was looking out the window with a blank stare, and did not see Frederick, whom he would have recognized as a slave. Then there was the "German blacksmith, whom I knew well," who gave Frederick the intense look of one reaching for a name—and then looked away: "I really believe he knew me, but had no heart to betray me."

At Wilmington, Delaware, still in slave country, he had to change again, to a steamboat for Philadelphia. Arriving in the free city, he did not tarry, even though he knew that many black members of the underground-railroad community, and a goodly number of white Quakers, were in the city. Directed by a black porter—no profession has done more for the mobility of black America than his—Frederick Bailey went straight on to a ferry, the night train, and a final ferry to New York.

His first morning as a free man was one of sharp contrasts. Walking from the ferry, he found himself "amid the hurrying throng, and gazing upon the dazzling wonders of Broadway," and he thought the "dreams of my childhood and the purposes of my manhood were now fulfilled. A free state around me, and a free earth under my feet! What a moment was this to me! A whole year was pressed into a single day. A new world burst upon my agitated vision." He found the "sensations . . . too intense and too rapid for words." He "was A FREEMAN" and was at peace.

Suddenly, he saw a familiar face; it was Jake—Allender's Jake—from Baltimore, on his way to work with his whitewasher's pail. But when Frederick greeted his fellow Baltimorean, he found that this free man, calling himself William Dixon now, was a defeated individual. Barely willing to speak, Jake brushed the bewildered newcomer aside, saying "it was not in his power to help me" and "I must trust no man with my secret." Jake, who had narrowly escaped being sent back to slavery, warned Frederick that slaveowners hired men of "my own color . . . for a few dollars" to spot runaways. Frederick, he insisted, must not go into any "colored boarding-house, for all such places were closely watched," nor onto the wharves in search of work. Close to terror, Douglass later recalled, "in the midst of thousands of my own brethren—children of a common Father . . . I was afraid to speak to any one for fear of speaking to the wrong one." And "a sense of my loneliness and helplessness crept over me."

His well-knit plans were unraveling. Frederick was supposed to go to the house of David Ruggles, on the corner of Lispenard and Church streets. Ruggles was the head of the Vigilance Committee, a group organized to usher fugitives north and to try to protect them while in the city. But presumably, after his encounter with Allender's Jake, Frederick trusted no one and was afraid to ask for directions.

That night, his second in freedom, he crawled behind some barrels stacked outside a wharf to sleep. The next day, hungry but still unwilling to ask for directions, he wandered the streets. Although he did not know it, he was close to Ruggles's house when, standing outside the newest and grimmest monument in town—the Tombs, the jail, with its Egyptian gates into hell—he looked across Centre Street and saw a sailor. Their eyes met, and the sailor, whose name turned out to be Stuart, came toward the stranger. "Compelled at last to seek some one who should befriend me," Frederick risked everything and "ventured a remark." Stuart responded—and took his new friend home for the night. The next day, knowing where to go, as any true ally of a runaway would, Stuart walked with him the four blocks to Ruggles's house.

David Ruggles, the remarkable, stalwart friend of all runaways, welcomed the Baltimorean. Once comfortably inside the Reading Room, as Ruggles called the headquarters of the Vigilance Committee, Frederick sat down to complete his plan. He chose "Frederick Johnson" as his new name and wrote Anna to join him in New York. The smoothness of Anna's trip north is further proof that their plan had been well crafted. She would have had free papers, but being illiterate, she must have been instructed carefully on how to negotiate the three trains and four boats that lay between the bride in Baltimore and the groom in New York. With Anna in a "new plum colored silk dress" and Frederick in the good suit that he had carried in his seaman's bag, the two were married by James W. C. Pennington, another Maryland runaway (he too was from the Eastern Shore), then just beginning his career as a Presbyterian minister and militant advocate of black equality. In the presence of David Ruggles and one other witness, the Reverend Mr. Pennington, as he recorded it, "joined together in holy matrimony Frederick Johnson and Anna Murray, as man and wife." With the preacher's certificate in hand and five dollars from Ruggles in his pocket, Frederick "shouldered one part of our baggage and Anna took up the other." The two set off for New England and forty-four years of marriage.

7

New Bedford

THE TWO words proclaimed bright promise. "New Bedford," written "in large yellow letters" on the side of the stagecoach that pulled up to the wharf in Newport, Rhode Island, was read aloud by the young man still as excited by the magic of words as he had been when he mastered the street signs of Baltimore. He and his bride had been told to look up a friend of Ruggles's in Newport if they lacked enough money to complete their trip, but they wanted to get right into this coach and go. As Frederick troubled over the fare, which he could not cover, an impressively somber man standing next to the coach looked him straight in the eye and "in a peculiarly quiet way, . . . said, 'Thee get in.'" Frederick and Anna obeyed.

Not by coincidence, William C. Taber, who spoke the welcome order, and another Quaker gentleman, Joseph Ricketson—the two were recognizable for their calling by their clothing's drabness, for their position by its fineness—also boarded the coach. Ruggles, in arranging for them to conduct the fugitives, had chosen wisely. Ricketson, though not as successful a businessman as Friends are proverbially supposed to be, was a leader in all manner of good works and intellectual endeavors in New Bedford, Massachusetts, while Taber was the proprietor of a thriving bookstore and a director of a private library society, with 3,200 volumes.

The coach stopped at Stone Bridge for breakfast, but Frederick and Anna skipped the meal, and when asked for their fares, they said they "would make it right" upon reaching New Bedford. When at last they drew up to the hotel in that bright, energetic city, their happiness was shadowed: with the fare still unpaid, the driver held their baggage,

At the wharf in Newport. From *Life and Times,* 1881.

including, to indelible memory, "three music books—two of them collections by Dyer, and one by Shaw." Ricketson and Taber, reassuring once again, sent them up Union Street to Seventh, and over to the corner of Spring, to the home of the man whom Ruggles had directed them to seek out. Unencumbered, the couple walked past fresh frame houses steady on formidable granite foundations, and divided from their neighbors by walks leading into neat gardens blurred with the yellows and lavenders of late-summer daisies and asters. In less than ten minutes, Anna and Frederick reached 21-23 Seventh Street, the large, double-doored house of Mary and Nathan Johnson, which had once been the Friends' meetinghouse.

The Johnsons were a remarkable couple; Mary Page Johnson, in her early fifties and ten years older than her husband, ran a confectionary shop in half the house and, more to the financial point, was the ranking caterer in well-fed New Bedford. The trade of Nathan Johnson, ebullient and gregarious, was listed in the city directory as "c. confectionary," but his labors were principally outside the kitchen, as he strove to build connections from the black community to the white. Johnson was the only African American member of Taber's library society; in its reading room (located in the Lyceum, whose lecture hall was closed to him), he sat in the company of the Rotches, the Rodmans, and other merchants of the whaling industry that had made New Bedford the richest city, per capita, in America.

Ironically, there was little meeting of the races in the Friends' handsome new meetinghouse, possibly because of its intimacy and austerity. (Sarah Mapps Douglass, a prominent black Quaker in Philadelphia forced to sit on a blacks-only bench in the Arch Street Friends Meetinghouse, had a different explanation: "I believe they despise us for our color.") But the Quakers, committed staunchly both to eradicating slavery as a sin against the free soul of man and to building great earthly fortunes, had made New Bedford, with its flourishing whaling industry, particularly attractive to black families in the 1780s, when the abolition of slavery in Massachusetts made that state seem more hospitable than nearby Rhode Island. In prospering New Bedford, as in the Quaker port towns of Salem and Nantucket, the commitment to equality of opportunity was strong enough to encourage people to develop self-confidence.

Elsewhere, free black people were forced to live on the margin of society, with the patterns of their activities largely derived from those of white people, to whom they deferred. The black people of New Bedford too were on occasion subject to discrimination and expected to show deference, but they had nevertheless achieved a measure of societal and psychological independence that made New Bedford the best city in America for an ambitious young black man.

When Anna and Frederick arrived, the town had a population of 12,354, of whom 1,051 were black. Not surprisingly in a port town with a highly transient population, two-thirds of the black people were men. One of the area's earlier sea captains and whaling merchants, Paul Cuffe, was himself black, and the legacy of his success, never fully repeated, lingered. Nathan Johnson held his head high, and so, that afternoon, did Frederick Bailey—or rather, as he now had to remember to call himself, Frederick Johnson. Borrowing two dollars from his host to pay his fare and retrieve his baggage, he strolled out, alone, to have a look at the town.

The streets and wharves of New Bedford were a study in a political economy very different from the one in which he had been so thoroughly schooled. In his *Narrative of the Life of Frederick Douglass* he stated, "I was quite disappointed in New Bedford"; the words he would seem to have wanted were "surprised by," but a bit of Baltimore snobbery, impossible to shuck, broke through into his prose. He was, perhaps, surprised and a little disappointed that this New England city could be prettier and more prosperous than his Baltimore. He had had "no proper idea of the wealth, refinement, enterprise, and high civilization of this section"; he had been "taught that slavery was the bottom-fact of all wealth" and had concluded, therefore, that "poverty must be the general condition of the people of the free states. A white man holding no slaves in the country from where I came, was usually an ignorant and poverty-stricken man." Now, as the former slave looked around him at "solid wealth and grandeur, . . . I found that even the laboring classes lived in better houses . . . more abundantly supplied with conveniences and comforts, than the houses of many who owned slaves on the Eastern Shore."

Back at the Johnsons', Anna and Frederick slept in a bed that night, the first they had been in since their marriage. Anna was a full-lipped, ample woman. Her skin was deeper and richer in color than Frederick's, and her eyes were softer and wittier than his, which seldom relaxed their watchful intensity. In a brilliant, probing essay, rich with ideas, the literary scholar Peter F. Walker has suggested that Frederick Douglass, forced to achieve greatness in a white society, engaged in a fundamental effort to escape from his blackness, from his African physiognomy—that he was pleased when, a few years later, as a young abolitionist, he was able to "forget that my skin was dark and my hair crisped." This analysis of Douglass invites critical examination on many levels, but on one basic level it is certainly flawed. There was no such repudiation in that New Bedford bedroom.

Over a breakfast of Mary Johnson's that can be assumed to have been excellent enough to make up for those the travelers had missed, Nathan Johnson, who himself came from Virginia, instructed the newcomers on both the practical problems faced by runaway slaves and the possibilities open to free black people in the North. He assured them that the local abolitionists were committed to preventing anyone in town from being returned to slavery. There was evidence that he was correct. Black churchgoers, using the pretext of a special meeting, had once lured into their church a man they knew to be an informer, and once they had him safely inside, told him that if ever again he tried to ply his ugly trade in New Bedford, they would kill him. He exited through an open window. White antislavery activists were equally determined. In one cliff-hanger of a case, when heirs of a slaveholder tried by subterfuge to get back a freed woman, the best of lawyers were hired and none-too-pacific Quakers guarded the house in which she was staying. The New Bedford abolitionists were prepared to defy the law if the court failed her (it did not), and take her to Canada.

This support was reassuring to Frederick, who had already taken the precaution of changing his name to elude identification. But the name he had chosen caused amused consternation at breakfast. It was perhaps a little too familiar, in a town with a full page of Johnsons in its directory; indeed, the new couple had by chance taken the name of the people who were now their sponsors. Nathan proposed another; the two men must already have confessed to their fondness for literature, for the host suggested to Frederick that a more heroic name could be drawn from Walter Scott's *Lady of the Lake*. Frederick, without looking to see what Douglas was up to in the poem, or how the name was spelled, liked its sound. With astonishing casualness, he gave himself the name, spelled as prominent black families in Baltimore and Philadelphia spelled it, that became one of the nineteenth century's most famous. Frederick Douglass now, he would never again be Frederick Bailey. Even when it would have been safe to do so, he did not reclaim Betsy's or old Baly's name.

Sounds had always mattered to Frederick, discordant ones as well as mellifluous. What he most vividly remembered about his first walks along the New Bedford wharves was that the free laborers spoke with quiet, republican self-confidence. There were "no loud songs heard from those engaged in loading and unloading ships. I heard no deep oaths or horrid curses." And there was no snap of leather: "Every man appeared to understand his work, and went at it with a sober, yet cheerful earnestness." Gangs of slave laborers working at tough, long jobs like loading lumber onto ships often, as they moved in unison, sang or chanted songs that simultaneously kept their work in rhythm and shouted mocking defiance of those who owned them and forced them to work. The very act of singing was a means of survival, even as its message was one of lamentation. Douglass had heard such "loud songs" on the docks of Baltimore and had been troubled by them. His appreciation of the silence of the New Bedford docks was private; he found it a welcome respite from the haunting dirges that reminded him, almost unbearably, of slavery's relentlessness.

Each free Northern worker, he thought, had a "sense of his dignity as a man." From the dignity of his position as a leading antislavery orator and editor, Douglass reported in *Life and Times of Frederick Douglass* that he soon "put on the clothes of a common laborer" and went down to the docks to try to join those men at work. These clothes, he was telling us, were inappropriate to their wearer. Perhaps he meant that they were not the clothes of the skilled journeyman caulker he knew himself to be, or perhaps, exhilarated by the self-reliance he observed in the workers of this free town, the twenty-year-old did not see himself as a laborer at all.

But he did have a living to make. The first dollar—"two silver half-dollars"—that he did not have to turn over to Hugh Auld (or feel guilty about keeping back) was earned shoveling a pile of coal into the Unitarian minister's cellar. It was lavish pay, and he was triumphant as he put the money in his pocket, but not all such encounters were as heartening. Well-cut wood was needed on the whalers for the fires under the great pots of fat that had to be boiled down, and Frederick borrowed a saw from Nathan Johnson so he could look for this work. While buying a length of cord to brace the saw, he used a Maryland expression that betrayed him as a stranger—perhaps a runaway. The store clerk was blunt: "You don't belong about here," but beyond glowering, he did nothing about his suspicion, and Douglass took his saw and went to work.

He wanted a better job than woodcutting, however, and set his sights on joining the ranks of the skilled laborers that he had observed. "Young . . . , strong, and active, and ambitious to do my full share," he got a job as a caulker in Rodney French's boatyard. (French was not as "distinguished . . . an antislavery man" as Douglass thought; he once fitted a boat to be a slaver, only to have the workmen on the job alert the Coast Guard that the ballast casks held not the usual salt water, which would not rot them, but fresh water for a human cargo, and the ship was seized as it was clearing the harbor.) Now Douglass would be practicing the skill he had learned in Baltimore and making two dollars a day, twice what he could earn with the back-straining work, miscalled manual labor, that he had been doing. But when he got to where the boat was cradled, he was "told that every white man would leave the ship . . . unfinished . . . if I struck a blow at my trade upon her." This proscription, pronounced not by a worker but by a foreman, did not extend to the unskilled work of hauling heavy fittings. Having been taught a lesson about bigotry in the free North, Douglass took the dollar-a-day job.

More day-labor jobs followed: "I sawed wood, shoveled coal, dug cellars, moved rubbish from back-yards, worked on the wharves, loaded and unloaded vessels, and scoured their cabins." The Douglasses were desperately poor the first winter. There was little work then for a male day laborer, and Anna, pregnant, was not working. In the spring, the docks grew busy and jobs were plentiful. For a time, Frederick worked the bellows in Richmond's brass foundry. Finally, he reached out again to the Quaker merchants and obtained a steady job with set wages in the whale-oil refinery of one of his companions on the coach, Joseph Ricketson. Moving the casks of oil "required good wind and muscle," which, Douglass proudly remembered, he had in full measure. He felt pride in his body as he gained the respect of his fellow "all white" workers: "I soon made myself useful, and I think liked by the men who worked with me."

Douglass was laid off during one slack time, but he soon found even more congenial employment on George Howland's wharf. Howland was "a hard driver, but a good paymaster," and Douglass liked him. Better still was the friendship of three men, John Briggs, Abraham Rodman, and Solomon Peneton, who worked with him there on the fitting of the whaling ships *Java* and *Golconda.* Douglass made it clear in his last autobiography, *Life and Times,* that his conversations with these men "imbued with the spirit of liberty" were important to him. Thinking back to those talks, however, he recorded not some affectionate moment of the men's interaction, but rather the lesson that he claimed to have learned from the three: "that all colored men are not light-hearted trifles, incapable of serious thought or effort." The contempt of Douglass half a century later for "working men," his amazement at finding them to be "intelligent," is as dismaying as his description of himself uncomfortably wearing "the clothes of a common laborer." The three men are not mentioned in his 1845 and 1855 accounts of his life in New Bedford, so it is difficult to know if there was any of this snobbish distancing of himself from black workingmen—from all workingmen—on Howland's wharf.

There may have been. Douglass walked apart. It is intriguing to speculate about the degree to which others took Douglass into account, while he took in all that was around him in New Bedford. His walks through New Bedford's few streets and onto its wharves, crowded along the short waterfront, were taken in the quiet of a world instructively set apart from the noise of slavery. There are no descriptions of chance encounters. It is intriguing to imagine the meeting that could so easily have taken place with that other prowler of New Bedford, Herman Melville. The novelist came to know the streets and wharves that he evoked so splendidly in the opening passages of *Moby-Dick* in the same months that Douglass was walking them daily. In 1841, the year Douglass was to make a short, fateful voyage to Nantucket, Melville crossed the narrow New Bedford harbor to Fairhaven and signed aboard the ship *Acushnet* for four years. It is pure conjecture, but not implausible, to imagine two of the nineteenth century's most striking men catching sight of each other one clear day in New Bedford.

The four men working on Howland's wharf and talking of liberty did know each other. All were married, or about to be. John Briggs had married Fanny Bassett in 1831, Frederick had married Anna in 1838, and Abraham Rodman had married Charlotte Wamsley the year following, while Solomon Peneton followed suit perhaps a bit later. One can easily imagine the four couples sharing the deadly serious, comic business of setting up families, but if they did, Douglass did not tell us about it; his autobiographies include almost nothing about his domestic life.

Children are born; dates are given—Rosetta on June 24, 1839, and Lewis Henry sixteen months later on October 9, 1840—but we are told little about the events. Except for its prettiness, there is no accounting for the name "Rosetta," nor is there any explanation for "Lewis"; "Henry," on the other hand, had been chosen four times in four generations of Frederick's family and was also the name of his closest (and lost) friend, Henry Harris.

Frederick and Anna Douglass seemed to be settling permanently into New Bedford's black community. Initially, maintaining his commitment to the Methodist church, Frederick attended the predominantly white Elm Street Methodist Church, even though he had to sit in the gallery. But one Sunday, having come downstairs and waited while the white communicants took the sacrament, he saw how the unctuous Reverend Isaac Bonney, looking toward "the corner where his black sheep seemed penned," called them forward separately and condescendingly. Thomas Auld's hypocrisy seemed on display once more.

Frederick then turned far in the other direction; he was drawn to the "deep piety" and the "high intelligence" of the Reverend William Serrington at New Bedford's Zion chapel, a congregation in the African Methodist Episcopal Zion denomination, founded by black Methodists in New York City late in the eighteenth century. The Zionists, like their fellow, and sometimes rival, Methodists in the African Methodist Episcopal Church, had broken away from the white Methodist churches because they were relegating blacks to back pews and generally and increasingly

making them unwelcome. The Zion chapel, which held its meetings in
a schoolhouse on Second Street, was to be the Douglass family's anchor
in New Bedford: "the days I spent in little Zion, New Bedford, in the
several capacities of sexton, steward, class leader, clerk, and local preacher,
. . . [were] among the happiest days of my life."

At Zion, Douglass met Bishop Christopher Rush, who gave him
"authority to act as an exhorter," and in 1840, there arrived at the little
church a remarkable new preacher, Thomas James. Born a slave in
Canajoharie, in upstate New York, in 1804, James was eight when his
family was divided for sale and his mother was dragged from the attic
in which she was hiding and forced onto a horse, to be taken away from
her children. James never saw her again. When he was seventeen, his
master was killed by a runaway horse, and James was among the assets
of the estate distributed to the heirs. Still later he "was bartered in
exchange for a yoke of steers, a colt and some additional property"; at
that point, he ran away, and for a time he supported himself by digging
canals and chopping wood. Eventually he reached Buffalo; he was working in a warehouse there when he discovered a Sabbath school for young
black men. He learned to read with that group and became a member of
a Methodist church in 1823; ten years later he was ordained a minister
in the African Methodist Episcopal Zion Church by Bishop Rush.

He was also already deeply involved in antislavery activity and at
several meetings in upstate New York towns was beaten for his outspoken
speeches. In 1833, he moved to Rochester. There he was the pastor of a
Zion chapel, and as part of his antislavery activities, helped edit a fort-
nightly, *The Rights of Man*. From 1835 on, he combined his labors as
pastor and as missionary of antislavery, organizing churches in Syracuse
and Ithaca in upstate New York, and in Sag Harbor, Long Island, and
finally moving to New Bedford, Massachusetts.

In his new church, James was deeply impressed by his young parish-
ioner's talks to the congregation and "licensed him to preach." Established
as a lay preacher, Douglass was beautifully positioned to be a leader in
the honorable, relatively safe, correct black community of New Bedford.
By 1841, the Douglasses had moved from a small house in the rear of 157
Elm Street into a larger house at 111 Ray Street. Secure employment,
even of an almost dignified sort, could be counted on in the prosperous
town, which provided schools for black children. The Douglasses already
had two; by the summer of 1841 a third was on the way. Anna had her
garden, Frederick his violin on which to play the Handel, Haydn, and
Mozart in the music books he had brought with him. This was a world,
shorn of slavery, not unlike the one Anna had been a part of in Baltimore,
a world into which she fit comfortably. Her husband, already respected

in the black community, could have reasonably aspired to being the second African American member of the library society. The Douglasses had the makings of an exemplary American family, one that was getting on well.

But soon Douglass was restless for something more than the respectability of black New Bedford. The churches not only gave their members religious nourishment but also provided them with the opportunities to raise their confidence by talking together of both personal and public concerns—moral improvement, it was called. Temperance, attractive less for its assault on alcoholism than as a mark of respectability, one accepted by proper white middle-class neighbors, was among the chief of the public concerns. So was antislavery, but many proper black church groups shunned it as too controversial.

This refusal to face what he knew from experience to be an evil troubled Douglass. On the one hand, he was eager to put his slave past behind him; on the other, he was aware that slavery was his story, and he was eager to tell it. Thomas James, who had always seen his own religious work and antislavery work as inseparably joined, urged him to do likewise. Douglass had already done just that, if a bit cautiously. On March 12, 1839, at a church meeting where the respectable subject of colonization was being debated, Douglass had risen and, assailing the idea of shipping slaves to Africa, had spoken of what slavery was like and why slaves should be set free, right here in America.

If making the speech, had felt good, reading the notice of it in William Lloyd Garrison's *Liberator* may have been even more exhilarating. With this brief item, the world took note of Frederick Douglass. At another meeting, attended largely by white antislavery New Bedford people, Thomas James was making an address when he spotted Douglass in the audience, and he called on him to "relate his story." This time Douglass did not simply assail colonization, but told of his own experiences as a slave.

People listened as Douglass spoke, and soon he, in turn, heard the most famous of all antislavery leaders. On April 16, 1839, William Lloyd Garrison spoke before an integrated audience in Mechanics Hall. Puffy-mouthed, sharp-nosed, balding, bespectacled Garrison had no right to be the charismatic figure that he was. But his voice was strong and passionately earnest; nearly half a century later, Douglass remembered seeing before him that rainy April evening "a young man of singularly pleasing countenance," and he heard a voice he could not forget.

William Lloyd Garrison, after his conversion to the antislavery cause by Benjamin Lundy, had become the leader of the abolitionists. He had published the first issue of the *Liberator* on January 1, 1831, and that year he was instrumental in founding the Massachusetts Anti-Slavery Society and the New England Anti-Slavery Society.

Garrison focused squarely on slavery, and unequivocally he said it was wrong. He ignored anti-abolitionist scoffings about his being a nigger lover; he paid no more attention to the feelings of antislavery people in his audience, who were often less cognizant of their black neighbors in the North than of the distant existence of black slaves in the South, and who usually failed to see the connection between the two. To make such people comfortable, some antislavery speakers, such as Edmund Quincy, unattractively and unsuccessfully tried for the common touch by making jokes about black people. Garrison ignored what to him were extraneous matters. He sought nothing less than a perfect world, and on his way toward his goal, he was determined to remove one of its greatest imperfections, human slavery. Douglass, always alert to any racial slur, was powerfully drawn to Garrison's focused attention on a fixed star of evil.

When Douglass had been in New Bedford only a few months, an agent for the *Liberator* persuaded the financially strapped workman to accept a trial subscription—free. No door-to-door salesman ever made a better deal for his employer. "I was," Douglass wrote, "brought in contact with the mind of William Lloyd Garrison."

Douglass was far from the only black person in New Bedford reading the *Liberator* or working against slavery. In 1837, Nathan Johnson had been chosen by a group of his black contemporaries to serve on a committee to screen candidates for the state legislature, ascertaining the extent of their allegiance to the movement, and in Worcester in October 1840, Johnson and Garrison were among the two hundred abolitionists crowded into a Methodist church—the only hall open to them—for the annual meeting of the Massachusetts Anti-Slavery Society. Douglass had ample opportunity to learn about the workings of this society, and to absorb gossip about its energetic, diverse members, from Johnson and a good many of his other New Bedford neighbors. He listened to everything but it was Garrison who made the difference.

In Garrison, that April night in 1839, Douglass had found what he himself would become. He would be an orator—not a playacting orator, privately declaiming the great speeches of other men learned from *The Columbian Orator,* but a man speaking out for himself. And he had his subject. It was not salvation or any other unsatisfying, and very likely hypocritical, preacher-man's subject—but slavery, which he knew to be a moral, public wrong, and which at the same time, in the deepest possible way, he hated personally.

Unlike Thomas James, Douglass found that he could not marry the two religions, Christianity and antislavery, though one led to the other:

"My association with the excellent men . . . [who preached at the New Bedford Zion chapel] helped to prepare me for the wider sphere of usefulness which I have since occupied. It was from this Zion church that I went forth to the work of delivering my brethren from bondage, and this new vocation, which separated me from New Bedford, . . . separated me also from the calling of a local preacher." Soon after he took to the field for antislavery, he wrote a candid letter to his fellow communicants of the Zion chapel, saying, as James reported, that he had had to "cut loose from the church" because he had found the American church, writ large, to be a "bulwark of American slavery." His affection for the chapel that had been his and Anna's never faltered, but Frederick Douglass was now committed to a new faith, one for which he would speak the word.

Hearing the man he now took as his mentor, Douglass looked down at himself: the body he saw was strong, and he knew his mind was as well; his voice was deep and clear. Garrison's words—"I will be heard"—could have been his. In the spring of 1841, at an antislavery meeting in his Zion chapel, Douglass was again speaking out against that evil. From his own experience, he told his neighbors what slavery had been like. In the congregation that evening was a white man, William C. Coffin, a book-keeper in the Merchants Bank, a trustee of the Social Library, whose rooms were above the bank on Water Street, a Quaker, and a member of the vast Coffin family of Nantucket. A staunch abolitionist, Coffin thought that a good many people ought to hear what the beautifully spoken, earnest young black man had to say.

8

Nantucket

FREDERICK called it his "holiday." Alone, away from his wife and two infant children, from the preachers, from the neighbors who, with some skepticism, had been watching him edging into his new calling, Frederick Douglass was on the steam packet to Nantucket. Once again he was crossing a beautifully shored stretch of coastal water, headed for a new beginning. Moving from the heat of town out into the glare that lay over the water, he sat on the deck, leaning into any breeze that reached him from the sea. His holiday was not solely hedonistic; it had to have moral purpose, and it surely did. He was on his way to a well-advertised camp meeting, one at which the business would be not the salvation of individual souls, but the rescue from slavery of people like him.

The Massachusetts Anti-Slavery Society was conducting a great midsummer meeting in one of the strongholds of abolition, the beautiful island of Nantucket. Its port, also called Nantucket, was a startlingly big and busy city, where great whaling fortunes had been made; the streets were gaudy with prosperity. As visitors left the dock and turned up Main Street, they passed the handsome brick customhouse, and walking up the steep first reach of the street, encountered the formidable Pacific Bank, standing guard over the splendid accounts of the shipowners who lived over its right shoulder on the hill behind. These brick mansions faced the street with a fresh and handsome dignity unsurpassed anywhere in America and allowed their proud owners to survey, from upstairs windows, the energetic harbor and the broad reaches of sea beyond.

Frederick Douglass, of course, had not come as a chance visitor. Nantucket, long the home of Quakers committed to the antislavery cause, had spawned perhaps the most remarkable antislavery family in the land, the prosperous, prolific Coffins. One of the clan, William C. Coffin, was the New Bedford bookkeeper who had urged Frederick to make the trip. Now, when Coffin spotted the young black man among the people walking in from the packet, he made his way through the crowd to welcome him, defying the unwritten rule of social separation of the races. As they walked along, Coffin invited him to rise in the meeting and, in the tradition of the Friends, to speak if it seemed right to him to do so. Coffin had already alerted the organizers of the meeting that the remarkable young runaway might be so moved.

Originally the meeting was to have been held in the Atheneum. But the trustees of Nantucket's elegant cultural meetinghouse became uneasy when word reached them that a flood of off-islanders could be expected, who practiced women's equality and God only knew what else and whose agitation for the freeing of African laborers in the far-off, benighted South seemed only to arouse dangerous people in the North (who might attack their valuable property). When the trustees learned in addition that two hundred people from Guinea, the black section of town, had been invited, and that a black speaker was to be imported for the occasion, they withdrew their permission for use of the hall. The meeting was then moved to the Big Shop, a solid, square building sheathed in weathered shingles that was owned by Reuben and George Coffin. Standing high up at the far end of town, just short of the Quaker cemetery, it was large enough for the crafting of harpooners' boats—or for a good crowd of slavery's enemies.

On the evening of Monday, August 16, 1841, Douglass, with Coffin and a "body guard" of loyal antislavery islanders that included Anna Gardner (the secretary of the local antislavery chapter) and several other young women, made his way inland to Nathaniel and Eliza Barney's house and then to the meeting. As the faithful were going through the stately ritual of convening, Quaker workingmen patrolled the perimeter of the Big Shop to warn away any who might disrupt the meeting. People from Guinea who had not gotten into the crowded building looked in through the windows; legs dangled from the twelve-by-twelve rafters and lofts where the nimble had found seats. Several of the great luminaries of the American Anti-Slavery Society were to be seen at the front of the congregation: Garrison—*"the Reformer* of this age," Lucretia Coffin Mott called him—and Wendell Phillips, the patrician orator whom some thought greater than Garrison, and a host of other abolitionist leaders, including Parker Pillsbury, Edmund Quincy, and John A. Collins, the society's general agent (executive director). It was a reflection of the local racial tensions that Garrison's opening resolution condemned not slavery directly, but the "cherishing and defending" in the North of "a cruel injustice against those whose skins are not colored like our own." Such attitudes, he claimed, were "putting arguments into the mouths of the Southern task-masters, and acting as the body-guard of slavery."

The resolution offered, it was seconded in speeches by local antislavery people as well as the famous visitors. The process was tedious, and while the decorous Quakers who made up most of the audience were patiently restrained, the boys and young men up on the rafters shifted their weight impatiently. Restless, too, for a different reason, was another young man in the audience. The summer evening's light was failing as Frederick sat summoning his courage to rise, to speak. It was a moment of great importance, of great emotion, for him when finally he did so. Everyone in the room strained to make out the chiseled features of the young man's face and to hear his words, which, in his unease, he was stammering. Some later recalled that he had been confused; others spoke of his embarrassment. He himself said in retrospect that of the hundreds of speeches he had made, it was the only one from which he could "not remember a single connected sentence."

His first phrases were the apologies of the novice, but then all that he had taught himself with *The Columbian Orator,* all that he had had within him from the start, poured forth. The Quaker quiet of the room was cut through with an electricity of excitement that everyone from twelve-year-old Phebe Ann Coffin to her most somber, senior relative would never forget. With intense concentration, these New Englanders heard Frederick telling them about his life. It was the story of a runaway slave, yes, but it was *his* story. He was telling it, he was calling himself into being, and people—people he had never seen before, white people, important people—were listening.

There are several accounts of this, Frederick Douglass's first great public speech. Samuel J. May, a Unitarian minister active in many reform movements, including abolition, spoke of its "intellectual power" and its "wisdom as well as wit," but other reports of the talk, including Douglass's own, focused less on what he said than on the response to it by Garrison. The great orator was never more eloquent as, deeply moved by Frederick's passionate words, he rose when the compelling young man had finished. "Have we been listening to a thing, a chattel personal, or a man?" he asked. "A man! a man!" the audience shouted "with one accord." "Shall such a man be held a slave in a Christian land?" called out Garrison. Anna Gardner, who was to be Douglass's loyal friend for the rest of their long lives, remembered the whole scene: " 'No! No!' shouted the audience. Raising his voice to its fullest note, he again asked, 'Shall such a man ever be sent back to bondage from the free soil of old

Massachusetts?' With a tremendous roar the whole assembly sprang to its feet and continued shouting, 'No! No! No!' " Garrison's voice was lost in their vehemence.

Garrison had made himself a master of antislavery propaganda. Early on, he had abandoned his initial espousal of colonization, with its goal of sending back to Africa people generations away from that homeland, and demanded instead the immediate and total ending of slavery; soon he was denouncing the more conservative advocates of colonization with almost the passion that he poured forth in his denunciations of the slaveholders. Having led in the organization of the Massachusetts Anti-Slavery Society and the New England Anti-Slavery Society in 1831, he joined with others equally committed to ending slavery, in New York and Philadelphia, to form the American Anti-Slavery Society in 1833. Under this umbrella, the state and regional organizations worked to force the nation to recognize slavery's evil. In time, some abolitionists espoused strategies different from those of Garrison and the Bostonians of the Massachusetts Anti-Slavery Society, who always saw themselves as the truest believers.

Nowhere was there greater use of evangelical fervor to gain converts to the cause than among the Garrisonians. Frederick Douglass was not the first former slave to be brought forward to arouse concern for his brothers and sisters, but this night on Nantucket, it was clear that a powerful new voice had been raised, one that demonstrated how high a former slave could stretch in a demonstration of his humanity.

As he sat there in the Big Shop, surrounded by standing, cheering champions, Frederick knew a triumph so intense, so total, that he would spend his entire life seeking to sustain it. He had spoken, he had been heard. What was more, the man in the world he most admired, "taking me as his text," had spoken words "of unequaled power, sweeping down, like a very tornado, every opposing barrier." And great men pressed forward to shake his hand—Garrison, Phillips, knew him, and he knew them. Never again would he be anonymous. He met Parker Pillsbury, who would be his friend for the rest of his life. John A. Collins, at the close of the meeting, capped it all with an invitation to him to become an agent of the Massachusetts Anti-Slavery Society and go out on the lecture circuit to tell the world of his experiences as a slave. A great career in the antislavery movement was born that evening, but no one, not even Douglass, has told us how the young man felt.

As the crowd finally left the Big Shop, Frederick, Edward J. Pompey (the local subscription agent for the *Liberator*), and the rest of the black people made their way back to the cluster of small houses, hugging the African Baptist Church, in Guinea, where Frederick must have spent the night. How he could have denied himself—while tormenting us—the satisfaction of telling of that night in his reminiscences is a mystery far greater than how he summoned the courage to make his speech. Guinea, scorning those who used its name scornfully, was a proud village, numbering among its citizens the whaling captain Absalom Boston, the Pompeys, the Godfreys, the Harrises—people of name, of substance. There can seldom have been more pride than on that August night, as they brought their young hero home.

9
Lynn

FREDERICK DOUGLASS had created a new world for himself and—though he may not have realized it—for Anna. He had lifted the smothering rug that frustrated his rage about slavery; now he breathed the fiery air of a great opportunity. As a speaker for the antislavery cause, as a witness for freedom's truth, he had something to do, something important. He would go wherever he would be listened to, wherever he was sent. He would commit himself totally to persuading America to expunge an evil he knew first hand.

But it was not quite as simple as talking from experience about what was wrong with slavery. Abolitionists, excoriating slaveholders, accused them of having made brutes of their slaves, and as if believing their own rhetoric, they required that Douglass exemplify the possibility of redemption from an animal state. "It is recorded in holy writ that a beast once spoke," said Garrison soon after Nantucket. Douglass had to be the creature made human, the chattel turned person, the delivered bondsman incarnate. People had to not only hear and see him, but—almost—feel him; he had to make his wounds bleed: "Yes, my blood has sprung out as the lash embedded itself in my flesh." And never could he appear less than totally noble.

This was a lot of christological weight for a young man from Talbot County to carry, but more than willingly, Douglass shouldered it. And neither he nor his fellow Anti-Slavery Society holy warriors had enough taste for blasphemy, or enough sense of humor, to recognize what they had brought forth. For the whole of his life, Douglass would have to appear as a man more admirable than other men.

Anna Murray Douglass, on the other hand, was mortal, and the man being handed up to the public was her man. She had helped Frederick escape. She had worked, as a domestic servant, as hard as he while they struggled to establish themselves as a respectable family in New Bedford. At the time he began his new career, she was carrying their third child. She had every reason to think it would be nice to have a man around the house.

It was not to be. Whether, as adulatory legend has it, she nobly sacrificed satisfaction of her personal wants so that he could fight slavery, or whether instead she resented being left with the diapers, we do not know. Illiterate, Anna Douglass wrote no letters, and few other reliable traces of her feelings can be found. In any event, left she was. Immediately upon returning home from Nantucket, Frederick began ceaselessly to tour, to speak, to appear. Late in the fall, elated by his prospects as agent for the Massachusetts Anti-Slavery Society, he moved his family, which had just begun to set its roots in New Bedford, to Lynn, Massachusetts. Members of the society appear to have made the down payment on the Douglass's small house beside the railroad tracks, and for the first time in his life, he was being paid a regular salary, the amount of which is not clear. Lynn, like Salem immediately to its north, was a Quaker town, only a few miles north of Boston. As a runaway, Douglass was safer there than in Boston, and yet he was only a short, direct train ride away from Garrison and his other employers in the Anti-Slavery Society.

But for a black man traveling, the trains could no more be counted on to run smoothly than they could be avoided. In the next two years Douglass was sent to speak at antislavery meetings in more than three score New England towns, and the trips to reach them were sometimes as eventful as the meetings he addressed when he arrived. For some time, black citizens in Massachusetts had been making a concerted effort to defy Jim Crow practices. John T. Hilton and William C. Nell were energetically struggling to achieve desegregation of the Boston schools, while Frederick Brinsley protested his exclusion from a pew, to which he held title through the collection of a debt, in the Unitarian Park Street Church. In New Bedford, Douglass had presided over a meeting protesting the beating of David Ruggles by a steamboat captain when he tried to purchase a first-class ticket. Now Douglass himself stepped into the classic scene of America's Jim Crow confrontations, the railroad car.

On September 8, 1841, Douglass and John A. Collins attempted to sit together as they traveled to an antislavery meeting in Dover, New Hampshire. The conductor ordered Douglass to go into the "negro car." When he refused, the conductor called for help, and four or five men dragged him away from his seat; Collins was also knocked around in the process. Toward the end of the month Douglass boarded a first-class car of the Eastern line (later incorporated into the Boston and Maine) at Lynn and was again confronted by a conductor—perhaps the same one, and certainly one with whom he had had an earlier discussion. When told to move, Douglass said quietly, "If you give me one good reason why I should . . . , I'll go willingly." The conductor, "trembling" with anger, said, "You have asked that question before," and Douglass retorted, "I mean to continue asking the question over and over again . . . as long as you continue to assault me in this manner," and he asked it again. The conductor hesitated before finally blurting out, "Because you are black." Then he called for reinforcements to "snake out the d——d nigger." Douglass clutched the bolted bench with his stevedore hands, and when he landed back on the Lynn platform, he still had his seat.

Antislavery people came to his support. At protest meetings in Lynn, threats were made to boycott the Eastern; the railroad's officials, for their part, ordered trains not to stop in that city when Douglass was known to be there. Douglass, who made the incident stock in trade for his lectures, was heartened by the response of his fellow townsfolk, but he was under no illusion that antislavery people could invariably be counted on to resist, or even to be conscious of, Jim Crow practices. One of his favorite Jim Crow stories was about the time he attended a communion service at the Elm Street Methodist Church in New Bedford and saw the "white people gathered round the altar, the blacks clustered by the door." After the whites had been served, the Reverend Isaac Bonney said—and here, in the frequent telling of the story, Douglass drew on his famous ability as a mimic—"Come up, colored friends, come up! for you know *God is no respecter of persons!*" Once, at the May 1842 meeting of the New England Anti-Slavery Society, when Douglass told this story Bonney himself was only a few feet away, in a prominent seat.

Like other black abolitionists smarting under indignities, Douglass devoted a large proportion of his speeches not to slavery, but to Jim Crow practices. The two injustices were inseparable in his mind. And the sting of the latter was, of course, what he personally was feeling now that he lived in the North. Douglass was also experiencing the tension inherent in more intimate encounters. Henry Ingersoll Bowditch, an abolitionist struggling to get past prejudice, saw himself as boldly ignoring what his neighbors would think when he invited Douglass to dine after a meeting at Marlboro Chapel. The walk home "by the side of a black man" through Boston streets "was . . . somewhat like a sponge bath . . .—rather terrible at the outset, but wonderfully warming and refreshing afterwards." One senses that Douglass too, in these often-accepted invitations, felt the chill and exhilaration of such social splashes of water.

In none of the antislavery leaders was the social ambiguity toward race more subtly wrought than in Wendell Phillips. The most aristocratic of the traveling antislavery lecturers, Phillips confided privately to his wife and to her cousin Anne Weston that he "had to sleep with all the cause" and was uncomfortable rooming with Douglass (and with the vulgar—and white—New Hampshirite Stephen S. Foster as well). And yet, unlike the supposedly genteel Edmund Quincy, who was fond of telling racist jokes, Phillips never permitted himself any overt expression of racial bias. Once, when Douglass was denied a berth on a boat to New York, Phillips paced and sat out the long night on deck with his black colleague. But Douglass needed nothing so blatant as the spectacle of Abbott Lawrence, having shaken his dusky hand, refuse a still darker one to make him keenly alert to the nuances of prejudice. He may have been more conscious of Phillips's (and other white men's) discomfort than his friend knew. Both were too gentlemanly to betray the least awareness of such matters, and with Wendell Phillips as a companion, one was a long way from the docks.

In the first of his speeches for which we have a recorded text, Douglass closed by saying, "Prejudice against color is stronger north than south; it hangs around my neck like a heavy weight. It presses me out from among my fellow men, and, although I have met it at every step the three years I have been out of southern slavery, I have been able, in spite of its influence, 'to take good care of myself.'" That prejudice was going to occupy a good deal of his attention. With vivid descriptions of beatings and of how families were torn apart by sales, he did establish that the South's treatment of his people was far worse than that meted out to him in the North, but unlike many white abolitionists, he seldom allowed his audiences the comfort of thinking their region was innocent.

In fact, particularly in his early speeches, he championed his old region and its people, in the face of the scorching anti-Southern attitudes expressed by Northern abolitionists. When he was not simply echoing standard but worn abolitionist rhetoric—as too often he was—he made it clear to his listeners that slaves, far from having been brutalized into stupidity, were consciously and acutely aware of their oppression. They only "pretend to be stupid," Douglass told the people of Hingham, as they "commit all sorts of foolery and act like baboons and wild beasts in [the] presence of their master; but every word is noted in the memory, and told to their fellow slaves." And he observed, "Waiters hear their masters talk at table, cursing the abolitionists, John Quincy Adams, &c.; the masters imagine that their poor slaves are so ignorant they don't know the meaning of the language they are using." Douglass knew that they heard, they understood, and they were watching and waiting.

If only his South could be granted the "quietness" of emancipation, it would be preferable to the North. Northern people, he told one audience, "say we [black slaves] could not learn if we had a chance . . . but . . . [Southerners] do not believe it, or they would not have laws . . . to prevent it. The northern people," he continued, "think that if slavery were abolished, we would all come north. They may be more afraid of the free colored people and the runaways going South. We would all seek our home and our friends, but, more than all, to escape from northern prejudice, would we go to the south." Another time, William Lloyd Garrison, introducing Douglass, proclaimed that by a "miracle," on this night a "chattel becomes a man." Douglass knew he had been a man for a good long time, since well back when he was still a slave in Maryland.

Despite such condescension, Douglass's loyalty to Garrison was great and their friendship real. Both men, for all their fierceness on the platform, could talk gently, particularly in their conversations and correspondence with women but also with each other, and there were moments, as on the trip out onto Cape Cod in the late spring of 1842 with Henry C. Wright, that talk must have turned to matters less grim than slavery. Wright, radical in many ways, was an unabashed exponent of the pleasures of a sensuous life, and walking the June beach at Hyannis, while not unmindful of the meeting to be attended in the village, these men— husbands, lovers, fathers—touched a gentle humanity.

The friendship of Garrison and Douglass later became jagged, but Douglass's loyalty to his mentor, wrenched though it was by controversy and, finally, their infamous estrangement, was never fully invalidated. When they broke, there were the bitter words that are sometime said—or thought—when a son must leave a father or a student a teacher, but in later life Douglass had in his library at Cedar Hill a fine drawing of Garrison as testament to his profound emotional and professional debt to the man he had heard speak in New Bedford and then come to know privately.

When Douglass, himself a speaker now, went out in 1841 as an agent of the Anti-Slavery Society, he paid no attention to Parker Pillsbury's advice that it was "better [to] have a *little* of the plantation" in his speech and to Garrison's that he should not sound too "learned" lest people not "believe you were ever a slave." Douglass was proud of the voice he was carefully training. And he was trained as well in the Garrisonian doctrine of opposing any approach to abolition through politics. Garrison was a devout champion of the efficacy of moral suasion, of changing people's hearts. Paradoxically, he argued for the political dissolution—once nicely recorded as "desolation"—of the Union as the way to liberate the nation from the evil of slaveholding. Garrison sought to expel from the garden the sinners—slaveholders—as well as the region they had tainted. How this would have helped the slaves who would be forced to go along with their masters, and would be further than ever from any prospect of a release from bondage, the purists did not say.

But from the start, Frederick's own common sense appears to have broken through to challenge the Garrisonian purity. For example, in the very first speech of which we have a transcript—in Lynn in the early fall of 1841—he betrayed positive feelings about politics. As his example of how the "agitation of this subject" gave the "highest hopes" to the slaves, Douglass chose the speech in which John Quincy Adams presented to Congress petitions for the abolition of slavery in the District of Columbia. Himself still a slave, Douglass had read Adams's speech to his fellow slaves in Baltimore. "My friends," he continued, in Lynn, "let . . . [that agitation] not be quieted, for upon you the slaves look for help. There will be no outbreaks, no insurrections, whilst you continue this excitement: let it cease, and the crimes that would follow cannot be told. . . . Emancipation . . . alone will give the south peace and quietness." If politics is the solution of social problems by nonviolent means, he would seem to be saying, the agitation of the slavery question in every forum, including those addressed by politicians, must be encouraged; other-wise—and here was evoked the old, white fear of being murdered in one's bed—violence will follow.

In November, in Hingham, Massachusetts, at the quarterly meeting of the Plymouth County Anti-Slavery Society, John A. Collins rose to oppose a motion to endorse Congressman Adams's strategy of petitioning Congress in order to break the gag rule and force the agitation of the slavery issue onto the floor of the House. Douglass responded that his "first knowledge of the abolition movements" came from reading about the petition to end slavery in the District of Columbia. Some had seen the proposal as designed simply to rid the nation of the embarrassment of slave markets, visible to foreign visitors, in the capital of the most advanced of the world's democracies, but Douglass considered it worth-while. Any agitation of the issue of slavery was desirable.

To be sure, the thought had occurred to him that the slaves might be lulled into inactivity by knowledge that the powerful in Washington were handling their problems. "They [the slaves] would get the vague idea that somebody is doing something to ameliorate their condition. Thus these petitions hold the slave in check. . . . I was myself contemplat-ing measures and making arrangements for my own emancipation, when learning of these petitions stopped me. But sir, the slaves are learning to read and write, and the time is fast coming, when they will act in concert, and effect their own emancipation if justice is not done by some other extraneous agency." For a moment, Douglass, rhetorically, was back inside the slave community. He knew that people learning of such petitions were more stirred into action in their own behalf than they were lulled into dependency. He called on the outsiders, the white abolitionists, to agitate the question in every possible forum. The still-slave saw that the value of Garrison's heretical condemnation of all activity sanctioned by a slavery-endorsing constitution lay not in directing the people of the republic toward greater moral purity, but in stirring them to do something about slavery.

In April 1842, about a month after the birth on March 3 of his second son, Frederick jr., Douglass paid his first visit to the utopian community of Hopedale, in central Massachusetts. So welcome was he made there that he extended his connection with these radical reformers by visiting the community of Florence, farther west, outside Northampton. There was, perhaps, no more progressive, integrated a community in America. Douglass credited Florence with being "from the first, a protest against sectarianism and bigotry and an assertion of the paramount importance of human brotherhood." There he was reunited with David Ruggles, who had helped him in his escape. Blind and destitute in New York, Ruggles had been brought to Florence by Lydia Maria Child. He was treated hydropathically, and in his wonderfully resilient way, went on to become moderately famous as a practitioner of his own therapy involving water and diet, which he credited with partially restoring his sight. One sufferer who came for the cure was Sojourner Truth—"that strange compound of wit and wisdom, of wild enthusiasm, and flint-like common sense," as Douglass described her, "who seemed to feel it her duty to trip me up in my speeches and to ridicule my efforts to speak and act like a person of cultivation and refinement." But she got his message; it was in Florence that she was converted to the abolitionist crusade, which she served well with her own unabashedly colloquial rhetoric.

Douglass was part of a wonderfully complex movement, and he reveled in that complexity. "It was a strange gathering," he wrote of one meeting, and went on, quoting a colleague, to describe it as "disgraceful, mortifying, alarming, divided, united, glorious, and most effective." Here, in Frederick's letter to the radical Abby Kelley, whom he much admired, was all the energy, all the exuberance—and all the exasperation—of the antislavery movement. And he was a part of it, body and soul. The meeting he described had been the annual gathering of the New Hampshire Anti-Slavery Society, and he was writing from Fall River, Massachusetts, where he was to lecture that evening, before going on, the next morning, to New Bedford. He had news as well of the annual meeting of the American Anti-Slavery Society and told of a proposed speaking trip to western New York, but he had yet to hear from its organizer; he was, therefore, going to conventions in Vermont, New York, Ohio, "etc etc." If ceaseless travel, meetings, speeches, could have broken the bonds of slavery—as these devoted people so much hoped those bonds would someday, somehow, be broken—there would have been nothing left of the peculiar institution but scraps of broken metal.

Unfortunately, all this activity was still far from enough quickly to smash the established system of labor. Larry E. Tise has recently pointed out how deeply entrenched was the concept that organizing a labor force around slave labor was rational and desirable. Ideas sometimes change, and do so at an unpredictable velocity. A concept of society that seemed impervious to futile abolitionist sparks in one decade could, two decades later, bend to a terrible heat. Not knowing when they would bring a change, these determined abolitionists, found the very intransigence of the problem to be the challenge. Stephen S. Foster, Abby Kelley (they married in 1845), Charles Lenox Remond, Wendell Phillips, Garrison himself, and a host of other agents of the society, would not be silent. They would go wherever twenty-five people could be found to listen; if few (or none) turned out to hear them speak, they were not daunted. Faced with a church's locked door or with no audience, Erasmus Darwin Hudson, an able orthopedic surgeon and an ardent foe of slavery, would find an alternative room and go "thro' the streets and ring the people out." And it was better that those people be "the publicans & harlots— rowdies & infidels . . . ," he added, "than those virtuous Christians & clergy, who were proved by their works to be practical infidels."

Hudson and Douglass first became acquainted in August 1842, when Frederick was in New York to meet Harriet, who came to live with his family in Lynn. The record of Harriet's life is exceedingly sketchy; she was known to Douglass's children as "Aunt Harriet," and in his letters Douglass addressed her as "sister," but in the 1850s, Rosetta referred to her as just an "adopted" aunt. Nevertheless, she could have been Douglass's youngest sister, "Harriet," of whom we know only that she was born about 1825; or she may have been not a blood relative of any sort, but simply a woman who escaped from slavery and whom the Douglasses, in the manner of fractured slave families, embraced as their own.

Somehow Harriet had found her way to Baltimore, and like Frederick, escaped to the North. That Frederick traveled to New York to meet her suggests that he had remained in touch with his friends on the underground railroad and had helped plan her escape. Erasmus Hudson, after a "boisterous time on the Sound" on his way into the city, encountered "Frederick Douglass and a sister on her way from slavery," and was one of the band of antislavery people who "saw them on their way to Mass." Harriet lived with Anna and Frederick in Lynn until her marriage four years later.

Of the whole band of antislavery speakers, it is hard to imagine a more startling, young, and attractive trio than the irrepressible, thirty-three-year-old physician, Hudson (who had probably preached a temperance sermon in a "pro-slavery rum tavern" on the way into town), his twenty-four-year-old black companion, Douglass, and the bold thirty-two-year-old Abby Kelley. Kelley was breaking strict taboos by traveling with two men (and one of them black), and she anguished over the constant sexual innuendos of critics of their "traveling seraglio." In 1842 they went from village to village in the burned-over region of New York State, seared by reform, where evangelism and antislavery met, and in 1845 they travelled together again, in western Massachusetts—Kelley was from Daniel Shays's rebel town of Pelham. The doctor's doctrine, Douglass's blackness, and, stranger than either, a woman speaking out radically in meetinghouses in which no woman had publicly spoken before, must have shaken up a good many farm families. Indeed, critics in cities as well as small towns were quick to pick up on the mixing of races and sexes that abolitionism engendered; in New York, at the Apollo Saloon (to which the the tenth-anniversary meeting of the American Anti-Slavery Society was moved after being barred from the Broadway Tabernacle), reporters took salacious note of what they chose to see as the "semi-flirtations" in a meeting "chiefly composed of members of the fair sex," but attended as well by "sable-complexioned sons of Africa."

As Douglass was particularly quick to note, clergymen, skittery as usual about issues that did not trouble their parishioners as they should have, were often the enemy. Hudson blamed both clergy and congregations: in Medina, New York, he found the "people stultified in conscience, full of worldliness, and the minister like the people—the people an index of the minister." On August 26, 1842, when Kelley began her address to an antislavery convention in Rochester, in the Third Presbyterian Church, the minister was appalled that a woman was speaking publicly, and ordered the small gathering—there were almost as many speakers as listeners—out of the building. After they had reassembled in the black Bethel church, Douglass and Hudson likened the banished to "Michaiah, Elijah, . . . Jesus Christ, Paul, & Martin Luther, all true reformers." Following the long session, Douglass stayed the night with Amy and Isaac Post, she a volunteer in countless causes, he a druggist, and both ardent Quaker foes of slavery. The visit was the beginning of two of the richest friendships of Douglass's life.

The abolitionist band was small but ceaselessly determined. Douglass alone made well over a hundred speeches a year, once he took to the road. And it would be entirely wrong to see this effort as foolish and futile, though a majority of their fellow Americans might have hoped that it was. Those who wanted to hear no more of the slavery question slowly came to realize that nothing would ever silence these antislavery people. They would keep up their agitation, against all odds, until—finally—slavery was ended.

As early as January 1842, only six months after his halting, then masterful, start in Nantucket, Douglass had found his full voice—and more. In Boston's hallowed Faneuil Hall—which Elizabeth Cady Stanton recalled as "a large, dreary place with bare walls and innumerable dingy windows"—he rose and achieved exultation. Half a century later, recalling this or a similar Boston meeting, Stanton told of the setting in which the mutual seduction of orator and audience was achieved. As the young man spoke, "Around him sat the great antislavery orators of the day [that January evening they included Garrison and Phillips] watching the effect of his eloquence on that immense audience, that laughed and wept by turns, completely carried away by the wondrous gifts of his pathos and humor. On this occasion, all the other speakers seemed tame after Frederick Douglass."

Looking up at the ceiling of the hall, Douglass made himself into a Southern preacher speaking up at the slave galleries of his church. In a reporter's careful account, "spreading his hands gracefully abroad, he says, (mimicking,) 'And you too, my friends, have souls of infinite value—souls that will live through endless happiness or misery in eternity. Oh, *labor diligently* to make your calling and election sure. Oh, receive into your souls these words of the holy apostle—"Servants, be obedient unto your masters." (Shouts of laughter and applause.) Oh, consider the wonderful goodness of God! Look at your hard, horny hands, your strong muscular frames, and see how mercifully he has adapted you to the duties you are to fulfil! (continued laughter and applause) while to your masters, who have slender frames and long delicate fingers, he has given brilliant intellects, that they may do the *thinking,* while you do the *working.'* (Shouts of applause.)" His voice and the movements of his body drew everyone to him. The physicality—the sexuality—reached round to encircle the audience as he reached out to them and they to him, making complete this ritual of oratory said and heard. Even after the emotion subsided, the memory lasted: Stanton was told that Douglass's "Servants, obey your masters" speech was by "some of our literary critics pronounced the finest piece of satire in the English language."

If fine speeches at great meetings were clearly putting Douglass into the public domain, there were times when he could hear the distant echo of a private past. Coming from Lynn one evening, he was late for a meeting, and the members of the Boston Female Anti-Slavery Society gathered in Armory Hall were anxious. Finally, "he *did* arrive though we were full of fears." His speech was "good," but having hurried from the train, he was not in his best form. With sarcastic stories about slaveholders, he "kept the audience laughing all the time," but there were few "chances for flowers of rhetoric."

Anne Weston, reporting privately on the talk, was more than usually attentive to Douglass's effect on his audience because she had as her guest a friend from below the Mason-Dixon line. "I expected Mrs. Tyler would be aggravated but she bore it very well, said she enjoyed the lecture amazingly & was wonderfully amused with the sermon but the most astonishing thing of all was that *she knew him*." Mrs. Tyler recalled having seen Douglass in Baltimore, and said that "his master was a Mr. Merriman," whose son attended the E. M. P. Wells School, and that the slave's "real name was Edward, that he was considered a very valuable servant."

After the lecture, Douglass "of course came home with Maria"— Anne's sister Maria Weston Chapman—and at the reception, their brother Warren Weston rather nastily "stepped up to" Douglass "quietly & called him 'Edward' at which he started as though he had been shot." Immediately, Douglass "took Warren into the back drawing room to learn where he got his information." When the chastened gentleman, aware that he had frightened and offended their guest, rejoined the ladies, "Mrs. T. said . . . she would keep her information to herself." Maria Chapman chose to interpret Douglass's reaction as a fear of being returned to slavery, a fear she regarded as groundless since "Douglass has made some arrangement with his master though he says nothing about it."

No record of a slave named Edward owned by a Merriman or Merryman has been found, but a slave could have been hired rather than owned by a wealthy Baltimorean, and even if the ripe gossip surrounding the incident is discounted, it is hard to see why the whole of the story—and Douglass's sharp reaction to the "Edward"—would have been made up. As suggested in the discussion of Douglass's years in Baltimore, it is not past possibility that dignified, well-spoken Frederick Bailey of Edward Lloyd's Wye House had at some point hired himself out as a house servant, and had been uneasy enough about the experiment to do so under another name, a name he may have wished were his own. The story of such a diversion from a relentless quest for freedom would not have fit the picture Frederick Douglass had painted of himself; it would have been logical for him to move instantly to suppress its telling. There were ghosts in Frederick's past, and if he was the only one troubled by them, he was not the only one who was curious about his identity.

Not all antislavery meetings ended in subdued drawing-room drama. In New Bedford the previous summer, Samuel Rodman had listened as the "col'd man C. L. Remond" spoke with "real power and eloquence" and Stephen Foster, "in the most radical style," denounced the ministers of the town "in no measured terms." This was all in the afternoon; when the meeting resumed in the evening, the hall was ringed with "disorderly rabble" who drowned out the speeches. "Females began to withdraw and got out with no difficulty"; the males were not so lucky. Many were struck as they left, although no one was seriously hurt save "one col'd man who was brutally attacked in making his way to the door."

In the annals of the antislavery movement, the throwing of rotten eggs is as commonplace as the tossing of custard pies in vaudeville. Garrison told his wife of one such episode in Syracuse that November: "Our friend S. S. Foster then took the platform, and . . . made his favorite declaration . . . that the Methodist Episcopal Church is worse than any brothel in the city of New York. Then came such an outbreak of hisses, cries, curses! All order was at an end. Several ruffians rushed toward the platform to seize Foster, but were not allowed to reach him. The tumult became tremendous. Several citizens . . . attempted to calm the storm, but in vain. Rotten eggs were now thrown, one of which was sent as a special present to me." It is easy to salute and to enjoy these Don Quixotes of the platform, but the organized groups of anti-antislavery people were serious and pervasive. The unnamed man beaten as he left the New Bedford meeting not only sustained injuries, but very likely also endured subsequent persecution, perhaps even the loss of his job. The price paid by the famous for their antislavery efforts is well known; the price paid by the anonymous working person often forgotten.

Many times, however, the meetings were greatly satisfying to Douglass. Meetings held in New Bedford in November were in sharp contrast to the one in August. For these, which Douglass and Remond attended, benches had to be brought into the town hall to accommodate the crowd. They were part of a series of meetings protesting Judge Lemuel Shaw's denial of a jury trial to determine whether a runaway slave, George Latimer, should be returned to his master. (The fugitive's freedom was subsequently bought with funds raised by Garrison and Douglass. The outcome of the protests was a Massachusetts law prohibiting judges and law-enforcement officers from participating in the return of fugitive slaves.) Douglass wrote, "I could see the entire audience [from the platform]; and from its appearance, I should conclude that prejudice against color was not there . . . ; we were all on a level, every one took a seat just where they chose; there were neither men's side, nor women's side."

This letter, which appeared in the *Liberator*, is one of the countless public letters that provide a vast record of Douglass's public life. On the other hand, the record of the Douglass family's life in Lynn is spare in the extreme. They arrived with two infants, and the next spring there was a third. Two women, whose last names are not recorded, lived with them at least for a time—Harriet and a young woman named Ruth (later Ruth Adams). All three women probably worked at home, on a piecework basis, sewing uppers to shoe soles; they could have completed a couple of pairs a day. Labor was in demand, despite the falloff of the economy in the wake of the financial crisis of 1837, and for those working at home, color was not a bar to employment. This work would have provided just about enough money to subsist on; to it would have been added what little was left from Frederick's salary after travel expenses had been paid. Less appealing, if not less necessary, were the checks for twenty-five or thirty dollars that came when Frederick reminded the rich ladies of the Boston Female Anti-Slavery Society that there was need at home. The Lynn Ladies' Anti-Slavery Society tried to bring Anna into their fold and once persuaded her (and paid her way) to attend the annual antislavery bazaar in Boston. But in the main, Anna shunned public life.

The only record we have—if that it is—of Anna's accompanying Frederick on a speaking trip is in Dr. Hudson's journal. On April 15, 1845, the Northampton physician, whose unpretentiousness put Douglass at ease, recorded that "A. K. [Abby Kelley] Mrs. D. & myself went to Petersham & left F. Douglass to give another lecture in Hubbardston." The identity of "Mrs. D." is not absolutely certain. In any event, these quiet interior Massachusetts towns would have been far less daunting than the bazaars and drawing rooms of the formidable antislavery ladies of Boston. But Anna was seldom comfortable appearing in public as the consort of the remarkable Mr. Douglass, and more and more she retreated to her house, her piece-work sewing, and her family. In January 1844, after a strenuous string of antislavery meetings across New York State and the Middle West, there was time to conceive another child. This time the movement reached all the way to the christening; the baby, born on October 21, was named Charles Remond, after the man who was then his father's closest companion in the crusade.

10

Pendleton

EIGHTEEN FORTY-THREE was to be the year of the Hundred Conventions—a hundred antislavery meetings planned by the American Antislavery Society. The goal of a hundred was never actually reached, but Douglass himself spoke at nearly that many meetings in 1843 as he traveled across New England, upstate New York, Ohio and Indiana, and back through Pennsylvania, gaining an increasingly strong and independent voice. While preaching against slavery as it existed in the South, he made constant references to what he was facing now in the North—a North that would not accord him equality. He believed fervently that the ending of slavery would mean the beginning of full manhood for his brothers and himself. With its end, they and he would be paid attention to, would be respected. Somehow, it was slavery that had bred the poison of racism. In the company of devoted proponents of universal reform, he did not waver in his belief that slavery was the one overriding evil that had to be gotten rid of before any other goals, however desirable, should be sought.

This single-mindedness led him into one of the myriad controversies in which he was to engage during his long life, and cost him the friendship of John A. Collins, with whom he had often traveled amicably. What drove them apart was a speech by Collins at a meeting in Syracuse at the end of July, in which, in Douglass's view, "the antislavery cause was wantonly assailed & by one to whom I had always looked up to as its warmest protector." Collins, a Fourierist opponent of all individual ownership of property—in interesting ways he anticipated Henry George—was the general agent, or executive director, of the American

Anti-Slavery Society. He found no incongruity in espousing more than one reform at a time, and as the antislavery team assembled in the city, Collins arranged for an anti-property meeting, to be held simultaneously with theirs. Abby Kelley, Charles Lenox Remond, and Douglass objected; he canceled the separate meeting, and they thought all was well. But when he addressed the antislavery gathering, Collins quickly turned the audience's attention from the 3,000,000 of his countrymen held in slavery to the 800,000,000 people worldwide whom he described as living with the evils deriving from property.

Douglass, seated beside Collins, "groaned, and looked sad." Remond, on the other hand, "assumed a more erect posture, his eyes flashed with the fire of excitement." As Collins put it, "No sooner had I closed my sentence, with a view to take my seat, than Remond was upon his feet, and with an agitated frame, half stifled, angry and furious delivery, disposed of the property question as humbug and moonshine." For an hour, the angry black man, who had never been a slave but was not about to let a white man divert attention from slavery, struck out at Collins "like a thunderbolt." He "hardly left enough of me to give the smell of fire," Collins reported, adding, with considerable candor, that Remond had accused him "of breach of confidence." When Douglass took the floor, he, "in a subdued and feeling manner, sustained Remond," and said, straight out, that if Collins were to continue in this vein, he would not continue with the carefully planned western tour.

Leaving Syracuse with the air anything but cleared, Douglass went to Rochester, where he stayed with the Posts while planning that city's meeting. He was joined by Remond and George Bradburn, a white Whig from Nantucket, but not by Collins, and the Rochester convention was a rousingly good one. But a reassuring word from Boston as to the primacy of the slavery issue was slow to arrive, and with accusations hanging over their heads that the trouble in Syracuse was the fault of the unbecomingly restless black men, Douglass and Remond began making good on their threat. Abandoning Bradburn, on his own way to Buffalo, the two made their way to that city, heading not for the Anti-Slavery Society convention, but, pointedly, for the National Convention of Colored Citizens.

This was the first major assemblage of African American men that Douglass attended. Amos Beman of New Haven, a champion of the vote—widely denied blacks in the North—was in the chair, but the great address of the meeting was given by Henry Highland Garnet. A descendant of the Mandingos of West Africa, and according to Alexander Crummell "a perfect Apollo, in form and figure," Garnet was, like Douglass, a slave who had escaped from the Eastern Shore. His father, on the pretext of taking his family to a funeral, had escaped with the lot, but in the North, they had been frequently pursued by agents of their former owner seeking to drag them back. As a boy, Garnet had carried a knife when walking through the streets of New York to the African Free School. Later, he and his friend Crummell were among twelve black students admitted to the Noyes Academy, in Canaan, New Hampshire. When the good farmers of the region took note of their presence, they brought in teams of oxen and pulled down one of the academy buildings. Not encouraged by this welcome, Garnet is reported to have gotten hold of a shotgun, which "blazed through the window" at threatening noises outside in the dark. Taken from their rooms, the twelve students were sent out of town in a wagon; the townspeople fired after them to hurry them along.

These experiences did not induce Garnet to champion moderation, but neither did they impede his determination to get on with his education, which culminated in a degree in theology from the Oneida Theological Institute. At the time of the Buffalo convention, Garnet, then twenty-eight years old, was the minister of the black Presbyterian church in Troy, New York, and one of the country's most militant spokesmen for equal rights and antislavery. In Buffalo, he gave a stirring address, "Call to Rebellion," in which he moved that the convention adopt a "motto of resistance" to slavery. It is a mark of the caution of the Northern black community, that the resolution failed of adoption in a close vote; it is a mark too of Douglass's commitment to Garrisonian principles that he undertook to debate Garnet. In what was said to be a sharp speech (no transcript exists), he opposed Garnet's militancy, and he and Remond cast the only two votes against cooperation with the recently organized Liberty party.

The city of Buffalo was not short on conventions that summer. Not coincidentally, both the National Convention of Colored Citizens, which supported the Liberty party, and the Anti-Slavery Society, which opposed it, met in the same month that the Liberty party held its annual convention. Founded in 1840, the Liberty party was committed to direct use of the political process in dealing with the slavery question. The basic tenet of Kentuckian James Gillespie Birney, the party's presidential candidate in 1840 and again in 1844, and of fellow party members like Gerrit Smith of New York, was precisely the opposite of that of Garrison and his followers. The Liberty party people saw the political system as a fact of life; to worry about whether the underlying document was corrupt was a waste of time. It did not follow, in their view, that if the Constitution was evil, as Garrison contended, because it countenanced slavery, participation in the politics to which it gave structure was also evil.

Instead, every effort should be made to bring issues relating to slavery into the arena of political decisions. As an agent of the American Anti-Slavery Society, Douglass was still committed to the uncompromising position that slavery must be damned as morally wrong, and people must be brought to the point of ending it by peaceful moral persuasion, but the events at the National Convention of Colored Citizens had reinforced his view that any and all attacks on slavery were worth making.

While Douglass was in Buffalo conducting store-front antislavery meetings—Bradburn had given up on him and on the town and had gone to his brother's in Cleveland—word of the controversy in Syracuse reached the Anti-Slavery Society headquarters in Boston. Or, to be more precise, word reached 39 Summer Street, the home of the secretary, Maria Weston Chapman. A woman "of victorious beauty," as one admirer put it, with a bearing, said Wendell Phillips, that "might befit a line of duchesses," Chapman ran the society. (William Lloyd Garrison and the rest of the male world always thought Garrison did, but Chapman knew better.)

The reports made it clear to Chapman that Collins, Remond, Douglass, and probably Kelley, had conducted a battle royal, in public, and the redoubtable secretary wrote admonitory letters designed to bring her divided troops back into line. Douglass, in a dignified but stern letter, protested to Chapman that "you labor under much misapprehension" with respect to the character of the public argument, and closed his restrained but unapologetic account, "These, Dear Friend are the facts in the case that have given rise to the rumors you have heard." In the letter, he repeated his threat to leave the tour if antislavery was not restored as its purpose.

Collins, in his letter to Chapman, struck a calm, rational tone. As a defense, he philosophized in a pre-Marxian vein, raising doubts that the ending of slavery would end the oppression of working people. He was candid about how greatly his remarks had upset Douglass and Remond, admitting that he had infuriated his colleagues. "Now Abby Kelley was there," he wrote, "and she hates the property question, as the slaveholder hates anti-slavery. She is," he complained, "intolerant beyond degree." He would not recant and agree to focus exclusively on slavery in the future.

Abby Kelley, concerned about the vulnerable black men, also reported in to Boston. Not only Remond and Douglass had lost their temper, she wrote, but also Collins. As she put it, there was little "cool Blood" during the exchange. She certainly did not think Chapman should dock Remond's and Douglass's pay (as she had said she might in her letters to them) because of their threats to leave the tour. Kelley contended that Collins was not fit for the work: "His nervous irritability alone was sufficient to disqualify him." In Boston, Chapman decided that Kelley was right; Collins (who was not well, his wife insisted) had strayed once too often from the true course and was dismissed as general agent. Several women hoped that Kelley would get his job, but her sponsor conceded that men in the West "have something of a horror of [the] Gyneocracy which would be constituted by having Miss Kelley in the field and Mrs. Chapman in the council." A woman would not do, and neither would a black man. Douglass, Remond, and the other black antislavery speakers were always treated as visiting artists in a production of which the white Bostonians never dreamed of losing the direction. From Northampton, Garrison sent his concurrence in the dismissal of Collins; it was, he told Chapman, just as well that he had "resigned," though, he added wistfully, he *"did* do good work."

Reflecting on the behavior of Douglass and Remond, Garrison did agree that their quarrel with Collins, in public, was regrettable, but he indicated to Chapman that he would like to hear their side of the story. He was countering the implication, in Chapman's criticism, that it was unseemly for the black men to be indecorous. To her it was bad enough when white Abby Kelley spoke her exceedingly active mind; for black men to challenge their betters in public simply would not do. "At best," Garrison concluded, somewhat wearily, "it is a painful affair." But the decision was that the two black orators were too valuable to lose; in Ohio they learned that their pay would continue if they would go on with the western tour—without Collins and with the understanding that slavery alone was the foe to be attacked.

Not everyone was as polite in replying to Chapman as Collins and Douglass had been. George Bradburn, defending himself against the apostasy of going to the Liberty party convention, even if it had been to attack its policies, complained of Chapman's "impertinent, impudent, insolent letter." He was also cross that he had had to go to Buffalo alone, Remond and Douglass having made their own way to the National Convention of Colored Citizens. These petty quarrels consumed—some would say provided—a great deal of the movement's energy. In this instance, Bradburn, who had fought an antimiscegenation law in the Massachusetts legislature and had difficulty eschewing things political, was induced to stay with the western tour, which did not grow less stormy.

In September, Remond remained in Ohio, while Douglass went on to Indiana with Bradburn and a new agent, William A. White, a Harvard graduate of Douglass's age whom Garrison thought "remarkable" and "full of promise." In Pendleton, the three men—one black, two white—were the house guests of a local physician. During the evening of September 14, 1843, they "learned that a mob had threatened to come down from . . . a miserable, rum-drinking place, about six miles distant," to drive the race-mixing abolitionists away. Warned but not deterred, the three went the next morning to the Baptist church. "Frederick spoke," reported White in a letter to the *Liberator,* "and there was no interruption, though I observed a great number of men, such as do not usually attend our meetings." The Baptists noticed them too; when the three speakers returned for the afternoon meeting, they were told they could not use the building because the church authorities feared it would be pulled down.

When the abolitionists tried to conduct their meeting from the steps outside the church, about thirty of the uninvited guests began to heckle. A local man reasoned with them and achieved sufficient quiet for Bradburn to be heard. His speech went on until a rainstorm abruptly did the hecklers' job for them. In the evening, the citizens of the town, opposed to slavery or simply embarrassed, met and passed a resolution that the men should be allowed to speak. "The next morning being pleasant," White continued, "we held our meeting in the woods, where seats and stands had been arranged." At the start of the meeting, White spotted only seven of their challengers among the hundred men and thirty women who had gathered. The scene was very like that of a camp meeting. The proceedings were opened with a song. Then Bradburn rose to speak, and as he rolled into his attack on slavery, White and Douglass noticed that "the mob continued to collect, but were quiet." The men were menacing, their faces fixed in sneers. White fixed his eyes on one man about his age who stood barefoot, a pair of homespun pants slung from his hips and a shirt slouched across his body so loosely that it bared his shoulders. The nakedness of this insolence fascinated and terrified the well-bred eastern gentleman. After several minutes, at a signal, the men got up and walked out.

"In a few moments we heard a shout, and saw the mob coming through the woods, thirty or more in number, two by two, armed with stones and eggs," and led by a man in a coonskin cap. The audience rose for a hasty exit, but White pleaded with them to sit down again. A few of the men and all of the women did. The cry from under the coonskin cap was "Surround them," and the thirty circled the audience, some stationing themselves at the foot of the speakers' stand. Stones were thrown at the speakers, but did no real damage. Old eggs were hurled and splattered on the speakers' faces; the three endured the drip and stink in stoical silence. The audience too was quiet, and the stymied hecklers were at a loss as to what to do next. The peacemaker of the day before tried again, but as he spoke, one man called out to the speakers, asking why they didn't go down south with their message. Bradburn replied: his challenger, James Jackson, offered a rebuttal; and White invited him up onto the platform to continue the debate. Jackson rose to the bait and made, said the Harvard man, "a most ridiculous spectacle, interlarding his speech with copious oaths, and ending off by saying he could not talk, but he could fight—that he had too much good blood in his veins to let us go on." At this point, another man jumped up onto the platform, saying that he saw that nothing would be done unless he did it, and seized hold of the table, overturned it, and began to pull the stand to pieces. His buddies now all joined in the wrenching of timbers, pushing protesting members of the audience out of the way.

Douglass was sandwiched between two antislavery people concerned for his safety, but thinking White was in danger, he ran into the midst of the pulling and prying and grabbed a piece of lumber to use as a club. In doing so, he violated not only the Garrisonian insistence on nonviolence, but also white America's stern law that black men were not to raise weapons except against other black men. There were screams: "Kill the nigger, kill the damn nigger." Furious men pursued Douglass, who ran for his life. White, not injured (and with his hat still on his head), followed in pursuit. The swing of one club broke Douglass's right hand. Running up, White was able to grab and slow another piece of lumber as it was swung with lethal force; it could have killed the downed black man. A stone hit White on the head; deflected by his hat, it nevertheless opened a gash that bled profusely.

Douglass never forgot those moments with William White. In what may be the most affectionate letter he ever wrote, he recalled it all (three years later) for his friend: "I shall never forget how like two very brothers we were ready to dare, do, and even die for each other. Tragic, awfully so, yet I laugh when I think how comic I must have looked when running before the mob, darkening the air with mud from my feet. How I looked running you can best describe but how you looked bleeding I shall always remember." Douglass went on in his reminiscence to salute White for leaving his "life of ease and even luxury . . . against the wishes of your father and many of your friends" to do "something toward breaking the fetters of the slave and elevating the dispised black man." Recalling White—"so warm so generous"—bleeding, he observed that "such noble blood . . . was too holy to be poured out by the rough hand of that infernal mob." And in conclusion, he wrote, "Dear William, from that hour . . . have you been loved by Frederick Douglass."

With White on the ground, his head gashed and his mouth bleeding from a blow that knocked out teeth, and Douglass lying nearby cradling his painful hand, the attackers got on their horses and rode off. Members of the antislavery audience helped Neal Hardy, "a kind-hearted member

An example of what F.D. risked when he abandoned speech making for action

Fighting the mob in Indiana. From *Life and Times,* 1881.

of the Society of Friends," ease the men into his wagon. Hardy took them home and with his wife got their wounds bandaged. (The fracture was not properly set; his right hand bothered Douglass for the rest of his life.) Two days later, they were on the platform in Noblesville, Indiana.

White behaved admirably in Pendleton, both as a friend and as an advocate of antislavery, but his letter to the *Liberator* reporting on the event vividly suggests why reformers so often go awry. Seeking a perfect America, they expose their scorn for the imperfect American. With the wearer of the "coonskin cap, tail and all" seen as representative of the great Whig party, the party of the recent log-cabin campaign that had put Tippecanoe and then Tyler too into the White House, and the barefoot man, "with nothing but a dirty shirt and pantaloons on, and the former half off his shoulders, [seen] as representative of the democracy of the country," White had disposed of the major political parties—the Whigs and the Democrats—so scorned by the American Anti-Slavery Society. But he had done much more. He had, twenty years before emancipation, given a clue to why the antislavery crusade did not translate into a pro-people crusade.

The four million ex-slaves turned out to be not well-tailored gentlefolk like Frederick Douglass, but more like the attackers at the Pendleton meetings. The black man and woman were barefoot too, and the rags they wore did not quite cover the nakedness of long deprivation. Nor had a gift of liberty wiped away the insolent looks with which, in self-defense, the freed people defied a callous world that cared no more for them than White had for his assailants—"devils in human form; men actuated by the passions of brutes, and using the intellects of men to carry out those passions." The thirty or so men in Pendleton were bad news, but no one at the *Liberator* office was asking why.

In Jonesboro, Indiana, the following week, Remond rejoined the Pendleton veterans for the annual meeting of the Indiana Anti-Slavery Society. When Bradburn spoke at too great length on what Douglass considered yet another tangential subject, his fellow orator interrupted him. Bradburn objected, and the chair ruled in his favor, "whereupon Remond . . . called the chairman a jackass, made a hot speech and appealed to the meeting." The meeting sustained the chair, and Remond remarked that they must be "a set of monkeys out here in the west." Such scraps prompted one white antislavery man, quoted in a letter to Maria Weston Chapman, to observe that if Douglass and Remond "do not [do] more hurt than good before they get out of the state," he would be thankful. The two black men were "a disgrace to abolition" in his judgment. "As near as I can find," he continued, "Remond and Douglass choose to be the lions of the party and are unwilling to be directed by others."

After Jonesboro, Douglass and Remond broke away from their fellow agents and proceeded by themselves. In Clinton County, Ohio, Douglass got into a fierce, public argument with Henry Brewster Stanton (husband of Elizabeth Cady Stanton) and another agent. Clearly, the kings of beasts had to be subdued. The black men were lecturing to large crowds "most ably and successfully," but nonetheless any further such meetings in the region were not advisable, in the view of the correspondent who had quoted an account of the Jonesboro affair to Maria Chapman: "These men[,] . . . talented and glorious specimens of the 'fallen' humanity as they are, still are but unregenerate men. The anti-slavery reform is but a partial reform after all." It was all well and good for Douglass and Remond to attack slavery, but they were forgetting that such attacks were only part of what should be expressions of "the higher sentiments and powers of our nature. The circumstances which continually surround our speakers are calculated to foster self-esteem—to beget pride where humility is needed."

Frederick Douglass felt no such need. He knew he was a glorious specimen, but not of fallen humanity, and he was tired of all the conjectures about his not having truly been a slave, and not being able to write his own speeches. He could damned well read and write; he had been a slave, but slavery had not left him a beast to be displayed; he was not a black dummy manipulated by a white ventriloquist. Some of his fellow agents, among them Sydney Howard Gay, with whom he traveled in Pennsylvania later in the fall, and Wendell Phillips, understood him and respected the independence of his voice. Douglass could write in a businesslike way to Phillips, as he did that winter, arranging for a salary of seven or eight dollars a week—twelve dollars would be "mercenary"—and insisting that the black agents should receive the same pay as the white. He was tired of pleading with Maria Chapman to see that his wife was "provided with $25 or $30" of charity.

In December, Douglass was in Philadelphia for the closing meeting of the Hundred Conventions, the tenth-anniversary celebration of the American Anti-Slavery Society. Philadelphia, with its large black and Quaker population, had a strong antislavery movement, which provoked some of the nation's most violent counterattacks. Proslavery people feared that the city and the region immediately to its south would be subject to an influx of blacks from Maryland and beyond if these people were no longer contained by slavery. The anniversary meeting was chaired by Robert Purvis, Sr., the richest black man in America, who lived in splendor in Byberry, outside the city. Purvis was the head of the city's active Vigilance Committee, which protected runaway slaves; his wife, Harriet Forten Purvis, a founder of the Philadelphia Female Anti-Slavery

Society, was also active in the crucial business of protecting fugitives who, like Douglass, came through their city from Maryland.

Douglass, in close touch with the black community in Philadelphia, was to speak there often in the years to come. In September 1844, he told of having to leave a "beautiful grove" in West Chester because of the rain, only to find all the churches and the courthouse closed to him, but the market house "fortunately for us and . . . [any runaway] slave, was doorless." He was depressed by how little antislavery fervor there was in Chester County, save from the "few women, almost alone in a community of thousands, asserting truths and living out principles . . . with a composure and serenity of soul which would well compare with . . . friend Garrison himself." One of these women, Lucretia Coffin Mott, reporting on a meeting in the Byberry Meetinghouse, was troubled both by the difficulty they had had in securing the room for a black speaker and by the fact "that Abolitionists are becoming so divided & subdivided." She regretted that "this political party movement is taking some of our most active members from us." Douglass tried to avoid the political realm, but he was not above the use of political puns—"people sunken almost inextricably into the mire and Clay." And he was acutely aware, as was Garrison for that matter, of the stances of various politicians on the question of slavery—of the accommodation to slavery of Henry Clay's Whigs, and of what he regarded as the too-feeble opposition of the Liberty party. Politics might be evil, but it was becoming increasingly absorbing for Douglass.

Some meetings went well indeed. In the yard of the Landon Grove Meetinghouse, he reported to abolitionist clergyman J. Miller McKim, "the day was fine, the heavens clear, the sun bright, the air salubrious, and the scenery by which we were surrounded extremely grand; all nature seemed redolent with anti-slavery truth." He was cheered as "men and women on foot, on horse back and in wagons, all press[ed] their way amidst dust and din, toward the great Quaker meetinghouse, under the eaves of which, we had to hold our meeting as it, like the strong hearts of its owners, stood locked and bolted against us." Not only were the Friends divided over the slavery question, but it was quite possible for them, like other white Americans, to despise both slavery and black people who had been—or might have been—slaves. As Douglass tactfully put it, the members of the Pennsylvania Anti-Slavery Society had not "yet quite rid themselves of what seems to be prejudice against color," but they were "advancing." As for himself, he was, he said somewhat disingenuously, "willing to be regarded as a curiosity, if I may thereby aid the high and holy cause of the slave's emancipation."

He was, in fact, determined to be something far beyond a curiosity

when in 1844 he began to write a story of his life that would make the
world pay him true attention. His book, he and his friends felt sure, not
only would reach readers who had not heard him, but would also
reinforce the picture in the mind's eye, the sonorous sound still in the ear,
of those who had. Wendell Phillips, in particular, urged him to write his
story, and in the spring of 1845 was telling his audiences to be on the
lookout for it. The *Narrative of the Life of Frederick Douglass* would be
a powerful antislavery tract, but it would also be far more than that.

In his writing, Douglass outran being a runaway. Never satisfied with
the degree to which a nineteenth-century white world took the ex-slave
seriously as an intellectual, he would have been profoundly gratified by
the attention paid his work in the twentieth century. Read now only
secondarily for what they tell us about slavery, his *Narrative* (1845) and
My Bondage and My Freedom (1855) have earned the regard of critics, such
as William L. Andrews, who see them as two in the series of great "I"
narratives of that most remarkable of all decades of American letters. The
Narrative carries none of the poetry of Whitman's first edition of *Leaves
of Grass* (1855), but it too is a song of myself. There is not the epic tragedy
of Melville's *Moby-Dick* (1851), and yet it is a story—not wholly unlike
Ishmael's—of survival in a world at sea with evil. On the other hand,
with its message of growing self-confidence, of self-reliance, the *Narrative*
is kin to Emerson's essays. But perhaps Douglass's telling of his odyssey
is closest cousin to Thoreau's account of his altogether safe escape to
Walden Pond. That quietly contained, subversive tale has reverberated
ever since its telling with a message of radical repudiation of corrupt
society. Thoreau heard a Wendell Phillips lecture describing Douglass's
exodus—and reporting that a written account was on its way—in the
spring of 1845 as he was planning his sojourn outside Concord. Robert
D. Richardson, Jr., who wrote Thoreau's intellectual biography, has said
that it is not "an accident that the earliest stages of Thoreau's move to
Walden coincide with . . . the publication of Douglass's narrative of how
he gained his freedom. *Walden* is about self-emancipation."

In all three of his autobiographies, Douglass tantalizes us with the
many things he leaves out; not the least of these is discussion of why and
how he wrote them. His correspondence is equally void of references to
what must have been a compelling exercise for him. We know that
Phillips and others in the Anti-Slavery Society urged him to put his story
into print, but whom did he talk to about the project, who helped, who
was its editor? His later quarrels with his British publisher make it clear
that he cared not only about the content—he resisted any censoring of
material thought to be offensive to Christians—but also about the appearance of the front matter and the cover. Such concerns must have been

with Douglass even at the time of the first printing of the first book.

But perhaps not. To a remarkable degree *Narrative of the Life of Frederick Douglass* does seem to have simply sprung from a man who had been telling the same story in much the same language from the antislavery platform for four years. And once he had created, with his voice and then his pencil, the Frederick Douglass of the *Narrative,* the author never altered either the character or the plot significantly. This, more than the fact that speaking came easier than writing for Douglass, explains why he wrote no books other than the autobiographies. He had but one character to craft, one story to tell. The two later books, *My Bondage and My Freedom* and *Life and Times of Frederick Douglass,* reveal important shifts in approach and detail, but the Frederick Douglass of the *Narrative* remains inviolate.

The *Narrative* is short and direct, from the "I was born" of its first line to its closing account of the Nantucket speech, describing how Douglass "felt strongly moved to speak" and was urged to do so as well: "It was a severe cross, and I took it up reluctantly. The truth was, I felt myself a slave, and the idea of speaking to white people weighed me down. I spoke but a few moments, when I felt a degree of freedom." The person we come to know in these brief pages is unforgettable. From the *Narrative* and the many other accounts of runaways published in Douglass's day, right down to Toni Morrison's *Beloved* in ours, there has been no escape from the slave in American letters. And for the fifty years following publication of the *Narrative* in 1845, there was no escape for the author from the runaway he had created.

It is easy when reading the *Narrative* to misjudge the reason for the author's many omissions—the nature of his relationships with his brothers and sisters, for example. His focused concentration on himself does invite the charge of insensitivity to others. But there were other, deeper reasons for such voids. We get a hint of them when he tells of slaves on a Wye House farm singing "most exultingly" when "leaving home: . . . they would sing, as a chorus, to words which to many would seem unmeaning jargon, but which, nevertheless, were full of meaning to themselves." There were some sounds of slavery that Douglass could not render in words that his readers would hear, private torments and horrors too deep in the well to be drawn up.

The book was published by the "Anti-Slavery Office" in Boston in June 1845 and priced at fifty cents. The *Liberator* had announced its publication in May, and Phillips and his allies in the literary world saw to it that reviews appeared promptly. By fall, 4,500 copies had been sold in the United States; soon there were three European editions, and within five years 30,000 copies were in the hands of readers. The inevitable charge appeared that a slave boy could not have written the book—Lydia Maria Child (also falsely credited with having written Harriet Jacobs's *Incidents in the Life of a Slave Girl*) was one of many suspected of having been the ghost writer. But anyone who had heard Douglass—and by 1845 thousands of people had—knew that the language of the *Narrative* was the same as that of the man who so passionately told his tale from the platform.

The famous "Preface" by William Lloyd Garrison and the "Letter" by Wendell Phillips, both preceding Douglass's text, had a double purpose. The great white fathers of the antislavery movement sought to authenticate the book—"Mr. DOUGLASS," Garrison wrote, "has very properly chosen to write his own Narrative, in his own style, and according to the best of his ability, rather than to employ someone else"—and to commandeer it for the cause. By 1845, the ex-slave they had sent out to carry their message was displaying troubling signs of independence, but the leaders of the American Anti-Slavery Society knew that his fiery oratory was an asset of incalculable value. "Go on, my dear friend," wrote Phillips in his "Letter," exhorting Douglass to carry the word to reach "every hut in the Carolinas, and make the broken-hearted bondman leap up at the thought of old Massachusetts." Phillips was sounding a bit as if he were running for governor.

With the book about to be published, Chapman, Garrison, and Phillips decided that Douglass's word was too good to waste on Pendleton, Indiana, or even on Massachusetts; there was an international audience that should hear him. The antislavery movement was not new in the 1830s and 1840s, nor was it confined to the sometimes parochial doings of the Bostonians (to whom it would never have occurred that they were parochial). Under the leadership of Toussaint L'Ouverture, blacks in Haiti had liberated themselves, and the British had succeeded in ending slavery in their West Indies colonies after a long and well-organized struggle—with Haiti as a reminder that if freedom was not granted, the blacks might seize it bloodily. West Indies Emancipation Day, August 1, 1833, was celebrated—as was the memory of L'Ouverture—every year by black American abolitionists, who thought it altogether appropriate that despite this emancipation in the West Indies the British had not disbanded their antislavery societies. Their organized antislavery movement remained strong and the immediate goal of the British was to get their American cousins to end slavery in North America.

Ties between abolitionists on opposite sides of the Atlantic had long been close, and the value of enabling people to see and hear a victim of the evil they were fighting was widely recognized. Douglass was far from the first former slave or black man to appear on British platforms, but in 1845 he was the one that ardent antislavery people most wanted to have a look at and to hear.

It was time for the runaway to go abroad.

11
Cork

IN A SMALL provincial city on the periphery of a society foreign to him, Frederick Douglass caught sight of a center for his life. He was only a house guest, but for a month in the fall of 1845 he was at home with a family innocent of those particular prejudices that had cut him to the quick almost everywhere he had stopped before. In Cork, with the Jenningses (six weeks after his arrival in Ireland), he sampled the special brand of equality, of social comfort that he was to champion for the rest of his life.

The Jenningses, Thomas and Ann, and their eight children were members of the Church of Ireland in a city of Roman Catholics whose English masters were, in the main, members of the Church of England. The hospitality of the house on Brown Street included the comfort Frederick could take from the realization that his hosts also knew what it was like to be thought odd. This awareness was coupled with the reassuring sense that, as they put right foot before left, the Jenningses had the self-confidence to assume that everyone else was out of step. In a household bustling with collisions and contradictions, theirs was an oddity that would have delighted an Austen or a Trollope, and did delight Douglass.

Jennings was a prosperous merchant of vinegar and mineral oil. The family firm had been in existence since 1797 in Cork, a market and port town from which preserved farm goods were shipped. Although Jennings was in trade, he provided for a gentle house in which music, talk of reform, and gossip easily mingled. At his hearth, his too many unmarried sons and daughters were their own companions, and therefore eager to stretch and take in a stranger. "We are," Jane Jennings wrote Maria

Weston Chapman just after Douglass's departure, "a large family[,] my mother, three brothers and five sisters, generally considered not easily pleased—but Frederick won the affection of every one of us."

In Cork, Douglass was at last in safe port. As he had hoped for a new direction for his life when he was sent back and forth across the Chesapeake and when he reached across the coastal waters of southeastern New England to Nantucket to accept a calling, so he had now come over the Atlantic filled with great expectations—and enough trepidations to make him wary. His Lynn neighbors had given him a reassuring farewell in the Lyceum, but when he left Boston, prejudice followed beyond coastal waters.

To begin with, he had been denied a cabin on the *Cambria;* in their eagerness for the trip, however, he and his traveling companion, James Buffum, had decided that being consigned to the least expensive accommodations—to steerage—could be chalked up as a victory for thrift. And staring out at the boundless sea, he had time for reveries about a world without barriers. These musings of triumphant freedom were broken in on. Douglass resented the curious stares of his fellow passengers on the *Cambria,* and as Benjamin Quarles aptly put it, with "Douglass on board ship, it was too much to expect a trip without an incident." On the last evening, the captain, no doubt at Buffum's urging, called on Douglass to speak. Biting the hand that fed him (but denied him a cabin), Douglass delivered a fiery oration denouncing the merchants who had used ships, like the one he was on, to haul human cargo from Africa. When two passengers, who had been drinking, tried to shout him down, the captain put his fist in the face of one and threatened the other with irons.

James Buffum, a successful carpenter from Lynn was deeply committed to the antislavery cause. He and Douglass had met earlier, in Nantucket. Politic enough to be elected by his neighbors years later to be their mayor, the amiable Buffums had been chosen by Chapman and Garrison, who recalled the rough passage of the Hundred Conventions tour, to smooth the way for Douglass. The incident on the *Cambria* suggested that his task would not be easy, but when they arrived in Liverpool, they spent their first night in a hotel without incident, and the next day Douglass had the pleasure of seeing the discomfort of several of his fellow passengers when he was admitted to the house of the marquess of Westminster, open to visitors, quite as readily as any other tourist. Next, he and Buffum crossed over to Dublin to see Richard D. Webb, a publisher and long-time worker in the antislavery movement, who had agreed to publish the British edition of the *Narrative.* Webb was an irascible, charming, cultured man, fond of literature and literary gossip. In the days that followed, he and Douglass, conducting the conventional warfare of writer and publisher, completed the business necessary for the successful marketing of the *Narrative.*

Outwardly, Douglass's relationship with Webb, the stalwart friend of all good causes—"we gather Wednesday nights to discuss Anti-Slavery, Teetotalism, Peace etc, etc."—was excellent. Within the house on Great Brunswick Street, the story was very different. "F. Douglass was a very short time in my house," Webb later wrote, "before I found him to be absurdly haughty, self possessed, and prone to take offense. Even my wife who is one of the sweetest tempered of women and full of allowance making (which I am not) was obliged to admit that this was the case."

The trouble began as soon as Douglass and his traveling companion arrived. It was, Webb told Maria Weston Chapman, "his offensive and ungrateful behaviour to James N. Buffum towards whom he has been absolutely insolent—not only in my house but elsewhere"—that first "battered my esteem for him." And Webb continued, "How Buffum has put up with the conduct from one for whom he has done so much, is past my comprehension—for I am not a model of meekness and forbearance myself." Neither was Frederick Douglass. When he discovered that Chapman had explicitly directed Buffum to tend to money matters as they traveled—that she thought these could not be entrusted to a black man was not hard for Douglass to deduce—he poured out his scorn on poor Buffum. Douglass had a stronger intellect than his companion, was by far a better orator, and, what was more, had written a successful book, facts that called into question Webb's word "insolent." Douglass refused to be a man Friday, to be deferential when the only reason for deference was the assumed superiority of a white man.

Douglass was being sour, in part because Buffum was so sweet. The carpenter's abundant goodwill—his "meekness and forbearance"—was seasoned with a pinch of racism, and his companion could taste it. Some white abolitionists were so eager to prove they bore no racial prejudice that they doused every relationship with a black person in excessive kindliness. It rankled.

Often short with the affable Buffum, Douglass paid a high price for his independence. People fond of both men saw in Buffum "an enormous degree of love[,] of affection"; and obtuse though he was, he appears truly to have been reaching out to Douglass as a friend. But Douglass could not see beyond what he took to be condescension. Nor could he let down another barrier he had raised against so close a male friendship. Webb saw the "enormous degree of Love, of affection" in Buffum's manner to be a "feminine" element of his maleness "that Douglass does not respect." A cold man was on guard. In sweeping condemnation of "the least loveable of the abolitionists," Webb said, "I think his selfishness intense, his affection weak, and his unreasonableness quite extravagant." Perhaps the most telling of these observations was about the want of affection. Somewhere in the ruined house of his relationship with Thomas Auld, in an obscure corner of the destroyed friendship with Henry Harris, Douglass had discarded his trust in himself wholly to be a man's friend.

Matters gradually worsened on Great Brunswick Street. Webb remembered the clashes vividly. "My cousin Lizzy Poole and my sister-in-law Maria Waring were here at the time," he wrote. "They are both young women—sensible and comely. They walked with him and treated him with respect and no condescension. Yet for some entirely groundless huff he took, he treated L.P. in such a contemptuous uncultured manner that I was and have ever since been perfectly indignant." But it had been Douglass's turn to be indignant. The ladies had taken their exotic guest out on a leash, for all of Dublin to see. They thought it unseemly when he barked. Douglass would have vigorously disagreed with Webb's later assessment that his "inexcusable behaviour" was "unprovoked."

The chief flaw in Webb's attack on Douglass lay in his assumption that there was no provocation for the ill behavior, but it would be a mistake to dismiss the whole analysis as racist. In fact, in his willingness to regard Douglass with his exceedingly critical eye, Webb showed himself innocent of the unwitting condescension of the Buffums of his world, who exempted black people from normal criticism. Webb kept his dislike of Douglass to himself for six months, but when he was chided for being rude by Maria Weston Chapman (who had received a "tirade" from Douglass), he sat down one evening in May 1846 to write a very long and damning reply. "In all my experience of men," he observed, "I have never known one not insane so able and willing as he is, to magnify the smallest cause of discomfort or wounded self esteem into insupportable talk of offense and dissatisfaction."

The next morning, as he looked over what he had written, he was worried lest he had been too critical: "I read what I wrote . . . to my wife, her sister & my cousin at breakfast—they agree to the truth of what I have said, but they do not think I made sufficient allowance. H[arriet, his wife] says 'He is a child—a savage.' M[aria] Waring says, 'he is a wild animal.' " The ladies' racist tolerance did not prevail; Webb mailed his letter, thereby giving Chapman fresh grist for her mill. Perhaps Webb should not have written as he did, but there is something to be said for his frankness. In the many monumental battles that Webb and Douglass fought, Webb was, in the main, an honorable foe. He was one of the few of Douglass's antislavery antagonists who did not prefer to smile benignly and then do their undercutting offstage. Webb was brave enough to disagree with Douglass to his face.

Commitment to the antislavery cause transcended these quarrels as Douglass made impressive antislavery speeches in Dublin. In a telling gesture, he visited the jail where Daniel O'Connell had been held in 1843, to salute the Irish patriot's opposition to African slavery. In October, Webb, Buffum, and Douglass went together by stagecoach down the east coast of Ireland. At the ancient port of Wexford, in the bright Georgian meeting room upstairs in the gaunt gray stone Assembly House, Douglass spoke to an audience composed largely of Quakers. The next night, he spoke in Waterford. Then, when he reached Cork, all of Douglass's hopes for his great adventure outside the United States were realized. His public and his private worlds came together.

In Cork, Webb turned Douglass and Buffum over to the Jenningses. If Webb whispered any of his misgivings about Douglass, the Jenningses evidently took them as a challenge to prove Webb wrong. Soon after his departure, Buffum left as well, and for three weeks, Douglass had the Jenningses to himself. They, for their part, had a celebrity to accompany to public meetings almost every evening and, better still, to interrogate in the privacy of their parlor. In a written assessment that would have troubled him and undercuts a bit the egalitarianism of their behavior, Isabel, perhaps the sharpest-tongued of the family, wrote to Maria Weston Chapman, "He is the very first intelligent *slave* who has ever visited Cork." (Charles Lenox Remond, never a slave, though one cannot be sure Isabel remembered that fact, had been there five years earlier.) But there is less wonder than admiration in her conclusion that Douglass had triumphed: "Never was [there] a person who made a greater sensation in Cork amongst all religious beliefs." He had, she triumphantly noted, even gotten Church of England people to come out to have a look at him, to listen, and more remarkably still, to dip into their purses for contributions to the cause.

As we have seen, when slavery ended in the British West Indies in 1833, the British antislavery societies turned their attention to other parts of the world, particularly the United States. For many reformers on both sides of the Atlantic, emancipation was but one great paving stone in the road to moral perfection. As Douglass himself put it, "All great reforms go together." He and his fellow reformers called for all the changes within the wide spectrum of their moral imaginations. They had no eye for class inequities, nor any thought that fundamental economic restructuring was the way to combat such imponderables as famine or pauperism—let alone slavery. Instead, they struggled toward the many goals they thought attainable by moral suasion.

Douglass, therefore, walked with the "anti-everythingarians"—with antivivisectionists, vegetarians, and, more frequently, with opponents of drink. Indeed, his first lecture on foreign soil, on August 31, had addressed the evils not of slavery, but of alcohol. In the prosperous inland town of Celbridge, west of Dublin, public houses split the distance between the fifty-year-old carpet mill—as gray of stone and stark as any Fall River mill or, for that matter, any New Bedford bank—and Castletown House, the Georgian splendor of which put Wye House in the shade. The temperance people reflected little upon the paradoxes of the political economy of mill and manor, which were enough to make the best of men, and women, reach for a pint. They preferred to see the downing of drink not as a societal reaction, but as a personal sin.

Mankind's redemption from the sin of slaveholding was, of course, Douglass's goal and he brought every talk around to that subject. Cork's Father Theobald Mathew was Ireland's greatest temperance advocate; when Douglass reached his city and spoke in the priest's St. Patrick's Temperance Hall, he turned alcoholism into a metaphor, and converted his talk into an antislavery sermon. *"Mankind has been drunk,"* he insisted, when it has allowed slavery to continue; sober, he contended with an optimism missing later on his tour, the slaveholder would "consider the sinfulness of his position" and repent. Garrisonian moral suasion was being put to a tough test before the first Roman Catholic audience that Douglass ever faced.

At the Wesleyan Chapel on October 17, with Cork's mayor, Richard Dawson, in the chair, Douglass spared not his Protestant hosts. He upbraided the Methodists for backsliding from their staunch eighteenth-century condemnation of slaveholding, and then went on, denomination by denomination, damning the churches for condoning slavery. These attacks on organized religion, which had failed him when he was a boy in Maryland, were the stamp of Douglass's antislavery oratory in Ireland and, later, in Scotland. But if his controversial comments were meant to make these devout people search their souls, Douglass knew as well how to excite other elements of their being. Drawing on the pornography of Theodore Weld's *American Slavery As It Is,* and adding tales from his own experience, he aroused his audience with graphic descriptions of physical maltreatment and torture. "Ran away a Negro girl called Mary," he read from an advertisement for a fugitive, "has small scar over her eye, a good many teeth missing—the letter A is branded on her cheek and forehead."

Mary's fate, the audience might have noted, was in sharp contrast to that of the runaway who stood before them. "He was," an American admirer later wrote, "more than six feet in height, and his majestic form, as he rose to speak, straight as an arrow, muscular, yet lithe and graceful, his flashing eye, and more than all, his voice, that rivaled Webster's in its richness, and in the depth and sonorousness of its cadences, made up

such an ideal of an orator as the listeners never forgot." As he completed
a speech that gave ample demonstration of these powers to an admiring
Cork Ladies' Anti-Slavery Society, he closed with a request that money
or handiwork for Mrs. Chapman's annual antislavery bazaar in Boston
should be sent to "the Misses Jennings, Brown Street, before the twenty-
third next." Then his audience pressed forward in a great "crush," or
reception, to greet him. Under the Imperial Hotel's chandeliers of Waterford crystal, Frederick Bailey from Tuckahoe firmly grasped scores of
eager hands and looked deeply into appreciative Irish eyes.

He could reach people in public with a skill so immense as to seem
almost easily come by, but he was less sure of reaching out to people
privately. When he did so, it was not to the Jennings brothers, but to one
of their sisters. He and Isabel, as their letters reveal, achieved an intimacy
that was essential to him in the precarious and exhilarating world into
which he had launched himself. After he left her house, Isabel Jennings
became the first in a long line of woman confidants with whom he
corresponded, and these letters to "My dear friend" have a comfortable-
ness that was seldom achieved in the letters he exchanged with men. There
was, and is, much prurient speculation—not always devoid of racism—
about the sexual component of Douglass's friendships with white women,
and lurking within are fantastical images of a not-so-noble savage turned
gleaming black beast and proving fatally attractive to pale virgins anxious
to yield their chastity to some imagined hugeness.

Such damp reveries do not fit. Douglass was not black enough to
gleam, even if he had wanted to, and it is exceedingly hard to imagine
the resolutely dignified Victorian gentleman ever trying. What is at least
as much to the point, all of the women in question were intellectuals
living long before, in a corruption of Darwinism, Western science codi-
fied Africans as animals—often imagined as dangerous and compelling—
swinging low on the human tree. When he had left the Freeland farm
and the athletics of his labors with the Harris brothers, Frederick Bailey
had left behind a certain kind of physicality. To be sure, the runaway was
for a time "rough—unpolished—just from the bellows handle in Richmond's brass foundry in New Bedford," but Frederick Douglass soon put
on the proper clothes of the bourgeois gentleman he had elected to be.
That these clothes made the body they hid more mysterious and compelling was no doubt true, but his attractiveness must be understood in terms
of the mores of his world. If he was a man proud of his ability to draw
emotional attention to what he had to say, he was also a man of discipline—a Darwin or a Palliser, rather than a Byron or a Heathcliff. The
path of some of his friendships may have led to a bed, but it is difficult
to imagine him springing upon it in wanton randiness. Douglass's undeni-

able sexuality was no less compelling for being made to smolder within well-tailored wool, tidied by crisp linen.

After his success in Cork, he traveled northwest across Irish farm country to Limerick, where, Jane Jennings reported, "one of the most popular soirees was given to him." He spoke to perhaps five hundred of the little city's "most respectable inhabitants." But the respectable were not the only people he noticed. On his way through Ireland, Douglass saw what his antislavery hosts seemed blind to. Reports of famine—the grim result of the first of the rotted potato crops—were in the newspapers. Thin-armed children and their defeated mothers huddled at door-stoops, as fathers tried, often unsuccessfully, to earn passage out of the ports of Wexford, Waterford, and Cork. The antislavery people stepped around these Irish poor as they made their way into Douglass's lectures about mistreated Africans in America. Abolitionists were generous in their concern for those who had been wronged, but in the late 1840s, a curious deafness to suffering at home accompanied their sympathetic response to what was endured across the Atlantic.

Douglass did not entirely miss this tragic irony, though he never brought it up in his public addresses. In one of his finest letters, he wrote to William Lloyd Garrison of a mud-walled, windowless hut with "a board on a box for a table, rags on straw for a bed, and a picture of the crucifixion on the wall" and of the "green scum" covering the pit, near the door, full of "garbage & filth. . . . I see much here to remind me of my former condition and I confess I should be ashamed to lift my voice against American slavery, but that I know the cause of humanity is one the world over."

The physical conditions he had observed were in fact far worse than any he had experienced, but in this moving letter to Garrison he demonstrated how real for him was the chain that linked all suffering people. He never was so rude as to call on his Irish hosts to look after the misery of their own island, and he had no plan with which to attack the starvation there. He had pity, but no cure for the desperate needs of the beggars he saw on the streets. In lieu of explanation, he resorted to the familiar dodge of blaming drunkenness. And with a chilling aloofness, he spoke of his pride in walking the streets of Dublin with Webb and James Haughton and Richard Allen—rich gentlemen all, yet "friends of the poor."

From Limerick, he had returned to Dublin; his next destination was Belfast. Winter had come and ice held up the horses, so that he missed the usual Dublin-to-Belfast train. When he reached Belfast, hours late, he was met by "a gentleman," who escorted him to the Victoria Hotel; there James Standfield, a merchant who chaired the Belfast Anti-Slavery

Committee, was waiting. His host admitted he had been "somewhat fearful" that Douglass would "disappoint him," but immediately made his guest welcome. "I have seldom seen any one that appeared more glad to see me," Douglass reported with considerable pride. But the words "that appeared" show his guard was still up.

There was a month's work to be done. As usual, his publisher had failed to get copies of the *Narrative* where they could be sold. "I shall need Books immediately," he ordered Webb. Two weeks later, he again wrote, specifically requesting fifty copies of the *Narrative* with or without the tipped-in portrait over which he and Webb had been squabbling. He added with startling candor (that suggests the two enjoyed their battles) that he had dined with one Belfast gentleman who "says you are an odd fish," and commented, "Tis no slander." But acknowledging receipt of letters from home that Webb had forwarded, Douglass reported with cold brevity, "My family are all well."

In December 1845 notices were posted throughout Belfast announcing seven lectures by Frederick Douglass. Of these the most fully recorded was the fifth, given two days before Christmas. As usual, its subject was slavery, but the particular target of Douglass's attack was not slaveholding but Christians who would not reject the fellowship of slaveholders. His speech was masterful; it was also very like scores that he would give in the months to come in Scotland. Like Ireland, Scotland was a country with no slavery and scarcely enough Africans to fill a church, but with a large number of people committed to the nineteenth century's greatest reform, the ending of slavery. What Douglass said that night in Belfast, and later in Scotland, was what he had been called to Great Britain to say. The nominally secular American Anti-Slavery Society was, as always, proselytizing among evangelical and nonconformist Protestants. Douglass called on these Christians on both sides of the Atlantic to join the abolitionist cause or be damned as unchristian for not doing so.

Belfast citizens paid their fee and crowded the Independent Meeting-house to hear Douglass. As soon as Standfield had introduced him, the black Savonarola went forward into battle: "Ladies and gentlemen, one of the most painful duties I have been called on to perform in the advocacy of the Abolition of Slavery, has been to expose the corruption and sinful position of the American Churches." Citing distinguished stateside clergymen by name, he exposed their equivocations on slavery to his heart's content and to a portion of his audience's discontent. Sarcasm about the pulpit was hard for pious Protestants to swallow.

Turning from the divines who condoned slavery to the slaveholders themselves, Douglass acknowledged that "some persons have taken of-fence at my saying that Slaveholders become worse after their conversion"; once converted, they regarded owning their labor force not merely as practical but as biblically right. Remembering the rural revival meeting long ago on the Eastern Shore where Thomas Auld had found religion—a meeting not all that different from this one in Belfast at which Auld's slave was the exhorter—Douglass roared out that religion was but an additional stimulant to Christian slaveholders as "woman-whippers, cradle-plunderers, and man-stealers." (As the tour progressed, the woman-whipper became a "woman-stripping" monster.) "The 'religious' slaveholder is a man from whom I have been myself happily delivered." And "when you tell me there are some Christian slave-holders in the States, I tell you, as well might you talk of sober-drunkards."

The rhetoric rose. "Slave-holders! Oh, my friends, do not rank the slave-holder as a common criminal—as no more than a sheep-stealer or a horse stealer. The slave-holder is not only a thiever of men, but he is a murderer; not a murderer of the body, but, what is infinitely worse, a murderer of the soul—(hear, hear, hear)—as far as a man can murder the soul of his fellow-creature, for he shuts out the light of salvation from his spirit." Then, in one of his most effective gestures, Douglass held up a newspaper clipping and read the announcement of an auction of the estate of a clergyman. For sale was land " 'together with twenty seven negroes—*some of them very fine*—a library *chiefly theological—two mules* and *an old waggon!' "* As his audience laughed, Douglass said, "We should be sadly weeping to think that such a man ever lived."

On he went until he reached his specific target; with false mildness he named "Dr. Chalmers, [who] looks on slavery as an evil, that though wrong in itself, nevertheless, is not sufficiently important to exclude persons from Christian Union." Everyone in the hall knew Douglass was referring to the campaign to force Thomas Chalmers's Free Church of Scotland, with which numerous Presbyterians in Ulster felt kinship, to repudiate their fellow Presbyterians who were slaveholders in the American South. Far from ignoring Christianity, the secular antislavery preachers were determined to unite all evangelical Christians in a redefinition of their faith that would force slaveholding Christians to decide between accepting Christ and owning slaves. However, from the start it was not clear whether the true aim was to free the slaves or to punish the slaveholders, and this ambiguity may have been the fatal flaw in Douglass's whole British campaign.

Thomas Chalmers was a Presbyterian clergyman deeply troubled by the extreme poverty of workers in Glasgow. Two years before Douglass spoke, he had, in the Disruption, led better than a third of his fellow Presbyterian clergymen out of the state Church of Scotland into the new

Free Church of Scotland. Chalmers sought to better the lot of people troubled in body and soul: he envisioned the establishment of a godly commonwealth on earth—the earth of his Scotland—which would be a model for the reforming of Christians everywhere, even those in that other city on the hill, America. Chalmers's dream was not unlike the secular vision of a world of moral perfection of William Lloyd Garrison. Not unlike—save in one dimension absolutely essential to Garrison; in 1826, Chalmers had written a pamphlet criticizing slavery, but he was not prepared to exclude from his commonwealth those who owned slaves. What was worse, he seemed to Garrison to be courting their company.

Chalmers was radical in his strong response to the real ills of capitalistic industrialism in cities like Glasgow. His aim was to make the Free Church independent of the unreliable voluntary weekly offerings, so that a structured missionary program, directed chiefly at the urban poor, could be maintained. To raise the needed funds, therefore, he sent agents to the United States; his goal was a penny from each Presbyterian. But, alas, except for a group in Princeton, New Jersey, most of the responding Presbyterians were in the slaveholding South. The three thousand pounds raised came mainly from South Carolina, and the money was accompanied by a gentle letter from the Reverend Thomas Smyth of Charleston (formerly of Belfast, Ireland), citing the Scriptures, so beloved by Chalmers, to the effect that as the biblical patriarchs had looked after their slaves, so too did the good Christians of the South. Chalmers replied to Smyth, in a public letter that set off the controversy, "I do not need to assure you how little I sympathize with those who—because slavery happens to prevail in the Southern States of America—would unchristianize that whole region." The Garrisons and Douglasses in America, and dedicated antislavery people in Great Britain, were outraged.

In his own defense, Chalmers in 1845 wrote a formal letter stating, "Slavery, like war is a great evil. . . . Yet, destructive and demoralizing as both are, and inimical as Christianity is to all violence, and to vice, it follows not that there may not be a Christian soldier, and neither does it follow that there may not be a Christian slave-holder." He did go so far as to declare that ministers "who hold slaves, not as masters of a household, who must have domestic servants, but as masters . . . holding slaves for profit," should be disciplined. Such slaveholding, he feared, would "brutalize" the preacher. But he was not sure that owning field hands would similarly affect the laity: "We resist the proposed excommunication of all slaveholders." Chalmers called on antislavery people, among whom he counted himself, "through the medium of the public mind" to "bring direct influence to bear on the American legislators." He gave the Southern Presbyterians no such assignment; at no point did he suggest that it was their Christian duty to ameliorate the slaves' condition, let alone work for emancipation.

James Standfield's Belfast Anti-Slavery Committee published Chalmers's letter in full in a penny pamphlet, with refutations in the margin. Douglas's task was to refute Chalmers from the lectern. His speeches in Belfast were the start of a crusade that he was to take on to Scotland; wherever he spoke, his cry was to "the Free church of Scotland and all other Churches" to "have no communion with the American slaveholders," for "the blood of the slaves forbade them" fellowship. To repudiate that fellowship, he thundered forth to a Christian audience on the eve of Christmas, would be to "give slavery a blow it would stagger under." The audience roared back its approval. That night in Belfast, Frederick Douglass had achieved one of the great emotional triumphs of his life. Two days later, he was almost certainly within the comfortable circle of a good antislavery household for the holiday. But we do not know for sure; there is no record of any Christmas letter home.

12

Edinburgh

"IT IS QUITE an advantage to be a 'nigger' here," wrote Douglass to Francis Jackson from the Royal Hotel in Dundee. "I am hardly black enough for the british taste, but by keeping my hair as wooly as possible—I make out to pass for at least a half a negro at any rate." The antislavery orator had arrived in Scotland in January 1846 to begin fifteen months' work there and in England, and was in a cocky mood. Jackson, the rich and generous president of the Massachusetts Anti-Slavery Society, had seen him off when he sailed on the *Cambria,* and Douglass was reporting on a trip that had become a personal triumph.

He was in Great Britain not merely as an emblem of redemption from American slavery, but to lead what the American Anti-Slavery Society people thought to be one of the most important battles of the movement. His task was to convince the Scots to give credence to a new sin. This would have been no problem except that it involved denouncing his hosts, or rather, those of his hosts who would not renounce their Presbyterian brethren in the American South who owned slaves.

Douglass was not alone in this crusade to free the Free Church of Scotland from sin; he and Buffum, with whom he had again teamed up, were soon joined by the gentle utopian Henry C. Wright, in whose garden of love a great many people found nettles, and George Thompson, "Garrison's most powerful antislavery ally" in Great Britain. The four, reported the Edinburgh abolitionist Mary Welsh in May, "have done wonders in opening the eyes of the public to this enormous iniquity." She was referring to the Free Church's acceptance of funds from evildoers. "Send Back the Money"—the money that Thomas Chalmers had raised from slaveholding Americans to help in his fight against Scotland's poverty—was the endlessly repeated cry of the antislavery orators, and Douglass's voice carried it more powerfully than any other. He was the one people came to hear—and to see.

His letter to Jackson was written confidently and confidentially, to one whom he felt comfortable crowing to about his success. He reminded Jackson that soon after their meeting in Nantucket, "you took me into your drawing room—welcomed me to your table, put me in your best bed, and treated me in every way as an equal Brother at a time when to do so was to expose yourself to the hot displeasures of nearly all of your neighbors." Now he told proudly of receiving welcomes in Scotland that were as warm as Jackson's had been. Gloating a bit, he noted that Buffum, of whom he once again spoke fondly as "my good friend," had found the racial tables turned; everyone wanted to hear the "negro."

Hear him they did—in Glasgow ("a proud week for our cause," with one antislavery and one antiwar address and two lectures on India by the ubiquitous Thompson), in Aberdeen, Perth, Arbroath, and then Ayr and Paisley (a "tremendous gathering"). As the dark winter opened into spring, he was in Kilmarnock, Greenock, Bonhill, Galashiels, and Kelso; in April, he was in the beautiful city of Edinburgh, with Arthur's Seat, the hill rising straight up from the town, in full green. "Everything," he wrote Amy Post, "is so different here from what I have been accustomed to in the United States. No insults to encounter—no prejudice to encounter, but all is smooth—I am treated as a man and equal brother. My color instead of being a barrier to social equality—is not thought of as such."

Later, in England, Catherine Clarkson, daughter of the famous old antislavery warrior Thomas Clarkson, worried about the paleness of that color: "I wish he were full blood black for I fear pro-slavery people will attribute his preeminent abilities to the white blood that is in his veins." One of Douglass's Dublin admirers had a somewhat different slant on the problem: "Faith, an' if half a Naigar can make a speech like that, whut could a whole Naigar do." At least one American knew the right answer to this excellent question: years later, Lizzie Lavender, a former slave herself, reflected "that if a man who is only half black can become great like that, what may not be achieved by a person who is all black like me."

Frederick Douglass was a celebrity. So impressive was he that he was absorbed into Scotland's abundant folklore. In a pamphlet of antislavery songs, a Scotsman who went to hear Douglass speak was quoted as saying: "On Munonday nicht our Jock gat me to gang doun an' hear that chiel Douglass. I had came away wanting ma specks: but frae the luik I gat o' him, he seemed a buirly fellow, ane I shouldna like to hae a tussle wi him either feeseecally or intellecktually." And, indeed, Douglass did carry the day; in a ballad set to the tune of "My Tammy Boy," a cleansed "Mother Kirk"—the Free Church—sings: "Heaven rings wi' Douglass' appeal/ An' thrills my heart like burning steel." The scene is set with *"Boy Tammy sitting at a table, scouring some suspicious looking Coppers with Intellectual Sand, and a Leaf of the Bible";* at the ballad's end, when Douglass enters and says "SEND BACK THE MONEY," Tammy overturns the table, spilling the coins as "MOTHER CHURCH and DOUGLASS cordially shake hands." It was Douglass, not his betters in the antislavery movement, who was immortalized in a ballad (which, one hopes, sang better than it reads), but the prophecy that he would succeed in converting the Free Church was not fulfilled.

For one thing, the slogan "Send Back the Money" was scarcely on the level of moral rhetoric of a later movement's "Freedom?" with its antiphonal response, "Now." Nevertheless, Douglass thundered the demand from scores of lecterns, and audiences shouted the words right back. The slogan caught on; it also brought retaliation. In Belfast, late one night while Douglass was there, bills were posted reading "Send Back the Nigger." This expression of free speech worked to Douglass's advantage. Like other antislavery people, Webb was outraged by the act of the "diabolical 'minister of christ' "—a Methodist named Smith, Webb was certain. Smith would, Webb reasoned, get his just reward, "for he has greatly promoted the cause he tried to injure." Triumphantly, Douglass chanted "Send Back the Money" wherever he went, and dignified middle-class audiences chanted it back; ragged children called it out to him as he passed them on the street; and in Edinburgh, he and two local antislavery women had the audacity to carve it into the sod of one of the city's lovely parks. The slogan and the increasingly vitriolic attacks on Chalmers made that man's last year on earth—he died in 1847—less than totally happy. One might have expected reformers committed to moral suasion to try to persuade Chalmers and his followers in the Free Church to send back the money in envelopes containing messages asking their fellow communicants to free their slaves. Instead, the slogan seemed only a chastisement, and Presbyterians in the American South who revered Chalmers were furious that a fellow Christian who had seemed to open a promising new avenue of fellowship should have had their generously given coins flung in his face.

Quite apart from what the campaign meant for Chalmers or Douglass personally, what did it have to do with getting rid of slavery? Nothing, if the goal was pacific emancipation. A good deal, if the goal was isolation of the slaveholding South. But shrewd observers were beginning to see that driving slaveholders into isolation drove them also into fiercely martial defensiveness. The year 1846 was crucial for the region that would become the Confederacy. It was the year the Mexican War began, the last time Southerners were able to spread their wings. Antislavery people in the North, including Douglass, spoke against the war with great vehemence, seeing it as nothing more than the manifestation of a slave-holding conspiracy to extend the geographical boundaries of slavery. Douglass bitterly opposed the sending of Massachusetts troops to the war by the governor, preferring a dissolution of the Union to such pandering to the slavocracy. The Mexican War gave the South its last relief from constriction. Thereafter it battled, successfully for more than a decade, against a movement that would result in the ending of slavery.

Long before 1846, slaveholders had felt squeezed not only by the nettlesome opponents in the North but by strong antislavery opinion in Great Britain and on the Continent. Southerners looked for ways of giving themselves a psychological boost. To the many Presbyterians among them, Chalmers offered a splendid opportunity for just such a sense of bettered self-regard. Chalmers's break with the state church—with central authority, as Stewart J. Brown has shown—his concern for the industrial poor, and most of all, his deep religious commitment, drew the Southern Presbyterians to him.

Many of these slaveholders believed their patriarchal slave-labor system, in which the workers were held to be securely cared for, was infinitely more humane than the wage-labor system, which left urban workers destitute. Chalmers's welcome to Southern Presbyterians gave them an international respectability they craved. It seemed that if, for example, the Reverend Mr. Smyth wrote a letter to Chalmers introducing Joseph H. Lumpkin as a distinguished jurist, the chief justice of the new Georgia Supreme Court, so often attacked at home as an apologist for slavery, could anticipate a greeting of respect rather than scorn when he visited Scotland.

The success of the Free Church and its embrace of the slaveholders also bolstered the Southerners in their battles to gain the recognition of other European Protestants for their now-separate Southern slaveholding denominations. With the establishment of the Methodist Episcopal Church, South in 1845, a vast gathering of Christians had said a formal no to the antislavery doctrine of Methodism. The Presbyterian split of 1837 had not been strictly along slavery–antislavery lines, but Southern Presbyterians too saw themselves as apart from any Northern brethren who embraced even the mildest antislavery sentiments.

Isolated at home, slave-owning Christians sought communion abroad, but a nonbelieving former Methodist from Maryland and Massachusetts was determined to keep them from the bread and the wine. As Douglass thundered "Send Back the Money," he thrilled the already converted and made a few Free Church people more critical of slavery, but his rhetoric was also an invitation to many other Scots to articulate an even more virulent hatred of the Free Church than they had expressed before. In all, Douglass achieved little beyond getting some very stiff backs up and shattering Southerners' hopes that they might share their communion with their Scottish brethren in quiet confidence-restoring comfort.

A good many antislavery people disapproved of Douglass's ferocity. Gentler souls still hoped that slaveholding Christians could be persuaded to work toward ending slavery. James Lenox, a Scot who had become a very rich New Yorker, believed as late as 1846 that Virginia would, of its own accord, institute gradual emancipation, and North Carolina and Tennessee would follow suit. Other people, concerned, as Chalmers was, with the very real industrial poverty suffered in the industrial cities of the antislavery world, sought to link together that poverty and the plight of the enslaved.

Douglass himself had made just such a connection in his long letter to Garrison describing the terrible poverty in Ireland, which Garrison published, but the public stance of the Garrisonian movement was that no wrong matched that suffered by the slave. Even if they privately acknowledged the kinship of slavery to poverty, the abolitionists knew that any depiction of the grim realities of industrial labor played into the hands of slaveholders. Apologists for slavery were fond of comparing the lot of their happy slaves with that of eight-year-old child laborers in the North and in England. But whatever the reasons, the cost of the failure to link the problems of the workers of Glasgow and the slaves of Georgia has been great.

Douglass's cold turning of his back on all slaveholders had its roots in his repudiation of the Aulds as well as in the Garrisonian policy of opposing all efforts to achieve gradual emancipation or amelioration of the slave's lot. Such an easing would only allow slavery to persist. In defense of this position, it must be added that none of the letters sent to Scotland by Presbyterian slaveholders, however gentle their Christian message, suggested that the writers had anything other than a steel-hard commitment to the retention of slavery as it stood. The 1846 attack on tainted money by Douglass and Garrison, who joined him that summer, was blamed for almost destroying the previously strong Glasgow Emancipation Society by pitting Free Church people against their critics. But the much-publicized, well-attended antislavery meetings conducted by Douglass and his colleagues won more converts to the cause than they lost. And while the stern message of the abolitionists may be seen as having driven Southerners into a position that they would go to war to maintain, evidence is hard to find, even in the years well before 1846, that any milder rhetorical attack on slavery would have produced any less staunch a defense of the institution.

In 1846, Douglass was the "lion" of Edinburgh. His bitterly critical publisher, Richard Webb (to whom Douglass no longer bothered to write), reported to Maria Chapman that "as a consequence of the stir he has made there . . . people of the highest rank in that eminently aristocratic & conceited metropolis contend for his company." This attention, Webb asserted, would put great strain on Douglass when he returned to America: "If he be able to tolerate with any degree of patience the immense change in his position that will then take place, he will give proof of extraordinary greatness of mind." But Webb was not anticipating such proof, and he added, "From what I hear of her, I wonder how he will be able to bear the sight of his wife—after all the petting he gets from beautiful, elegant, and accomplished women in a country where prejudice against colour . . . is laughed at." Douglass, he concluded, "is a sharp man—but I am sure he needs such ballast . . . as Garrison alone can supply."

The ballast was being brought on board. In Boston in the spring of 1846, Garrison was planning a summer trip to England while Douglass was off to London in May. He spoke there before the London Peace Society, the Complete Suffrage Association, the National Temperance Society, and the British and Foreign Anti-Slavery Society. He was feeling so heady about life in Great Britain that he was giving thought to staying. In the summer of 1846, the great men and women of the American movement were making new decisions about Douglass; they did not know that some of the women in Britain were helping him realize that he should make some decisions for himself. The American plan was to keep Douglass in Britain for another year of proselytizing. He agreed to stay, and began seriously to make plans for settling permanently there. James Buffum, who returned to Lynn at this time, agreed to care for the Douglass family's affairs during Douglass's additional year abroad. Douglass may also have asked him to arrange for the family's emigration.

While Buffum was en route, Douglass wrote a letter to his family in Lynn, proposing the move to Britain. That letter has been lost, but not his follow-up letter. Contrite that he had missed a mail steamer—which suggests that he seldom did so, and that many of his letters to Anna have been lost—he wrote "My own Dear Sister Harriet" asking that she, as one of the "beloved ones of my family" and Jeremiah Sanderson, an amiable young man who was also part of the Douglasses' Lynn household, persuade Anna to consider moving. They were to read aloud both his letter to Harriet and the one enclosed for Anna "over and over again until Dear Anna shall fully understand their contents." The "Dear Anna" has a disingenuous ring; the "over and over again" almost suggests that his wife was dim. When the letters had been carefully read, Harriet was to "write me by the next steamer what you think of coming to this country. Speak dear Harriet," he implored, "just what you think even though [you may] differ from me. I will love you the more for speaking out."

Later in July, as he contemplated the idea of settling permanently in Edinburgh or some other place in Britain, he wrote a letter to William A. White. "I dreamed last night," he said, "that you would not be angry at receiving a letter from your friend Frederick Douglass. It may all be a dream, yet for once I felt like acting under the direction of a dream." The dream had taken him back to Pendleton, Indiana, in 1843, and the savage attack the two had helped each other survive. After recounting that story, Douglass closed, as we have seen, by saying that he had ever since "loved" White. Then, with a beautiful description of Edinburgh, he invited White to join him there, and also expressed the hope that White was by now married: "I want to see more William A. Whites in the world as well as to see happy those who are already here." In the quiet of a foreign city, Frederick Douglass was happy, but wistfully contemplated something that was impossible to achieve. He missed his friends—"I long to see a face which I have seen in America"—and wanted them to come to him, though he must have known they could not, except on rare visits. And the idea of bringing his family across the Atlantic was just as unrealistic.

Three days later he was in Newcastle upon Tyne, visiting Ellen Richardson and her brother and sister-in-law Henry and Anna Richardson, Quakers with whom Charles Remond had stayed in 1841. Ellen Richardson, about a decade older than the twenty-eight-year-old Douglass, was the headmistress of a girls' school. She had long been active in the antislavery cause, and cognizant of the personal problems that ex-slaves faced. She and her brother took Douglass to the seaside, and there, "sitting on the sand," he may have begun to see that moving his family to Britain could not work. Douglass himself, enjoying the "democracy of the intellect," could be oblivious to any racist sentiment, but he must have realized that his illiterate, black wife and his dark children could never be at home in this foreign country. Looking out at the water, he pondered, as he had in his letter to White, if "it would be safe for me to come home" now that he was so notorious and so easy for the Aulds to find. "Observing his sadness," Ellen Richardson made up her mind to arrange to buy him his freedom.

The dream of a new life in Britain died hard, however. Harriet had been asked to speak "just what you think." When she did—actually in an August letter that crossed his of July—it was to say that Frederick was not the only one in the family with a life to lead. She was to be married. Frederick was devastated by the news and furious that Harriet did not even tell him the man's name: "All you wish from me is a dress a light silk dress—a wedding dress." Since she hadn't identified the groom, he declined to send the dress. Realizing that the marriage would mean Harriet would not be on hand to keep things going in Lynn, let alone to arrange for the family's emigration, he nevertheless claimed that he would not put a "straw" in the way of her marrying. "I should rejoice to see you married tomorrow if I felt you were marrying some one worthy of you," he added. "It would spread a dark cloud over my soul to see you marry some ignorant and unlearned person. You might as well tie yourself to a log of wood as to do so. You are altogether too refined and intelligent a person for any such marriage." Then he closed with a blessing that scarcely erased his damnation: "God bless you. You are of age." She need not, he concluded, wait for him to get back.

How much Douglass, consciously or subconsciously, felt himself tied to a log he never again betrayed. But he knew now what his choices were: he could abandon his family and stay in Britain alone, or he could go home. A strong person, who had had no choice, had once abandoned him; now he was the strong person of the family. And he did have a choice. Ellen Richardson was working to make it a safe one. At the end of the summer, after he had journeyed to London to join Garrison in August for what he thought was to be the conclusion of his mission, he wrote Anna that he was coming home.

In London, Douglass and Garrison made a start at forming the link that Karl Marx always thought was a natural one—between the working classes in Europe, Britain, and the American North, on the one hand, and laborers in the American South on the other. It is one of the great missed opportunities of Douglass's life and of the history of black Americans that this promising effort at cooperation did not bring about a true international working-class movement. The two Americans had conversations with William Lovett, one of the most important radicals in Britain, and many of his most ardent associates. Lovett—a Cornishman whose father had drowned at sea and whose resolute mother came from a family of blacksmiths—had come to London in 1821. He had tried his hand at many jobs before establishing himself as a cabinetmaker. Lovett was a tireless speaker in the cause of his fellow workingmen. With another radical reformer, Henry Vincent, he had organized the small but influential London Working Men's Association; R. H. Tawney has credited their efforts with being the start of the political labor movement "which . . . developed into Chartism." For twenty years, in jail and out, Lovett had championed the cause of the working class.

Douglass, too, was a craftsman, and he and Garrison had spent a bit of time in jail themselves; there were ties that did bind, and the three men were eager to make common cause. On August 17, 1846, at the Crown and Anchor, with the ghosts of Johnson and Boswell hovering over the teetotallers, abolitionists Douglass and Garrison joined Chartists Lovett and Vincent to launch publicly their new Anti-Slavery League. The room in which they met had been the scene of a meeting in 1838 that had been critical in the development of Chartism. The new organization stood quite deliberately as an affront to the British and Foreign Anti-Slavery Society, which neither concerned itself with issues other than slavery nor repudiated cooperation with those who countenanced religious communion with slaveholders.

That venerable society, whose meetings Douglass had recently addressed, considered itself to have a great deal of pressing work; there was lobbying to be done, to prevent the government's tariff policy from working to the extreme detriment of recently freed people in the West Indies, and there was, in 1846, an upsurge in the slave trade to Brazil to be combated. Adopting a viewpoint not unlike that of Douglass and Remond in their battle against John A. Collins's anti-property agitation, members of the British and Foreign Anti-Slavery Society were to claim that the new league had perfectionist aims far removed from the cause of the slave. Most of the few members of the old society who came to the Crown and Anchor were appalled.

George Thompson, the radical, much-traveled antislavery leader, was in the chair, and Henry C. Wright gave the opening address. Garrison followed with a long speech (and was deeply moved by the exceedingly warm response); then, as Garrison generously reported, Douglass, following "one of his very best efforts," was "even more rapturously received." Indeed, Garrison said that he "never saw an audience more delighted." Two men were not delighted. The Reverend John Howard Hinton, an English Baptist minister and author of *History and Topography of the United States,* rose to defend the American and Foreign Anti-Slavery Society, a counterpart of the British group. And an American "alluded to our friend Douglass as *'that colored man,'*" whereupon "the whole audience burst out in such a thunder-tone of disgust and indignation, that [the speaker] sunk upon his seat as if a thunderbolt had smitten him." Douglass's Dublin friend James Haughton hastily offered a resolution welcoming the new organization to the family of reform, and Henry Vincent, head of the London Working Men's Association, closed the six-hour meeting with a speech firmly linking the cause of the British working class to that of the slaves.

Even reformers need to relax after efforts like these. Lovett recalled "a very delightful evening" he spent with Douglass, Garrison, and some other friends. "On that occasion we had not only a very interesting account of the Anti-Slavery movement and its prominent advocates in America, but our friend Douglas, who had a fine voice, sang a number of negro melodies, Mr Garrison sang several anti-slavery pieces, and our grave friend, H. C. Wright, sang an old Indian war song. Other friends contributed to the amusement of the evening, and among them our friend Vincent sang 'The Marseillaise.' " In the next few days there was another, more businesslike meeting with Vincent, in Stoke Newington; a breakfast with a reform member of Parliament, John Bowring; a Sunday with William Ashurst, who contributed regularly to the *Liberator;* and a visit at Muswell Hill—which Garrison pronounced "as charming a spot as the earth presents"—with the Unitarian minister and politician William Johnson Fox, a member of the Anti-Corn Law League and an advocate of compulsory education.

In Clapham, Douglass visited the Quaker writers Mary and William Howitt. Mrs. Howitt, a translator of Hans Christian Andersen, declared the "runaway slave" to be "one of the most interesting men I ever saw." The sight of him fascinated her; "I can talk of nothing but the 'dear blacks.' " Her observation may be a clue to why these promising discussions bore so little fruit; Douglass was seen not as an organizer of a movement or even as truly an individual, but as a marvelously compelling representative object of wonder. That he might be the American who could transform antislavery into a movement concerned with the welfare of all workers, whether slave or "free," was not seriously pursued. There was to be in the 1860s a critical linkage between workers in Britain and their fellows in the American South, in the form of opposition to the Confederate cause during the Civil War, but no such connection between workers was established in the United States.

The problem lay not merely in the way Douglass was perceived but in his own perception of himself. Nowhere in his letters or Garrison's is there any account of their visiting the working-class districts of the great city to talk to the people who lived there. (The one exception is Garrison's reference, in a letter to his wife, to the many prostitutes—including one "with a sweet countenance, almost pensive, and a beautiful form"— who gave him "the most earnest glances.") Socially, Douglass reached upward, rather than outward to the laborers, one of whom he had been not so long ago. If only because he liked good clothing, Douglass might have looked up William Cuffey, a former slave, a master tailor, a highly respected member of the Chartists, and a talented musician into the bargain. Cuffey too had come a long way, and the two men might have found they had a good deal in common.

In Bristol, later in August, Douglass made the most explicit connection he was ever to make between Chartist concerns and his own. Reiterating, less strenuously than he sometimes did, his long-held view that actual chattel slavery was worse than the wage "slavery" of industrial Britain, he referred approvingly to the recent formation of the Anti-Slavery League, which his listeners knew had Chartist support, saluting it for "having for its object the overthrow of slavery throughout the world." In one of his rare metaphoric uses of the word "slavery," which a reporter took down with care, he "spoke of 'political slavery in England' " and of "slavery in the army, . . . the navy, and, looking upon the labouring population, he contemplated them as slaves. He then asked, 'Why does not England set the example by doing away with these forms of slavery at home, before it called upon the United States to do so?' " This odd, upside-down bit of anti-anti-Americanism was coupled with a firm declaration of common purpose with the Chartists.

His remarks would have delighted his avowedly radical friend Elizabeth Pease, in Darlington, in the industrial north of England. In 1842 she had complained when Joseph Sturge refused to bring the word "Chartist" into the name of the British and Foreign Anti-Slavery Society. "Why," she asked Ann and Wendell Phillips, "succumb to the prejudices of the middle classes by rejecting an appellation which tells you their principles at once?" She might have been less delighted with the way Douglass and Garrison succumbed if not to the prejudices then surely to the charms of middle-class Bristol. Indeed, their visit to Bristol severely diminished the radical commitment they seemed to have been making in London.

Douglass and Garrison were met at the station by John B. Estlin, a Unitarian ophthalmological surgeon whom Garrison regarded as the "main spoke in the anti-slavery wheel, in all this region." In his fine phaeton, the doctor drove the two to the handsome houses where they were to stay—Douglass with George Thomas, a prosperous Quaker, and Garrison with the Estlins. The next afternoon, Douglass, with London Chartism still ringing in his ears, gave his radical speech attacking "slavery" in England. Mary Estlin, the doctor's daughter, was there with her friend Mary Carpenter, who thought Douglass's speech impressive for its "powerful reasoning, facts impressively brought out, touching appeals and," as so many observers noted, "keen sarcasm," combined with "graphic description." Bristol had been the center of investment in and trade with the slaveholding West Indies, and Garrison was uneasy for a time about how the good merchants of the city would react to Douglass's speech. But they seemed not to take offense at his branding of all slaveowners—and many Bristol families had been absentee owners—as "vagabonds" and "villains." "How the mayor," who chaired the meeting, "really felt at such plain talk, I cannot say," Garrison reported. The mayor had "concluded the meeting with some commendatory remarks;—and, to my surprise, Mr. Estlin took exception to nothing." Garrison knew that the "gentle" Estlin, in private, was urging Douglass to avoid radical working-class politics, to stop hammering at the churches, and to avoid the sexual innuendos he claimed to find in the *Narrative of the Life of Frederick Douglass.* Under the influence of the pious, conservative Bristol Quakers, the Americans, concentrating again solely on slavery, were ducking away from Chartism.

One morning Mary Estlin took Frederick to "our asylum for the blind," where she had been reading the *Narrative* aloud, and "there was much shaking of hands." Just two years younger than Douglass, Mary Estlin—like so many of the other antislavery women he met in Britain—was fascinated by the runaway. Something other than his sexual attractiveness drew these women to Douglass; in some way his quest for liberation urged them on in their repressed quest for their own. Talented and devoted to a worthy cause, these women encountered great frustration; they were often not allowed to sit downstairs at the public meetings, or to speak, despite their undoubted grasp of the issues. Even the most outspoken of them, like Elizabeth Pease, were forced to defer to the men and to sit home expending their energy on handicraft monstrosities to send to Maria Chapman for her antislavery bazaars in Boston. They were capable of much more, and Douglass, by his attention to them, gave evidence of his understanding of their frustration. For their part, the women—a good many of them, at least—were peculiarly attuned to the way the male leaders of the antislavery movement unconsciously neglected to consult the black man about strategies and decisions. When, after Garrison had departed, Douglass decided to begin his own newspaper upon his return to America, to find his own voice, these women encouraged him.

That return to America, which he had told Anna would come in the fall, was delayed again. It had taken only a call from on high to change his mind. (He knew the change in plans would "cost . . . some pain" to "my Anna," he told Isabel Jennings, whom he was also disappointing by not going home by way of Cork, but "disappointment is the common lot of us all.") On August 18, Douglass had accompanied Garrison and George Thompson on a pilgrimage to Playdon Hall to call on Garrison's "dear and venerated" friend Thomas Clarkson, the grand old man of British antislavery. Clarkson, who had once had to fight his way through a gang trying to walk him off the end of a dock, had battled slavery all his life. Douglass, he insisted, must continue the unfinished work in Britain. Garrison's letter thanking the old man for an hour of "unspeakable happiness" was flooded with the "cheering light of heaven" as he imagined Clarkson entering the "valley of the shadow of death!" Perhaps without the help of this hastening along, Clarkson did die a month later, but the Americans could remember that he had admonished them "not to mix up any extraneous matters with our sacred cause." Garrison concurred: "The American Anti-Slavery Society is . . . unswerving in its course, and single in its object—to wit, the abolition of Slavery." The incipient linkage to Chartism was abandoned.

No one better exemplified that sacred cause than the magnificent slave. Garrison recognized this, and so, reluctantly, did Richard Webb: "I take back nothing I have said of his defects . . . but I admire and value him so much for the cause's sake that I would bitterly regret if anything occurred to end his usefulness." Douglass seemed all but indispensable, and though, as one shrewd historian has noted, Garrison was jealous of his protégé's success, they continued to serve the common cause together. They spoke jointly before huge audiences in Edinburgh and in Glasgow. In October, Douglass traveled to Liverpool for a sentimental parting with Garrison, who was sailing for home. The two were to take to the road together again the following summer for a speaking tour in Pennsylvania and Ohio; in Harrisburg, as if in confirmation of the solidarity of their friendship, they would be stoned by an angry crowd.

By the time Douglass was to go back, Ellen Richardson's campaign had worked. Her plea for money to buy his freedom had brought a check for fifty pounds from John Bright; she knew that with this money, and the prestige of Bright's support, her efforts would succeed. Douglass was still legally the property of Thomas Auld, as the thousands of readers of the *Narrative* knew. Arrangements for his trip to Britain had already been made when the book came out; indeed, Douglass would have been out of the country on publication day if his trip had not been delayed by an illness. Opponents of the antislavery cause might well urge Thomas Auld to try to retrieve his insolent property. Any such effort by either Thomas or his brother Hugh would have met with an extraordinary outcry and would probably have failed, but as long as Frederick Bailey was owned the possibility of his return to slavery did exist. This situation was intolerable to Ellen Richardson—and, of course, to Douglass.

With John Bright's check in hand, Richardson confided in her sister and her sister's husband, a lawyer. The way arrangements were made for the purchase and manumission of Frederick Bailey is a perfect demonstration that some, at least, of the abolitionists were able to marry their social concerns to their successful endeavors within the world of commerce and the law. Exactly how the negotiations proceeded is not clear, but we do know that Douglass wrote about the problem to William A. White, who could find those in Boston who could get things done. The man in the American Anti-Slavery Society who got the job was Ellis Gray Loring, long a stalwart of the antislavery movement. Though they might choose not to employ him as their lawyer, not even the most conscienceless Cotton Whigs on State Street could ignore a Loring, let alone a Gray, and neither could lawyers and bankers in New York and Baltimore.

Loring engaged the services of a New Yorker, Walter Lowrie, who in turn arranged for a Baltimore lawyer to ask Hugh Auld, the brother available in the city, for a price—or, more probably, to suggest one to him, since a ship's carpenter would probably not have known what price in pounds to stipulate. The figure agreed upon was £150 sterling— roughly $1,250—and when Hugh consulted him, Thomas Auld agreed to it. In December, the transaction was completed: Hugh passed the money to Thomas Auld, who in Talbot County on November 30, 1846, had filed a bill of sale of "Frederick Baily or Douglass as he calls himself" to Hugh Auld; Hugh, in turn, on December 12, 1846, had formally registered a deed of manumission in the Baltimore County courthouse for "Frederick Bailey, otherwise called Frederick Douglass." The lawyers had made sure that there could be no misunderstanding about who was being set free.

Douglass's freedom had been obtained in the most unsensational way. Thomas Auld had not been forced to assume a mantle of guilt by selling his slave to abolitionists—foreign abolitionists, at that—and Frederick Douglass could not wave a bill of sale in the air showing that he had bought himself. But moralists bent on purity—someone else's purity— will not allow anything to be accomplished quietly. There were harsh outcries (not unlike those that greeted Moncure Conway when, in the midst of the bloody stalemate of the Civil War, he proposed that the Confederacy be allowed its independence if it freed the slaves; at that time, the harshest screams of outrage came from abolitionists who would not hear of accomplishing a goal they had sought for decades unless the evil slaveholders were made to suffer). Douglass and his friends, the moralists claimed, were trafficking with slaveholders. His rich friendship with Henry C. Wright was weakened now by Wright's criticism of what he had done, and people in Britain who had recently been singing his praises, like Mary Welsh in Edinburgh, deplored the action. So did a great many members of the American Anti-Slavery Society. Presumably he would have been beyond criticism—and they would have wept over his fate—if he had gone back to Covey's fields or had been shot while struggling to escape from those dragging him there. Douglass, who responded to the attacks with more dignity than they deserved and more patience than was to be expected, preferred to be a free antislavery worker rather than a martyr. To his credit, William Lloyd Garrison shared his viewpoint, and helped defuse the criticism.

After Garrison's departure in October, Douglass undertook a five-month speaking tour, largely in the strongly antislavery and nonconformist north of England. He spent Christmas 1846 in Newcastle upon Tyne with the Richardsons; there he met another articulate, intelligent antislavery worker, Julia Griffiths, and talked to her of his plan for starting a newspaper on his return to America. The two developed a friendship that was intense and lasting. Julia Griffiths loved Frederick Douglass from their first meeting until they both died, nearly half a century later.

In Britain, Douglass had achieved an independence that he would never be willing to yield. In Cork with the Jenningses, in the rest of Ireland, and in Scotland and England as well, he had come to know himself. He had gained enormous self-confidence from being treated with public respect. He had been paid full attention. As Nathan Huggins has said, he was "his own man" now. To be sure, this strong self-regard was accompanied by an arrogance that could be exposed by the smallest slight. But his confidence could also be expressed with great warmth and intelligence, as in his letter to William White about their experience in Pendleton and in the letters he wrote to Isabel Jennings. The trip to Britain had brought a man not yet thirty a very long way toward becoming the person he wanted to be, but had separated him fatally from the domestic life he and his wife had achieved back in New Bedford. After his return to Lynn, he reported to the Richardsons, "My dear Anna is not well, but much better than I expected to find her, as she seldom enjoys good health. She feels exceedingly happy to have me once more at home. She had not allowed herself to expect me *much* for fear of being disappointed; but she was none the less glad to see me on that account." The return could not straighten a misshapen marriage.

When the *Cambria* docked in Boston, Frederick Douglass, ignoring his luggage, "lept" onto the wharf, and scarcely nodding as he ran through a crowd of admirers, he raced for the train to Lynn. "In twenty five minutes, I reached Lynn, the train passing my door from which I saw my family five minutes before getting home." Having waited impatiently for the train to finally stop, he rushed out of the station: "When within fifty yards of our house, I was met by my two bright-eyed boys, Lewis and Frederick, running and dancing with joy to meet me. Taking one in my arms and the other by the hand, I hastened to my house."

13

4 Alexander Street

ROCHESTER was a brash new city, bright and ready for a man eager to claim his own place in the world. In 1847, it was a prosperous manufacturing center of fifty thousand people. Situated in upstate New York at the fall line of the north-flowing Genesee River just short of where it reached Lake Ontario, Rochester was across the lake from Canada, the last—the safe—stop of the underground railroad. That famous conduit to freedom, so compelling to the American imagination that it sometimes seems to dwell only in legend, was real indeed in Rochester; from the city, many runaways from slavery made their way out of the United States and into freedom, with the help of a vigorous group of antislavery citizens. The route to liberation led due north, and Frederick Douglass chose the richest image of the resolute, hopeful trek of runaways to freedom when he named his new antislavery newspaper *North Star.*

Rochester offered promise to another runaway as well. For Douglass, going there meant a new start. He would be leaving Lynn and breaking free of the Garrisonian fold. Initially, it had appeared that the traveler had returned not only to hearth and home but also to his old relationship with his mentor. The two had parted affectionately in Liverpool the previous fall, when Garrison had left for America, but when Douglass returned, he brought with him ideas and ambitions that the American Anti-Slavery Society found hard to contain—notably his plan to have his own newspaper, with which to bring his own words in his own way to a public concerned with the slavery question. "I still see before me a life of toil and trials . . . , but," he pledged, "justice must be done, the

Frederick
Douglass in his
twenties. This
daguerreotype
is perhaps his
earliest portrait.

Tuckahoe
Creek. Betsy
Bailey's cabin
stood on the
bank to the left.

Frederick Bailey's Baltimore at about the time he left, 1838.

Frederick Douglass's New Bedford in the 1840s.

Nantucket, where
Douglass gave his
first great antislav-
ery speech, August
16, 1841. He walked
along Main Street,
above, to the meet-
ing in the Big Shop,
left. The African
Baptist Church, *be-
low*, was in Guinea,
the black commu-
nity where he
probably spent the
night.

Women in the antislavery movement. *Clockwise from the upper left:* Susan B. Anthony, leading feminist; Lucretia Coffin Mott, Quaker abolitionist; Anna Dickinson, dynamic orator in the cause of equal rights; Maria Weston Chapman, powerful secretary of the American Anti-Slavery Society; Sojourner Truth, irrepressibly articulate abolitionist.

William Lloyd Garrison, *above*, inspired Douglass. Wendell Phillips, *above right*, was an ardent champion of the antislavery cause—and of Douglass. Douglass joined Abby Kelley (later Abby Kelley Foster, *below*) on many antislavery platforms. In a tribute to Harriet Tubman, *below right*, who risked returning to Maryland, where she had been a slave, to bring runaways to safety, Douglass said, "I have had the applause of the crowd. . . . The midnight sky and silent stars have been the witnesses of your devotion to freedom and of your heroism."

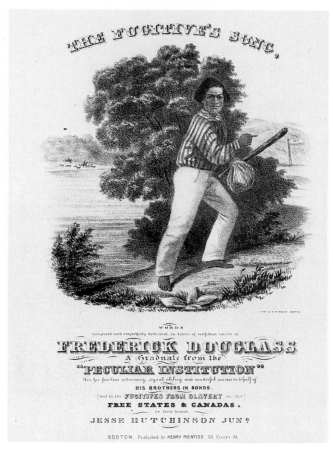

The cover page of a piece of antislavery sheet music.

In 1847, Douglass moved to Rochester, his home for the next twenty-five years. The view is from the west.

A note sent by Douglass (reversing his initials in a feeble effort at disguise) to Samuel Porter, his Rochester neighbor and fellow worker on the underground railroad, who escorted many fugitives, at dawn, onto boats for Canada.

My Dear Sir
there are three men now at my house who are in great peril. I am un well, I need your advice Please come at once.
D. F.

S. D. Porter

Above, Amy Post, who with her husband Isaac, a druggist, also hid runaway slaves. She was a sustaining friend to Douglass and to many other active antislavery people, among them Harriet Jacobs.

A rare daguerreotype of an outdoor antislavery meeting. Douglass is seated at the table; the man standing at his left shoulder is believed to be Gerrit Smith.

This portrait was the frontispiece for *My Bondage and My Freedom*.

truth must be told. . . . I will not be silent." When he returned to Boston, he carried with him a draft for five hundred pounds, raised by British friends to enable him to start his paper.

At 39 Summer Street in Boston there was consternation. Maria Chapman knew full well how effective Douglass was on the speaker's platform, and she was determined to keep him there. He was, in her eyes and the eyes of most of her colleagues in the Anti-Slavery Society, an emblem, a superbly articulate emblem, of the cause, but he could not be permitted to become a rival entrepreneur in the movement. He had to be made— though she would not have said this in so many words—to keep his place. Along with Garrison, Quincy, and Phillips, she tried to dissuade Douglass, saying that no new paper was needed and that his talents lay in speaking, not in editing. The *Liberator* had never been self-sustaining; it already depended on funds raised by Chapman's annual bazaars as well as on black subscribers. A rival paper, with Douglass as editor, might pose a real threat.

Whistling past the graveyard, they announced firmly in the July 9 issue of the *Liberator* that Frederick Douglass had abandoned his plan to start a newspaper. He hadn't, and neither had skeptics in the American Anti-Slavery Society given up their fears that he was still untamed. To deflect Douglass from too unseemly ambition, they gave him a chance to write regularly for the society's official publication, the *National Anti-Slavery Standard,* which originated in New York City. He accepted the offer, but not in a sufficiently generous spirit to suit Edmund Quincy, editor of the *Liberator* when Garrison was out of town and an official in the society; writing to Maria Chapman's sister Caroline Weston, he registered a complaint: "Talking of unconscionable niggers [he had been complaining about Charles Remond], I wrote to Douglass to ask him what he should consider a fair compensation for the letters that he had proposed he sh'd write for the Standard. In due time I rec'd an answer, saying that he sh'd think *two dollars & a half* about right! I consulted Wendell about it & he thought we had better not beat him down; but tell him that $1[.]oo was as much as we could afford." Despite his annoyance, Quincy thought it better to pay Douglass twenty or thirty dollars for twenty or thirty letters than to have him defect to some other publication.

Quincy's problems were not over. Later in the month, he wrote, "I am afraid we shall have trouble about Douglass's compensation [for his work as a touring speaker]. I suppose he thinks that his services are worth more than any one's else & sh'd be higher paid. This is probably true enough, in a sense & yet to pay him more than others would set all the flax to flame—or, at least, all the *wool.* " He anticipated that Remond would object if Douglass was paid more than he—and wished both were as agreeable as William Wells Brown, whose "intellectual power" he judged inferior to Douglass's, but who was, Quincy was sure, of a "much higher cast of character." Samuel J. May, on the other hand, taking Douglass's intellect fully into account, recognized the power of his thinking: "Allow me to thank you for the sermons you gave me before parting. . . . the one on woman's rights is the best thing I ever read on . . . the oneness of our common family."

Similarly, William Lloyd Garrison retained his esteem for Douglass, whose friendship he deeply cherished, despite the fact that now his protégé was often the commanding figure at meetings they both addressed. As he was introducing Douglass at the annual meeting of the American Anti-Slavery Society in New York City on May 11, 1847, the crowd, the largest ever at one of these meetings, interrupted Garrison with cries for "Douglass, Douglass." The fugitive was getting to be more than Boston could contain or be comfortable with.

During this same visit to New York, Douglass addressed a rally of black citizens that Amy Post, down from Rochester, attended. Afterward, she shared with her husband her dismay at the "work Jealousy Sectarianism and Envy does make with otherwise bright and good men." That meeting ended "tumultuously" and unhappily because black leaders too resented Douglass's enormous celebrity. If Post had been at 39 Summer Street she would have recognized similar emotions there. Maria Chapman was receiving so many letters from women in Britain praising "our beloved friend Frederick Douglass whom we love & cherish as a dear brother" that she had begun to wonder if her discipline could be sustained (and to suspect that Douglass had not discouraged the writers from rushing to the mailbox).

When one of these women, assuming that her American colleague would share her enthusiasm for the new venture, asked Chapman if she had talked to Douglass yet about the printing press for which they were busy raising money in England, the cat was out of the bag. Douglass had not given up the idea of having his own newspaper. Chapman made inquiries and confirmed that this was so, but her annoyance was still in no way shared by Garrison. As he and Douglass traveled together in Pennsylvania and Ohio that summer, they seemed as close as ever. On a canal boat, Garrison insisted that Douglass be served at the same table as he, and reported proudly that the captain, reluctantly, to be sure, had agreed. Stones were thrown at them in Harrisburg, but they had agreeable meetings with new antislavery friends. Among these were Martin Delany, editor of the *Mystery,* in Pittsburgh, whom Garrison described as "black as jet and a fine fellow of great energy and spirit," and Sarah Jane Clarke, a "handsome and interesting young woman." As a successful newspaper reporter and columnist, writing under the name "Grace Greenwood," she was to be for decades a champion of Douglass's.

In his letters to his wife, Garrison showed not a trace of doubt about Douglass's loyalty until after the two parted in the fall. From Cleveland, where he was recuperating from an illness caused at least in part by a far too demanding schedule, he wrote, "Is it not strange that Douglass has not written a single line to me . . . inquiring after my health, since he left me on a bed of illness? It will also greatly surprise our friends in Boston to hear, that, in regard to his project for establishing a paper . . . , to be called 'The North Star,' he never opened to me his lips on the subject, nor asked my advice in any particular whatever."

Most of those friends would not have been the least bit surprised. They had already closed their minds to him. Neither they nor Garrison were able to see how hard it was for Douglass to break with a mentor who had meant so much to him, but who, by his very encouragement, had made it impossible for him to remain in a subservient role. Sadly, like many a father and son, the two men found no way to talk about the painful rift that had developed between them. Instead, Garrison simply offered a lament: "Such conduct grieves me to the heart. His conduct . . . has been impulsive, inconsiderate, and highly inconsistent with his decision in Boston [not to start his own paper]." Garrison regretted that Quincy had not been more firm with Douglass in *Liberator* editorials. In the issue of October 1, which announced that Douglass was starting a paper, the *Liberator* editorial somewhat disingenuously wished him well, while expressing regret that the Anti-Slavery Society was losing his services as a lecturer. The price for being free to be an editor was being fired as a lecturer.

On October 28, 1847, Frederick Douglass, back from his tour, wrote to Amy Post—"My Dear Amy"—to tell her, "I have finally decided on publishing the *North Star* in Rochester and to make that city my future home." The prospectus for the paper was issued in Lynn, prior to the move, and went out in firm defiance of Garrisonian loyalists. Frederick Bailey, slave field hand turned skilled caulker; Frederick Douglass, free laborer and then agent of the American Anti-Slavery Society, was taking another giant step upward in the social structure of the antebellum republic. From the days of Benjamin Franklin to those of the politically powerful newspaper editors of Andrew Jackson's America, journalism had been a potent calling. Only a rare black man was a doctor or a lawyer; none was a merchant chief. A black man who would be heard became a man of the cloth, but Douglass had firmly turned his back on that correct calling. What he could be was an editor.

At least four other newspapers edited by African Americans were in existence when Douglass announced that the *North Star* would be published. As early as 1842, he had aspired to being a newspaperman; in August of that year he asked Sydney Howard Gay, a lawyer who was also one of the editors of the *National Anti-Slavery Standard,* to look into the financial situation of the *Ram's Horn,* a New York City paper which wanted him to contribute pieces as a corresponding editor. Nothing came of that prospect, but the idea of having a newspaper of his own lingered with Douglass, not least because his mentor, Garrison, had one.

"Mr. Editor, if you please," Douglass answered, once the paper was established, when asked how he wished to be addressed. Proudly, this reply said that he was a gentleman—not a gentleman of leisure, but one with a profession. As Henry James noted in his essay on Emerson, a man without a profession—in Emerson's (and Douglass's) case, a preacher without a pulpit—was in an ambiguous relation to the public. Emerson created for himself a profession as a lyceum lecturer and sage; Douglass, as an agent of the American Anti-Slavery Society, was still an employee, beholden to others, however great his oratorical powers. As Mr. Editor, Frederick Douglass would have not only a position in society but also his own place in public affairs. He was determined to make the most of both.

Douglass went to western New York without his family and with almost no assets of his own available to underwrite the venture. But he did have better than $4,000 he had brought back from Britain, as well as the promise of further financial support from friends there: Isabel Jennings in Cork, Maria Webb in Dublin, the Richardsons in Newcastle upon Tyne, the Reverend R. L. Carpenter in Halifax, in the north of England, all solicited subscriptions from people who had heard Douglass speak. With a check for £445.17.6 from J. D. Carr, he bought an "elegant press" (which proved to be a mistake), and he had on the books sufficient subscriptions to allow him to begin printing. He also had the backing of a rich upstate New Yorker. "I welcome you to the State of New York," wrote Gerrit Smith in December. He enclosed his check for five dollars for a two-year subscription and informed Douglass that he and his friends William C. Nell, William Wells Brown, and Charles Lenox Remond were to receive forty acres of land each (not in Rochester). He closed his letter, "With great regard, your friend and brother, Gerrit Smith."

Smith was a most generous philanthropist who had a great deal to be generous with. His father, Peter Smith, building on a partnership with an Astor and a marriage to a Livingston and skillfully manipulating the payment of taxes and purchases of land, had acquired land in all but six of New York's counties. Unhappy and unstable, the father sold his son his lands in 1819, whereupon Gerrit moved into Peter Smith's house in

Peterboro, New York—and the old man moved out. Gerrit was a good deal more comfortable with his conscience when disposing of his largesse to strangers than he had been when acquiring it quarrelsomely from his father, and in 1846 he asked three prominent antislavery people to help him locate 1,985 (of a projected 3,000) landless (and liquorless) "colored people" to receive from forty to sixty acres of land each.

"I could not put a bounty on color," he wrote. "I had not come to it [a decision to give the land only to blacks], were not the colored people the poorest of the poor, and the most deeply wronged class of our citizens. That they are so, is evident, if only from the fact, that the cruel, killing, Heaven-defying prejudice of which they are the victims, has closed against them the avenues to riches and respectability;—to happiness and usefulness." These particular lands were all in eastern—and largely down-state—counties, but Smith, with plenty of acres to work with, also established the black community of North Elba in the remote, unfertile country back of the Adirondack Mountains. He used grants of land to induce black leaders to settle in upstate New York cities as well; as owners of property, they would qualify to vote. What disposition Douglass made of his forty acres is not known; he probably sold the land.

Much was insinuated about Smith's patronage of Douglass and the *North Star;* indeed, Douglass's enemies tried to portray him as nothing but a toady to his patron. A good deal of this came from the Garrisonians, who thought Douglass an ingrate for beginning a rival paper, and disliked Smith, a Liberty party man, as a rival antislavery leader who had carried the issue of slavery firmly into politics. Nothing in the dignified, affectionate, extensive (and, on Smith's part, barely legible) correspondence between Douglass and Smith supports a charge of subservience on the part of one, or ascendancy by the other. One indication of Douglass's autonomy with respect to Smith is his choice of Rochester rather than Syracuse, ninety miles away, the city nearest Smith's home. Another is the fact that Smith did not underwrite the *North Star:* he did not supply its capital. This is not to say that his frequent contributions were not essential to the paper's survival. The large, sturdy entries in the ledger—"Gerrit Smith, $100," "Gerrit Smith, $200"—were made at crucial moments.

That ledger was itself a declaration of independence: "Leger No. 1 The Property of Douglass & Delany. Rochester, N.Y. November 3rd, 1847." The two men were picking up an acquaintance made only the previous summer, but the partners seemed well matched. Martin Delany, born in 1812 of a free mother and slave father, was black and proud of it; he "boasted not only pure African ancestry but noble blood as well." Delany had trained himself to be a medical practitioner—there was almost no line of endeavor he was not willing to have a go at, during an extraordinarily varied career—and was an ardent participant in antislavery activities in Pittsburgh, helping to move fugitive slaves north and joining in efforts to restore the vote to black people in his state. Douglass thought he was exactly right for the new publishing venture. Delany was one of the nineteenth century's most interesting men, but the very range of his activities proved a disadvantage for Douglass. Although he was listed as an editor on the masthead of the *North Star* until 1849, he never moved to Rochester, and despite repeated pleas from Douglass, he contributed only occasional letters.

William C. Nell, the third man listed on the masthead—he, in fact, as publisher—was as different from Delany and certainly from Douglass as a person could be. Although he had written for the *Liberator* for fifteen years, he was irrepressibly boyish; he was playing blindman's buff in the Posts' parlor almost as soon as he reached Rochester. Isaac and Amy Post, at the center of a large Quaker family, were involved in a myriad of reform movements in the city, and comfortably linked the black and white communities. Nell was greatly fond of them, and in letters to Amy Post, and to his friend Jeremiah Sanderson, he was able to be completely relaxed and candid. Nell was a man who had missed his calling. A born reporter, he carried his writing pad with him wherever he went; in the middle of one of Douglass's speeches, or alone at night in bed, he would toss onto the page his immediate thought. Then he would draw a line under it and—the next moment or the next day—leap to a totally different topic.

Nell's letters are rich with news of "Mr. Garrison" (for whom he later worked once again, in the *Liberator* office); gossip about all of his buddies, who, unlike him, seem to be finding brides; tales of daring attempts to rescue captured fugitives; and nostalgic reminiscences of family times at the Posts', which he much missed after moving to Boston. If he had written for the *North Star* as he did for his friends, we would have a far better humored, candid account of the antislavery movement than any that has come down to us. And Frederick Douglass would have had a real newspaper rather than a rather solemnly polemical journal. But Nell, instead of acting as a reporter—or publisher—was the paper's printer, and one whose spelling put the *North Star*'s text in grave jeopardy.

The three proprietors of the *North Star,* along with John Dick, an English printer who had met Douglass abroad and now joined him to help get the paper out, charged themselves not only with assembling the paper, but with raising subscriptions to support it as well. A good many familiar names were on the lists, with payments of $2.00 (the stated yearly rate), $1.00, or $1.50 noted next to them; Lucretia Coffin Mott, Lydia and Abigail Mott, "Mrs. H. E. B. Stowe, Andover, Mass.," were there. So was Sydney Howard Gay, editor of the American Anti-Slavery Society's *National Anti-Slavery Standard,* who would need to keep his eye on the new rival, but few other members of the society subscribed. Significantly, the journal was read by Lewis and Arthur Tappan of the American and Foreign Anti-Slavery Society, an organization, formed in 1840, that challenged the Garrisonians' claim that they and they alone possessed the antislavery cause.

Copies of the *North Star* were sent to Canada, Mexico, and Australia, and to several of Douglass's admirers in Great Britain, among them Lady Byron, the poet's widow, who had been committed to American abolition since conversing with Garrison and Remond in the balcony of the World's Anti-Slavery Congress in London in 1840. *The Statesman,* in Wilmington, Delaware, and the *Virginia Telescope,* in West Columbia, Virginia, are listed but crossed out, suggesting that Douglass had sent his paper to their iconoclastic editors, hoping they would pick up some of his items, but was rebuffed. Perhaps the most surprising name listed is that of John C. Breckinridge, of Lexington, Kentucky, who was to be James Buchanan's vice-president and, later, a Confederate general. It too is crossed out. The explanation for its appearance in the first place may lie on the same page of the ledger: Robert J. Breckinridge, who was antislavery, is listed as a subscriber, and it would have been just like him to arrange for his nephew to get a copy. Another of the rare slave-state subscribers was the Reverend J. C. Young, president of Danville College, who was not afraid to have his copy sent to him at the college, in Danville, Kentucky. Two Purvises subscribed, as did Douglass's friend from Chicago meetings, Henry O. Waggoner, but there were surprisingly few other black subscribers.

The first issue of the *North Star*—the name is reminiscent of Feargus O'Connor's *Northern Star,* the leading paper of Chartism—was published on December 3, 1847. Almost immediately Dick pronounced inadequate the expensive press the inexperienced Douglass had bought, and the printing was given out to William Clough, whose weekly charge ran from $19.00 to $20.75 during the paper's life. The cost of foreign and domestic postage was also relatively stable. Subscriptions must have barely covered the printing costs, leaving other expenses and an occasional modest amount given to Douglass for "sundries" to be covered by intermittent small contributions from friends, and Smith's more substantial contributions. How Nell, Dick, and Douglass subsisted is not clear from the account book. Perhaps each was receiving free room and board from a Rochester supporter. Douglass boarded with Charles Joiner while he was getting the paper started.

In February 1848, Douglass went back to Lynn to tell Anna that once again she must follow him to a strange town. Still illiterate—as she was to remain for the whole of her life—Anna was a totally domestic woman. In Lynn, with her husband off making himself famous, and with the sewing of shoes, at home, the only work at hand, she had little beyond her house and her children to command her attention. In addition to her husband, a second member of the family was missing. At her father's insistence, Rosetta had been sent to Albany to live and study with the formidable Mott sisters, Abigail and Lydia, cousins of Lucretia Coffin Mott's husband, James Mott. This separation had proved costly for both mother and daughter. To Anna, the move to Rochester would mean having Rosetta back, but it would also mean tearing herself away from a home once again. Lynn had been her town—though scarcely Frederick's—for six years; now she who had given up a known place as a free person in Baltimore to help her husband escape from slavery, who had left comfortable New Bedford, was told she must move again.

The move was not made easier by the fact that in Rochester they had to board until they could find a house. Late in February, Douglass wrote the Mott sisters that he was a "most unhappy man." His "house hunting" had not been successful and "Anna has not been well—or very good humored since we came here. She," he added, a bit less gloomily, "however looks better." In April, things looked up. A local abolitionist—to the consternation of all the neighbors on the block, save the Parkers next door and one other antislavery family—sold Douglass a pleasant, narrow city house at 4 Alexander Street, with a front porch and a small yard for the garden. Douglass had a "little den-like upstairs study . . . with its small table and few books," according to Douglass's neighbor Jane Marsh Parker. She recalled "how he used to keep there a list of the words he found it hard to spell." There was nothing wrong with the Douglasses' physical setting; there was everything wrong with their psychological arrangements.

Only the dimmest light is thrown on the Douglasses' home life by the letters of those who knew them well enough to see how great was the strain. Anna's garden seems to have been her greatest solace, and friends like Ann Smith (who, despite her vast wealth—she was Gerrit Smith's wife—knew another green thumb when she saw one) thoughtfully sent seeds and cuttings. Amy Post, trying to bring Anna into the community, urged a neighbor to ask her to contribute the pumpkin for the school's pantomime of "Cinderella," but such overtures were fruitless; she could not enter a world she found alien.

Anna did not take her lot in life in silence, and her anger can only have been increased by the fact that she could not make her husband see or do anything about the discomfort she felt. To formal visitors—white visitors—the husband and wife presented the image of decorum. She greeted them, then retreated to the kitchen, emerging only to serve her husband as if he, like his friends, were a guest in her house. Almost certainly her New Bedford neighbor the Reverend Thomas James, himself a former resident of Rochester, would have alerted the black women in the social groups connected to the Zion chapel there, but whether they reached out to Anna we do not know. (James himself was away from Rochester until 1856.) Indeed, everything we know about the tightly knit small black community of 162 households suggests that they must have tried to reach her. The Douglasses themselves, however distant their concerns had become, had not retreated totally into separate spheres; in the summer of 1848 they conceived another child.

Despite or perhaps in part because of the discord at home, Douglass was never long away from the antislavery lectern. Edmund Quincy had been premature in assuming he had left the fold. In the spring of 1848, again traveling with Remond, Douglass made the circuit of upstate New York, and completed the tour by attending the May meeting of the American Anti-Slavery Society, in New York City. And now he had a new cause to plead for—his paper; everywhere he went, Douglass urged his listeners to subscribe.

On July 19 and 20, 1848, the editor was hawking his wares at perhaps the most remarkable and important of the hundreds of meetings of nineteenth-century reformers that he was to attend. The Seneca Falls convention had been planned by Elizabeth Cady Stanton, who had moved to the remote Finger Lakes region of western New York when, to her regret and exasperation, the exhilarating pace of Boston proved too strenuous for her husband, lawyer and abolitionist Henry Brewster Stanton. The indestructible woman, five feet three inches tall, had little to do in Seneca Falls except raise her children, come to the aid of the wives of battering husbands (". . . . if a drunken husband was pounding his wife the children would run for me. Hastening to the scene of action, I would take Patrick by the collar, and, much to his surprise and shame, make him sit down and behave himself"), and arrange to reshape the world. Sitting next to Lucretia Coffin Mott in a special section, behind a skirted railing, at the World's Anti-Slavery Congress in London in 1840, where "only half of humanity was represented" by the delegates, she had been converted to the cause of women's rights. Walking arm in arm from the meetings, Stanton and Mott had resolved one day to convene a gathering that would begin breaking the chains that bound women.

Now, eight years later, they were ready. They issued their call—in the *Seneca County Courier*—on July 14, 1848, leaving the faithful little time to find excuses not to be present. About forty responded, including, from Rochester, both Amy Post and Frederick Douglass. At the first session, in the Methodist chapel, the famous Declaration of Sentiments was read; at the second, Stanton's controversial resolution declaring it to be the "duty of women of this country to secure to themselves their sacred right to the elective franchise" was debated. Stanton knew that her husband and their much-admired feminist friend William Lloyd Garrison—as well as most of the rest of Christendom—disapproved. Even Lucretia Mott disappointed her. "Why, Lizzie," said the good Quaker, "thee will make us ridiculous." All the other resolutions were carried unanimously, but it was only, Stanton reported, "with the help of Frederick Douglass"— the lone male in favor—that after "heated discussion" her suffrage resolution passed "by a small majority."

During the debate, one delegate, reaching for a piece of paper on which to scrawl her thoughts before speaking, picked up a flier advertising the *North Star;* the blank space on the back was just what she needed. Sixty-eight women and thirty-two men, many of whom had not been at the convention, signed the Declaration of Sentiments and the resolutions. Douglass was among them. On July 28, in his article on the convention, he wrote, "We are free to say that in respect to political rights, we hold woman to be justly entitled to all we claim for man."

There was not a great deal of point in having the vote if it was not to be used. Douglass was beginning tentatively to recognize that the Garrisonian rejection of all political activity countenanced by an evil constitution had its limitations. Already in 1846, back in England, he had condemned the Mexican War in unequivocal terms and applauded the Wilmot Proviso, the proposal of Congressman David Wilmot that slavery be prohibited in the vast territory that would be taken—as spoils of war—from Mexico when the United States invasion succeeded and the war was won. In years past, as a staunch Garrisonian, Douglass had ridiculed members of the antislavery Liberty party for sullying the cause by engaging in a political process—in elections—in which slaveholders had so long flourished. But Gerrit Smith was active in the Liberty party, and with the move to Rochester and his new tie to Smith (whom David W. Blight aptly calls Douglass's "mentor," as distinct from William Lloyd Garrison, a "fatherly figure"), the editor found himself in conversation with politicians. Soon Douglass was attending their meetings, and instead of condemning them out of hand, he tried to make them more resolutely antislavery.

At about the time Douglass became comfortable goading politicians within their own arena, the stadium seats were beginning to fill. The single-issue Liberty party, dedicated to ending slavery, was far from achieving majority status; its sole victory on a national level had been the diversion in 1844 of sufficient votes from the Whigs in New York State to defeat one slaveholding candidate, Henry Clay, thereby, ironically, ensuring the victory of another, James K. Polk, who went on to take the nation into a war with Mexico that abolitionists saw as nothing more than a scheme to extend slavery. But even this negative achievement indicated the potency of slavery as a political issue.

In 1848, an antislavery majority seemed within reach when Liberty men, Conscience Whigs (antislavery members of the Whig party, which included also the proslavery Cotton Whigs), and Democrats who did not want slaves (or, for that matter, ex-slaves) in the territories, met in Buffalo to create the Free Soil party. Douglass was among the black leaders who attended, and he took heart at the excitement engendered by the gathering. He could muster little enthusiasm for the presidential candidate, former Democratic president Martin Van Buren, but in September, when John P. Hale, the Liberty party nominee, dropped out of the race, the *North Star* uneasily endorsed the Free Soil party.

Douglass was nipping at the heels of the politicians, hoping to drive them nearer and nearer to actually doing something about abolishing slavery. Since they kept adroitly stepping out of his way, it was a frustrating business. As we look at the frustration of the abolitionists and the sense of being under siege that was growing among the slaveholders, we do well to recall that beyond this impasse lay a civil war. The participants in the politics of the 1840s and 1850s had no such hindsight available to them; still, it is intriguing to speculate on what might have happened if the Gerrit Smiths and Douglasses had had their way, and Congress, rather than ducking, had pressed earlier into strong measures against slavery.

In November 1848, the Free Soil party seemed to accomplish nothing but the election of yet another slaveholder to the presidency: New Yorker Van Buren diverted enough votes in his home state from the Democratic candidate, Lewis Cass, to give the victory to the Louisiana Whig and Mexican War hero Zachary Taylor. About the time of Taylor's inaugural in 1849, Douglass drew as hopeful a picture as he could of the Free Soil party: "What good has the free soil movement done? Much in many ways but not every way. It has for once rallied a large number of the people of the North in apparent hostility to the whole system of American slavery; it has subjected this vile abomination to wide-spread exposure; it has rebuked and humbled quite a number of corrupt and cringing politicians, by driving them to change their positions on this subject, and driven them from office. It has awakened the whole south to a sense of danger, and perhaps has checked the proud and arrogant pretensions of the slaveholder with respect to the extension of slavery. So far so good."

Douglass was, of course, unaware that ultimately war would be the result of that awakening of the South, but from the days of the Wilmot Proviso, past the terrible disappointment of the passage of the vile, abominable Fugitive Slave Act, the foulest component of the loathsome Compromise of 1850, through to his abandonment in 1856 of what was left of the Liberty party, the Radical Abolitionist party of Gerrit Smith, in favor of the rising Republican party, Douglass was exhilarated by the thought that men of goodwill like Gerrit Smith—and Frederick Douglass—would somehow persuade legislators to use the law to end slavery. Eventually, the politicians would have to step into line. The Garrisonians had been wrong, he declared: "There is no question . . . that the anti-slavery movement will always be followed to a greater or lesser distance by a political party of some sort. It is inevitable."

In the *North Star,* Douglass relentlessly pursued the great public issues that touched on slavery, but his personal quarrel with one particular slaveholder was never absent from his thinking about the subject. In September 1848, on the tenth anniversary of his escape, he published an open letter to his old master, Thomas Auld. The eight-page document, which Douglass later published in an appendix to *My Bondage and My Freedom,* is one of the strangest pieces in the literature of American slavery. "Sir," he began, "The long and intimate, though by no means friendly, relation which unhappily subsisted between you and myself, leads me to hope that you will easily account for the great liberty which I now take in addressing you in this open and public manner." Continuing in this elaborate and ostensibly polite vein, he contended that Auld, as a thief—having stolen Douglass's labor—had forfeited his right to have his former slave's grievances kept private.

After having boasted, reasonably enough, about his accomplishments and those of his free children "going regularly to school," Douglass turned to a recital of his grievances. He had plenty, but what is strange about his account is its peculiar distortions. Initially, Auld is made to stand in for all slaveholders, who are vilified for wrenching children from parents. This was, of course, one of the ugliest aspects of slavery, but there is little evidence that Auld ever instigated the separation of a family. When, about ten years after Douglass's attack, Auld "sold" the slave "Clary Baily" (for a term to end in 1871), he included in the transaction her infant child.*

---

*Certain of Douglass's Aunt Milly's children, inherited by Auld, are not accounted for in his household in St. Michaels, and it is uncertain whether he sold or freed them. On Jan. 12, 1859, Auld granted manumission, to take effect on their thirtieth birthdays, to four slaves: Charles ("who was born Toby"), born Feb. 7, 1840; Mary Elizabeth, born Jan. 2, 1843; Clary Baily, born Aug.

Turning to particulars, Douglass described vividly and accurately how "you, while we were brothers in the same church, caused this right hand, with which I am now penning this letter, to be closely tied to my left, and my person dragged, at the pistol's mouth, fifteen miles, from the Bay Side to Easton, to be sold like a beast in the market." That had been a terrifying experience, and Douglass had every right to recall it, but he pointedly ignored the fact that it was Auld and Auld alone who prevented him from being lynched by having him jailed, and who refused to sell him.

Douglass also accused Auld of mistreating his grandmother—of turning her out "like an old horse to die in the woods." Concern for an aged grandmother is totally understandable—and some of his expression of it suggests that Douglass felt rather as if he too had deserted her—but why did he point the accusation at Auld when he knew that one of the Anthonys, not Auld, owned his grandmother? Stranger still is the fantasy of the rape of Amanda, the daughter of Thomas and Lucretia, whom Douglass remembered both as a child Auld cherished and as one who had been a kind young friend to Frederick Bailey in St. Michaels. "How, let me ask, would you look upon me, were I, some dark night, . . . to enter the precincts of your elegant dwelling, and seize the person of your own lovely daughter, Amanda, and carry her off from your family" and "make her my slave . . . ?" Not only might he force her to work as he willed and deny her the right to learn to read and write; he might also "clothe her scantily, and whip her on the naked back occasionally; more, and still more horrible, leave her unprotected—a degraded victim to the brutal lust of fiendish overseers, who would pollute, blight, and blast her. . . ."

Douglass knew that—as Theodore Weld had shown in *American Slavery As It Is*—lusty stories could arouse a Northern antislavery audience. Countless times in his speeches Douglass had used events out of his own experience to make telling points about slavery, and he was not above altering details to make his story better. But why, in a letter explicitly and formally addressed to Thomas Auld, did he misrepresent Auld's actions? There were other villains he could have pointed to, such as the murderous overseer Austin Gore, or Edward Covey; instead, all calumny was vested in his owner—who no longer owned him.

Douglass's loathing of Auld did reach its mark. One of the most interesting items in the Maryland State Archives is a copy of *Narrative of the Life of Frederick Douglass* with marginal comments—more per-

<hr />

29, 1841 (she, with her child, had been "sold," for a term, to Charles Willie); and Clary's infant child. The adults could have been Milly's grandchildren. (Manumission Lists, Maryland State Colonization Society, Maryland Historical Society, Reel 17.)

plexed than angry—written by a member of the Auld family who went through that book noting where it errs as to fact. Douglass's score settling is understandable, but there is absurdity in his reference to Auld's "elegant dwelling" and in the ludicrous rhetoric of "Just ten years ago this beautiful September morning, yon bright sun beheld me a slave—a poor degraded chattel—trembling at the sound of your voice, lamenting that I was a man, and wishing myself a brute."

Douglass pushed his polemical point hard. He seemed to feel that in pressing Auld, the master to whom, to his disgust, he was beholden, he had to create a monster, one he would not spare. He told Auld that as he traveled, "I . . . have invariably made you the topic of conversation—thus giving you all the notoriety I could." And later he added, "I intend to make use of you as a weapon with which to assail the system of slavery." There is in this tormented letter a hint that the legacy of slavery that Douglass could not shake was a trace of hatred of himself. A note of redemption for them both comes in Douglass's closing statement that he holds no personal animosity toward Auld—"There is no roof under which you would be more safe than mine"—and in the letter's famous last line: "I am your fellow-man, but not your slave."

If Rosetta read her father's glowing report of her prospering in school, she must have been surprised. In August, her father had taken her along Alexander Street to Miss Lucilia Tracy's Seward Seminary, and when she had passed an entrance quiz, and her tuition had been arranged for, Rosetta was admitted. The Mott sisters had prepared her well, and the nine-year-old no doubt went off to school with the standard mixture of terror and expectation. Her father was in Cleveland at the National Convention of Colored Citizens during the first days of school; when he returned, eager for her affirmation, he asked Rosetta if school was going well. She replied, "with tears in her eyes, 'I get along pretty well, but father, Miss Tracy does not allow me to go into the room with the other scholars because I am colored.' "

"Stung to the heart's core," Douglass went the next morning to see the principal—and no teacher can ever have confronted a more ferocious parent. How, he demanded, could she admit the child and then treat her as she had? Tracy's defense was that when she reported the admission to the trustees, they remonstrated with her. She told Douglass that at first she had thought of defying them, but "then she remembered how much they had done for her in sustaining the institution." Her thought had been that if Rosetta was taught in a room alone "for a term or more," the "prejudice would be overcome." Douglass could not share her faith in the theory that time cures and stated that he and his wife were going to take Rosetta out of the school. Implied as he left was the threat that the entire nation would hear of Tracy's "unwomanly conduct."

Trying to relieve herself of responsibility for the actions to which Douglass had so vigorously objected, Tracy polled each of her other pupils on the matter; when one girl said she didn't care if the black girl stayed, Tracy asked, "Did you mean to vote so? Are you *accustomed* to black persons?" To her immense credit, the "young lady stood silent; the question was so extraordinary, and withal so ambiguous, that she knew not what answer to make to it." Flustered, the principal then asked the students where Rosetta would sit if she were admitted to the classroom. "By me, by me, by me" was the chorus of replies. With the students undercutting her defense, Tracy turned to the parents; that afternoon notes were carried home.

The next day, when Rosetta got to school, she was handed her books and pencils and told to go home; one father had objected. Before the day was out, Douglass had arranged for her acceptance by another school, but he did not let the matter drop as the school year progressed. One of the disagreeable features of Rochester, as of other towns with an active antislavery group, was the strong prejudice against the black citizens, whose presence was suggestive of the change in the polity that would occur nationally if slavery was to end. Douglass was doubly troubled that this attitude was encouraged by a fellow editor, and in the *North Star* he treated H. G. Warner of the *Rochester Courier* to immortal scorn for being the sole parent—"a *despised minority*" of one—to object to Rosetta: "We differ in color, it is true, (and not much in that respect,) but who is to decide which color is most pleasing to God, or most honorable among men? But I do not wish to waste words or argument on one whom I take to be as destitute of honorable feeling, as he has shown himself full of pride and prejudice."

The week before Douglass publicly defended his oldest child, his youngest was born. On March 22, 1849, just over a year after the family's move to Rochester, the Douglasses' fifth and last child was born. The baby was named Annie.

That same spring—on a "2nd Day," as the good Quaker put it, early in May—Isaac Post looked up as his friend Frederick Douglass walked into the drugstore. He had just come from the train station after a "comfortable" trip from New York. He could only stop for a moment, but he wanted to be sure Isaac would come to tea to meet his "English friend" and her sister, who had come with him. Frederick was in an exuberant mood and made a remark about how pleased he was with the railroad's considerable powers. "And with your own, too," Post shot back. Then, Isaac wrote Amy (who had not yet returned from the American Anti-Slavery Society annual meeting that she and Douglass had both attended), "he grasped my hand and laughed as nobody else can."

Post felt a bit awkward about going to the Douglasses' house, but when he arrived that afternoon, he discovered that the travelers, rather than resting, had been for a long walk, and now, in the parlor, he "found the older sister with the children arranging their presents." With her bonnet still on, the woman "was so intent to have matters arranged with the children" that she did not immediately look up, and Post "thought she was a coloured woman." But "I took another look," he wrote his wife, and "saw I was mistaken & about . . . [then] Rosa introduced me to her." Scarcely noticing the caller, "she continued on[:] Rosa must have such [,] Lewis that [,] Frederick these two & Charles the remainder & giving them the reasons why each should have the ones picked out for them, that they saw the reasonableness of her explanations."

Julia Griffiths had arrived and taken charge.

14

25 Buffalo Street

NO SELF-RESPECTING reform movement is complete without a scandal. Frederick Douglass and Julia Griffiths, earnest and devoted, supplied that ingredient for the antislavery cause. Critics and even some admirers of the movement have been quick to describe the more fervent of the abolitionists as eccentric. And indeed, like Virginia Woolf, the English-woman seems to have had something in her dress and demeanor that caused people, for no apparent reason, to turn and stare as they passed her on the street. There was nothing eccentric about her companion, but Douglass was indisputably attractive. As the famous spiritualist medium Margaret Fox put it, "Frederick is as fine looking as Ever." Meaning no disrespect to her adopted town, she added, "I think he is the finest looking gentleman i have seen since I have been in Cincinnati." A lecture here by him, she reported to her friend Amy Post, "would set the people *Crazy.*"

But it was something far simpler in their appearance that set people talking about the two. He was black and she white. The Posts were among the few of their friends who resolutely chose to attribute no meaning to such a distinction, to make it not a fact. Indeed, the Posts' affection and respect for Douglass was unshakable, and yet even they found that mapping the contours of his friendship with Griffiths challenged their unorthodoxy. When Isaac Post walked into the Douglass house that first day, he found the Englishwoman hard to read. A father himself, he was not sure that the children, despite the presents, had "submitted with tolerable good grace" to the newcomer. But when their father came into the room and Julia explained her distribution, Frederick pronounced it "admirable." He and Julia, ignoring the children (and Isaac) then launched into a discussion of "their writings." With no sign of the tea for which he had been invited, Isaac decided it best "to make a short call," and left.

A few evenings later, the party reassembled at the home of Post's daughter and son-in-law William Hallowell. That day, the Griffiths sisters, their countryman John Dick, now Douglass's assistant at the paper, and Douglass had walked all the way to the lower falls of the Genesee River; the forthright Englishwomen, Isaac realized, were "real ramblers." Resuming his assessment, the druggist, with not entirely successful tact, observed that Julia was "older than I expected"; her sister Eliza, he noted, had a "round faced" prettiness.

The Griffiths sisters, Amy Post, and Amy's sister Sarah had already met, in New York at the American Anti-Slavery Society annual meeting, and Isaac reported to his wife that Julia was "very much in love with thee" and with Sarah. He also noted that Frederick had said Julia was "very talented," and in a subsequent letter, he showed in his own admiring evaluation of the quality of Julia's mind that he agreed. "It was," he concluded, "a talent beyond common." Isaac found it intriguing "to hear her & F. D. talk[;] they happened to get talking about Adventism [and] the Question was asked if Gerrit Smith had become a convert. F. would be sorry if he had[;] she did not see that should be regretted[,] for some of the best or many of the best and learned of Episcopalians were of that view[,] which led to quite an argument." Isaac was impressed with the way she stood up to Frederick, and with how he reacted: "I wish F.D. would treat all that differ with him in public as kindly as he did her."

The Posts, for all their interest in every road that seemed to open to perfection, did not forget that the work before them was the opposition to slavery. They honored Douglass and the Griffiths sisters for their commitment to the cause: "Julia and Eliza . . . are seting a glorious example." Harriet Jacobs, a zealous antislavery advocate, and herself a runaway, agreed. "I suppose we shall have Frederick and the Misses Griffiths here on sunday to draw a full house," she reported to Amy Post from Massachusetts. The Posts knew that Julia Griffiths had come to America not only to speak against slavery, but to help Douglass edit the *North Star.* The two worked opposite each other at a table and a desk in the newspaper's office at 25 Buffalo Street. The building, in the center of downtown Rochester, was opposite Reynold's Arcade, at the end of which was Corinthian Hall, the site of many of Douglass's greatest speeches.

Douglass's ceaseless lecturing trips, and his disinclination to bother with business, meant that the paper's practical aspects were neglected, and it was soon in a precarious position. But when the Posts moved to provide help on this front, they, the gentlest of his colleagues, ran up against his sensitivity to criticism. Knowing the paper's dire financial trouble, the Posts had reported to him that people like his rich and prominent abolitionist neighbor Samuel Porter would continue to back it only if sound— for which Douglass read "white"—businessmen in Rochester audited the books. They quickly retreated when they found what an affront to his independence Douglass saw this proposal to be. Douglass had reacted the same way in Dublin, a few years earlier. As he explained in September 1850 in a letter to Richard Webb, in which he tried to patch up their damaged friendship, some of the fury he had displayed in Dublin had been occasioned by his awareness that Maria Chapman "commended me to your watchful care" because she did not trust a black man with money. The Posts were relieved when they realized that Julia Griffiths, with her good head for business, had turned her attention to the paper's problems.

When it came to Douglass's private life, the Posts, unlike a good many vicious gossips, simply chose not to write about what they did not know. In their frequent family letters, they alluded to the gossip about Frederick and Julia, but made no adverse judgments of their own. More than enough of these were being made, and there can be little question that the breaching of racial lines, rather than the breaching of conventional marital ones, was what caused the decibel range among antislavery people to reach the level of a screech.

The more loudly the abolitionists deplored the interracial relationship, the happier their opponents became. To be sure, since Douglass traveled with both sisters, he could not be accused of sexual impropriety, except by the truly prurient, but simply the sight of a black man escorting white women on the street was enough to raise hackles. Walking along the Battery in New York City after attending the 1850 May meeting of the American Anti-Slavery Society, the three were accosted by a gang of white men; shouting obscene racial epithets, the men dragged Douglass away and beat him, until a policeman, hunted up by the women, drove the attackers off. Assaults like this were painful and terrifying, but there was considerable solace in the support they engendered. After this incident, Gerrit Smith wrote, "*My outraged and afflicted brother,* . . . I sympathized with you and loved you before, but much more now."

The Smiths were undaunted by the interracial nature of the friendships and welcomed Douglass and the Griffiths sisters to Peterboro. Most of their colleagues in the movement, however, were far from welcoming the new editorial team, and when Eliza Griffiths, hitherto always present as chaperone, was no longer available for that assignment, the criticism of the two candidly unorthodox friends grew. Late in the summer of

1850, romance had bloomed elsewhere in the office; John Dick ("Lucky Fellow," noted William C. Nell) married Eliza and took her off to Toronto, where, in time, he would work on another antislavery paper, the *Provincial Freeman*. Now Julia Griffiths and Douglass had no protection against the gossips.

The business of race and color was inescapable for Douglass, even though he refused to regard his personal life as comprised of transactions in a dishonorable commerce. In early September 1850, as if to say that now he could ignore color, he spoke of "a very pleasant visit from Fredrika Bremer—the Swedish authoress"—and James Russell Lowell. The year before, the American poet had tried to persuade his friends in Boston's Town and Country Club, founded for a "better acquaintance between men of science, literary, and philanthropic pursuits," to admit Douglass as a member. Lowell hoped Douglass's membership would help rid "many worthy people of a very unworthy prejudice," but—his biographer Martin Duberman tells us—Emerson "black-balled" the black abolitionist, who, presumably, was never told about the matter.

When Lowell and Bremer arrived at the Alexander Street house, they were greeted by Mr. and Mrs. Douglass and then had a long conversation with the editor. If Douglass was delighted with the visit, Bremer had a different view. Writing to friends to correct an earlier and presumably even more racist description of the Douglass family, she declared that "Fr. Douglas, dear Rebecca, did not seem black to me. He is a fine-looking man of the couler and caste of countenance I should suppose to belong to Arabs. It was *his wife and and little daughter* I spoke [of] in my letter as being very black. Douglas I liked very much and wish to see more of him under more favourable circumstances." Douglass's distinguished friend was not prepared to include Africans from below the Sahara in her vision of the human family. How Anna, putting her baby to bed that evening, felt about pink-skinned red-whiskered poets and Swedish authoresses can be guessed.

Another writer, an American trying hard to understand her compatriots, wrote to Douglass for help. In the summer of 1851, Harriet Beecher Stowe, doing a series of sketches she intended to call *Uncle Tom's Cabin*, felt a "need to hear from a laborer in the cotton fields." With his reply, politely omitting the fact that a Marylander did not qualify, Douglass placed himself on the long list of inaccurate guesses about who the model was for the chief character in Stowe's immediately and immensely popular 1852 novel. The exchange of letters also began a long friendship.

In the fall of 1850, the antislavery people were, with the rest of the nation, consumed with dismayed interest in the attempt in Congress to minimize sectional conflicts over slavery, which had been exacerbated by the question of whether to extend slavery into the lands won from Mexico in the Mexican War. The result was the Compromise of 1850, which provided that California would come into the Union as free state, the status of slavery in the territories of New Mexico and Utah would be decided later, and the national government would support slavery where it was already established. A major element of this support was the Fugitive Slave Act, which required federal authorities to participate actively in the return of runaway slaves.

"Oh! that cursed 'Fugitive Bill' is it not vile enough to make the vilest spirits blush?" exclaimed one of Douglass's friends, summing up the feelings of the whole antislavery community. And that community grew larger as a result of the enforcement of this legislation. The spectacle of people being condemned by federal commissioners and marched by federal troops to ships that would carry them back to slavery in the South aroused Northern opposition to slavery as nothing else had. Slavery had become visible—as Douglass, with his verbal descriptions, had long sought to make it. Rather than being paralyzed by the passage of such reactionary legislation, Douglass was stimulated by the increasingly outspoken support of the antislavery cause by politicians. As his Rochester neighbor Jane Marsh Parker put it, "Frederick Douglass had his education in four great schools, graduating from one to the other in natural sequence and with honors—Methodism, Garrisonianism, Journalism, Political Campaignism."

Douglass was honored when William Henry Seward subscribed to the *North Star* and, typically, used his note of acknowledgment to open a correspondence; by 1853, writing to thank the New York senator for a copy of his *Works,* he offered some advice: "I long to see the day when . . . *Wm H. Seward* is no longer a member of the old Whig party—but is at the head of a great party of freedom." As editor of the *North Star* and then of *Frederick Douglass' Paper,* Douglass urged everyone, moral suasionists as well as politicians, to join in what was called the Common Family of people committed to ending both slavery and the concomitant denigration of those who were, in the eyes of many white beholders, branded with the coloration of slaves. Acknowledging a subscription from Salmon P. Chase, he took the occasion not only to thank the Ohio senator for his opposition to slavery, but to chide him for adopting the old colonizationist position that it would be well to separate the two races. Although the political climate of 1850 did "not appear very favorable to our remaining here," Douglass declared, ". . . yet I think there has been no time in the history of our [it was, firmly, "our"] country when there were more favorable indications than can be seen at this day."

In the winter of 1851, Douglass had extensive conversations with

Gerrit Smith about merging the *North Star* with the *Syracuse Standard,* the journal of the faltering Liberty party. But Smith made it clear that his would have to be the dominant voice in the new paper, and when the rival editor understandably held on to his own prerogatives, the merger did not take place. Douglass had long ago pointed out to Smith, as he had tried in vain to indicate to the Garrisonians, that the *North Star* "is not a party paper and looks with grateful friendship upon all classes of abolitionists." Smith's support of the *North Star* increased after this episode, so he appears not to have been dismayed by Douglass's insistence on his own independence. Neither was Julia Griffiths, who was now fully in place as Douglass's right hand on the paper.

For Smith, Douglass's unwillingness to merge the newspapers was more than offset by his friend's conversion with respect to the Constitution. Ever since moving to New York State, Douglass had been wrestling with the question of whether it was truly moral to participate in politics—an activity, after all, that was sanctioned by a constitution that Garrisonian dogma held to be a covenant with the devil. The document did indeed take slavery into account, and purists regarded it as making inviolate the slaveholders' power to hold onto slavery.

Other abolitionists, most notably James Gillespie Birney of the Liberty party, Arthur and Lewis Tappan, who, rebuking Garrison, had founded the American and Foreign Anti-Slavery Society, and Gerrit Smith, contended that moral suasion was clearly not enough and that politics was precisely the arena in which slavery should be fought. They insisted that the Constitution allowed for such an effort. Douglass, in whom seethed an implacable hatred of slavery, had found purgative Garrison's scathing dismissal of the core of the nation's political structure on the grounds that the Constitution, with its demonstrable accommodations to the existence of slavery in the nation, immorally enshrined that institution. But Gerrit Smith, who despised slavery as heartily as did Garrison, argued with Douglass that this doctrinal position was far from practical.

In May 1851, Douglass went to Syracuse for the annual meeting of the American Anti-Slavery Society, held for the first time outside New York City, where no suitable auditorium was open to the abolitionists. George Thompson had come to America for the meeting, and his presence, a reminder of the heady days the three had spent together in London, presented Garrison and Douglass with the opportunity to reassert their old comradeship. They did not take it.

In his speech at the meeting, having lauded Thompson and the British abolitionists, Douglass referred to Edmund Quincy's characterization of the South as "impudent," saying it was "a word with which he and his people were very familiar." After mimicking a white Southerner demanding deference, Douglass (who knew perfectly well whom Quincy really thought was impertinent) neatly made all Southerners one; if to "assert their rights was to be impudent," then his people were just as good at behaving impudently as their masters. When Douglass went on to say that he couldn't have quite the same view of these matters as Quincy because "he [Quincy] was white, whilst he [Douglass] was black," there was, nervously, "(Laughter.)"

If the audience was amused, the leadership of the society was not. Douglass had had the audacity to point out that antislavery people in the North drew their own color line and that he was on the other side of it. The "ungrateful"—that was their word for his behavior—runaway had had the nerve to start his own newspaper and now he was about to go his own way on the question of the Constitution. During a debate chaired by Garrison, Douglass asserted (in what Samuel J. May described as a "hesitating and embarrassed" manner) that the document might be consistent with abolitionist aims.

This was too much; the delegates passed a resolution forbidding support by any member of the society of any paper that did not specifically condemn the Constitution. Two weeks later the proscribed *North Star* carried an item headed "Change of Opinion Announced." Openly defying the American Anti-Slavery Society, Douglass embraced the Constitution, which "construed in the light of well established rules of legal interpretation, might be made consistent . . . with the noble purposes avowed in its preamble." He demanded that the document "be wielded in behalf of emancipation." In June 1851, flushed with this new assertion of independence, Douglass discarded one of the nation's most reverberant newspaper names: the *North Star* became *Frederick Douglass' Paper.*

To Douglass's great satisfaction Gerrit Smith ran for Congress in 1852 as an avowed foe of slavery and won. "The election of *Gerrit Smith*— what an era!" he exulted in a congratulatory note. (Unfortunately, the era lasted only one term.) Douglass would not let his friend rest on his laurels; the new congressman was admonished to keep up the agitation, for they "must carry the state for freedom in *1856.*" Similarly, Douglass sought to push Whigs toward the cause. In November 1851, when a move was made to nominate him for a seat in the state legislature, he not only declared that he could not be a candidate of a party that countenanced the Fugitive Slave Act, but preached a rather hortatory sermon on the need of that party to move firmly into the antislavery family.

That family now extended far beyond the nucleus of those loyal to the Garrisonian creed. Slavery was, in Douglass's view, unquestionably a moral evil, but he no longer thought that Americans could simply be brought to a state of morality that would waft slavery away. He wanted to use every conceivable ounce of leverage to dislodge the institution. His sense of the inclusiveness of the antislavery cause meant that he wanted to hold his old friends in the American Anti-Slavery Society within the family, but he knew that as he had moved far from their severely narrow view of the cause, he had also moved painfully away from these old friends. Every effort he now made to keep the Bostonians with him ran up against their feeling that they should do the keeping. The old guard still smarted under what they saw as his ingratitude, expressed by his starting his own paper and going his own way in matters of antislavery policy, and now they found a focus for their irritation. Samuel J. May, Jr. (a Leicester, Massachusetts, minister, not to be confused with Douglass's friend Samuel J. May), complained about the unhumble black man and that "ordinary looking" white woman whom he insisted on having at his side.

Some of the criticism of Julia Griffiths seems to have been justified. She took upon herself the role of defender of the Great Man, and wrote Douglass's old allies demanding letters that purported to pass along his instructions to them. This practice, quite naturally, was resented by his loyal friends. Isabel Jennings complained to Mary Estlin that she had "heard only once" from Douglass in the two years that Griffiths had been in Rochester. The only communication had been a request from "Miss J.G." for money for the newspaper. Jennings suspected that "her injudiciousness" was hurting the cause; having seen Griffiths and Douglass together in Manchester, she thought them to be of very different temperaments and ideas, and this conclusion made Jennings "fear her going to his house." The Irishwoman did recognize that Griffiths had cleared seven hundred dollars of the paper's debt by her fund raising, and that she had made herself indispensable to the paper as an editor, but nevertheless Jennings concluded, "I know well that all this had better be left undone than accomplished at too great an expense." One such expense was that she no longer felt she could write candidly to her old friend, for she suspected that "Miss G. reads all F.D.'s letters." Then, trying to put the best face on her disappointment, she added, "I am sure he thinks anti-Slavery zeal is the strongest emotion she is capable of."

Others were convinced that other emotions dominated, but their appeals to Douglass to end his friendship with Julia Griffiths because it was harming the antislavery cause went unheeded. Indeed, his right to that friendship was, in his mind, indivisible from the right of his people to be liberated and given a chance to reach their full humanity. When Samuel Porter, with whom he had long worked in moving fugitives into Canada, wrote him that the scandal was undercutting his effectiveness, Douglass replied, in January 1852, "Individuals have rights not less than society." He was "a husband and a father—and withal a citizen," he declared, implying that as a citizen, a responsible member of society, he alone could decide if he was properly discharging his familial duties while he maintained his friendship with Griffiths.

Douglass chided Porter for writing to him of the "scandalous reports" instead of speaking to him face to face: "You and I have been friends during the last two or three years—on as intimate terms as can . . . subsist between the Rich man and the Poor." This bit of sycophancy behind him, he went on to say that "Miss Griffiths—is a free woman—and [acknowledging that they had indeed felt the sting of criticism], of her own free will" had moved out of his house to board elsewhere two months earlier. Rebutting Porter's allegations, he denied responsibility for her words, deeds, or dress, or "her thinking me a *'God'*— if she is so foolish or wicked as to think so."

He would not allow Porter or anyone else to undercut his friendship by making fun—"speaking lightly"—of Julia, whose forthright ways and eccentric clothes made her an easy target. "She has a just claim upon my gratitude, respect, and friendship," he declared. Julia Griffiths had built something like a satisfactory relationship with Anna Douglass, sharing tea with her in the kitchen, and had even, unsuccessfully, tried to teach her to read. Douglass, reflecting his awareness of the criticism he and Griffiths faced, insisted that "when she was in my family—I was necessarily in her society—our walking and riding together was natural. Now we are separated and meet at my office at business hours and for business purposes—where we are open to the observation of my printers and the public—from ten o'clock or earlier in the morning until four o'clock in the afternoon." Then, after wandering into conjecture as to whether she would stay on at the paper or go back to England, as she talked of doing, he brought himself up short: "But I am doing what I had no intention of doing, when I took up my pen and therefore, bring this letter to a close at once." He would neither try to read her mind nor apologize.

A few months later, in the summer of 1852, Ann Smith, to the consternation of the critics, made a point of climbing the steep, dark stairs to the newspaper office to surprise and delight Julia with the offer to ride out together to Frederick's new house two miles south of the center of the city. When Douglass got the idea of buying a farm high on a hill outside of town, and where he got the money to buy it, is not known. The Monroe County records shed no light on the original purchase, but do document his acquisition in 1863 and 1865 of two adjacent lots. The Alexander Street house was not sold; it was held as the first of several real-estate investments, which became for the Douglasses, as for many prosperous African American families, the foundation of financial security. (There was, for example, the speculative purchase for the considerable sum of $2,500 of lots in the town of Ogden, west of Rochester, in 1865.)

Douglass's new house stood in "a neighborless place, its only roadway at that time the private road leading to his door." In time, Douglass cleared a wide area, which gave him a view of Rochester and allowed him to put in fruit trees. The farm's roadway connected with the dirt road leading into the city from the southeast, and soon the Douglass place became a reliable stop for fugitive slaves making their way to Canada. There, in the house or the barn, runaways could spend their last night in the slaveholding United States or wait to be taken by wagon downtown after dark, to be hidden in E. C. Williams's sail loft or Isaac Post's barn on Sophia Street; "the most we ever had at one time was twelve," Amy Post recalled. She once estimated that 150 fugitives a year moved through Rochester. If they stayed at the Douglasses', a note, often carried by one of the Douglass children, went to Isaac Post or Samuel Porter— "Two weary people here; need transportation in the morning." The signature, in a perfunctory effort at disguise, would be "D.F." At dawn, a wagon would take the refugees to town, where they would be led down below the lower falls and put aboard a boat headed for Canada and safety.

As Ann Smith and Julia Griffiths made their way out of the city on the St. Paul Road that summer day, Julia reported that Frederick was working hard on a speech, and pronounced it excellent. Douglass was writing the speech in response to an invitation from the Rochester Ladies' Anti-Slavery Society to give an oration in Corinthian Hall on the Fourth of July. He agreed to speak, but not on that date; on the day after Independence Day, staunchly antislavery Rochester crowded into the hall to hear what came to be known as Frederick Douglass's Fifth of July Speech. "This Fourth [of] July," he reminded his audience, "is *yours,* not *mine. You* may rejoice, *I* must mourn. To drag a man in fetters into the grand illuminated temple of liberty, and call upon him to join you in joyous anthems, were inhuman mockery and sacrilegious irony. Do you mean, citizens, to mock me, by asking me to speak today?"

But he did speak. "Would you have me argue that man is entitled to his liberty? that he is the rightful owner of his own body? You have already declared it. Must I argue the wrongfulness of slavery? Is that a question for Republicans?" Then, expounding on the republican philosophy of those who had not only declared independence but also constituted a nation, Douglass proclaimed, "Fellow-citizens! there is no matter in respect to which, the people of the North have allowed themselves to be so ruinously imposed upon, as that of the pro-slavery character of the

Constitution. In *that* instrument I hold there is no warrant, license, nor sanction of the hateful thing; but, interpreted as it *ought* to be interpreted, the Constitution is a GLORIOUS LIBERTY DOCUMENT."

He surprised an audience used to speaking of "chains" as characteristic of slavery by stating, "The 4th of July is the first great fact in your nation's history—the very ring-bolt in the chain of your yet undeveloped destiny." With a bold mixing of metaphors, he mused on how that day's philosophy had been ignored, and offered only an Ishmael's hope of survival: "From the round top of your ship of state, dark and threatening clouds may be seen. Heavy billows, like mountains in the distance, disclose to the leeward huge forms of flinty rocks! That *bolt* drawn, that *chain* broken, and all is lost. *Cling to this day—cling to it,* and to its principles, with the grasp of a storm-tossed mariner to a spar at midnight."

It was in the Fifth of July Speech that Douglass not only gave his searing prophecy of what the nation's fate would be in less than a decade, and what would ensue in the decades toward the end of his life, but also pointed a haunting finger at our own day, a century after his death: "There is consolation in the thought that America is young. Great streams are not easily turned from channels, worn deep in the course of ages. They may sometimes rise in quiet and stately majesty, and inundate the land, refreshing and fertilizing the earth with their mysterious properties. They may also rise in wrath and fury, and bear away, on their angry waves, the accumulated wealth of years of toil and hardship. They, however, gradually flow back to the same old channel, and flow on as serenely as ever. But, while the river may not be turned aside, it may dry up, and leave nothing behind but the withered branch, and the unsightly rock, to howl in abyss-sweeping wind, the sad tale of departed glory. As with rivers so with nations."

When the long, learned, carefully crafted speech was over and Douglass took his seat, the audience rose to cheer him. His Rochester neighbors had heard perhaps the greatest antislavery oration ever given.

The Rochester Ladies' Anti-Slavery Society was one of the most active in the movement. To raise money for the cause, Julia Griffiths, its secretary, in 1852 hit on an excellent scheme. She asked celebrities to submit antislavery statements, and these were printed, each followed by a facsimile of its author's signature, in a book called *Autographs for Freedom*. There were to be two volumes, to double the profits. In volume one, William Henry Seward led off, followed by Harriet Beecher Stowe. Most of the entries were, like John Greenleaf Whittier's poem, brief, but Douglass's contribution was a sixty-five-page novella called "The Heroic Slave." This, his only attempt at fiction, is a curious mirror of his *Narrative of the Life of Frederick Douglass* and a way station on the road to his second telling of his own heroic life, *My Bondage and My Freedom.*

In "The Heroic Slave," a Northern traveler, Listwell, listens attentively to the ruminations of a slave musing over the philosophical problems that confront him. He moves from despair over his "aimless" life to a passionate pursuit of *"Liberty."* The slave in this work of historical fiction is named Madison Washington, after the leader of a revolt on the brig *Creole* in 1841. (Irony in American history knows no bounds.) Physically, the slave resembles if not Douglass himself, then Henry Harris: "Madison was of manly form, tall, symmetrical, round, and strong. In his movements he seemed to combine, with the strength of the lion, a lion's elasticity. His torn sleeves disclosed arms like polished iron." For him, "those distant church bells have no grateful music"; he wants to run away, and is held back, he tells the Northerner, only by the thought that he would have to leave his wife behind.

Five years later, back in Ohio, Listwell finds at his door a tall, weary traveler—Madison, on his way to Canada. The fugitive is invited into the best bedroom rather than the barn, and helped on his way to a successful escape. A year later still, Listwell is back in Virginia, in a tavern that in its decrepitude is a metaphor for the decay of the slaveholding society—it is a meeting place for "gamblers, horses-racers, cock-fighters, and slave-traders." He hears the doleful sound of chained slaves marching, and looking out, he sees Madison among the miserable people pressed on by loathsome slave traders. Unable to enjoy freedom without his wife, Madison had returned to try to rescue her, and had been caught and sold south.

As the slaves are driven onto the "Baltimore built American Slaver," the *Creole,* for the journey to New Orleans, Listwell slips three sharp files to Madison, whom, he has confessed, "he loved as well as admired." Off the Virginia coast, the files are put to good use; the slaves, led by Madison, attack, and the captain and the slaves' owner are killed. Madison spares the life of the first mate, and after stalwartly facing a great storm, orders him to take the ship into Nassau, in the Bahama Islands. There, when Madison is confronted with the responsibility for the deaths, he replies, "You call me a *black murderer.* I am not a murderer. . . . Liberty . . . is the motive of this night's work." Hearing his cry, the black officials in the British West Indies port refuse to send this "property"—these "barrels of flour"—back to Virginia: "Uttering the wildest shouts of exultation," the mutineers and the island's armed black soldiers march "amidst the deafening cheers of a multitude of sympathizing spectators, under the triumphant leadership of their heroic chief and deliverer, MADISON WASHINGTON."

There are echoes here of Nat Turner, with Madison having a sojourn in the Dismal Swamp, in which Turner hid after the failure of the uprising he led in 1831. And in addition to the *Creole* revolt, the story recalls the *Amistad* mutiny of 1839, when black slaves on board a ship seized it and sailed to New England in quest of their freedom. All of these actions had deep resonance for black Americans; Martin Delany's novel *Blake,* published in 1859, is another work telling of a black revolt. Such events stirred and somewhat frightened white abolitionists as well; in 1856 Harriet Beecher Stowe's *Dred: A Tale of the Great Dismal Swamp* appeared, as did Herman Melville's *Piazza Tales,* which includes "Benito Cereno," with its hauntingly ambiguous portrait of a black mutineer threatening a captured white ship captain. Douglass's Madison, with no ambiguity and far less depth than Melville's rebel, is in part the philosophizing slave that he remembered from *The Columbian Orator.* But there was more than memory; "The Heroic Slave" was its author's fantasy of his own heroism.

Douglass was still mourning the loss, or rather the gradual losing, of his own hero. In the winter of 1853, William C. Nell reported to Amy Post from Boston that Douglass had just been to the *Liberator* office and had gone "upstairs for a few minutes to see Mr. Garrison." The conversation was brief, and that evening, breaking a date to visit an exhibition based on the already vastly popular *Uncle Tom's Cabin,* Douglass went instead to Andover to seek the advice of Harriet Beecher Stowe on how to restore his relationship with the Boston antislavery group. Nell suspected that there was no way his old friend could do so: "I do not think he enjoys himself here as formerly." Ten days later, Douglass failed to appear to speak at an antislavery meeting in Worcester.

The Garrisonians, despite their official secularism, regarded any deviation from their leadership as heresy: theirs was the only way; all others were wrong. They left no room for the view that all who were opposed to slavery were engaged in one united enterprise. Douglass, like Gerrit Smith, was trying to unite the whole of the antislavery movement, but in the view of the Garrisonians, he was trying, as William C. Nell put it, "to ride two Horses." Nell, the proper prodigal, had left Rochester and Douglass's editorial office to return to Boston and the *Liberator,* where he had worked before joining the *North Star.* He thought now that there was but one mount for the true crusader. Nell was dismayed when Douglass accepted an invitation from Lewis Tappan to address the May meeting in New York of the rival American and Foreign Anti-Slavery Society after having agreed to speak before Garrison's American Anti-Slavery Society, which was also to meet in that city. Douglass wanted none of the exclusivity some insisted on. After attending both meetings, he reported to Gerrit Smith that "the Garrisonians could not say that I deserted them, nor the new organization that I failed to recognize them."

Mary Post Hallowell wrote to her stepmother, Amy Post, that the American Anti-Slavery Society meeting went "gloriously," but at the evening session, "Frederic sat on one side of the platform looking quite sad during the reading of the report." He should, she thought, have been seated next to the presiding officer, since he was the chief speaker of the evening. Rising to speak, Douglass showed that the old powers were as great as ever; "when he got about half thro' he threw [down] his notes and spoke extempore." She went on to report, "The faces on the platform were all strange to me"; Garrison, Quincy, Phillips, who had been at the afternoon session had stayed away.

The black abolitionists, not above their own jealousies, nevertheless tried to help each other keep the faith. Douglass and Amos Beman exchanged bantering notes, and in August 1853, William C. Nell, one of the most gregarious of men, having "breakfasted at William Lloyd Garrison's in the company of William H. Ashurst of London," traveled alone to New Bedford, there to have "very pleasant times with Fredk Douglass," both "public and private." As they rode in a barouche through Frederick's old town, Nell tried to bring his friend back to his old feelings about the New England abolitionists. For an hour, all seemed as it once had been, but when the two went on to a meeting in Framingham, a nasty "scene Occurred" between Frederick and Wendell Phillips. Nell "felt it" his "duty to ask him" to forgo his "hostility direct and indirect against his old friends." Frederick would not be contrite: "He disposed of the matter in a characteristic manner—professing his love for Mr. Garrison but no love for Wendell Phillips, Edmund Quincy—and regarding Mrs. Chapman as his inveterate enemy—He brought all kinds of charges against the abolitionists & acquit[ed] me of any dishonorable motives in bringing the matter up."

Quick-tempered, alert to the smallest slight, Douglass excoriated in private and in public people whom he had once immensely admired, and who, in turn, had admired him, though he had come to see that they did so through the glass of unconscious racism. He could not find a polite way to make them understand how important to him was his independence, to make them see that he could no longer be their agent, but must be taken into account as a leader in his own right. Nell, by contrast, could be content with playing the part Chapman and Garrison assigned him, that of the grateful child pleased with the privilege of breakfasting with a famous visitor from England, with having first-class accommodations when traveling with his employers, and receiving gratitude for a job well done on the *Liberator*. Nell had a world of black friends as well, among them Jeremiah Sanderson, who for a time had lived with the Douglasses. Nell had the great satisfaction of having Sanderson name a son after him and the comfort of an easy companionship with the man, while Douglass cut himself off from a good many men like Sanderson, to whom he had once been close, in his quest for a grander, more intellectually searching world. He knew he had achieved eminence, and he refused to apologize for the fact. He would make no excuses for his friendship with Julia Griffiths, nor would he back off from his sense that it was perfectly proper for him to preach to his former mentors that a unified attack on slavery must be achieved. He would never acknowledge a break with Garrison, but neither would he accept what he now regarded as a dead-end approach to ridding the country of slavery.

Other men had that job in hand better than the Garrisonians. While Gerrit Smith was in Congress, Douglass wrote frequently to him, commending him for his political attacks on slavery and urging him on. In Boston, Douglass "had a long talk" with Ellis Gray Loring, the lawyer who had arranged for his manumission. He found Loring a man of "much learning" and good practical political sense. Loring thought Smith could be much more effective in Congress if he would master parliamentary procedures and avoid the "mantraps" which the proslavery people were laying for him. The now politically astute Douglass hastened to pass the advice along to Smith, and not without a sarcastic reference to how others in the cause perceived him: "Now hear the impertinence of this runaway slave!" Then, to exclude Smith from such ranks, he added, "Ah! but he knows who he is talking to."

If he was feeling a bit guilty about his behavior in Massachusetts, he was big enough to discuss it. He told his friend Smith, "I am expecting a letter from you pretty soon about my late behavior . . . and yet I think [you] would not have blamed me had you been present. But give [me] a lecture—I have ears to hear." Not waiting, he gave his own: "Indeed I am greatly desirous of keeping out of quarrels with Boston. Nevertheless, I think, on the score of downright bigotry and pride of position, Boston deserves just such a 'going over' as you gave Mr. Quincy a few years ago. They talk down there as if the antislavery cause belonged to them—and as if all antislavery ideas originated with them—and that no man has a right to 'peep or mutter' on the subject who does not hold letter patent from them."

Smith did more than peep. In December 1853, he gave a powerful speech refuting President Franklin Pierce's State of the Union message, which was scarcely helpful to the antislavery cause. Delighted with what he read in the summary sent over the telegraph Douglass asked for a copy of the full speech: "My readers love the slave, love the truth, and love

Gerrit Smith the friend of both." On the personal front, Smith gave evidence of the richness of his friendship with the editor who wrote those words. When in Boston that month, he stopped in at the office of the American Anti-Slavery Society to try to patch up Douglass's friendship with William C. Nell. He was only partially successful; Nell reported that his old friend had a way of "coming down upon me in Battle axe state." Harriet Beecher Stowe too tried to mend New England fences. Garrison, calling on her in Andover, complained of Douglass's pandering to Smith and called him an "apostate." Stowe, who later admitted that she had engaged in some unseemly gossip about Douglass both with Garrison and with one of the Westons, invited the sinner to her house so she could see him for herself.

"I enjoyed the pleasure of a personal interview with Mr. Douglass," she reported to Garrison, "and I feel bound in justice to say that the impression was far more satisfactory than I had anticipated. . . . There did not appear to be any deep stratum of bitterness; he did not seem to me malignant or revengeful. I am satisfied that his change of sentiment was not a mere political one but a genuine growth of his own conviction. . . . he holds no opinion which he cannot defend, with a variety of richness of thought and expression and an aptness of illustration which shows it to be a growth from the soil of his own mind with a living root, and not a twig broken off other men's thoughts and stuck down to subserve a temporary purpose."

Turning to the personal dimensions of the quarrel: "You speak of him as an apostate. I cannot but regard this language as unjustly severe" and, she asked Garrison, "Why is he any more to be called an apostate for having spoken ill-tempered things of former friends than they for having spoken severely and cruelly as they have of him?" Then she continued, warming to the real point, "where is this work of excommunication to end? Is there but one true anti-slavery church and all others infidels?" Stowe was echoing Douglass's own passionate conviction that all antislavery people must pull together; she therefore made no bones about the need for Garrison to stop the gossip about Douglass's "family concerns" and other allusions "more unjustifiable still." She was "utterly surprised" by Garrison's indulgence in such talk: "As a friend to you and to him, I view it with the deepest concern and regret." She sternly advised that he make no further contributions to the "controversial literature," the swirl of malicious letters sailing through the antislavery mail slots: *"Silence* in this case will be eminently—*golden."* Then, reflecting on her own reaction to her visitor, the novelist wrote, "What Douglass *is* really, time will show."

The events of the 1850s seemed scarcely to permit such introspection.

In January 1854, Senator Stephen A. Douglas of Illinois was arguing for his Kansas-Nebraska bill, which called for organization of the Kansas and Nebraska territories, with decisions on slavery in them to be made by their respective inhabitants, in accordance with the doctrine of "popular sovereignty." The democratic ring of the words fooled no abolitionist. Adoption of the measure would end the Missouri Compromise, which called for no slavery in territories that—like Kansas—were north of Missouri's southern border. If Congress enacted the bill, it would be relinquishing its power to hem in slavery by preventing its spread north and west.

In the winter and spring of 1854, that bill caused excitement over slavery greater than at any time since the passage of the Fugitive Slave Act four years earlier. Julia Griffiths, visiting the Gerrit Smiths in Washington, was made "ecstatic" by the drama, and her host's role did not go unapplauded by Douglass: "Of your speech on the Nebraska Bill, aside from all my admiration and love for the friend of my poor people—I must pronounce it the mightiest and grandest production ever before delivered in the House or Senate of this nation." Other antislavery legislators were equally firm in response to the Illinois senator, and when Senator Charles Sumner made a powerful speech in February, Douglass thanked him for his passionate opposition, without which "this wicked measure will pass." But despite their vigorous efforts, the antislavery opponents of the bill failed to block its passage.

As organization of the territory of Kansas began, rival governments, for and against slavery, were formed, and vicious guerrilla warfare broke out. Back east, previously pacific antislavery people began raising money to send arms to those who sought to terrorize settlers favoring slavery. With the turn to violence, the rhetoric of abolition became increasingly apocalyptic. In October 1854, Douglass delivered a speech focused entirely on the Kansas-Nebraska Act and its consequences. Despairing of his fellow men, he reached toward religion, contending that the whole chain of pro-Southern actions, from the annexation of Texas to the proposed opening of Kansas to slavery, "vindicated the wisdom of that great God, who has promised to overrule the wickedness of men for His own glory." This was strange, unsettling talk from one who had placed such great trust in human beings; it pointed toward nothing save violence. But the fifteen hundred people crowded into Chicago's Metropolitan Hall cheered the speech.

Few of the skirmishes and none of the battles of the political war over slavery were being won by the antislavery people, but the worse the still-bloodless conflict went, the more fierce became the determination of some of the warriors to reverse its course. Although many black abolitionists had begun to despair of the country's ever setting things to rights, Douglass, for one, seemed only to gain energy for the effort of pushing the stone up the hill. He spoke, he wrote, he exhorted others to act, and in 1855, he published the strongest of his three autobiographies, *My Bondage and My Freedom.*

His crisp 114-page telling of his story in the *Narrative of the Life of Frederick Douglass* ten years earlier has so grasped the imagination of American readers that the richer, deeper, and far more ambiguous *Bondage* has not been fully appreciated. But students of literature, William L. Andrews prominent among them, have now taken the lead in a reevaluation of Douglass's autobiographies; Andrews views *Bondage* as far more than just an extension of the *Narrative,* bringing up to date the account of Douglass's life after he reached the North. Rather, it is a different and much more penetrating look into the heart of slavery. And yet, *Bondage* suffers from some of the constraints and distortions that have beset virtually all works that seek to convey the experience of slavery from within the consciousness of the slave. Even Harriet Jacobs's *Incidents in the Life of a Slave Girl* (1860), with its extraordinarily candid telling of her sexual strategies for coping with slavery, is cloaked so tightly in the rhetoric of reform that for well over a century—until literary historian Jean Fagan Yellin made us look at it afresh—we did not see the immense psychological complexity of the slave experience that Jacobs struggled to express.

Douglass's problems had several sources. In the first place, there was the absurd but real business of white readers either refusing to believe that a black person could be a writer or being so amazed at the performance that all they could see was the ball on the seal's nose. In the second place, there was the political necessity of making the book work in the antislavery cause, which resulted in his unavoidable urge to climb onto a hortatory soapbox. Furthermore, when he told the story of slave experiences with graphic particularity—with names and descriptions of the things that happened to these real people—he could not be sure how much intellectual response he would get. His account of his aunt's whipping by their owner, Aaron Anthony—the woman bared to the waist, the taunts, the snap of the whip, the screams at the slicing of the leather into her "plump and tender" flesh—went not to his readers' brains, but to their groins. The long reach of racist sexuality made the story for them an exercise in sadomasochistic eroticism, rather than an exploration of the complexities of the sadistic but also self-interested lustful motivation of the man who did the whipping. In *Bondage,* Douglass gave three full pages to this episode, which occupied just one paragraph in the *Narrative,* but it seems unlikely that he succeeded in getting many readers to credit fully the humanness of the dilemma of a woman so determined to have her own man that she would defy—and be cruelly tortured for defying—another.

When it came to appealing to the other emotional response that his friend Harriet Beecher Stowe had so brilliantly exploited in *Uncle Tom's Cabin*—sympathy with the trauma of forcible separation of a child from its mother—Douglass was at a loss. Unlike Eliza, his mother had not crossed a river on ice floes to hold onto him; he was forced to report that he had scarcely known his mother, saying now not that she had been a stranger, but that they were "separated . . . when I was but an infant." When his grandmother, for whom he professed a great sense of closeness, had been forced to abandon him, she did so. And he could not point to successful, heroic deeds. Even his own escape didn't fill the bill; the first try, potentially heroic, was aborted; his actual escape from slavery came almost as an anticlimax. He hinted at the psychological scars of slavery in his descriptions of the Harris brothers and Sandy Jenkins (who, technically, was free), but he could not fully explore this realm of the slave experience. Had he done so, he would have played into the hands of two contradictory white audiences, both of whom saw African Americans as inferior beings. Members of the first group seized on any evidence of deficiency to justify slavery's continuance. A person forced to repress immense grief can become psychologically injured, but these white observers often saw—or chose to see—in the resulting seemingly submissive behavior only proof of black inferiority. Other white observers, opposed to slavery, preferred to think of the slaves as helpless victims, whom only white Northern benevolence could carry toward a happier existence. But if in Douglass's time readers distorted the book into just another runaway's tale, it stands today as one of the most suggestive inquiries into the heart of slavery that we have.

Bondage was also its author's declaration of independence. Douglass recanted none of the heartfelt praise for William Lloyd Garrison that was in the *Narrative,* but gone, now, were the prefatory essays by Garrison and Wendell Phillips that had introduced the earlier book. And there was in the saccharine effusion of a long dedication celebrating the "Honorable Gerrit Smith" for his "Genius and Benevolence" and for "Ranking Slavery with Piracy and Murder" and "Denying It Either a Legal or Constitutional Existence" a not very subtle slap at his former champions, who deplored Smith's political activities and his belief that slavery could be ended through constitutional means. This dedication scarcely leaves the impression of an author unimpeded by obsequiousness, but the reader who leaps past it into the text will find a Frederick Douglass of a far more critical and analytical mind than the one in the *Narrative.*

Strangely, for a man not loath to stand in the full light of praise for his accomplishments, Douglass has left almost no record of how he went about writing his books. We have no notes, no correspondence, concerning the travails of composition, though we can be sure that Julia Griffiths urged him on and probably helped with the editing of *Bondage,* their last collaboration. The best clue we have to the process of creating the work lies in its tone; it carries the voice of the best of Douglass's speeches, particularly those which have been described for us by people who heard them given. A surging, probing imagination is at work in *Bondage;* an "I" cries out and is heard.

Back in the fall of 1853, Amy Post, away from Rochester visiting an ill son, received a letter from Julia Griffiths that was typical both in its expression of her proprietary affection for Frederick Douglass and in the inevitable comment on controversial political matters: "I miss you very much, I assure you—for although we do differ on 'The Constitution' "—the Quaker Posts, had not deserted Garrison on that issue—"we agreed to differ & that is a good thing!" She went on to report that while Frederick "looked greatly worn and fatigued" from a trip, she was, just then, sitting in the parlor with him, and he was "rather merrily playing the violin & singing, by turns, which will show you that he is in good spirits." During his absence, there had been considerable excitement over renewed enforcement of the Fugitive Slave Act in Rochester; "we have," she reported, "started quite a number of Fugitives off to Canada lately."

Julia closed the letter when Frederick, in a welcome interruption, began to read aloud. Two years later, this domesticity was over. The Posts had been understanding of their friends' friendship, but almost no other antislavery people were. By 1855, the criticism had become so shrill that the two could no longer withstand its pressures. Julia packed her bags and went back to England, where she continued her antislavery activities. Later, she wrote a regular column, "Letters from the Old Country," for *Douglass' Monthly,* the handsomely produced journal, originally a supplement to *Frederick Douglass' Paper,* which appeared as a separate publication starting in January 1859. As always, she ruffled feathers. Her outspoken advocacy of political strategies and her criticism of the American Anti-Slavery Society were but "the machinations of that double-and-twisted worker of iniquity" in the judgment of William Lloyd Garrison. In time, Julia married the Reverend H. O. Crofts, a stolid clergyman with whom she moved from parsonage to parsonage in England. After he died, she conducted, for twenty years, a school for young women in St. Neots. Until the death of Frederick Douglass, three months before hers, she never ceased corresponding with her "beloved friend." But she was never again to sit with him in his parlor.

15

South Avenue

THE FOREIGN LADY, calling at the newspaper office in 1856 and finding that the editor was not in, was directed to his house. Making the half-hour trek up the hill, Ottilia Assing was tired, but her expectations were restored as she reached the house, with its lovely garden and fine view over the city. She was more excited still when she was greeted by the man she had come so far to meet. He was, she discovered, a "rather light mulatto of unusually large, slender and powerful build." The curiosity of the visitor from Berlin was great, and his appearance answered a good many of her questions: "His features are marked by a distinctly vaulted forehead and with a singularly deep indentation at the base of the nose. The nose itself is arched, the lips are small and nicely formed, revealing more the influence of the white than of his black origins. His thick hair is mixed here and there with grey and is curly though not woolly." If she had felt the need to establish that his features were not markedly Negroid, this keen observer had an even stronger urge to take in the whole of the man she met.

As the two began to be acquainted, Assing found that Frederick Douglass had a "talent" for "conversation through which he stimulates and elevates and shows himself to be both learned and ingenious and highly cultivated." The handsome German woman, speaking careful, correct English, was as intriguing to Douglass as he to her. They began a friendship that day which was to last for a quarter of a century.

Ottilia Assing was born in Hamburg, the daughter of Rosa Maria Varnhagen Assing and David Assing, a surgeon who had converted from Judaism to Lutheranism. After her mother's death in 1840 and her father's two years later, Ottilia and her sister Ludmilla moved to Berlin to live with their uncle, Karl August Varnhagen von Ense. Varnhagen, who explained his somewhat casual appropriation of "von Ense" with the quip "As long as one nobleman exists, one must also be ennobled," was a former diplomat and a man of letters, deeply involved in liberal politics in the Prussian capital. While still relatively young, he had married the much older Rahel Levin, a brilliant woman fascinating to him both for being a Jew and for resolutely refusing to be Jewish.

By the time Levin married, her salon, conducted with perverse grandeur in a garret, had long been a center for fashionable literary and political conversation; Hannah Arendt credits her with being the "originator" of the "Goethe cult." Rahel had been dead for a decade when the Assing sisters arrived, but the tradition of a woman as cultural mentor in the household still lingered; Ludmilla soon took up the role of hostess for her uncle and dedicated her life to editing and publishing his writings. Ottilia, whose relationship with her sister was stormy, would eventually leave for America.

Ottilia had come to know about Frederick Douglass by reading *My Bondage and My Freedom.* In view of her espousal of other liberal causes, it was entirely fitting that she should become an ardent advocate of the emancipation of America's slaves. If the tale of liberation in *Bondage* was compelling, so too was the elegant frontispiece showing its handsome author, and with Germanic determination, she traveled to Rochester to meet him.

Perhaps conscious of the relief with which his friends had celebrated the departure of Julia Griffiths the year before, Douglass did not, once their friendship was established, invite Assing to move to Rochester. She settled, instead, in Hoboken, a pleasant town with a sizable German American population, across the Hudson River from New York City. There she taught German (and perhaps English) and wrote articles for German American journals and for the liberal Frankfurt journal *Morgenblatt fuer gebildete Staende,* which published over a hundred of her reports from America.

The distance between Hoboken and Rochester did not impede the friendship. Assing began making summer visits to the Douglasses' home on South Avenue, as the St. Paul Road was now called, at least as early as 1857. The two friends, seemingly so different, had a great deal in common. As Varnhagen's biographer, Terry H. Pickett, has observed, Assing "belonged to a family in which high cultural ambitions were taken as a matter of course." The American public generally may not have taken such ambitions as a matter of course for a runaway slave, but Douglass did. Pickett's observation that the "state of being educated and cultured cannot be . . . [overestimated] as a primary value in [Assing's] native milieu in Germany," applies to Douglass's personal values as well. Douglass was delighted when his friend took it as her calling to put him in touch with European culture. Assing's friend the princess Helene von Racowitza insisted that intellectually "dark, handsome Fred" was the "handiwork" of Ottilia's "spirit," but as much as Assing enjoyed the role of mentor, the two friends would have seen their relationship as a partnership.

There was no yielding of intellectual primacy when Frederick, as author, discussed with Ottilia the translation into German of *My Bondage and My Freedom,* which she had undertaken. After she had finished, expertly, he wrote to Ludmilla Assing asking her help in finding a publisher. (In his letter, he adopted a manner that he apparently took to be European; he was extravagant with the word "extravagant"—and became obsequious. As he put it, Ottilia's "interest in the Book and in the Cause it was designed to promote has led to an acquaintance and a friendship for which I have many reasons to be grateful.") His quest for a publisher was successful; *Sklaverei und Freiheit: Autobiographie von Frederick Douglass* was published by Hoffmann and Campe in Hamburg in 1860.

How soon—and, indeed, whether—their friendship led to a sexual relationship is impossible to determine. Helene von Racowitza stated in her memoirs that Ottilia was *mit leidenschaftlicher Liebe* (which is to say, passionately in love) with Frederick, but Racowitza decorously if not persuasively claimed that her friend "respected the bonds of wedlock." Ottilia, writing to her sister eighteen years after meeting Frederick, said of their connection, ". . . if one stands in so intimate a relationship with a man as I do with Douglass, one comes to know facets of the whole world, of men and women, which would otherwise remain closed, especially if it is a man whom the entire world has seen and whom so many women have loved." One could conjecture that a sexual union was only Ottilia's fantasy, but it would be credulity to do so. Indeed, given Ottilia's eagerness in seeking to meet Frederick, and given his charm, which women had never been slow to note, it is hard to imagine that they took very long to achieve such a relationship.

The two met at a crucial period in the evolution of Douglass's response to the intransigence of slavery's proponents. More and more militancy was in the air. Black Americans were as despondent as they had ever been. Efforts to end slavery seemed to have been frustrated on every side. For those who were free and able to act, and unwilling to give up on America altogether, the only alternative seemed to be to push stagnant politics to some new life. Neither Douglass nor Assing was ignorant of this dangerous excitement. She came from a world that had fostered liberal revolutions; their only flaw was that they had failed. She was eager to be party to a revolution that succeeded, and she thought the Americans were about to give her that opportunity. For Douglass, the heady energy of antislavery and women's rights conventions had collided with the harsh realities of stubborn resistance. The hope of ending slavery through an appeal to peoples' better nature or through political means was dimming. In Kansas, the flame had gone out entirely—snuffed, a good many people believed, by Douglass's friend John Brown.

The two had first met in 1848, when Brown, then living in Springfield, Massachusetts, invited the famous young black orator and editor to stop and visit on his way to Rochester from Boston. Douglass had been told that Brown was staunchly antislavery and that he was a tanner by trade. As he walked from the station, Douglass expected a richly furnished middle-class house, like those of the many other antislavery merchants he admired. Instead, the house, in a working-class neighborhood, proved as spare as the man who lived there. Like so many others, Douglass found Brown's appearance unforgettable: "Straight and symmetrical as a mountain pine. His bearing was singularly impressive. His head was not large, but compact and high. His hair was coarse, strong, slightly gray, and closely trimmed, and grew low on his forehead. . . . His eyes . . . were full of light and fire."

Served by his wife and children at a plain pine table, this patriarch—old, though still in his forties, and "lean, strong, and sinewy, . . . built for times of trouble"—talked with ease with his ex-slave guest. Unlike many white abolitionists, Brown did not regard black men as easily forgotten artifacts of the cause; rather, they were people to whom he was deeply drawn. It is a measure of both men's often overlooked ties to the black community, that the suggestion that they meet had come from two black men, Henry Highland Garnet and Jermain Wesley Loguen, not from white antislavery people. Brown already loathed slaveholders and thought they had "forfeited their right to live," but the image he evoked in these pre-Kansas days was not that of white people murdering other white people, but of his comradeship with black men in a common effort.

The basic lines of that effort, the raising of an insurrection and the establishment of a black state in the Appalachian Mountains, were already in his mind as he and Douglass talked. Douglass remembered well how it felt for an escape to fail, but Brown assured him that once the slaves began to rise, a steady stream of their escaping fellows would follow them into the mountains. There, he claimed, in armed squads of twenty-five men each, they could successfully resist efforts to retake them. Slaveholders captured trying to prevent their slaves from escaping would not be killed, but would be held as hostages; nonslaveholding whites would not be touched. What Douglass and other runaways told Brown about the practicality of his plan is not known. In 1848, it probably seemed so remote from reality that no critical scrutiny was called for. There was no need to dampen the ardor of one white man who was ready to take action against slavery.

For Douglass, any scheme for getting rid of slavery was worth hearing about; any foe of slavery was worthy of friendship—and certainly one as wholly committed to the cause as Brown was. Brown wanted the trust and help of the rising young black leader, and Douglass always responded well to a white man who took him seriously. At its most attractive, Brown's tie to black people was devoid of racial condescension; in 1849 he settled his family in North Elba, the black community on remote and barren lands given by Gerrit Smith in the far northern reaches of New York State.

Less appealing was Brown's obsession with being the black bondsmen's savior, their Moses leading his people out of bondage and into a black mountain kingdom that would, somehow, float free of its mooring in the Appalachian Mountains of the slaveholding American South. And violence was not then, or ever after, absent from his mind. Brown was consummately a warrior. In perhaps the most telling judgment in his perceptive biography *John Brown,* Oswald Garrison Villard notes that Brown conceived of "slavery as *war,* thereby establishing the context for his martial opposition to it."

Brown's battlefield shifted in the 1850s from its imagined place in the Southern mountains to the bloody reality of Kansas. There, on the frontier, the white nation's quarrel over slavery was focused. The Kansas-Nebraska Act, which Senator Stephen A. Douglas had pushed through Congress in 1854, had destroyed the federal government's authority to determine whether or not slavery should exist in the various territories. This had been the prerogative of Congress since the Northwest Ordinance of 1787, which kept slavery out of the territories that eventually formed the states of Ohio, Indiana, Illinois, Michigan, and Wisconsin. Now, under the Kansas-Nebraska Act, the settlers themselves were to decide if slavery was to be permitted. Douglas championed this fair-sounding "popular sovereignty" as the essence of democracy, but his rhetoric did not persuade the furious abolitionists, including his near-namesake.

When the senator died seven years later, Douglass wrote to Susan B. Anthony, "I rejoice not in the death of any man, but I cannot but feel, that in the death of Stephen A. Douglass [*sic*], a most dangerous man has been removed. No man of his time has done more than he to intensify hatred of the negro."

During the turmoil over the passage of the Kansas-Nebraska Act, and the bloody events in the territory that followed, mass protest meetings were held by antislavery people across the North. Douglass himself went to Senator Douglas's state of Illinois, where his friends tried to arrange a debate between the two. There can never have been much hope that Douglas would share a platform with any black man, let alone this one, but Douglass, in Chicago in October 1854, relished the idea: "Ebony and ivory are thought to look better standing together than when separated. A white Douglas, canvassing the State for slavery," might meet his match in a black rejoinder for "freedom." Stephen Douglas knew how much controversy he had stirred; returning to Illinois a few months earlier, he had noted sardonically, "I could travel from Boston to Chicago by the light of my own effigy."

In a famous Douglas debate that did take place, with Abraham Lincoln in 1858, the senator told the people of Freeport, Illinois, that while he was addressing an earlier crowd there, "I saw a carriage—and a magnificent one it was,—drive up and take a position on the outside of the crowd; a beautiful young lady was sitting on the box-seat, whilst Fred Douglass and her mother reclined inside, and the owner of the carriage acted as driver." There was laughter in the crowd, but also a cry from one listener: "What of it?" The senator replied, "All I have to say is if you, Black Republicans, think that the negro ought to ride in a carriage with your wife, whilst you drive the team, you have a perfect right to do so."

Both supporters and opponents of slavery in Kansas had begun moving into the territory by the the spring of 1854, when President Franklin Pierce signed the bill leaving the decision up to the settlers. Since Kansas was due west of slaveholding Missouri, whose residents felt proprietary about the territory, it was readily accessible to the supporters of slavery, but antislavery men were not long in challenging them, and soon both were conducting vicious guerrilla attacks. Civil war, pale beside the great war it presaged, but war nonetheless, had broken out.

America has never been short of men and women driven by vision, but it is difficult to imagine that John Brown would have had any followers if not for the psychological state to which the nation had brought itself over Kansas. Many antislavery leaders who had been pacific, in action if not always in rhetoric—Henry Ward Beecher, Gerrit Smith and Douglass himself among them—now called on their followers to send guns to the Kansas abolitionists, and among some highly incendiary guerrillas, John Brown was the most fiery. No modernist he, Brown did not rely on guns alone to do his killing. At Pottawatomie, Kansas, in May 1856, after he and his band had dragged three proslavery men named Doyle, from their cabin, Brown shot the father in the head with a pistol while the two sons were hacked to death and their bodies mutilated with broadswords. Broadswords! Whether Frederick Douglass ever wondered about the sanity of John Brown we do not know. If anything might have induced him to do so, it should have been the use of medieval weapons—"odd-shaped cutlasses, the gift of General Lucius V. Bierce of Akron, Ohio"—on the American frontier by men caught up in a fantasy of sadistic ritual murder.

Douglass, a fervent opponent of capital punishment—"Murder is no cure for murder"—had little taste for violence. During the days of "Bleeding Kansas," in the summer of 1856, he was still contending that black Americans need not take up arms. In "the noble work" of redeeming "an entire race from the . . . scorn of the world . . . the strife we are called upon is not . . . a war-like one," he wrote in his paper in September. Unlike republicans in France and Italy, he did not think that the friends of freedom here would have to resort to "slaughter": "With us the only hardship is, the industry and persistence with which our efforts must be made. The right of petition, the right of the press, and free speech, are left to us, and the use of these is all that is required for the acquisition of our rights in the northern States." This position of course begged the question of how slavery was to be gotten rid of in the South; the self-proclaimed radical abolitionist, choosing not to speak of the act of violence, declared that "the open sesame for the colored man is action! action!! action!!"

The most incendiary act of which the anti-antislavery people could accuse the abolitionists was that of inciting a slave insurrection—a rising of African savages. The opponents of abolition made every effort to get Douglass, the most famous and articulate black leader, to come out in favor of violence; he countered with equal determination not to play into their hands. But the humiliations African Americans faced were provoking. In his 1852 novella, "The Heroic Slave," he had had slaves use their broken fetters to kill the captain of a slaver and a slave owner; now, in the fall of 1856, he was pressed into saying that a black man had as much right forcibly to resist attack as a white man; and when it came to Kansas, where violence was an everyday occurrence, his sympathies were unequivocally with those doing battle with proslavery forces.

Lewis Tappan, writing to Douglass after the 1856 presidential election, lamented the defeat of the Republican candidate, John C. Frémont, but agreed that the absence of an affirmation of equality made the Republican party's platform one "no coloured man could stand on." He soon found it necessary, however, to reprimand his friend. Things did not add up for him as they now did for Douglass: such "means [violence] in either case are abhorrent to my mind & heart. I am truly sorry you cherish such sentiments." Perhaps "cherish" was not exactly the right word, but there can be no doubt that Douglass was condoning the means employed by John Brown and other war makers.

That same month, December 1856, Brown himself climbed the hill south of Rochester to visit Douglass. He was on his way east, ostensibly to raise more money for his war in Kansas. In confidence, Brown told Douglass of at least two schemes. One, with considerable appeal to a person who had long worked on the underground railroad, was known as the Subterannean Pass Way. Under this scheme, a corridor running roughly north from the Valley of Virginia through Pennsylvania and New York to Canada would be opened; guarded by men in frequently spaced armed stations along the way, slaves could move in a mass exodus into freedom. The other plan was Brown's old dream of an Appalachian state.

After leaving Douglass, Brown continued on to Boston, where Franklin B. Sanborn, the young secretary of the Massachusetts Kansas Committee, arranged for him to visit a phalanx of antislavery leaders. William Lloyd Garrison sternly rebuked Brown for his killings and would have none of his gun-money campaign, but many of the others had abandoned the creed of nonviolence. They wanted to hear what the warrior proposed. In Kansas, where the fighting over slavery had been savage, there were few slaves. Virginia, by contrast, was the state with the largest number of slaves, and these were the ones Brown pledged to lead in revolt. The Bostonians listened with fascination; soon a cabal, known later as the Secret Six, began to form. These eminently respectable divines, intellectuals, businessmen, and landed gentry were mesmerized by the fifty-six-year-old revolutionary and his grand design. Not since Aaron Burr's dream of a separate Western republic had there been an American enterprise more bizarre.

Brown may have seen Douglass as the most important of the black leaders he had gained as brothers, and may have hoped to enlist him as a comrade in arms, but it was the six white men who were to become famous, or infamous, as his allies. One scrupulous observer, David Potter, has challenged the correctness of regarding the six, safely away from the action, as true allies. What is undoubtedly correct is that, somewhat unreliably, they supplied the money. Samuel Gridley Howe, who had fought in Greece for that land's independence, also supplied a modicum of military legitimacy to the scheme. He recalled that mountain guerrilla activities had worked against the Turks. (He also had a restless young wife, who would later write the most martial hymn in musical literature—"The Battle Hymn of the Republic." The words were sung to the tune of an old hymn that by then had been appropriated for "John Brown's Body," the dirge widely sung almost immediately after Brown's death.)

Julia Ward Howe reported that she was much taken by the penetrating gaze of the revolutionary. So were Mary Stearns and her husband, George Luther Stearns; he and Brown were "like the iron and the magnet." Stearns, a rich Massachusetts linseed-oil manufacturer, had long been a gunrunner for the Kansas fighters whom his friend Thomas Wentworth Higginson had recently visited and talked of joining. Higginson (who was to be the colonel of a black regiment in the Civil War, and later, as editor of the *Atlantic Monthly,* an encouraging friend to Emily Dickinson) occupied the pulpit of a major Unitarian church in Worcester, from which he advocated the most radical of antislavery positions.

Higginson's fellow Unitarian Theodore Parker, perhaps the most erudite man in the land, was so independent that he had left the staid Park Street Church to found his own congregation of radicals. Sanborn, the youngest of the group, was the fatuous master of a fashionable school in Concord and much given to seasoning his hyperbolic letters with dashes of Latin and Greek. In due course, these five New Englanders would be joined by Douglass's immensely rich friend from upstate New York, Gerrit Smith.

If evidence is needed that many antislavery people had become convinced that neither moral suasion nor governmental action would ever end slavery, the participation of these erstwhile pillars of Northern society in a slave insurrection provides it. They—to say nothing of black abolitionists—needed no justification for such an action beyond that provided on March 6, 1857, when Chief Justice Roger B. Taney declared in *Dred Scott* v. *Sanford* that a slave, an ex-slave, or a descendant of slaves could not be a citizen of the United States, and that Congress, being constitutionally required to protect property—including slaves—could not prohibit slavery in the territories. And yet, these white radicals had little sense that the oppressed black people could be agents of their own destiny. (That they could be, Higginson learned from his soldiers during the war.)

The white New Englanders did not take Frederick Douglass into account any more than they did Garnet or Loguen. They had learned from their Garrisonian friends to distrust Douglass, but the paucity of references to him in their letters mainly indicates not distrust arising from doctrinal disagreements, but simply the invisibility to them of any black person in so serious a matter as planning an insurrection.

Talking of Kansas while thinking of Virginia, Brown toured the North in search of support for the war on slaveholders. But in January

1858, he was busy at the most authentic and rational of all American occupations, the drawing up of a constitution. On the twenty-eighth, he arrived at Douglass's secluded house, this time not just for a quick visit. He had come to stay with the black leader while he perfected his revolutionary design. So determined was Brown that Douglass's house be regarded as his place of work that he insisted on paying a modest board. (Or perhaps Anna was the one who had the grip on reality.) It was all business, serious business, and there can be no doubt that Brown intended to make Douglass an integral part of his developing plan. Douglass, for his part, must have been intrigued by the energetic work of the driven man laboring in his house. Years later, he spoke proudly of having a copy in Brown's hand, perhaps the original, of the constitution written under his roof, and it is impossible to believe that Brown did not tell a curious Douglass the details of the complex scheme that he now devised.

John Brown proposed to create a separate state in the mountains. Having drafted the constitution, he was deciding who would initially govern this unnamed state, which would need a commander in chief of the army, cabinet members, and a president. Even if Douglass thought the scheme farfetched, he may, in private, have liked to imagine himself as that president. In any case, there is no evidence that he tried to block this boldest-yet plan to end slavery.

As early as 1849, in an uncharacteristic endorsement of violence, Douglass had said, in a speech in Faneuil Hall, "I should welcome the intelligence tomorrow, should it come, that the slaves had risen in the South, and that the sable arms which had been engaged in beautifying and adorning the South, were engaged in spreading death and devastation." Once again, "I" was talking about "they"; he did not envision his own arms as wielding a weapon. And in 1858, he did not go along when Brown, the man planning insurrection, went to Canada to establish a rebel state in exile. On May 8, in what purported to be a gathering of a fraternal organization, thirty-five black men and twelve white met in a black schoolhouse in Chatham, a town in Ontario in which many fugitives had settled. The Reverend William Charles Munroe, a black minister from Detroit, was in the chair. Having been greeted by Martin Delany, Brown presented his constitution, proclaimed his provisional government, and named himself commander in chief, to lead the war he was to start. The record suggests that there was no specific mention of a raid on Harpers Ferry.

John Henry Kagi, a journalist of Swiss descent who was adamantly opposed to slavery, was made secretary of war; Kagi was white, as were all the other officials chosen at that meeting. Villard claims that two black men were offered the presidency—presumably Delany was one of them—but both declined. Delany was, in fact, the only truly prominent black supporter of Brown to attend; Garnet, Harriet Tubman, Loguen, and Douglass, all people that Brown had been talking with and claimed as allies, were conspicuously (and sensibly) absent. Any black person would have realized that no matter who was at the actual head of the conspiracy—in this instance, Brown, of course—the ones most at risk would be those who were black. Also absent were all of the Secret Six.

The revolution was off to a thin start, and yet clandestine news that it was coming discharged a current of energy into the ranks of radical opponents of slavery in both the white community and, even more strongly, the black. Those who met in Chatham had taken an oath of secrecy, but the secret was soon an open one among blacks in Canada and the United States. Most of the white members of the conspiracy seemed to be lovers of intrigue; Brown's military strategist was an Englishman named Hugh Forbes, at one time a merchant in Vienna, who had fought with Garibaldi in the failed revolution of 1848 and had come recently to an America that seemed ripe for its own revolution. When Forbes, passing through Rochester in November 1857, stopped off to meet Douglass, the editor was immediately dubious about the man, but, as he recalled it later, Forbes "conquered my prejudice"; at the end of a later visit, in 1858, Douglass gave Forbes carfare to New York, and arranged for Ottilia Assing to introduce him to her liberal German friends in the city.

Excited by the presence of an international revolutionary, Assing was dismayed when she saw Forbes's efforts to raise funds for Brown's expedition turn into extortion in his own behalf. "Using God knows what kind of tricks," she wrote in an article for the *Morgenblatt,* he began irritating her friends with his constant begging. Assing soon recognized that Forbes was a blackmailer, prepared to expose Brown unless he received the money that, he plaintively claimed, was desperately needed by his wife and child stranded in Paris. Assing reported to Douglass in dismay that Forbes had also talked to Horace Greeley. The two journalists knew that if charged with a secret, one did not discuss it with the editor of an aggressive New York newspaper. When Forbes, confirming her fears, informed antislavery senators Henry Wilson of Massachusetts and William Henry Seward of New York of Brown's plans, Wilson told Sanborn that the insurrection must be forestalled.

Brown's target was the federal arsenal at Harpers Ferry, a picturesque town on the Potomac River well west of Washington and due south of Chambersburg, Pennsylvania, in what was then Virginia. Arms seized at the arsenal would be given to the slaves, who, Brown was sure, would instantly rise to join his insurrection. (There were less than 5,000 slave men in the immediate region, which was also inhabited by more than

100,000 white people.) If Brown had thought about it, he might have recalled from his Springfield years tales of Daniel Shays's brave, ill-fated attempt to seize that city's arsenal some seventy years earlier. But there is no evidence that this or any other cautionary signal ever deterred the determined Brown for long. However, aware that if two senators knew their secret, half of Washington probably knew it, the Secret Six insisted that Brown go to Kansas. He did so, and while in the area, made an attack on a proslavery community in Missouri to cloak the fact that his true target was still in Virginia.

The maneuver worked. Forbes disappeared from the scene, and though Brown remained a hunted man, the War Department, led by the extraordinarily inept John B. Floyd, dropped its guard. In the spring of 1859, rejecting any further postponement, Brown secretly led his tiny band of followers to a farm near a quarry outside Chambersburg, to prepare for the campaign to free the slaves.

Lost in all the attention paid to the Secret Six, and to the effect of Brown's martyrdom on white America in general, is an appreciation of the deeply ambiguous but nonetheless passionate feelings in the black community. Garnet, Loguen, Tubman, Delany, and Douglass were but five of the great many black people who were intensely curious to know what the man was up to. And anyone familiar with the outpourings of the radical wing of the antislavery movement knew he was up to something. For example, in *The Roving Editor,* a white writer's account of his tour of Southern states and his interviews with slaves, published in 1859 before the events at Harpers Ferry, and dedicated to Brown, the author, James Redpath, spoke openly and admiringly of an insurrection. His participation in the bloodshed in Kansas had demonstrated that "Old Brown" was serious about the antislavery cause, although the fact that almost no black people lived in Kansas gave that struggle a certain remoteness. On the other hand, the black community, linked north and south by a remarkable grapevine, and kept informed by leaders like Loguen, Tubman, and Douglass who spoke of Brown as one white person who took black people into account, was intensely drawn to him. And his message, his promise of action—however vaguely it was understood—was appreciated in a period in which black Americans were profoundly frustrated.

The rumors that Brown would bring the drastic cure of an armed revolt were enticing. Toussaint L'Ouverture remained the most revered figure in the imagination of black people who wanted to find a way not only out of slavery but out of deference to a white world; this white man seemed to have a dream—of a state apart—that had the ring of a Haiti. What the skeptical Americans thought Brown lacked was any notion of how swift retribution had been in this country when slaves, like those who marched with Nat Turner, had revolted. And did he understand how the nonslaveholding North felt about black people gaining power? Black Americans had learned to be cautious. Slave and free, they were exceedingly reluctant to risk bringing down upon themselves the lethal vengeance of white society by actively participating in an insurrection. But that did not keep them, in the privacy of their own homes and meeting halls, from cheering Brown on.

At no point in the eleven years that he had known of Brown's hopes for an insurrection did Douglass repudiate the plan; indeed, there is no evidence that he even counseled caution. It was very much in character for Douglass to be flattered by Brown's repeated insistence that as a leader of his people, he was crucial to the enterprise; curiosity at the very least compelled him to go and have a look for himself. Early in the fall of 1859, John Brown, Jr., called on Douglass, and other black leaders in northern New York State and Canada, in the attempt to build a phalanx of antislavery support for the insurrection. Brown, his son insisted, greatly needed Douglass's help. Undeterred by the younger Brown's strangely wild talk, Douglass set out from Rochester with Shields Green, who had met Brown at Douglass's house. The two stopped in Brooklyn, where Douglass gave one of his customary lectures. When they left the meeting, Douglass carried with him a contribution of twenty-five dollars from the Reverend and Mrs. James Gloucester. The gift, generous in and of itself, suggests both the meagerness of the funding that Brown was receiving for his war and the widespread hope the black community held for its success.

Going next to Philadelphia, Douglass met in private with a church congregation; there, alone with black people, he could talk openly and forcefully about Brown's operation. Fearing with good reason the retaliation likely if Brown failed, the black Philadelphians, who had experienced armed attacks by racists, were extremely uneasy about committing themselves to whatever it was Brown was up to. Douglass, who loved to be in the know about important events, was probably able to hint that Brown definitely had plans of some kind for an insurrection. If Douglass did so, his audience must have been skeptical about the likelihood that Brown's scheme might succeed, even while hoping that it would. With the community's endorsement and some of the money which was quietly being raised, Douglass then set out for his meeting with Brown.

Traveling west, Douglass and Green arrived in Chambersburg—and immediately aroused suspicion among the white citizenry. Douglass would not normally have come to such a town except to give a lecture, and none had been announced. In the absence of the usual antislavery reception committee, the two men followed the standard procedure for a black person in a strange town; they went to the barbershop. Henry Watson was busy, but he put down his scissors to confer with his distinguished visitor. Douglass confided to this black man (who probably already knew) why he was in town, and in short order, Watson began making arrangements for a public lecture, which would give legitimacy to Douglass's presence in Chambersburg. He then directed Douglass and Green to the quarry at the edge of town, for their scheduled clandestine meeting with Brown and Kagi.

On the dusty walk, Douglass may have remembered the terror of Frederick Bailey being dragged down the road into Easton, for reality finally caught up with him. Years later, he recalled, "I approached the old quarry very cautiously, for John Brown was generally well armed, and regarded strangers with suspicion." Douglass, always recognizable, was in any case no stranger to Brown, and yet he was uneasy as he walked into sight of his old friend and the suspicious, watchful captain (as Brown was familiarly known) acknowledged that he had been recognized. A warrant had been issued for Brown's arrest, because of his activities in Kansas, and he was living under one of his several aliases. Suddenly, Douglass felt himself also to be a fugitive: "I was on a dangerous mission, and was as little desirous of discovery as himself, though no reward had been offered for me."

They sat down on the rocks to talk, and Douglass soon discovered that Brown seemed to have forgotten his plans for establishing communities of fugitive slaves in the mountains and for perfecting a more efficient armed channel northward from Virginia through which runaways could reach Canada. Now Brown was obsessed with the idea of taking the Harpers Ferry arsenal, which he viewed both as the emblem of the military power of a government he had learned to hate and as a source of arms with which to wage war against the slaveholders protected by that power. Suddenly Douglass saw the whole enterprise in a different light: he was convinced it was doomed.

When, later in the day, Douglass met the pathetically small group of brave but, he now thought, deluded men who were determined to follow their leader's bidding, he was still more dismayed. (The sight of the disturbed, one-eyed nephew of his old abolitionist friend Francis Jackson must have simply saddened him.) Douglass told Brown that he was "going into a perfect steel trap, and that once in he would not get out alive." Douglass saw no safety in Brown's plan to protect himself by taking civilian hostages; "Virginia," he later claimed to have declared, "would blow him and his hostages sky-high, rather than he should hold Harpers Ferry an hour."

Undaunted, Brown continued for two days his attempts to persuade Douglass to join his force, saying, "I want you for a special purpose." But his image for Douglass's essential role in bringing the slave revolt into being was a disconcerting one: "When I strike, the bees will begin to swarm, and I want you to help hive them." Brown's likening a rising of human beings to a swarm of stinging bees, with Douglass as the queen bee who could control them, must have made the whole enterprise seem mad. When Douglass tried to persuade the man to return to his scheme "of gradually . . . drawing off the slaves to the mountains," he found that Brown "had completely renounced his old plan" and was zealously and singlemindedly committed to the armed attack and the raising of an insurrection.

Douglass said no to Brown's final plea that he join him, and left. But it is a mark of the captain's extraordinary hold on others that Shields Green, a "man of few words," as Douglass recalled, felt otherwise. Brown had been at once drawn to the "stuff" Green "was made of," and the runaway, whose "speech was singularly broken," was drawn to the captain. Green had come with Douglass from Rochester determined to join the cause, and he stood firm in his resolve. "I b'leve I'll go wid de ole man," he told Douglass and the two black men parted.

On October 16, 1859, leading an army of twenty-two, Brown moved on Harpers Ferry; with expert reconnoitering and extraordinary nerve, they did manage to seize the arsenal. Shields Green and Jeremiah Sanderson, another of Brown's black soldiers, were sent out to rally the slaves in the region to the revolt. As the two left on their futile assignment, they saw Robert E. Lee's detachment of marines surrounding the arsenal. Anderson said to Green that they had better keep going; they could do nothing now to save Brown, but Green went back into the arsenal, saying he "must go down to de ole man." The rebels were all either captured or, like Green, killed.

The second edition of the *Philadelphia Evening Bulletin* for October 17, 1859, carried two telegrams, one from Baltimore and one from Frederick, Maryland, reporting "wild rumors" of a slave insurrection. The next day, with the paper full of news of Brown's raid, there appeared a notice: "Frederick Douglass lectures on 'Self-Made Men' this evening at National Hall, Market below Thirteenth." As if he did not want to face the fact that Brown had gone through with his plan, as if he were innocent of any knowledge of it, Douglass proceeded to give his best-known stock-in-trade lecture. The following morning, with the papers still burning with news of Harpers Ferry, he opened a "very elegantly written note." Amanda Auld Sears, the daughter of his former master, had heard him in National Hall, and asked if they could meet. As children,

Amanda and Frederick had shared the wrath of her stepmother; now, some twenty-five years later, she was the wife of John Sears, a coal merchant living in Philadelphia.

Choosing, whether consciously or not, to ignore the storm over one of the most sensational events in the nation's history, an event in which he knew he was implicated, Douglass went to Sears's office in response to the invitation. Presumably, Amanda Sears had given Douglass her husband's business address, but at first Sears resisted talking to Douglass at all; when he relented, he remained distant, saying that he greatly resented the attacks Douglass had made on his father-in-law, Thomas Auld, in his books. Only reluctantly did he at length permit Douglass to call on his wife. When the slave went to visit the mistress, he was dismayed to find the Sears's parlor full of people, curious about the caller. Douglass had been afraid that he might not recognize Amanda as a grown woman, but he did so immediately, and the two fell into an intimate conversation. Amanda ignored Douglass's years-old hortatory attacks on her father, referring instead to his affectionate recollection of her mother, Lucretia Aaron Auld, in the *Narrative.* Forthrightly, she told him that she agreed with him that slavery was a wrong. After more than two decades Douglass was pulled back into one of his families. Years later he found out that soon after his reunion with Amanda, her father, Thomas Auld, learned of the visit and told her that she had been right to reach out and bring Frederick back.

Members of another of his families, the black and radical antislavery group in Philadelphia, knew, if Douglass did not, that he had no time for sentimental journeys. He had to get out of town. Among the papers seized with Brown was a brief note from Douglass dated December 7, 1857: "My dear Cpt. Brown, I am very busy at home. Will you Please, come up with my son Fred and take a mouthful with me?" The note—newspapers wishing Douglass ill omitted "1857" to make the invitation seem more recent—was quickly published. It scarcely proved conspiracy, but Governor Henry Wise of Virginia followed up the apprehension of Brown with requests to President Buchanan to assist in arresting Brown's allies, including, explicitly, "Frederick Douglass, a negro man . . . charged with . . . inciting servile insurrection."

In Philadelphia, Douglass learned that authorities had possession of his note to Brown and knew that it could be proved that he had brought money, and Shields Green, to Chambersburg to assist Brown. Furthermore, though Douglass did not know it, Lind F. Currie, a teacher near Harpers Ferry from whom Brown had commandeered a schoolhouse, was aware that Brown had boasted that Gerrit Smith and Douglass knew of the insurrection. The danger of capture was real—and imminent.

James Hern, an operator in the telegraph office, took down a message from Washington directing the sheriff of Philadelphia County to arrest Douglass. Delaying delivery for three hours, the antislavery Hern hurried to the home of Thomas J. Dorsey, where Douglass was staying, with the news. They rushed Douglass to the Walnut Street wharf, from which he could take the ferry to Camden, New Jersey. Douglass "was sure the arrest would be made" in Camden. He urged his friends not to leave him, but "upon one ground or another, they all found it best not to be found in my company." One man, Franklin Turner, as Douglass never forgot, remained with him while he waited what seemed an eternity for a start toward "a more northern latitude." His account suggests that instead of taking the train from Camden, as he had originally planned, he boarded a steamer for what must have been an achingly slow trip to New York. There was still no arrest, but the city held terrors he had not known since he walked its streets twenty-one years before. Hastily, he took the Barclay Street ferry across the Hudson River to Hoboken and walked to the boarding house where Ottilia Assing was living, to spend, as he recalled, "without undue profession of timidity, an *anxious* night."

His friend told him that the New York papers were full of fury over Brown's raid and his apparent complicity in it. In his anxiety, Douglass recalled that some of Brown's papers, including drafts of his constitution, were in his study at home. In the morning, Assing went out to send a telegram from Douglass addressed specifically to B. F. Blackall, a telegraph operator in Rochester whom he trusted: "Tell Lewis to secure all important papers in my high desk." Then she hurried back to help Douglass on his way. The train he would normally have taken for Rochester left from New York City; to escape the dangers there, and avoiding even Jersey City, Douglass and Assing borrowed a carriage and drove to Paterson, New Jersey, where he boarded a train that went north on the west side of the Hudson River, to a connection with the Rochester train. Finally back on his hillside, Douglass hoped he was safe, but on October 22, the day a Rochester paper carried his seemingly incriminating letter to Brown, Amy Post hurried up South Avenue with a message from William Still, a Philadelphia African American active in helping runaway slaves, and later a famous chronicler of the operation of the underground railroad.

No one knew better than Still the ways of fugitives and their pursuers. In his letter, he explained to Post why his message to Douglass was addressed to her: "I am very sorry to trouble you with a letter that I am very anxious for Frederick to get quickly & safely, but owing to the excitement just now in consequence of his name being connected with the 'Harper's Ferry' difficulties, I feared to trust to the mail least it be intercepted. You will therefore greatly oblige me by seeing that he gets it at your earliest convenience." Post was asked to "confirm that you have done so." Still's concerns were well placed; Governor Wise of Virginia was determined to prove a nationwide—indeed, a continental—conspiracy, one involving the community of black fugitives in Canada. Brown had been charged with treason and likely would be hanged, and his accomplices were being sought as well. From Massachusetts, three of the Secret Six fled to Canada; Stearns and Higginson alone refused to flee or even to burn the letters that did, indeed, tie them to Brown. Lydia Maria Child tried to get to Charles Town to care for Brown in prison, while Higginson and James Redpath were engaged in a hopeless plot to rescue him. But a good many other white antislavery people seemed in an almost indecent hurry to send him into martyrdom, while vulnerable black abolitionists went underground. Gerrit Smith, whose family had a long history of mental illness, was so distraught that he entered a lunatic asylum.

Historian David Potter, at the close of his account of John Brown's raid in *The Impending Crisis,* writes, "To Brown and the abolitionists, the plan seemed perfectly reasonable, and the literati of Boston admired him extravagently as man of action for attempting it. But to Frederick Douglass and the Negroes of Chatham, Ontario, nearly every one of whom had learned something from personal experience about how to gain freedom, Brown was a man of words trying to be a man of deeds, and they would not follow him. They understood him, as Thoreau and Emerson and Parker never did." Douglass's understanding, however, had come late in the day; he had flown close to the flame and his life was in danger.

When Post reached Douglass's house, they conferred over Still's letter and decided to follow his advice—that Douglass should leave the country secretly; it proved both wise and effective. The next day, United States marshals were said to be in Rochester, looking in vain for Douglass; two weeks later, Governor Wise thought he was in Michigan. After dark on the day that Amy Post delivered the letter, she and Isaac had conducted Douglass to the wharf below the lower falls, near the mouth of the Genesee, to which he had taken so many runaways, and he was, himself, put on a boat for Canada.

16

Tremont Street

FREDERICK DOUGLASS could not allow himself to think he was
taking flight, but he had every reason to be frightened. Governor Henry
Wise was determined to hang John Brown and would have liked nothing
better than to have the most arrogant black man in America swinging
beside him. And probably most of white America agreed.

Fear of the nonexistent slave revolt seized the South; white men rushed
to arms at every accidental burning of a barn, but could "find the enemy
only with a magnifying glass," wrote Ottilia Assing for her German
readers. Particularly in Texas, rumors of slave uprisings were rampant,
and to this imagined "horror" was added the real knowledge that abolitionists were saying "there were men in the North who were not content
with fighting slavery with words and . . . a country which could produce
twenty-two such heroes, could easily produce thousands more and
would." A "kind of insane anxiety gripped the whole population"; a
"lightning bolt had awakened Virginia and the whole South," Assing
claimed.

In truth, she overestimated the support for Brown in the North, but
emotions did ride high there too. While those determined to put down,
with finality, any insurrectionary action, were aroused, the abolitionists,
for their part, were now more devoted to the antislavery cause than ever.
They saw in Brown's brave effort, and in his trial at the end of October,
the makings of a martyr. (At moments, some of them seemed almost as
eager as Wise that the occasion for achieving that goal take place.) One
of America's more pacific thinkers, heretofore a nonviolent subversive,
was so moved by Brown's cause that with a forceful address, he aligned

himself with militant abolitionism. The occasion was provided by Douglass. On October 31, 1859, a lecture-series booking agent sent a telegram to "Henry Thoreau or Ralph Waldo Emerson, Concord," specifying that "Thoreau must lecture . . . Tuesday Evening—Douglass fails." The stand-in did well: Henry David Thoreau's "A Plea for John Brown" was the most powerful address of his life.

With similar enthusiasm, members of the American Anti-Slavery Society, which had once condemned Brown's call for violence, now eagerly embraced a new hero, but they stood clear of their old ally, Douglass. Samuel May, Jr., never an admirer of articulate runaways, was not in a benign mood when he wrote to Dublin publisher Richard D. Webb (he would bring out a life of John Brown after the captain was safely dead), telling him that "F. Douglass leaves here [the United States] by a circuitous route. He is implicated in the Harper's Ferry business, and took refuge in Canada. We all agree with you—to give him a wide berth, & take no notice of him. He is wholly selfish and unworthy of our trust for a moment."

Since before Brown's raid, Douglass had been planning a trip to England. He had intended to leave from Boston after the scheduled lecture in Concord; instead he was now in Canada, moving from town to town, trying to decide what to do. His Rochester friends kept in close communication with him, and Douglass almost returned with two who crossed Lake Ontario to visit him. Fortunately, he did not do so, for he "should have walked into a trap." Moving on to New Brunswick, he received a note from Lucy N. Coleman, who was worried lest his property be seized. "I am about convinced that nothing is to be feared at this point," he told her friend Amy Post. "It [the property] cannot be lost unless I am convicted; I cannot be convicted unless I am tried, I cannot be arrested unless caught, while I keep out of the way." In New Brunswick, he stayed in the remote town of Clifton, where Amy Post's letters were "like good news from a far country." She offered to visit him and urged him to stay safely hidden away. This, he intended to do for a time: "It will take many months to blow this heavy cloud from my sky." But, he told her in a letter sent by a friend, he could not for long "consent to an inactive exile."

In November, he set out for England on the *Nova Scotian,* from which he wrote an open letter to the readers of *Douglass' Monthly,* saying that he was relinquishing his editorial duties for a time, to go on a long-planned overseas lecture tour. The tour had indeed been announced before Brown's raid, and Douglass's posture in the letter was that he was simply making good on earlier arrangements. He mentioned Brown only far down in his text, where he struck out at his vengeful countrymen who had made it unsafe for him to travel to a port in the United States. The letter was posted from Halifax, Nova Scotia; the ship arrived in Liverpool on November 24. The deliberate, calm tone of the piece reflects the conscious effort Douglass had made to regain his composure.

Once he was across the Atlantic, that process was greatly enhanced by a visit with Julia Griffiths, now Julia Griffiths Crofts. She had been married in the spring of 1859, and after a wedding trip to Paris, had settled in with her minister husband in England's Halifax, a town in Yorkshire. Frederick's reunion with Julia, after almost five years, must have been a richly emotional experience for both; a tolerant spouse stood by as the American settled in to spend December—Christmas—and January with them. At least in the public domain, the friendship picked up where it had left off, with Julia urging Frederick cautiously to resume speaking and writing against slavery, as if he had never been connected with John Brown.

On December 7, five days after John Brown was hanged by the "Virginia hyennas," as Rosetta put it in a letter to her father, Douglass shared the platform in Mechanics' Hall with old abolitionist friends, as well as the Reverend Dr. Crofts. His address was remarkably optimistic, and out of respect for his host, he gave it a more biblical tone than usual, speaking of those truths which go from "everlasting to everlasting." He went on to declare, "Such a truth was man's right to liberty—he was born with it—it entered into the very idea of his creation." Douglass spoke warmly of John Quincy Adams, "long gone in his grave" (he had died in 1848), as one who "stood up for the right of petition of the slave." Adams had been elected to Congress after completing his term as president, and now Douglass compared Adams's time, when he was the sole member of Congress to declare himself an abolitionist, with 1859, when from twenty-five to a hundred representatives and senators could be counted on to "lift up their voices for the abolition of slavery—(cheers). This was progress." And it was not entirely an exaggeration. Douglass believed that the political ball was rolling toward the ending of slavery, and he was right. He said not one word about John Brown.

The hanging of John Brown made Frederick Douglass more law-abiding than he had ever been. In grave danger from the law, with his life in jeopardy for the first time since he had faced possible hanging after his failed escape from the Freeland farm, Douglass, in his first speeches in Great Britain, steered clear of any kind of revolutionary rhetoric that might seem traitorous. Instead he contended more ardently than ever that the Union must not be dissolved and that slavery could be eliminated constitutionally.

At the end of January he was back in Edinburgh for the first time since

1846 and had regained sufficient boldness to give a lecture called "John Brown and the Slaveholders' Insurrection." To frequent bursts of applause, like those of fourteen years ago, he championed the "martyr" and excoriated those who held in bondage the people Brown had sought to free. Now Brown was that "brave, heroic, and Christian man"; it was the slaveholders who were in insurrection against a nation that, awakened by Brown and the antislavery crusade, could find a way to end slavery without splitting in two.

In March, when the radical antislavery leader George Thompson rose in Glasgow's city hall and delivered a blistering attack not only on slavery, but, as Britons are fond of doing, on all things American, Douglass was roused to something very like patriotism. In the Queen's Rooms, with the hall only half filled, he began a long speech in which the old 1846 bombast of "Send Back the Money" was replaced, perhaps to the consternation of his audience, by a learned analysis of the American Constitution. Referring to Thompson, he acknowledged that: "he who stands before a British audience to denounce any thing peculiarly American in connection with slavery has a very marked and decided advantage. It is not hard to believe the very worst of any country where a system like slavery has existed for centuries. This feeling towards every thing American, is very natural and very useful. I refer to it now not to condemn it, but to remind you that it is just possible that this feeling may be carried to too great length."

Of Thompson's accusatory litany, he declared, "This jumbling of things is a sort of dust-throwing which is often indulged in by *small men who argue for victory rather than truth.* Thus, . . . the American government and the American constitution are often spoken of . . . as one and the same thing." It was, he claimed, only that government—the Buchanan administration, most recently—that was "mean, sordid, mischievous, devilish."

In a somewhat schoolteacherish way, Douglass reminded his audience—which probably needed the reminder—that not all things constitutional were British. Their unwritten constitution was an accruement of laws and customs; the American version was a fixed, formal document. The Constitution did not include the Fugitive Slave Act or authorize the African slave trade so abhorrent to Thompson. Indeed, Douglass contended, far from being guaranteed by the Constitution, slavery was a violation of it. Brown's co-conspirator was now sounding exceedingly legalistic as well as optimistic. In the face of *Dred Scott,* he argued that "whereas slavery has ruled the land, now must liberty; whereas pro-slavery men have . . . given the constitution a pro-slavery interpretation against its plain reading, let our votes put men into that Supreme Court who will decide, and who will concede, that the constitution is not [pro-]slavery."

As legal scholar Milner S. Ball has pointed out, Douglass was insisting that African slaves had always played a role in the nation's legal story. They had been given a negative part. Fractionally, insultingly, African Americans—unlike those even earlier native Americans, the Indians— were counted into the Constitution; in *Dred Scott* they were made pariahs, but they were there. Douglass simply wanted to turn the story around and affirm the black people's positive place at its center. He was harking back to his conversion to Gerrit Smith's position on the Constitution. And he was displaying a remarkably sanguine enthusiasm for the American legal system, as if rallying all the lawyers in the United States to argue this position aggressively in every American courtroom in which they could force a case to be heard.

It is a shame that Douglass was not one of those lawyers. Given the legal profession's less formal nineteenth-century requirements, he might well have found a way to read with an antislavery lawyer and gain admission to the bar. By 1860 he had lost whatever patience he had had for the seclusion of the editorial office; he needed an audience (which the courtroom would have provided) to rouse him to his best rhetorical efforts. Douglass did not know it yet, but he would always be denied elective or important appointive office. As a lawyer—and he sounds mighty like one in his pamphlet *The Constitution of the United States: Is It Pro-Slavery or Anti-Slavery?*—he could have argued civil-rights cases in lower courts, and after 1865, when the first black lawyer was admitted to practice at its bar, before the Supreme Court. It is fascinating to speculate on how Douglass might have argued alongside such civil-rights lawyers as Thomas Jefferson Durant for the protection of black Americans under the Fourteenth Amendment. And one can readily imagine his brief in the Civil Rights Cases of 1883.

To credit Douglass with being an original legal thinker would be an error; his arguments were those of Lysander Spooner and William Goodell as he had acknowledged at the time of his change of heart about the Constitution in 1851. Constitutional scholar Sanford Levinson has suggested that Douglass nevertheless made a significant contribution to legal history. Just as it mattered that affirmation in *Gideon* v. *Wainright* (1963) of the right to counsel in a criminal trial resulted from a jailed man's penciled appeal, so did the fact that Douglass was a runaway slave—a fact that his deliberately learned discourse did not disguise—underscore his argument.

In 1860, in his role as a constitutional historian, Douglass drew on the lawyerly tradition of admitting the worst before insisting on the best. He faced up to the four provisions of the Constitution that Thompson had insisted perpetually enshrined slavery. Thompson was, Douglass contended, fifty-two years late in worrying about Article 1, Section 9; it did prevent Congress from excluding "such Persons as any of the States . . . shall think proper to admit," but only until 1808, when the slave trade was ended. Douglass conveniently ignored the efforts being made by leading politicians in the South, at the very time he was speaking, to reopen the trade.

Turning to Article 4, Section 2, the constitutional provision that seemed to demand federal enforcement of the Fugitive Slave Act, he boldly relied on textual criticism. That section says that a person who has fled to another state must be delivered up to the party to whom "Labour may be due." No one, Douglass declared with wonderful simplicity, is "due" slave labor. Similarly, he dismissed out of hand the nasty and tricky business in Article 1, Section 2, under which a slave was counted as only three-fifths of a person in the determination of how many representatives a state would have in the House of Representatives. Did that mean that the descendants of these three-fifths persons were perpetually less than whole people as observers ranging from William Lloyd Garrison to Roger B. Taney read the Constitution as saying? Douglass did not even consider so absurd a proposition; instead he chose to point out that if they refused to accept black people as full citizens—with each ex-slave counted as a whole person, not three-fifths of one—white Southerners would be denying themselves the power that full representation would bring their states when they set down the burden of slavery.

Douglass was still more cavalier in disposing of the idea that Article 1, Section 8, which grants Congress the power "to provide for calling forth the Militia to . . . suppress insurrections," was aimed primarily at uprisings of slaves. His audience knew that just such a course had been followed—by the executive branch, however—when the marines were sent to put down John Brown's insurrection. Douglass did not, on that account, argue that this governmental power should be curtailed. On the contrary, he proposed that its use be expanded and turned against the slaveholders, for, he insisted, "slavery is itself an insurrection." He was, of course, predicting what would happen almost exactly a year from when he was speaking, when a force vastly larger than the word "militia" brings to mind, was called out to put down the nation's biggest insurrection.

Far from wanting "to burn up" the Constitution and dissolve the Union, as Thompson and the Garrisonians did, in order to banish slavery (and, as Douglass put it, to be "rid of the responsibility"), he would enhance the power of the government and put it to a new use, the ending of slavery: "The American people in the Northern States have helped to enslave the black people. Their duty will not have been done till they give them back their plundered rights." He was arguing for the legal status of African Americans as citizens on the grounds that as far back as an English-speaking American community of any size had existed, they had been part of it. They wanted their countrymen to return their nation to them.

While he was in Glasgow, Douglass was pulled sharply back from his comfortable escape. In Rochester, on March 13, 1860, bright, lithe Annie Douglass died, nine days before her eleventh birthday. She had been ill since December. Anna, alone with her children, was desolate; Annie, a charming scamp, happier about the house than her tense older sister, Rosetta, was gone. Annie, her namesake, the last child of her troubled marriage, was dead. And she was unable to articulate her despair.

Rosetta read to her mother a letter of condolence from Harriet and then sat down to reply. "My darling sister is now an angel," she wrote, and added, "I have just asked Mother what I should say for her. She sends her love to you and thanks you as heartily as myself for your sympathizing letter, and she as she is unable to write will allow my letter to be in answer for both. . . . She is not very well now being quite feeble though about the house." And then Anna called out that Harriet should—"if you desire," as Rosetta politely put it—write to her brother and tell him to come home.

Word of Annie's death reached her father just after he had received an affectionate, cheerful letter from his son Charles, and as he was indulging himself in the satisfying business of visiting congenial Scottish friends. Annie herself had written in December, telling proudly of her good work in school. Douglass's anguish was intense, not the less so, no doubt, for being mixed with remorse and anger that he had not been on hand when the illness struck—he, the self-made man who could accomplish everything, could surely have prevented this tragedy. But he had not been there. "We heard from dear father last week," Rosetta told Harriet, "and his grief was great. I trust the next letter [neither that one nor the first survives] will evince more composure of mind." Rosetta, for her part, claimed to take some comfort in the thought that Annie "has gone to Him whose love is the same for the black as the white."

Ignoring the uncertainty about his safety, Douglass started back to Anna and his four remaining children. He returned cautiously, taking a ship to Portland, Maine, and trains to Montreal and westward before crossing Lake Ontario. He had been directly implicated in testimony given before the Senate's inquiry in January 1860, but to his good luck, congressional leaders, seeking to minimize its divisiveness, had moved to close off the Brown affair rather than to pursue possible accomplices and create some more martyrs. Some black radicals had seen the instant repression of Brown's insurrection as the low point of the antislavery cause. Douglass, on the other hand, shrewdly guessed that even those Northern moderates who had firmly distanced themselves from Brown were not prepared to support further protection by the federal government of the slaveholders' interests. John Brown had overstepped the bounds, but Southerners would not be allowed to do the same.

Once back in Rochester, Douglass resumed publication of *Douglass' Monthly* in April, but waited several months before making any public appearances. When, in August, he again took the platform, he discovered that for the first time in his life, he was in the political mainstream. The Republican party, opposed to the extension of slavery, was in imminent peril of winning the presidential election.

Douglass could see that ideas he had helped spread were beginning to move the nation. Tired of purity, he reminded voters who were skeptical about Abraham Lincoln that votes diverted from the less-than-perfect Henry Clay had elected James K. Polk, who was far worse. In fact, although by doing so he was disagreeing with his old friend Gerrit Smith, running for president, with no hope of winning, on the Radical Abolitionist ticket, he gave the Republicans an endorsement of sorts: " While I see . . . that the Republican party is far from an abolition party, I cannot fail to see also that [it] carries with it the antislavery sentiment of the North, and that a victory gained by it in the present canvass will be a victory gained . . . over the wickedly aggressive pro-slavery sentiment of the country." And he went on to declare to his audience in Geneva, New York, "Abolitionist though I am, and resolved to cast my vote for an Abolitionist, I sincerely hope for the triumph of that party over all the odds and ends of slavery combined against it."

On November 6, 1860, Douglass was in Rochester, hoping for a Republican victory in the national election and for repeal of the galling $250 property requirement that black men had to meet in order to vote in New York State. With no help from the Republican party organization, he had stumped upstate New York for the repeal movement, led by James McCune Smith. The effort was in vain; the stigmatic qualification was not repealed, even though New York's votes went to Abraham Lincoln.

Any dream that Douglass may have had that the Republican victory in November would bring a ground swell of antislavery sentiment vanished on December 3, 1860, in Boston. He was there to address a meeting in the Tremont Temple to mark the anniversary of the "martyrdom" of

John Brown. As the morning session began, an organized group of supporters of the defeated Constitutional Union ticket—men of substance—came into the hall and outnumbering the abolitionists, elected their own man, Richard Sullivan Fay, to the chair. These Unionists, with South Carolina's secession imminent, were still trying to find some compromise that would skirt the slavery issue and avoid disunion. In their view, abolitionists, and particularly black abolitionists, were the cause of the nation's faltering unity.

When Franklin B. Sanborn, a white abolitionist, and J. Sella Martin, a black one, defiantly tried to speak (and to take back the meeting), they were hissed down. So tumultuous did the meeting become that police, already alerted by the anti-antislavery mayor, Frederick Walker Lincoln, Jr., entered the hall. When Douglass rose to speak, the chair reluctantly recognized him, but telling the Niagara not to fall, admonished him to be brief. As the black man headed for the rostrum, gentlemen blocked his path; his head down like a "trained pugilist," Douglass battered his way to the platform. Trying to be heard, he was interrupted constantly by hecklers, now standing on their chairs. Douglass thundered his fury at this "barefaced, (knock him down! Sit down!) outrageous" attack on free speech. His voice rolled louder as his opponents tried to roar above him. The chair, Fay, continually called, "Time"; the exasperated orator snarled, "Keep quiet"; and Fay snapped back, "We cannot stand you all day." Douglass, quite prepared to stay all day, went on orating until someone called out, sarcastically, "Go on nigger."

At this point, Douglass's temper broke totally. "If I were a slave-driver, and had hold of that man for five minutes," he pealed, pointing to the culprit, "I would let more daylight through his skin than ever got there before." Fay responded, "He has said the truth, for a negro slave-driver is the most cruel in the world." Douglass, up out of that gutter, shouted above it all, "It seems to me as though some of the white men of the North [have] gone to the devil. They'd murder liberty—kill freedom."

This verbal assault precipitated a rush onto the stage. Men seized chairs from one another, and the furniture ended up "all thrown in a heap" at the back of the platform. By now the antislavery women in the balcony had crowded to the front corners the better to see the fray. When order, in very small measure, had been restored, the chair declared the meeting adjourned. Unionists began leaving, and Douglass called out, "Good bye, good riddance." For this, he got three cheers from his supporters, particularly those in the balcony. When one lingering gentleman called out, "You black fool, don't you know the meeting's dissolved?" an antislavery man yelled, "Go out"; the first then replied, "Faith and I'm going out." Douglass, momentarily in charge, called on his people to stay, and the result was a new rush onto the stage and the addition—with a toss—of a man to the pile of chairs.

Douglass struggled to his feet, while the police began ejecting the black men. When Joseph Hayes and other antislavery men protested, Unionists screamed, "Nigger Hayes." One black man stood on the very edge of the platform, leaned far out into the crowd, and pointing his finger at one after another white man, pronounced, "You are the niggers, you are the niggers!" Now the women came downstairs and entered the splendid battle: "In the centre of the room stood several ladies, a young one attracted considerable attention by carrying on an excited and loud discussion with a Union man." She was not alone in having her say; the excellent reporter who captured it all, did not miss the scatology that rang in the air: "Douglas[s]—I feel no more embarassment by this uproar than if I had been kicked by a jackass. Voice—It is dinner time Fred."

Amidst cries of "Put all the niggers out!" "All out!" "Blow them up!" a bit of order was restored, with the Unionists again in control of the meeting. A businessman, James Murray Howe, preparing to take over the

"Expulsion of Negroes and Abolitionists from Tremont Temple, Boston, Massachusetts, on December 3, 1860." From *Harper's Weekly.*

chair, had just removed his coat, "when a collision occurred between him and Mr. Fred Douglas[s]" and the battle was on again: One gentleman had retrieved from the pile the chair that Douglass had been sitting on, and set it down for Howe; Douglass ran after him and grabbed it back. To wrest the chair from the ex-stevedore took several Unionists and a policeman. One man grabbed Douglass by the hair while another called out gleefully, "Wool won't save him." After this rough handling, Douglass and his followers were hurtled out of the hall by the police.

Those who remained now began to pass resolutions praising Brown's execution, while the women, back in the balcony, hissed and shouted and refused to obey the policemen's commands to leave. At this point, there were more policemen than any others on the platform, and the women began laughing at them. Meanwhile, Douglass came back by another door, and for an hour more, the arguing raged. Finally, the police lost their tempers and began clearing the antislavery people from the hall; even Judge Thomas Russell was grabbed by the arms and dragged from the room. As a policeman forced one woman down the stairs, "she turned round to him and said 'I am a mother, but if I had you in a good place wouldn't I give it to you.' (Down the stairs she went with a jump.) A young girl, apparently about nineteen, resisted for a while, 'Now officer,' said she, smiling, 'will you produce your authority?' Officer—'You see my buttons.' Girl—'they look so much like your face I cannot tell the difference.' Officer—'How so?' Girl—'they are all brass.' The girl was hurried out with a lot of masculines."

That night a tired group of veterans of the day's battle (along with some allies) held yet another meeting, this one in the Reverend J. Sella Martin's Joy Street church. Wendell Phillips first bitterly assailed the morning's attackers, who had seriously injured five black men. Then Douglass rose, shedding caution, and advocated a course of action even more subversive than John Brown's insurrection: "We must . . . reach the slaveholder's conscience through his fear of personal danger. We must make him feel that there is death in the air around him, that there is death in the pot before him, that there is death all around him." Acknowledging that any hope for a general insurrection was vain, he called for encouraging more slaves to run away, and revived the old dream that the Appalachian Mountains could become a haven for them. "I believe in agitation," he thundered. And with uncharacteristic bitterness, he declared, "The only way to make the Fugitive Slave Law a dead letter, is to make a few dead slave catchers." Ominously, in a call for "all methods of proceeding against slavery," he included "war."

All through the day, a year after the hanging, John Brown had been present. Douglass was but one of the many who then and since have kept this bloodied saint's martial cause before us. Indeed, it was the acceptance of Brown's martyrdom in the North that made it safe for Douglass to return after his self-exile; very quickly, to have known Brown made one honorable. When Douglass took the platform again after his return from Great Britain, he made the most of his tie to his martyred friend. "Wonderful orator that he was," wrote a shrewd observer in Lynn, describing Douglass, "after telling the story, he folded his hands penitently before him, hung his head humbly and, in the saddest of voices, said: 'And I, my friends, was not there.' It was a confession that he had not been courageous enough to join Brown's daring band; that he failed to meet the occasion. He was doing penance as best he might for his weakness. He thrilled us all and it was impossible not to grant him absolution."

The December near-riot in Boston underscores the fact that the stoning of Union troops by pro-Confederates in Baltimore four months later was not the only evidence of unrest in the North. Abraham Lincoln was sworn in as president in March 1861, and after the firing on Fort Sumter in April had begun the Civil War, he successfully called on the Northern states for troops, but he still had to ensure that the whole of the North was with him in the war—including those Boston anti-black, anti-antislavery men who had staunchly called themselves Unionists as they attacked Douglass. It was to the loyalty of people like them that the president successfully appealed with his pledge that the war was being fought to preserve the Union. He did not make it a war to end slavery.

Douglass and the other abolitionists were determined to change his mind. In a speech in Rochester on June 16, 1861, "The American Apocalypse," he criticized those who would be silent on the divisive slavery issue in order to unite the people of the North. The war should become as a "war in heaven" between the archangel Michael and the dragon; when it was over, he insisted, "not a slave should be left a slave in the returning footprints of the American army gone to put down this slave-holding rebellion. Sound policy, not less than humanity, demands the instant liberation of every slave in the rebel states."

The archangel was slow in arriving. When 1861 closed after deeply discouraging defeats and frustrations, Douglass took stock of the crusade. In a January speech, he vigorously objected to the Lincoln administration policy of returning runaway slaves to their masters, and to the president's rescinding of General John C. Frémont's order emancipating slaves in Missouri. He also questioned the tactic of the ingenious Union general Benjamin F. Butler, who at Fortress Monroe, on the Virginia coast, refused to return escaping slaves to their masters on the grounds that they were contraband of war. Douglass had to approve of the Massachusetts man's action, but not without noting that "contraband" was "a name that will apply better to a pistol, than to a person." He insisted that when "slaves are referred to, they must be called persons held to service or labor" and not referred to as things. He had a plan for those escaping persons: his speech was called "Fighting the Rebels with One Hand," and in it he argued, introducing an image he was to use time and time again, "We are striking the guilty rebels with our soft, white hand, when we should be striking with the iron hand of the black man."

Douglass was addressing a self-improvement society that evening. His audience was largely black, and it is intriguing to imagine how that powerful call to black pride, that call to combat, must have sounded. Twentieth-century recordings of famous speakers are often surprising; an unexpected high-pitched squeak can seem out of harmony with the sonorous rhetoric of the written text. But in Douglass's case we would not have been disappointed. Some of those who heard him speak wrote extensively of how he sounded. A reporter for the *Christian Recorder* left one of the richest accounts we have of "the magnetism and melody of his wonderfully elastic voice." The reporter allowed that the printed text gave a "fair view of the *ideas,* but no printed sentences can convey any adequate idea of the manner, the tone of voice, the gesticulation, the action, the round, soft, swelling pronunciation with which Frederick Douglass spoke, and which no orator we have ever heard can use with such grace, eloquence and effect as he." There was elasticity in Douglass's rhetoric as well. He could go up to the mountain; he could plunge into the valley: "In thinking of America, I sometimes find myself admiring her bright blue sky—her grand old woods—her fertile fields—her beautiful rivers—her mighty lakes and star-crowned mountains. But my rapture is soon checked. When I remember that all is cursed with the infernal spirit of slaveholding and wrong;—when I remember that with the waters of her noblest rivers, the tears of my brethren are borne to the ocean, disregarded and forgotten; that her most fertile fields drink daily of the warm blood of my outraged sisters, I am filled with unutterable loathing."

In 1862 the job for this elegant vocal instrument was agitation. Douglass was constantly pressing the president and everyone else in Washington to stop downplaying the slavery question and turn the war into a crusade to rid the land once and for all of the hated institution. On March 25, after word that the Union had finally made a forcible and successful invasion of the Confederacy—the navy under Flag Officer Andrew H. Foote took Fort Henry on the Tennessee River, and the army under General Ulysses S. Grant took Fort Donelson on the Cumberland—Douglass gave a bellicose assessment of the war. With bitter wit, he talked of how far the Union had come since "[Secretary of War—from Virginia—John B.] Floyd had stolen all the arms, and [Secretary of the Treasury—from Georgia—Howell] Cobb had stolen all the money." Now the traitors were beginning to get their due. His call was for blood; he would allow the rebels no credit: "[General George B.] McClellan . . . is careful to tell us that the Southern army is composed of foemen worthy of our steel. I do not like this. . . . they are traitors worthy of our hemp." The only echo of old-fashioned reform that this audience in Rochester's Corinthian Hall heard was in Douglass's giving credit to a teetotaler—"Tennessee is under Foote"—while omitting mention of Grant, whose reputation ran in another direction.

And he saw clearly how to put the greatest pressure on the Confederacy. With humility at its falsest, Douglass told his neighbors, "I stand here to-night to advocate in my humble way, the unrestricted and complete Emancipation of every slave in the United States whether claimed by loyal or disloyal masters. This is the lesson of the Hour."

The president seemed to Douglass more than a bit behind in his lessons; perhaps Union victories would help get him there. The president, he stated, "is tall and strong but he is not done growing." To encourage this growth, Douglass chose to interpret the president's action as recognition that "the highest interest of the country will be promoted by the abolition of slavery." But the next step toward emancipation seemed slow in coming, and in his annual Fourth of July address in New York, Douglass castigated Lincoln for stubbornly refusing to make emancipation the aim of the war. In a blistering rebuke of the man whose election he had applauded, he declared, "Jefferson Davis is a powerful man, but Jefferson Davis has no such power to blast the hope and break down the strong heart of this nation, as that possessed and exercised by Abraham Lincoln." We have, he insisted, "a right to hold Abraham Lincoln sternly responsible for any disaster or failure attending the suppression of this rebellion." Like his fellow abolitionists who were that spring and summer conducting a series of lectures at the Smithsonian Institution, in Washington, he was keeping the president under ceaseless pressure. And though none of the speakers yet knew it, their message was getting through. On July 22, Lincoln presented to his cabinet a draft of a proclamation of emancipation.

Julia Griffiths Crofts would have been disappointed that the antislavery politician she had most admired was the one who stayed Lincoln's hand. Secretary of State Seward cautioned the president to wait for a battlefield victory, in a war that was not going well, before announcing his intention to end slavery, so that the administration would not appear to be taking the step out of desperation. After the bloody battle at Antietam, in September 1862, which was sufficiently helpful to the Union cause to be labeled a victory, Lincoln did announce that on January 1, 1863, he would issue a proclamation freeing the slaves in the rebellious states.

When that great day came, black Americans could scarcely endure the wait for word that the Emancipation Proclamation had, indeed, been signed. Douglass, for one, never forgot the delicious agony of anticipation. In New York's Cooper Union, at the close of a long, rambling speech on February 6, 1863, he told a huge integrated audience what the waiting had been like. And in doing so, he skated on the thin ice of good taste to achieve truth. There are many moments of oratorical greatness in his speeches, but none of more emotional veracity than his reminiscence of the Boston celebration on January 1 of the signing of the Emancipation Proclamation. Douglass, over the years, contributed hundreds of florid recollections of Jubilee Day, but that night, before the Cooper Union audience, his risky words brought him all the way home. It was sad, perhaps, that the only place where he could get back to his own, to those who like him were slave people, was in a grand auditorium—but back he got that night.

After a learned review of the struggle against slavery, after appropriate warnings that the job was far from done, Douglass told his audience, now with him at every word, what he had done on the great day of emancipation. "We had two machines [mass meetings] running—at Music Hall and Tremont Temple—more than three thousand at each." There had been an all-day vigil, which his old friend William C. Nell had opened; other great friends spoke—among them Anna Dickinson, an antislavery orator whose effectiveness rivaled his; so did Douglass himself. In the evening Whittier and Stowe and Emerson were at the Music Hall—and the Philharmonic, playing Beethoven's "Ode to Joy"; from seven-thirty on, messengers waited at the telegraph office for word that President Lincoln had signed the proclamation (he had done so that afternoon) and for its text. By ten o'clock, the suspense was unbearable; at eleven, "We . . . waited on each speaker keeping our eye on the door. No Proclamation. . . . And I said, We won't go home till morning." Finally, Judge Thomas Russell went himself to the telegraph office and rushed back into Tremont Temple with the text in hand. The words were read: "I do order and declare that all persons held as slaves within said designated States and parts of States are, and henceforward shall be, free. . . ." "I never saw Joy before," Douglass recalled. "Men, women, young and old, were up; hats and bonnets were in the air."

For a great portion of the crowd, which was "mainly black," the wonderful tumult of Tremont Temple was not enough, Douglass reported as he continued his narrative. These people adjourned to the Twelfth Baptist Church, Boston's leading black church. "There was shouting and singing, 'Glory Hallelujah,' 'Old John Brown,' 'Marching On,' and 'Blow Ye, the Trumpet Blow!'—till we got up such a state of enthusiasm that almost anything seemed witty—and entirely appropriate to the glorious occasion." And then, patronizing, even perhaps a touch racist, but at last himself, Douglass told his respectable black and white Cooper Union audience a story. It was a watermelon story about "one black man who stood in a corner, . . . I never saw a blacker man and I think I never saw whiter teeth. Occasionally he would bound up like a fish out of water, and as he was standing in a dark place, you could see nothing going up but a little white streak." Using his notorious skill as a mimic and dropping his voice into the South, Douglass spoke the man's speech: " 'Brethern,' said he, 'I was born in North Carolina, where my brother Douglass was born, thank God!' I didn't happen to be born there, but I could not for the life of me interrupt him. Said he, 'I was born there, and was born and held a slave there, thank God! (Laughter.) I grew up from childhood to manhood there, thank God!' And the audience shouted. And said he: 'When I got to be grown up to man's estate I wanted to marry a wife, thank God!' (Laughter.) And said he: 'I courted no less than sixteen women, thank God!' (Great laughter.) And said he: 'The woman I married is here to-night, thank God!' We all rose up to see this little woman, and she was told to get up, and we looked at her, and she was nothing extraordinary (laughter); but still it was all in place."

The tale had no point, it posed no moral (though Douglass squeezed in a non sequitur of a lesson about the willingness of black people to fight). But that night it was not Frederick Douglass's story; it was Frederick Bailey's. And it was, simply, an expression of pure joy by one who knew from experience what it was to become free. At last, the runaway had come home.

17

Fort Wagner

FREDERICK DOUGLASS all but snatched the Emancipation Proclamation from Abraham Lincoln's hands to make of its flat rhetoric a sharpened call for freedom and equality. Douglass had never regarded the ending of slavery as enough, either for himself or for his people; it had to be the beginning of an embrace of the black individual's fullness as a person, a beginning that would point straight toward an end, within quick reach. For Douglass, each gain in the struggle, and the Emancipation Proclamation decidedly was one of the greatest, simply meant that America must move on to the next gain—right away. No one, including President Lincoln, would be allowed to rest on his laurels.

Now Douglass and his people had their Fourth of July. In February 1863, he told a Cooper Union audience that henceforth January 1 would be black America's independence day. And as he spoke, no one could miss the fact that a great war was in progress. There was martial energy in the air. The opportunity for black American males to achieve the fullness of being, said the white orators and patriotic essayists, lay in their becoming warriors. For his part, Douglass was eager to send black men off to war, not only to bring victory, but also to ensure the nation's respect for, its indebtedness to, black men who had taken up arms for what was now their country. But he displayed no eagerness to lug a rifle across a muddy or bloody field himself.

Douglass was, after all, only forty-four when his fellow abolitionist Thomas Wentworth Higginson led the First South Carolina Volunteers on the regiment's first raid on the mainland, from its sea-island base. Despite the still-troublesome old injury to his right hand, a result of his beating in Pendleton, and his occasional respiratory troubles—as early as 1842 he seems to have harbored the widespread nineteenth-century fear of tuberculosis—he was still a powerful man. He was no less well qualified to command than Higginson, a Unitarian preacher, and had he, like Higginson, been offered the colonelcy of a black regiment, he would probably have been no less eager to accept, seeing a colonelcy as a major symbol of racial achievement. But he was much too far advanced into dignity to indulge any urge to become an overage soldier boy, subject to the will of a drill sergeant.

Needless to say, Douglass was having none of the nonsense that Africans, deficient in manliness, had to prove that they were more than the sluggish beasts that abolitionist rhetoric insisted the slaveholders had made of them. What he did advocate that black men should do—what, he insisted, they were eager to do—was to participate in the achievement of their own freedom: "The colored man only waits for honorable admission into the service of the country.—They know that who would be free, themselves must strike the blow." His goal was to press the government into admitting black men into the army and navy; then he would recruit volunteers.

This world of war was a man's world, but even as Douglass plunged energetically into it, he was called back into the woman's world of his own domestic life by a letter from his oldest child: "I think my position in the family rather a singular one . . . ," Rosetta told her father in October 1862, "for I wish to be all you would have me be and I wish also to do some thing to make *mother* happy and if both were interested in the same pursuits it would be easier for me." Rosetta's life had been one of constant tension; she, more than her brothers, bore the brunt of the disparity between her parents. Her father pressed her to excel intellectually, to rise; her mother saw in Rosetta's efforts a repudiation of her, and of her attempts to keep the family sound and level.

What Rosetta's father would have her be was one of the resourceful, intellectual, active women, at work at important business, that he so much admired. When only seven, she had been sent away from her mother to study, in Albany, with Abigail and Lydia Mott. Rejoining her family in Rochester, Rosetta soon had the indefatigable, dedicated Julia Griffiths to look up to. Julia never ceased asking after the girl in her many letters to Douglass after she returned to England; "it is seven years . . . since I saw Rosetta—& in that time she will be much changed and much improved, without doubt," she wrote in December 1862. Soon after Julia left, there was the formidably learned Ottilia Assing to try to emulate.

Meanwhile, uneasily, Rosetta herself was a teacher. Her mother could "read a little"—Anna had mastered the checkbook—but larger works were beyond her. "I was instructed to read to her," Rosetta recalled in her troubled reminiscence of her mother, written years after her parents' death. She not only had to read to Anna the letters that Frederick wrote home when he traveled, and to keep her mother abreast of the news, but also to read literature to her, in an effort at education. The latter did not work; Anna remained essentially illiterate. This dependence on her daughter put Anna in an awkward position for imparting the maternal wisdom that Rosetta desperately needed. After leaving home she did speak to her father of her mother's "sure counsel," but all too often, instead of receiving help, Rosetta encountered in her resentful, insulted mother a "strict disciplinarian—her *no* meant *no* and *yes, yes,* but more frequently the *no's* had it," as she later recalled.

When Anna's youngest child, Annie, died in 1860, she lost a daughter not only young and cheerful, but also obviously still needing a mother's care. Cruelly deprived of that emotional bond, Anna seems not to have realized how much her thornier oldest child still needed her—and re-spected her. After both her parents had died, Rosetta wrote an article not about her famous father, but about her mother, whose name she hyphen-ated: Murray-Douglass. Proud of the female line, Rosetta gave her youngest daughter the name Rosabelle Murray. But when Rosetta herself was a child, she and her mother argued rancorously—when she left home in 1862 there were rumors that she had gone, even had been sent away, because "of my quarrelsome disposition towards my mother." The twenty-three-year-old young woman went to Philadelphia to become, as a respectable single young woman might, a schoolteacher. But boarding with a formidably correct black family, Rosetta was soon bitterly un-happy.

Maturing in her father's extraordinary household, Rosetta had received exceedingly contradictory signals, which made it hard for her to function in either the black community from which her mother had come (and in which, psychologically, she remained) or the studiedly nonracial world of intellectual activism that her father had created. He and Ottilia Assing (after whom Rosetta asked affectionately in her letters home) had encour-aged her to disdain churchgoing and to be a freethinker. She therefore found it difficult to teach Sabbath school, as she did, even though she knew how essential that institution was to a great many black people. In addition, her father and Ottilia had set an example of extraordinary disdain for propriety and for any infringement on their independence of action. But when, fascinated by the city of Philadelphia, Rosetta tried her wings as the assertive woman she had been taught to admire, she was roundly rebuffed.

Rosetta was staying with the achingly respectable family of Thomas

J. Dorsey, a leading Philadelphia caterer. In a long, anguished letter describing some of her problems, she revealed to her father her bafflement and her bitter unhappiness. One difficult situation began when "Mr. Dorsey who is quite genial told me he would like to see me go out and walk." Noticing her restlessly wandering about the house, he had admonished her that "white ladies walked out but colored ones were too lazy to dress and go." Rosetta eagerly accepted this advice, in part because, as she told her father, Dorsey "talked much the same as you do." Telling Mrs. Dorsey she was going out, Rosetta put on her best dress and went to pay a call on a recent acquaintance.

Emboldened by this expedition, she went out again the next day, this time to mail a letter. She had not thought this simple errand required Mrs. Dorsey's permission. Once away, she went on to the home of Mrs. Dorsey's sister-in-law, and accepted an invitation to stay for the noontime dinner. Arriving back at the Dorseys for tea, she was promptly told by Mrs. Dorsey, in front of guests, that she was a *"road runner. . . .* I asked what she meant by that term and she said I know devilishly well." Rosetta was not one to let that kind of insult pass; she insisted on her respectability and added that "I had no idea of being a hermit." Unyielding, Mrs. Dorsey was also disapproving when Rosetta received a call from the son of the head of the school where she was expecting to teach, even though he was accompanied by one of the male teachers.

Mrs. Dorsey was trying to teach Rosetta that a world that gave excessive value to respectability expected a black girl to appear twice as virtuous as a white one. If she did not, she would be the victim of the racist assumption that black people were sexually promiscuous. This charge haunted the young woman. So often was it intimated that she was sexually eager, that her tormentors almost succeeded in converting her defiance in the face of their charges into a sense of guilt.

In Philadelphia, Rosetta had too much pride to accept Mrs. Dorsey's castigation, but over the long pull, lacking her father's commanding presence and his intellect, she faced great obstacles in achieving the independence he cherished and she admired. Not tall, she was growing stout, and she could not shed her mother's dark skin, as a daughter in the Dorsey family had reminded her. "Sarah herself told me . . . she did not like too dark a face to come in their house," she wrote her light-skinned father.

Abandoning Philadelphia (none too soon), and failing to get a job in Myrtilla Miner's well-known school for black children in Washington, Rosetta moved, that summer, to Salem, New Jersey. Back in 1854, Rosetta had been a student in Oberlin College's "Young Ladies' Preparatory" department, studying arithmetic, English grammar, geography, and beginning Latin; now she was enrolled in the Salem Normal School. In August, she proudly reported that she had passed an examination in "Arithmetic, Geography, Grammar [,] reading and spelling" and was licensed to teach in the Salem schools. She taught not only during the day but also in the evenings, as many of her students were domestic servants and were free only after work. It is hard to imagine Rosetta as a good teacher. In addition, as she tried to establish herself, difficulties of a different kind arose.

She was boarding with Uncle Perry, her mother's brother,* and his wife, Lizzie, who were poor. "When I went there I found they had but one towel and everybody used it." Unable to get used to this, she "bought three towels." After taking her time undressing by candlelight, she discovered that the rest of the household went to bed in the dark, and thereafter, tactlessly, she bought her own candles, with money her father sent her. During the eight weeks before taking her examination she had taught in nearby Claysville, and had often gone without a noon meal. When teaching in Salem, she sometimes went to bed without supper, while enduring the taunts of her aunt, who thought it a hardship to have her staying with them while "Perry was struggling to pay for his house."

And there were worse humiliations: "Everything that is vile has been said of me by persons living here and strangers coming here pretending to have known me." One thoughtful soul quoted another as having said "that Fred Douglass himself was a very nice man but this daughter of his is one who has become low"; another rumor had it that she was not truly Douglass's daughter, but an impostor. Particularly odious were the Gibbonses, Quakers who "questioned me, where was thee born, was thy father married to Perry's sister before he left Slavery? and many more inquisitive questions"—insinuating that Rosetta had been born out of wedlock. On another occasion, when one of the Gibbonses spoke disgustedly about what degraded creatures ex-slaves were, Rosetta's temper flared: "I was quite indignant . . . and tried to show as well as I could that much of [the] degradation was owing to the whites."

"Much was said on both sides," she added, summing up that encounter in a triumph of succinctness. So fierce was the exchange, that afterward her uncle upbraided her for speaking harshly "to people who were his friends." And so furious was the argument that then ensued, that Rosetta tried to bolt the room, only to be barred by Aunt Lizzie, who "jumped

*Once again, family relationships are difficult to establish with certainty. Frederick had a brother Perry, but the two were out of touch until after the war, when the latter moved north from Texas, so if Perry was, indeed, an uncle, as the context of Rosetta's letters suggests, he must have been Anna's brother. (The possibility that he was a courtesy uncle seems unlikely in view of his poverty: the Douglasses would hardly have imposed on so poor a family unless they were actually related.)

up and dodged me first one way and then another to prevent my going upstairs." At last she did get away, and slammed the door in her aunt's face, only to have the enraged woman open it again and thrust a fist at her. Just in time, Rosetta found a "new home" in which to board.

Amidst all this turmoil (and scarcely disguised homesickness) Rosetta remained always the "affectionate daughter" of her letters. There is no question that she felt a deep emotional tie to her father: "I often think of your loneliness for you perceive the necessity for congenial companions[.] I have felt it since I have left home[.] I flatter myself if I were at home I might in a measure contribute to your happiness as well as to mothers." She wrote this in the face of her father's hints that she herself might have caused Sarah Dorsey's outburst, and of criticisms that impelled her to write, in the same letter, that he was "mistaken in supposing I spread family differences."

Nor did she lack affection for her siblings, with whom she was forced to compete. In her letters, she asked eagerly about her brothers, who, also somewhat slowly, were coming of age. "I am glad to know he is fine looking." Rosetta said of Lewis. "I did not think he was," she added with sisterly frankness, "but I noticed within the last year or two a change, a little of the sharp edge taken off . . . he will do." Remembering the not-always-tranquil days on the hill in Rochester, she added, "I can see him give me a green look at this criticism of his manners." She took note, too, of Lewis's frequent railroad trips to Syracuse to court Amelia Loguen, the beautiful daughter of Jermain Wesley Loguen, a prominent Methodist minister and himself a runaway slave. In 1863, Rosetta, too, turned to marriage; giving up her faltering career as a teacher, she went back to Rochester and, almost defiantly, married Nathan Sprague.*

Her husband, on the surface, seemed cut from the same cloth as her father. According to family legend, he was descended from a Maryland governor, Samuel Sprigg. One of his female ancestors, Peggy Rideout

---

*Rosetta and Nathan Sprague were to have five daughters—Anna (always called "Annie"), Harriet, Estelle, Fredericka, and Rosabelle—and one son, Herbert, according to the notes for a family history left by Rosabelle Murray Sprague Jones (Frederick Douglass Collection, Library of Congress, Reel 27). Annie died as a young woman; the four surviving sisters were all active in the organization of black women's clubs. Amelia and Lewis Douglass had no children. There is scant information on the offspring of Frederick and Virginia M. Hewlett Douglass and of Charles and Mary Elizabeth Murphy Douglass ("Libbie"). Each of these couples appears to have had six or seven children, but many of them died while still young. Late in life, on March 20, 1894, Douglass wrote to Ruth Adams, "I have about twenty grand children, *nine* only are living." The best known of Libbie and Charles's children was Joseph Douglass, who became a concert violinist. Charles and his second wife, Laura Antinette Haley Douglass, were the parents of Haley George Douglass.

A study of the Douglass family would yield rich returns in social history; no attempt has been made here to provide a thorough account.

(either his grandmother or his great-grandmother), had been remarkably resourceful, and her grandson (either Nathan or his father) had been a runaway slave. If Rosetta was not to have a career that met her father's expectations, she would at least have a husband that matched him. But in this respect she was to be bitterly disappointed. In Nathan, the feistiness of the runaway did not translate into talent; he proved as inept as her father was able. But like her mother, once married, Rosetta never gave up on her man.

As Rosetta settled down, her brothers (who, surprisingly, received no higher education) found themselves vulnerable to their father's newest great cause. At twenty-two, twenty, and eighteen, all three were the right age to respond to Frederick Douglass's call to arms. Douglass had been urging the inclusion of black soldiers in the Union army since the war began, and with Lincoln's announcement, in September 1862, that he would issue the Emancipation Proclamation, he had become increasingly vehement. Shortly after the proclamation was issued, Governor John A. Andrew of Massachusetts called for volunteers for what became the famous Fifty-fourth Massachusetts Volunteers. Still marching, on the Boston Common, in that greatest of American sculptures, Augustus Saint-Gaudens's depiction of black men on the way to war, these soldiers were recruited not only in Boston, but in black communities all across the North.

George Luther Stearns, one of the six whites who had backed John Brown, was now a major and headed the recruitment effort. In the eyes of bitter Southern planters, by putting guns in black men's hands, Stearns was making good on his mentor's promise of raising an insurrection. As in Brown's day, however, the black men were skeptical about serving in a white man's army. In 1862, on the Union-held Sea Islands, off the coast of South Carolina and Georgia, they had resisted General David Hunter's attempts to forcibly enlist them; they found unappealing the idea of changing one white master for another, particularly when they were being recruited to do a potentially lethal job. Thomas Wentworth Higginson, another of the Secret Six, on the Sea Islands to raise the First South Carolina Volunteers, warned a Worcester neighbor who wanted to enlist, *"If taken prisoner by the rebels . . . you would probably be sold as a slave."* Stearns, recognizing the problem of recruiting free Northern black soldiers, went to Rochester early in February 1863 to seek Douglass's help.

The editor needed no persuading; in the March issue of *Douglass' Monthly* appeared his call for volunteers, bearing the famous title "Men of Color to Arms." Joining such other black leaders as Martin Delany, Henry Highland Garnet, George T. Downing, William Wells Brown, and Jermain Wesley Loguen in recruiting, Douglass traveled across upstate New York, persuading young men to enlist, and he proudly informed Gerrit Smith that the first man he had signed up was his youngest son, Charles. In all, Douglass sent over a hundred young men from upstate New York, to the famous Fifty-fourth Massachusetts. On March 27, Douglass arrived in Boston with one contingent, including Charles and his oldest son, Lewis, and escorted them to the encampment in Readville, outside the city, where the first recruits had been since February.

Lewis Douglass became the first sergeant major of Colonel Robert Gould Shaw's regiment, in which the commissioned officers were white—and aristocratic. Charles Douglass was a private in Company F; his physical description, in his service record, reads, "eyes, black; hair, black; complexion, black; height, 5 feet 10 ½ inches"; Lewis was "five feet nine inches high, Brown complexion, Brown eyes, Black hair." Both were shorter in stature and darker in color than their father; some of the men in the regiment were of lighter color than either, but most were not. The commissioned officers had separate quarters, so for the first time in their lives, the brothers were living entirely with other black men.

Lewis Douglass found the struggle of the recruits to get along with one another both troubling and exciting. Writing to Amelia Loguen, he told of men fighting among themselves—and with their officers, even though, he claimed, such behavior brought threats of death as a punishment. Colonel Shaw and Lieutenant Colonel Edward N. Hallowell put their young recruits, their numbers augmenting more slowly than had been hoped, through drills that began to make a group of strangers into a band of fighters. But they did not often have a full day to themselves. Boston was too curious; the city's legendary reserve yielded before the chance to glimpse the wonderful happenings in the bleak barracks in Readville. On April 21, the Ladies Committee, the auxiliary of the group of men sponsoring the regiment, came out for a look; on April 30, the Fast Day called by President Lincoln to bolster the Union's determination, Governor Andrew was there, with Secretary of the Treasury Salmon P. Chase. And on May 18, the governor was back, to present the regiment with its colors.

Frederick Douglass was one of the distinguished guests who filled the carriages and extra trains that brought the crowd to Readville that day. Not surprisingly, William Lloyd Garrison (whose pacifism had yielded in the face of war) and Wendell Phillips were there; less surprising still was the presence of a large number of Boston's black citizens. The day was clear and warm, a relief after the rains of March, which had brought bronchitis and pneumonia to a good many of the recruits, Charles Douglass among them. Governor Andrew, as he addressed Colonel Shaw, was surrounded by the men, drawn up in formation. "Now," he said, "in the

Providence of God, [they have] given to them, an opportunity which, while it is personal to themselves, is still an opportunity for a whole race of men. With arms possessed of might to strike a blow, they have found breathed into their hearts an inspiration of devoted patriotism and regard for their brethren of their own color, which has inspired them with a purpose to nerve that arm, that it may strike a blow which, while it shall help to raise aloft their country's flag—*their* country's flag, now, as well as ours—by striking down the foes which oppose it, strikes also the last shackle which binds the limbs of bondmen in the Rebel States."

What the soldiers had to say about this simple assignment, Captain Luis F. Emilio, in his splendid history of his regiment, does not tell us, but we know that because the dignitaries had to be well fed, the men too, that day, got a good lunch.

At six-thirty in the morning of May 28, 1863, with orders to ship out of Boston for the Sea Islands, the Fifty-fourth traveled by train from Readville into the city. Charles Douglass was not with his comrades; illness kept him, and some others, in Readville. A crowd cheered as the men of the ten companies left the cars. (The police, whatever their personal reactions to black men with guns, must have been relieved that there was no repeat of the kind of assault Douglass, armed only with words, had faced in Boston just two Decembers earlier.) The companies formed into marching order and, behind solemn-faced drummer boys, started through the streets of the city. From the sidewalks and windows the curious watched, and much of patriotic Boston—and all of antislavery Boston—cheered. Handkerchiefs fluttered, the cheering rose, and so did the spirits of the new soldiers stepping steadily forward. Somehow bigger, stretching to fill their still-new uniforms, they were now truly the men of the Fifty-fourth Massachusetts.

Reaching the statehouse, they were greeted by Governor Andrew, who then marched with them down Beacon Street and onto the Common. There, Colonel Shaw led them past the reviewing stand, filled with white men who were sending them off to war, and past a cheering crowd. About noon, marching to the music of "John Brown's Body," they moved out along Tremont Street and the streets of downtown Boston to the Battery Wharf. Boarding an unpromising transport ship, the *DeMolay,* the regiment steamed out past the harbor islands. Frederick Douglass was one of those who stayed on the dock until the ship, bearing his oldest son, was out of sight.

Arriving first at Beaufort, South Carolina, the headquarters of the Union force that occupied the islands along the South Carolina and Georgia coast, the Fifty-fourth was soon sent farther south, to St. Simons Island, in Georgia. There the men participated in their first military actions, guerrilla raids against the mainland led by Colonel James Mont-gomery. The colonel had learned his nasty trade as a Kansas Jayhawker, raiding pro-Southern communities in Missouri. A similar raid, on the coastal town of Darien, with the looting and burning of houses, did not endear the Union forces to white Georgians; when black soldiers were spotted among the troops, the outrage grew. Northerners joined in con-demnation; Charles Russell Lowell, who was engaged to Colonel Shaw's sister, said that instead "of improving the negro character and educating him for civilized independence," they were, by introducing the black soldier to such practices, "re-developing all his savage instincts." A gentle-man always, Shaw was troubled by these ugly assignments and was pleased when his regiment was ordered to strike a military target—Fort Wagner, an artillery post on Morris Island, guarding the Charleston harbor. Now, like the black units that had been fighting well at Milliken's Bend in the Mississippi Valley campaigns that June, his men would truly be at war.

On July 18, 1863, buoyed by word of the great Union victories at Gettysburg and Vicksburg, Shaw led the Fifty-fourth in an attack on Fort Wagner. The defenders of the fort had repelled an attack on July 11; now the Fifty-fourth, with other regiments following, moved up the beach. There was a salt marsh on the left; the men on the right marched through the lip of surf from the ocean as they moved across the flat sand in a frontal assault. The first attackers made it to the parapet; in hand-to-hand fighting, they were forced back, but not yet routed. "This regiment has established its reputation as fighting regiment not a man flinched, though it was a trying time," wrote Sergeant Major Lewis Douglass. "Men fell all around me. A shell would explode and clear a space of twenty feet, our men would close up again, but it was no use we had to retreat, which was a very hazardous undertaking. How I got out of that fight alive I cannot tell, but I am here."

Lewis, writing two days after the assault on Fort Wagner, was waiting for orders to be sent on another raid: "Should I fall in the next fight killed or wounded I hope to fall with my face to the foe. . . ." Having told Amelia, "You are as dear as ever, be good enough to remember it as I no doubt you will," he closed: "My Dear girl I hope again to see you. I must bid you farewell should I be killed. Remember if I die I die in a good cause. I wish we had a hundred thousand colored troops we would put an end to this war."

At Fort Wagner, 174 of the Confederate defenders were killed or wounded; 1,515 Union men fell; the next morning the defenders saw "live and dead men strewn in piles and windrows, their bodies horribly man-gled. . . . detached arms and legs and heads were splattered all about."

The Confederates buried the Union dead: the black soldiers went into a common grave; their colonel, killed in the battle, was thrown in with them. In Robert Gould Shaw, the North had gained another saint. But the recruiters of black troops, Douglass among them, faced a growing problem. Enthusiastic after the Fifty-fourth's triumphant exit from Boston, Douglass had accepted eagerly the War Department's request, arranged by George Luther Stearns, that he travel across the North in the effort to recruit black volunteers. The recruiting was slow work, made all the more difficult by the contempt, and worse, shown toward black people in the North. Douglass was in Philadelphia when, on July 13, 1863, the ugly draft riots broke out in New York and other Northern cities. Poor white men and women, furious about the federal government's new conscription of troops, from which rich men could exempt themselves by paying a substitute, took out their anger not on the rich but on scapegoats: the niggers had caused the war; they could suffer for it. As not-so-poor haters of blacks joined in, houses were burned and scores of people killed. Brains were dashed out against lampposts; a crippled black man was tortured and hanged; a colored orphanage was burned. Quiet had not been fully restored by July 16, and as Douglass headed for New York, a "friend," probably Ottilia Assing, met him in Newark, New Jersey, and warned him against going into the heart of the city. Once again, New York held terrors, and after a night in Hoboken, he took the ferry to the downtown railroad station, many blocks below the area that had seen the worst of the rioting, where he could board a train for Rochester.

The commitment to end slavery was strong in black communities in the North, but Douglass and other recruiters had to recognize that despite the valor black soldiers had displayed at Milliken's Bend and Fort Wagner, they were still treated with scorn and were paid less than other soldiers (including the newest immigrant). More sobering still to would-be recruits was the thought that if taken prisoner, they would not be treated like other soldiers. Horrified by the prospect of white Southerners being killed by black men—the ultimate act of intimacy in their eyes—members of the Confederate Congress on May 1, 1863, put through a formal declaration that black men bearing arms would be subject to the laws of the state where they were captured; in other words, they would be treated as insurrectionary slaves. The punishment would almost certainly be death.

General Grant told Confederate general Richard Taylor, "I cannot see the justice of permitting one treatment for them, and another for the white soldiers," but his logic did not persuade Taylor's government. Northern advocates of sending black troops into battle, aware that their recruits would face double jeopardy—death on the battlefield or if taken prisoner—called upon Union generals and the president himself to take stern action. Douglass was loud in his denunciation of this latest expression of slaveholding barbarism. On August 1, he wrote Stearns a letter, clearly intended for the eyes of official Washington, saying he would no longer work at recruitment. Such work required complete commitment to the government's cause, and that government had done nothing to protect captured black soldiers and black civilians who had assisted the invading Union armies. Douglass's letter was among many similar expressions of horror; Jefferson Davis and his congress could have done nothing more conducive to gaining sympathy for black Americans from those who had never before cared about them.

President Lincoln had already gotten the message. On July 30, 1863, he signed an order requiring that "for every soldier of the United States killed in violation of the laws of war a rebel soldier shall be executed." The barbarism of the war was escalating, but the president's action took him one more step toward a recognition that there could be no turning back to the *status quo ante bellum* on slavery. The abolitionists were not slow in pressing their advantage and pushing Lincoln to take yet another step.

Later in the summer, at Stearns's request, Douglass made a "flying visit" from Philadelphia to Washington. He went first to Capitol Hill, to get the advice of allies in Congress. One of them, Senator Samuel C. Pomeroy of Kansas, then accompanied him to the War Department for an interview with Secretary Edwin M. Stanton, whose "manner was cold and business like throughout but earnest," Douglass reported to Stearns. "I told him," said Douglass, "that the negro was the victim of two extreme opinions. One claimed for him too much and the other too little[;] that it was a mistake to regard him either as an angel or a devil. He is simply a man and should be dealt with purely as such." Some were brave, some cowardly; some "ambitious and aspiring," some not.

Douglass candidly pointed out that the greatest barriers to recruitment were the low pay received by black soldiers, as compared to white ones, and the fact that they were denied ranks above noncommissioned officer. Nevertheless, "I told Mr. Stanton that I held it to be the duty of Colored men to fight for the Government even though they should be offered but subsistence and arms considering that we had a cause quite independent of pay or place." Stanton, with an eye on Senator Pomeroy, replied that he had helped write a bill calling for equal pay, which had been passed by the House only to fail in the Senate, and he made a pledge, which he was a long time fulfilling, to give "the same pay to black as to white soldiers" and to open the way for promotion into officer ranks.

Stanton then turned intently to Douglass, and reminding him that General Lorenzo Thomas was "vigorously engaged in organizing colored troops along the Mississippi, said that he . . . wished me to report to Gen. Thomas and cooperate with him." In response, Douglass told the secretary that he was already at work in Pennsylvania, under—and here he must have orally underscored the word—*Major* Stearns. Stanton interrupted, saying that the black man was needed in the South and, as Douglass understood it, that he would prepare the papers for Douglass's commission as an officer in the army.

Cautiously, Douglass reported to Stearns that his stiff conversation with the "imperative" secretary "was free of compliment of every kind." By contrast, he found the tone of his next conversation—one that has been given enormous importance in the history of black Americans—to be vastly different: "I went directly to the White House [and] saw for the first time the President of the United States. Was received cordially and saw at glance the justice of the popular estimate of his qualities expressed in the prefix *Honest* to the name Abraham Lincoln." If there were other people in the room, the two ignored them. Douglass began the conversation by thanking the president for extending protection to black soldiers with the retaliatory order. His aim in introducing this subject was to provide a "hint for a discussion from Mr. Lincoln himself. In this I was quite successful for the President instantly . . . proceeded with . . . an earnestness and fluency which I had not expected . . . to vindicate his policy respecting the whole slavery question and especially that in reference to employing colored troops."

Douglass saw "one remark" of Lincoln's as "of much significance. He said he had frequently been charged with tardiness, hesitation and the like, especially in regard to the retaliatory proclamation, but had he sooner issued that proclamation such was the state of public popular prejudice that an outcry would have been raised against the measure. It would," Lincoln told Douglass, "be said, 'Ah! We thought it would come to this: White men are to be killed for negroes.'" Lincoln went on to deny that he was guilty of "vacillation" and implied that what Douglass was seeing was steady, if perhaps slow, progress, rather than any indecision on his part. Douglass came away convinced that once Lincoln had taken a position favorable to the black cause, he could be counted on to hold to it.

And he came away elated. Abraham Lincoln—with his seeming candor, his "transparent countenance"—had charmed his black visitor totally. Douglass felt at ease in his presence, with no sense of inferiority.

This call on the president of the United States, in the Executive Mansion itself, was a crowning achievement for the boy who had once sneaked into Wye House.

At least at the familial level, Douglass's trust in Lincoln would prove justified a year later. Charles was ill much of the time he was in the service—more men died of disease than were killed on the battlefield in the Civil War—and, staying behind in Readville with a remnant of the Fifty-fourth, he did not find the going smooth. In March 1864, Governor Andrew interceded with Secretary of War Stanton to get Charles transferred to another black regiment, the Fifth Massachusetts Cavalry—by then dismounted—where he would be promoted to sergeant. (Jumping from one regiment to another in order to advance in rank was not normally permitted.) Douglass, Andrew pointed out to Stanton, was Frederick Douglass's son, had joined early, and because of a "lung complaint" had been prevented from "ever taking the field with the Fifty-fourth."

In May, Charles was stationed with his new regiment at Point Lookout, Maryland, where the Potomac River joins the Chesapeake Bay. He appears not to have been sent into the grim battles across the way in Virginia that spring and summer—the Wilderness campaign and the battle of Cold Harbor—but Charles did take advantage of being stationed in Maryland to cross the Chesapeake, becoming the first Douglass to get back in touch with Bailey cousins in St. Michaels.

At Point Lookout, Charles was again ill, so seriously this time that his father wrote to the president: "I hope I shall not presume to much upon your kindness—but I have a very great favor to ask. It is . . . that you will cause my son Charles R. Douglass . . . to be discharged." This request was sent into the president's office on August 29; it came back on September 1 bearing the simple endorsement "Let this boy be discharged. A. Lincoln." On September 15, Charles Douglass became a civilian.

Charles's service record makes no mention of his having seen action; life in the army did not match the glory of his father's recruitment rhetoric. But if his military career was a disappointment, his father's was nonexistent. In the late summer of 1863, fresh from his visits with Lincoln and Stanton, Douglass returned to Rochester, eager to take up his commission as the first black officer in the United States Army. He was to join General Thomas in recruiting black soldiers in occupied Tennessee and northern Mississippi, and so sure was he that the orders would come, that he announced that he was suspending *Douglass' Monthly.* When at last word came from Washington, it was from Stanton, directing him to report to Thomas, with nothing said about the commission. When Douglass inquired, he received no satisfaction. He blamed Stanton for the humiliating lapse; he could not bring himself to blame Lincoln. But Benjamin Quarles's shrewd guess is that it was in fact the president, not vacillating but once again going slowly, who decided to deny the black man his rank; in February 1865, with the war almost won, Martin Delany, was made a major. Frederick Douglass was too proud to take the job of recruiting within the occupied rebel states without a commission. He returned to the lecture circuit to plead for a victory that would not only end slavery but guarantee equal treatment for his fellow black Americans.

In February 1864, at Cooper Union before the Women's Loyal League, Douglass delivered an address called "The Mission of the War." The mission, as he was also to define it in many other speeches before the war was won, was to bring about "simply those great moral changes in the fundamental condition of the people." That war had "filled our land with mere stumps of men, ridged our soil with 200,000 rudely-formed graves, and mantled it all over with the shadow of death." To be worth such sacrifice, the war had to achieve abolition—and he proudly proclaimed the word. He was aware of the strong movement, in this election year, for a negotiated peace, one that might leave slavery in place: "While the Democratic party is in existence . . . we are in danger of a slaveholding peace, and of Rebel rule. There is but one way to avert this calamity, and that is to destroy Slavery and enfranchise the black man while we have the power." Further, he told his audience, "You and I know that the mission of this war is National regeneration." As George Fredrickson has shown, Douglass was not alone in having traveled the road from belief in individual moral commitment as a medium for reform to profound and conservative belief in the nation state as the agent for such change. A national government, not a morally persuaded citizenry, was needed now to end slavery and ensure the safety and the well-being of the freed slaves.

"I end where I began," he concluded; "no war but an Abolition war; no peace but an Abolition peace; liberty for all, chains for none; the black man a soldier in war; a laborer in peace; a voter at the South as well as at the North; America his permanent home, and all Americans his fellow-countrymen. Such, fellow-citizens, is my idea for the mission of this war."

Toward the achievement of this mission, Douglass flirted with every move within the Republican party to press it away from compromise. If a man like Salmon P. Chase or John C. Frémont would hold more firmly to the faith than Abraham Lincoln, Douglass believed, then he should be put forward. If the president was to be renominated, he should first have been pushed toward a radical understanding of those fundamental changes that Douglass so fervently believed in. In June, Lincoln was indeed renominated, but during the summer, with the war dragging agonizingly on, the president was as despairing as he was ever to be. Late in August, he sent his famous memorandum to the cabinet asking how, if he was defeated for reelection, they could best save the Union between election day and the inauguration, since the winner—the Democrats would probably nominate General George B. McClellan—"will have secured his election on such ground that he can not possibly save it afterwards."

On August 19, 1864, just four days before Lincoln wrote this memorandum, Frederick Douglass was sitting in the White House waiting to see the president. So were two men from Wisconsin, Joseph T. Mills and former governor Alexander Randall. Mills, who fancied himself a humorist, later told the president, "I was in your reception room. . . . It was dark. I suppose that clouds & darkness necessarily surround the secrets of state. There in a corner I saw a man quietly reading who possessed a remarkable physiognomy. I was rivetted to the spot. I stood & stared at him. He raised his flashing eyes & caught me in the act. I was compelled to speak. Said I, Are you the President. No replied the stranger, I am Frederick Douglass." Douglass had given Mills his usual response to someone pulling his leg with a racist jerk: he had advanced into immense dignity.

In the president's study, Mills, going on to Lincoln's delight—the president's "elasticity of spirits" was in play—inquired whether Douglass had not converted him to a new view. "Now Mr. P.," Mills asked, according to his diary, "are you in favor of miscegenation?" Replied the president, "That's a democratic mode of producing good Union men, & I dont propose to infringe on the patent."

Turning to politics, Lincoln told Randall and Mills that he expected General McClellan to be nominated by the Democrats and that McClellan would insist he could crush the rebellion. But he would attempt to do so by abandoning the promise to emancipate slaves in the states still within the Confederacy. This strategy, which played to antiblack sentiments among Northern voters, was a prescription for disaster. "There are," the president said, according to Mills, ". . . between 1 & 200 thousand black men now in the service of the Union. These men will be disbanded, returned to slavery & we will have to fight two nations in stead of one. [Just what Lincoln meant by this is not entirely clear; presumably he was referring to the white South, reinforced by the labor of a once more enslaved black South.] I have tried it. You cannot conciliate the South, when the mastery & control of millions of blacks makes them sure of ultimate success. You cannot conciliate the South, when you place yourself in such a position, that they see they can achieve their independence."

Warming to his subject, Lincoln told Randall and Mills, "Abandon all the posts now possessed by black men surrender all these advantages to the enemy, & we would be compelled to abandon the war in 3 weeks. . . . Freedom has given us 200,000 able bodied men, born & raised on southern soil. It will give us more yet. . . . My enemies condemn my emancipation policy. Let them prove by the history of this war, that we can restore the Union without it." There is no similar memorandum recording Douglass's conversation with Lincoln, but Douglass later reported that he had found the president in an "alarmed condition," and the letter he sent to the president on August 29, ten days after their interview, makes it clear that what Lincoln was proposing was a stepped-up effort to persuade slaves within the Confederacy to make a break for freedom—and to do so in time to help win the war prior to McClellan's inauguration. Lincoln feared that if the war was not won by the time McClellan entered the White House, the freed black people would be returned south to their masters as part of a negotiated peace.

As Douglass notes in his letter, Lincoln had asked him to consult with other black leaders and tell them that "something should be speedily done to inform the slaves in the Rebel States of the state of affairs in relation to them, and to warn them as to what will be their probable condition should peace be concluded while they remain within the Rebel lines; And more especially to urge upon them the necessity of making their escape." Just how such a mass escape was to be engineered, Lincoln seems not to have determined, but, shrewd politician that he was, he could scarcely have said anything that would have ensured the support of black leaders more than the intimation that his opponent would end emancipation. Douglass was asked to come up with a plan, and it was suggested that he should also be the "general agent" to carry it out.

Douglass must have left the White House with deeply ambivalent feelings. On one hand, the man that he had to trust to push the war through to a victory over slavery seemed to expect that the voters would not give him a chance to do so. On the other hand, once again, the president had charmed Douglass, and held out the hope of an important governmental assignment aimed at rescuing slaves.

In his formal letter of August 29, Douglass outlined how such an effort might be implemented. He knew why it should be: "That every slave who escapes from the Rebel States is a loss to the Rebellion and a gain to the Loyal Cause, I need not stop here to argue. The negro is the stomach of the Rebellion." He then went on to outline "the ways and means by which many such persons may be wrested from the enemy and brought within our lines." The general agent put in charge of the undertaking should, in turn, appoint twenty subagents who should "have permission to visit such points at the front as are most accessible to large bodies of slaves." These local agents, Douglass indicated, should be people who knew the territory, but he did not make clear whether they were to go behind the rebel lines to proselytize, or were simply to be advertised as available to receive runaways. Douglass was skeptical enough to stress that the subagents should be assured of pay and the commanding generals should be told to give explicit permission for them "to pursue their vocation unmolested."

By the summer of 1864, with Lewis reporting from Hilton Head, "We still keep banging away at Sumter," large numbers of black refugees were crowding Union posts, some of which, like Camp Nelson in Kentucky, had in effect become displaced-persons' camps. In their conversation, the president and Douglass may have been edging toward a concept of the general agent as responsible for helping individuals make the transition from slave to soldier or citizen (as the postwar Freedmen's Bureau was to do). But if such a vision of the general agent's functions did come into their conversation, Douglass did not embody it in the recommendations in his letter. He did, however, advise placement of the office of general agent—a post he did not need to say he would be happy to hold—firmly within the framework of the government. He proposed that the general agent should have "a salary; sufficient to enable him to employ a competent clerk and . . . be stationed in Washington."

Thanks to Sherman's and Sheridan's military victories in September 1864, which ensured Lincoln's reelection, nothing came of the conversation between Douglass and the president. What lasted, never to be tested, was Douglass's sense that Lincoln held him in respect. But he still retained his wariness of the president. In October, he told the radical editor Theodore Tilton, "When there was any shadow of a hope that a man of a more decided anti-slavery conviction and policy could be elected, I was not for Mr. Lincoln." After Lincoln had beaten back Chase and Frémont, radicals had no alternative but to support him as the nominee of the National Union Party. And after the Democratic party nominated McClellan, Douglass—with the president's predictions ringing in his ears—supported Lincoln's reelection. But he was not allowed any visible role in the campaign: "I am not doing much in this presidential canvass for the reason that the Republican committees do not wish to expose themselves to the charge of being the 'N——r' party. The Negro is the deformed child, which is put out of the room when company comes."

Where the still-tentative relationship between Lincoln and Douglass might have taken the nation after the war cannot be known. It is one of the might-have-beens that lie in the shadow of Lincoln's assassination. Lost in the speculation of how Reconstruction might have been different if only the president had lived is the fact that he had only two private conversations with Douglass—and none with other black leaders, except for the famous meeting with *creole de couleur* gentlemen from New Orleans just before the president's death, in which the franchise of black leaders like themselves was discussed. Perhaps Douglass's insistence that the franchise be granted to all black males seemed so radical to Lincoln that he wanted to avoid appearing to listen too closely. In any event, the president sought almost no counsel from his black constituents with respect to the postwar problems of the freedmen.

In the winter of 1865, with the prospect of peace and another four years in the White House in which to give that peace shape, Lincoln might have had much to gain by talking matters over with Douglass. And the president might have been able in short order to break through Douglass's reverential deference to "your excellency" and get down to some good earthy mimicking. Overly pious preachers, for example, would have been fair game for both. After his first visit, Douglass claimed that he felt comfortable with Lincoln; had they indeed achieved a way to talk comfortably, the president could have learned a lot from his visitor. And there is evidence that Lincoln was not as slow a learner as Douglass, with his well-placed impatience, sometimes thought. Douglass was in Lincoln's debt for Charles's discharge, but Lincoln would not have had to call in that chit. By 1865, Douglass's loyalty to the president was complete. Lincoln could have had this fervent ally as an adviser for the asking. He did not ask.

Soldiers on their way home from war sometimes find just the right celebrations. In the spring of 1865, Lewis, on his way north from Morris Island, from which Union artillery trained on Fort Sumter had hammered that symbol into rubble, was stationed briefly, with a detachment of the Fifty-fourth Massachusetts, in Royal Oak, Talbot County, Maryland. On June 9, he wrote his father of walking eight miles into St. Michaels, four more than he had reckoned the distance would be. On the way, he stopped to ask directions, and only later learned that he had been talking to his cousin John Mitchell, his aunt Eliza's son. In the town, as he was looking for her, his aunt came up to him; she had been expecting him and recognized Lewis "from my resemblance to Charles," who, earlier, had come over from Point Lookout. Eliza Mitchell was Frederick Douglass's older sister nearest in age; she was two years his senior.

It was Pentecost, and "the streets were full of colored people, my aunt introduced me to the crowd and I soon became a lion! Before going to her house she made several calls with me just to show the people that her brother's family were not too proud to come and see her." Eliza Mitchell's place was half a mile out of town, "toward's Capt. Auld's place;" Auld had moved out from St. Michaels. The Mitchells, on "about an acre of ground," which was rented, "raise vegetables enough for the family" and "there own meat." Lewis's three adult cousins, John, Peter, and Edward—there are Mitchells still in St. Michaels—were all farmers nearby; Susan, the oldest daughter in the area, "lives out to service." (Lewis made no mention of Eliza's two much older children, born in 1834 and 1835.) Three children were still living at home—the oldest, Mary Douglass, named "after you." An illiterate sister had proudly heard about and paid tribute to an honored brother in 1856.

While Lewis was visiting Aunt Eliza—who asked him to thank his father for presents sent her—Tom Bailey, the son of Frederick's favorite aunt, Milly, "called on me." When Lewis showed him photographs of Frederick, Tom "remembered the scar over your nose." Although he stammered badly, he took the trouble to remind Lewis that his great-grandmother "was of Indian descent." More and more family members crowded into Eliza Mitchell's house; among them was the daughter of Frederick's brother Perry, who informed Lewis that her father had been sold away three years before. John Mitchell reported that "Ned Hamilton" [Hambleton] was saying in town that he was the last white man to get "you to jail." (Presumably he had been a member of William Hambleton's posse.) And the last caller Lewis mentioned was a "white woman by the name of Harriet Auld . . . [where in the sizable Auld family this member belonged is uncertain], she said she used to know you."

"I kept pretty quiet in St. Michaels," Lewis continued, "because I knew it to be one of the worst places in the South. A colored was mobbed there about two weeks ago for advising the colored people to do business for themselves[;] those who were not able to work to open stores and the rest should trade with them. [T]he white shopkeepers took offense at that and broke up his meeting. The white people will do anything they can to keep the blacks from advancing. There seems to be a combination among the white people to keep the blacks from buying land. Large tracts of woods that the whites will neither use nor sell to the blacks is idle, and wasting. There are a great many colored people who would buy land if the whites would sell. The whites think to get [illegible word] labor by not selling land to the blacks. The highest price paid on farm land here is fifteen dollars, a month. A large number of colored men make from eighteen to twenty dollars a week oystering. They have surplus money and can't use it to any advantage around here and they do not want to move away."

Lewis could not have more accurately summarized the dilemma that faced the emancipated Baileys and Mitchells of America in the aftermath of the war. No more fathers were going to be sold away, and in St. Michaels, Maryland, people could be proud that a now-famous relative and neighbor had helped with that first essential achievement. But for these people, making their land theirs was a job still to be done. Whether their Rochester cousin could help much with that simple yet immense effort was not yet clear.

18

Philadelphia

THERE WAS TO BE a brave new world. "Revolution," Ottilia called it; "Reconstruction" was the politicians' word. To the German revolutionary, the war had been worth the cost; it had brought about a step forward "which even fifty or even a hundred years of peace could not have produced." Indeed, she wrote, "in the whole century" nothing in Europe or America had been "more important" than the "revolution" which had been taking place "here in the last five years." She was eager for its consummation.

The war was over, emancipation had been won, and America would rebuild itself into a place of newer, greater equality and opportunity. Looking back, most observers would say that Assing had overstated her case. In our national embarrassment over having so firmly slammed the door on the freed people so soon after this moment of triumph, we tend to say that hopes were too high; the usual excuse is that times were not yet right for racial equality. Frederick Douglass and Ottilia Assing thought they had never been more right.

The Douglasses in their forties and their children in their twenties were eager to enter the city of which the family patriarch was not the least of the architects. African Americans, slave and free, were to be simply Americans. William Lloyd Garrison, another of the builders, thought no further construction was needed. For him, the job was done; liberation was the whole of it. In the spring of 1865, he called for the disbanding of the American Anti-Slavery Society. But others, Wendell Phillips and Douglass among them, knew that things were not yet secure enough for that.

Despite this latest disagreement, Douglass and Garrison were more alike than they were different. Each had come from an obscure, unstable family; each had struggled to make a profession of being an editor; each had made himself heard as a superb orator; each had achieved economic security and lasting fame. And each had every reason to expect that he could stretch his success so that it would embrace his children. But there was a difference, which became apparent not so much in what befell them as in what became of their sons and daughters.

Douglass named his third son after his fellow abolitionist leader Charles Remond; Garrison named six of his children after antislavery workers. The seventh, Frances (Fanny), was named for her grandmother. Both Fanny Garrison and Rosetta Douglass had the world of abolition as their schoolbook; their mentors were some of its greatest luminaries. Fanny Garrison married a liberal newspaperman, Henry Villard, who became one of the late nineteenth century's most successful railroad entrepreneurs. For a time she lived in a beautiful mansion in New York. She was actively concerned for the freed people, and early in the twentieth century, with her son, helped to found the National Association for the Advancement of Colored People. But Rosa Douglass's husband set out to drive a hack, only to be scorned by his fellow hackmen. Francis Jackson Garrison became an editor at the publishing house of Houghton Mifflin, but Charles Remond Douglass wrote with forced pride that he had become one of two "colored" clerks in a government department, and Frederick Douglass, Jr., son of a well-known author and editor, struggled to get into the typographical workers' union. These young people were different one from another, of course, but the greatest of the differences was that the Garrisons were white and the Douglasses black. The fame of their fathers did not change that fact.

In 1865, the Douglasses were not prepared to acknowledge that there was such a fact. Young Charles Douglass, working at the war's end at Freedmen's Hospital in Washington, savored the changes victory brought. He enjoyed sitting in the gallery listening to the "smartest man in the U S Senate," Charles Sumner, and better still, he reported to his father that he was planning to call on "Father Abraham and Secy Stanton" with his superior at the hospital. But not even the prospect of a black army private's calling on the president of the United States suggests as powerfully the faith people had that their America had been profoundly changed as does Charles's proposal for his future. In February 1865 he wrote to his father, "I want to go off . . . and go it on my own hook as every young man does. . . . I mean to make a bold start for myself in some direction." What the ambitious young black man had in mind, in this world turned upside down, was to go to Tennessee with his roommate, Thomas J. White, who had studied at Wilberforce University, to invest in cotton lands.

Charles never became a planter. When Douglass arrived in Washington two weeks later for Lincoln's second inaugural, he must have advised his son against Tennessee. Lee's surrender early in April was followed in a few days by Lincoln's assassination. Douglass was back in Rochester when the news came. With his neighbors, he crowded into City Hall the next day for a service of mourning. Although not scheduled to speak, he was called on, and reaching far past mere admiration, he delivered a eulogy that along with countless others given by black Americans that day and in the years to follow, lifted the fallen martyr into sainthood.

From England, Julia Griffiths Crofts brought things back down to earth. When she heard of the assassination and the nearly fatal attack on her old friend Secretary of State William Henry Seward, she sent Douglass a stern warning: "I fear this [is] but the beginning of a new & cowardly style of vengeance." Douglass had written to her that he was thinking of moving back to Baltimore—of making the triumphant gesture of going home. Now, on April 28, she wrote, "Pray, my dear old friend, stay in the *Northern* states & leave Baltimore an untried field of labor—do not throw your valuable life away by venturing near the *old home*—think of *realities* and let those romantic visions remain in abeyance for the present. . . . Dreadful murders are never anticipated by the sufferers." Affectionately, and yet formally, Julia closed her letter: "With fervent prayers for your safety, I remain, as ever, unchangeably your friend, Julia G. Crofts."

Her advice heeded, Douglass, instead of moving to Baltimore, returned to his task as monitor of those who would prescribe for his people. White reformers looked sympathetically at the thousands who had fled hated masters, had left plantations and farms ruined by the armies that traversed them, or sought to reunite their families. These black refugees required basic shelter and food. Douglass, more sensitive to the tone with which the benevolence was to be bestowed than to the desperate need for assistance, recoiled from the reformers and placed optimistic faith in the freed people themselves.

It was no surprise to Douglass that all across the South black people were demonstrating a fierce interest in politics. They wanted all that emancipation meant was due them. The Bureau of Refugees, Freedmen, and Abandoned Lands, established in March, was soon called by everybody the Freedmen's Bureau. A great many white people intended that this agency should keep the ex-slaves in line, but black people saw it differently. The Bureau was theirs, and they came together in informal political meetings to insist that it work in their behalf. When they found that it did not, they went on to plan efforts—including strikes—that would force recognition of their right to live safely, to work on their own, and to be free of coercion by former masters seeking to reestablish control over a cheap labor force.

Senator Charles Sumner, for whom Douglass's admiration was great, had wanted the Freedmen's Bureau to be a separate department, of cabinet rank, that would protect the interests of the freed people. Cabinet status was not achieved, but in the spring of 1865, Douglass was not alone among black leaders in having great expectations that the Bureau's mission would remain what Sumner intended it to be. General O. O. Howard, the commissioner of the Bureau, had seen the successful working farms of the freed people on the Sea Islands of South Carolina, and there was reason to believe that he would support land redistribution across the South. To Douglass, the Bureau represented not an exercise in the patronizing charity of the several freedmen's aid societies (volunteer relief organizations, often church-related), but a commitment by the government to attend to the interests of his people.

In April 1865, as the Bureau was being organized, Douglass wrote to Senator Sumner asking for a post, not for himself, but for his son Lewis. There was genuine fatherly pride in his extolling of the veteran's battle record, but surely Douglass would not have been dismayed if the senator had sponsored himself as well as his son for a position in the Bureau. The hint had been made.

But Charles Sumner was so controversial that he could not have gotten an appointment of any kind for the even more controversial Frederick Douglass, and probably could not even have helped get Lewis into the Freedmen's Bureau. To begin with, the Douglasses were black; and the father was insisting, loudly, that blacks should have the same right to vote as whites everywhere in America. Nothing in Douglass's record would have suggested to anyone making appointments to federal agencies that he could be counted on to keep a bureaucrat's discreet silence when matters of principle arose—as, daily, they did arise for Douglass.

On May 2, 1865, in response to an invitation, Douglass sent a carefully drafted letter to the Reverend J. Miller McKim, head of the largest of the private relief agencies, the American Freedmen's Aid Society. Taking a lofty tone, he stated that he would attend a mass meeting at Cooper Union, but would not speak. "I ought to tell you frankly," he wrote, "that I have my doubts about these Freedmen's Societies. They may be the necessity of the hour . . . but I fear everything looking to their permanence. The negro needs justice more than pity, liberty more than old clothes." In his zeal to see that the freed people were not brushed aside as impotent victims, he overlooked the damage slavery had done to many of them—damage he had escaped. Wary of the missionaries, he insisted that his people needed "rights more than training to enjoy them." He was committed, as he had long been, to the proposition that all any black person needed was to be treated like any other person: "Give him Equality before the law and special associations for his benefit may cease."

He was as skeptical as ever of Christian charity, and his criticism of it was highly perceptive; such "special efforts, shall furnish an apology for excluding us." If the ex-slaves were to be turned, even if only in the thinking of other people, into a class of pathetic—and worse, impotent—victims, they might be left out of society's conception of who was included in the America that mattered. (Much the same thing, we might add, has happened to the homeless and very poor of the twentieth century.) Douglass was determined to prevent this: "My mission for the present is, to ask equal Citizenship for the negro—in the State: and equal fellowship for the negro in the Church."

When it came to the church, Douglass himself did not want to get caught inside the door, but, just as surely, he did not want anyone else kept out. Turning to places where he was more interested in guaranteeing admission for all, he called yet again for equal treatment on the streetcars and in the public schools. He was dubious about the private church-run schools that McKim's Christian missionaries proposed to open for freed people in the South. (Many of these schools, it turned out, became the South's black colleges, the immense value of which proved Douglass to have been wrong.) He was, he said, willing to support the schools only under "protest." Indeed, taken as a whole, the efforts of the church-sponsored American Freedmen's Aid Society seemed patronizing to him. To drive his point home, and to call once again for equal treatment for all, he proposed that if the missionaries were determined to bring light to a benighted region, they should consider their would-be black scholars "in common with all other ignorant and destitute people (white as well as colored) of the South."

In "reading over this note," preparatory to sending it, Douglass found it "pretty strong," but send it he did. As he had stated in the formal portion of the letter, he believed that until black people were accorded full equality, rather than charity, "we shall be a crippled people . . . grateful for crutches to hobble along with." Frederick Douglass, for one, intended to do no hobbling. He was, however, displaying a degree of callousness toward the displaced, destitute, and confused Southern farm workers—with whom he had once shared a field.

He was ignoring as well the opposition that freed slaves encountered when they began asserting themselves as independent citizens. Those who had successfully established farms of their own on lands abandoned by white planters fleeing Union armies found that when the former owners were given political pardons by President Andrew Johnson, they were given back their lands as well. The fact that the Freedmen's Bureau Act of March 3, 1865, mandated the distribution of these lands to the freed people did not deter Johnson. During the spring and summer, while Congress was out of session, the president reestablished in the states of the former Confederacy governments that were committed to white supremacy. White landowners and entrepreneurs were eager to reassert dominance over the region's black labor force. The freed people, equally eager for farms of their own, were told to make contracts with their former masters to work for wages, which they doubted would be paid. By the fall of 1865, a sobered Douglass had lost some of the confidence in progress that had prompted him to scold the Freedmen's Aid people.

In September he declared, "I once flattered myself that the day had happily gone by when it could be necessary for colored people in this country to combine and act together as a separate class. . . . I would have had them infuse themselves and their works in all the political, intellectual, artistical and mechanical activities and combinations of their white fellow countrymen. It seemed to me that colored conventions, colored exhibitions, colored associations of all kinds . . . had answered the ends of their existence and might properly be abandoned." Douglass had had to change his position because of the "persistent determination of the present Executive of the nation, and also the apparent determination of the portion of the people to hold and treat us in a degraded relation."

Douglass made this statement before a black audience gathered to honor him. The occasion was the dedication in Baltimore of the Douglass Institute. Located in the heart of the city, on Lexington Avenue a half block north of Monument Square, the Institute was intended to "promote the intellectual advancement of the colored portion of the community." A group of black men had persuaded white benefactors to buy and renovate a wartime hospital.* The result was a handsome cultural center, with a hall for concerts and lectures upstairs, an office for the black newspaper *The Communicator* on the first floor, several meeting rooms, and a dining room. On September 29, 1865, with the paint on the walls barely dry but a full-length portrait of Lincoln firmly in place behind the lectern, Douglass rose to speak.

Thanking the founders for the honor paid him in their choice of a name, he added, "When I left Maryland, twenty-seven years ago, I did

---

*The Institute always had black managers, but ownership of the building remained in white hands. In 1888, after one owner sued for its dissolution on the grounds that no profits had accrued, the Institute was closed and the building sold.

so with the firm resolve never to forget my brothers and sisters in bondage, and to do whatever might be in my power to accomplish their emancipation," and, he declared, "in whatever else I may have failed, in this at least I have not failed." The dedication of the Institute was a proud moment for Douglass, and he made it the occasion to evoke what was to be called, a century later, black pride. He knew full well how high was the wall that had been erected against that pride: "A Benjamin Franklin could redeem, in the eyes of scientific Europe, the mental mediocrity of our young white Republic, but the genius and learning of Benjamin Banneker of your own State of Maryland, the wisdom of Toussaint, are not permitted to do the same service for the colored race to which they belong."

He then went on to deride the only acceptance that a white world seemed prepared to extend. "Wealth, learning and ability made an Irish-man an Englishman. The same metamorphising power converts a Negro into a white man in this country. When prejudice cannot deny the black man's ability, it denies his race, and claims him as a white man. It affirms that if he is not exactly white, he ought to be." This sarcasm doing its work, Douglass pursued his point by pointing to a parade of black achievers: if "Robert Smalls, the gallant captain of the Planter" (a ship the slave sailor had piloted out of Charleston harbor under the noses of the Confederates), or "Garnet, Remond, Martin, Rock, Crummell," are credited with talent, "they are treated as exceptions," whose abilities come from intellectual association with white people. And, by implication, from genetic association as well: "They [of the white world] contend that [our] race, as such, is destitute of the subjective original elemental condition of a high self-originating and self-sustaining civilization." Forgotten had been the culture and accomplishments of Ethiopia, Egypt, Carthage, and the lands of Africa to the south; ignored too were Haiti and the emancipated islands of the West Indies. "Where under the whole heaven," he asked, "was there ever a race so blasted and withered" by three centuries of the "unfavorable influence" of "Christendom"? "Our history has been but a track of blood." Now, redemption was at hand. Here, at the Institute, he declared, "we who have been long debarred of the privileges of culture may assemble and have our soul thrilled with heavenly music, lifted to the skies on the wings of poetry and song. Here we can assemble, and have our minds enlightened. . . ."

The oratory rolled forth; there were subtle moments when Douglass sounded much as W. E. B. Du Bois was later to sound: "The mind of man has a special attraction towards first objects. It delights in the dim and shadowy outlines of the coming fact." Douglass had, too, that almost miraculously perennial African American faith that a great day would dawn. Closing with an image Langston Hughes would use in perhaps the greatest of his poems, Douglass pronounced that in this hall "the loftiest and best eloquence which the country has produced, whether of Anglo-Saxon or of African descent, shall flow as a river, enriching, ennobling, strengthening and purifying all who lave in its waters." A Negro had spoken eloquently of rivers.

If Douglass read the account of his triumph in the *Baltimore Sun* the next morning, he must have noticed an item immediately below it that was, in a sense, about him too. At a meeting the previous Thursday, white shipyard mechanics had voted to levy a fine of twenty dollars against anyone who worked in a yard employing black caulkers. The result had been "what might be called a general strike, the workers in all the yards having stopped work." Frederick Bailey, as a slave, had been a caulker in those yards, but in free New Bedford he had not been permitted to work at his craft. Over the years free blacks in Baltimore too had been driven from many of the skilled jobs in the yards, including carpentry, but black caulkers, perhaps because they were still slaves, had managed to stay on. Now, ironically, with emancipation and all of its bright promises, these black artisans were threatened with the loss of their valuable trade.

There is no record of one-time caulker Frederick Bailey going down to Fells Point in 1865 to see what he could do to help his brothers keep their jobs. A year later, after these determined black workers organized their own yard, they were "mobbed and beaten." Douglass was outraged, but did not rush to Fells Point to protest. Instead, he took the rhetorical highroad. "But a better day dawns," he told James Lynch, the author of the article exposing the violence. "Baltimore shall be released from this barbarism. Mad as we have seen her in the past, shaking aloft a bloody hand, and scowling wrath on the unprotected black mechanic and laborer, we shall yet see her at the feet of Eternal Justice." And then he urged Lynch, "Follow up the Work."

Back in the fall of 1865, an elegant Frederick Douglass had paused in Baltimore neither to enter the workingmen's dispute nor to imbibe the culture of the Institute. Instead, he moved on in his new crusade. Obtaining the vote for black people was his passion. His slogan, as pronounced in his dedication speech, was, "They gave us the bullet to save themselves; they will yet give the ballot to save themselves."

There was deliberate ambiguity in the latter "themselves"; the obvious word, which he sometimes used, was "ourselves," but Douglass contended that all loyal Unionists, white and black, needed the black vote to protect the nation. He and other radicals, such as Anna Dickinson and Theodore Tilton, held that leaving the freed men without the ballot would leave them in the absolute power of the old master class—and would leave the Confederacy in the hands of the Confederates. Douglass was persuaded that his people, with the vote, could not only protect themselves but rise to a new level. And in granting the vote to their black brothers, white Americans too would rise. The franchise was for him an emblem of a higher order of civilization.

That summer Douglass had written Lydia Maria Child, "I am just now deeply engaged in the advocacy of suffrage for the whole colored people of the South. I can see little advantage in emancipation without this." In public speeches, he stressed the same point: "Without the elective franchise the Negro will still be practically a slave. Individual ownership has been abolished, but if we restore the Southern States without this measure, we shall establish an ownership of the blacks by the community among whom they live." Hindsight makes it easy to charge that Douglass put too much faith in the vote as a guarantor of freedom, but his prediction that in the absence of a safeguard of some kind, whites within local communities would seize control of African Americans was to prove all too accurate.

It quickly became clear that things were not fitting into place for all of the freedmen. In the summer of 1865, in Washington, Charles came upon a thirteen-year-old Georgian boy, Henry Strothers, who had followed Sherman's army all the way to the capital and was now adrift in the city. On August 2, Charles asked his father if he could send Henry to Rochester. The answer was yes, and on the eighteenth, he put the boy on the train, with ten dollars in his pocket, instructions in his head about the complicated transfers from train to ferry to train, explanatory letters to the train conductors he would encounter en route, and a letter to Frederick Douglass, to whose home anyone in Rochester could direct him when he got off the train.

The plight of this orphan boy was evidence, if any was needed, that freed people, dislocated by the war, were badly in want of assistance, but there were distressing signs that help was not to be forthcoming from President Johnson. When a delegation of black veterans presented to the president a petition asking for assistance, they were told to go home to work for their masters—and prove they deserved to be free. Douglass was furious. The concept of having to prove one's right to be free was absurd. He was disgusted with Johnson, who simply was not doing the job Congress had given him to do. By the end of 1865, the president had completed the emasculation of the Freedmen's Bureau Act, restoring to pardoned Confederate landowners the acreage that this legislation had marked for redistribution.

In February 1866, the president vetoed a bill strengthening the Freed-

PHILADELPHIA   *2 4 7*

men's Bureau. That veto was sustained, but in April, his veto of the excellent Civil Rights Bill of 1866, which made illegal the systems of involuntary labor that were being introduced to replace slavery, was overridden; the radicals had fought back. They harbored no illusions that Johnson would work to enforce the rights of black people. Indeed, the newly organized state governments that Johnson had sponsored in the South had recently passed the restrictive Black Codes.

To protest these codes, the Convention of Colored Men met in Washington in February 1866, and chose a delegation to take their grievances directly to the president. Both Douglass and his son Lewis were members of the delegation. It was headed by George T. Downing, formerly a rich hotelkeeper in Newport, Rhode Island, and now the manager of the House of Representatives dining room, where he could give ear to the richest of political gossip, and by the same token, could keep the white radicals in Congress informed on the thinking of the black community, operating as a formidable lobbyist. At the delegation's meeting with Andrew Johnson, on February 7, Downing began with deferential greetings to "your Excellency"; Douglass, as chief spokesman, followed. He did not help his case by stressing how "noble and humane" had been Johnson's predecessor. Invoking patriotism, he said that just as Lincoln had called on the black people to join in the war to save the Union, so now they should be given the vote "with which to save ourselves." Johnson, with "repressed anger," replied that he had already "periled" more than he should have for the black people and he was not about to be "arraigned by some who can get up handsomely-rounded periods." He was, he guessed, willing to play Moses in leading a people from bondage to freedom, but, he declared, moving "very near to Mr. Douglass"—no one was sitting—the poor whites and the poor blacks had always been bitter enemies and if they were "thrown together at the ballot box" a race war would ensue.

When Johnson invoked the Jacksonian belief that the majority will should prevail, Downing reminded the president that in South Carolina, black people were the majority. Johnson chose to ignore this point, wandering off, instead, to the old concept, so doggedly held by Lincoln and many others, that the black people should emigrate. (He would have been delighted to load the first ship with the delegation he was addressing.)

The president knew that bringing up this idea was insulting to Douglass, who (save for a brief flirtation with James Redpath's plan for settlement in Haiti in the black days after *Dred Scott*) had fought colonization all his life. And Douglass countered with a suggestion that struck at the heart of all that was tragic in Andrew Johnson—and in his

South—saying that if poor black people and poor white people were given the vote, they would unite to achieve the justice denied them by the rich. Johnson, once an indentured servant learning the craft of tailoring, had himself smarted under such denial of justice, but he was not going to have a former slave tell him so. He had been willing to advocate black rights during the war as a way to affront rich Confederates of western Tennessee; he could not take the next step—a step back, the tailor thought—and stand equal with the caulker, achieving a true democracy. The meeting ended, according to Douglass, "not without courtesy," but with nothing more.

While their father ranged forth calling for the vote—for equality—the Douglass children were coming back together in Rochester. Rosetta's husband, Nathan Sprague, who had been on army duty at Hilton Head, South Carolina, while she awaited the birth of the first Douglass grandchild in 1864, rejoined her at her parents' home. Once the baby came, Rosetta, always glad to get out of the house, tended to her father's business in his office while her mother took "care of little Annie." Julia Griffiths Crofts, hearing the news, wrote to say how glad she was that "Rosa's baby" would "form a source of interest to Grandmama, as well as to Grandpa!" and be the focus for the family reunited on the hill, with its beautiful peach orchard. "Will all the sons and son in law come home now, I wonder? Are all the troops to be disbanded at once?" she asked in May 1865. She again counseled against a move to Baltimore and added, "Tell Mrs. Douglass I would give a great deal to see her & Rose nursing her baby & to have a good cup of tea with her & a nice 'Maryland biscuit.'"

The young men did come home, but not to pursue an education. Douglass seems never to have contemplated college for his sons; Rosetta completed her course in normal school, but did not go on to work for a college degree. Lewis, the most able and ambitious of the Douglass children, did not get the job in the Freedmen's Bureau that his father had sought for him, but, like thousands of other mustered-out war veterans, went on looking for a way to make a strong start in peacetime America. For a time, he was back in the Rochester house, while he taught school. Charles disliked leaving the excitement of Washington, where returning black troops were the pride of the swelling black population, but he too was disappointed in his quest for a permanent job and returned to Rochester. There he tended the family gardens, which amounted to a small farm, while planning to get back to Washington as soon as he could.

In 1866, Lewis and Frederick jr. went west, to Denver, to seek their fortunes. There, they had the help of their father's old friend Henry O.

Waggoner. Writing as one father to another, this wise observer commented on a letter of encouragement that Douglass had sent to Lewis: "As you have well said . . . he and his brother have *'a future'*, but you and I have very little more left than *'a past'*. Waggoner was rushing himself to the grave prematurely, but had his eye on what the younger generation should aspire to. (Years later, his own son, with Douglass's help, was to get a job in the American consulate in Lyons, only to have the promise of a truly bright future snuffed out by his early death.) Writing to his friend in 1866, Waggoner gave his assessment of the two Douglass boys: "Lewis is a young man of strong, clear good sense. He seems to drive right ahead at the object aimed at. Frederick, however, seems to be more cautious, reflecting, hesitating, and, as *you say, 'practical.'* I can easily discover that they are both very desirous of succeeding." Soon they were engaged in a venture that had the ring of postwar America's promise, the Red, White, and Blue Mining Company.

In his letter to Douglass, after speaking of his optimism for his region—"the great Pacific R R is progressing well"—Waggoner turned to politics. He reflected on "the 'clouds' which have risen in high places, and seem to darken the political horizon." Despite them, he wrote, he was "as firm as ever in the belief *that bad Men,* or devils, can do a very little more than cause a sort of vibration to the car of progress, in its onward March." The optimism of these black men who had so long been struggling for that progress was profound; their faith was secure even in the face of steadfast opposition not only from President Johnson but from a great many of their countrymen.

Douglass, determined to keep the engine of progress on the track by working for the vote, thought he had a splendid ally. In February 1866, he wrote to an old antislavery comrade, Elizabeth Cady Stanton, thanking her for "the launching of the good ship 'Equal Rights Association.'" Now, he thought, the women's quest for the vote would lead them to support also his efforts to gain the vote for the freed black people. There had been, he said, "no vessell like her . . . since Noah's Ark." Then, thinking about his metaphor, he added, "Without the presence of woman the ark would have been a failure. I have about made up my mind, that if you can forgive me for being a negro—I cannot do less than forgive you for being a woman."

In March, in New York, he met with her and Susan B. Anthony at the Beekman Street office of the *National Anti-Slavery Standard,* which, with the demise of Garrison's *Liberator,* Anthony regarded as the "only anti-slavery [that is, reform] paper left." However, a letter Anthony wrote to Ottilia Assing soon after this meeting sounded a note that was ominous for the new alliance. With respect to the proposed wording of a constitutional amendment that would guarantee the vote for blacks, Anthony said, "We have at least saved the nation from disgracing the Constitution by inserting the word *male.*" There was more than a hint here that if "without regard to sex" did not accompany "without regard to race" in the description of who might vote, Anthony would work to block passage of an amendment enfranchising black Americans.

In the summer of 1866, Thaddeus Stevens, of all people, demonstrated the fragility of the support for equal rights for African Americans. Along with Charles Sumner, Stevens was one of their most dependable allies in Congress, but when the radicals decided to hold a convention, Stevens urged Rochester Republicans not to send Douglass as a delegate. The convention was called to counter a National Union convention, which met in support of President Johnson and the white-supremacist state governments in the South and in opposition to ratification of the Fourteenth Amendment, which was designed to establish that black Americans were citizens. Stevens's personal ties to his black friends were real. After his death in August 1868, hundreds of mourners, including Charles Douglass, wept as his body was put on a train for the burial he had requested, in an unsegregated paupers' cemetery. But in 1866, Stevens urged caution.

Stevens knew Douglass was an outspoken proponent of black enfranchisement, which he thought to be an essential element of citizenship. He knew also that a great many Americans (including Douglass, despite his denials) equated full political equality with full social equality and, unlike Douglass, were repelled by the latter. Stevens was aware that radical congressmen who would be at the convention were afraid their white constituents would reject them in the fall election if they even appeared to support such equality.

At the meeting of Rochester Republicans, a staunch egalitarian, John Van Voorhis, moved that Douglass be selected—to the consternation of the chair and of the other delegate, already chosen, who said he would not serve with the black man. The motion was carried, and Douglass was elated. Ignoring the pleas of Stevens and others, he set off for Philadelphia with a declaration of independence: "*If* this convention will receive me, the event will certainly be somewhat significant of progress. *If* they reject me, they will only identify themselves with another Convention," the one that supported Johnson. He had laid down a challenge, and stopping in New York, he found that his good friend Theodore Tilton had taken it up. In his newspaper, the *Independent,* Tilton declared that Douglass must be seated. When other Republicans, who strongly disagreed, called on Douglass and asked him to go back to Rochester, he refused.

Douglass arrived in Philadelphia on the same day as two war heroes, Generals Benjamin F. Butler and Ambrose E. Burnside—and caused more excitement than either. The Johnsonian National Union convention had taken as its symbol of reunion the entrance, arm in arm, of South Carolina's Governor James Lawrence Orr, who had served in the Senate of the Confederacy, and Major General Daniel E. Sickles of the Union army. Now, Theodore Tilton, white, and Frederick Douglass, black, offered a different statement of fraternity when, arm in arm, they walked in the procession to Independence Hall. Stevens regarded the gesture as "foolish bravado," and Senator Henry Wilson of Massachusetts, heretofore friendly, shied away in embarrassed pique; of the dignitaries, only bluff, irrepressible (and totally unembarrassable) Benjamin Butler greeted the two cordially.

When they had formed ranks to march to the hall, Douglass's old friend Anna Dickinson had called out a warm greeting, and during the walk there were cheers from some of the Philadelphians, black and white, who lined the street. The enthusiasm of the welcome surprised even Douglass. His address to the convention later that day, demanding an end to Johnson's blocking of black rights, was so similar to the addresses of the other speakers that it seemed to demonstrate, by its very existence, that black people within the body politic need not be feared. This was the first time Douglass had been a full participant in an out-and-out political convention, as opposed to an antislavery or women's rights meeting. He saw the occasion—mistakenly, it turned out—as an augur of things to come.

Another of the speakers was Anna Dickinson. That a woman addressed such a meeting—one that was in grave danger of backing full political equality—was probably even more alarming to the fainthearted than that a black man had done so. Douglass proclaimed her to have been magnificent in her advocacy of the black vote. "Hers was a speech, not of a brilliant declaimer, but the solid logic of a statesman," he declared much later. At the time, he wrote to her, "My heart is full to overflowing"; and he thanked her for "rescuing the great convention of the unreconstructed states from moral and political destruction and of whirling, by your eloquence, its powerful ranks into the great Army of Equal Rights." The not-so-advanced radicals listening to the two wondered just what kind of egalitarian box they had allowed to pop open.

"The victory was short, signal, and complete," Douglass wrote in *Life and Times of Frederick Douglass,* long after he knew how incomplete it had really been. But on that day in 1866 he experienced nothing save exhilaration. He had been among great politicians as an equal. And, what was more, there had been a splendid private moment. As Douglass walked to the convention, he spotted Amanda Auld Sears and two of her children standing in the crowd along Chestnut Street. Shouting over the cheers, he asked what had brought her to Philadelphia—she now lived in Baltimore—and she called back, "I heard you were to be here."

19

Mount Vernon

EXHILARATED by the 1866 convention, Douglass wanted a place in the constructing of his new America. There was a world of work to do, and he was ready. As a citizen who had long championed full citizenship for his fellow black Americans, he was convinced that what they most needed was the vote. To achieve that goal the constitution he revered needed only an amendment. He was confident that he was the man in America who could best exemplify, in his person, the soundness of enfranchising his people.

This national goal pointed Douglass toward the nation's capital. But, curiously, he was a long time getting there. While at the 1866 Philadelphia convention, Douglass was invited to move to Alexandria to edit a paper that would address issues not only in Virginia but also in Washington, across the Potomac. John Curtiss Underwood, who made the proposal, was one of the most interesting figures in Reconstruction America. Born in upstate New York, Underwood had been a planter in Virginia since 1839. He was also an outspoken opponent of slavery. In 1864, he was named United States district court judge, and after the war he presided over some of the most important cases to be tried under the Civil Rights Act of 1866. He was also deeply involved in interracial Republican politics. Underwood's invitation was powerfully reinforced by Chief Justice Salmon P. Chase, at that time still an advocate of enfranchising the freed people, who urged Douglass to make the move.

Douglass declined, but his reason for doing so was not a shunning of position. Ever since he first spoke in Nantucket, he had been pushing himself further and further into the light. Now, in the heady days of

Reconstruction, he could reasonably assume that some high office would come his way if he remained in the public eye. Having so recently been chosen a delegate to the convention, he was optimistically (and unrealistically) hoping that high office would come to him not through a new job or an appointment, but through election, in upstate New York. In Syracuse, Samuel J. May was predicting "confidently" that Douglass would be chosen for either the House of Representatives or the Senate. This was not to be, and each time a post eluded him, he grew more hungry to obtain one. Recognition became almost an obsession; he always believed it was just around the corner.

In his letter to the judge declining the offer, with thanks, he made a strange assessment for 1866, a time when great political change was taking place in the South: "The sceptre has passed from Virginia," he wrote (in words that must have hurt Underwood, who, against great odds, was wielding a gavel in his home state with considerable effectiveness). "The loyal North and West must now and for sometime to come control not only the destiny of the Negro but that of the nation. . . . I am probably doing as much to disseminate sound views of human rights [here] as I could were I to place Baltimore between me and the North and West." Surely, curiosity alone would have made him want to see what ex-slaves like Robert Smalls in South Carolina and Tunis Campbell in Georgia, both already political leaders in their low-country districts, were up to. It is hard to know why Douglass, unlike so many other ambitious men in 1866, failed to move south, at least as far as Washington, until in a sense it was too late.

Perhaps one reason was his "fear" (reminiscent of Julia Griffiths Crofts's warning against Baltimore) that moving to Alexandria in "defiance of the old residents" would "render me an object of unusual hostility and . . . render me less likely to gain their attention than almost any other Colored man. It is not my duty to court violence or Martyrdom or to act in any manner which can be construed into a spirit of bravado." Only when he could be assured of the protection of "a more reliable man than our present Commander in Chief" would it be "safe for me to attempt to establish a press in Virginia."

Having shaken off the dust of the South nearly thirty years earlier, Douglass did not want to go back. Baltimore remained a barrier, not a home to be reclaimed. (When he addressed his old neighbors at the opening of the Douglass Institute, he had spoken of Baltimore as "your," not "our," city.) His reticence about the city made some of his friends curious. Ottilia Assing was once in Baltimore on her way to Washington and, she told her sister, "would have liked to take a couple of hours . . . if I could have found an old Negro who could locate the places where

Douglass spent his youth and later worked as a caulker in the shipyards. Since I could not find such an individual, I went straight through." An inquiry or two of porters in the railroad station could not bring back her friend's past. But for Ottilia, there was also the immense pull of the political present: "Gerrit Smith's wife thinks she has never known another woman with as much interest in politics as I." And she yearned to see her greatest friend in the center of politics in Washington, which "enchanted" her.

If Douglass was not in the capital, he was nonetheless concerned with national politics and acutely aware that President Andrew Johnson was blocking all that should go forward. In the December 1866 and January 1867 issues of the *Atlantic Monthly,* Douglass set out to assess Reconstruction. The question before the nation was: "Whether the tremendous war so heroically fought and so victoriously ended shall pass into history a miserable failure, barren of permanent results, . . . a strife for empire, as Earl Russell characterized it, of no value to liberty or civilization, . . . or whether . . . we shall . . . have a solid nation, entirely delivered from all contradictions and social antagonisms, based upon loyalty, liberty, and equality."

He was discussing the 1866 session of the Thirty-ninth Congress; this body has been accused of a good many things over the years, but seldom has anyone claimed that "it really did nothing." What Douglass meant by this impatient statement was that the Civil Rights Act of 1866 and the proposed Fourteenth Amendment did not give a "final" answer to his immense question. Curiously, he did not view the answer as coming from vigorous federal enforcement of those remarkable measures. Instead, this black abolitionist looked to states' rights, of all things: "The arm of the Federal government is long, but it is too short to protect the rights of individuals in the interior of distant states. They must have the power to protect themselves." The power would be theirs when African Americans had the vote and could elect sympathetic local and state officials.

Douglass's view of states' rights was of course different from that of "treacherous" President Johnson, who saw them as a means to perpetuate white supremacy. What Douglass contended was that the shadow of slavery was so strong that "when you add the ignorance and servility of the ex-slave to the intelligence and accustomed authority of the master" it becomes "impossible for the Federal government to wholly destroy" the supremacy of the latter "unless the Federal government be armed with despotic power, to blot out State authority, and to station a Federal officer at every cross-road." The answer, he contended, was "to give to every loyal citizen the elective franchise,—a right and power which will be ever present, and will form a wall of fire for his protection." He refused to acknowledge that this wall might be insufficient in the face of the murderous intimidation of black voters.

The freed people, while scarcely happy to hear a brother talk of their "ignorance and servility," appreciated any help they could get in protecting or enhancing their position, but Douglass's rhetoric in these articles, aimed at a white audience, demonstrates his distance from Southern black people struggling politically and economically. He and they did not speak the same language. Both did, however, share a faith in what the vote would bring. Until the Fifteenth Amendment was ratified in 1870, and, indeed, for the rest of his life, Douglass was committed fully to achieving and holding the power of the ballot.

In 1867, Douglass was vastly encouraged by the actions of the radicals in Congress: William D. Kelley, a Pennsylvania congressman, and Senator Henry Wilson of Massachusetts were "doing important service," he reported to Anna Dickinson in May. He rejoiced in his restored friendship with Wendell Phillips, who, along with the "bright and Young" Theodore Tilton, was "gloriously and beautifully" working for radical reconstruction of the South and for the vote for blacks nationwide.

If Douglass did not move south, neither did he sit home on the hill in Rochester. From there, in the cold December of 1866, Charles—married now to Mary Elizabeth Murphy ("Libbie")—reported that they had been grading the hill, as his father had asked, that his mother had "in safe keeping" Ticknor and Fields's check for a hundred dollars for the *Atlantic* articles, that "Mr. Remond took tea with me last night after calling on Mother," and that arrangements had been made for the Plymouth, Massachusetts, meeting scheduled for the nineteenth. Douglass, as usual, was hurrying from one lecture to another.

So busy was Douglass, in his almost perpetual traveling in behalf of black enfranchisement, that his family sometimes knew nothing about him save his itinerary. In the winter of 1867, he was gone for three months, lecturing in Pittsburgh, Louisville, and St. Louis. From Rochester, Nathan reported that he and Rosetta had left the South Avenue house and moved into town. Characteristically, Nathan was engaged in a quarrel over the title to the house, and not surprisingly, three-year-old Annie was bewildered by the move and "cries to go home." Rosetta, in a postscript, added that theirs was "a neat little house on a nice street," and went on to comment, "On one side of us are three American families and on the other two Irish families those I do not like so near still we need not have any trouble from them." The baby (Harriet, her second child) was well, she reported, and "Mother seemed in very good spirits [perhaps at the prospect of having her difficult daughter and son-in-law out of the house] and wished when I wrote to you to send her love."

In the new house on Pearl Street, life went as smoothly as it ever was to go for the couple, but downtown Nathan ran into trouble. "His hack," Rosetta wrote, "is the finest that can be found on either stand and he has a handsome span of greys." Nathan had bought it for $640, with a $200 down payment, from a seller willing to extend credit only because he knew Douglass. When Nathan went to the Osborn House to look for his first customers, however, he encountered "some trouble" from the other hackmen; "they insult him and threaten his hack. A Policeman came up and told him he had better go to the other stand in front of the Courthouse. . . . Nathan refused as the Mayor told him he could stand any place where hacks were allowed. The policeman said I shall have to move it then." Nathan was losing the argument when another policeman, who knew who his father-in-law was, interceded and let Nathan remain. But the taunts from the other hackman remained in the air as well. This news must have made Rosetta's father seethe: not only was his son-in-law a hackman, but he was being discriminated against. Soon driving a hack joined what was to become a long list of Nathan's abandoned enterprises.

Traveling in the Middle West in the spring, Douglass heard from Charles that he had been given a job in the Freedmen's Bureau—at a hundred dollars a month. Short of cash, Charles reported that he would leave his wife in Rochester and go on to Washington, lest he lose the post. Libbie would stay with his mother, who was ill again, until Frederick returned home; then she would board with Rosetta. From his desk at the Bureau, he reported in May that "Genl. Howard is very well pleased with me thus far and I mean to keep on his right side if possible." (The general later confided to Charles that when the other clerks protested the hiring of a black man, he had threatened to fire them and "fill their places with colored men.")

Charles was determined to make Washington his permanent home. The clerks in the Bureau, who had soon accepted him, had organized a building association and were having modest houses built for themselves. Wouldn't his father like to "invest $1800 in one of these?" Charles asked. This was one of a hundred times when the father and his children tilted over money. Douglass struggled between the roles of patriarch provider (with limited resources) and aloof mentor inspiring his children to be independent; they (and he) were never quite sure where they stood. This time Douglass told Charles to wait until his job was secure and he could make his own down payment on the house before bringing his wife to Washington.

Charles was boarding with James T. Wormley, Washington's famous black hotelkeeper (who sent a message that he hoped Douglass, too, would soon stop with him). Charles liked the capital, and was enjoying himself thoroughly: "I can get along better here than in Rochester and have more rights, for next year I will become a voter here." Congress had granted blacks the vote in the District of Columbia in 1866. Charles was fascinated by the first election in which black men voted in the District of Columbia and was delighted by the election of candidates favorable to black citizens, who were moving into the capital in huge numbers. There was even talk of the election of a black councilman. News like this was verification for Douglass of the value of the vote and of the benefits that would derive from it. Charles went on to report that newcomers from the South were impressed to find fellow black men in white-collar jobs. So was Charles Douglass, who held one: "I am the second colored man in the Government that has been given a first class clerkship," he proudly declared. In a later letter, he reported that Fred, now in the East, was working in a printing office and that Lewis, still in Denver, had been "chosen secretary of his mining company."

Charles may have been keeping his father up to date about his new career, but he was, in his sister's view, leaving his pregnant wife and his mother in the lurch. Rosetta told her father that Anna was deeply hurt that Charles had left home so abruptly, and added that every reaction of her mother's was exacerbated by her poor health. One day Anna fell while working at the sink, and Libbie had to help her to a couch. This was but one incident in a long illness that eventually ended in her death. Just what was wrong is difficult to determine; she experienced recurring episodes of what appear to have been progressively more severe neurological problems. Rosetta, without medical training but with considerable common sense, talked to another woman who claimed to have the same condition, "except that she has strong fits—but she is much better, she diets and does not over exert herself." That came to be about all that anyone could prescribe for Anna.

Douglass, home again in June 1867, received what one might guess would have been an irresistible invitation. "Your letter comes from *Easton, Talbot County, Maryland,*" he wrote in his reply, and began reminiscing: Easton had seemed "a grand seat of commerce, a center of law and learning." When he was about eight, he "had already learned to think that any slave that had been there was vastly superior" to one who had not. But then he recalled that his own stay in Easton had been in its jail, where "the gentleman who kept the house" had protected him from a lynch mob. The invitation was for the Fourth of July, and the thought of making an address that would reclaim his old slave county for himself and for future black voters must have had some appeal, but Douglass declined, saying he had already accepted an engagement to speak elsewhere, in a flowery letter obviously designed to be read to the audience. Had he wanted to go back, he could easily have rearranged his schedule or asked for another date. Once again, in some way his Maryland home powerfully repelled him.

Talbot County had not, after all, been for the Baileys a total "vision of human greatness." It was a place from which a lot of them had been sold south. In February 1867, Frederick Douglass had received a letter from his elder brother Perry—Perry Downs now—who had followed his wife to Texas after she had been sold by one of the Anthonys. Wanting to see his famous brother, Downs, with his wife and four children, started east. In New Orleans, Thomas Conway, one of the most helpful of the Freedmen's Bureau officials, arranged for the New York philanthropist James J. Spelman to pay for their trip to Rochester. When Frederick got back from his first venture into the South, a speaking tour in Virginia, he found his brother waiting to greet him in the house on the hill. Thanking Spelman, Douglass wrote, with a formality that cloaks his feelings, "The meeting with my brother after nearly forty years separation is an event altogether too affecting to describe." Such reunions of separated members of families, occurring across the land, were occasions of the "deepest pathos," he added.

Black Americans had a nicely literal understanding of the possessive in the term "Freedmen's Bureau." The agency was theirs—or should have been. In the summer of 1867, with black men attending state constitutional conventions and being elected to office in a region in which two years earlier they had been slaves, the energetic, growing black community in the nation's capital made a move to secure their Bureau. On July 18 a friend of Charles Douglass's, Carter Stewart, stopped at the Bureau office. He told Charles that he was there at the request of Ward Hill Lamon, who had been Abraham Lincoln's bodyguard and friend and knew Andrew Johnson as well. Having served as marshal of the District of Columbia for several years, Lamon had become well acquainted with the black leaders in the city. Now he wanted Charles to see, "in a quiet way," if his father would be interested in heading the Bureau. Charles immediately championed the idea, not, as he hastily explained to his father, because it would mean the firing of Commissioner Howard, who was treating him well, but because Frederick Douglass would be so good at the job.

While Charles was about his father's business, he received a letter from Rochester reporting the birth of his first child. In response he wrote, "I am very glad to hear the news and also that it is a boy. I know that Libbie is glad that it is over. I hope that she will come out all right. I have no fears that she won't, knowing she is in good hands and well cared for." He closed with, "My love to Libbie, Mother, and all. I am very well satisfied with the name [Charles Frederick] you have given the boy."

Black leaders soon stepped up their maneuvering to get Douglass appointed head of the Freedmen's Bureau. With encouragement from Charles, conveyed by Stewart, William Slade (the dignified, elderly steward of the White House, who was in a position to pick up a great deal of useful gossip) wrote an informal letter—on Executive Mansion stationery—urging Douglass to take the post. Commissioner Howard, he declared, "is a good man, yet one at the same time that lacks moral courage."

There was no job, short of president or pope, that Frederick Douglass would have liked better, and his reply was a shrewd attempt to draw President Johnson out. He said no to Slade, but left open the possibility that he might say yes if he could have the assurance of the president that the offer was a real one, that he was being appointed to help the "emancipated people" and not, he implied, to cover up Johnson's neglect of their needs. He would, he wrote, have been glad to serve "especially if [inquiringly in the conditional tense] I should be assisted—as I undoubtedly should be—by President Johnson."

Douglass knew how much Johnson disliked Howard, who reluctantly followed his orders, but remained a thorn in his side with constant reminders of the brutal mistreatment of black people in the South. He knew too that Howard was his son's employer, and had been generous in his encouragement. Ambiguously, Douglass added that he was declining the offer "without pronouncing at all upon the character and fitness of the present incumbent of the Bureau."

Risking that he might be playing into the hands of a rival, the Bureau's inspector of schools, John Mercer Langston—the two black leaders were to keep a wary eye on each other for the rest of their lives—Douglass urged that Johnson appoint a "colored man," and thereby become the "Moses of the colored race." He closed with personal regards to Mrs. Slade, just as Slade had asked after "Mrs. D."; the movers and shakers of the nation's black community, who sometimes, to Douglass's immense distaste, had to use the back stairs, all knew one another.

Douglass's letter was not the kindest he could have written with respect to Howard, whom he knew to be beleaguered and who was widely reported to be on his way out. But he realized that Slade would show it to the president, whom he suspected of concocting the whole appointment scheme. Andrew Johnson was sometimes a shrewd politician, and for him to approach a man about a post just below cabinet rank through one of his servants was not as bizarre as it sounds—not when both men were black. Slade, who must have been aware of his employer's negative attitude toward the use of the Freedmen's Bureau to serve the freedpeople, may have agreed to being intermediary in the hope that Douglass could subvert the president's tendency, as Charles put it, to "play mischief in all quarters."

Eager as Douglass was for black people to achieve any positions that could be seen as enhancing their standing, he was exceedingly doubtful about this offer. Johnson was clever enough to see the advantages of putting a gullible or flatterable black man in charge—nominally—while he undermined a government program designed to assist black people. Douglass was flatterable, but not always gullible. In his tough mind, he knew that Johnson would not give him, or any other black man, the job if doing so meant giving him also the power that should go with it; in his eagerness to have such power, he kept hoping he was wrong. Saying no, he left open the door.

But he certainly did not wait breathlessly, or even patiently, for a formal summons to the White House. Only three weeks after writing to Slade, who begged his "dear friend" to reconsider, Douglass told Theodore Tilton that he had turned down a proposition from the "White House" that he "take charge of the Bureau." In a cheerful, domestic letter to his friend, he reported that he was keeping a "hotel": Perry's family of six had been there (he had gotten them a cottage), Ottilia Assing still was, and the Joneses from Chicago had been to visit as well. Then, turning to the Bureau, he said that "among the strange things" of the summer had been the tantalizing offer that Slade had been sure he could *procure.* But "of course," he added disingenuously, "I refused at once to facilitate the 'Removal'—of a man so just and good as General Howard." Douglass went on to ask whether they had "reached the end of Johnson's wrath or may we look for more?"

Tilton and Douglass did not have to look very hard for examples of the president's callous disregard of the welfare of the freed people, which raised their own wrath against him. When the president's downfall began, Charles Douglass, in Washington, watched with undisguised pleasure. In February 1868, he reported to his father that this "city is in the wildest excitement in consequence of Johnson's last drunk. Before you receive this, Johnson will be impeached. Rumors are afloat that [Maryland governor Thomas] Swann's militia from Baltimore are preparing to march on this city to sustain Johnson." In Hoboken, Ottilia Assing was equally exhilarated at the prospect of a "coup." But Charles reassured his father: "Should such a course be adopted, we are ready to meet them."

The reporter for the *Morgenblatt* journeyed to Washington in the spring of 1868 for the impeachment trial of Andrew Johnson, and savored every delicious moment. She went to the Capitol with Charles Douglass, who delighted in identifying the participants in the drama. The actors, from the black janitors sitting in the halls with their feet propped up on the wall to the dubiously dignified chief justice, Salmon P. Chase, delighted the Berliner, who had never encountered such casual disregard of class at home. Chase, she reported, "burns with desire" for the presidency. When Chase, presiding over the trial, appeared to her to be setting the stage for acquittal, she called him a "traitor." Returning to the capital in July, she avoided a White House reception lest she have to shake President Johnson's hand and "be grinned at by him," but her hopes for the future did not flag. Ulysses S. Grant was sure to be elected in the fall, and just as surely, once the general was in office, things would go better for her friend. "Real radicals" with whom she had talked had persuaded her to overcome her skepticism and "trust and hope" in Grant's commitment to the cause of equality.

From Washington in July, Assing, Amelia Loguen Douglass (Lewis's wife, with whom she had traveled from New York), and Libbie and Charles Douglass set out on an expedition that tested the nature of that equality. They packed a "picnic" and took the excursion boat down the Potomac to Mount Vernon. Assing, a bit chagrined to be going to the shrine of a lifelong slaveholder, nevertheless took it all in—in her own inimitable way. Her long letter to her sister says not one word about the famous house, but fully describes the "minstrel" singers on board the boat; unlike such singers in New York, who were white people in black face, these were "genuine" Africans singing their own songs.

At Mount Vernon she encountered a gardener who claimed that as a fifteen-year-old he had been a slave of Washington, just before the general died. Assing thought he looked suspiciously young for his eighty-three years. As they talked, a fellow tourist came "marching in" and "pompously" said, "I must shake hands with you! I think there is no position more valuable and honorable in the country than to have been the slave of General Washington." In response, "the old man made a dubious face," and Assing, gleefully taking up the cudgels, pronounced, with Prussian authority, "And I will shake hands with you because we are so lucky to meet here on free soil." The gardener smiled; the other tourist left in a huff.

In full armor now, Assing reveled in the "notoriety" of being a white woman sitting on equal terms with the black couple and their strikingly handsome sister-in-law on the boat trip back to Washington. She "was addressed on the subject very curiously" and was eyed as "striking" from all directions by her fellow white tourists. Personally triumphant, she nonetheless had to report to her sister that though blacks enjoyed all civil rights, including, in the District of Columbia, the right to vote, "social prejudice is not at all gone."

Ottilia was in Rochester when she wrote the letter describing this excursion. She had gone there by train, riding through the hill country of central Pennsylvania before turning north. That summer of 1868 was one of contentment and hope. As Frederick worked at his desk in the morning, Anna was busy with her lush flower beds, while Ottilia strolled in the orchard, picking peaches. "I don't get to see a lot of the outside world," she told her sister, without a touch of regret. In the afternoon, she and Frederick would sit outside as she read Goethe and Feuerbach to him. They were also reading *Hard Times,* which she considered "one of Dickens's best novels" (and too little known), and Motley's *Rise of the Dutch Republic.* "I am so completely satisfied with life in the garden here that I don't have any desire for anything else, especially because this garden encloses a whole world for me." But it was a world neither she nor Frederick could make stand still: "Summer is passing for me as a green island of enchantment, with incomprehensible speed."

Among the things that Douglass wrote in the quiet of that summer was a tribute to another of his friends. A book was being published about Harriet Tubman, the fugitive slave—also from Maryland's Eastern Shore—who had made nineteen trips back into slave territory and led three hundred people to freedom, and Douglass was asked for a comment to be used in an advertisement. The famous orator, who was ambitious and could be vain, could also be generous—and eloquent: "I am glad to know that the story of your eventful life has been written. . . . You ask for what you do not need when you call upon me for a word of commendation. I need such words from you far more than you can need them from me, especially where your superior labors and devotion to the cause of the lately enslaved of our land are known as I know them. The difference between us is very marked. Most that I have done and suffered in the service of our cause has been in public, and I have received much encouragement at every step of the way. You on the other hand have labored in a private way. I have wrought in the day—you in the night. I have had the applause of the crowd and the satisfaction that comes of being approved by the multitude, while the most that you have done has been witnessed by the few trembling, scarred, foot-sore bondmen and women, whom you have led out of the house of bondage. . . . The midnight sky and silent stars have been the witnesses of your devotion to freedom and of your heroism. . . ."

The battle against slavery had been a time for heroic action. Now emancipation had been won, and black Americans, differing as much as Harriet Tubman differed from Frederick Douglass, struggled to persuade their nation to reconstruct itself in such a way as fully to include them. They could not know that the door would be slammed shut. Despite bitter resistance, the prospects for success seemed real, almost palpably so.

Charles Douglass, just a clerk, but an optimistic one, dreamed of great things for his father. In 1870, he wrote to Rochester that he had gone to the crowded visitors' gallery of the Senate to listen to the debate as Democrats, even resurrecting *Dred Scott,* tried to block the seating of Hiram Revels as a senator from Mississippi. It was a great day when the effort failed and Charles saw the black man escorted to the front of the chamber and sworn in. The new senator was "dignified, . . . but I fear . . . weak," Charles wrote his father. "If it could only have been Fred. Douglass," he mused, regretfully. But "the door is open and I expect yet to see you passing, not through as a tool as I think this man is, to fill an unexpired term . . . but from your native State." The son was telling the father to come to Maryland, to Washington—to walk through the door.

20
Kansas

THE TRIUMPH of a black man achieving a seat in the Senate, and another's dream of joining him there, did not hide the scars of slavery. Black Southerners were burdened with handicaps that the vote alone would not cure. To be sure, they had heard enough about politics from their white folks to know of its potency, and when the polls were open to them, they voted with an eagerness that was astonishing. But people like Harriet Tubman, with their memory of destitute, terrified fugitives, knew that a legacy of deprivation called for more than just the vote. Douglass, on the other hand, wanted to think that all his people needed to do was stand tall and free, that everything could be cured by codification of the equality of which he himself seemed the perfect emblem.

In the heady days immediately after the Civil War, with radicals pressing strenuously for the enfranchisement of black Americans, equality was in the air. And there was another group, long engaged in the antislavery struggle, who called for equality too—American women.

Their leader was Susan B. Anthony, an old friend of Douglass's, herself from Rochester. She was absolutely determined that the drive for the equality—the enfranchisement—of black men was not to be put ahead of the drive for women's suffrage. The two goals had to be reached as one. As Anthony's closest ally, Elizabeth Cady Stanton, put it, "I would not talk of negroes or women, but of citizens." Philosophically, Douglass was in complete agreement with this old friend.

In 1866, Wendell Phillips, Elizabeth Cady Stanton, and Theodore Tilton formed the American Equal Rights Association. They hoped to make it an organization that would incorporate both the energy and the goals of the American Anti-Slavery Society, which had as its postwar aim the achieving of African American equality, and those of the new National Woman Suffrage Association, in quest of the vote for women. Anthony, a founder of the suffrage association, agreed initially to be the corresponding secretary of the umbrella organization, but when Tilton, viewing conditions in the South, declared this to be "the Negro's hour" and called for achieving the vote for black males before trying to gain it for women, Anthony announced that she "would sooner cut off my right hand than ask the ballot for the black man and not for woman."

In December, Anthony called a convention in Albany, New York, to prepare for the lobbying necessary to persuade the New York legislature to amend the state constitution in a way that would not only end the prejudicial property qualification for black voters—which Douglass detested—but also enable women to vote. Douglass was present at the convention, and Anthony saw his participation as crucial to the work ahead. But he was sensing the dilemma that he would soon have to face. Susan B. Anthony had every right to claim that women were equal to men—or, as in her own case, even superior—and that they were capable of voting and holding office. But she, who had been steadfast in her opposition to slavery, crossed the line into racism when she said that women were more intelligent than the black men who, she now saw, were competing with her and her fellow women for the vote.

That competition resulted in the one of the saddest divorces in American history. Since Seneca Falls, if not earlier, the antislavery movement and the women's rights movement had been seen by a good many people as one. Opposition to slavery, these perceptive observers remembered, also implied achieving equality for people once they were no longer slaves. Now a breach was in the making, and it has never fully healed. The two movements have run parallel courses at times since, but they have never been joined as they were before the quest for the vote during Reconstruction.

In 1866, the prospects for gaining the vote for black men, particularly in the South, looked fairly good. Radicals in Congress thought the only way black Americans in the former Confederacy could protect themselves was by having the power that the vote brought. Galling as it was to Douglass, there was also the argument that had been so persuasive in the debate that resulted in passage of the Civil Rights Act of 1866—that if black people in the South were not given protection and rights, they would move north. Douglass was pragmatic enough to accept even that reasoning if it would facilitate black enfranchisement. But at the Albany convention, he began to realize that although white men might reconcile themselves to the idea of black men coming to the polls, particularly if not too many black men were in the neighborhood, they were not yet up to facing the threat of having half the population—the women—elbowing their way in.

Offering no excuse, Douglass left the convention, but his departure did not go unnoticed. "Not one lisp from you," wrote Anthony, "since you suddenly and mysteriously disappeared at Albany—but to the *Work.*" The work was the lobbying of the New York legislature, and the chastised student knew he must do as he was told. "Will you go the first week in January," Anthony asked, or rather, instructed. "And if so, which department will you take?" Douglass, along with Stanton and Parker Pillsbury, was being sent to talk to legislators, and to give no quarter. They needed "*grand* utterances," she continued, "so *prepare* this *bombshell.*"

Another state also needed attention. Kansas had come into the Union in 1861 with a constitution that permitted women to vote on school matters. In 1867, a campaign was mounted to amend the constitution to extend the full franchise to women and to black people. Here was the opportunity for the two causes to move together toward a victory. Instead, they divided. The suffragist leader Lucy Stone and her husband Henry Blackwell went out ahead of Stanton and Anthony, still busy in New York. They soon discovered that a good many Republicans in Kansas wanted to drop the campaign for women's suffrage on the grounds that it endangered the effort to get the vote for black citizens. The editors of the *Weekly Monitor,* the Republican paper in Fort Scott, knowing the conservative county board was vigorously opposing black suffrage, ran a powerful editorial in its support, but did not even mention women's suffrage. Horace Greeley in the *New York Tribune,* Theodore Tilton in the *Independent,* and Wendell Phillips in the *National Anti-Slavery Standard* all similarly dismissed the women's claim as they called for votes for black men.

The Republicans were abandoning the cause of votes for women; in October, the *Weekly Monitor* declared that it would have been logical for woman to vote if she did not already hold a "nobler position than she could possibly acquire as a voter." Anthony and Stanton stumped the state attempting to counter such arguments. In Fort Scott, male Republicans conceded that Stanton had made a good speech for "impartial suffrage." Sharing a page in the *Weekly Monitor* with a strong editorial endorsing black suffrage was a description of Stanton as a "jolly looking woman, fat and probably forty." Ridicule, as usual, was at work. Unfortunately, the supporters of women's suffrage countered with ridicule of their own. George Francis Train, a Democrat, joined in the campaign with an assurance to a crowd that the vote for women was sure to come:

"... thank God, we are now out of the woods, (laughter) in this suffrage question, and Sambo must wait a while for Sarah, (cheers and laughter) for the women are bound to win on the fifth of November." After many compliments to Anthony, the flamboyant Train summed things up: "Women first and negro last, is my slogan." In closing, he described himself as "your modest, diffident, unassuming friend, General Geo. Francis Train, the future President of the United States. (Loud laughter and cheers for several minutes)."

Champions of Anthony and Stanton insist that they were right to accept any ally, but Train's racist opposition, which was echoed by many others, cannot have been unknown to them. Anthony's argument that surely the vote should not be denied to intelligent women while being given to black men—with the implication that the men were lesser in intellect—may have been subtler in tone, but it was scarcely less racist than Train's diatribes. The result, in November, was that neither women nor black men gained the vote. In one sparsely settled county, Republican legislators won by 300 votes, while black suffrage lost by 100 votes and female suffrage by more than 150 votes. Douglass, Tilton, and other radicals now saw the federal government as their best hope, provided a sympathetic man could be voted into the White House.

General Ulysses S. Grant was the Republican candidate for president in the fall of 1868, and the freed people looked to him. Douglass, for one, counted on Grant to support universal suffrage for black men, particularly as he was sure to win the votes of those black men who were already voters in the reconstructed South. When Douglass was invited to a women's suffrage meeting in Washington in the fall of 1868, he declined. Irritated, the organizers of the meeting declared Douglass ungenerous, given the support his antislavery cause had received from women. Josephine Griffing, who had run a camp for destitute black refugees in Arlington, Virginia, during the war and whose commitment to the cause of African Americans was undoubted, was given the role of persuading him to change his mind.

She failed. His letter to her read: "I am impelled by no lack of generosity in refusing to come to Washington to speak in behalf of woman's suffrage. The right of woman to vote is as sacred in my judgment as that of man, and I am quite willing at any time to hold up both hands in favor of this right. It does not however follow that I can come to Washington or go elsewhere to deliver lectures upon this special subject. I am now devoting myself to a cause [if] not more sacred, certainly more urgent, because it is one of life and death to the long enslaved people of this country, and this is: negro suffrage. While the negro is mobbed, beaten, shot, stabbed, hanged, burnt and is the target of all that is malignant in the North and all that is murderous in the South, his claims may be preferred by me without exposing in any wise myself to the imputation of narrowness or meanness towards the cause of woman. As you very well know, woman has a thousand ways to attach herself to the governing power of the land and already exerts an honorable influence on the course of legislation. She is the victim of abuses, to be sure, but it cannot be pretended I think that her cause is as urgent as . . . ours. I never suspected you of sympathizing with Miss Anthony and Mrs. Stanton in their course. Their principle is: that no negro shall be enfranchised while woman is not. Not considering that white men have been enfranchised always and colored men have not, the conduct of these white women, whose husbands, fathers and brothers are voters, does not seem generous." The unconscious sense that the male comprehension of a problem was the correct one pervaded Douglass's letter to Josephine Griffing. He spoke with the voice of absolute patriarchal assurance. But patriarchal or not, his was a realistic appraisal of the realities of 1868.

A good many feminists—Anna Dickinson, Ottilia Assing, and Amy Post among them—were castigated for being untrue to the women's movement because they did not follow Anthony and Stanton. Women such as these disagreed with the two great leaders not because of timidity or servility, but because they believed, however reluctantly, that for the time the vote for women would have to wait; the argument that Douglass articulated in his letter to Griffing seemed to them unassailable. They could not know how brief would be the empowering of Southern black men by the Reconstruction grant of the vote to freedmen or foresee that it would take half a century to achieve the right of women to vote. Immediately upon the ratification of the Fifteenth Amendment, early in 1870, Douglass called for an amendment enfranchising women. Stanton, Anthony, and their National Woman Suffrage Association may have opposed the Fifteenth Amendment, but its very existence made the logic of enfranchising women unassailable, at least in the long run.

Although Douglass could not stop to take women into the brave new world in 1868, he had high hopes for black Americans as he campaigned for their Republican party and its nominee, General Grant. Lincoln's assassination and the disasters of Andrew Johnson's administration, it appeared, had been but unnatural barriers to the fulfillment of the true promise of the North's victory. A member of the Carpenter family wrote from England in 1868 that "one cannot altogether regret" your "horrible war," for "so much good has come of it." When the nation in November elected the greatest hero of that war, the hopes of black leaders like Douglass would have been hard to overestimate.

In February 1869, nine of those leaders, Douglass among them, announced that they would soon be publishing the *New Era* "in the interest of the colored people of America; not as a separate Class, but as a part of the WHOLE PEOPLE." Sending in his $2.50 for a subscription, Douglass's friend Henry O. Waggoner wrote from Denver that he rejoiced, as he had a quarter of a century earlier "on seeing your name" on "the old North Star." Holding Douglass to his task, Waggoner reminded him that "words are only valuable as they conduce to action."

When President Grant took office, black leaders were hoping for a good deal of action. They were pleased by Grant's unequivocal call for ratification of the Fifteenth Amendment in his inaugural address. More personally, they were hoping to be recognized with presidential appointments. In particular, it was assumed that a black man would be appointed minister to the black republic of Haiti. These leaders, including Douglass, each aspiring to the post, one after another claimed disinterest, and while waiting to hear who would get the nod, politely deferred to their brothers' claims. But when the fairly obscure Ebenezer D. Bassett of New Haven was chosen, some were highly discontented. George T. Downing asked Senator Sumner, chairman of the Senate Foreign Relations Committee, to urge that Bassett be withdrawn as nominee in favor of Douglass. When the request went to the White House, Grant, laconically and accurately, reported that he was having too much trouble getting other appointments confirmed to withdraw one that seemed safe, and refused. After Bassett's appointment was confirmed, Douglass sent him warm congratulations and wrote to Downing denying that he had ever sought the post.

Even with no presidential appointment in the offing, Douglass was spending more and more time in Washington. (Back in Rochester, Rosetta returned with her family to the South Avenue house, to be with her mother.) In January 1869, Douglass presided over what Philip S. Foner has called the "first truly *national* convention of the Negro people in the United States." There were delegates from the reconstructed South as well as from the old free black groups in the North. When Douglass confronted the needs of this national gathering, he was turning all of his attention to the political future of black Americans, and in so doing he was obscuring—perhaps inadvertently, perhaps not—the energy of a nascent black labor movement and the readiness of black men to identify themselves as workers. For Douglass, the goal was always to rise above what Thoreau has called this "mean moiling life." There is some evidence that he took pride in his skill as a caulker, and even in the physical strength he had gained in part from his work in the fields and on the docks, but when he spoke of his days as a worker, his aim was to describe how he had been denied the opportunities for loftier work that were open to white men, rather than to suggest a solidarity with other black artisans or manual laborers. His workingman friends in New Bedford had been attractive to him because they were using their minds to reach a bit into another realm, the realm of learning that so powerfully drew Douglass himself.

Douglass believed that to organize black unions was to capitulate to the racism that he saw in too abundant evidence in the general American labor movement. That attitude had recently struck close to home; in 1869, his son Lewis was accused of being a scab. Lewis, back from Denver, was working in the Government Printing Office, and the union claimed that he had obtained the job "improperly" and had had no regular apprenticeship. "It is alleged," Douglass told a Rochester audience in August 1869, "that he is an improper person to be allowed to work; that he has . . . worked at a lower rate of wages than that fixed upon as the proper one by the Printer's Union." The father (who had overseen Lewis's training on his newspaper in Rochester before the war) was furious; his son, he told the audience, "is made a transgressor for working at a low rate of wages by the very men who prevented his getting a high rate. He is denounced for not being a member of a Printer's Union by the very men who would not permit him to join such Union" simply because he was black. "Suppose it were true that this young man had worked for lower wages than white printers receive, can any printer be fool enough to believe that he did so from choice?"

Lewis, who had "stood on the walls of Fort Wagner with Colonel Shaw," had, back at the war's end, "week after week, month after month . . . sought work, found none, and came home sad and dejected. I had," his father recalled, "felt the iron hand of Negro hate before, but the case of this young man gave it a deeper entrance into my soul than ever before." Now, in Washington, Lewis was being publicly criticized for union-busting practices. Where are we, asked Douglass (who pointed out that he employed white men on his newspapers), when "a young man of good character . . . [is] unable to find work at his trade because of color or race?"

Douglass wanted racial barriers ended, but more and more, he was driven to working from behind them. He was becoming a part of the growing, self-conscious African American establishment of the capital, even though he steadfastly refused to see himself as having been segregated into this group. Indeed, when the *New Era,* of which he was a sponsor, began publication in January 1870, its offices were in Uniontown, a part of the District of Columbia across the Anacostia River; the number of black citizens in Washington was growing, and a good many of them were building houses there. The paper, intended to be a weekly journal for "Colored America," had J. Sella Martin as editor. Its first issue carried a full account of a black labor convention held in Washington early in December 1869. George T. Downing, the leading black citizen of the capital and one of Douglass's co-publishers, had been in the chair, and Lewis Douglass had been elected one of the meeting's four secretaries.

In his various newspapers, Douglass had covered the meetings of black workingmen, but he had done so to record the group activity of black Americans, to demonstrate the equality of these groups with white volunteer associations, rather than to endorse the concept that it was as laborers that black Americans should take their stand. He despised the fact that he had been part of the enforced-labor system that slavery was, and still felt somehow that to identify oneself as part of a laboring class was to perpetuate one's inferiority. But the vast majority of his fellow black Americans were manual laborers, and many of them were willing—indeed, proud—to acknowledge that identity. These men were different from Douglass, with his ceaseless, eloquent rights-of-man insistence on the destruction of any barriers that would prevent a black man from attaining any position open to a white one. His goal was opportunity for the individual, not the collective action advocated by the laborers at their 1869 convention who resolved "that we recommend the establishment of co-operative workshops, land, building and loan associations among our people as a remedy against their exclusion on account of color and as a means of furnishing employment, as well as protection from the aggression of capital, and as the easiest and shortest method of enabling every man to procure a homestead for his family. . . ."

At the meeting, Lewis Douglass proposed another resolution, which was quickly passed. It called not on the government, or on reformers, but on the "colored union" to press for equal recognition of colored mechanics and laboring men in the workshops of the country. Black workers were not leaving to others the struggle for a chance to work, and Lewis, now a printer in Washington, had workers in his own family in mind. Charles wrote to his father a few weeks later, "Fred is fighting the Printers in one of the city offices, and he has been promised that he shall commence work today, he having secured a card from the Typographical Union in this city." But Charles's report turned out to be optimistic, and as he had done ever since his return from the West, Frederick Douglass, Jr., struggled on to obtain that union card. (In 1873, both Lewis and Frederick would join their father's newspaper.) Charles, too was in a precarious position. In the spring of 1869, he had been fired from the Freedmen's Bureau when, despite the supposed ascendance of the radicals, its staff was drastically cut.

While his sons fought to establish themselves, Frederick Douglass was celebrating an event that he thought would be the salvation of his people. Nothing since emancipation itself was as important, he believed, as the ratification of the Fifteenth Amendment. Now his people would not need help from such sources as the charitable freedmen's aid societies and the Freedmen's Bureau. Empowered as voters, as full citizens, they would, he chose to believe, be able to go it on their own.

On March 20, ten days before Grant formally announced the Fifteenth Amendment to be in effect, Ottilia Assing wrote to her sister, "In politics things are more felicitous than ever; . . . the radical equal rights of the Negro have been secured through the ratification. . . . A Negro has been appointed to West Point. . . . Grant is doing more than he promised and is loved by the radicals and by the masses. . . . The next thing to be undertaken is to improve the position of the Indians and the Chinese, whose circumstances are still awful." She too regarded the Fifteenth Amendment as the capstone of the revolution. In city after city, black citizens celebrated what they saw as a culminating victory. On April 20, 1870, Douglass was in Richmond for the Colored National Labor Union salute to the new era, and in May, in splendid voice, he addressed a vast rally in Baltimore's Monument Square. In New York, in April, at the American Anti-Slavery Society's annual meeting, Wendell Phillips declared the work done, and the venerable group—its "purpose . . . achieved and more"—disbanded. Douglass, who was staying in Hoboken with Assing, was one of the "courageous old guard" who attended the sentimental occasion. Garrison was absent, but Abby Kelley Foster, Stephen S. Foster, Lucretia Coffin Mott, and many of Douglass's other old comrades in the thirty-seven-year-old society were there. All shared the euphoric hope that the former slaves were now in a safe position, ready to move ahead.

On September 1, 1870, the *New Era* ran an announcement that Frederick Douglass had bought a 50 percent interest in the paper; the following week the first issue of the *New National Era* appeared. He was once again Mr. Editor, and as the word added to the title suggested, he had in mind holding the nation to its commitment to a new age of equality.

21

1507 Pennsylvania Avenue

IN THE LATE-SPRING NIGHT, "flames lit up the horizon for miles around and cast lurid shadows on the surrounding trees, rendering their foliage intensely beautiful." The Douglass house was on fire. Rosetta "was awakened by the odor of smoke and a bright light in her room" and, rousing Nathan, ran from the house. With smoke already filling the halls, he awoke his mother-in-law and his three older children, snatched up the already coughing baby, and got them all out. Running to the barn, which was close to the house, Nathan managed to lead the horse from its stall even though the loft above was the fierce torch that had carried the fire to the house. A cow died, and all the "carriages, sleighs, harnesses, farming implements, &c. were destroyed."

Guided by the light in the night sky, a fire company raced up the South Avenue hill. The water supply proved maddeningly and totally inadequate, and the firemen joined the family and neighbors in hauling whatever they could out of the burning house. Books—an astonishingly large number of them—pictures, and furniture were rushed into the yard. Even the piano was pushed and shoved down the porch steps. (Left inside—and lost—were the only existing complete runs of the *North Star, Frederick Douglass' Paper,* and *Douglass' Monthly,* as well as hundreds of personal letters.) By morning, nothing remained of the lovely house on the hill but charred bricks, foundation stones, and ashes; the gardens and some of the trees of the orchard were badly scorched. The morning paper stated flatly, "The fire is attributed to an incendiary."

The telegram of June 3, 1872, to Douglass in Washington said that there had been a fire and the family was safe, but did not say where they

With sentiments of highest regard

Very truly yours

Frederick Douglass

Douglass gave copies of this portrait to admirers.

Facing page, Rosetta Douglass. *Above*,
Anna Murray Douglass.

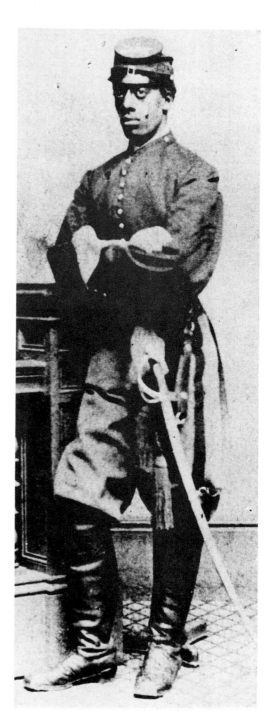

Above, Lewis Henry Douglass, sergeant major of the Fifty-fourth Massachusetts Volunteers. *Right*, Private Charles Remond Douglass.

Frederick Douglass, Jr.

The Douglass house on A Street, on Capitol Hill, Washington, D.C. The family is gathered in front.

When Douglass was president of the
Freedman's Savings and Trust Company,
his office was in this building, which
stood across Pennsylvania Avenue from
the White House, on the east corner of
Lafayette Square.

Facing page: Cedar Hill, *top,* the Douglass home in Anacostia, across the river from Washington; *below,* Douglass sits at his desk in the library.

Above, Douglass's violin sits on top of the piano in the west parlor, or music room; the portrait on the easel is of Wendell Phillips. In Douglass's bedroom, *left,* his bed stands to the left; a dumbbell lies on the floor; a shirt and suspenders are on a chair. *Below,* the table in the dining room is set for four. Most of the furniture and pictures in Cedar Hill are as they were when Douglass lived there, from 1878 until his death in 1895.

Helen Pitts Douglass.

Frederick Douglass.

Frederick and Helen Pitts Douglass at Niagara Falls on their honeymoon trip, 1884. Below is the Haitian pavilion over which Douglass presided at the Chicago world's fair, 1893.

Three more woman opponents of slavery. *Above left*, Elizabeth Cady Stanton, staunch ally, sometime foe, and always fascinating friend; *above*, Harriet Beecher Stowe, who supported Douglass at a crucial moment in his quarrel with William Lloyd Garrison. These two portraits hang at Cedar Hill. Sarah Remond, *left*, sister of Charles Lenox Remond, Douglass's fellow black abolitionist, was herself a forceful antislavery orator and the Douglasses' host in Rome in 1887.

Douglass in his seventies with Joseph Douglass, who, to his grandfather's delight, was a concert violinist. *Facing page*, Ida B. Wells, leader in the antilynching crusade, who inspired Douglass to return to battle.

The house at Highland Beach, south of Annapolis, Maryland, where Douglass planned to spend his summers. He died before it was finished.

The view from the upstairs window, which would have been Douglass's, looking toward the Eastern Shore—and back to his boyhood.

had gone. When he arrived in Rochester twenty-four hours later, to the mocking accompaniment of a drenching rain, he hurried up Mill Street to the Congress Hall Hotel to dry off, rest, and plan how, in the morning, he would find the family and face the spectacle of his ruined house. At the desk, the clerk told him the hotel was full; when Douglass went around the block to the Waverly House, he was again told that no rooms were available.

Frustrated and furious, Douglass assumed that he was being told the hotel had no rooms for a black person, and blurting out his name, demanded that he be accommodated. The clerk, realizing he had the town's most famous man on his hands, still insisted that the hotel was full, but offered to try to move guests about to accommodate Douglass. Embarrassed by the possibility that perhaps it was not racism after all that was keeping him from a bed (it turned out later that "four colored people" from a circus company were at the Waverly), Douglass declined the offer and blustered out. He splashed his way to the police department to learn where the family was, and then walked out to South Avenue, to join them at a neighbor's.

Characteristically, Douglass recorded only a trace of his private grief: when he and his family went back up the hill the next morning, the scarred skeletons of the trees "planted by my own hands and of more than twenty years of growth" were what most saddened him. The rest of his account of the fire, in the *New National Era* (an account which the *Rochester Union and Advertiser* found to have been written "in bad temper") was an indictment of public injustice. His slights at the hotels loomed as large as the arson that he, and the fire company, took to be the cause of the fire. Even in one of the "most liberal of northern cities . . . that Ku Klux spirit . . . makes anything owned by a colored man a little less respected and secure than when owned by a white citizen," he wrote. No one denied that "incendiarism" was the cause of the fire, but the *Rochester Union and Advertiser,* acknowledging that Douglass blamed "Northern colorphobia," claimed on June 17 that "testimony thus far obtained points strongest to colored persons as the guilty party." Not surprisingly, the arsonist was never identified.

Douglass reported that $11,000 in securities had burned (he later found the identifying numbers of these and was able to effect recovery) and that a monetary loss of $4,000 to $5,000 remained after he received payment on his insurance. He said nothing of the friendship of the Posts and Porters, or of the neighbors who had carried out the lamps and chairs— nothing of almost twenty-five years of an extraordinarily rich life in Rochester.

Weeds took over Anna's flower beds; brush choked the orchard. Rejecting the pleas of friends, including Susan B. Anthony, that he rebuild, and turning his back on the town that had been home for a quarter of a century, Douglass moved his family irrevocably to Washington. Writing about the fire for his Washington paper, he asked his readers to accept his "apology for absence from my post of public duty, which after all will not be long." His *New National Era* firmly supported the Republican party; its masthead proclaimed, "Frederick Douglass, Editor; Douglass Brothers, Publishers: For President, U. S. Grant."

Even more enticing for Douglass than this entrance into the journalistic world of the capital was his side-door entrance into federal service. President Grant had been engaged in a struggle with the Senate in general, and Senator Charles Sumner (chairman of the Senate Foreign Relations Committee) in particular, over the annexation of the Dominican Republic, then usually called Santo Domingo. The republic occupied the eastern two-thirds of the island of Hispaniola, which it shared with Haiti. Grant envisioned the island as a haven for black Americans, who, he knew all too well, were subjected to increasing oppression in the Southern states. Unfortunately, some of his subordinates and supporters of the annexation plan saw it mainly as a way to open the door to lucrative real-estate transactions. Senator Sumner regarded the whole project as sordid; for the United States to export its racial problems to a Caribbean island instead of guaranteeing the rights of African Americans within the Southern states would be, he thought, to declare moral bankruptcy.

His opposition to the treaty designed to bring about annexation eventually cost him his chairmanship of the Foreign Relations Committee— fellow Republicans loyal to the president voted him from the post—but in June 1870, Sumner persuaded the Senate to reject the treaty. At this point, David Donald has written, "annexation was surely dead, and everybody knew it except Grant and Sumner"; Sumner continued to excoriate the president for his determination to pursue annexation, and Grant, rising to the bait, appointed an investigative commission to visit the island. Its members were former senator Benjamin F. Wade of Ohio, Andrew D. White, the president of Cornell University, and, surprisingly, Sumner's old friend Samuel Gridley Howe of Massachusetts. And to further embarrass Sumner, who had long had cordial relations with his fellow abolitionist, Douglass was named the commission's secretary.

Douglass gave his support of annexation in defiance of Sumner, for whom he had great respect. Sumner, disappointed at the desertion, argued fervently that black citizens should be protected and encouraged to succeed right at home, not shipped off to the Caribbean. It would have been entirely consistent for Douglass to feel precisely the same way, but the attraction of a presidential appointment, even to a secondary post as secretary to the commission, was so alluring that he simply looked past Sumner's objections, choosing to see the presidential assignment as an honor.

Before embarking with the commissioners from the Brooklyn Navy Yard in January 1871, Douglass stopped in Hoboken to visit with Ottilia Assing. She reported to her sister that he was "enchanted at the prospect of visiting a tropical island."

When the commissioners returned with, as predicted, a report favoring annexation, the Senate, just as predictably showed no interest in reconsidering it. President Grant, still trying to save the doomed treaty, gave the commissioners a dinner party at the White House. Frederick Douglass was not invited. A good many black leaders were insulted, and the next year, Horace Greeley, on the campaign trail as the presidential candidate of the Liberal Republican and Democratic parties, chastised Grant, the hero of black Americans, for his hypocrisy. This was the kind of insult that cut Douglass to the quick (as had the steward's refusal to serve him in the main dining room of the ship returning from Santo Domingo), but, publicly, he was at pains to say he took no offense. "There is something so ridiculous about this dinner affair," he wrote Charles Jervis Langdon, an upstate New York friend (and Samuel Clemens's brother-in-law) in a "private" letter—that was widely published. He would have been happy to be invited, he added, but Grant had as much right not to invite him to his table as Langdon had to welcome him to his dining room thirty years earlier.

This turning of the other cheek, Douglass calculated, would make Grant grateful. To ensure that the gratitude was of sufficient magnitude to produce the important appointment he so badly wanted, he campaigned hard for Grant's reelection in 1872. Douglass's stalwart loyalty to the Republican party separated him from many of the reformers, such as his old Rochester neighbor Samuel Porter, with whom he had worked in the antislavery cause. Sumner was not the only major national figure to join the Liberal Republicans, and Douglass had to work hard to counteract abolitionist Horace Greeley's efforts to bring in black voters. By winning the war that ended slavery, Grant had become a hero to black Americans second only to Lincoln, but Greeley's antislavery credentials were in good order. Grant's attorney general, Amos Akerman, who had fought the Ku Klux Klan firmly and with some success in 1871, had been driven from the cabinet by the combined pressure of railroad interests and white supremacists, and his departure encouraged talk of bolting Grant's party.

In April 1872, before the political conventions, but with Grant's renomination assured, Douglass, his son Lewis, and George T. Downing

The commissioners to Santo Domingo. From *Life and Times,* 1881.

had boarded a Baltimore and Ohio train for the first leg of their trip to a national convention of black citizens in New Orleans. As he left, Douglass recalled his fears long ago in the Easton jail that he would be shipped to that dreaded city and sold amid the noise of the notorious slave auctions. All went well until Cincinnati; then, as their section of the train headed south, the three were barred from the dining car and forced to rely on the provisions (no doubt excellent; since Downing was one of the nation's leading caterers) they had brought along in a basket. At the meeting, Douglass, who had expected the legendary *creole de couleur* citizens of New Orleans to be in command, took special note of the fact that "jet black" delegates were just as prominent in the deliberations.

One of the goals of many of the Southern delegates was to organize black laborers into a national union, which could then exert pressure on the government by threatening to withhold the members' votes from the Republicans. A good many working-class black Americans, particularly in Georgia and South Carolina, had already organized into unions, and made it known that if the Republicans did not give more believable promises of protecting their rights, they would withhold their support. Douglass challenged this strategy, saying that it would only play into the hands of white-supremacist Democrats at the local level and of Liberal Republicans at the national level—both groups that for the most part were indifferent or even opposed to black interests. Loyalty to the party of Lincoln and Grant was, he insisted, the only course for black Americans.

Many conservative Republicans had grown weary of the frustrations inherent in dealing with the woes of the freed people, and as Americans often do when frustrated by a fundamental problem, had turned to the more genteel posture of horror over corruption in high places. The Grant administration supplied plenty of that, and the stealing of fistfuls of money was easier to comprehend than the tangle of race and class presented by the plight of the former slaves. Stealing money was wrong, the reformers had said as they picked up their marbles and stomped off to form the Liberal Republican party.

Paradoxically, some of the thieves were also the freed people's best friends. These eager, grasping men, for whom the urge to gain power was so great that they would even steal money in the process, understood the freedmen's intense need to advance. Aristocrats in the government, like Hamilton Fish, who deplored such grasping by their colleagues, were blind both to the freed people's aspirations and to the unfairness of racism which made the things hoped for so hard to obtain. But the scoundrels tended to be more sympathetic. These white men, perhaps uncomfortable about themselves, were frequently comfortable with black Americans in ways that others were not. The president's private secretary, Orville E. Babcock, who had reached up to his shoulder into the barrel of Whiskey Ring tax-fraud money, could cut the dahlias in his Capitol Hill garden and take a bunch around to a neighbor's door. "Dear General Babcock," wrote Frederick Douglass, "A thousand thanks for a fresh fragrant and beautiful bouquet. As I am something of an Irishman as well as a negro I send with my thanks my best wishes for your health and happiness."

After the Rochester fire, the Douglasses had moved into a small, charming Queen Anne style house on A Street, N.E., in a neighborhood of pleasant new blocks just back of the Capitol. Douglass's study, soon filled with books added to those saved from the fire, was in the rear of the first floor. Front and back there were little city gardens, but not the long flower beds that had held Anna's attention and sustained her in Rochester. As for Douglass, unlike his neighbor Babcock, but like most men in the ceaselessly political town of Washington, he found that campaigning, organizing, gossiping, and office seeking took precedence over dahlias. But for Douglass, not even lending his prestige to Grant's scheme to annex the Dominican Republic, nor his many campaign speeches in the fall of 1872 resulted in an appointment from the White House. Instead, a different door opened.

In March 1874, Frederick Douglass walked into one of the most splendid offices in Washington, sat down in its finest black-leather chair, and began presiding over, of all things, a bank. The trustees of the Freedman's Savings and Trust Company, the first interstate bank since Andrew Jackson had destroyed the second Bank of the United States three decades earlier, had chosen Douglass as its president. It was a "National Savings Bank," that was "Chartered by the United States," the advertisements and passbooks proclaimed, and judging by as handsome a new headquarters building as the capital could boast, the institution, in its ninth year, appeared to be flourishing. The elegant tall structure at 1507 Pennsylvania Avenue, flanking Lafayette Square, had been built at a cost of over a quarter of a million dollars. Inside, filigreed walnut cages encased the fastidiously attired tellers who received the customers' minute but regular deposits. President Douglass could look over to President Grant's White House diagonally across the street; to his left, on the other side of Pennsylvania Avenue, was the Treasury building, with its classical columns, still imposing, though in 1874 thought a little dowdy.

Not even Edward Lloyd had had a front door like his. The slave boy stood tall. Frederick Bailey, once chattel—something owned—was now president of the Freedman's Savings and Trust Company. Never, it seemed, had capitalism cooperated better with the makers of the American dream. The only problem was that the bank was insolvent.

Congress had chartered the Freedman's Bank, as it was known, on March 3, 1865, the same day it established the Freedmen's Bureau. The two agencies were, in the view of many, intended to work in tandem. The Northern concept of free labor, of working for wages, with the attendant, if often merely theoretical, freedom to advance and to be mobile, was being exported to the South, and the newly freed people were urged to put the fruits of their labor safely aside—hard-working black people were encouraged to deposit their pay in the bank that, like the Freedmen's Bureau, they were invited to think of as their own. Congress had not established any federal responsibility for the solvency of the institution, but with the congressional charter, the endorsement of the commissioner of the Freedmen's Bureau, and the images on the passbooks, like that of Lincoln holding a broken chain in one hand while the other rested beatifically on a sturdy "Freedman's Safe," everything suggested that the government stood behind the bank. As long as it was solvent, many in government were happy to maintain that fiction.

Branches were opened not only throughout the former Confederacy, but in cities across the nation, among them Louisville, Baltimore, and New York, that had significantly large black communities. Nickel by nickel, freed women and men, hoping one day to buy the farm they were working on shares, or a house in town, made their deposits. Their passbooks became a source of pride and assured them that they had not labored in vain; the money put by promised comfort and advancement in a not-too-distant future.

"Every piece of Freedman's Bank literature revealed the officers' missionary zeal," comments an astute student of the bank; several of these first officers and trustees—white people—had in fact been preachers among the freed people. John W. Alvord, an abolitionist Congregational minister and formerly the Freedmen's Bureau's superintendent of education, had been the bank's first president. The aim of those who had created the bank was to have a secure institution in which these new citizens could build assets that they could then invest in a house, a farm, or a business—thus entering the ranks of financial respectability.

But banks are tricky things. The money supplied by depositors piles up and must be invested; those who decide where the funds are to be placed have a great deal of power. Given the Freedman's Bank's purpose, a highly conservative investment policy was indicated, but Washington, growing rapidly in the postwar years, was ripe for speculative loans, and the assets of the new bank caught the eye of eager promoters. One of them, Henry D. Cooke, also seemed to have the freed people's interests at heart; recommending him for election to the board of trustees, Alvord wrote that Cooke and his associate William S. Huntington were "excellent men of high business reputation, & *friends of the Negro.*" Henry Cooke was the president of the First National Bank of Washington; he was also the brother of Jay Cooke, who had played a leading part in the financing of the Civil War and whose investment-banking firm, Jay Cooke & Company, was one of the leading houses in New York. Henry Cooke represented his brother in the firm's relentless lobbying on Capitol Hill. Once elected to the board, he persuaded his fellow trustees to make Washington, not New York, the headquarters city for the bank.

With the black population of Washington growing—it had increased from 14,312 in 1860 to 38,663 in 1867—people were in need of jobs and houses, so loans to the construction industry seemed to make excellent sense. Furthermore, General Howard of the Freedmen's Bureau argued that the depositors deserved a higher interest rate than was possible with the returns from the safe securities the bank was required to invest in, and in 1870, Congress amended the bank's charter to permit mortgage loans, provided they were covered by collateral double the value of the loan. But loans to good employers and honest builders were one thing; money supplied to corrupt firms, which often did not put up collateral of much value, was another. Henry Cooke was chairman of the bank's finance committee, which made its loans; his own Seneca Stone Company, financed by the bank, was later described as a "monstrous fabric of credit." The "excellent Christian man, warmly the friend of the Freedmen" proved an even better friend of himself.

Also risky was an investment of $100,000 in bonds of the Union Pacific Railroad; railroad securities were notoriously susceptible to nose dives. And equally distressing to cautious members of the board—among them Charles Burleigh Purvis, a bright young surgeon on the staff of Freedmen's Hospital and member of one of the nation's most distinguished African American families—was a loan of $50,000 to Jay Cooke & Company. The loan was accompanied with an agreement that the bank serve as an agent for the sale of bonds of the Northern Pacific Railway underwritten by the firm, and Purvis urged that the Freedman's Bank get out of the business of selling securities.

As early as 1872, the worthlessness of some of the larger loans made by Henry Cooke's finance committee became known to the other trustees, and that year Cooke and William S. Huntington, also of the First National Bank, left the board. In 1873, with the Northern Pacific Railway in grave financial difficulties, Jay Cooke & Company collapsed. A major panic ensued; banks failed across the country. The Freedman's Bank was in serious trouble, but because many of the bad loans, as later investigations and audits were to show, had been made surreptitiously, the trustees did not know how serious that trouble was. (The full board of trustees probably never met; when the bank was organized the names of fifty men, including some of the most impressive businessmen in the nation, were on a figurehead list of trustees. By 1874, only the thirteen trustees in Washington, some of them recently appointed, took responsibility for the bank.)

And by 1874, the majority of the trustees who attended meetings and voted were black. There have been conflicting assessments of what that fact signified. On one hand, the white trustees can be viewed as deserting a sinking ship and cynically consigning responsibility for the predictable demise of the institution to black men, whom the public would assume had insufficient intelligence to run a bank. On the other hand, one can see able and dedicated black men at last making the bank truly theirs, with determination to save it for the benefit of their brethren, the depositors. The intelligence of trustees like Dr. Purvis and John Mercer Langston, who had been dean of Howard University's law school, was certainly not in doubt, and the sensible running of a bank is not as arcane an art as is sometimes thought. But it does require some experience, and until they took command in early 1874, none of these men had had any experience in banking; as Purvis put it at a later investigation, "as the thing was, we, trustees—meeting but once a month, and then only hearing statements— could really know nothing about the affairs of the bank."

Once those affairs were in their hands, they took decisive action. They removed Alvord from his job as president; he remained a trustee. A minister and not a banker, Alvord had not been scrutinizing the loans made by the finance committee. The trustees then looked around for a new president who could best fill one particular requirement: ordinary black people who had entrusted the bank with their savings had to be made to believe that the bank was sound; they had to have enough confidence in it to refrain from withdrawing their money. To ensure this state of mind, the trustees turned to the most visible African American in the country, Frederick Douglass.

He took office believing that the restoration of confidence was the crucial—indeed, his only—task. Had the trustees been willing to make a searching audit of the bank, they might have concluded that it needed a president with financial acumen, or that Douglass should have as his ally an officer who would keep continuous watch over the bank's investment and lending activities. Purvis was selected as vice-president and Langston as chairman of the finance committee, but neither was a banker and both had other duties that prevented their attending to the bank's day-to-day operations. That Douglass would have resented a white man in a watchdog post is likely; he had balked at efforts by white friends to shore up the finances of the *North Star* and to supervise his expenditures when he was in Great Britain. In any case, the bank had no such official, and the trustees may have been wary of inviting one in. They, like some of the departed trustees, had real-estate interests that had benefited from the dubious loans on the books.

Douglass presided over the bank grandly, but not meticulously. He always maintained that he had been unaware of the bank's actual situation when he became its president. This was no doubt true, but there was more than enough gossip around Washington to make him highly skeptical, had he chosen to be. Once again, the desire for position overwhelmed good sense. As president, he seems to have devoted all of his attention to reassuring the depositors; there is no evidence of his exercising daily supervision over the loan portfolio. One of the most blatantly unsound loans, revealed in the audit ordered by Congress after the bank failed, was put on the books in June 1874, three months after Douglass took office. That loan was said to have been made "secretly" by a subordinate officer acting without any other official's knowledge; had the bank's president been doing the whole of his job, he would have been reviewing each day's loans before the money was actually turned over to the borrowers, and he would have asked the bank's actuary, George W. Stickney (successor to D. L. Eaton, who had flagrantly abused his office to the benefit of his personal business interests), why he believed that Juan Boyle, already on the books with shaky notes, should receive $33,366.66 more. And Douglass would have checked into the collateral put up, which was worthless.

Instead, all his effort went into attempts to stay the runs on the various branches of the bank in the South. He met with considerable success, but only by taking drastic action. Money was borrowed to meet demands for withdrawal, and thus to persuade customers, it was hoped, that their deposits were safe. When the Montgomery branch could not be rescued, it was sold; the Chattanooga branch was closed, with no payment to its depositors.

Douglass may have truly believed that he inspired such immense confidence in the black community that his mere presence as president of the bank would cause depositors to keep their money on account long enough for it to be soundly invested. But he could have achieved that belief only by closing his eyes to hard business facts—facts that were a matter of public record when he took office. Indeed, in one of his earliest statements designed to shore up the confidence of his customers, he let fall that his daughter had told him not to take the job. Rosetta Sprague had been battered by the world enough to make her wary in a way her father refused to be. He did not want to think that his America—that he himself—could possibly let his people down. But let them down both did. On July 1, 1874, Douglass joined with his fellow trustees in voting to close the failed bank.

The Freedman's Bank could have been rescued. A government flexible enough to support the financing of a vast railroad system could have found a way to supply the capital needed to match the amount owed depositors. Renewed adherence to the original policy of investing in safe government securities could have maintained that parity and provided modest interest on the accounts. George Boutwell, who had been Grant's secretary of the treasury and, since Charles Sumner's death in 1873, senator from Massachusetts, was one of only three members of the shifting Grant cabinet who showed any true responsibility for the black community. Astute in money matters, he might have been the one to make such a rescue. But the idea apparently did not occur to Boutwell, or to any other public figure.

For decades afterward Congress was called on, futilely, to make good on the deposits recorded in the passbooks of carpenters and laundresses and day laborers, whose trust in the nation's economic system had been lost along with their poignantly small savings. The state has committed larger crimes, but the failure to secure the five-dollar and fifty-dollar deposits in the Freedman's Bank was one of the nastiest.

During his tenure as bank president, Douglass did urge that the government fulfill its moral obligation, but only in muted tones. The House committee that conducted the original investigation (not with great skill) reported having "examined the management of this institution," and recommended that the commissioner who would be hired to oversee liquidation of the bank be "assisted by a competent attorney," with an eye to instituting "civil and criminal proceedings." (A legend persists in Washington that money for the purchase of Cedar Hill in 1878 came from a Freedman's Bank loan. No evidence for this has been found.) As the investigation got under way, Douglass moved to protect himself, adopting a defensive position that included protestations that he had not known the true condition of the bank when he took over and avoidance of aggressive efforts to rescue his depositors, for fear that he would irritate the litigious members of the subcommittee.

Indeed, deeply embarrassed by his impotence in the face of the bank's problems, Douglass in the spring of 1874 devoted more energy to asking others in Washington to do their various jobs than to doing his own. His letters to senators (on the Freedman's Bank's handsome stationery) did not concern financial rescue plans, but instead were eloquent statements in support of the civil-rights bill they were debating. His heart lay with such advocacy rather than with the bank, whose sad failure he seemed eager to forget. He refused to acknowledge any responsibility for its demise. On July 3, 1874, at the end of a letter to Gerrit Smith about the faltering civil-rights bill and Smith's efforts to sustain a harassed black cadet trying to integrate West Point, he wrote, "Despite my effort to uphold the Freedman's Savings and Trust Company it has fallen. It has been the black man's cow, but the white man's milk. Bad loans and bad management have been the death of it. I was ignorant of its real condition till elected its president." The doorway at 1507 Pennsylvania Avenue was one Douglass should never have gone through.

The black historian George Washington Williams, writing in 1888 to key figures to get their accounts of their work during Reconstruction, found Douglass "the first and only one that has declined to answer." Frustrated, the mercurial historian (who in time got over his anger and resumed his friendship with Douglass) had his secretary notify Douglass that "as a professional writer of history . . . [who] always goes to the authentic records," Williams had had "free access to the records of the Freedman's Savings Bank," which showed the bank to have been insolvent when Douglass became president. What then, he asked, "were the motives of Mr. Douglass in accepting the Presidency of an insolvent bank . . . [?]"

Williams knew the kind of criticism Douglass had been getting ever since the bank's failure. "Black washerwomen have been throwing dimes in Fred Douglass's pocket because he's colored," sneered John Mercer Langston ten years after the institution went under. Now, somewhat disingenuously, the historian's scribe asked Douglass to respond "in order that history might do him justice." The accusatory question posed was, "That the acceptance of the Presidency of the abovementioned bank by Mr. Douglass revived confidence in its solvency, [the breakdown] of which Mr. Douglass as a trustee was duty bound to know [about]; or if he did not know, then Mr. Williams would like to know the reason why." There is no record of a reply; by then Douglass had given up trying to account for himself as a banker.

Eighteen seventy-four was not Douglass's year. Not only was there the bank debacle, but in October he had to close down the *New National Era*. The newspaper, designed as a beacon for a reformed, racially integrated nation, had found few white readers; for it to become a journal read only by the African American community in Washington would have defeated its original purpose and, in the absence of a shift to a more parochial focus, would have doomed it to unprofitability as well. And along with these defeats in the public forum, Douglass had to face private woes. One day a year earlier, Charles's wife, Libbie, "all fired up" burst in to tell her father-in-law that she had caught her husband and another woman talking alongside the barn in the backyard of the small house in Washington that Charles had bought. In a long letter to his father, who was right there in town, Charles defended himself. Libbie was incurably jealous, had been since the day they were married—so much so that he could not even help female relatives and friends get jobs in the auditor's office of the Treasury Department, where he now worked. (The younger Douglass men changed jobs constantly in search of an elusive security.) As he had done when confronted with the tensions in Nathan and Rosetta's marriage, Douglass sought, successfully on the whole, to keep the family going along a path of somewhat uneasy gentility.

Three years later, Rosetta, still in Rochester, wrote her father of being besieged by her husband's creditors, of seeing all her household goods hauled out into the rain. Lewis had come down from Syracuse to help—he had been visiting Amelia's family—but she was still in despair: "It is a wild night—a cold rain has fallen all day and as I write . . . the wind [is] howling around the house. . . . Good night—dear father. I wish I could be with you to night—and be out of this turmoil. I never knew so little what to think in my life." Soon after, she and Nathan moved their growing family to Washington. Rosetta's despair, and Charles's earlier brush with impropriety while in his own backyard looking after the chickens underscored the huge gulf that existed between Douglass's style of life and that of his children.

But painful circumstances were to be found at Douglass's own level as well. Just a few days before he had to calm Libbie and Charles, he received a letter from Dr. Gustave Frauenstein, Ottilia Assing's physician, whom he knew well. The doctor was concerned about Assing's psychological condition, but predicted that with the warmer weather, she should "recover her philosophical calmness within the cranial cavities of her auditory system for at least the summer months." He added, however, that they needed to recognize that "she has, as well as every-one of us, an Achilles' heel in her body. Her self-slaughterous tendencies remain unabated, notwithstanding her improvement and it is useless to reason with her on that nonsense: for it is nonsense itself to reason on nonsense." Soon Ottilia began her summer visit with the Douglasses, which lasted this time until October. The following spring, urging her sister, Ludmilla to tell her what had gone wrong with her marriage, she commented, "If one stands in so intimate a relationship with a man as I do with Douglass, one comes to know facets of the whole world, men and women, which would otherwise remain closed to one, especially if it is a man whom the entire world has seen and whom so many women have loved."

The physician's clinical analysis of Assing raises more questions than it answers. Her "self-slaughterous tendencies" were to prove real, but does her want of "calmness" indicate that the "intimate" relationship with Douglass was a fantasy? This is possible, but if so, why did he indulge her long visits, particularly in view of the anguish they caused in his household? In her letter to her sister, Assing reported that Douglass was adding a wing to the A Street house and wanted her to move in permanently: "You can imagine how happy that would make me, but I must consider if it is advisable to be in the constant companionship of his amiable wife. Until now I have managed through diplomacy and the giving of many gifts to maintain the best of relationships with her, but one can never know what can come into the head of such an unknowledgeable and illiterate creature. What should one say, for instance, if one were charged with having bewitched a person?"

Assing was implying that Anna Douglass, lashing out at the bewitcher, had reached back to savage African superstitions in her fight to hold her man. Nothing could have disturbed the German rationalist more than an appeal to supernatural forces, particularly those out of blackest Africa. But "bewitched" was not an altogether inappropriate term for the way Anna's husband was affected by Ottilia. Ill and inarticulate, Anna Douglass was trying to hold fast to the man who had led her into a world she could compete in only with her own primal tenacity.

Anna may have reached into an African past for survival, but Frederick went right on being the great figurehead of racial advancement in America. His ceaseless lecture tours caused his family to worry about his health; Assing commented sarcastically, "He would be doing all right if he did not have his dear family worrying him to death and consuming everything he manages to earn." Her nasty charge had some justification. Charles, Frederick jr., and Rosetta were constantly asking their father for financial help. He had pressed them to live according to a standard of dignity that was hard to maintain for a clerk in government office, a printer who had a sure job only as long as his father's newspaper employed him, and a son-in-law (for whom Douglass showed true affection and understanding) who had trouble holding any kind of job.

Never was the incongruence of family relationships better displayed than when Frederick Douglass went to Kate Chase Sprague's elegant place in the city to play croquet, while his son-in-law was in her employ as a stableman. That Nathan later, to Douglass's embarrassment, seems to have cheated Mrs. Sprague on the purchase of a horse suggests the level of frustration and subconscious revenge that this confused man was driven to.

At the Centennial Exposition in Philadelphia in 1876, a bust of Douglass by J. M. Mundy was on display. It was a great tribute to the runaway, but a tombstone for Reconstruction. The effort to rebuild the nation along a fundamentally more egalitarian line was over, and the bust an ironic memorial to a job not done. But if symbolically Douglass was already part of a dead past, the Republicans knew there were still black voters who liked a look at him, alive. In April 1876, Ottilia Assing, who had long wanted to take Douglass to Europe with her, wrote to her sister, "No, Douglass cannot come this summer, for he is completely taken up in the service of the Republican party during the campaign."

The campaign was successful—in a measure. When the disputed election had been decided by an electoral commission (with members from both houses of Congress and the Supreme Court), Douglass's beloved Republicans held the White House. And its new occupant appeared to be most respectful of Douglass's position and personal dignity. Douglass seemed comfortable about Rutherford B. Hayes and almost totally oblivious to the concessions to white supremacists in the South that had put him into office. Hayes's election spelled the end of federal responsibility for the rights of black people in the South, a responsibility that Douglass had committed his life to furthering. But he did not see what was happening—did not allow himself to see it. And he accepted with great pride the presidential appointment that had so long eluded him.

Hayes named Douglass marshal of the District of Columbia; this appointment was the first requiring Senate approval to be given to a black man. Harriet Jacobs wrote from Cambridge, Massachusetts, "to tell you how anxiously I have perused the papers the last few days and how happy I was made this morning . . . to see your nomination confirmed." She spoke for many old friends who sent their congratulations when she added, "There is not man living that I should so rejoice to see hold this position at the Capitol of the Nation." From Nantucket, Mary G. Wright, one of the three survivors of the group of woman abolitionists who had "formed your body guard" as Douglass walked to the Big Shop to speak, rejoiced that now "colorphobia has been cured by real merit, superior intellect and culture."

Ottilia Assing, whose revolution was now dead, though she did not yet know it, was proud as well. She had not yet figured out that the appointment was part of Hayes's shrewdly constructed screen to conceal the cessation of truly significant federal action in behalf of black people. For her the new post meant that for four years, at least, Douglass would not be able to accompany her to Europe. "I do not feel the least disappointment," she told her sister. Rather, "I have pure pleasure in that which has canceled our common travel plans. He has been named marshal of the District of Columbia. . . . I do not yet know exactly what responsibilities are connected with this office, but I know that it is honorable and lucrative, and that it relieves him of the necessity of undertaking each winter those dangerous, difficult, and unhealthy lecture tours. . . . He has served the Republican party for the past twenty years so well that such an acknowledgment could hardly have been put off any longer. Since he will now be in the immediate vicinity of the president, one might hope that he will win his way to a beneficent influence."

22

Uniontown

OTTILIA was wrong. Frederick Douglass was not to have a "beneficent influence," or any other kind, on Rutherford B. Hayes and his administration. And the stances on various issues that Douglass was to take between 1877 and 1881 were the least honorable and least helpful to his fellow former slaves of any in his long life. They were, in fact, entirely consonant with the betrayal of promises that ended Reconstruction.

The most positive thing that can be said about his service as marshal is that by occupying the post and distributing jobs, Douglass continued and strengthened the hold of black civil servants on minor government positions. These positions with the federal government were the cornerstone of the staunchly middle-class black community in the capital. So firmly set was that stone, that the wiliest of twentieth-century segregationists could not dislodge it.

At the time Douglass was named marshal, however, the black community was dismayed that he did not get the whole of the job. Abraham Lincoln had made his close friend Ward Hill Lamon the marshal, and Ulysses Grant appointed his brother-in-law; during these administrations, the marshal attended formal receptions in the White House, stood next to the president, and presented each guest to him, by name. Douglass was excused from this chore, and not a black person in America, among those who cared about such things, was unaware that this duty had been eliminated to prevent too great a black presence in the Republican palace.

Douglass was exceedingly defensive about his failure to resign over this slight. Ponderously, he justified Hayes's decision in *Life and Times of Frederick Douglass,* and then observed, "I should have presented . . . a most foolish and ridiculous figure had I, as absurdly counseled by some of my colored friends, resigned the office . . . because President . . . Hayes, for reasons that must have been satisfactory to his judgement, preferred some person other than myself to attend upon him at the Executive Mansion." He would have been more persuasive if he had added that any man, and certainly any black man, had better things to do than act the obsequious servant performing the unctuous job of managing receiving lines. Douglass's friend the columnist Grace Greenwood wrote in the *New York Times,* "Could he be dressed in gaudy livery and stand at the door of the Blue Room . . . ," he might have been acceptable. He was not acceptable, he privately told her, as "the *insolent Negro*" that those in charge of the White House took him to be.

Douglass had scarcely occupied the post of marshal before he came close to losing it. Speaking in Baltimore, in March 1877, he forgot to be the noncontroversial officeholder. Resorting to his old platform tricks of mimicry and sarcasm, he made fun of the white old guard of Washington's embarrassingly long slaveholding days. The speech was widely reported, and a petition calling for Douglass's removal, and signed by a hundred businessmen, soon reached President Hayes. With dignified letters to newspaper after newspaper, Douglass justified his absence from the city to attend a perfectly legitimate meeting in Baltimore and defended his right to express his feelings even though he was an officeholder.

In the *Times,* Grace Greenwood gave not only a vigorous defense of Douglass's fitness for the post (or a better one) but a brilliant insight into his character. In reply to the charge that Douglass was as "guileless as a child . . . [with] no more knowledge of business than a child," Greenwood said, "A Pickwickian simplicity is not his strong point. The expression of his peculiar, long eyes, sleepy but wary—Moorish or Malayan eyes—is shrewd to subtlety. Among other things which men of brains learned in the primal hard school of slavery were craft, reserve, circumvention, and repression." And she added sarcastically, "If these valuable acquirements, joined to even an irregular course of finesse, address, adroitness, mental reservation, and moral irresponsibility, pursued in Freedom's High School of politics, will not fit a man for an important Federal office, I don't know what will."

Hayes did not yield to the pressure; Douglass kept his job and felt more beholden to the president than ever. On a personal level, Douglass was to find the mild Civil War general from Ohio, who consulted him on the reliability of black petitioners, the most comfortable to deal with of the eight presidents he came to know. And yet, one of his observant friends detected "something in your way of speaking of Pres. Hayes which suggests you do not feel quite at ease in regard to him." Whether knowledge that he was part of a cover-up of the administration's anti-black policies caused Douglass's discomfort, he never said, and he took pride in being able to take English friends to "the White House and introduce them to the Pres't and sometimes Mrs. Hayes—and they go away delighted with the warmth, cordiality, and simple dignity of the President."

With the federal appointment came sufficient confidence to go home again. In June 1877, Douglass took the train to Baltimore, and on June 16, from a Fells Point dock, he set out on the excursion boat *Matilda* for St. Michaels. The deck was crowded with other Eastern Shore people going home; their excitement was increased by the presence of a celebrity, but "the most famous black man in the world" wasn't happy. He kept hearing the noise of slavery; "the one hundred colored people aboard made as much noise as five hundred whites would have done," he imprudently said to a *Baltimore Sun* reporter. As Dickson Preston described it, "Soon bottles were being passed around; food baskets were opened; banjos were produced; dancing and stomping began. Old *Matilda,* a stern-wheeler built during the war, had only primitive accommodations; her passengers relieved themselves over the rail, and since there was nowhere for most of them to sleep, kept up the shouting, singing, and stomping all night long." Douglass "sat through the night in grim disapproval."

The wharf at St. Michaels looked much as it had forty-one years earlier. The boats at the dock were of a newer design, the houses he passed as he walked into town sported a bit more paint, but none of his people had moved—as he and some others had been able to do in rapidly growing Washington—into the proper part of town. Instead, they lived in shanties on its outskirts; men working as day laborers and women as domestics or in the fish canneries eked out their insufficient wages with the meager additional pay they received in kind and the produce of their small gardens. It was Douglass's first close look at how former slaves were living in the rural South. With a burst of nostalgia, he proudly announced to a crowd around him later in the day, "I am an Eastern Shoreman," and stretched his chest, saying, "Eastern Shore corn and Eastern Shore pork gave me my muscle."

The rest of the speech, if the *Baltimore Sun* reporter is to be believed, consisted of the worst elements of his pull-up-your-socks sermon: "We must not talk about equality until we can do what the white people can do. As long as they can build vessels and we can not, we are their inferiors. ... If twenty years from now the colored race as a race has not advanced beyond the point where it was when emancipated, it is a doomed race. The question now is, will the black man do as much now for his master (himself) as he used to do for his old master?" The St. Michaels day laborers, with their white neighbors looking on, were told to work and save their money. "Without money," Douglass declared, according to the *Sun,* "there's no leisure, without leisure no thought, without thought no progress." The latter two-thirds of the doctrine was Thoreauvian, but the audience was a long way south of Concord.

The proudest people standing in the confused crowd must have been the nine children of Frederick's older sister Eliza Mitchell, who had recently died. One of the nine, Peter Mitchell, Jr., was to have a great-grandson, James E. Thomas, who a century later would become the first black town commissioner of St. Michaels. In 1877, the old Bailey clan was still very much a presence in Talbot County, but Douglass, in his memoirs, made no mention of the family that his son Lewis had spoken of so fondly when he visited the town just after the war. Whether the reunion, like the meeting with his brother Perry ten years earlier, was an occasion too emotional to record, or whether he and his sister's family were now so different in the way they lived and talked that they found nothing that was satisfying to say to each other, Douglass never revealed.

But there was another reunion that Douglass could describe. Walking into a brick house on Cherry Street, Douglass was taken straight to the room of his old master, Thomas Auld, now a dying man. "Captain Auld," he said; "Marshall Douglass," Auld replied. "Not *Marshall,* but Frederick to you as formerly," Douglass corrected. Auld, shaken with palsy, wept; Douglass was so choked up that he could not speak. Then, regaining their composure, the two old adversaries talked. Auld, his mind clear and any bitterness gone, corrected Douglass: he had not inherited Douglass's grandmother Betsy Bailey; his brother-in-law had, but he had brought her in her old age to St. Michaels to be cared for until she died. Douglass apologized for having accused Auld, in his "Letter to His Old Master," of having "turned out [my dear old grandmother] like an old horse to die in the woods." Then he resumed his lifelong quest for information about his birth. Douglass had calculated that he had been born in 1817; Auld, his memory firm, said it had been in February 1818; this fact was only verified a century later, when Dickson Preston examined the records of Aaron Anthony's slaves.

The conversation lasted just twenty minutes, for Douglass could see that the old man was exceedingly weak. He noticed too that there had, after all, been something genuine to Thomas Auld's conversion at that revival more than four decades earlier; "he felt himself about to depart in peace." Douglass's reserved account in *Life and Times of Frederick Douglass* of this final meeting has an elegiac tone. He and Auld had had a relationship of vast extremes; it closed with quiet satisfaction.

We do not have the letter Douglass wrote to Ottilia Assing a week after his return from St. Michaels, but we do have her reply; from Munich, she wrote, "If only I for once could see the Eastern Shore in your company!" but along with her regret at missing a trip with him into his past went a warning. "Loaded with honor" though he was, she was uneasy about his being so deferential to Auld. She was particularly dubious about such behavior in view of what she saw as the betrayal of blacks by the Republican party: "At a distance matters look terrible." Then she turned her attention to recent depressing events in Germany. Troubled by a court decision denying "the equal rights of the Jews," she went on to observe, "It is an ugly feature of human nature that the lower . . . a race or an individual has reached, the more it is oppressed; the more it will yearn to oppress some one more humble in its turn. The Jews and the Irish, so long downtrodden in their own country are foremost among the negro haters and the slaves used to vent their superiority on poor defenseless animals."

Members of the black community who read about the visit to Auld in the press criticized Douglass for what was seen as obsequious obeisance to a slave master he had once denounced. Worse, perhaps, was his misunderstanding of the plight of his black Eastern Shore neighbors. Indeed, in all the years of the Hayes administration, Douglass never fully acknowledged—publicly, at least—how devastating had been the blow to his dreams of moving the nation toward a commitment based on moral principle to afford all black people equal protection under the law and equal opportunity. It is not a matter of twentieth-century twenty-twenty hindsight to accuse him of this myopia. One after another of his friends, particularly his black friends, wrote warning him to "beware of Compromise." Amid the flood of congratulatory letters that Douglass received in March and April 1877 was one from a "Citizen," warily not giving his name, who damned Hayes's recognition of Governor Wade Hampton's government in South Carolina, which had gained power with the help of the armed Red Shirts, groups organized by white supremacists to intimidate Republicans in general and black voters in particular. He called the governor "the worst enemy a race battling for freedom can find." Indeed, this writer went on, "the race was more endangered than anytime since slavery." Another spoke of "these days when it appears to be growing dark again to the colored man."

Ottilia Assing was equally pessimistic. Her initial euphoria at Douglass's appointment as marshal soon disappeared, being replaced by her usual political acumen. "I should give up Republicanism not exactly as for dead but for paralysed at least for many years, thanks to Hayes, Schurz [she was no admirer of her fellow German Carl Schurz, who had abandoned radicalism once he realized it meant attending to the needs of black people]—if it were not for your hopefulness," she told Douglass. "Every number of the paper records now deeds of crime and violence."

One word that Assing used to describe her friend's new post—one that got straight to the point—was "lucrative." Douglass's salary was a respectable one, and he was in a position to know what was going on in the Washington real-estate market, in which he invested. Also, because as marshal he was in close contact with many government-bureau officials, he could help people get jobs; these, as always, were badly needed, particularly in the black community. His salary meant that Douglass was able, for the first time in thirty-five years, to stop his arduous speaking tours. He could also afford a new house. In September 1878, the Douglasses left A Street behind for a beautiful place, high and alone, on a hill in one of the most interestingly integrated areas of the District of Columbia, Uniontown in Anacostia.

The city of Washington lies in the V formed by the junction of the Anacostia and Potomac rivers; across the Anacostia, to the east, lay the village of Uniontown, surrounded by the Anacostia hills, some wooded and some cleared for farms. On one of the hills was the house of John Van Hook, a prosperous local real-estate man. With the help of a loan from Dr. Charles B. Purvis, Douglass bought the house and nine acres, with a barn and large vegetable and flower gardens like those he and Anna had had in Rochester. The next year, he bought fifteen adjacent acres. Frederick and Anna Douglass had achieved a country seat.

The ample, white frame house, all the more handsome for being unpretentious, had been built in the 1850s. Visitors climbed the steep steps up Cedar Hill, as Douglass called it, crossed a comfortable one-story porch, and entered by a fine front door. The formal east parlor was to the left; behind it was Douglass's spacious, book-lined library. To the right, bright in the afternoon sun, was the more casual west parlor, or music room, with Douglass's violin resting on the piano. Behind this room was the comfortable square dining room, with its good but not grand china and German silver, and in the rear of the first floor was a big, sensible kitchen.

Upstairs, along the west wall were the guest room, the bedroom that became Anna's when she was ill, and at the front a small sitting or sewing room. Across the hall was the large, patriarchal master bedroom, behind which, separated only by velvet porticres, was a second guest room. Up the back stairs were small bedrooms for grandchildren and servants. From the front porch or, better still, from the front windows above, one could look down on the whole of the capital city. Whatever Douglass's frustrations with the job he held in that city, including the unacknowledgeable fact that the position was not equal to the pride he felt duty-bound to express in holding it, Cedar Hill was his. Walking the long way home in the afternoon, across the bridge and up the hill, Douglass could know that when he gained its crest, no one had a finer prospect of Washington than he.

The winter before moving to Cedar Hill, Douglass lost a cherished member of his "family." John Sears, who had long ago overcome his resentment at Douglass's criticism of his father-in-law, wrote with the ease now of an old friend that Amanda was gravely ill. Douglass immediately took the train to Baltimore for a final visit with "Mrs. Lucretia's" daughter. On January 10, John reported her still alive and thanked Frederick for his visit; on February 1, Thomas (named for his grandfather, Thomas Auld) wrote that his mother had died. The following month Douglass received a sad brave letter from his old friend Henry O. Waggoner in Denver. His only son, Henry, whom Douglass had helped obtain a job in the consulate in Lyons, had died there of tuberculosis. One father pressed on another the whole of the story; ridding himself of documents too painful to keep, Waggoner enclosed his son's final letter, describing his cough, his whispering voice, his skeletal legs.

In February 1878, Douglass was sixty, and laurels were on his brow. When the marshal of the District of Columbia rode in to the city and picked up Senator Blanche K. Bruce to go to a government office about a job for a friend, he did so behind a fine trotter. All seemed to be well, but appearances deceived. These first years after Reconstruction, which saw the dashing of so many of Douglass's public dreams, were also a time of great and unsettling confusion in his private life. Old friends, most of them speaking with a good deal less acidity than Ottilia Assing, repeatedly urged him to cut loose from his children and allow them to have lives of their own. But by now, they were irrevocably dependent on him.

He was damned if he did and damned if he didn't. Not to help them when they were indeed in trouble seemed cruel; his assistance, on the other hand, only made more pronounced the sense that he could accomplish anything, and they, nothing. In 1879, Douglass, who had lost, he claimed, ten thousand dollars on his failed newspaper, the *New National Era,* had three families to support, in addition to his own: Rosetta and her children (Nathan was in Omaha, briefly, trying once again for a start in life); Charles and his children (his wife, Libbie, had died and he needed help in caring for them); and Douglass's brother Perry, and Perry's daughter, who had come to Cedar Hill to live. Perry was dying; Douglass told Amy Post, "He is a dear old fellow, and I am glad to have a shelter for him."

Anna's health too was deteriorating, and as it did, her smoldering resentment of her husband grew. At the same time, Ottilia Assing was making greater and greater emotional demands. The remarkable balance that she and Douglass had maintained for so many years—with the summer visits and the occasional times together in Hoboken and New York—had broken down. Having failed to persuade him to leave Anna and go to Europe with her, Assing had gone alone in 1877. On her return, she attempted to pick up where she and Douglass had left off. A visit to Cedar Hill in the fall of 1878 for a moment recaptured the times on the hill overlooking Rochester, but once she had left, her letters were filled with rancorous remarks about old friends. More and more, her bitterness was moving into true mental disturbance. For Douglass, responding to her fully would have meant becoming engulfed by her overpowering distress. Instead, he increasingly withdrew, which only made her the more eager to have him respond.

Frederick Douglass did not take Ottilia Assing with him when, later in the fall of 1878, he once again went back to the Eastern Shore. This time, he was to visit Easton; this time there was a stateroom on the steamer. In the little city, he stayed in the hotel, now renovated, across from the jail where covetous slave traders had prowled about as Frederick Bailey endured the terrible uncertainty of possible lynching or sale. The *Gazette,* eager to please black voters, who had just helped elect a Republican to Congress, greeted him warmly; the Democratic *Star* made a sneering point of almost ignoring the visitor. At the African Methodist Episcopal church, Douglass once again gave, not a political speech, but— as if to elevate the proceedings—a version of his most familiar lecture, "The Self-Made Man."

Personal matters took command when he hired a horse and carriage, rode out to Tuckahoe Creek, and with Louis Freeman, who had been a slave in the region, found the site of Betsy Bailey's long-gone cabin, the scene of his first memories: there was a cedar tree that, somehow, seemed to be in the right place; he put his hands into the soil, gathering fistfuls of it to carry back to Cedar Hill.

In the summer of 1881, Ottilia Assing returned to Germany, apparently committed to writing regularly there for the *Morgenblatt.* But her restlessness did not cease; she challenged in the courts her exclusion from her sister's will and wandered about the continent so aimlessly that her newspaper once tried advertising to find out where she was. She and Douglass were still in correspondence as late as June 1884, but after 1879 he no longer saved her letters as he had done in closer days. In 1881, and again in 1882, she had a friend in New York send him large boxes of his favorite cigars, the ones whose lingering aroma had reminded her of him when he had left after a visit.

Preoccupied as he was with his personal life, Douglass somehow loosed his hold on the excellent equilibrium he had for decades maintained between his own need to be with white people, not permitting race to determine the boundaries of his existence, and his commitment to the black community to which he belonged and whose interests he had so long and staunchly defended. The shift was evident, for instance, in his view of the Exodusters, black people in Louisiana and Mississippi who sought to make a new start in the West. Standing on the levees with bundles of their slight belongings at their feet, fearful that posses of whites would drag them back to work in the fields, they waited for boats that might carry them up the river. They were destitute. Douglass's good mind let him down as he examined their plight, and so did his sense of sympathy. He refused to see that something had changed—for the worse.

The most important and enduring provision of the Compromise of 1877, the deal cut in the Republicans' successful effort to hold the White House following the contested election of 1876, had been the clearly understood, if not explicitly stated, agreement that the federal government would no longer attempt to guarantee the rights of black people in the South. The fate of these people, who formed the largest segment of the South's nonindependent laboring class, was to be left in the hands of white people committed to white supremacy. The Redeemers, as the white leaders liked to think of themselves, had quickly regained control of Southern state and local governments.

Reassured that they would not be interfered with, these keepers of the social order made haste to complete the intimidation, already well under way, of black Southerners, who as farmers and as citizens, had been making a good thing of Reconstruction. These black farmers understood, as the marshal of the District of Columbia did not, what damage the compromisers who had ensured President Hayes's election had done to their cause. As Richard T. Greener, then dean of Howard University's law school, put it in a brilliant analysis of Hayes's policy of returning "home rule" to the South, "With the downfall of reconstruction a new lease on life was given to Southern barbarity and lawlessness. As usual the negro was the principal sufferer. Negro representation went first; next, the educational system . . . was crippled by insufficient appropriations. Majorities were overcome by shot-gun intimidation, or secretly by the tissue [disposable] ballot." These actions, and more, had made the condition of "the negro tenant class worse than at any period since slavery."

Profoundly disillusioned, a good many of these freed people, who had been so committed to places they had always known as home, prepared to leave; like so many disappointed white Americans before them, they would look for better luck in the West. Kansas was the goal of the desperate pioneers known as Exodusters, and some would actually reach it, to found all-black settlements and begin farming. If these pioneers were to truly find a promised land, a great many of their brothers and sisters might follow. The movement was never huge, but in the late 1870s it was strong enough to get the landowners of the South worrying about who would chop the cotton when all the hands had gone.

To make matters worse, many of the emigrants and would-be emigrants were destitute. Long ago, Douglass had chastised Garrison for contending that once the nation had ended slavery, the ex-slaves could make their way, unassisted, in the world of the former slaveholders. Now he was being blind to exactly such a situation. Black workers, in the wake of a ruined Reconstruction, needed his help, but Douglass could not give it. He was blind because the passage of these people into exile was a tragic rejection of what his story stood for. His people, relieved of their single disability, slavery, and protected by a benevolent government, were to rise self-confidently into freedom as he had done, to become respectable citizens of their own country, not wander off into a wilderness of destitution. His dream, his fantasy, was that each person should be his or her own Moses and confront Pharaoh on equal terms. Douglass saw the Exodusters—the slanginess of the name grated—to be like immigrants just off the boat, whose arrival would "cast upon the people of Kansas and other Northern states a multitude of deluded, hungry, homeless, naked and destitute people." He was, he said, "opposed to this exodus" (a phrase he repeated six times in a public letter), "because I see in it a tendency to convert colored laboring men into traveling camps."

The image of his people as miserable refugees was more than Douglass could face. For the first time in his life, he found himself hissed and shouted down by black audiences. And he did not quiet his critics when he spoke of the exodus as "a wretched substitute for the fulfillment of the national obligations" of the federal government, or a "concession to the idea that colored people and white people cannot live together in peace and prosperity." Those with their eyes open to the oppression of black laborers in Mississippi and Louisiana in 1879 saw Douglass as simply wrong when he claimed that "the conditions . . . in the Southern States are steadily improving." His prediction "that the colored man there will ultimately realize the fullest measure of liberty and equality" was cold comfort in 1879.

If Douglass's sense of compassion was failing him, so was his intellectual grasp of a new problem. In the end it did matter that he had no formal education. In the experiential sense that Henry Adams used the term, Douglass's education had, of course, been splendid. But Douglass's self-confidence, his sense that as he talked, he concomitantly came to know, sometimes kept him from systematic intellectual analysis. He had not had training in such analysis. He loved to read and to converse about books with others, particularly women, whom he never found intimidating. (With men, he was somewhat intellectually insecure, and hence deferential and even, at times, dangerously malleable.) Well-read friends like Ottilia Assing enriched his mind. But his thinking lacked a truly critical dimension. Perhaps he began with too much moral certainty; he knew without the least doubt that slavery was wrong and that what we today would call racism was wrong. He tended to project that certitude into other realms, and never more disastrously than when he ventured into social science.

The American Social Science Association was to hold its annual meeting in Saratoga Springs, New York, in September 1879, and would be considering the structure of the laboring classes in the American South. In particular, some of the social scientists were troubled that an alarming number of members of one of those classes seemed eager to get out of the South. To explore the issue, two leading black thinkers were asked to give papers: Douglass was to speak opposing the emigration from the South, and Richard T. Greener was to defend the Exodusters. Greener, Harvard's first black graduate, had taught at the University of South Carolina during Reconstruction and now, in addition to teaching at Howard University, was an active sponsor of an organization that sought to help the emigrants.

Greener, along with a great many other black leaders, sought to raise money to alleviate the suffering of the Exodusters and to prevent them from being returned forcibly to the Southern fields. Unlike Douglass, Greener saw their emigration as a perfectly appropriate effort by American citizens to better their condition.

In the end, the two black leaders did not confront each other at Saratoga. As a trustee of Howard University, Douglass had already had serious conflicts with Greener, who over his long and richly varied career was to gain a reputation for being exceedingly hard to get along with. Douglass sent his paper ahead, to be read by someone else on September 4, and planned to arrive at the famous spa only on the tenth. He was hoping, as he told Franklin B. Sanborn, his one-time ally in John Brown's cause and the founder of the American Social Science Association, that he would be greeted "in the spirit of social science and not in a spirit of controversy." Clearly, he subsequently decided the spirit of controversy would prevail if he appeared with the argumentative, persuasive dean. On September 9, he wired that he was not coming at all.

In his essay, Douglass began with a disarmingly sympathetic rendering of the Exodusters' plight: Rather than slaughter the oppressors "by fire and sword" as emancipated slaves did in Haiti, the American freed person "has adopted a simple, lawful and peaceable measure. It is emigration—the quiet withdrawal of his valuable bones and muscles from a condition of things which he considers no longer tolerable." With this seeming approval of the removal of "a few thousand freedmen" to Kansas, he turned his attention to "the sober thinking minds of the South," focused now on this "new and startling peril to the welfare and civilization of that section of our country." Already, he continued, "apprehension and alarm have led to noisy and frantic efforts . . . to arrest [the exodus] and put an end to what it [the South] considers a ruinous evil." His explanation of the alarm is interestingly put: "This Exodus has revealed to the southern men the humiliating fact that the prosperity and civilization of the South are at the mercy of the despised and hated Negro." But Douglass's response to those landowners' fears was perverse.

Having correctly credited black laborers with the clearing and tilling of the South's land, he declared, with a peculiar sense of botany, zoology, and geography, that if they were to cease their laboring, the region would succumb to "noxious weeds" or return to "dense forests and impenetrable jungles, natural hiding places for devouring wolves and loathsome reptiles." Turning next to ethnology, he asserted that "neither Chinaman, German, Norwegian nor Swede can drive him [the African] from the sugar and cotton fields of Louisiana and Mississippi." He alone can do the work, as "the climate of the South makes such labor uninviting and harshly repulsive to the white man. He dreads it, shrinks from it and refuses it. He shuns the burning sun of the fields, and seeks the shade of the verandas. On the contrary, the Negro walks, labors, or sleeps in the sunlight unharmed."

Such reasoning, he acknowledged, was the "standing apology for slavery," but then he drew a bizarre picture of the meaning of emancipation. It was to be the glory of the emancipated that "however galling and humiliating to Southern pride and power," they would hold the South in their thrall—by doing the labor that must be done and that only they could do. Since the white men would not "take off their own coats, cease to whittle sticks and talk politics at the cross-roads, and go themselves to work," the black men would: "Neither natural, artificial nor traditional causes stand in the way of the freedman to such labor in the South. . . . he stands today the admitted author of whatever prosperity, beauty, and civilization are now professed by the South. He is the arbiter of her destiny."

An arbiter is one who has power. But the Exodusters knew, even if the gentlemen in the rows of seats at the social scientists' convention did not, that the black people were losing whatever power they had held during Reconstruction. Work would be their lot in the South, but it would be work under subservient conditions that did not fit the promise of freedom, a promise that had never been articulated better than by the author of this appalling paper. Douglass did have a sense of the hardships the emigrant faced as "he stands mournfully imploring hard-hearted steamboat captains to take him on board; while the friends of the emigration movement are diligently soliciting funds all over the North to help him away from his old home to the modern Canaan of Kansas." But Douglass's solution was for the would-be emigrants to stay in the South and face the hardships there: "Suffering and hardships made the Saxon Strong,—and suffering and hardships will make the Anglo-African Strong." Frederick Bailey had thought that Anglo-Africans had already had more than enough hardships, and he had not liked the idea of doing the work of the Coveys of this world. Frederick Douglass, in 1879, believed the vote would cure all: "The South must let the Negro vote, or surrender its representation in Congress. The chosen horn of his [the white Southerner's] dilemma will finally be to let the Negro vote, and vote unmolested." (This from a man who knew full well what had been done to break the political power of his beloved Republican party all across the South.) "Let us have all the indignant and fiery declarations which the warm hearts of our youthful orators can pour out against Southern meanness, 'White Leagues' . . . and other 'Dark Lantern' organizations, but let us have a little calm, clear reason as well."

Douglass's was the reasoning of the white Redeemers. Although he acknowledged that the "fever of freedom is already in the negro's blood" and declared that to "forcibly dam up the stream of emigration would be . . . madness as well as oppression," he hoped that emigration would cease voluntarily as a result of improved conditions. But the conditions he was willing to settle for were those of white Southern agricultural entrepreneurs. The South is "the best market for the black man's labor," he declared. Casting down the bucket from which he as a runaway slave had long ago resolutely refused to drink, he concluded with a warning that landowners would be wise to be alerted by revolutionary crises in Russia, and the almost unbelievable suggestion that workers should be content to be bought off with kindness: "The cry of 'Land and Liberty,' the watchword of the Nihilistic Party in Russia, has a music in it sweet to the ear of all oppressed peoples, and *well* it shall be for the landholders of the South if they shall . . . adopt such a course of just treatment towards the landless laborers of the South . . . as shall make this popular watchword uncontagious and unknown among their laborers, and further stampede to the North wholly unknown, indescribable and impossible."

Betsy Bailey would have washed out his mouth with soap. Figuratively, a good many of his fellow blacks did. They did not want to settle for working someone else's land on shares, trapped by perpetual debt and forced to accept the white man's discipline out of fear of eviction or physical harm. Nell Irvin Painter credits Douglass with predicting the twentieth century's Civil Rights Movement when she states that his position was that when "the level of violence against nonviolent Black protesters . . . [reached] a level intolerable to the rest of the country," the nation would take action. But the people desperate to get to Kansas could not wait seventy-five years for this to happen. And the idea that the Southern worker should wait docilely for that day was totally antithetical to Douglass's repeated insistence on immediate full equality. With his words to the social scientists, he had let his black brethren down. More than four decades earlier, a band of young men on the Freeland farm had planned their exodus. Frederick Bailey had mourned the return of his comrades to the fields while he, later, made good his own escape. In 1879, Frederick Douglass was abandoning not only the Henry Harrises of the South, but Frederick Bailey as well.

23
Niagara Falls

"WHEN THE REPUBLICAN PARTY loses 'Fred' Douglass' voice, it will be a heavy loss." Marshall Jewel, writing in the name of the Republican National Committee, was worried not about the orator's loyalty, but about his temporary hoarseness, as plans were laid for the 1880 presidential campaign. Douglass was needed to help keep the black vote in line and lure back the reform vote. James A. Garfield, an intellectual Civil War general from Ohio, was Douglass's kind of politician, and he stumped for him in the South and the Midwest. In the exhilaration of the campaign, Douglass had great hopes that he would be rewarded with a far grander post than he had yet held, perhaps even a place in the cabinet. But after Garfield was elected and while the quadrennial speculation over cabinet selection raged, he issued a Uriah Heep of a disclaimer, saying he was "altogether too modest" to hope for so high a post.

Douglass did, however, let the president-elect know that the "colored people of this country want office not as the price of their votes . . . , but for their recognition as a part of the American people." Samuel Clemens, for one, agreed. Douglass, at the least, should keep his job as marshal. Clemens's brother-in-law, a fellow abolitionist, admired Douglass, and Clemens, who was soon to bring Huck and Jim into being, did too. In January, as jobs were being parceled out, the nation's most popular author, not using his clearest prose, wrote to Garfield in Douglass's behalf: "He is a personal friend of mine, but that is nothing to the point, his history would move me to say these things without that, and I feel them too." The marshal was sent a copy of the letter by Clemens's brother-in-law; buoyed by this support, he wrote to thank Clemens, saying that his letter would "put the President elect in good humour, and that is very important." But Garfield was not to be humored. Marshal Douglass led the inaugural procession through the rotunda of the Capitol, but this was his last ceremonial task. The new president went back to the old practice of giving the job of marshal to a personal friend and shunted Douglass off to the insulting post of recorder of deeds. One more time, Douglass swallowed his pride, and with bitter disingenuousness claimed that the new job was better suited to his tastes.

In one sense it was; there were jobs for clerks in the recorder's office that Douglass could fill, and after warding off efforts in Congress to restructure the office, fill them he did, with a splendid disregard for any embarrassment about nepotism. His patronage power was limited, however. After Garfield's death in the fall of 1881, the new president, Chester A. Arthur, accused of corruption himself and therefore a convert to civil-service reform, declared that he would receive no delegations of job seekers or job brokers. Douglass knew that Arthur felt no obligation to him; when asked by John Sears, Amanda Auld Sears's widower, who was, for "the first time since the War of the Rebellion[,] . . . under the necessity of asking" for help getting "a place where I can earn a living for myself and family," he had to reply that he could promise nothing. As he told George T. Downing, for him to ask the president for a post for a friend would be to ensure being "snubbed at the White House." But in his own office, patronage was exercised in quite literal fashion: at one time or another Frederick jr., Lewis, and Rosetta were all employed there. Charles had a similar clerkship in the Treasury Department. The family seemed secure again.

The member of his family of whom Douglass was most proud was Charles's son Joseph, who had begun to study the violin. Joseph proved talented, and later, in the 1890s, having studied in Baltimore and New York, he appeared on the concert stage in Chicago, New York, and other cities. (It is, perhaps, just as well that his grandfather did not live long enough to learn that in the twentieth century, Joseph Douglass could rarely be heard playing his violin, that emblem of European culture, except in segregated concert halls in the South, shunned by those claiming untinged European ancestry.) But while the boy was growing and learning, he and his grandfather could play Schubert together in the music room at Cedar Hill.

From that fine house, Frederick Douglass could go back to another. Once more, he went to the Eastern Shore, this time to Wye House. In June 1881, with John L. Thomas, the collector of the port of Baltimore, Douglass set out on the latter's official cutter, the *Guthrie,* for the trip across the Chesapeake. As they came into the neck of the Miles River where Wye House stands, he "saw once more the stately chimneys of the grand old mansion which I had last seen from the deck of the *Sally Lloyd* when a boy." Of that departure, fifty-five years earlier, he had written in his *Narrative of the Life of Frederick Douglass,* "I walked aft, and gave to Colonel Lloyd's plantation what I hoped would be my last look."

Grandly, a seaman in a small boat was sent ashore with an invitation for the present Lloyd of Wye House to come aboard the *Guthrie;* he returned with a request that Recorder Douglass come to the old place. "Colonel"—as they all were—Edward Lloyd VII, the grandson of the

Douglass as marshal at the inauguration of President Garfield.

proprietor of Wye House whom Frederick Bailey had held in such awe, had conveniently been called to Easton on business. He had left his sons, Howard, aged eighteen, and DeCourcy, eight, with the intriguing, bewildering task of showing the vastly dignified black man around the country seat where he had once been a slave and from which hundreds of slaves had been sold south or sent to the Lloyd's other huge holdings in Arkansas, Mississippi, and Louisiana. None of that ugliness was in Frederick Douglass's line of vision that day; what he saw were the beautiful grounds and woods which he had roamed with Daniel Lloyd: "Very little was missing except the squads of little black children once seen in all directions."

Missing too were the slaves in the fields; the farms, far out of sight of the house, had been mechanized—ten men did the work of sixty, which simply meant, had Douglass stopped to think about it, that fifty descendants of those slaves had to scratch out a living some other way. But present realities were not on his mind, only a nostalgic recreation of things past. Aaron Anthony's square, sturdy brick house was still there, on Long Green; the closet Frederick had slept in had been incorporated into the kitchen, and its dirt floor "had disappeared under plank." Gone too was the memory of Hester being whipped in that kitchen; similarly, all he said now about the brutal overseer Austin Gore was that his house still stood. So did "old Barney's" stable and the wonderful carriage house once filled with coaches, phaetons, gigs, and even an almost-never-used sleigh; "Uncle Abe's" shoemaker's shop was still standing, and so was "Uncle Toby's" blacksmith shop. And there was the great barn where a little child had once watched swallows ceaselessly sweeping the air.

The poplars that the red-winged blackbirds had favored were gone, but not the oaks and elms whose shade had cloaked Daniel Lloyd and Frederick Bailey, eating the food the young lord had brought from his kitchen to compensate for the meagerness of Aunt Katy's fare. And in the graveyard, crowded now with two hundred years of Lloyds, lay "Mr. Page, a teacher in the family, whom I had often seen and wondered what he could be thinking about as he silently paced up and down the garden walks." Joel Page, brought down from Massachusetts by a grand Maryland family that ultimately left him in the care of the child in his charge, had opened mysterious worlds to Daniel Lloyd—and to young Frederick Bailey, who said back the words Daniel said to him. The teacher, apart from the overseers and other white subalterns, had moved in restless loneliness through the Wye House gardens under the curious, watchful eye of a child who, being a slave, was unapproachable. Now he lay in this stately grave far from his New England hill town, unknown even

Douglass revisiting his old home. From *Life and Times*, 1881.

to his family: "I have had intimation that they knew little about him after he once left home."

It was June, beautiful and warm. Douglass was carrying a bouquet of wild flowers "Mr. Howard" had picked in the graveyard, to be carried home to Cedar Hill to dry, as they came through the profusion of the now-unkempt gardens, onto the verandah bordered with boxwood, and into the great house. There the once-slave sipped madeira with a great-grandson of the lord of Wye House, whose portrait, still on its walls, the slave child had once surreptitiously studied with wondering imagination.

Where had the anger gone? The Lloyd boys (and their great-aunt Ann Catherine Buchanan, married to a former Confederate admiral, who received Douglass in her Wye River house the next day) had, with the most exquisite manners, and—one senses—genuine affection, smothered the wrath of a black man who had once thundered against their kind. With cloying faith in "a new dispensation of justice, kindness, and human brotherhood . . . dawning not only in the North, but in the South," he wrote of being given a bouquet of "many colored flowers" by Mrs. Buchanan's granddaughter: "I never accepted such a gift with a sweeter sense of gratitude." Referring to slavery, Douglass spoke of the "sunset of decayed institutions" that had yielded to "the grand possibilities of a glorious future"; he had, for the moment at least, been wholly seduced by too ripe a sunset.

Back in the recorder's office in Washington, in 1882, he hired a new clerk. Helen Pitts had been born in 1838 in Honeoye, New York, a farming community in Ontario County, some forty miles south of Rochester. Her farmer father, Gideon Pitts, and her mother, Jane Wills Pitts, were abolitionists, and the household fostered feminism as well. Helen, the oldest daughter, graduated from Mount Holyoke Seminary in 1859, while her sister Eva was one of the first female graduates of Cornell University.

In the 1860s, following the Civil War, Helen Pitts taught at Hampton Institute, later Booker T. Washington's alma mater. Ill-health, perhaps coupled with discouragement, sent her back to Honeoye, where she remained for several years. In 1880 she moved to Uniontown to live with her uncle Hiram Pitts, who had considerable investments in land in that growing community. Pitts's place, high on an eastern slope of the town, was adjacent to Douglass's Cedar Hill.

Women still held the toehold they had gained during the Civil War in the expanded government agencies. Pitts was at first employed in the pension office, but when she heard of an opening in the recorder's office, she applied there, and was taken on. Both positions were routine. Being single, she had to support herself, but an educated woman was unlikely to find a post equal to her ability. Pitts became active in the women's rights movement in Washington, and collaborated with Caroline Winslow in the publication of a radical feminist newspaper, the *Alpha.*

Helen Pitts and Frederick Douglass met in Uniontown as neighbors, and immediately had the cause of women's rights to talk about. Douglass's sensitivity to women's aspirations, born, no doubt, in his own struggles to pass an unfair barrier, was genuine. In a long, frank letter to the successful journalist Grace Greenwood, for example, he had written, "I have even flattered myself . . . that I helped to remove your . . . distrust of your own ability as a writer—and encouraged you to venture into the arena of literature where you have . . . [shone] for thirty years." Cedar Hill was something of a gathering place for members of the movement; when the National Woman Suffrage Association met in Washington in January 1881, several of the delegates called on Douglass in his home. Douglass attended the meetings and wondered in admiration at the incongruity of the "profusion of flowers and music" at the tribute to his old friend Lucretia Coffin Mott, who had recently died. Recalling the stern Quaker, he wrote, "I am quite sure Lucretia would have objected."

Helen Pitts must have had childhood memories of Douglass. Her father had met him in the 1840s, when he was lecturing in the antislavery region of western New York, and she herself, as a child, may also have met him. When she became a clerk in his office, Douglass soon found that he could trust her to keep things going during his frequent absences. He was lecturing under the aegis of James Redpath and was also completing a new autobiography.

In 1881, Douglass published *Life and Times of Frederick Douglass.* In many ways, including the vanity of the title, the work was tired. Its time had passed—or so thought the public, which did not buy it. Douglass must have been aware that he was cranking out many-told tales yet again; his expression of frustration with his publisher over the poor physical quality of the volume suggests a more general dissatisfaction. But the book does have interesting differences from his *Narrative of the Life of Frederick Douglass* and *My Bondage and My Freedom,* and he brought his story up to date with observations on the Civil War, its coming, and its aftermath. Despite his distance from workers in the postwar world, it also includes curious, valuable insights into his experiences as a day laborer and a skilled caulker.

But the book's real message—which few people received—was that the story of slavery should not be purged from the nation's memory. White America wanted to hear no more of the subject; emancipation had taken care of it. Many black Americans, reacting to this weariness, had become almost apologetic about their slave past. His friend Harriet

Beecher Stowe had once awakened the nation with a great saga of slavery. Now his story might rouse people to the plight of the former slaves who were not fully free. He saw his life as a metaphor for a second emancipation, but he offered no plan that would meet the needs of a desperate people. Even if he had had a plan, few would have learned of it; the book sold few copies. And yet that book remains a cry from the heart that his slave experience, and the experiences of all American slaves, must not be forgotten.

Several of his friends had been encouraging him to branch away from autobiography in his writing. Ottilia Assing had urged him to tell the John Brown story, write of his relations with "Lincoln, Grant, Sumner, and other prominent men," describe his returning to Baltimore and the Eastern Shore, and tell of his trip to the Dominican Republic. All of these subjects found their way into *Life and Times,* but as part of his self-narrative. His own was, in the end, his only story.

In Rochester on July 9, 1882, Amy Post, the best of the Douglasses' friends, received a postcard from Frederick jr.: "Mother had a paraletic stroke yesterday. She is dangerously ill." Post immediately wrote to Douglass, who replied on July 14: "I am glad to be able to report a favorable change in Anna's condition. . . . She is not yet out of danger and is very feeble, but her mind is clearer and her speech and appearance is better. All that Medical skill and good Nursing can do will be done." All the children were joining him in caring for their mother, he added. To another old friend, Parker Pillsbury, he wrote on July 18 that for the last twelve days Anna had "been pressing near the gates of death." Her left side was completely paralyzed. "It is a marvel that she is still alive, but alive she is. . . ." But at four o'clock in the morning of August 4, 1882, Anna Murray Douglass died; she was sixty-nine. "It is especially sad to you," wrote Douglass's old friend Henry O. Waggoner, "because she was the choice of your youth."

In his grief, Douglass wrote, "My dear friend Amy, You kindly said come to me in your trouble." And so he did. The Saturday after the funeral, he, Rosetta, and his oldest granddaughter, Annie Sprague, were on the train for Rochester, where Anna was to be buried. They would stay with the Posts. "When death comes into ones home—a home of four and forty years, it brings with it a lesson of thought, silence, humility and resignation," Douglass wrote Grace Greenwood, who was in Paris. "There is not much room for pride or self importance in presence of this event." His first thought had been to "break up my home and possibly go to Europe—but upon reflection—I felt it too late in life to . . . become a wanderer." After returning from Rochester, Douglass stayed on at Cedar Hill. Nathan Sprague's sister Louisa, who had long been living there to care for Anna, served as a kind of housekeeper, assisted by Rosetta's daughter Annie, now eighteen.

While he struggled to pull himself together emotionally, Douglass also began to regain his political bearings. His proper stance was always as a critic, as one crying in the wilderness, rather than as a practical politician. Douglass had had his brief moment in the pale sun of the Hayes administration, but after being slighted by Garfield and ignored by Arthur, he was now more impotent than ever when it came to power derived from public office. His voice could still be heard, however. In the fall of 1882, with Republican stalwarts in trouble in a good many congressional elections, he wrote to Grace Greenwood, "You will see by American papers . . . a determination to annihilate Conkling in New York, and Cameron in Pennsylvania: and from present appearances there is a fair promise of success." Reflecting on antislavery days, he wrote, "I find . . . a great comfort in the thought that I have had, as you have had, some agency, in ridding this country of Slavery—and in restoring to freedom millions of the human race—but the evils that remain are so multitudinous and so powerful [as] to dwarf what has already been done and leave little room for complacency. . . . It is sad to see . . . the once great and powerful Republican party—which had done so much for our country, for humanity and civilization being now literally stabbed to death— assassinated by men who have hitherto been its staunch defenders. A spirit of rule or ruin is abroad here."

In the summer of 1883, Douglass appears to have been depressed almost to the point of a breakdown. He was under the care of a physician, who prescribed complete rest. This the sixty-five-year-old widower sought with his friends Martha and Frank Greene. Martha Greene, witty and outspoken, not only knew Douglass from the old antislavery days but knew his children as well. When the Greenes took him off to the beautiful and quiet inland Maine resort of Poland Springs, Douglass received such a flood of uncharacteristically upbeat mail from his children and grandchildren that one suspects Martha Greene of having inspired the outpouring in an effort to cheer him.

From Poland Springs in July 1883, he wrote Lewis a formal letter— clearly designed for publication—expressing his thanks to a Washington gathering for choosing him as a delegate to the National Convention of Colored Men, to be held in September. He was particularly sorry "that the condition of my health [had] compelled me to be absent" from the Washington meeting, as the invitation represented a rebuff to young rebels who, for a time, had taken over the proceedings and attempted to disqualify the delegates already chosen, including him. For public consumption, he wanted Lewis to know that while he did "not approve the sentiment which would exclude all gray heads from the counsels of any class of people," he was willing, in the hope of "cool, cautious, and wise deliberations" to stand aside and "allow some younger man to come to the front and thus secure union and harmony where there now seems to be discord and even bitterness." And he continued, with more candor than usual on this subject, "Places of honor and responsibility are as pleasant to me as to most men, but to be acceptable they must come freely and without harm to any." Therefore, he authorized Lewis to make an "absolute and final" withdrawal of his name—thus virtually assuring that he would be retained as a delegate.

Douglass, Richard T. Greener, George Washington Williams, and twenty-three other activists, had issued the call for the September meeting, originally scheduled for Washington. (Antagonisms among black leaders, aggravated by their frustration at not having any other way of using up their political energy, often did not last.) Delegates were allotted on the basis of the black population of the several states; 243 of the 282 delegates were from the former slave states. In the call for the meeting the leaders announced, "We are not given a fair remuneration for our labor in the south. . . . We are not allowed fair and equal educational advantages in the public schools in most parts of the country. . . . our political rights are now almost wholly ignored." The time to meet was right, they declared, as "the country is on the eve of a great political revolution."

In May, as plans were still being made, the black journalist T. Thomas Fortune accused Douglass in his *New York Globe* of acceding to a White House request that the convention be moved out of the capital. Loud calls for a renewed commitment to civil rights would embarrass the Republicans, and Fortune wanted them embarrassed. He asked what President Arthur had to do with the arrangements anyway: "Is Arthur a Negro?" Douglass denied that he and the president had ever "uttered one word" on the subject, and did not mention the concern of several shrewd, cautious black leaders who wondered if having a great many black people in the capital's hotels might alarm Supreme Court justices just then considering the constitutionality of the Civil Rights Act of 1875. The question before the justices was whether the Fourteenth Amendment protected the right of black people to enter privately owned public places such as theaters, restaurants, and hotels, or whether the owners' rights to their property permitted them to exclude black patrons. Not knowing that the Court would make a mockery of their discretion, the chary organizers, with Douglass's concurrence, had moved the meeting to Louisville.

Douglass closed his letter to Fortune with the hope that "the time will never come when you and I may not differ in opinion in respect to public measures, without assailing each other's motive." This last statement was not cant; it is essential to an understanding of Douglass to recognize that while he could say in harsh and unequivocal terms what he thought of old allies who disagreed with him on an issue, he seldom lost a friend for long. He was too much respected, and solidarity in the face of adversity kept reasserting itself. Once, he branded George Washington Williams a liar, in print—"I do not see how you can expect to win a reputation to . . . veracity while you allow your pen to write deliberate falsehoods"—for what Williams had said about his opposition to Garrison and his battle with Greener over the Exodusters; privately they remained close. He had attacked both Elizabeth Cady Stanton and Susan B. Anthony over their opposition to the Fifteenth Amendment, yet Anthony wrote immediately after Anna Douglass's death, offering him badly needed help, and when, later, he was criticized for taking too strong a stand on interracial marriage, Stanton wrote him the kindest and wisest of notes.

Despite his ostensible reluctance, Douglass was in Louisville in September, confronting, among the 280-odd delegates, a good many young, angry black men disgusted with the betrayal of their cause. They saw the Republican party, sacred still to their elders, as a participant in that betrayal. Neither invocations of the Republicans' sainted Lincoln nor reminders that the Democrats were even worse on racial matters impressed them. Independence was in the air; the early stirrings were felt of a new way that in the 1890s would take many of these black rebels into their uneasy alliance with the People's party—the Populist party.

Douglass rose to speak as mentor to the young rebels. To give his words universality, he called his talk to the black men "Address to the People of the United States," and he acknowledged his uneasiness about attending what was, in effect, a segregated meeting: "We are asked not only why hold a convention, but, with emphasis, why hold a *colored* convention?" Answering his question, he declared that it was "our lot to live among a people whose laws, traditions, and prejudices have been against us for centuries, and from these they are not yet free. . . . Though the colored man is no longer subject to be caught and sold, he is still surrounded by an adverse sentiment which fetters all his movements. . . . He is rejected by trade unions, . . . and refused work where he lives, and burial where he dies, and yet is asked to forget his color, . . . [to] forget that which everybody else remembers." Everywhere, "he is sternly met on the color line."

Douglass was deeply ambiguous in his relation to working-class black people; he could not think of himself as one of them, but he could not accept anything that suggested that they were apart from him. He resisted their attempts to form either racially defined unions or political parties. He knew that black people, save in a few parts of the Deep South, were in a minority in America and therefore probably could not force their will on the nation, even if they organized. What was more, he would not have welcomed such a separatist undertaking because he remained philosophically committed to the concept of all people being part of a common family.

But those members of the family who were doing the work in the South were in grave trouble. In maddeningly general terms, Douglass told their representatives in Louisville that he favored unions as long as they did not exclude his people, but his wording suggested sternly, if obliquely, his objection to black unions: "It is a great mistake for any class of laborers to isolate itself and thus weaken the bond of brotherhood between those on whom the burdens and hardships of labor [fall]. The fortunate ones of the earth, who are abundant in land and money and know nothing of the anxious care and pinching poverty of the laboring classes, may be indifferent to the appeal to justice at this point, but the laboring classes cannot afford to be indifferent. What labor everywhere wants, what it ought to have, and will someday demand and receive, is an honest day's pay for an honest day's work. As the laborer becomes more intelligent he will develop what capital he already possesses—that is the power to organize and combine for its own protection." It is hard to see what the working-class people in his audience were supposed to make of this brief analysis, as Douglass, in his talk, moved on to present-day echoes of ancient animosities with a condemnation of a grandson of John C. Calhoun, who had recently accused blacks of being "indolent."

The younger men in the audience (who might have had to be told who John C. Calhoun was) took small comfort from his expressions of disappointment in the Republican party and even smaller comfort from his insistence that any third-party activity would only play into the hands of the Democrats. And, to his exasperation, they said so. "For the life of me," he told the press, "I cannot see how any honest colored man, who has brains enough to put two ideas together, can allow himself, under the notion of independence, to give aid and comfort to the Democratic Party in Ohio or elsewhere." He also contended that black people would be in great jeopardy if, following the departure of those among them who insisted on independence, the Republicans were to discover that they could win without black votes. Unlike many of his fellow delegates in Louisville, he still believed a properly chastened Republican party could be counted on.

In addition to holding his young colleagues in line, Douglass had to check his own vehemence. Recently he had called for a black vice-president, and the response had been accusations that he wanted offices to be granted according to race, without regard to merit. Now he stated that "no class or color should be the exclusive rulers of this country." Racists had made a red herring of the burst of oratory, perhaps self-interested, in which, in imagination, he elevated a black man to the vice-presidency. With the nation's second presidential assassination a matter of very recent memory, white supremacists could be counted on to pounce on such an idea with particular speed. His final advice to those who had attended the convention and to African Americans in general—advice from which he never swerved—was to "stick to the Republican Party. Tell your wants, hold the party up to its professions, but do your utmost to keep it in power in state and nation."

While Douglass was in Louisville, he was sent a letter, from a resident of that city, that suggests how far he was from totally escaping his past, or, for that matter, how far from escaping the consequences of slavery our country is ever to be. Sarah O. Pettit, signing herself "your affect. sister," wrote, "I again write to you a few lines to let you know that I am still on the enquire for you—as it has been a number of years since we met still I have never forgotten that you are my Brother." Pettit then alluded to some important business and to an earlier visit in Louisville, giving the address where the meeting had taken place. The bleak note closes, "All's well, all is well." At that earlier meeting, if such there was, Douglass may have concluded that Sarah Pettit was not his sister, but he had had a sister Sarah, four years older than he. In the division of the Bailey family in 1827, Sarah had been awarded to Andrew Anthony, and in 1832, he sold her and an infant son, Henry, to one Perry Cohee, of Lawrence County, Mississippi, for nine hundred dollars. No response to Pettit's letter has been found, and nothing in the record suggests that it resulted in any sort of reconstruction of her family, or of Douglass's.

On October 15, 1883, the Supreme Court handed down a decision that "came upon the country like a clap of thunder from a clear sky." The blow, Douglass was later to say, "was dealt us in the house of our friends. The bench was composed of nine learned Republican judges, and of these nine honorable men only one came to our help, I mean honorable John Marshall Harlan. He [and Douglass might have noted the irony that Harlan was the only one of the nine to once have owned slaves] stood up for the rights of colored citizens as those rights are defined by the fourteenth amendment of the Constitution. . . ." In the ironically named Civil Rights Cases, the justices held that the owner of a place of public accommodation could not be required to admit black patrons, because such a requirement would violate the owner's right to private property under the Fourteenth Amendment's due process clause. And what was more, only the state legislatures, not the United States Congress (which had passed the Civil Rights Act of 1875) had jurisdiction over a citizen's rights. The Fourteenth Amendment, adopted, as an earlier Supreme Court had said, for "that race and that emergency," was now, with this new decision, of virtually no use to "that race" in its continuing emergency.

A week later, Douglass rose wearily, sadly, in Lincoln Hall in Washington: "We have been, as a class, grievously wounded, . . . and this wound is too deep and too painful for ordinary measured speech." The decision had "swept over the land like a moral cyclone," and he likened it to the Missouri Compromise, the Fugitive Slave Act, and *Dred Scott:* "I look upon it as one more shocking development of that moral weakness in high places which has attended the conflict between the spirit of liberty and the spirit of slavery." But not even this "heavy calamity" that left "seven millions of the people of this country . . . naked and defenceless against . . . malignant, vulgar, and pitiless prejudice," could drive Douglass to revolt against a union that had ended slavery: "government is better than anarchy, and patient reform is better than violent revolution." Turning his attention to the Supreme Court, he described it as "the autocratic point in our National Government. No monarch in Europe has a power more absolute over the laws, lives, and liberties than that Court has over our laws, lives, and liberties." With sorrow rather than anger, with regret rather than bitterness, he accepted the dictum of judges who "live, and ought to live, an eagle's flight beyond the reach of fear or favor, praise or blame, profit or loss." This said, he did not neglect to praise Justice Harlan for dissenting in the face of "criticism from which even the bravest man might shrink."

Looking beyond the decision, Douglass went on to declare, "Color prejudice is not the only prejudice against which a Republic like ours should guard. The spirit of caste is dangerous everywhere. There is the prejudice of the rich against the poor, the pride and prejudice of the idle dandy against the hard handed working man." Then, noting that "Catholic Irish fellow citizens" were guilty of a good deal of color prejudice, Douglass launched into an attack on England's tyranny over Ireland, and called out, "Fellow Citizens! We want no black Ireland in America. We want no aggrieved class. . . . The power and friendship of seven millions of people scattered all over the country . . . are not to be despised." And "far down the ages," he predicted, the court's decision would be overturned—as it essentially was, eighty-one years later, with the adoption of the Civil Rights Act of 1964. Meanwhile, "in humiliating the colored people of this country, this decision has humbled the Nation."

On January 24, 1884, the recorder of deeds of the District of Columbia went to City Hall, called a clerk aside, paid a one-dollar fee, and quietly obtained a marriage license. If Douglass was trying to avoid notice, he failed. Another clerk alerted a reporter for the *National Republican,* and he rushed to the recorder's office for background on what he knew would be a sensational story. When he asked Rosetta about her father's coming wedding, she was "visibly affected" by the question, and the reporter discovered that everyone else in Frederick and Helen's office was surprised too.

The determined reporter failed to make his way, later that afternoon, into Douglass's home, "where his family was assembled," and the nature of the discussion that followed we do not know. At best it was probably frosty; more likely it was rancorous. Later, Rosetta, in particular, made no secret of her disapproval of her father's marriage, and that day, none of the children accompanied Douglass when he left for town (with the reporter again in his wake). He waited for a time at a friend's house, and shortly after six, "called for a carriage and drove to the residence of Miss Pitts."

He was not the day's first caller at 913 E Street, N.E., where Helen Pitts was now living; earlier, the energetic reporter had talked his way into the parlor of the "copyist in Mr. Douglass's office," whom he found to be "petite in figure, with dark eyes and hair, and . . . about 36 years of age." (She was forty-five.) "After submitting to persistent questioning for awhile," Pitts confirmed that she was to be the bride.

When Douglass arrived, the two drove to the parsonage of the Fifteenth Street Presbyterian Church, the home of Francis and Charlotte Forten Grimké. The choice of who would marry the couple had not been left to chance. The Reverend Mr. Grimké was not only the minister of perhaps the nation's most distinguished African American church, but also the acknowledged product of the best-known and most honored interracial union in the land. The son of a slave mother, Nancy Weston, and her aristocratic South Carolinian planter-owner, Grimké had come north after serving as a valet to a Confederate officer during the war. With his brother Archibald, he attended Lincoln University; later, with the assistance of his two white aunts, the abolitionists Angelina and Sarah Grimké, he studied law and then, at Princeton Theological Seminary, prepared for the ministry. Grimké's performance of the ceremony was an assertion not only of the sacred blessedness of this interracial marriage, soon the nation's most famous, but of its secular correctness as well.

The ceremony was witnessed by the minister's wife and, simply, "two members of the household." Afterward, on the steps of the house, reporters were ready with questions, and the appropriately "nervous" bridegroom gave the *National Republican* reporter "all the information he could in good spirit, but finally hinted that his questioner was rather 'cheeky.' " Breaking away, the couple drove to Cedar Hill, where a stiff reception from the Douglass children was followed by "an elegant wedding supper."

Soon after the wedding, the two traveled to Honeoye to see Helen's family. They were hoping for a warmer reception than they had received at Cedar Hill, but Helen's abolitionist father, who had once been proud to know Douglass, was not to give them his blessing. Instead, Gideon Pitts was so adamant in his objection to the marriage that he refused his house to his son-in-law, and thereafter would visit Washington only when he was sure his daughter and her black husband were out of the city. Similarly, his brother Hiram Pitts, Douglass's neighbor, broke off all relations with his niece and her husband. Helen refused to knuckle under to her father, and refused, as well, to accept a full break with her family. Her sisters Jennie and Eva remained loyal to her, as did her nieces (who grew fond of their "Uncle Fred"), and when their mother became ill in 1887, Helen returned early from a trip to Europe to care for her; later Jane Pitts came to live with her daughter and son-in-law. Quickly, Helen Douglass had established that Cedar Hill was her home.

The marriage caused great strain within Douglass's family. With the wonderful adaptability of children, the young Douglasses had been able to accept their father's friendships with Julia Griffiths and Ottilia Assing, and the long stays of these friends in their parents' house, but the idea of marriage to someone other than their mother, to someone who was not black, was anathema to them. They had always known of the importance to their father of his many close white friends, but it was only with his marriage that he seemed formally to have repudiated his family—his children, their mother, and their mother's people—all black people. Marrying a white woman seemed a public confirmation of his children's heretofore private grievance, their sense that they, being darker than he, were of less value. In this feeling the Douglass children were joined by many black Americans, who felt betrayed by a leader they had so long admired. Their criticism was loud and clear: "Fred Douglass has married a red-head white girl . . . ," wrote a correspondent to the *Weekly News*. "Goodbye, black blood in that family. We have no further use for him. His picture hangs in our parlor, we will hang it in the stables."

In contrast, at the close of January, Douglass received a letter from Elizabeth Cady Stanton congratulating him and expressing the "wish that all the happiness possible in a true union may be yours." She had heard, she wrote, "much criticism on your condescention in marrying a *white woman*. After all the terrible battles and political upheavals we have had in expurgating our constitutions of that odious adjective 'white' it is really remarkable," she added with rich-sarcasm, "that you of all men should have stooped to do it honor." Then Stanton, taking majestic exception to both sexism and racism, added, "In defense of the right to pilot ships [the solicitor of the Treasury had recently ruled against employment of a female pilot on a Mississippi steamboat], or marry whom we please—we might quote some of the basic principles of our government"; we might, she continued, "suggest that in some things individual rights to tastes should control." Warming to her cause, Stanton declared, "If a good man from Maryland sees fit to marry a disfranchised woman from New York, there should be no legal impediments to the union." With such encouragement, and with immense dignity, the Douglasses chose not to notice being constantly noticed.

Douglass's second marriage, so simple and direct for him, was to spin a troubling and complex web of personal relationships. He married, confident in his belief that the universality of the experience would sustain all of the people to whom his comradeship reached. He did not know how little his confidence was shared. He had arranged the marriage secretly to avoid the public outcry that prior announcement would surely have raised, but he did not stop to realize how startled old friends might be. Worse, he never quite understood how ill-equipped his children were for the emotional reach his way of life imposed on them.

In another direction, Douglass seems not to have taken into account how demanding his own sense of his rightness was, or how vulnerable was the seemingly most sophisticated of his friends, Ottilia Assing. He was aware that she was susceptible to deep depression and for a decade he had known that her physician was conscious of her "self-slaughterous tendencies." Douglass must have recognized that his marriage would affect Assing deeply, and apparently tried to reconcile her to it; their correspondence during this period is lost.

From The Cross, St. Neots, in February, Julia Griffiths Crofts wrote, "I have this morning received from the kind hand of . . . [a] mutual friend a copy of the Rochester *Democrat* which makes mention of your marriage & I as one of your truest and warmest friends hasten to send you (& Mrs. Douglass) my most sincere congratulations." Later, in the spring, Martha Greene wrote from Fall River, "It seems to me Frederick that it is right for me to say that I believe you misjudge public sentiment when you insist the sole cause of your being as you express it 'under the ban of public displeasure' is because you married a white lady. It is because of the *way you did it.* Had your courtship been open and above-board, your marriage announced, and consummated in the presence of your children and friends, yourselves conducting the whole affair with the dignity and propriety which have ever before marked all your public proceedings

. . . all would have said 'God bless him,' and made up to him all he has lost in the past."

Mrs. Douglass was also being called on to be public about her marriage. That spring, at Mount Holyoke, an indefatigable arranger of seminary events was eager to have Helen Pitts attend her twenty-fifth reunion, bringing along the one who could be counted on to be the most-noticed spouse. Helen sent her "sincerest thanks for your noble letter with its generous invitation," but said that other travels would make it impossible for them to be in South Hadley. In June, Helen wrote to her classmate again: "I feel like putting on my hat and going right along when I think what good times you will have together." But she did not attend; instead, she informed her classmate proudly that if anyone should care to call, her address was "Mrs. Hon. Frederick Douglass, Cedar Hill, Anacostia, District of Columbia."

On August 21, 1884, Ottilia Assing dressed carefully in a monogrammed blouse and skirt, put on her hat, dropped her key, a brooch with a picture inside, and a bit of money into her red leather wallet, and left her Paris hotel. Walking in the Bois de Boulogne, she stopped to pick a leaf from an oak tree and carefully put it into her purse; shortly, from that same purse, she took out a container of poison and swallowed its contents. Under her will, dated November 9, 1871, a $13,000 trust fund was established, the income from which was to be paid semiannually to "Frederick Douglass for and during the term of his natural life, in recognition of his noble labors in the Anti-Slavery cause." The final (scrupulously honored) stipulation in this document was that "all the letters that will be found in my possession, are to be destroyed immediately." In a last, minor alteration to the will, made in Florence a year before her death, Assing wrote, "My large album I give to Hon. Frederick Douglass. He may besides select among my books those that will please him."

That same August, the Douglasses were on their wedding trip. "Helen and I have had a delightful tour," Frederick wrote, on their return. "From here to Chicago to Battle Creek, Niagara Falls—Rochester, Geneva, Syracuse, Oswego—Thousand Islands—Montreal, White Mountains—Portland, Boston, Fall River—Plymouth—New Bedford—and what is remarkable and gratifying not a single repulse or insult in all the journey," he reported to Amy Post, whom they had missed seeing in Rochester. "I return home with a higher estimate of the progress of American Liberty and civilization than I started out with. You will be glad to know that my marriage has not diminished the number of the invitations I used to receive for lectures and speeches—that the momentary freeze of popular disfavor caused by my marriage has passed away. I have had very little sympathy with the curiosity of the world about my domestic relations. What business has the world with the color of my wife? It wants to know how old she is,? how her parents and friends like her marriage,? how I courted her? whether with love or with money? Whether we are happy or miserable now that we have been married seven months? You would laugh to see the letters I have received and the newspaper talk on these matters—I do not do much to satisfy the public on these points—but there is one upon which I wish you as an old and dear friend to be entirely satisfied and that is: that Helen and I are making life go very happily and that neither of us has yet repented of our marriage. I give you, thanks my dear friend, for your congratulations and good wishes."

24
Africa

"WELL HERE I AM IN EGYPT. I have not seen pharaoh yet," Frederick wrote his son, "but I have seen at a distance the tops of the Pyramids, leaning their lofty heads mountain like against the soft blue sky." The Douglasses were at the farthest point of their trip to Europe and the eastern Mediterranean. It was the most conventional of upper-class trips abroad, and as one is apt to do when traveling, both Helen and Frederick had begun diaries when they left New York, in September 1886. Helen had made the arrangements for Stateroom 2 on the *City of Rome,* and they encountered none of the embarrassment and abuse that had marred Douglass's first Atlantic crossings. When they boarded, Helen was intrigued with the ingeniousness of the compact arrangement of their quarters, and both were busy visiting with the people who had come to see them off. Among them was Gustave Frauenstein: "We talked of Miss Assing & as the genial Dr. left he threw his arms around Frederick's neck in a good old fashioned hug & kissed him, kissed me, and ran off the steamer."

"In the evening, Frederick went on deck, but I was tired and undressed and mounted my perch, the upper berth," wrote Helen; "though we had pulled close on the dock and were all night receiving and loading freight just outside our port-hole, I slept all night." At sea, Frederick wrote of the rows of deck-chaired ladies with books "peacefully closed on their laps," held "more as ornament" than otherwise, dozing or peering at their fellow passengers while the men "walk the deck and smoke, smoke and smoke, looking as solemn as if they were on the way to a funeral."

"I had thought to cross the ocean quietly and without being recognized by anybody," he wrote, describing the impossible. The "English passengers all agreeable," he noted, "and mind their business and [are] not disturbed by our presence." Helen Douglass found they had as a fellow passenger "a real live 'lord,'" Lord Porchester, a wan young man who had been traveling in the United States with his tutor; when introduced to Douglass, he "showed, I thought, a possibility of there being something to him after all." Also aboard were "the Rev. Henry Wayland, son of old Dr. Wayland" (Francis Wayland, president of Brown University), and his companion George Bulloch, both of whom Douglass had met before. They were eager to talk politics, and Helen thought "there was the smell of mugwumpery" in their remarks. The two Americans were eager to arrange for Douglass to address the passengers—not very many altogether—but for a time he put them off.

Four days later, on September 19, 1886, in a "saloon . . . furnished in dark green plush," with a long writing table, Douglass wrote, "This is Sunday—and one of our fine men is dead and is to be buried in the sea today"; the ceremony was "more solemn . . . than on land." The next day, Douglass was on deck; the weather had cleared and he watched a "large school of porphoses . . . playing with our powerful ship by diving under its bow as if she were a fish." Sitting in his deck chair, Douglass was reading *English Traits* by Emerson to ready himself for his tour, happily oblivious of the author's having blackballed him from a Boston club almost forty years earlier.

On September 22, Douglass saw "the mountain coast of dear old Ireland . . . come into view" and called Helen to join the passengers at the rail. "Poor, barefooted Ireland!" he said to her, as he gazed "sadly upon those shores he first saw forty-one years ago." After a stop in Queenstown, they set out across the Irish Sea; Helen found that the "Fastnet light" at twilight reminded her "of Sankaty Head tower on Nantucket." Having passed the coast of Wales, they arrived in Liverpool. "Everything about the Docks much the same as forty years ago," he noted; "no sign of decay." The people were "full of life and activity." When the two went walking in streets crowded with "omnibuses, carts carriages and people," they found a "throng . . . made up of working people" who walked "as if hurried along by an irresistable pressure. Boys girls men and women, some in plain clothing and some in scarcely any clothing at all barefooted and bareheaded. . . . Once in a while a family begging a woman with a babe in arms and two or three small children at her skirts—she singing, in mournfully heartbroken and heart breaking strains." Douglass must have been reminded of the beggars, abandoned children, and cripples he had seen in Dublin in 1845. Helen saw "little begrimed children in tatters, and great bare-legged bare-headed girls" hurrying along in the crowd. "The faces of many are tolerably cheerful but not happy in expression. Life is certainly a struggle here." Douglass, too, noted that the "crowd is cheerful. . . . One sees in this moving mass the immense energy there is in this English nation. I was however struck by the number of short men and women among the working people." Helen noted that as they walked, "people will look at Frederick wherever we go, but they wear no unpleasant expression. Many have a decided appearance of interest."

On September 24, Douglass wrote, "Today we are making ready to go to St. Neots," but then, tantalizingly, there is a gap of several weeks in his diary, so we are deprived of an account of his reunion, after a twenty-six-year separation, with Julia Griffiths Crofts. The two had corresponded regularly over all these years, and in conversation about each other's activities, they probably could have picked up almost as if they had seen each other a day or two before. But the emotional weight of the meeting is harder to assess. Frederick came to Julia, who had been a widow since 1880, with a wife so much like the one she would have been that it cannot have been easy for either old friend to talk. After a meandering trip, including a stop in Chester, they had come "unannounced to Mrs. Crofts," Helen wrote. She was charmed by the "quaint little English town hidden away from the R.R. station," with its "4000 inhabitants and no newspaper." There "Mrs. Crofts met us with open arms." And, whatever the two who had not seen each other in so long may have been thinking, they all "had tea," Helen recalled; then she and Frederick "went to bed in a cosy chamber, and I spent my first night in a real English home."

The visit took on the form of a totally commonplace reunion with friends from far away, and the deliberate elimination of drama was not without its value. By relying on restrained good manners, Frederick and Julia avoided an emotional outpouring that might have been so intense as to require them to make this meeting a final one. Instead, the friendship endured for a lifetime. Helen suggested the shape the relationship now took when she wrote, "In the morning a walk with Mrs. Crofts & Frederick (the trio) . . ." Months later, Frederick wrote of Julia that it "was a great happiness to see her so fresh and vigorous—we had much talk of old Rochester days—and of the good people who stood by us in the midst of popular prejudice."

They walked to the old church in the village, going around the cemetery and then back "through lovely lanes" to the "everlasting eating" of an English household. "After dinner," at noon, one day, Helen continued, "a donkeyish looking diminutive horse & I think a 'fly,' with Frederick driving, took us to Buckden, an old coaching town, to the

Towers, the palace in which Catherine of Arragon spent some time." Then they stopped in the Buckden cemetery, where two of Julia's nephews lay. They had died while students at nearby Cambridge. Back in St. Neots, they went to the high-church service on Sunday; Helen, "like an American barbarian, could not find a single place in the ritual." In the evening, "Frederick went with Miss Crofts to Wesleyan meeting." Next the two Americans went on a "pilgrimage" to Cambridge; they loved the gardens, the Bridge of Sighs, and a five o'clock service in King's College chapel, with its "slim wax tapers, the fading daylight coming through the grand painted windows, the noble organ, the magnificent anthem, the solemn echoing of the vaulted roof."

They went next to London, then to Paris, which Douglass had longed to see. Staying at the Hotel Britannique, on the right bank, they walked and walked along the recently carved-through boulevards of the beautiful city, and discovered the worn, more wonderful old streets as well. "I find the people here," Douglass wrote to his son Lewis, "singularly conscious of their Liberty, independence and their power. They show it in their whole carriage and in every line of their faces. . . . To show their contempt for the religious superstitions of the day they work or play on Sunday as it suits them—and even work on Sunday the better to take a holiday on Monday." He was not, he added, "in love with the french character. It is a strange mixture of kindness and cruelty[,] of politeness and rudeness—of fondness for animals & . . . perpetual use of the [whip] on the backs of their horses—There is more appearances of drinking here than I have ever seen anywhere and less drunkedness."

Douglass was troubled, he wrote to friends, to find that the "leprous distilement of American prejudice" had been exported to Paris, "in the shape of Ethiopian singers, who disfigure and distort the features of the negro and burlesque his language and manners in a way to make him appear . . . more akin to apes than to men. This mode of warfare," the constant battler insisted, "is purely American." On the streets, "colored faces are scarce. . . . I sometimes get sight of one or two in the course of a day's ramble. They are mostly from Haiti and the French Colonies."

In his letter to Lewis, Douglass also told of increasing trouble with his eyes and mentioned seeing in the newspaper "that our friend Robert Ingersol is [ill with] something like the trouble which took of[f] General Grant. I am very sorry." The letter also betrayed Douglass's anxiety about family business affairs: "Are you still in the Recorder's office? Is Rosetta and Fred still there? Has Smith paid or taken up his note: Does he pay his rent? Has my interest from the treasury come to hand? Has Mrs Howard paid her interest? I depend on you to keep my affairs straight and to make prompt collections when rent or interest is due—retaining for yourself five percent. . . . But do write at once." He closed by sending "love to Amelia Frederick Charley and all our little circle."

The Douglasses' guide in Paris was Theodore Stanton, the amiable, gregarious son of Elizabeth Cady and Henry Brewster Stanton, who wrote for American newspapers and with his elegant French wife, was active in the intellectual and social life of liberals, American and French, in the city. Stanton took Douglass to call on Victor Schoelcher, the French politician who, as Douglass wrote, "in the final hours of the Revolution of 1848 drew up the decree and carried through the measure of Emancipation to the slaves in all the French colonies." Douglass and Schoelcher had a rich conversation; the senator praised Jefferson, but condemned Washington, who, he held, could have ended slavery in the United States. Schoelcher, to Douglass's delight, was writing a biography of Toussaint L'Ouverture. But he destroyed Douglass's illusions about the novelist Alexandre Dumas. Douglass had long held up the black author as an exemplar the race's capacity for genius; now, Douglass reported, Schoelcher said he was "a clever writer, but . . . nothing in morals and politics." Unlike Victor Hugo, who championed emancipation, Dumas had "never said one word for his race."

Moving south into Burgundy, the Douglasses stopped in Dijon. "Helen did the town pretty thoroughly," Douglass told Stanton. "I stayed in to save my boots." In Lyons, where Henry O. Waggoner's son in the consulate had died of tuberculosis, they tried in vain to find a record of his having been a patient in a hospital, and they discovered "no trace of his grave." Douglass was left with nothing to report to his old friend about a son whose loss he much grieved. In Avignon, "one of the oldest, quaintest, crookedest and queerest places I ever visited," he was reminded powerfully of the popes who had reigned there. His reverie about them brought forth a judgment: "What a horrible lie that Romish church has palmed of[f] upon the people . . . pretending that its Pope, is the vice regant of God, the creator of the universe, and how strange it is that . . . millions of sane men have believed this stupendous . . . lie." At Marseilles, despite Schoelcher's comments, they hired a boat and were "rowed out to the old Chateau D'If made famous by the story of Monte Christo by Alex. Dumas."

From France, the Douglasses went on to Italy. They were charmed by Pisa, and as their train carried them to Rome, they took note of women, in fields bordered by olive trees, plowing behind long-horned oxen. In Rome they stayed at the Palazzo Moroni, the home of Caroline Remond Putnam and of her son Edmund Quincy Putnam and his English wife. There Douglass visited with Caroline's sister Sarah Remond, whom he had not seen in forty years; like her brother, his old friend Charles Lenox Remond, who had died in 1873, Sarah had been a speaker in the antislavery movement. "Like myself, the Remond sisters [there was a third in Rome as well] with the exception of Caroline have grown quite old but in all of them I saw much of the fire of their eloquent brother Charles." The Palazzo was a center of an interesting interracial group that included the sculptor Edmonia Lewis, the daughter of a Chippewa mother and an African American father. Her work was in museums and galleries in the United States and Europe. Although Lewis had received considerable appreciative notice at home—especially for a woman, and a black woman at that—she had for the past twenty years chosen to live in Rome. Douglass was intrigued that Lewis's constant use of Italian had "somewhat impaired her English."

The sculptor traveled with the Douglasses to Naples; another member of the party was a Miss Gates, whom Douglass described as "an artist and philanthropist." And he observed, as if excluding himself from the category, that she had "done a great deal for the Colored people." With Edmonia Lewis they went to a museum to see some of the "pictures and statuary and many objects of interest taken from the ruins of Pompeii and Herculaneum. The perfection of some of these in form, color and utility was remarkable considering their antiquity. In some respects they transcended modern art." Like so many tourists of the time, Douglass found Pompeii itself totally absorbing: "It was almost worth the voyage across the Atlantic to see the part of Pompeii already unearthed and to think of the two thirds of it still underground." He did not fail to emphasize that some of the Pompeians who had lived in such great luxury "were wealthy and powerful slaveholders."

On February 11, 1887, Helen and Frederick decided to extend their tour: "The thought of this trip to Egypt and Greece will probably keep me awake to night." He would get to see the "Land of the Pharaohs." The history of Egypt that came to mind as he contemplated the experiences ahead of him was almost entirely biblical: "It is no small thing to see the land of Joseph and his brethren and from which Moses led the children of Abraham out of the house of Bondage." As their ship sailed toward the Strait of Messina from Naples, Helen, early in the morning, called Frederick to the rail "to catch my first view of Stromboli, a volcanic mountain . . . [rising] abruptly from the sea. There were white clouds about its base, but the morning light rested upon its summit—and made it beautiful." Looking at the mountains along the shore, Douglass was moved to a solemn judgment that suggests the emblematic mode in which he saw himself: "I could but congratulate myself that born as I was a slave marked for a life under the lash in the cornfield that . . . [I] was abroad and free and privileged to see these distant lands . . . which those of the most highly favored by fortune are permitted to visit."

On another day—in February, which was accurately fixed in his mind as his month of birth—he mused, "If right in my estimate of the length of time I have been in the world, I am now 70 years old." And he was feeling fine, he reported—one of the few "able to go at the sound of the Bell." Once again, he was not seasick, despite the "wild behavior of the Mediterranean" on a "trying day for Helen and many other ladies on board."

On February 16, they arrived at Port Said: "The queerest of queer places." Douglass had written from Paris that he had "long been interested in ethnology, especially of the North African races. I have wanted the evidence of greatness, under a colored skin to meet and beat back the charge of natural, original and permanent inferiority of the colored races of men. Could I have seen forty years ago what I have now seen, I should have been much better fortified to meet the Notts and the Gliddens . . . in their arguments against the negro as a part of the great African race. Knowledge on this subject comes to me late, but I hope not too late to be of some service; for the battle at this point is not yet fought out, and the victory is not yet won." J. C. Nott and George R. Glidden were ethnologists who, Douglass recalled, had in their 1854 book denied that the "inferior" blacks of interior Africa were kin to the people of the advanced societies of Egypt and other parts of North Africa. Thinking on this subject had progressed little. Indeed, for Douglass a good deal of the battle was still to come, six years later, at the Chicago world's fair. Now, in Port Said, he had a chance to look at these people for himself. "All nations are here represented—a place to study ethnology," he wrote in his diary.

"Forty or fifty small boats" surrounded their ship in the harbor. Scows stood by with the coal for refueling, and were "soon boarded by a perfect swarm of Arab laborers, frocked, hooded, or fezed, barefooted and bare-legged to the knee, to bring in baskets on their heads the coal on shipboard. Heavens! What a clamour—what a confusion of tongues, all going at once and each endeavoring to drown the voice of the other—but the work goes bravely on—and one is astonished at the strength[,] cheerfulness and endurance of these sable children of the desert. I saw among them several genuine Negroes—and they seemed not a whit behind their fellow workmen either in noise or physical ability." Writing to Lewis, he reported, "It was wonderful to see how this dirty and disagreeable work was done. The men seem to revel in it. As I looked upon them, I thought of the time when in New Bedford I was, nearly fifty years ago, glad to do the same kind of work."

The refueling complete, they proceeded "slowly and noiselessly on a narrow stream of pure, blue water"—the Suez Canal—down to Ismailia, where they took the train to Cairo. From the window, they saw "outspread fields, of green vegetation," and men working ancient plows of the kind "used ten thousand years ago." Douglass described the land in Egypt well, but once in the city, he turned his attention to the people.

"Everything we see reminds us of the days of Moses. I do not know of what color and features the ancient Egyptians were, but the great mass of the people I have yet seen would in america be classed with mulattoes and negroes. This would not be a scientific description, but an american description. I can easily see why the Mohomidan religion commends itself to these people, for it does not make color the criterion of fellowship as some of our so called Christian nations do. All colors are welcome to the faith of the Prophet."

They arrived in Cairo on a holiday. The crowd in the street was so dense that their carriage could not move for half an hour: "Our patience however was rewarded by seeing the Khedeive—and having from him a gracious bow—and what is better to see the struggling, jostling noisy and eager mass of his turbaned subjects pushing there way between carts, carriages, donkeys . . . at risk of life and limb. We could not have a better chance of seeing an Egyptian crowd—Though noisy and without form, utter[ly] chaotic, it was good natured—each one took the push of his neighbor without offense. The officer that endeavored to clear the way for the Khedeive used a whip instead of a sword or Bayonet. The sound of the whip upon some of the long skirts was sharp and loud, but no body was hurt."

"You did not think, I did not think, nobody thought, that I would venture so far from home as I am this Sunday morning. 'Go down Moses, way down in Egypt land and tell old Pharaoh to let my people go.' " Douglass was writing to his son Lewis on February 20, 1887, and he leapt to ethnography, an intellectually active field in the 1880s. His library at Cedar Hill contained a good many books on the subject—studies, richly illustrated, that focused on the physical differentiation of groups of humankind, called races. "I was glad to see the Negro displaying equal muscle with the Arab in this work," he observed, "for there is no better physical man living than the Arab." And he reminded his son, "You know, I have long been interested in the Science of races, and especially interested to know something about the colors and features of Egyptians." Forty years earlier, he had found in James Cowles Prichard's *Natural History of Man* the picture of a pharaoh that reminded him of his handsome, lost mother, and now he had a chance to see the pharaoh's people for himself. "It has been the fashion of American writers, to deny that the Egyptians were Negroes and claim that they are of the same race as themselves. This has, I have no doubt, been largely due to a wish to deprive the Negro of the moral support of Ancient Greatness and to appropriate the same to the white race."

"Well what," he asked rhetorically, "have I to say on the subject? Why this, that in color, features and conduct, I see a much stronger resemblance to the Negro than to the Europeans. They are not the genuine crisp-headed Negro, but they are very much like the mulatto, and would be taken for such in the United States." Douglass, like other students of ethnology, was viewing the specimens from a detached perspective, while at the same time looking in the mirror. He too was a product of complex genetic linkages, not unlike those that had produced the people who had been living in Egypt for centuries. For Douglass, the most striking fact about this most ancient of the civilizations he was to encounter was that it demonstrated the early existence of such linkages, and he was not unhappy about having resulted from a more recent instance.

Traveling out into the country, the Douglasses were troubled by the "squalor, disease and deformity" and "all manner of importunate beg-gary." In the city, they found the bazaars fascinating and like other tourists they made their purchases, but their eyes were seldom off the people: "The most painful feature met with in the streets are the hooded and veiled women. It is sad to think . . . that one half of the human family should be thus cramped, kept in ignorance and degraded—having no existence except that of ministering to the pride and lusts of the men who *own* them as slaves are owned—and worst is they seem to like to have it so."

They drank it all in; Douglass's diary entries are fuller for Egypt than for any other place they visited. In March, after close to a month in Africa, they moved on to Greece. On their first afternoon in Athens, they went up to the Acropolis and "saw the great Parthenon." The next day, "we ascended by a zigzag path to the top of Lycabettus 919 feet above the level of the sea. I could look down . . . [; it] was a scene never to be forgotten. The Plains of Attica were spread out at our feet. Over the mountain, we could almost see the fields of Marathon—off towards the Sea we could see dimly the Mountains of Sparta."

Late in March, Helen received word that her mother was ill, and cabled, "Shall I come?" The answer was "favorable," and they continued on to Rome, arriving in time for Easter. At their hotel, one day, "a great surprise came to me . . . a lady of very fine appearance who introduced herself as Mrs John Beddulph Martin, of 17 Hyde Park Gate S.W. She frankly—and I thought somewhat proudly told me that she was formerly Mrs Victoria Woodhull—I am not sure that I quite concealed my surprise." All that he had heard about the most flamboyant and controversial American woman of his century flashed through Douglass's mind. "I however soon began to think, what do I know about this lady—that I should think her otherwise, than merely holding strange . . . opinions." He was in no position to think poorly of her for her espousal of free love or any other egalitarian view, but similar lack of license to chastise had not kept many others from vehemently criticizing her. Douglass, for his part, concluded, "I do not know that she is not in her life as pure as she seems to be. I treated her politely and respectfully—and she departed apparently not displeased with her call."

In Florence, they found the grave of Theodore Parker, whom Douglass revered not only for his stand against slavery but for his liberal views on religion. With less luck, they tried to find the home of "Miss Ludmilla Assing, the sister of my friend of many years Miss Ottilia Assing. Alas! How soon are the dead forgotten." In Venice, in a nicely incongruous twist, Douglass took special note of letters of John Adams, Jefferson, and Franklin in the archive there. Then, more traditionally, out in a gondola on the Grand Canal, "I saw the house where Desdemona resided when wooed by Othello."

On their way back to England, they again stopped in Paris. Grace Greenwood was there, as was Theodore Tilton; the Douglasses visited too with Elizabeth Cady Stanton, at work on "her woman's Bible—and . . . more radical than ever—She is a noble woman—and has no snobbery about her." Another feminist, Laura Hayes, meeting Douglass there, found him an "extremely handsome and amiable man . . . and so American in his speech and dress; and in the cheerful enthusiasm that pervaded his manner." She noted with distinct pleasure that he "handled the woman question with an ease and fearlessness that could only have come from deep conviction and early training."

Back in England, Helen received another cable, this time saying that her mother was gravely ill. Douglass took her to Liverpool and sent her on alone. As he told Amy Post, he knew the time would be difficult for her, but he was unwelcome in Helen's father's house. "She is a strong woman," he said, and she "bore" the separation "bravely." After giving the lectures that had been scheduled—no Frederick Douglass trip was complete without these—he too sailed for home. Helen's mother's illness proved not to be fatal, and in August the travelers were back at Cedar Hill.

25

Port-au-Prince

"DEAR ONES," wrote Helen Douglass on October 12, 1889, "with trunk closed and bonnet ready, I, while waiting must give a little account of ourselves since leaving the good ship Kearsarge." Frederick Douglass, the new minister to Haiti, and his wife had arrived on the famous Civil War battleship; once again, maddeningly to the others, Douglass alone of the party was not seasick. In calm water two miles offshore at Port-au-Prince, having taken "very pleasant leave of the officers," the Douglasses stepped down into a steam launch and "puffed" their way into the harbor.

"One of our first sights," continued Helen, "was a little fellow with a tray of molasses cake, or what looked like it, upon his head and one short garment on. He lifted the front of this to wipe his face, and the natural man was revealed. We all started to walk a little way to the carriages and there stood another brave youth describing a vigorous curve into the adjoining water, very composedly looking around at us the while." It was Columbus Day, and the Douglasses of Cedar Hill were discovering a new America.

The runaway slave from North America was now the minister to the black republic that Toussaint L'Ouverture had wrested from slaveholders close to a century before. In 1888, yet another Republican for whom Douglass had campaigned had been elected president; again it was time to hope for an appointment. In the winter of 1889, before Benjamin Harrison's inaugural, Douglass visited Arkansas for the first time, staying in the homes of several of the state's leading black citizens. Asked what position was likely to be given to a black man, he answered—saying the opposite of what he thought—that it would be presumptuous for a black person to aspire as high as a cabinet post. In point of fact, the only federal job in Washington securely in the hands of African American Republicans was Douglass's old one as recorder of deeds. Douglass would have liked to get it back, but in an appointment that showed how the tide was running for once-powerful black politicians, it went instead to Blanche K. Bruce, formerly a United States senator.

Black Americans still had the claim they had staked to the ministries to the black republics of Haiti and Liberia. Ebenezer D. Bassett of New Haven had been minister to Haiti during the Grant administration (and he too would have been happy to have his old post back). John Mercer Langston had succeeded Bassett, serving from 1877 to 1885. Even Grover Cleveland, a Democrat, had honored the tradition, sending John E. W. Thompson to Port-au-Prince. For nearly three months after Harrison took office, neither this nor any other appointment came Douglass's way. During this time, the loyal campaigner (while carefully not antagonizing Harrison) sought to persuade the president to return the federal government to the desperately needed work of protecting the lives of black citizens in the South and upholding the right to vote. Douglass's friends feared that simply by raising the issue of Republican backsliding in the old Confederacy, he would lose favor with Harrison.

Black leaders could find little evidence that the president wanted to reverse the policies that had been established following the Compromise of 1877. Jeremiah E. Rankin wrote to Douglass, "I have never believed that President Harrison will prove untrue to you. But, the movement for a White Republican Party in the South does not augur well. The party must be Black as well as White: and no more White than Black." The first of Rankin's prophecies proved accurate. Douglass was given a post; but it was not related to the grave problems in the South. Despite strong pressure from New York merchants, with allies in the cabinet, to get a white man appointed, President Harrison had Secretary of State James G. Blaine send to Cedar Hill an offer of the ministry to Haiti. On June 25, 1889, Douglass replied that he would "accept the mission thus tendered me by his Excellency, the President."

In a sense, this was a somewhat thoughtless reward for the loyal Republican. Douglass was seventy-one. Haiti was hot for at least a third of the year; torrential rains hit in September. And the troubled nation was in the midst of one of its recurring revolutions. (Of the four heads of state to whom Bassett had been accredited between 1869 and 1877, one had fled the country, one was murdered, and a third had received asylum in the minister's house.)

Perhaps Harrison was simply discharging a campaign debt in a harmless way. On the other hand, if the president wanted to resist the pressure in his own administration to intervene in Haiti at the expense of that country's independence, having Douglass in Port-au-Prince might help. The Haitian minister to Washington thought that Harrison did indeed seek to preserve Haiti's independence and that Douglass, who, he said, was "not to be bought" by any would-be violators of that independence, would have a large assignment on his hands, one perhaps no other black man in America could carry out.

Both Martha Greene and Julia Griffiths Crofts counseled Douglass against taking the post—the offer was, they thought, a bit insulting, and the position possibly even dangerous—but Bassett, when the job did not come his way, urged Douglass (not, it turned out, for completely disinterested reasons) to accept it. Both he and Douglass knew that Haiti symbolized the liberation and autonomy of black people. Haiti's Toussaint L'Ouverture was the greatest of black heroes. And they both insisted that his Haiti, the only independent black nation in the Western Hemisphere and, along with Liberia and Ethiopia, one of only three in the world, must not be exposed to the contempt of an insensitive white minister. They were determined that despite its bloody revolutions and its poverty, the black republic not lose its sovereignty.

Always vulnerable, independent Haiti was now under the particularly avaricious eyes of white powers seeking bases for their growing navies— bases that in the Caribbean would support them in their rivalry to build a canal across the Central American isthmus. Other Caribbean islands, among them Spain's Cuba and the British West Indies, already belonged to competing European empires; Haiti, once part of the French empire, wanted no infringement of its independence. In fact, the Haitians were so protective of their autonomy that no non-Haitian was allowed to own property there. They knew that as a black republic their nation was viewed with much contempt and that it was judged fair prey by those wishing to annex any or all of it.

Initially, the Haitians saw Douglass as suspect because some twenty years earlier he had participated in President Grant's effort to annex the Dominican Republic, which shared the island of Hispaniola with Haiti. Now Douglass repudiated the idea of annexing any Caribbean nation; his statement to this effect, but his own African heritage even more, laid Haitian fears to rest.

Before going to Haiti, Douglass waited for the revolution to end. (Apparently, he learned only later that in part it was of North American manufacture.) Two black generals, François D. Légitime and Florvil Hyppolite, having participated in the 1888 revolution that ousted the mulatto government of President Louis-Étienne-Félicité Salomon, were now contending for leadership. Légitime had proclaimed himself president, and with the support of the French had isolated his rival in the northern corner of the country and was maintaining a blockade that prevented Hyppolite from receiving arms and other supplies. In June, President Harrison recognized the Légitime government.

Hyppolite, not surrendering, sought popular support by accusing Légitime of favoring the mulattoes over the blacks who had backed them both in their revolt in 1888. He courted help from abroad as well, and it was soon clear that he and his band in the northern hills had the support of both the United States navy and the New York mercantile world. Chief among the merchants was William P. Clyde, who sought to sell guns to the rebel general not only for the immediate profit, but to obtain concessions from Hyppolite that would be valuable once he had command of the country: Clyde, who owned Clyde's Coastwise and West India Steam Lines, was after the predominant trading position as carrier of the mails, and an arrangement whereby he would receive a kickback of 20 percent of any tariffs on goods brought into the country.

The gun merchant loaded ten ships with arms and other supplies for the Hyppolite forces; he also contacted his lawyer, Benjamin Franklin Tracy, a partner in one of the most important law firms in New York, and, conveniently, also secretary of the navy. (While in the government, he stayed on his firms's list of partners.) In an action that must have had President Harrison's sanction if not his full comprehension, Rear Admiral Bancroft Gherardi led the North Atlantic Squadron into warmer waters. Off the Haitian coast, he broke the Légitime blockade, permitting Clyde's shipments to be landed. The reward for the navy—and for the American imperialists, led by Secretary of State James G. Blaine—was to be the Môle St. Nicolas, a harbor of a magnificent bay on the extreme northwestern tip of Haiti, which was envisioned as the primary United States naval station in the Caribbean. With this assistance, Hyppolite drove Légitime from office, and on October 7, 1889, he became the president of Haiti.

During the summer of 1889, as Hyppolite consolidated his position militarily and politically, Douglass, waiting to be sent to Port-au-Prince, received a remarkable series of letters from Ebenezer Bassett, who now proclaimed himself an old friend. Denied the post of minister, Bassett was so eager to get back into the political life of Haiti that he was willing to go, at $850 a year, as the minister's secretary. But he saw himself less as a secretary than as Douglass's mentor and translator. His French was good, a product of study at Yale and eight years of practice in Port-au-Prince; Helen's Mount Holyoke French stood her in modest good stead; Douglass's was virtually nonexistent.

Bassett was an astute observer of politics. He knew what Hyppolite

was up to: "The usual proceeding on the triumph of a revolution is
1.) to put out of power every vestige of the fallen government, thus producing . . . a temporary state of anarchy; 2.) to organize the several cities
and communes into revolutionary committees, who come by delegations
to the Capital and name what is called a Provisional Government." This
provisional government, he went on, would then call for an election that
would be arranged to go in Hyppolite's favor. The amnesty promised
during the revolution would be forgotten, and the adherents of the fallen
government would be persecuted and forced into exile. Bassett predicted
that by the time Douglass reached Haiti, Hyppolite would have in place
a government in full command.

In addition to his own assessment of the political situation, Bassett
passed along excerpts, in translation, from letters he received from Stephen Preston, the Haitian minister to the United States. Preston, who
despite his Anglican name was a Haitian, had been known since the days
of Hamilton Fish as an astute diplomat committed to defending Haiti's
sovereignty regardless of its many changes of government. Speaking as
one black man to another, Preston was, through Bassett, charging Douglass with the duty of defending black Haiti. He declared himself (before
Gherardi broke the blockade) encouraged by Harrison's position—the
"great dangers that menaced our independence have disappeared"—and
delighted "by the consternation of the merchants" and by the prospect
of having Douglass in Haiti's capital, Port-au-Prince. "The Môle St.
Nicolas will not be occupied either by France or the United States—vive
Haiti!"

Citing conversations with Blaine, Preston passed along to Douglass his
assessment that Harrison was a noninterventionist, that unlike the navy,
he did not want special commissioners sent to demand a naval station or
otherwise interfere with Haiti's autonomy, and that he had, personally,
picked Douglass to be the minister. Harrison, Preston pointedly added,
"does not regard lightly the colored vote as Mr. Blaine does." Preston
was delighted by the thought of Douglass as minister, not least because
the appointment was powerfully criticized in the New York press by
commercial leaders whom he regarded as so predatory toward Haiti as
to threaten its independence. The minister called the merchants "petit
blancs" (which Bassett translated as "worthless whites") and said, "Not
a single merchant in N.Y. favors the sending of a colored man" to Haiti.

One would never have guessed that such was the case from the letter
that, as he was packing to leave, Douglass received from William P.
Clyde. Dated September 30, 1889, the letter was replete with fulsome
references to Douglass's great opportunity: "I consider it a circumstance
of no small significance that our Country, the older republic, should at

this time be sending its congratulations, its sympathy and the expression of its desire for the most cordial relations with Haiti, the younger republic[,] by you, pre-eminently the representative man of your race among us." Clyde went on to describe the urgent need for roads to transport coffee and other crops that could be grown in Haiti's fertile interior; their exportation might then end the island's terrible poverty. He also spoke of the unique opportunities for Americans engaged in commerce with Haiti; while the Europeans had been backing a loser, General Légitime, the American navy, by keeping the northern ports open, had enabled his rival's army "to procure food, arms, and ammunition when they greatly needed them and contributed largely to General Hypolite's success as he knows." Clyde was sure too that the general would "recognize the brilliant and masterful manner in which Rear Admiral Gherardi [in charge of the United States naval squadron] prevented bloodshed, robbery and the usual destruction of property by fire in the transition of the capital from the Government of General Légitime to that of General Hypolite." In short, Douglass was being flatteringly encouraged to capitalize on a revolution largely of American manufacture.

With Hyppolite in the ascendancy, the State Department ignored Harrison's recognition of Légitime, and early in the fall of 1889, Blaine ordered Douglass to Haiti. The Douglasses were accompanied on their journey by Jane Marsh Parker, a Rochester reporter and a friend since Alexander Street days. Driving away from the Port-au-Prince harbor, with its casual males, the Douglasses, in the rear of an open barouche, sat facing John E. W. Thompson, the retiring minister, and Miss Parker. On her face, Helen reported, "the consternation . . . was almost enough to quite upset any dignity." The new diplomat and his lady put up in the city's best hotel and immediately began house hunting; then the capital's more sinister mood began to intrude. Everywhere they went, they saw soldiers in the streets, and some of the places they were shown to rent were those abandoned by quickly fleeing mulattoes, who in their haste had left behind "red damask parlor furniture, gilt clocks," and other bright, rich furnishings that Helen Douglass found so garish that not even the lovely flowers spilling out over enclosed patios redeemed the houses. Up in the country, they "secured [temporarily] a cottage, in the midst of flowers and trees; with a broad verandah, bath, and good water." Then the Thompsons helped them in their search, and soon they were settled in the lushly gardened Lucie Villa.

The open behavior of a black working class, in evidence on the wharf, and the gaudy discards of the richer, lighter-skinned citizens, many of whom had fled into exile, presented the Douglasses with indications of

Haiti's extraordinary variety of cultures. And the broad spectrum of color made delicious mockery of the use of the words "black" and "white" to describe people; for the first time, the two Americans had the luxury of living without the constant back-home irritation of being looked upon as the white woman with the black man. In Port-au-Prince, they fit comfortably into an international group of diplomats (of no particular distinction) and local residents and dealt with an intelligent secretary of state who saw the Americans as simply two lightish people who happened to be cultivated, dignified, and charming. When they reported to the family in Washington about this pleasant way of life, Amelia Loguen Douglass, Lewis's sensitive and perceptive wife, who was herself light-skinned, responded in a letter to Helen, "How delightful it must be to be able to live for a time at least where the question of color as you say is sunk clear out of sight where it belongs."

The Douglasses may have been less content when they looked beyond the diplomatic corps and the society of the presidential palace. That there was an immense range of hues did not mean that differences were ignored. Stratification, with the lightest at the top and the darkest at the bottom, permeated Haiti's social structure and its politics. In a penetrating study of Haiti, David Nicholls contends that the Haitians, virtually all of whom were of acknowledged African descent, saw their common race as what united them against the world, while variations in color divided them from one another.

In the United States the opposite was true, at least in public. Americans were divided by the racial animosity between those of European and those of African descent, while the people of color of whatever shade, seemed united. This solidarity existed not only because the dominant white society held that all people of African descent were black but also because after the Civil War black Americans had made a political decision that regardless of shade, they must stand together. For example, in Louisiana in 1865, the *creoles de couleur,* a long-free and well-established group, gave up the chance to establish themselves as a politically separate caste, and instead called for universal suffrage. Solidarity in the long, unended struggle for equality with "white" Americans required that no distinction on account of color be recognized publicly. Colored people stuck together; color united in North America. Race, on the other hand, was sharply divisive.

Both of these propositions gave Douglass trouble. To be sure, his whole public life had been based on the conviction that black people must stand together politically. But he was also convinced, paradoxically, that race must not be acknowledged as affecting citizenship; America, oblivious to white and black, must be one. And despite his public advocacy of black solidarity, Douglass had always felt, in private, different from his darker siblings and—with deeply troubling consequences—from his first wife and his children. In this respect he was not alone. The matter of color that caused open political unrest in Haiti caused unacknowledgeable discord in the United States. Douglass was resented by many of his fellows for being too light, too white. But for a time, in Port-au-Prince, the Douglasses were away from categorizations they hated.

From Haiti in the fall of 1889, Douglass reported to Blaine, a bit uneasily, about the cabinet that Hyppolite had chosen; some crucial groups seemed not to be represented. On the whole, however, he was impressed by the young men—most "under forty years of age"—led by Secretary of State Antenor Firmin, who he accurately predicted would prove able. It is not clear whether Douglass was aware that Blaine may not have welcomed the news that the Haitian administration appeared able. There was to be a change too in the ministry to Washington; Preston, who had supported Légitime, was to be replaced by Hannibal Price.

In November—Thompson had held onto his post as long as possible—Frederick and Helen Douglass rode in an open carriage between ranks of brilliantly uniformed, saluting soldiers into the palace grounds, where a band played the "familiar strains of the 'Star Spangled Banner,' . . . with remarkable skill and effect." Then, "ascending to the audience chamber, we were ushered into the presence of President Hyppolite." Douglass described him to Blaine (with an uncharacteristic reference to color) as "a man of . . . medium height, of dark brown complexion and grey hair," who was "not to be trifled with."

In December, Secretary of State Firmin called Douglass in to ask just what the United States warship *Yantic,* purportedly studying the exact longitudinal position of the French cable from Cuba to Haiti, was doing prowling about in the Môle St. Nicolas. Douglass sought an answer from Blaine. "In view of the numerous articles which have appeared especially within the past few months, in the American journals relative to an alleged purpose of the United States to gain some sort of a foothold at the Môle, and in view also of what appears to me to be an extreme sensitiveness of the Haitien people generally on the subject of any possible alienation of their territory, it is," he gently warned the secretary of state, "but natural that the presence of the 'Yantic' . . . should occasion some comment in Haitien circles." The navy's hovering made both the Haitians and Douglass uneasy.

As predicted in Bassett's analysis of revolutions, Hyppolite had his authority confirmed by an election, and Douglass, who flourished amid so much dignity, had the honor of transmitting President Harrison's formal letter of recognition to the president of the sister republic on December 14. Neither Great Britain nor France accorded such recognition, and the American minister kept a close eye on his French counterpart, who was still accredited to the previous president. Douglass predicted to Blaine that the French minister would "become the center of all the elements of discontent in the country," since he had been an ally of President Légitime, who was hovering nearby in Jamaica. In January, local elections in Haiti were marked "by considerable disorder and violence," but though Douglass was acutely aware of too many "soldiers in uniforms at the polls," he insisted—with more hope than conviction—that the government stood for "stability" and "peace." The greatest discord was in the capital, Port-au-Prince, where martial law was declared. In February 1890, a major fire that destroyed twenty-two houses near the palace seemed, in the overly restrained words of the American minister, to be "evidence of discontent."

As Douglass went about the business of courting President Hyppolite's government and reporting on its problems—the business of the diplomat—a family tragedy was developing back home. From Washington, Nathan Sprague, once again restored to the family, reported to "Dear Father" in November that Frederick jr.'s wife, Virginia, was dying. Amelia and Rosetta were able to do little more than try to prepare Fred for what that bewildered man would not see was coming. They were also trying to care for Virginia's two small children, Charley Paul, a boy with a paper route and an unsettling propensity for running away, and a toddler, Robert. In January, when they brought Robbie to see his mother, she was too weak to hold him. The family did not know how to steady Fred; one hope was that Blanche K. Bruce, now recorder of deeds, might give him a job.

That grim winter, as Virginia grew weaker, there was an epidemic of influenza in the city. A leading black physician died; so did two of Secretary Blaine's children. To add to the private tragedies within the official family, a fire in the home of the secretary of the navy killed Tracy's wife and daughter. Among the Douglasses, Lewis had the most serious case of influenza; from Meridian Hill, the new suburb where she was now living, Rosetta reported that her "house appeared like a hospital." Everyone recovered except Virginia; at the start of February, in Port-au-Prince, Helen opened a letter from Frederick jr.: "Dear Mrs. Douglass, Thanks for your kind words of sympathy. . . . Virginia was my all." The letters she and Frederick had sent when Virginia died have been lost.

In Haiti, too, there were funerals. At a vast, solemn service for a dead archbishop, President Hyppolite, seated in splendor, sent Secretary of

State Firmin across the cathedral to offer two bemused Protestants his "private carriage. But," Douglass reported to Blaine, "I thought it best to decline the proffered courtesy." Douglass's love of pomp was balanced not only by his sense that the black president was courting his favor but also by his anti-Catholicism; dryly he reported that the "death of the eminent prelate"—which closed down all business in the capital—is "regarded here as an event of public importance." So too was the choice of Monseigneur Hillion's successor. According to the Concord of 1860, as Douglass understood it, the new prelate would be chosen by Hyppolite, "subject to the approval of the Holy See." Acting with the wholly political aim of further consolidating his control over the country, the president chose a compliant priest. The following week, Douglass reported that Hyppolite, strong in the north, was in the south attempting to overcome prejudice against him: "As usual he has gone with a strong body guard, and has taken into his company several whom popular rumor credits with Presidential aspirations and revolutionary predilections, it being deemed safer to have them under his eye than to have them left at home." High coffee prices, Douglass shrewdly noted, "are here accounted favorable to peace."

In April, Louis D. Brandeis, the lawyer for an American firm that sought to regain a ship seized by Légitime for running his blockade with guns, told Blaine that the British, French, and Germans were sending a joint fleet to collect their claims against Haiti for debts contracted by the Légitime government. Blaine instructed Douglass to ask Firmin about the rumor. Douglass not only checked with Firmin, who promised to tell him if he heard of any such European maneuver, but also sounded out all the other representatives of foreign countries. He told Blaine that he thought if such a report were true, gossip about it would have reached other capitals—but none had been picked up. Meanwhile, Douglass too was instructed to collect a debt—this one due an American citizen, Charles Adrian Van Bokkelen—and, by implication, to do so before the American navy had to be sent in to get the $60,000. Firmin was annoyed at Douglass's insistence on the payment, which had been agreed to before Hyppolite took office, and Douglass urged Blaine to let Haiti pay in installments over a six-year period. Aware of European threats of military intervention, Douglass pointed out that this forbearance by the United States would work no harm, but rather would enhance the favorable standing of the United States with Hyppolite's government.

When Hyppolite had summoned an elected legislature to sit, the consolidation of his government was deemed complete, and an elaborate inaugural ceremony was arranged for May 26, 1890. There was the "thunder of cannon, the inspiring notes of martial music," and a great shuffling of assembled dignitaries; as the president entered the room, all rose in elaborate deference. Addressed by the legislature's presiding officer, Hyppolite replied "in a calm and serious tone" with "wise and patriotic sentiments." The chamber then "resounded with the huzzas: *Vive le Président Hyppolite! Vive la Constitution! Vive la République d'Haïti!*" Then there were more speeches, including one by Douglass as dean of the diplomatic corps. Douglass had a grand moment, but Haiti had another dictator on its hands.

In June, with summer upon him, Douglass asked for a leave of absence for August and September. Unless Blaine objected, he and Helen would sail for New York on July 20. Before he left, Douglass and Firmin signed a protocol that implemented the plan for payment of the Van Bokkelen debt over time. In addition to this achievement, Douglass had the satisfaction of reporting to Washington that Great Britain, France, and Italy had all recognized the Hyppolite government. Concluding what seemed to them a successful stretch of diplomatic duty, the Douglasses went back to the United States for the rest of the summer. In the fall, ready to return to Haiti, the two were in New York with their trunks packed when they received a note from Blaine——black-bordered in memory now of his wife as well as his children: "For public reason request that you will not return to your post at least for the next twenty days."

Douglass had been caught in a crucial struggle between the secretary of state and the president over the course of empire. Americans had always been involved in international relations. This had been true since before they had their name, since far back in the pre-Columbian past, as one Indian society dealt with another. And, since the first European incursions, nations of the Eastern Hemisphere had squared off one against another in the Western Hemisphere. Once the United States was itself a nation, it largely heeded George Washington's warning against entangling alliances while expanding westward across the North American continent, at the expense of the native Americans. During the years of this expansion, there had been little reason to compete with European nations in the areas where they sought power. The War of 1812, with its threat to American independence, had shown the wisdom of avoiding European quarrels; the Mexican War was a conflict only with a North American neighbor, and the diplomacy of the Civil War was intended to keep Europe out of the fray. To be sure, Americans had never been innocent in the world. Before the Civil War, there had been the jingoism of the filibusterers who had their eyes on the Caribbean, and in 1867 the expansionist secretary of state William Henry Seward had purchased Alaska. But now, in Haiti, with a canal to the Pacific as the prize, the

United States, led by Secretary of State Blaine, was entering the new and dangerous waters of world balance-of-power politics. And President Benjamin Harrison, who unlike Blaine had seen war at first hand, was wary.

26

Môle St. Nicolas

IN 1890, expansionists in Washington no longer saw Haiti as a peculiar little republic to which a loyal black supporter of the party could be sent in order to placate the black electorate. It had become a prize in the game of empire building, of adjusting and readjusting the international balance of power. With the British still in firm control of their West Indian islands and Cuba still in Spanish hands, the island of Hispaniola, with Haiti on the western part and the Dominican Republic on the eastern, was the barbell waiting to be pressed high by North American muscular Christians vying now with other Western powers for domination of the Caribbean.

The big boys were not going to war, but they were flexing their biceps as if they wished they were. Thirty years before, the Civil War had been for Americans—the slaveholding Confederates as much as the Douglasses of the land—a war that had to be. But now there was no particular reason for a war; three centuries of assaults against the Indians ended in December 1890 with the merciless ugliness of Wounded Knee, which completed control of the continental empire. At the close of the nineteenth century, in an ominous line of thinking essentially new to America, war would have to be its own reason for being, not the last resort for occasions when peaceful politics failed. "War is one of the great agencies by which human progress is effected," Admiral Stephen Bleecker Luce was to declare in the same volume of the *North American Review* in which Douglass defended his own more pacific 1891 exercise in diplomacy. "The ancient and 'immovable civilization' of China," Luce wrote, ". . . shows the stagnation of a people unaccustomed to war with a superior race. China, to day, presents a picture of what the modern world would have been without war. The rights of man are there unknown." (If this was what he thought of China, it is not hard to guess how Haiti would have been judged.) "The truth is," Luce added, "that war is an ordinance of God."

It was from this world of God-obeying admirals that Frederick and Helen Douglass finally returned to Port-au-Prince in December 1890. Once again, Helen found the place wonderfully beautiful; at Tivoli, their new villa, "many and many a night Mr. Douglass would arise &, while others slept, stand beneath the open sky & commune with the stars. Here I learned the mystery of the dawn & saw the night flee away—Down the mountain it would come audibly—the great banana leaves would begin to stir—& the air would be filled with a sense of life—and lo! great diverging rays of rose & blue, perfect in their symmetry, would fill the east from horizon to zenith." As she looked out over the sea and back, "up the sun would bound and day would be born. The moment the sun would peer above the mountain, he would strike one as with a blow. Many times I dodged him & shut the blind to escape being hit."

The Douglasses were back even though Secretary of State Blaine and Secretary of the Navy Tracy had tried to persuade President Harrison that Douglass would frustrate their efforts to establish a United States naval base at the Môle St. Nicolas. President Hyppolite had, they claimed, promised to yield this area in return for the help he had received from Tracy's client William P. Clyde, and from the American navy. But a year had gone by and neither the entertaining of the Haitian president aboard a visiting United States admiral's flagship nor the polite attentions paid by the American minister had brought the Haitian government any nearer to keeping the promise.

President Harrison, with a quiet strength of will for which he is seldom credited, stayed the hand of the imperialists in his government by refusing to fire Douglass. The president was concerned about keeping black voters safely within his Republican party at a time when the Democrats were making a surprisingly successful bid for the support of flatterable black leaders, but also genuinely ill at ease with the notion that the nation's destiny lay in building a world empire. But he did, in January 1891, agree to have Rear Admiral Bancroft Gherardi negotiate directly for the base. Douglass was to join him in this effort.

Gherardi was the son of Jane Bancroft, historian George Bancroft's sister; his father had been a teacher in Bancroft's experimental Round Hill School in Northampton, Massachusetts. A graduate of Annapolis, Gherardi had been with Admiral David Farragut when the Union fleet wrested Mobile Bay from the Confederates, led by Admiral Franklin Buchanan. He was a man of fierce, even sadistic, temper and monumental arrogance. In 1878, he had come close to being cashiered for flogging seamen in defiance of the law prohibiting corporal punishment. That he had survived to achieve the command of the North Atlantic Squadron had not diminished his self-confidence.

By 1890, the admiral's attention was directed not to the cold waters of the North Atlantic, but to the Caribbean—and to the Pacific. As Ebenezer Bassett explained to Douglass, there was to be a "white men['s] . . . canal" through the Isthmus of Panama; and Americans like Blaine and Gherardi were determined that their nation's interests would not be superseded by those of any European power. Toward that end, black Haiti had to be made to see that Môle St. Nicolas, the magnificent harbor on the northwestern tip of the island, must become a coaling station for Gherardi's fleet.

Anchored at Port-au-Prince, the admiral sent a launch to bring the American minister to a meeting. Both men knew that protocol had been breached—the admiral should have been calling on the minister—but Douglass, having "long since decided to my own satisfaction that no expression of American prejudice or slight on account of my color could diminish my self-respect or disturb my equanimity," went out to the *Philadelphia*. It was a meeting of two of the century's least humble Americans, and Gherardi came out ahead on that particular day. "He told me," wrote Douglass some six months later, "in his peculiarly emphatic manner that he had been duly appointed a United States special commissioner; that his mission was to obtain a naval station at the Môle St. Nicolas; and that it was the wish of Mr. Blaine and Mr. Tracy, and also of the President of the United States, that I should earnestly cooperate with him in accomplishing this objective. He further made me fully acquainted with the dignity of his position, and I was not slow in recognizing it."

Douglass had already been told by a representative of Clyde's firm (a man whom he loathed for his condescending manner) that Gherardi had been given this assignment and, what's more, that he—Douglass—would be recalled. The meeting with Gherardi suggested that things were "not quite so bad as the New York agent had prepared me to expect"; he had not been fired. Dutifully, Douglass set out to assist in the negotiations by arranging a meeting with President Hyppolite and his secretary of state, the able Antenor Firmin.

When the two Americans entered the presidential palace two days later, on January 26, 1891, Gherardi immediately realized that Douglass was treated with considerable respect by the heads of the Haitian government; he also learned that the president was not prepared to hand over the harbor. According to Douglass, Gherardi was "the principal speaker" at the four-hour meeting. And the master of oratory found the admiral wanting in persuasiveness: "If anything was omitted or insisted upon [that could be] calculated to defeat the object in view, this defect must be looked for in the admiral's address." With embarrassing candor, Gherardi told President Hyppolite that he was in office because the United States navy had protected Clyde's shipments of arms to him, and had kept away the French and British, who supported his rival, Légitime. Perhaps accurately, but certainly not tactfully, Gherardi reminded the president of his promise that in return for the first of these services, the harbor would be turned over to the navy.

Douglass tried for a higher road. He claimed that "the concession asked for was in the line of good neighborhood and advanced civilization, and in every way consistent with the autonomy of Haïti." Then getting down to realpolitik brass tacks himself, he suggested to the president that "national isolation was a policy of the past," and that by openly agreeing to a lease of the harbor, the Hyppolite government would forestall the rumors "afloat in the air that it was about to sell out the country." He pointed out that everybody in Haiti knew of Hyppolite's indebtedness to the United States, and in a masterful bit of nonsensical diplomatic rhetoric, suggested "that a fact accomplished carries with it a power to promote acquiescence; and I besought them to meet the question with courage."

Not surprisingly, Hyppolite and Firmin chose not to meet the question at all. Firmin, conceding that "the offer of certain advantages had been made to our government," denied that the harbor had been promised in return, declaring that a letter saying that it had been was "only a copy" and, what was more, that the original document was "never accepted by the American Government." This position "was resisted by Admiral Gherardi . . . with much force," Douglass reported dryly. Shouting now, the admiral told the president that he was "morally bound" to give up the harbor because he owed to the United States navy his victory over Légitime.

At this point, Douglass interrupted, for he "plainly saw the indefensible attitude in which he [Gherardi] was placing the government of the United States in representing our government as interfering by its navy with the affairs of a neighboring country, covertly assisting in putting down one government and setting up another. . . . It did not strike me that what was claimed by Admiral Gherardi to have been done—though I did not say as much—is the work for which the United States navy is . . . supported by the American people." Gherardi declared that although "our government" had not "authorize[d]" him "to overthrow Légitime and to set up Hyppolite as President of Haïti, it gave him

[Gherardi] the *wink*" to do so. Mortified by Gherardi's contention, Douglass came right out and said that he could "not accept this as a foundation upon which I could base my diplomacy." Of this interjection, he later wrote, "If this was a blunder . . . , it was a blunder of which I am not ashamed."

None too soon, Firmin terminated the meeting by asking that the American request be put in writing. Thereupon, the two diplomats left, taking their separate ways. On board the *Philadelphia,* Gherardi wrote out the terms of a lease and signed the request for the turning over of the harbor for a naval station. Douglass reported later that he "neither signed it nor was asked to sign it, although it met with my full approval."

At a second meeting, on February 16, the formal letter of request was politely presented to Firmin; had the Haitian agreed to the request, wrote Douglass, not without a certain disingenuousness, "the credit for success . . . would have properly belonged to the gallant admiral." However, Douglass continued in his account of the meeting, at "this point, curiously enough," Firmin, who was "an able man and one well skilled in the technicalities of diplomacy, asked to see the commission of Admiral Gherardi and to read his letter of instructions. When these were presented to Mr. Firmin, he, after carefully reading them, pronounced them insufficient." Gherardi exploded, and while "earnestly and stoutly" arguing with Firmin, stepped over the line; he accused the secretary of state of being "insincere." Firmin's frosty response was that his objection to handing over part of his country was "honestly taken." At this point, Douglass noted, the "negotiation was brought to a sudden halt."

Out on the street, the Americans now had three choices: to insist that Gherardi, with his ships riding at anchor, was indeed authorized to demand possession of the harbor and would seize it by force; to give up altogether the attempt to get the Môle St. Nicolas; or to ask Washington to send the letter of credence that Firmin insisted on. Exasperated by Gherardi's complaints about the negotiations he had himself bungled, Douglass made the mistake of sputtering that if the navy simply took the Môle St. Nicolas, all of this negotiating could end. Seizing on Douglass's gaffe, Gherardi wrote to Washington that the minister had agreed to such a move; Douglass then wrote to Blaine to complain that the "Rear Admiral" was being "amazingly inaccurate." What Douglass did say to Gherardi after he had caught his breath was that they should get from President Harrison a letter with an explicit request that Haiti cede the harbor to the United States. Their message asking for this letter went by cable, so that a reply could be obtained almost immediately. (The cable to Cuba ran from the Môle St. Nicolas; hence, whoever was in control of the harbor also largely controlled Haiti's contact with the outside world.) Gherardi, in no mood to take any more advice from Douglass, had sent an officer to his house to help write the message. Two days after it was sent, the admiral received a cable in response telling him that the letter would come shortly—on a Clyde steamer to the island of Gonâve, in the waters off Port-au-Prince. But the letter did not arrive, and Gherardi moved his squadron restlessly, from the island, to the Môle St. Nicolas, to Jamaica—and back. To the Haitians, these movements of the fleet suggested that the United States was about to take over not just a harbor but the whole country.

In Washington, President Harrison resisted Secretary Blaine's request that he immediately authorize Gherardi to demand that the harbor be ceded to the United States. Instead, he finally signed a letter specifying that not Gherardi, but Gherardi and Douglass together, arrange for a lease of the harbor. The letter, dated April 9 and sent to the admiral, arrived only on April 16. Harrison ordered the two men to make application for a naval station "pure and simple," as Douglass put it, "without limitations and without conditions." They were, in short, not authorized to try to bring any more of Haiti than the harbor into American hands, nor were they to bargain for the concessions to Clyde. When the negotiations were resumed, Gherardi assumed that his squadron's puffing in and out of Haitian waters must have intimidated the Hyppolite government into compliance. The opposite proved true. The Haitian resolve to remain independent had strengthened. Worse still for the cause of the admiral and his expansionist allies, the skillful Haitian minister to Washington had informed Firmin that Harrison had forbidden the use of coercion by the armed forces. Firmin therefore knew he was safe in refusing the lease.

Refuse he did; Douglass's cable to Blaine read simply, "Haiti . . . declined lease of Môle." Douglass, though he had dutifully conducted the negotiations for the lease, was not surprised. He had come to know that the Haitians were fiercely proud of their independence, gained in a revolution that had brought them not only political freedom but emancipation from slavery, and were correspondingly fearful that their neighbors were not ready to truly honor their republic's autonomy. Cuba had abolished slavery only in 1886; on the other colonial islands and in the United States, there was virulent anti-black prejudice. The Haitians were vulnerable—and wary. Douglass hoped to redefine his position as minister. If instead of participating in attempts to take over a valuable part of their territory, he could appear as a defender of Haitian independence, he would, as the American minister, gain for the United States the trust and allegiance of the Haitian people. And he would be doing just what he had always tried to do at home—assisting fellow Africans who had been held in bondage to defend their freedom.

What he did not recognize was that white imperialism was not the only threat to the freedom and safety of these people. At nine o'clock on Thursday, May 28, 1891, the streets of Port-au-Prince were filled with people celebrating the Feast of Corpus Christi. President Hyppolite and his entourage were in the crowded cathedral when shots outside were heard through the sounds of the service. Seventy armed men had rushed down into the streets from the mountains south of the city and fired on the poorly guarded jail, freeing two hundred political prisoners, along with the "common criminals." Some of the rebels and the allies they had released started for the arsenal. In the cathedral, "the great congregation started up in alarm," but the president "counseled the audience to calmness," before going out into the square to join his troops, already confronting the rebels.

Like everyone else in the city, the Douglasses were terrified when the shooting erupted. At their house, Frederick and Helen secured the louvers and dragged a mattress into place against the window wall, propping it up with a bookcase. They could hear "the stray bullets that were flying past" the house. In the streets, Douglass reported, "there was a sharp fight for a few minutes and then the troops won and the others fled for their lives. There were no great numbers involved, but the execution was terrible while it lasted." Hyppolite, "a man naturally humane and just, under this tremendous provocation, was changed almost from a lamb into a lion." Raging through the streets of his capital on his horse, the president "ordered the killing of every one of his enemies that he found" and himself led the massacre. After the firing ceased, Helen Douglass recalled, "the air was rent by the wailings, from various cottages, of women bereft of those they loved."

In the quiet of the evening, Douglass walked into town. Sitting in the cafe of a hotel, Ebenezer Bassett spotted his chief: "It was the first time I had seen him that day. I got a chair for him and he sat down, but scarcely had he done so when the sound of firing was heard. This time it was from a Gatling gun. I took Mr. Douglass by the arm, and said: We will have to get out of here." The two American diplomats (who hurried away) were much criticized by writers for the New York papers—the same critics who roundly denounced Douglass for not acquiring the naval base—for not stopping the massacre. How they could have done so, the critics did not say.

Bassett's reply to the charge was that "we could not prevent the massacre of May 28 any more than any of the other foreign ministers who were present and were not blamed." That four men who had gained asylum in the Mexican consulate were dragged out by troops and shot in the Champ de Mars certainly suggests that Hyppolite could not have been held to moderation by the diplomatic corps. On June 2, the various ministers and consuls together called on the president to protest this outrage. It was a strange meeting; Hyppolite was reported to have been so enraged at one point that the diplomats thought they might be shot right there in the palace. Instead, the president retired to another room; soon they heard the sound of a flute. His equilibrium restored, Hyppolite returned, apologized for the breach of asylum, and resumed his posture as a constitutional head of state.

Hyppolite had restored order in Port-au-Prince, but the threats to his rule were not over. He was greatly suspicious of everyone; Secretary of State Firmin resigned on May 4, when his loyalty was doubted, and soon went into exile. For a week after the revolt in the capital there were uprisings in the country, which were mercilessly put down. As guards tortured and killed prisoners in the port town of Jacmel, "all the people . . . assembled to see the execution. The wives and daughters of the condemned were there also, sobbing. . . . It seems that no one in the crowd protested, so great is the fear of Hyppolite."

Neither accounts of brutal torture and murder nor the image of General Hyppolite savagely attacking civilians seems to have been allowed to alter Douglass's satisfaction at being able to stand equal with the president of a republic. The relationship between Douglass and Hyppolite was an intriguing one, in part shaped by what lies in the eye of the beholder. The ear of the listener was not much help. Hyppolite's excellent French was Parisian; his father was said to have been a linguist. His English was nonexistent. Douglass knew no French, but, eager to bridge a cultural gap and to impress the Haitians with his intellectual standing, he pressed on them the French translation of *My Bondage and My Freedom*. All that the two said to each other was filtered through Bassett's translations. On formal occasions there were courtly exchanges between these two men for whom dignity was a prized possession.

A white reporter for the *New York Herald* wrote of calling on Hyppolite in his blue and yellow palace in September, after Douglass had left Haiti. He was struck by the "contrast between . . . [the president's] ebony skin and his silver white hair. . . . his features are well cut, with straight nose and lips not over thick, but what strikes you most in Hyppolite's appearance are his eyes, which you feel but never see, screened as they are behind a pair of gold-rimmed blue glasses, which allow him to study you at his ease without betraying anything of his thoughts or expression." The president was dressed "entirely in white," the reporter noted, adding that as "you watch this remarkable man you see frequently playing about his mouth a curious smile, which half reassures, half disconcerts you. Is it a smile of benevolence or of hatred, of good or of evil? . . . The voice, the polished speech, the courteous manner—everything is calculated to dispel the idea of a blood-thirsty tyrant, everything save the eyes, which a stranger never sees."

The Douglasses chose to ignore the blue glasses and the smile in favor of the dignified manner. There was a half-truth in the criticism leveled against Douglass that he was "so absorbed in the contemplation of the experiment of black men governing themselves that he has forgotten his duties." The duties were not actually forgotten, but they were carried out by one predisposed to find all the good that could be found in a government of black men. The Douglasses would have liked their fellow Americans to think of the black head of state as, simply, a head of state—one, as Helen put it, whose "suavity and politeness, & dignity" were impressive. She was disgusted when "one of the great papers of N.Y. city" spoke of Hyppolite "as a very 'intelligent darkey.' "

What Helen Douglass was trying to see in Hyppolite was another Frederick Douglass. She, and Frederick, wanted the memory of the president's dignity to win out against that newspaper's "coarseness and vulgarity." To carry this image of a man they so much wanted to admire, the two Americans had to overlook the fact that he was a bloody tyrant. Douglass was not the first American diplomat—nor the last—to turn a blind eye to appalling human-rights violations; that they were not alone does not dispel the chill of Helen Douglass's summary of her impressions of Haiti: "Short shrift is given in military executions, and I recall the calm of a Sunday morning being suddenly pierced when the sharp rattle of musketry on the Champs de Mars, by order of the President. It was thus that, Hypolite, with a firm hand held the reins of government, and made it possible to institute reforms and to encourage programs and stability which lead to peace."

Helen Douglass had been seriously ill in Port-au-Prince in the spring of 1891, and was still convalescing when they made plans to go home for the summer. In June, convinced that President Hyppolite, who was to rule Haiti until 1896, had ridden out the worst threats to his ascendancy, Douglass arranged for them to leave. On board the *Prinz Willem III* with the Douglasses were a good many Haitians on their way into exile in France. When the ship docked in New York, reporters were immediately busy interviewing as many of these Haitians as they could, trying to discover what was behind the conflicting rumors circulating about the revolt and its suppression. Douglass sought to minimize the sensational (but not necessarily inaccurate) nature of the reports on the violence, and insisted that the Hyppolite government was stable. He also insisted that he was taking a purely routine leave of absence from his duties in Haiti. But he was fully aware that neither the commercial houses in New York nor the expansionists in Washington were going to forgive him for what they saw as a black man's deliberate scuttling of the effort to acquire the Môle St. Nicolas.

Actually, it had taken more than the actions of one man, even one black man, for the United States not to get its naval station. In the reasoned judgment of Rayford W. Logan, a careful student of Haitian-American relations, the expansionists had, for the time, overreached themselves. Douglass's "failure," Logan concludes, "was due . . . to the fact that there was no real public demand for the Môle, that Harrison was not prepared to use force and that Tracy, in spite of his many obligations to Clyde, could not or would not force the administration." (On September 10, 1891, Secretary Tracy telegraphed William Clyde, "Can do nothing more, will explain fully when I see you.") Even Secretary Blaine, who by that time had relinquished active leadership of the State Department because of what was to prove to be his fatal illness, wrote the president in August 1891, from Bar Harbor, Maine, that Hawaii, Cuba, and Puerto Rico were the "only three places of value enough to be taken." It would appear that Douglass was exceeded in lack of enthusiasm for a predatory move on the Môle St. Nicolas by President Harrison, but the scorn of those who had wanted their way in Haiti did not fall on Harrison's shoulders. Instead, the New York newspapers vehemently attacked Douglass for a key failure in what they held to be the program for the future of America.

The *New York Sun,* a Democratic newspaper, canvassing the possibilities of American "manifest destiny," if "not [in] this century, . . . surely early in the next," looked at Cuba, Newfoundland, Hawaii, and Samoa, as well as Haiti. Of the last, the editorial said, "Hayti? No, we don't want it, because it has too many cheap voters. Yet we should like to lease a small piece of it for a coaling station. At the same time we don't want any European powers entrenched there, raking Cuba and right there at the gateway of the Gulf." "Cheap voters" was a euphemism for "black voters"; Republican expansionists might have had less scruples about taking over the country. (It is interesting that imperialism then presupposed that new territories would become states with voting citizens.) Douglass had been standing in the way of progress in the Caribbean and the *Sun* joined the *New York World* and the *New York Herald* in trying to push Douglass out of office by predicting that he would be fired. Gleefully, they described the efforts—and many there were—of black politicians to succeed him.

On the stationery of the New Haven, Connecticut, Republican League, his secretary and colleague Ebenezer Bassett wrote, "I think you owe it to Haiti and our whole race to hold on right where you are. No man of our race could fill just the breach that you now fill. You hold the fort. You stand between a handful of our people—a mere hand full as compared with other people and the roaring wolves gnashing their teeth in all the panoply of race hatred." Bassett, ever the exhorter, added, "Don't stir, don't move an inch. . . . Don't even whisper about resigning, for the moment you do the jig is up for Haiti." On the other hand, a much older friend—one who remembered Douglass from his great evening in Nantucket fifty years earlier—wrote that he should not go back to "that fearful theater of cruelty." The Frederick Douglass she knew, Anna Gardner went on to say, should not be tarnished by having anything to do with "that 'mindless monster' Hyppolite."

Douglass was torn. Helen had been dangerously ill in Haiti, and, as he told the journalist T. Thomas Fortune, instead of rejuvenating him, the lush island had made him feel old. He knew he had lost the confidence of the State Department. He even had to submit to humiliating negotiations to prevent the department from deducting a portion of his salary for what it considered inappropriate expenditures for office furniture. Late in July, he wrote Bassett that he had decided to resign; Bassett replied that he should not do so until he had gotten to the president to explain his side of the controversy. And, never one to beat around a bush, he asked Douglass to put in a word for him as his replacement.

On July 30, 1891, Douglass sent to the State Department the most formal of notes: "Sir: I have the honor to respectfully render to Honorable Benjamin Harrison, President of the United States, my resignation of the office of Minister Resident and Consul General . . . to Haiti. . . ." He closed with "every sentiment of respect, confidence and esteem towards the President." He said not a word about Blaine or any of his colleagues in the State Department. Warned that black voters would take flight to the Democratic party if this office, a somewhat pathetic symbol of black significance, was denied them, Harrison chose as Douglass's successor the journalist and diplomat John S. Durham, of Philadelphia—to the disgust of Wall Street and of black voters in Ohio, who had had their own candidate and now threatened to withhold their votes from William McKinley, then running for governor. Durham was the man a reporter had described to a relieved Hyppolite as a "yellow man."

Douglass, as sick of color as ever, did not take lightly his having been pushed out of office. To be sure, he had had enough of Haiti, but his pride had been hurt, and, worse, his loyalty to his country had been challenged. Even before resigning he had begun negotiations with Lloyd Stephens Bryce, editor of the *North American Review,* to write an article giving his views on the controversy. The result was some of the best writing of Douglass's career. The article, which appeared in the *Review* for September and October 1891, presented succinctly and clearly his version of the negotiations for the base. He contended, for example, that he had had no orders to try to secure it during his first year in Haiti and therefore could not be charged with delay in the months immediately following Hyppolite's assumption of power. Discussing the negotiations that did take place, Douglass was candid in suggesting that Admiral Gherardi had been condescending and hence insulting to Antenor Firmin, Haiti's secretary of state. (After the article appeared, Firmin, from exile in Paris, wrote Douglass that his resignation was a great loss to both Haiti and the United States.)

To establish that his efforts to obtain the base had been genuine, Douglass said that he had favored overseas expansion ever since slavery's abolition—most notably in the 1870s with his support of the attempt to annex the Dominican Republic "against the powerful opposition of my honored and revered friend Charles Sumner." But the invocation of Sumner, with its hint that the senator might have been been right, is a clue to the article's true importance; it could have served as a position paper for the beleaguered anti-imperialists who, unsuccessfully, sought to restrain the expansion of the American empire at the turn of the century. Douglass's exposure of Gherardi's dangerous bellicosity and, more mutedly, the hint of the rapacity of those with commercial designs on the Caribbean, made a cautionary tale.

The *North American Review* article also admirably reveals the quality of Douglass's mind. His opening—"I propose to make a plain statement regarding my connection with the late negotiations"—is quietly forceful and direct. Telling why he had decided to state his case, after "six months" of restraint while under withering attack, he acknowledged without using the word that he had been accused of treason. To respond, therefore, had become "a duty which cannot be omitted without the imputation of cowardice or of conscious guilt. This is especially true in a case where the charges vitally affect one's standing with the people and the government of one's country. In such a case," he continued, in one of his most powerful and revealing sentences, "a man must defend himself, if only to demonstrate his fitness to defend anything else." Douglass was once more calling himself to duty; nothing could be allowed to impair his ability to defend the rights of people who need defending.

Next, he forthrightly stepped up to confront the racist assumption that a black man was less competent than a white one: "One of the charitable apologies [my critics] are pleased to make for my failure is my color; and the implication is that a white man would have succeeded where I failed. This color argument is not new. It besieged the White House before I was appointed.... At once and all along the line the contention was raised that no man with African blood in his veins should be sent as a minister to the black republic. White men professed to speak in the interest of black Haïti; and I could have applauded their alacrity in upholding her dignity if I could have respected their sincerity. They thought it monstrous to compel black Haïti to receive a minister as black as herself. They did not see that it would be shockingly inconsistent for Haïti to object to a black minister while she herself is black. Prejudice sets all logic at defiance."

27

Chicago

THE PATRIOT went to work for foreigners, in an America grown strangely alien. In 1892, Frederick Douglass accepted appointment as the commissioner of the Republic of Haiti pavilion at a world's fair celebrating the four hundredth anniversary of Columbus's discovery of America. In 1492, the explorer had set foot on Haiti's island, Hispaniola; in 1893, a year late, Chicago staged the World's Columbian Exposition, perhaps the most famous of America's world's fairs, to commemorate—without a trace of doubt—the blessedness of four hundred years of the New World.

That world was not looking as good as it might to Douglass when he returned from his diplomatic post in Haiti. Values that he had struggled to make firm for half a century seemed to be slipping away. He clung to old banners and despaired as they faded and were dropped into the dust. A Republican to the death, he was aware of the party's defection from commitments to black Americans, but blind to the energy of the Populist movement that some courageous, hopeful blacks risked entering in the belief that their joint action with whites caught as they were in poverty could lead to basic economic change. Almost out of habit, Douglass campaigned for President Harrison's reelection in 1892, ignoring the Populist party. A year earlier, feeling his years, he had written to a younger black leader who also shunned the Populists, Booker T. Washington, "I fully intended to hear your lecture . . . but for the state of my health," and sent the note across the city of Washington in care of his granddaughter Estelle.

Discouraged, Douglass felt all the more the imperative of keeping his personal story going. Disingenuously, he told an old friend that he was bringing *Life and Times of Frederick Douglass* up to date only at the "bidding of my publisher"; there was a painful compulsion within him that drove the narrative on. "When I laid down my pen a dozen years ago I thought . . . I had reached the end, not of life, but of autobiographic writing, and was glad to have done with it. I have always found it easier to speak than to write. These ten or twelve years have not been cheerful," he wrote to Marshall Pierce, another old abolitionist who understood that the needs of the generation born since slavery were being ignored in the way that the slaves' needs had once been. "They have been years of reaction and darkness. The air has been filled with reconciliations between those who fought for freedom and those who fought for slavery. We have been . . . morally obscuring the difference between right and wrong. The Ship of State has been swinging back to its ancient moorings."

This doleful assessment led inevitably to a task: "I am now seventy five years, and though my eyes are failing and my hand is not as nimble as it once was I hope to do some service in writing [of] this period." The assignment sent his mind back to better, more vigorous periods and a sad reverie: "Three men [older than he] are now left of the old guard: John G. Whittier, Robert Purvis and Parker Pillsbury. They stand in the open field where once was forrest. Dear battered and scarred Parker, though he is now over eighty three, is still erect and active. You [Pierce] and I have seen the trees falling all around us."

After aggravating delays, his book, again called *Life and Times of Frederick Douglass,* was published in the fall of 1892. Douglass had added better than a hundred pages to the 1881 autobiography, telling of his trip to Europe and Africa and of his personal accomplishments. There was again an eloquent call for civil rights, but no direct attack on the new evils of the decade in which he was now living. There was nothing to match the fervor of the antislavery message of *Narrative of the Life of Frederick Douglass* or *My Bondage and My Freedom,* nothing, for example, on the scourge of lynching that had fallen on his people.

Douglass was disappointed in the appearance of the book, finding the paper "inferior and the binding slovenly, imperfect and unattractive," and it did not sell well. This telling of his story, his valedictory, did not invigorate him as the first two autobiographies had. It took something—someone—else to give him new life.

In March 1892, the *Memphis Free Speech* published a stinging piece by the brilliant thirty-year-old writer Ida B. Wells describing a triple lynching. This daughter of slaves, who had been an eager student at Rust University, wrote fearlessly of the killing of three male friends; they had been lynched, she asserted categorically, not for raping white women, as alleged, but for competing with white storekeepers. While she was in Philadelphia in May, speaking at protest meetings, her neighbors destroyed the office and plant of the newspaper, in which she owned a one-third interest.

Even before the Memphis paper was silenced, the editor of the *North American Review* asked Douglass to write on the subject, and "Lynch Law in the South" appeared in the July 1892 issue. Getting right to the point, a recent "case in the so-called civilized State of Arkansas," he wrote, "Think of an American woman . . . mingling with a howling mob, and with her own hand applying the torch to the fagots around the body of a negro condemned to death without a trial." He was revolted by the cruelty, but did not condemn the punishment as strongly as he did the fact that it was administered outside the law. "While not denying that the negro may, in some instances, be guilty of the peculiar crime so often imputed to him," he nevertheless felt that if a man was guilty of rape, a proper trial would confirm the fact and punishment would follow.

Douglass had his doubts about that guilt; "there is good reason to question these lynch-law reports. . . . The crime imputed to the negro is one most easily imputed and most difficult to disprove, and yet it is the one the negro is least likely to commit." There had been, he pointed out, no rapes reported during the Civil War, when white women were often alone with their slaves. Turning to the case about which Wells had written, he noted that just as the "Jew is hated in Russia, because he is thrifty," so the "negro meets no resistance when on a downward course. It is only when he rises in wealth, intelligence, and manly character that he brings upon himself the heavy hand of persecution. The men lynched at Memphis were murdered because they were prosperous." Inquiring into what lay behind the summary killings, Douglass shrewdly observed that "responsibility for the lynch law . . . is not entirely with the ignorant mob. . . . they simply obey . . . sentiment created by wealth and respectability."

The analysis was acute, but Douglass offered no solution beyond calls for a Southern change of heart—"Let the press and the pulpit unite . . . against the cruelty"—and for an "emphatic condemnation and withering reproach" from the North. What was more, his article did not fully disavow the widely accepted assumption that the victims of the horrible executions were to blame for their fate, that black men were indeed a sexual threat to Southern white women. It took a Southern black woman to fully discredit such an idea.

While Douglass was writing, Wells had a fiery piece in the June press, a seven-column article in the *New York Age* "giving names, dates, and places." Douglass, in New York, came to call on the brash new editor and writer to tell her "what a revelation of existing conditions" her writing had been for him. Distanced as he was, he "had begun to believe it true that there was increased lasciviousness on the part of Negroes." Now he wrote her a letter—which appeared as a preface to her 1892 pamphlet *Southern Horrors*—"Brave Woman! You have done your people and mine a service which can neither be weighed nor measured. If the American conscience were only half alive . . . a scream of horror, shame and indignation would rise to Heaven. . . ." Ten thousand copies of Wells's pamphlet were printed and distributed, many of them in Memphis.

Shortly afterward, Wells visited Cedar Hill. Driving her to the train for her trip back to New York, Douglass said to her, "I want to tell you that you are the only colored woman save Mrs. Grimke who has come into my home as a guest and has treated Helen as a hostess has a right to be treated. . . . Each of the others, to my sorrow, acted as if she expected my wife to be haughty and distant . . . , and they all began by being so themselves."

Wells began to speak about lynching, often before small groups but always effectively, in cities in the Northeast. When only a handful of people, including Frederick and Helen, Charles and his second wife Laura, and Lewis and Amelia Douglass, showed up for a meeting Wells was to address at the Metropolitan African Methodist Episcopal Church in Washington, Douglass "apologized for Washington's seeming indifference" and promised to arrange a larger meeting for her. The following February (1893), he made good on his promise; the big church was filled; Douglass presided and had Mary Church Terrell, another of the new generation of leaders, introduce Wells. Deeming the meeting, with its "donation of nearly two hundred dollars," a great success, Wells went on to note in her autobiography that at the very time it was held, a man was being burned alive in Paris, Texas: "The dispatches told in detail how he had been tortured with red-hot irons searing his flesh for hours before finally the flames were lit that put an end to his agony. They also told how the mob fought over the hot ashes for bones, buttons, and teeth for souvenirs."

Despite his admiration for Wells, Douglass did not urge young people to protest as she and also black Populists were doing. On May 23, 1892, he stepped down from a carriage drawn by "four handsome bays" and strode majestically into Ware Chapel, at Atlanta University, to listen to "some of the 'old time' plantation songs and some of the more classic music" and then to tell the students, "Be not discouraged. There is a future for you and a future for me. The resistance encountered now predicates hope. The Negro degraded, indolent, lazy, indifferent to progress, is not objectionable to the average public mind. Only as we rise . . . do we encounter opposition."

Referring to the men lynched in Memphis, he declared that they were killed not because "they were low and degraded, but because they knew their business and other men wanted that business." And then, after employing a curiously heartening commencement-speech cliché—"I am delighted to see you all"—he spoke directly to this particular audience: "Don't be despondent. Don't measure yourself from the white man's standpoint; but measure yourselves from the depths from which you have come. . . . Boys, you will be men some day. Girls, you will be women some day. May you become good men and women, intelligent men and women, and a credit to yourselves and your country."

From Atlanta, Douglass traveled to Alabama to give the eleventh commencement address at Booker T. Washington's Tuskegee Normal and Industrial Institute on May 26. After a parade, Douglass stood up in the shade of a temporary pavilion to make his old "Self-Made Man" speech. The *Southern Workman* reported that the "tenor of the speech, so far as it touched upon race questions, was calm and dispassionate. He urged economy, thrift and common sense, and declared that the Negro had no right to live unless he could live honestly, giving a fair equivalent for everything he received." Washington himself could not have been more cloying. "Let us alone, and give us a fair chance," Douglass added. "But be sure you *do* give us a fair chance."

The next month, still traveling, Douglass gave a speech in Rochester, and then went on to Minneapolis for the Republican convention. There, a ghost of old commitments, he pleaded futilely for a renewal of his party's assistance to black Americans; he found the handshaking (to which he was almost compulsively drawn) tiring, and the references to him as the "old man" undeniable. And he was a long way away from the group of people in Terrebonne, Louisiana, who wrote to him to say that "the facts have never been told how the Poor colored People have Suffered and are Suffering for the want of Protection. . . . If we register as Republicans we are driven from home as dogs." They urged Douglass to Publish this in the paper," and being "afraid to Sign our names," they closed their plea: "from your friends now and for always." Such letters, in Douglass's assessment, were what made the discouraging efforts in Minneapolis necessary.

Black solidarity in and of itself was not always possible or even desirable, in Douglass's view. He had long been distrustful of John Mercer Langston (at one time dean of the law school and vice-president of Howard University, where Douglass was a trustee) and had stood with Senator William Mahone, the head of the Republican party in Virginia, in opposition to Langston's unsuccessful campaign for Congress in 1888, his successful bid in 1890, and his failed try for reelection in 1892. In refusing Langston his support, Douglass was both settling old scores with a rival leader with whom he had often disagreed and being true to his belief that race should not be the determining factor in political decisions. But he did not disagree just with Langston; increasingly, the "old man" was finding himself estranged from other black leaders. Their quarrels, gleefully pointed to by white supremacists as proof of the blacks' humorous incompetence, were largely a product of frustration. Blocked from the responsible posts they were capable of holding, and becoming instead members of a kind of racially defined shadow government, able men were reduced to futile debate, often acrimonious, about policies over which they had no influence.

At the Republican convention in Minneapolis that June, Douglass still tried to have some influence. He wanted a strong commitment to federal protection of the lives and civil rights of blacks in the South, but here he ran into the opposition of an old foe, James G. Blaine. The former secretary of state, though dying, was still a power in the Republican party, and he chose to focus not inward on the dreary domestic scene in the South, where there were 550 lynchings and 332 "legal" executions in the years 1890–92, but rather outward on the possibilities, under continued Republican rule, of greater power for the United States in world politics. Disappointed that the Republicans gave no assurances of a federal program to stop the lynching, Douglass nonetheless campaigned for his old boss Benjamin Harrison.

After Grover Cleveland won the election, Douglass wrote that the "first and natural effect of the restoration of the Democratic party to power will be to make the white people of the South still more indifferent to the claims of justice toward their colored fellow citizens." He placed the blame for the Democratic victory on the Republicans themselves, and particularly on his enemy "the Hon. James G. Blaine," who, he contended, had "divested the campaign of every humane sentiment" by blocking Republicans from making passage of a bill calling for the enforcement of civil rights a part of the party's platform. "If the Republican party had become tired of its own ascendancy," he pronounced, "it could not . . . have adopted a more effective plan of campaign."

While Douglass was at the convention in Minneapolis, Helen had remained behind at Cedar Hill to care for her dying mother. Increasingly, the Anacostia house had become home to the Pittses as it had once been to the Douglasses. Frederick was "Uncle Fred" to Helen's nieces; she remained, resolutely, "Mrs. Douglass" to his children and grandchildren. When her grandfather censured Estelle after he heard that she had spoken disrespectfully of his wife, Rosetta's daughter forthrightly replied that she would own up to what she had actually said, but not to what she hadn't: she had told her parents that when she visited Cedar Hill, "Mrs. Douglass could have treated me better if she tried."

Others were even less charmed by the integrated domesticity in Anacostia. At the Populist convention in Atlanta, the Reverend Sam Small, a one-time alcoholic and now an ardent prohibitionist, discovered a unique way to attack the Democrats: "Grover Cleveland invited that leader of niggerdom, Fred Douglass, to his dinner table. I might excuse him for getting the nigger into his house for supper, but when he invited the low wife to go there, it is more than I can stand." What the two black delegates, John Mack and R. J. Mathews, thought of the good reverend's (inaccurate) social note, the reporter did not say.

At the time Douglass tucked a clipping of the Small speech into his files, he was facing one of the occasions of engulfing personal grief that he found it impossible to write about. In July 1892, his son and namesake died after a lingering illness. Frederick jr. had always been the most vulnerable of the Douglass children. Articulate—his letters to his father, always in an elegant hand, were infrequent but perceptive—and committed to journalism work, Frederick jr. was remembered fondly by fellow writers and printers at the *National Leader,* the Baltimore church journal where he had been working. But he was the only Douglass son who did not enlist in the army, and after the war he was the one that Henry O. Waggoner most worried about as he tried to help Frederick and Lewis establish themselves in business in Denver. Frederick's own son, the third Frederick Douglass, had died at fourteen, and several other of Virginia and Frederick's children had died at a young age. After Virginia's death in 1890, the family despaired. Rosetta found her brother to be so forlorn that he could cope with nothing.

And now Frederick jr. too was gone, and his troubled eleven-year-old son, Charley Paul, was put in the charge of the family lawyer, E. M. Hewlitt. The following winter, after the boy had once again run away, this time to a neighbor's house, Hewlitt took him to the K Street police station and persuaded the officers to lock him up for the night. Defiantly, the child told the lawyer his grandfather would look after him. "He seems," Hewlitt reported to Douglass, "to think he can stay around your place, and not run away." But regardless of where Charley Paul was going to be, the lawyer wanted no more of him. He went to court to have himself removed as the "ungrateful" child's guardian. Uncle Lewis would have to take over in his stead.

Surrounded by unhappiness within the family and by the deteriorating condition of his people in an indifferent America, Douglass sought to escape by entering the strangely unreal world of the Chicago world's fair. He had agreed to serve as Haiti's commissioner in February 1892; his assistant commissioner was Charles A. Preston, whose father had been the Haitian minister to the United States and had passed along valuable advice to Douglass when he headed for Haiti. During 1892 young Preston, reporting to Douglass, conducted the frustrating but ultimately successful negotiations with fair officials and contractors over the site, design, and building of the Haitian pavilion. Cheerfully and deferentially, but with a disconcerting tendency to ask for small personal loans and to give himself overgenerous expense allowances, Preston did the actual business of readying the pavilion.

The fair was dedicated on October 12, 1892; in January, the Douglasses were in Chicago, staying at the Palmer House, for the dedication of the Haitian pavilion. In April the commissioner returned to the city to take up residence and preside over his odd palace. His hosts were Fannie Barrier Williams and S. Laing Williams. Fannie Williams was a stunningly beautiful and light-skinned woman from upstate New York—*"je suis française,"* she would assert to avoid being removed to a Jim Crow car. She was active in Chicago society as a clubwoman and lecturer and by 1895 would make it into the Chicago Woman's Club as its first black member. S. Laing Williams, a Georgian with degrees from the University of Michigan and the Columbian School of Law (later the George Washington University School of Law), was the partner of Ida Wells's future husband, Ferdinand Lee Barnett. The Williamses were as delighted with their distinguished guest as he was with their hospitality, and they provided a bright black buffer against some exceedingly silly white darkness that lay ahead.

Douglass needed the protection. There were banquets for Spanish dukes to attend, and any number of other grandees to receive, but there was also the galling reality that the America he wanted exhibited was not to be seen. Indeed, in one realm, it came close to being entirely invisible. The Board of Lady Managers, headed by the formidable Bertha Honoré Palmer (wife of the fair's president, Potter Palmer, of Chicago), was composed of representatives from the several states and the District of Columbia. These women were in charge of the exhibits of women's work, and since none of them was black, work done by black women would probably not be displayed unless pressure was brought. One group of black women, headed by Lottie L. Trent, urged a separate black exhibit. Another group, averse to any appearance of acquiescence to segregation, demanded that the board members pledge to encourage black craftswomen to present their work for possible inclusion alongside that of white women. (When the pledges came in, they were accompanied by such patronizing letters that the protesters wondered why they had bothered.) Both groups urged that some black women be allowed to participate in the planning of the fair. To meet—or rather, avoid—this problem, Bertha Palmer, who was also warding off criticism from professional white women who resented the fact that the board was in the hands of socialites, turned to Fannie Williams.

Chosen for her presentability as much as for her neutral position (she did not belong to either of the contending groups), Williams was given a desk in Palmer's office, but no salary and no authority. That this appointment did not entirely meet the more important of the problems at hand was demonstrated by Williams's appeal to the white lawyer and author Albion W. Tourgée for help in preparing a speech, "The Progressive and Present Status of the Colored Women of the United States and Their Progress since Emancipation," that she was to give at the World's Congress of Representative Women, to be held in conjunction with the fair. Williams wrote Tourgée, "If there be any literature upon this sex phase of the Negro question that you can refer me to or any accessible data that tell unmistakeably of the steady and sure development from a degraded peasantry toward noble womanhood, I would be duly obligated." Disgusted by the whole business that could produce thinking like this from a fellow black woman, and that had resulted in no more than a couple of display cases of black women's work, Ida Wells wrote a powerful condemnation of the fair, *The Reason Why the Colored American Is Not in the World's Columbian Exposition,* and with Douglass as one of the sponsors, published it while the fair was still under way.

Douglass had hoped that the fair would say something positive about the accomplishments of black people both in Haiti and in the United States, but from the start, there were the sounds of a new day uncongenial to a nineteenth-century liberal who believed in the transcendent worth of the individual and of individual freedom. His appointment, uncritically accepted, had come from President Hyppolite, whose flattering attention blinded the commissioner to the fact that he was a ruthless dictator. The post seemed to Douglass's enemies a payoff for having taken Haiti's part, at the expense of the United States, in the negotiations for the naval station. Douglass saw it otherwise; his assignment was to represent "our common race," as his letter of commission from the Haitian government had put it. But he could not claim the black republic as an example of a just democracy. And science too was leaning away from his old ideal of universal opportunity for all to grow into fully realized human beings.

The fair was designed to be a metaphor for human progress. Harlan Ingersoll Smith, an assistant to Harvard anthropologist Frederic Ward

Putnam, the man in charge of the ethnological exhibits, declared that they "from the first to the last . . . will be arranged to teach a lesson; to show the advancement of evolution of man." Otis T. Mason, the curator of the Smithsonian Institution's Bureau of American Ethnology, proudly announced, "It would not be too much to say that the World's Columbian Exposition was one vast anthropological revelation."

All that was to be revealed of the progress of the human race lay along a road—the midway—that led to the central cluster of formal display pavilions. The throngs of visitors taking the instructive stroll along the midway advanced from the grass huts of the Dahomey village peopled with half-naked Americans in "native" skirts upward to a Teutonic village where the germ of true civilization was to be encountered. They encountered, too, sword swallowers and belly dancers, and stalls where goods from around the world were for sale, side by side with the ethnographic exhibits. Shopkeeper Isaac Benyaker, whose letterhead proclaimed him the proprietor of "Over 40 Different Bazaars" in Cairo, sent a note reminding Commissioner Douglass that he had served him and Mrs. Douglass on their trip to Egypt. He asked for an autograph and enclosed a photograph "of myself and our Nubians and Sudanese."

Once the honky-tonk—and fun—of the fair had been fully savored, visitors were ready to cross the bridge into the White City. On that alabastered island stood the national pavilions and those dedicated to the display of machines, scientific devices and discoveries, and artistic work, thematically arranged. Much has been made of the fact that the Palladian architecture—in sterile white—seemed to many critics to be not in the spirit of aesthetic progress, but a stale and stalled statement of discredited design, but black Americans had another reason to be dismayed by the celebration of the White City. To them, it was an all-too-powerful metaphor of the dominance of white people over those of color.

To be sure, in some of the formal exhibit halls, work of scholarly value was to be seen. In the Woman's Building, Mason had African artifacts that, in his words, showed in part what America "has done and undone" to African American women. The exhibits emphasized "women's role in peacemaking," but the women's "rude arts" were arranged so as to exemplify "the three modern types of savagery, namely: the [native] American, the Negroid and the Mayalo-Polynesian." Some of the anthropologists were careful in their use of the term "race" and recognized that differences among groups arise from cultural and temporal influences, but in the view of the scholars who dominated the fair, race as a scientific and hence inescapable fact was firmly established. Douglass himself had been partially in step with this kind of thinking, and had correspondingly undercut his own sense of the oneness of human experience, when on his trip to Egypt, he took careful note of what he saw as racial characteristics. Here in Chicago, he was abruptly reminded of how pernicious the concept of race could be.

He was not alone in the African American community in this respect. The *Cleveland Gazette* declared the fair to be "the great American white elephant," and the *New York Age* stated that "if the matter was left to our determination we would advise the race to have nothing whatever to do with the Columbian Exposition." Two people almost congenitally unable to wash their hands of anything, Frederick Douglass and Ida Wells, now firm allies, wanted the world to know how their people were faring in the United States. With Douglass's help, Wells wrote a pamphlet describing both the accomplishments of black Americans and their plight in a nation plagued by lynchings. In a call "To the Friends of Equal Rights" for funds to pay for the pamphlet, which they hoped to publish in French, German, and Spanish, as well as English, and to distribute widely to visitors at the fair, Wells and Douglass asserted that the "absence of colored citizens from [the planning of the fair] will be construed to their disadvantage by the representatives of the civilized world there assembled." When insufficient funds came in, they issued the pamphlet in English only, with prefaces in German and French. Day after day, from the desk in the Haitian pavilion that Douglass had given her, Wells put a copy into the hands of every visitor who would take one. The fair, these two embattled black warriors wrote, had become the "whited sepulcher."

When it came to exhibits, Douglass himself was the one that best refuted the melange of hokum and highly respected science. Presiding with monumental dignity over the pavilion of a black republic, he drew more visitors than did Toussaint L'Ouverture's sword or what was purported to be Christopher Columbus's anchor—they had dropped the pot holding the dust of the great admiral while removing it from the cathedral, and he had blown away. The antique abolitionist was as much a relic as any on display, but this foreign citadel was a sad home for a man who in the ethnographers' own terms might be said to be the quintessential example of human progress. In lonely splendor, "Mr. Douglass held high court," as Ida Wells put it, receiving the homage of curious tourists. And yet, Frederick Douglass as message was largely ignored; he was seen only as a runaway from his natural habitat, the savage village. Henry Adams, long after his visit to the fair, declared that "Chicago was the first expression of American thought as a unity." Douglass, had he been alive to read *The Education of Henry Adams,* would have recognized with infinite sadness, that his own thought—his concept of human oneness—was excluded; Adams's unity did not transcend the denigrating divisiveness of race.

It all came down to watermelons. August 25 was to be Colored People's Day. Douglass's granddaughter Fredericka Sprague warned him of what was coming: "So, one day has really been found for the colored people at the 'World's Fair.' And the very idea that they are going to the trouble of supplying them with watermelons is enough to draw every dusky American from his castle and land him at the Fair ground gates." Will Marion Cook, a brilliant young violinist back from studies in Berlin with Joseph Joachim and in New York with Anton Dvořák, had been urging that there be a special day at the fair when young black artists like himself and his friend Joseph Douglass—a grandson in whom Douglass took great pride—could perform. He had pled with Douglass to support such an event, and the commissioner, charmed by the young artists who had congregated in the city, overcame his doubts. He knew what such a day was likely to turn into, but he still had sufficient vanity to look forward to being the centerpiece of a celebration, and he overrode the objections of other black leaders, who feared mockery would outdo Mozart.

When Colored People's Day came, Douglass arrived at the grounds early and found that Fredericka's prediction had been accurate. Vendors had their watermelons ready; the day was to be a joke. Disgusted, he went back to the Williamses', leaving the pavilion in the charge of the young poet Paul Laurence Dunbar, whom he had hired to help out. Soon that bright, aspiring writer was confronted by a reporter in search of a humorous story, unaware that *Puck*'s cartoonist would take care of the humor; Frederick Burr Opper's drawing "Darkies' Day at the Fair" had fat-bellied, barefoot spear carriers in grass skirts and thick-lipped, ornately uniformed soldiers lined up to buy their watermelon from a checked-pants sharpster with his top hat atilt.

Not finding Douglass in, the reporter began interrogating Dunbar. He wanted to know who was distributing the "No Watermelon" leaflets protesting the day, and why so few black people were coming through the gate. Perhaps realizing he would be wasting his breath if he explained that the leaflets came from a people capable of something beyond spitting seeds, Dunbar attempted to turn the reporter's attention to an event planned for that afternoon that was expected to restore some dignity to the day. "He believed Mr. Douglass wished no publicity in the matter," he told the reporter, but there was to be a program at Festival Hall at two-thirty. Ignoring that event, the reporter's story in the afternoon edition, beginning with the watermelons, was headed "Few Colored Folks There, Negroes Apparently Not Interested."

He was wrong. At two-thirty a throng of sober black citizens, ringed by some white spectators, gathered for an achingly formal occasion. Douglass, presiding, introduced clergyman after clergyman, among them Bishop Henry McNeal Turner; another honored guest was Harriet Beecher Stowe's sister Isabella Hooker, one of the few white women who had taken a nonpatronizing part in trying to get black American crafts exhibited.

The introductions over, Douglass rose once more, put on his glasses, and began somberly reading a paper, "The Race Problem in America." Suddenly he was interrupted by "jeers and catcalls" from white men in the rear of the crowd. In the August heat, the old man tried to go on, but the mocking persisted; his hand shook. Painfully, Dunbar witnessed his idol's persecution; the great orator's voice "faltered." Then, to the young poet's surprise and delight, the old abolitionist threw his papers down, parked his glasses on them, and eyes flashing, pushed his hand through his great mane of white hair. Then he spoke: "Full, rich and deep came the sonorous tones, compelling attention, drowning out the catcalls as an organ would a penny whistle." "Men talk of the Negro problem," Douglass roared. "There is no Negro problem. The problem is whether the American people have loyalty enough, honor enough, patriotism enough, to live up to their own Constitution." On he went for an hour: "We Negroes love our country. We fought for it. We ask only that we be treated as well as those who fought against it." The applause when he stopped was the welcome thunder of old times. And then the young had their day: Joseph Douglass played, there was a duet from an opera Cook was composing, and Dunbar read "Colored Americans," which he had written for the occasion. Douglass, together with the musicians and the poet, had redeemed the day.

After reading about the speech in the newspaper, Ida Wells hurried to the fair and "begged his pardon for presuming in my youth and inexperience to criticize him." She and Douglass had quarreled over Colored People's Day; she had argued for a boycott. Now she declared that his speech "had done more to bring our cause to the attention of the American people than anything else which had happened during the fair." He had not had much competition.

The land in which Douglass now spoke his mind was not the one he had worked so hard to achieve. He and all of black America had long known about the monstrous happenings in the South—the terrorism, culminating in lynchings—and the refusal of the federal government to do anything effective about them; black Americans knew that white America was deflecting its guilt by seeing them as comic figures; that so-called scientific thought was consigning them to a lower position on the evolutionary scale. What black America had not previously experienced was the humiliation of seeing these attitudes and beliefs all together, on display at a vast celebration of "progress" spread out before the whole world. The White City took no account of the inhumanity endured by black Americans; the Midway was a parade of insulting buffoonery; the ethnographic displays seemed to validate all that the Frederick Douglasses had stood against for the whole of their lives. The Chicago fair was a world gone sour. Booker T. Washington made his speech accommodating to this world two years later, at another fair; Rayford W. Logan has placed the nadir of American regard for other Americans two decades later; but the cold white shoulder had been given at the World's Columbian Exposition.

Happily, younger voices called out for the old man's attention: "Dear Grand Pa[,] . . . I go out fishing and crabbing almost every day. I have learned to swim well and I can swim over a hundred yards without stopping to rest." This was the best of letters to receive in the midst of a hot, trying summer. Haley George, Charles's young son, was at Highland Beach, a bayside community his father was developing on the Chesapeake below Annapolis. With the streets named "after prominent colored men so far as there are streets enough to go around," this was to become the summering place—it is now reaching its centennial—for the old guard of black Washington. Douglass disliked the self-segregation, but white exclusivity, particularly at watering holes, invited the defensive move.

Lewis and Nathan Sprague too were now in the real-estate business, that firm undergirding of the black bourgeoisie. Indeed, all of the family, save Frederick jr.'s blighted branch, seemed reasonably well placed by the spring of 1893, though Rosetta's daughters were often unhappy in their teaching jobs in the South, and Nathan, as always, bore watching. But Annie, twenty-eight now and married to Charles S. Morris, a student at the University of Michigan, had almost a premonition of disaster as she and her grandfather parted in April. She had been staying at Cedar Hill—the grandchildren were more comfortable there than the children—and in the fifteen minutes between his and Helen's departure and her own, she experienced a terrible loneliness. She went on to Hampton Institute, in Virginia, and later in the summer, to Harpers Ferry. In July, her sister Fredericka received a postcard from Douglass asking her to go to Annie, who was pregnant and ill. In October, against his better judgment, Douglass agreed to lend Annie's husband three hundred dollars to move her to Ann Arbor (where, Charles Morris claimed, his bootblack parlor should prove profitable enough to pay for his education); there, the husband was sure, "free from worry," his wife would recover. On November 11, in Washington, Rosetta took a sheet of Nathan's business stationery and wrote her father, then on a lecture tour, "Annie is dead. . . . I am utterly dazed and crushed." On November 27, which would have been Annie's twenty-ninth birthday, she wrote again: "If only she hadn't gone to Ann Arbor she'd be alive; the doctor had said she shouldn't travel." Rosetta's grief, like most of her accounts of unhappiness, carried with it a reproach.

That same day, Helen, who had not been told the news, wrote "Dear courageous weary Frederick," telling him "it is 'awful lonesome' " at Cedar Hill and urging him to come home as soon as the lecture tour ended. Charles too had made Cedar Hill sound inviting; earlier in the fall he had written that the ground there was covered with apples and pears; the trees were laden with russets. Cedar Hill sounded fine, but going home meant going back to all the sorrows of the family. And first there were, as always, lectures to give. Douglass went to Des Moines and then to Omaha, where he had another errand.

He had heard that an old friend from Lynn days, one he had lost track of, was in Omaha. But "my search was in vain"; no one had heard of Ruth Adams. He was afraid that the handsome woman who had lived with them in Lynn had died, that one more link to a rich past was gone. Then, early the next year, he learned to his relief that she was in Virginia: "I am now very glad to know that you still live and have not forgotten what we were to each other in our younger days." When she replied, he wrote her an oddly revealing letter, one the very few letters that give glimpses of his emotions. "The reason of your inability to have correspondence with me of late years is easily told. Our lives have been for a long time running in different channels," he said. Then, turning to metaphor, he continued. "I have for years had no constant abiding place [he had been at Cedar Hill for fifteen years]—been a 'stranger and sojourner as all my fathers were'—sometimes at the North—sometimes at the South—sometimes on the land and sometimes on the sea. I am still a traveler," wrote the runaway, "but cannot hold out much longer."

He reported that he was "still among active workers for the improvement and elevation of our people," and then, turning intimately to her: "I notice that you tell me about the color of your hair. I am sure you are growing beautifully. . . ." It was somehow wrong that she should not be young, that a whole other world existed for her that he had not been a part of: "It seems funny to have you tell me of your grandchildren"; he retaliated by telling her about his. Then, reaching back to when they were in their twenties, he added, "Rose and Lewis remember you—Charley was too young. . . . All our old friends in Lynn have passed away—and sometimes I think it strange that I am yet in the land of the living. . . ."

28

Cedar Hill

THERE WAS THE PAST and there was the future. Times had not been so discouraging since the *Dred Scott* decision. Now, in the 1890s, even fewer allies seemed to be at hand to try to reverse the nation's course. In 1893, Governor John Peter Altgeld of Illinois, reviewing the trial of the Haymarket anarchists that had resulted in the hanging of four of them, had the courage to declare that a miscarriage of justice had occurred, and pardoned those remaining in prison. But he was noticeably absent from the platform at Douglass's program for Colored People's Day. Shrewd black observers were not surprised.

One of Douglass's supporters accused Altgeld, along with President Grover Cleveland, Secretary of State Walter Q. Gresham, and Henry Watterson, editor of the *Louisville Courier-Journal,* of being among the "enemies . . . of the South & the Afro as well, [who] have been persuading colored leaders, that striking out their vote, will stop their persecutions." Douglass's anonymous correspondent added, "It will do *no such thing.*" Douglass emphatically agreed. The move to disfranchise black Southerners violated everything he had struggled for since emancipation and before.

From a great distance, in time and place, came another recognition that things were going badly indeed for former slaves and their offspring, born since emancipation and coming into maturity. Simultaneously with the fair, religious and intellectual leaders had been conducting in Chicago the World Auxiliary Congress on Evolution (an offshoot of the World Parliament of Religion), intended by religious leaders and other moralists to sanctify the work of Herbert Spencer. From Edinburgh, a group of ancient Quakers, greatly troubled that black Americans were being placed too low on the evolutionary scale to attract the benevolent attention of these worshippers of progress, sent a petition. "We, old workers in the *Anti-Slavery Cause,* being deeply grieved by the Prejudice against the negro race still prevailing in the United States of America," it began. The stern reminder of grievances closed with the quaint old un-Spencerian message "All men are created equal." The signatures formed a list of women Douglass had known in Scotland in 1846: Priscilla Bright McLaren; Eliza Wigham, identified as a "worker in 1832"; Jane Melville Aberdeen; Mary Burton; and, probably most touching of all to Douglass, Elizabeth Pease Nichol, who, said the appended notation, "from 1830 worked for colonial and American abolition; Huntly Lodge, Edinburgh; now blind, signature *authorized.*" For Douglass, to whom the old ladies entrusted the petition, these were wonderfully heartening voices out of the past, but the day of these remarkable women, and of Douglass himself was passing.

Still, nothing but the grave would silence them. And there was Ida Wells; there was a new generation. Small battles could even now be won by great warriors. One day as the fair was winding down, Douglass invited Wells to join him for lunch. Asked where they should go, she said there was a nice place across the street, but, she told him, they did not serve colored people: "Mr. Douglass, in his vigorous way, grasped my arm and said, 'Come, let's go there.'" She said she was game and they "sauntered into the Boston Oyster House as if it were an everyday occurrence, cocked and primed for the fight if necessary." Douglass strode to a table, held a chair for Wells, and took his seat, as "paralysed" waiters looked on—and gave no sign of coming over with a menu. A classic standoff seemed in the making until the proprietor, recognizing Douglass, came over and greeted him. From then on, waiters hovered, while the proprietor kept up nonstop reminiscences of a visit Douglass had once made to his hometown. "When he finally went to another part of the room," Wells recalled, "Mr. Douglass turned to me with a roguish look and said, 'Ida, I thought you said that they didn't serve us here. It seems we are getting more attention than we want.'" Not until they took a walk after the meal—probably an excellent one—were they free to have the conversation he had looked forward to.

Ida Wells was remarkably like her friend. Both were editors, both orators, both began their careers passionately committed to righting the worst form of injustice that, in their respective times, was inflicted on their people. Wells wrote against injustice in newspapers and pamphlets as Douglass had done; after the *Memphis Free Speech* was silenced, she had begun contributing to the *New York Age.* Then, in 1893 and again in 1894,

Wells, like Douglass before her, took her crusade to Great Britain. She carried with her letters from Douglass introducing her to people he had known there nearly half a century earlier. As he had done with his descriptions of slavery, she aroused great sympathy with her vivid depictions of the horrors of lynching. Douglass and Wells were similar too in their conviction that their determination to be unembarrassably outspoken about the evil of their day did not mean that they must look as disreputable as many people found their views to be. Nor did they see any virtue in pretending to be simple folk. Both loved to dress well, to speak elegantly, and both could be snobbishly scornful of those who did not keep their socks pulled up.

Unlike her mentor in his battle against slavery, Wells did not see her cause succeed. No law was passed making lynching a federal crime, the poverty that still oppresses her people had not been addressed when she died in 1931, and the gains of the far-off Civil Rights Movement could only be imagined. While she lived, neither her marriage to Ferdinand Lee Barnett nor the raising of four children curtailed the range of her work. Wells-Barnett—she surrendered nothing, not even her name—chastised Republican presidents for their imperialism and for their disregard of the rights of black Americans, as in the outrageous Brownsville incident. (Theodore Roosevelt discharged "without honor" 167 black soldiers because the unidentified gunmen in a recent shooting were assumed—falsely, it turned out—to be members of their battalion.) Infuriated by Democrat Woodrow Wilson's segregation of federal offices, she was a member of a protesting delegation. With Jane Addams, she fought against the segregation of Chicago's schools, and, no doubt chafing at the adherence to Jim Crow, she led members of the black Alpha Suffrage Club in the great 1916 march for the franchise. In 1918 she was one of eleven chosen as a delegation to protest the condition of black Americans at the Paris Peace Conference, but then unable to attend because they were denied passports. And Wells, an admirer of W. E. B. Du Bois, had been at the 1906 meeting of the Niagara Movement, of which he was a founder, and from which came the National Association for the Advancement of Colored People. If Frederick Douglass left a legacy for the twentieth century, no one bore it forward with more fervor or grace than she.

Early in her life, Ida Wells may have been inspired by Frederick Douglass, but he, near the end of his, was driven back into the fray by Wells. On January 9, 1894, at the great Metropolitan African Methodist Episcopal Church in Washington, Douglass delivered what was to be his last great speech, "The Lessons of the Hour." "Friends and Fellow Citizens," he began. "No man should come before an audience like the one

38

FREDERICK DOUGLASS

by whose presence I am now honored, without a noble object and a fixed and earnest purpose." There were, he told them, Southern white views of the issues he would address, and there were the views of Northern white people, but "I propose to give you a colored man's view of the unhappy relations at present existing between the white and colored people of the Southern States of our union. . . . The presence of eight millions of people in any section of this country constituting an aggrieved class, smarting under terrible wrongs, denied the exercise of the commonest rights of humanity . . . is not only a disgrace and scandal to that particular section but a menace to the peace and security of the people of the whole country."

There was, as he had told the people of Chicago, no Negro problem; the problem lay on other shoulders, white Southern shoulders. He did not duck around the psychological core, the sexual core, of the device being used in the South to justify the subjugation of the black people: "A white man has but to blacken his face and commit a crime, to have some negro lynched in his stead. An abandoned woman has only to start the cry that she has been insulted by a black man, to have him arrested and summarily murdered by the mob. Frightened and tortured by his captors, confused into telling crooked stories about his whereabouts at the time when the alleged crime was committed and the death penalty is at once inflicted, though his story may be but the incoherency of ignorance or distraction caused by terror."

He then cited three defenders of the white Southern course. The first was Bishop Atticus G. Haygood, author of *Our Brother in Black* and an advocate of education for black people. Although he had recently written, "The most alarming fact is, that execution by lynching has ceased to surprise us," Haygood had gone on to blame the victim, saying that "unless assaults by negroes come to an end," there would be many more burnings. Next, Douglass pointed the finger at another sometime friend of African Americans, Daniel Henry Chamberlain, who had been a Reconstruction governor of South Carolina. Chamberlain, whom he quoted, had recently criticized Douglass for denouncing the lynching while not denouncing the "assault on white women" that had caused black people to be "tortured and burned," and he had exhorted, "As you value your own good fame and safety as a race, stamp out the infamous crime."

Third, with his lethal sarcasm in full use, Douglass turned to "the sweet voice of a Northern woman, of Southern principles . . . the good Miss Frances Willard, of the W.C.T.U." The leader of the Woman's Christian Temperance Union had written, and he quoted, " 'I pity the Southerner. The problem on their hands is immeasurable. The colored race' "—and here Douglass paused for emphasis—" 'multiplies like the locusts of Egypt. The safety of woman, of childhood, of the home, is menaced in a thousand localities at this moment, so that men dare not go beyond the sight of their own roof tree.' "

Next, having inserted the obligatory denunciation of rape—"The crime they allege against the negro, is the most revolting which men can commit"—Douglass proceeded to analyze the matter: "This charge . . . brought against the negro . . . is not merely against the individual culprit, as would be the case with an individual culprit of any other race, but it is in a large measure a charge against the colored race as such. It throws over every colored man a mantle of odium." He then set out to remove that veil: "I can and will show that there are sound reasons for doubting and denying this horrible and hell-black charge of rape as the peculiar crime of the colored people of the South. . . . The first is the well established and well tested character of the negro. . . . The second ground for my doubt and denial is based upon what I know of the character and antecedents of the men and women who bring this charge against him."

Douglass did not at that point lapse into reverse racism; instead, he skillfully brought into question the trustworthiness of the word "of men who justify themselves in cheating the negro out of his constitutional right to vote." Subtly, Douglass had introduced the idea that guilt was a motivating force, if not among the lynchers, then among those who defended them. He went on to attack the spurious literacy tests and the various other "obstacles and sinuosities" used to keep the black man from voting. "That this is done," he continued, "is not only admitted, but openly defended and justified by so-called honorable men inside and outside of Congress." He had, he related, heard such actions condoned in a "solemn paper" given by a professor at the religious "World's Auxiliary Congresses at Chicago."

Turning to the character of the black man, Douglass cited the fact that when Southern men had been away from their homes during the Civil War, there had been no rape of the women by the slaves left behind. And then he got down to the heart of the matter—the utility of accusing a whole group of a propensity for rape to justify the practice of lynching as a means of social control. He identified "three distinct periods of persecution," each with its own excuse for violence. "First you remember it was insurrection," seen as a threat during slavery. "When that was worn out, [the danger of] negro supremacy" was the excuse, during Reconstruction. "When that is worn out, now it is assault upon defenseless women" that is seen as the threat justifying violence. "Now, my friends, I ask what is the rational explanation of this singular omission of this charge [rape] in the two periods preceding the present?" Answering his own question, Douglass said that the third accusation had not been necessary as long as the threat of insurrection or of negro supremacy could be invoked to justify severe measures of social control; now "altered times and circumstances have made necessary a sterner . . . justification of Southern barbarism."

Douglass acknowledged that he had been criticized by many for not agreeing to the "new departure"—the withdrawal of black people from politics and the acceptance of segregation. This, in his view, would bring peace to the South only at the cost of the "ruin [of] the negro's character as a man and a citizen." It was no happenstance, he was persuaded, that the tarnishing of the whole race with a charge of carnal savagery was occurring "simultaneously with well-known efforts now being . . . made to degrade the negro by legislative enactments, and by repealing all laws for the protection of the ballot, and by drawing the color line in all railroad cars and stations and in all other public places in the South." Douglass was convinced that these developments, taken together, were "paving the way for our entire disfranchisement."

He had returned to his favorite cause: "It has come to be fashionable of late to ascribe much of the trouble at the South to ignorant negro suffrage. The great measure . . . recommended by General Grant and adopted by the loyal nation is now denounced as a blunder and a failure." He took issue with those, black and white, who would restrict suffrage to the educated. "Among those who take this view are Mr. John J. Ingalls [former senator from Kansas] and Mr. John M. Langston. They are both eloquent, both able, and both wrong." Nothing must impede the whole of the black people, and yet everything was being done to stand in their way. "I have sometime thought that the American people were too great to be small." Now, he was not so sure: "I cannot shut my eyes to the ugly facts before me. . . . He is a wiser man than I am, who can tell how low the moral sentiment of this republic may yet fall. . . . The Supreme Court has surrendered. . . . It has destroyed the civil rights Bill, and converted the Republican party into a party of money rather than a party of morals."

The idea of deporting his people received his greatest scorn: "All this native land talk is nonsense. The native land of the American negro is America. His bones, his muscles, his sinews, are all American. His ancestors for two hundred and seventy years have lived, and labored, and died on American soil, and millions of his posterity have inherited Caucasian blood." Shrewdly, he counted on the fact that the white South did not want to expel its workers: "The land owners of the South want the labor of the negro on the hardest possible terms," terms including perpetual debt and a lien system by which "he is fastened to the land as by hooks of steel."

"Words are things," dangerous things, and the words "Negro Problem" were false, pernicious. "Even the noble and good Mr. Lincoln . . . told a committee of negroes . . . 'they were the cause of the war.' " This thinking had to end. The problem was the nation's problem; if it could not be solved, the nation was doomed. But, Douglass insisted, there was still a solution and he thundered forth a stream of correctives: "Let the white people of the North and South conquer their prejudices . . . ," and, in the skillfully quoted words of former senator Ingalls, " 'Let the nation try justice and the problem will be solved.' " Well over an hour into his speech, the old man paused: "But, my friends, I must stop. Time and strength are not equal to the task before me." And then, with a peroration only Mahler could have bested, he closed by rejecting "the idea that one class must rule over another," and sat down.

The trip from the Tuckahoe, from Nantucket, was complete. He had said all the words; he had taken action. The speech was handsomely printed, with a fine photograph of the orator on the cover, and was much praised. William E. Chandler of New Hampshire rose on the Senate floor to commend it to his fellows, and sat down to write a note congratulating Douglass on his splendid defense of the Fifteenth Amendment and his assault on lynching. "The Lessons of the Hour" was a magnificent success. It did absolutely no good.

ON FEBRUARY 20, 1895, Douglass rode into the city to attend a women's rights rally. When he entered the hall, the presiding officer interrupted the meeting, and the women rose as Susan B. Anthony and Anna Shaw escorted him to the platform. Later, in the hotel parlor, a British delegate confronted a "commanding figure six feet high, a splendid head with large and well-formed features, soft, pathetic eyes, complexion of olive-brown, flowing white hair," who rose to greet her. As they were chatting—the visitor told him of having once broken *Uncle Tom's Cabin* in two so that she and her sister would not fight in their eagerness to read it—Douglass gave her "that look of keen enjoyment that is so often noticed in those whose spirit does not grow old."

He was back at Cedar Hill for an early supper, and that evening, while he waited with Helen for their carriage to take them to a meeting in a neighborhood black church in Anacostia, he began to mimic one of the day's grandiloquent speakers, rising from his chair and then sinking to his knees in a heroic gesture. In an instant, Helen's delight became horror. Frederick crumpled to the floor.

Telegrams of condolence were delivered to Cedar Hill in batches: from John W. Hutchinson, a voice from the first great trip to Ireland, "I wish to sing at the funeral"; from the former South Carolina congressman Robert Smalls, "The greatest of the race has fallen." The feisty radical Henry O. Waggoner—a friend for better than half a century—telegraphed from Denver, "Can I get there in time takes four days."

Four days later, they closed the colored schools in Washington, and thousands of children filed past Douglass's open casket in the Metropolitan African Methodist Episcopal Church. There had been a Baptist service at Cedar Hill earlier that morning, and in the afternoon—Ottilia would have been scandalized—a vast service was held in the church. Justice John Marshall Harlan attended, and Senators John Sherman and George Hoar; the whole faculty of Howard University came to honor Douglass. That evening, Helen, Rosetta, Lewis, and Charles traveled with the body on the train to Rochester. Again, the body lay in state—in City Hall—and there was another great service, in the Central Church.

They took Frederick Douglass's body to the city's vast Mount Hope Cemetery, where his wife Anna and his daughter Annie were buried. Fifty years earlier his staunch antislavery friend Erasmus Darwin Hudson, with a fine nineteenth-century eye for the rightness of things, had called it a "delightful place for a burial ground—full of forest trees & shrubbery, with fine roads meandering among the hills." But "even here," the resolute reformer had seen "the spirit of caste—the potters field, where all are crowded together in republican style, & the expensively laid out grounds & tombs of the rich in the beautiful grove." "Christianity," he pronounced with finality, "is a leveling principle & none of this aristocracy can go to heaven." Douglass probably would not have wanted to go there in any case—unless he could have been sure of a good crowd—but his modest gravestone, secure from both potter's field and plutocratic extremes, would not have disqualified him. Marred only by slavery's error, which, ironically, had given him an extra year, the inscription read, "To the memory of Frederick Douglass, 1817–1895."

Later, a heroic statue was placed near the site of his Rochester house; it is one of the finest of hundreds of memorials to Douglass. But perhaps his best monument lies quietly in the diary of another of the titans of the nineteenth century, one with whom Douglass had done ferocious battle. On February 21, Elizabeth Cady Stanton wrote, "Taking up the papers to-day, the first word that caught my eye thrilled my very soul. Frederick Douglass is dead! What memories of the long years since he and I first met chased each other, thick and fast, through my mind and held me spellbound." She recalled his "burning eloquence" before a Boston antislavery meeting when "with wit, satire, and indignation he graphically described the bitterness of slavery and the humiliation of subjection to those who, in all human virtues and powers, were inferior to himself." It was the first time she had seen Douglass: "Around him sat the great antislavery orators of the day, earnestly watching the effect of his eloquence on that immense audience, that laughed and wept by turns, completely carried away by the wondrous gifts of his pathos and humor." For Stanton, "all the other speakers seemed tame after Frederick Douglass." He "stood there like an African prince, majestic in his wrath."

29

Chesapeake Bay

EXCEPT TO RUN FREE, Frederick Douglass never ran away from anything. There were things he reached past as he strode into a full engagement with life. He pressed excellence on his children and did not see that they needed something simpler, deeper; he looked beyond his wife, and scarcely seeing her, left her almost invisible; he lost touch with the men in the Freeland fields and in the shipyards, and so lost as well his closeness to ordinary people. There was anger within him—always. The world would not let him shrug off that burden. But even as he incurred and endured these disadvantages, he was amassing a richness of experience, a fullness of living.

It has been said that he ran away from being black. The opposite is true. Every time he walked up to a lectern to speak, he was seen: by his very presence he not only announced that he was black but also instructed all who looked at him that they were not to see that fact pejoratively. As Whitman did, Douglass sang of himself, and he did so just by standing on the platform. His simple appearance was a proud assertion that neither color nor previous condition of servitude was relevant to his aspirations, either for himself or for others.

His light skin and aristocratic mien have long suggested the same distancing from color of which much of the upper-class black community in America is accused. What has been missed has been Douglass's struggle to bridge that distance with his intellect, with an unswerving commitment to human dignity and equality. More than some of us with a different sense of society would have preferred, he sought to draw his people over to his side of the span instead of crossing back and engaging them in their own world. But the reality and grandeur of the bridge cannot be denied.

Yet it has been. The work of Douglass's mind has not until recently received serious attention. He once told James Redpath, "I shall never get beyond Frederick Douglass the self-educated fugitive slave," and indeed the American public never let him escape from being thought of as a runaway slave. Most white people could not see him as other than that remarkable colored fellow; in this Douglass shared an experience that every black intellectual in America has faced.

Frederick Douglass was one of the giants of nineteenth-century America. And in the end, he stood as tall as any. He had not found it necessary to rein in his sexuality as Melville had. With great dignity on his part—as well as his partners'—he openly dared to embrace intimacy in a way few Americans did. His principles did not slacken as fully as did those of so many would-be statesmen. In an age of oratory, some judged him to have had the greatest voice. As a writer, he created an unforgettable character named Frederick Douglass; as a citizen, he struggled in a winning cause to rid his homeland of its most grievous social flaw, only to see slavery replaced with injustice and terror. If he had been denied great public office, he could always walk out the fine front door of Cedar Hill and look down on the Capitol, down on the White House. Not even Henry Adams scornfully gazing across Lafayette Square could achieve quite this disdain.

There were lovelier, nobler sights than the castles of politicians to look out on. Of these, for Frederick Douglass, as once for Frederick Bailey, the Chesapeake Bay was the best. In his seventies, he planned to go back into his past in the sad way that rich, famous old men sometimes do. Behind a gatehouse built to exclude outsiders (and—as the residents were black—to guard against them), in the tight little community of Highland Beach, which his son Charles had developed south of Annapolis, Douglass was building a house facing on the bay. From its tower, he would have looked across the wide expanse of water to the Eastern Shore—the shore that he and Henry Harris would have passed had they made it to their canoe; the shoreline broken to the south by the Miles River, on which Wye House still faced in lordly arrogance; and farther south, the shore's high bank where, turning his back on Covey's bleak cruelty, Frederick Bailey, at sixteen, looked out at the Chesapeake.

In his *Narrative,* telling of that most tormenting time of his life, when a slave cabin on Covey's farm was home, Douglass wrote, "Our house stood within a few rods of the Chesapeake Bay, whose broad bosom was ever white with sails." As Frederick Bailey sat on the bank and looked out, those white sails were both a metaphor for freedom and "so many shrouded ghosts, to terrify and torment me." He poured out his "soul's complaint" to them, and as if to show that it was a reverie, perhaps in part culled from his reading, and surely committed to memory, he placed this apostrophe to the ships within quotation marks. So important was the passage, that when he was retelling his story in *My Bondage and My Freedom,* Julia Griffiths would not let him change a word. It was inviolate.

"Nothing reminds me of my dear f[rien]d Frederick so much as *'the Sea'*!" she wrote a decade after the two had parted, describing a warm late-fall day on the Welsh coast. It made her "think of the Chesapeake Bay!"—which she had never seen, except through Douglass's eyes. Beautiful before him, the bay had been his path, its ships his passage. "You are loosed from your moorings," he had had himself say, "and are free; I am fast in my chains, and am a slave! . . . Why am I a slave? I will run away. I will not stand it. Get caught, or get clear, I'll try it." As he looked far out over the brisk water, Frederick Bailey saw a sloop catch the wind, curve, and carry him swiftly forward.

Notes

Except where otherwise noted, citations of letters to or from Frederick Douglass are from the photostatic copies of his correspondence in the Yale University Frederick Douglass Papers.

CHAPTER 1

p. 5   *Frederick Augustus Bailey:* See Dickson J. Preston, *Young Frederick Douglass: The Maryland Years* (Baltimore, 1980), 32.

p. 5   *Belali Mohomet:* See Charles Joyner, *Remember Me: Slave Life in Coastal Georgia* (Atlanta, 1989), 22.

p. 5   *"footsteps before me":* Quoted in Anson P. Atterbury, *Islam in Africa* (1899; reprint, New York, 1969), 81.

p. 6   *for a spoon:* Frederick Douglass, *My Bondage and My Freedom* (1855; reprint, New York, 1969), 42.

p. 6   *"fork improperly":* Ibid., 40, 41.

p. 6   *"bright sunshine":* Ibid., 42.

p. 6   *running "wild":* Ibid., 41.

p. 6   *to see him:* Frederick Douglass, *Narrative of the Life of Frederick Douglass, an American Slave* (1845; reprint, Garden City, N.Y., 1963), 2.

p. 6   *"in her manners":* Douglass, *Bondage,* 52.

p. 6   *likeness to her:* See James Cowles Prichard, *The Natural History of Man,* 3d ed. (London, 1848), 157.

p. 6   *"to my mother":* Douglass, *Bondage,* 52.

p. 7   *"of her child":* Ibid., 53.

p. 7   *"no adequate expression":* Ibid.

p. 7   *"of a stranger":* Douglass, *Narrative,* 3.

p. 7   *"heartfelt sorrow":* Douglass, *Bondage,* 57.

p. 7   *"love of letters":* Frederick Douglass, *Life and Times of Frederick Douglass* (1892; reprint, New York, 1962), 36.

p. 8   *calculated:* See Preston, *Young Frederick Douglass,* 32.

p. 8   *"of my parentage":* Douglass, *Narrative,* 1.

p. 8   *"darker" mother:* Ibid.

p. 8   *"was my father"*: Ibid., 2.
p. 8   *"and happy"*: Douglass, *Bondage*, 42.
p. 8   *from the Tuckahoe:* Ibid., 33.
p. 9   *nutritious food:* Ibid., 36.
p. 10   *"yelling around me"*: Douglass, *Life and Times*, 32.
p. 10   *"grandmammy gone!"*: Douglass, *Bondage*, 49.

CHAPTER 2

p. 12   *"such a master?"*: Douglass, *Life and Times*, 58–60.
p. 13   *"latest generation"*: Preston, *Young Frederick Douglass*, 195.
p. 13   *a white father:* Douglass, *Narrative*, 2.
p. 13   *"was my father"*: Ibid., 1, 2.
p. 13   *Harriet Bailey:* Douglass, *Bondage*, 53.
p. 13   *"to penetrate"*: Ibid., 51.
p. 13   *"I know nothing"*: Douglass, *Life and Times*, 29.
p. 14   *clearly resembled:* See ibid., 62–63.
p. 14   *hence his father:* See, for example, Douglass, "An Appeal to Canada," April 3, 1851, in John W. Blassingame et al, eds., *The Frederick Douglass Papers*, 3 vols. to date (New Haven, Conn., 1979–) 2:328.
p. 17   *"any other fault"*: *Bondage*, 102.
p. 17   *"hateful whip"*: Ibid., 87. In *Bondage*, Douglass calls the victim of this whipping his "cousin Esther," but in *Narrative*, 5, and in the records of Aaron Anthony's slaves she is identified as his aunt Hester.
p. 18   *Anthony household:* Ibid., 74.
p. 19   *"got most"*: Ibid., 133.
p. 19   *powers as well:* See Preston, *Young Frederick Douglass*, 81.
p. 19   *"very industrious"*: Douglass, *Life and Times*, 34.
p. 19   *"mother gone"*: Douglass, *Bondage*, 56.
p. 22   *bachelor:* See *Vital Records of Conway, Massachusetts, to the Year 1850* (Boston, 1943), 79.
p. 22   *"to the back"*: William Faulkner, *Absalom, Absalom!* (New York, 1936), 233.
p. 25   *"to Baltimore"*: Douglass, *Bondage*, 136.
p. 25   *"was leaving"*: Ibid., 135.

CHAPTER 3

p. 26   *"Sophia Auld"*: Douglass, *Narrative*, 32.
p. 26   *"as a child"*: Douglass, *Bondage*, 142.
p. 26   *"with fear?"*: Ibid.
p. 26   *docks close by:* Douglass, *Narrative*, 33; see also Matchett, *Baltimore City Directory*, 1829.
p. 27   *there was bread:* Douglass, *Bondage*, 144.
p. 27   *"her affections"*: Ibid., 143.
p. 27   *"a slaveholding mistress"*: Ibid., 142.
p. 27   *earliest recollections:* Ibid., 174.
p. 28   *ear and nose:* See Douglass, *Narrative*, 49.
p. 28   *"kindly treated"*: Ibid., 48.
p. 29   *sister Eliza:* "Distribution of Negroes in Estate of Aaron Anthony, Sept. 24, 1827," in *Talbot Co. Distributions, 1825–1845*, Maryland Hall of Records, Annapolis.
p. 29   *"teach me to read"*: Douglass, *Bondage*, 145.
p. 30   *" 'away with himself' "*: Ibid., 146.
p. 30   *"oracular"*: Ibid.
p. 30   *a slave trader:* See William Calderhead, "The Role of the Professional Slave Trader in a

Slave Economy: Austin Woolfolk, a Case Study," *Civil War History,* 23 (Sept. 1977): 195–211.

p. 31 *south in 1825:* See Preston, *Young Frederick Douglass,* 78, 206.

p. 31 *to Woolfolk alone:* See ibid., 78.

p. 31 *"human shape":* Calderhead, "Role of the Professional Slave Trader," 205.

p. 31 *greatly provoked:* See Merton L. Dillon, *Benjamin Lundy and the Struggle for Negro Freedom* (Urbana, Ill., 1966), 118–20.

p. 31 *Vermont newspaper:* See John L. Thomas, *The Liberator: William Lloyd Garrison* (Boston, 1963), 107–13.

p. 31 *in Maryland:* See Walter M. Merrill, *Against Wind and Tide: A Biography of William Lloyd Garrison* (Cambridge, Mass., 1963), 27.

p. 31 *slave markets:* See Thomas, *The Liberator,* 101; and Leroy Graham, *Baltimore: The Nineteenth Century Black Capital,* (Washington, D.C., 1982), 297. Jacob Greener was the grandfather of Richard T. Greener, later dean of the Howard University law school and a rival of Douglass's.

p. 32 *his goal: Liberator,* Jan. 1, 1831. See also Wendell Phillips Garrison and Francis Jackson Garrison, *William Lloyd Garrison, 1805–1879,* 4 vols. (New York, 1885–89), 1:174–218.

p. 32 *"very little about":* Douglass, *Narrative,* 43–44.

p. 33 *"fellow-slaves":* Ibid., 44.

p. 33 *were caught:* See Douglass, "I Have Come to Tell You Something about Slavery," Oct. 20, 1841, in Blassingame et al., eds., *Frederick Douglass Papers* 1:4.

p. 33 *"to their masters":* Douglass, *Bondage,* 169.

p. 33 *"as the worst":* Douglass to Benjamin Auld, Sept. 15, 1891.

p. 34 *"the slave system":* Douglass, *Bondage,* 156.

p. 34 *"in his hand":* Caleb Bingham, comp., *The Columbian Orator,* 18th ed. (New York, 1816), 9.

p. 34 *"an orator's province":* Ibid., 7.

p. 35 *farewell:* See Douglass, *Bondage,* 158.

p. 36 *"RIGHTS OF MAN":* "Slave in Barbary," in Bingham, comp., *Columbian Orator,* 112, 115, 118.

p. 36 *"between master and slave!":* "Dialogue between Master and Slave," in ibid., 242.

p. 37 *"not have 'Fred' ":* Douglass, *Bondage,* 182.

p. 37 *Nathaniel Turner:* See ibid., 165.

p. 37 *"different roads":* Ibid., 307.

p. 38 *written manuscript:* Report of Douglass's speech at the forty-ninth-anniversary celebration of the Sabbath school of the Dallas Street Methodist Church, *Baltimore Sun,* Dec. 8, 1879, quoted in Graham, *Baltimore,* 216.

p. 38 *to press his cause:* See Preston, *Young Frederick Douglass,* 92, 96.

p. 38 *"of their sins":* Ibid., 97.

p. 38 *"holy affection":* Ibid.

p. 38 *"seeking knowledge":* Douglass, *Bondage,* 167; and *Life and Times,* 94. Douglass referred to the man as "Lawson" in 1845 and 1855, and as "Charles Lawson" in 1881. The only black drayman listed in Baltimore city directories for the years in question was a Solomon Lawson.

p. 38 *" 'Uncle Tom' ":* Douglass, *Life and Times,* 101.

p. 38 *for the Lord:* Ibid., 91, 157.

p. 39 *"brandy":* Douglass, *Bondage,* 183.

CHAPTER 4

p. 40 *the wrong way:* See Douglass *Bondage,* 184.

p. 41 *"intense selfishness":* Ibid., 191.

p. 42 *"on earth":* Ibid., 186.

p. 42   *"within the circle":* Ibid., 193–94.
p. 42   *"Master Thomas":* Ibid., 194.
p. 42   *" 'more kindly' ":* Ibid.
p. 42   *"come through":* Ibid., 195.
p. 43   *his lead:* See ibid., 198–99.
p. 43   *the school:* Ibid., 200
p. 43   *from Christianity:* Ibid., 201–2.
p. 44   *reputation:* Douglass, *Narrative,* 59.
p. 44   *"his switches":* Ibid., 62.
p. 45   *"in our midst":* Ibid., 63.
p. 45   *"of the slaves":* Ibid., 64.
p. 45   *"fanning wheat":* Ibid., 68.
p. 46   *"at every turn":* Douglass, *Bondage,* 242.
p. 47   *"walked off":* Ibid., 244–45.
p. 47   *"that morning":* Ibid.
p. 47   *"I held him":* Ibid., 243.
p. 47   *"two hours":* Douglass, *Narrative,* 74.
p. 47   *"broad bosom":* Ibid., 66.
p. 47   *"resurrection":* Ibid., 74.
p. 48   *"A FREEMAN":* Douglass, *Bondage,* 246.

CHAPTER 5

p. 49   *"among the slaves":* Douglass, *Bondage,* 253.
p. 49   *as energetic, as he:* Ibid., 261.
p. 50   *"for the race":* Ibid., 261–62.
p. 50   *recalled:* Ibid., 264.
p. 50   *"spelling books":* Ibid., 265.
p. 50   *"as possible":* Ibid.
p. 50   *"to my brother slaves":* Ibid., 274.
p. 51   *"on this farm":* Ibid., 268–69.
p. 51   *"with and for them":* Ibid., 274.
p. 51   *"running away":* Ibid.
p. 51   *"oppression and slavery":* Ibid., 275.
p. 51   *"revolutionary conspirators":* Ibid., 280.
p. 51   *"our opinions":* Ibid., 275.
p. 51   *"to be done":* Ibid.
p. 52   *"hired kidnappers":* Ibid., 283. The literary critic Herbert Leibowitz has said, "As a piece of extended storytelling" this passage "cannot be surpassed" (Herbert Leibowitz, *Fabricating Lives: Explorations in American Autobiography* [New York, 1989], 6).
p. 52   *"if we failed":* Bondage, 284.
p. 52   *"became troubled":* Ibid.
p. 52   *"for my chains":* Ibid., 275–76.
p. 52   *"indeed, honey":* Ibid., 284–85.
p. 53   *"to look back":* Ibid., 288.
p. 53   *"to be slaves":* Ibid., 289.
p. 53   *"just as you do":* Ibid.
p. 53   *"surely betrayed":* Ibid., 290.
p. 53   *"No I won't":* Ibid., 292.
p. 53   *subdued and bound:* Ibid., 293.
p. 54   *into St. Michaels:* Ibid., 293–94.
p. 54   *behind her:* Ibid., 294.
p. 54   *"Own nothing!":* Ibid., 296.

p. 54 *"from my back"*: Ibid., 295.
p. 54 *"our betrayer"*: Ibid., 297.
p. 54 *"shoulders"*: Ibid.
p. 55 *"to be sold"*: Ibid., 298.
p. 55 *"pretty quick"*: Ibid., 299.
p. 55 *apprehension:* Ibid., 300.
p. 56 *"had now fled"*: Ibid., 301.
p. 56 *out of the county:* See Preston, *Young Frederick Douglass,* 140.
p. 56 *to release Frederick:* Douglass, *Bondage,* 306.

CHAPTER 6

p. 58 *"surpassing it"*: Douglass, *Bondage,* 136.
p. 59 *"desired to live"*: Ibid., 306.
p. 59 *"his slave"*: Ibid., 307.
p. 60 *"American freemen"*: Ibid., 311.
p. 60 *" 'brains out!' "*: Ibid., 309. Douglass was deliberately quoting from *Narrative,* 94.
p. 61 *" 'to be killed' "*: Douglass, *Bondage,* 312.
p. 61 *"my eyeball"*: Ibid., 313.
p. 62 *"a white person"*: Ibid., 313–14.
p. 62 *"rights of property"*: Ibid., 316.
p. 62 *"has been done"*: Ibid., 316–17.
p. 62 *"disgusted"*: Ibid., 317.
p. 63 *"without hindrance"*: Ibid., 309–11.
p. 63 *a journeyman caulker:* Douglass, who frequently misremembered first names, referred to Asa Price as "Walter Price" (ibid., 312).
p. 63 *the grim business:* See Howard I. Chapelle, *The Search for Speed under Sail, 1700–1855* (New York, 1967); and Preston, *Young Frederick Douglass,* 146–47.
p. 64 *"Master Hugh"*: Douglass, *Bondage,* 319.
p. 64 *" 'Is that all?' "*: Ibid., 325.
p. 64 *"into repose"*: Ibid., 327.
p. 65 *"calking tools"*: Ibid., 328.
p. 65 *"before known"*: Ibid., 329.
p. 65 *"as by day"*: Ibid.
p. 65 *48 Calvert Street:* See handwritten "extract" from a letter of March 6, 1843, Weston Sisters Letters, Boston Public Library. Helen Weston, in compiling this material around 1900, attributed the letter to "Ann W. Weston." Anne Bates Weston and Warren Weston had daughters Anne, Deborah, Caroline, and Maria, and a son Warren (Helen Weston's father). Other letters suggest that it was their daughter Anne who wrote this account. The occasion on which this story became known is discussed in chapter 9. See also Walter Fisher to the author, Dec. 26, 1985.
p. 66 *the same street:* Rosetta Douglass Sprague, "Anna Murray-Douglass—My Mother As I Recall Her," *Journal of Negro History* 8 (Jan. 1923): 94.
p. 66 *before her birth:* See ibid., 93.
p. 67 *to 2,788:* See Barbara Jeanne Fields, *Slavery and Freedom on the Middle Ground: Maryland during the Nineteenth Century* (New Haven, Conn., 1985), 13.
p. 68 *"these young men"*: Douglass, *Bondage,* 319.
p. 69 *"happily for me"*: Ibid., 331.
p. 69 *"by a slave"*: Ibid.
p. 69 *"disloyal purposes"*: Ibid., 332.
p. 69 *"underground railroad"*: Ibid., 333.
p. 70 *his own plan:* See Douglass to Wilbur H. Siebert, March 27, 1893, quoted in Wilbur H. Siebert, *The Underground Railroad from Slavery to Freedom* (New York, 1899), 99.

p. 70   *"left slavery?":* Rosetta Douglass to Frederick and Anna Murray Douglass, quoting the questions of her tormentors, September 24, 1862.

p. 70   *"than courage":* Douglass, *Life and Times,* 197.

p. 71   *"than did mine":* Ibid., 200.

p. 71   *"an 'old salt' ":* Ibid., 199.

p. 71   *"from justice":* Ibid., 200.

p. 71   *"to sea with me":* Ibid., 199.

p. 71   *"his business":* Ibid., 200.

p. 72   *"to betray me":* Ibid., 201.

p. 72   *at peace:* Douglass, *Bondage,* 336–37. Douglass's several accounts of his arrival in New York vividly exemplify the ways his three works differ, and these pages in *Bondage* provide an excellent illustration of its superiority as autobiography.

p. 72   *"my secret":* Ibid., 338.

p. 72   *"closely watched":* Douglass, *Life and Times,* 203.

p. 72   *"the wrong one":* Douglass, *Narrative,* 106.

p. 72   *"crept over me":* Douglass, *Bondage,* 338.

p. 73   *Ruggles's house:* Douglass, *Life and Times,* 204. Once again, Douglass's memory of a name was uncertain. In *Bondage,* he called the man "Stewart."

p. 73   *black equality:* Rosetta Douglass Sprague, "Anna Murray-Douglass," 93, 95.

p. 73   *"man and wife":* James W. C. Pennington, quoted in Douglass, *Narrative,* 108.

p. 73   *"took up the other":* Douglass, *Narrative,* 108.

CHAPTER 7

p. 74   *Anna obeyed:* Douglass, *Life and Times,* 205.

p. 76   *"one by Shaw":* Ibid.

p. 76   *"c. confectionary": Annual Advertiser: The New-Bedford Directory,* ed. Henry H. Crapo (New Bedford, Mass., 1839), 93.

p. 76   *"for our color":* Sarah Mapps Douglass to William Bassett, Dec. 1837, quoted in Sarah W. Thomas, "Lionesses or Sheep for the Slaughter? A Comparative Study of the Transatlantic Experiences of Two American Abolitionists" (B.A. thesis, Amherst College, 1989), 34.

p. 77   *were men:* See *Annual Advertiser,* ed. Crapo; and "Compendium of Black Citizens of New Bedford, 1850," recently compiled by Carl Cruz (Typescript, New Bedford [Mass.] Public Library, n.d.).

p. 77   *"in New Bedford":* Douglass, *Narrative,* 110.

p. 77   *"on the Eastern Shore":* Douglass, *Life and Times,* 207.

p. 77   *"my hair crisped":* Ibid., 216; see also Peter F. Walker, *Moral Choices: Memory, Desire, and Imagination in Nineteenth-Century American Abolition* (Baton Rouge, 1978), 244 and passim.

p. 78   *most famous:* There were many African American Douglasses in Baltimore, and both Sarah Douglass and William Douglass in Philadelphia were well enough known for Douglass likely to have seen their names, spelled as he was to spell his. See C. Peter Ripley et al., eds., *The Black Abolitionist Papers,* 2 vols. (Chapel Hill, N.C., 1985–86), 1:77n, 571.

p. 78   *"cheerful earnestness":* Douglass, *Narrative,* 111.

p. 79   *forced them to work:* See Arthur S. Rosenbaum, "Songs of the Coastal South" (Paper read at Conference on Race and the Law, Sapelo Island, Ga., March 3, 1989).

p. 79   *"dignity as a man":* Douglass, *Narrative,* 111.

p. 79   *"a common laborer":* Douglass, *Life and Times,* 209.

p. 79   *"half-dollars":* Ibid.

p. 79   *went to work:* Ibid., 210.

p. 79   *"my full share":* Ibid., 212.

p. 79   *"antislavery man":* Ibid., 210.

p. 79   *clearing the harbor:* Philip F. Purrington (curator, Old Dartmouth Historical Society, Whaling Museum, New Bedford, Mass.) to the author, June 16, 1984.

p. 79   *"trade upon her":* Douglass, *Life and Times,* 211.

p. 80   *"their cabins":* Ibid.

p. 80   *"worked with me":* Ibid., 212.

p. 80   *"a good paymaster":* Ibid.

p. 80   Golconda: In *Life and Times,* Douglass spelled the name "Pennington"; there is no one with the designation "c" and the surname "Pennington" in the New Bedford records, but a "Solomon Peneton (c)," living at 19 Eighth Street, is listed in the 1850 New Bedford census, New Bedford (Mass.) Public Library. The *Java* was in port from March through May 1839, when it left on a two-year voyage; the *Golconda* was fitted between March and December 1839 and returned in June 1843. See Alexander Starbuck, *History of the American Whale Fishery* (1878; reprint, New York, 1964), 354.

p. 80   *"intelligent":* Douglass, *Life and Times,* 212.

p. 81   *a bit later:* See *Vital Records of New Bedford to 1850,* New Bedford (Mass.) Public Library.

p. 81   *October 9, 1840:* See Preston, "Genealogy of Frederick Douglass," in *Young Frederick Douglass,* 207. Rosetta's birth date has not been confirmed; the gossip that she was born on March 12, 1839, is partially refuted by the fact that her father gave a speech on that date.

p. 81   *condescendingly:* Douglass, *Bondage,* 353.

p. 81   *"high intelligence":* Douglass to James W. Hood, 1894 (no month or day), in William L. Andrews, "Frederick Douglass, Preacher," *American Literature* 54 (Dec. 1982): 596.

p. 82   *unwelcome:* See Samuel S. Hill, ed., *Encyclopedia of Religion in the South* (Macon, Ga., 1984), 6–8.

p. 82   *"days of my life":* Douglass to James W. Hood, 1894 (no month or day), in Andrews, "Frederick Douglass, Preacher," 596.

p. 82   *"an exhorter":* Thomas James, "The Autobiography of Rev. Thomas James," abridged, *Rochester History* 37 (Oct. 1975): 8.

p. 82   *"additional property":* Ibid., 3.

p. 82   *"to preach":* Ibid., 8.

p. 83   *too controversial:* See Frederick Cooper, "Elevating the Race: The Social Thought of Black Leaders, 1827–50," *American Quarterly* 24 (Dec. 1972): 604–25.

p. 83   Liberator: See *Liberator,* March 29, 1839.

p. 83   *"relate his story":* James, "Autobiography of Rev. Thomas James," 8.

p. 83   *Mechanics Hall:* See *The Diary of Samuel Rodman,* ed. Zephaniah W. Pease (New Bedford, Mass., 1927), 191. Rodman, who attended, does not establish without question that black people were at the meeting, but Garrison refused to speak before segregated audiences, and if permitted, Douglass would certainly have attended. The next day Rodman was at a meeting at which a black delegation was definitely present.

p. 83   *"pleasing countenance":* Douglass, *Life and Times,* 213.

p. 84   *"Garrison":* Douglass, *Bondage,* 354.

p. 84   *Massachusetts Anti-Slavery Society:* See William Lloyd Garrison to "My Editorial Chair," Oct. 6, 1840, William Lloyd Garrison, *The Letters of William Lloyd Garrison,* ed. Walter M. Merrill and Louis Ruchames, 6 vols. (Cambridge, Mass., 1971–81), 2:711.

p. 85   *"local preacher":* Douglass to James W. Hood, 1894 (no month or day), in Andrews, "Frederick Douglass, Preacher," 596.

p. 85   *"American slavery":* James, "Autobiography of Rev. Thomas James," 8.

CHAPTER 8

p. 86   *"holiday":* Douglass, *Bondage,* 357

p. 87   *slavery's enemies:* Robert F. Mooney to the author, Aug. 11, 1986. See also Robert F. Mooney and André R. Sigourney, *The Nantucket Way: Untold Legend and Lore of America's Most Intriguing Island* (Garden City, N.Y., 1980), 142; "Interesting Facts Regarding the 'Big Shop' and Its Old-Time Habitues," *Inquirer and Mirror* (Nantucket, Mass.), Aug. 30,

1913; and Arthur H. Gardner, "The 'Big Shop,' " *Inquirer and Mirror,* Nov. 15, 1913.

p. 87 *to the meeting:* Mary G. Wright to Douglass, April 1, 1877.

p. 87 *rafters:* See Gardner, "The 'Big Shop.' "

p. 87 *"of this age":* Lucretia Coffin Mott to Nathaniel Barney, May 21, 1841, Foulger Library, Nantucket Historical Association, Nantucket, Mass.

p. 88 *"of slavery":* William Lloyd Garrison, quoted in "Anti-Slavery on Nantucket, Frederick Douglass' Visit," *Inquirer and Mirror,* Oct. 22, 1932.

p. 88 *"connected sentence":* Douglass, *Bondage,* 358.

p. 88 *Phebe Ann Coffin:* See Phebe A. C. Hanaford, introduction to *Harvest Gleanings in Prose and Verse,* by Anna Gardner (New York, 1881).

p. 88 *"as well as wit":* Samuel J. May, *Some Recollections of Our Antislavery Conflict* (Boston, 1869), 294.

p. 89 *vehemence:* Anna Gardner, quoted in undated fragment clipped from *Proceedings* of Nantucket Historical Society, [1938].

p. 89 *"barrier":* Douglass, *Bondage,* 358.

p. 90 *Absalom Boston:* See Lorin Lee Cary and Francine C. Cary, "Absalom F. Boston, His Family, and Nantucket's Black Community," *Historic Nantucket* 25 (Summer 1977): 15–23.

CHAPTER 9

p. 91 *"once spoke":* William Lloyd Garrison, introducing Douglass at public meeting of the Massachusetts Anti-Slavery Society, Boston, Jan. 28, 1842, in Blassingame et al., eds., *Frederick Douglass Papers* 1:15.

p. 91 *"in my flesh":* Douglass, "I Have Come to Tell You Something about Slavery," Oct. 20, 1841, in ibid., 3.

p. 92 *not clear:* See Benjamin Quarles, *Frederick Douglass* (1948; reprint, New York, 1968), 24.

p. 93 *had his seat:* Footnote to Douglass, "American Prejudice and Southern Religion," Nov. 4, 1841, in Blassingame et al., eds., *Frederick Douglass Papers* 1:10.

p. 93 *"respecter of persons!":* Douglass, "American Prejudice and Southern Religion," in ibid. 11.

p. 93 *a prominent seat:* See Douglass, "The Church Is the Bulwark of Slavery," May 25, 1842, in ibid., 19.

p. 93 *"refreshing afterwards":* Henry Ingersoll Bowditch, quoted in Irving H. Bartlett, *Wendell Phillips: Brahmin Radical* (Boston, 1961), 85.

p. 94 *Anne Weston:* See Anne Weston to Deborah Weston, [184?], quoted in Bartlett, *Wendell Phillips,* 102.

p. 94 *his black colleague:* See Bartlett, *Wendell Phillips,* 91.

p. 94 *" 'care of myself' ":* Douglass, "I Have Come to Tell You Something about Slavery," Oct. 20, 1841, in Blassingame et al., eds., *Frederick Douglass Papers* 1:5.

p. 94 *"they are using":* Douglass, "The Union, Slavery, and Abolitionist Petitions," Nov. 4, 1841, in ibid., 8.

p. 95 *"quietness":* Douglass, "I Have Come to Tell You Something about Slavery," Oct. 20, 1841, in ibid., 4.

p. 95 *"to the south":* Douglass, "The Union, Slavery, and Abolitionist Petitions," Nov. 4, 1841, in ibid., 5.

p. 95 *"becomes a man":* William Lloyd Garrison, introducing Douglass at public meeting of the Massachusetts Anti-Slavery Society, Boston, Jan. 28, 1842, in ibid., 15–16.

p. 95 *a gentle humanity:* See *Letters of Garrison,* 2:xxx.

p. 95 *"ever a slave":* Parker Pillsbury and William Lloyd Garrison, quoted in James Brewer Stewart, *Holy Warriors: The Abolitionists and American Slavery* (New York, 1976), 138.

p. 96 *"and quietness":* Douglass, "I Have Come to Tell You Something about Slavery," Oct. 20, 1841, in Blassingame et al., eds., *Frederick Douglass Papers* 1:4.

p. 96 *District of Columbia:* Douglass, "The Union, Slavery, and Abolitionist Petitions," Nov. 4, 1841, in ibid., 8.

p. 97 *"extraneous agency":* Ibid.

p. 97 *"human brotherhood":* Frederick Douglass, "What I Found at the Northampton Association," in *The History of Florence, Massachusetts,* ed. Charles A. Sheffeld (Florence, Mass., 1895), 136.

p. 97 *"refinement":* Ibid.

p. 97 *"most effective":* Douglass to Abby Kelley, June 19, 1843.

p. 98 *and desirable:* See Larry E. Tise, *Proslavery: A History of the Defense of Slavery in America, 1701–1840* (Athens, Ga., 1987).

p. 98 *"practical infidels:* Erasmus Darwin Hudson, Journal, August 26, 1842, University of Massachusetts Library, Amherst, Mass.

p. 98 *"adopted" aunt:* Rosetta Douglass to "Dear Aunt," March [185?].

p. 98 *about 1825:* See Preston, "Genealogy of Frederick Douglass," in *Young Frederick Douglass,* 206.

p. 99 *"to Mass":* Hudson, Journal, Aug. 4, 1842.

p. 99 *"rum tavern":* Ibid., Aug. 13, 1842.

p. 99 *"seraglio":* Abby Kelley to Maria Weston Chapman, Aug. 15, 1843, Weston Sisters Letters.

p. 99 *"sons of Africa":* Quoted in headnote to "The Anti-Slavery Movement, the Slave's Only Earthly Hope," May 9, 1843, in Blassingame et al., eds., *Frederick Douglass Papers* 1:20.

p. 99 *"the minister":* Hudson, Journal, Aug. 15, 1842.

p. 99 *"true reformers":* Ibid., Aug. 26, 1842.

p. 100 *"dingy windows":* Theodore Stanton and Harriot Stanton Blatch, eds., *Elizabeth Cady Stanton, As Revealed in Her Letters, Diary and Reminiscences,* 2 vols. (1922; reprint, New York, 1969), 1:128.

p. 100 *after Frederick Douglass":* Ibid., 2:311.

p. 100 *"of applause":* Douglass, "The Southern Style of Preaching to Slaves," Jan. 28, 1842, in Blassingame et al., eds., *Frederick Douglass Papers* 1:17. The texts of Douglass's speeches in the *Frederick Douglass Papers* are more often than not taken from reporters' transcripts, which may include parenthetical notations of the listeners' reactions, rather than from manuscripts prepared by Douglass. Some are from reports of his speeches that Douglass printed in his own newspapers. Where several accounts were available, the editors of the *Papers* were careful to select the one that seemed the most complete and reliable. The headnotes to the speeches frequently provide valuable contextual material, including quotations from Douglass and his contemporaries.

p. 100 *"English language":* Stanton and Blatch, eds., *Stanton* 2:312.

p. 101 *"of rhetoric":* Handwritten "extract" from a letter of March 6, 1843, Weston Sisters Letters. Helen Weston, in compiling this material around 1900, attributed the letter to "Ann W. Weston," evidently her aunt Anne Weston.

p. 101 *"valuable servant":* Ibid.

p. 101 *"nothing about it":* Ibid.

p. 102 *his identity:* See Ibid.

p. 102 *"to the door":* Rodman, Aug. 9, 1842, *Diary,* 237–38.

p. 102 *"present to me":* William Lloyd Garrison to Helen Benson Garrison, Nov. 27, 1842, *Letters of Garrison* 3:113. See also Leonard L. Richards, *"Gentlemen of Property and Standing": Anti-Abolition Mobs in Jacksonian America* (New York, 1970).

p. 102 *fugitive slaves:* See *Letters of Garrison* 3:48n.

p. 103 *"women's side":* Douglass to William Lloyd Garrison, Nov. 8, 1842.

p. 103 *later Ruth Adams:* See Ruth Adams to Douglass, March 9 and March 20, 1894.

p. 103 *thirty dollars:* See Douglass to Maria Weston Chapman, Sept. 10, 1843.

p. 103 *"in Hubbardston":* Hudson, Journal, April 15, 1845.

CHAPTER 10

p. 104 *"warmest protector":* Douglass to Maria Weston Chapman, Sept. 10, 1843.

p. 105 *western tour:* John A. Collins to Maria Weston Chapman, Aug. 23, 1843, Weston Sisters Letters.

p. 105 *"form and figure":* Alexander Crummell, quoted in Sterling Stuckey, "A Last Stern Struggle: Henry Highland Garnet and Liberation Theory," in Leon Litwack and August Meier, eds. *Black Leaders of the Nineteenth Century* (Urbana, Ill., 1988), 129.

p. 106 *in the dark:* Stuckey, "A Last Stern Struggle," in ibid., 132.

p. 106 *"resistance" to slavery:* Henry Highland Garnet, quoted in Earl Ofari, "Henry Highland Garnet," in Rayford W. Logan and Michael R. Winston, eds., *Dictionary of American Negro Biography* (New York, 1982), 252.

p. 107 *"of duchesses":* Quoted in Jane H. Pease and William H. Pease, *Bound with Them in Chains: A Biographical History of the Antislavery Movement* (Westport, Conn., 1972), 28, 31.

p. 107 *knew better:* One man who did not share this blindness was Lewis Tappan, who, disapproving of the Chapman, Garrison, Phillips, and Quincy brand of antislavery, wrote that "with the disposition of a fiend," Chapman "manag[e]s . . . [them] as easily as she could 'untie a garter' " (quoted in ibid., 29).

p. 107 *its purpose:* Douglass to Maria Weston Chapman, Sept. 10, 1843.

p. 107 *in the future:* John A. Collins to Maria Weston Chapman, Aug. 23, 1843, Weston Sisters Letters.

p. 108 *"disqualify him":* Abby Kelley to Maria Weston Chapman, Aug. 28, 1843, ibid.

p. 108 *general agent:* See Eunice M. Collins to Maria Weston Chapman, Aug. 15, 1843; ibid; and John A. Collins to Maria Weston Chapman, Aug. 23, 1843, ibid.

p. 108 *"in the council":* A. Brook to Maria Weston Chapman, Oct. 5, 1843, ibid.

p. 108 *"good work":* William Lloyd Garrison to Maria Weston Chapman, Sept. 9, 1843, ibid.

p. 108 *"a painful affair":* Ibid.

p. 108 *"insolent letter":* George Bradburn to Maria Weston Chapman, Aug. 31, 1843, Weston Sisters Letters.

p. 108 *"of promise":* William Lloyd Garrison to Francis Jackson, Aug. 2, 1843, *Letters of Garrison* 3:186.

p. 108 *a local physician:* See Quarles, *Frederick Douglass,* 32; William A. White, letter, *Liberator,* Sept. 22, 1843; and *Liberator,* Oct. 13, 1843.

p. 109 *pulled down:* William A. White, letter, *Liberator,* Sept. 22, 1843.

p. 109 *walked out:* Ibid.

p. 110 *out of the way:* Ibid.

p. 110 *bled profusely:* Ibid.

p. 110 *"by Frederick Douglass":* Douglass to William A. White, July 30, 1846. In the quotations from this letter, the spelling stands as written. This practice is followed throughout; in general, *sic* has been omitted.

p. 112 *"of Friends":* Douglass, *Life and Times,* 231.

p. 112 *Noblesville, Indiana:* See "Partial Speaking Itinerary," in Blassingame et al., eds., *Frederick Douglass Papers* 1:CII.

p. 112 *"of the country":* William A. White, letter, *Liberator,* Sept. 22, 1843.

p. 112 *"those passions":* Ibid.

p. 112 *"by others":* A. Brook to Maria Weston Chapman, Oct. 5, 1843, Weston Sisters Letters.

p. 113 *"is needed":* Ibid.

p. 113 *as the white:* Douglass to Wendell Phillips, Feb. 10, 1844.

p. 113 *"or $30":* Douglass to Maria Weston Chapman, Sept. 10, 1843.

p. 114 *"Garrison himself":* Douglass to J. Miller McKim, Sept. 5, 1844.

p. 114 *"members from us":* Lucretia Coffin Mott to Nathaniel Barney, Sept. 17, 1844, Foulger Library, Nantucket Historical Association.

p. 114 *"and Clay":* Douglass to J. Miller McKim, Sept. 5, 1844.

p. 114 *"slave's emancipation":* Ibid.

p. 115 *lookout for it:* See Robert D. Richardson, Jr., *Henry Thoreau: A Life of the Mind* (Berkeley, Calif. 1986), 316.

p. 115 *American letters:* See William L. Andrews, introduction to *My Bondage and My Freedom* (Urbana, Ill., 1987), xi–xxviii.

p. 115 *"self-emancipation":* Richardson, *Henry Thoreau*, 316.

p. 116 *"of freedom":* Narrative, 1, 114.

p. 116 *"to themselves":* Narrative, 13, 14.

p. 117 *of readers:* See Quarles, *Frederick Douglass,* 55; and Houston A. Baker, Jr., introduction to the Penguin edition of *Narrative of the Life of Frederick Douglass* (New York, 1982), 20–21.

p. 117 *"some one else":* William Lloyd Garrison, preface to Douglass, *Narrative,* xiv.

p. 117 *"old Massachusetts":* Wendell Phillips, introductory letter in ibid., xxiv.

CHAPTER 11

p. 120 *"every one of us":* Jane Jennings to Maria Weston Chapman, Nov. 26, [1845], Weston Sisters Letters.

p. 120 *"an incident":* Quarles, *Frederick Douglass,* 38.

p. 121 *marketing of the* Narrative: See Douglass to Richard D. Webb, Dec. 7 and Dec. 22, 1845.

p. 121 *"was the case":* Richard D. Webb to Maria Weston Chapman, May 16, 1846, Weston Sisters Letters.

p. 121 *of a white man:* Ibid.

p. 121 *rankled:* Ibid.

p. 122 *a man's friend:* Ibid.

p. 122 *"unprovoked":* Ibid.

p. 122 *"and dissatisfaction":* Ibid.

p. 122 *to his face:* Ibid.

p. 123 *contributions to the cause:* Isabel Jennings to Maria Weston Chapman, [Oct. or Nov. 1845?], Weston Sisters Letters.

p. 123 *"go together":* Douglass, "Intemperance and Slavery," Oct. 20, 1845, in Blassingame et al., eds., *Frederick Douglass Papers* 1:58.

p. 124 *opponents of drink:* See C. Duncan Rice, *The Scots Abolitionists, 1833–1861* (Baton Rouge, 1981), 93.

p. 124 *and repent:* Douglass, "Intemperance and Slavery," Oct. 20, 1845, in Blassingame et al., eds., *Frederick Douglass Papers* 1:58.

p. 124 *"and forehead":* Douglass, "Slavery Corrupts American Society and Religion," Oct. 17, 1845, in ibid., 52.

p. 125 *"never forgot":* David N. Johnson, *Sketches of Lynn* (Lynn, Mass., 1880).

p. 125 *"twenty-third next":* Douglass, "American Prejudice against Color," Oct. 23, 1845, in Blassingame et al., eds., *Frederick Douglass Papers* 1:70.

p. 125 *"in New Bedford":* Douglass to Francis Jackson, Jan 29, 1846.

p. 126 *"respectable inhabitants":* Jane Jennings to Maria Weston Chapman, Nov. 26, 1845, Weston Sisters Letters.

p. 126 *"the world over":* Douglass to William Lloyd Garrison, Feb. 26, 1846.

p. 126 *"of the poor":* Ibid.

p. 127 *was still up:* Douglass to "Dear Friend [Richard D. Webb]," Dec. 5, 1845.

p. 127 *"Books immediately":* Ibid.

p. 127 *"are all well":* Douglass to Richard D. Webb, Dec. 22, 1845.

p. 127 *"American Churches":* Douglass, "Baptists, Congregationalists, the Free Church, and Slavery," Dec. 23, 1845, in Blassingame et al. eds., *Frederick Douglass Papers* 1:104.

p. 128 *"man-stealers":* Ibid., 109.

p. 128 *monster:* Douglass, "An Account of American Slavery," Jan. 15, 1846, in ibid., 138.

p. 128 *"sober-drunkards":* Douglass, "Baptists, Congregationalists, the Free Church, and Slavery," Dec. 23, 1845, in ibid., 109.

p. 128 *"ever lived":* Ibid., 111.
p. 128 *"Christian Union":* Ibid., 112.
p. 129 *of Scotland:* See Rice, *Scots Abolitionists,* 124; and Stewart J. Brown, *Thomas Chalmers and the Godly Commonwealth in Scotland* (New York, 1982).
p. 129 *"whole region":* Thomas Chalmers to Thomas Smyth, Sept. 24, 1844, in *The Character of the Late Thomas Chalmers, D.D., LL.D., and the Lesson of His Life,* pamphlet (Charleston, S.C., 1848).
p. 130 *for emancipation: Letter of the Rev. Dr. Chalmers on American Slave-Holding with Remarks by the Belfast Anti-Slavery Committee,* pamphlet (Belfast, 1846), 11, 15, 16.
p. 130 *"stagger under":* Douglass, "Baptists, Congregationalists, the Free Church, and Slavery," Dec. 23, 1845, in Blassingame et al., eds., *Frederick Douglass Papers* 1:118.

CHAPTER 12

p. 131 *"at any rate":* Douglass to Francis Jackson, Jan. 29, 1846.
p. 131 *"ally" in Great Britain:* Ripley et al., eds., *Black Abolitionist Papers* 1:57n.
p. 131 *"enormous iniquity":* Mary Welsh to Maria Weston Chapman, May 16, 1846, Weston Sisters Letters.
p. 132 *"negro":* Douglass to Francis Jackson, Jan. 29, 1846.
p. 132 *"tremendous gathering":* Douglass to Richard D. Webb, April 25, 1846.
p. 132 *"as such":* Douglass to Amy Post, April 28, 1846.
p. 132 *"in his veins":* Catherine Clarkson to Maria Weston Chapman, Aug. 2, 1846, Weston Sisters Letters.
p. 132 *"Naigar do":* Quoted in Lawrence Levine, *Black Culture and Black Consciousness: Afro-American Folk Thought from Slavery to Freedom* (New York, 1977), 325.
p. 132 *"black like me":* Lizzie Lavender, quoted in Levine, *Black Culture,* 492n.
p. 132 *"intellecktually":* *Anti-Slavery Songs* (Edinburgh, 1846): eight-page pamphlet, British Museum, cited in George Shepperson, "Frederick Douglass and Scotland," *Journal of Negro History* 38 (July 1953): 314.
p. 133 *"shake hands":* Ibid., 315–17.
p. 133 *"to injure":* Richard D. Webb to Maria Weston Chapman, June 26, 1846, Weston Sisters Letters.
p. 134 *Presbyterians to him:* See Brown, *Thomas Chalmers.*
p. 134 *antislavery sentiments:* See Donald G. Mathews, *Slavery and Methodism: A Chapter in American Morality, 1780–1845* (Princeton, N.J., 1965), 206–8, 279.
p. 136 *"can supply":* Richard D. Webb to Maria Weston Chapman, Oct. 31, 1846, Weston Sisters Letters.
p. 136 *year abroad:* See Catherine Clarkson to Maria Weston Chapman, Aug. 2, 1846, ibid.
p. 137 *"speaking out":* Douglass to "My own Dear Sister Harriet," [July 1846].
p. 137 *"in America":* Douglass to William A. White, July 30, 1846.
p. 137 *in 1841:* See Ripley et al., eds., *Black Abolitionist Papers* 1:92, 225, 404n.
p. 137 *to find:* Douglass to William A. White, July 30, 1846.
p. 137 *his freedom:* Ida B. Wells, *Crusade for Justice: The Autobiography of Ida B. Wells,* ed. Alfreda M. Duster (Chicago, 1970), 162.
p. 138 *to get back:* Douglass to "sister" Harriet, Aug. 18, 1846.
p. 138 *"into Chartism":* R. H. Tawney, preface to William Lovett, *Life and Struggles of William Lovett* (1876; reprint, London, 1967), vii.
p. 139 *development of Chartism:* See Dorothy Thompson, *The Chartists: Popular Politics in the Industrial Revolution* (New York, 1984), 30.
p. 139 *to be combated:* See Howard Temperley, *British Antislavery, 1833–1870* (Columbia, S.C., 1982), 161–63, 182.
p. 139 *were appalled:* See William Lloyd Garrison to Edmund Quincy, Aug. 18, 1846, *Letters of Garrison,* 3:378–79.

p. 139 *"rapturously received"*: Ibid., 379.

p. 139 *"more delighted"*: William Lloyd Garrison to Helen Benson Garrison, Aug. 18, 1846, ibid., 377.

p. 139 *"smitten him"*: William Lloyd Garrison to Edmund Quincy, Aug. 18, 1846, ibid., 379.

p. 139 *Working Men's Association:* See Thompson, *Chartists,* 61.

p. 140 *" 'The Marseillaise' "*: Lovett, *Life and Struggles,* 267, 268.

p. 140 *John Bowring:* See William Lloyd Garrison to Edmund Quincy, Aug. 14, 1846, *Letters of Garrison* 3:369–73.

p. 140 *"earth presents"*: William Lloyd Garrison to Helen Benson Garrison, Sept. 3, 1846, ibid., 394.

p. 140 *"I ever saw"*: Mary Howitt, quoted in Temperley, *British Antislavery,* 215.

p. 140 *"earnest glances"*: William Lloyd Garrison to Helen Benson Garrison, Aug. 11, 1846, *Letters of Garrison,* 3:365.

p. 140 *into the bargain:* See Thompson, *Chartists,* 189.

p. 141 *with the Chartists:* Douglass, "Slavery As It Now Exists in the United States," Aug. 25, 1846, in Blassingame et al., eds., *Frederick Douglass Papers* 1:343–44.

p. 141 *"at once?"*: Elizabeth Pease to Ann and Wendell Phillips, March 29, 1842, quoted in Thompson, *Chartists,* 151.

p. 141 *"this region"*: William Lloyd Garrison to Henry C. Wright, Aug. 26, 1846, *Letters of Garrison* 3:387.

p. 141 *"graphic description"*: Mary Carpenter to William Lloyd Garrison, Sept. 3, 1846, quoted in Quarles, *Frederick Douglass,* 48–49.

p. 142 *Life of Frederick Douglass:* William Lloyd Garrison to Henry C. Wright, Aug. 26, 1846, *Letters of Garrison* 3:387.

p. 142 *"shaking of hands"*: Mary Estlin to Maria Weston Chapman, Sept. 1, 1846, Weston Sisters Letters.

p. 142 *"lot of us all"*: Douglass to Isabel Jennings, Sept. 22, 1846.

p. 143 *"of death!"*: William Lloyd Garrison to Thomas Clarkson, Aug. 26, 1846, *Letters of Garrison* 3:385.

p. 143 *"sacred cause"*: Thomas Clarkson, quoted in ibid., 386.

p. 143 *"abolition of Slavery"*: William Lloyd Garrison to Thomas Clarkson, Aug. 26, 1846, ibid.

p. 143 *"his usefulness"*: Richard D. Webb to Maria Weston Chapman, Sept. 1, 1846, Weston Sisters Letters.

p. 143 *his protégé's success:* See Temperley, *British Antislavery,* 219.

p. 143 *a lawyer:* See Wells, *Crusade for Justice,* 162.

p. 144 *roughly $1,250:* "Commercial and Money Matters" (rates of exchange), *New York Tribune,* June 6, 1846.

p. 144 *"called Frederick Douglass"*: Bill of sale, Nov. 30, 1846, and deed of manumission, Dec. 12, 1846, both in Frederick Douglass Collection, Library of Congress, Reel 1. See also *Frederick Douglass Papers* 1:482n.

p. 145 *"his own man"*: Nathan Irvin Huggins, *Slave and Citizen: The Life of Frederick Douglass* (Boston, 1980), 38.

p. 145 *"on that account"*: Douglass to Ellen Richardson, April 29, 1847.

p. 145 *"to my house"*: Ibid.

CHAPTER 13

p. 147 *"not be silent"*: Douglass, quoted in headnote to "Country, Conscience, and the Anti-Slavery Cause," May 11, 1847, in Blassingame et al., eds., *Frederick Douglass Papers* 2:57.

p. 147 *"we could afford"*: Edmund Quincy to Caroline Weston, July 2, 1847, Weston Sisters Letters.

p. 148 *"cast of character"*: Edmund Quincy to [Caroline Weston?], July 30, 1847, ibid.

p. 148 *"our common family"*: Samuel J. May to Douglass, Sept. 27, 1847.

p. 148 *"Douglass, Douglass"*: Headnote to "Country, Conscience, and the Anti-Slavery Cause," May 11, 1847, in Blassingame et al., eds., *Frederick Douglass Papers* 2:58.

p. 148 *enormous celebrity*: Amy Post, quoted in Isaac Post to Amy Post, May 19, 1847, Post Family Papers, University of Rochester library.

p. 148 *"as a dear brother"*: Eliza Whigham to Maria Weston Chapman, April 2, 1847, Weston Sisters Letters.

p. 148 *"interesting young woman"*: William Lloyd Garrison to Helen Benson Garrison, Aug. 16, 1847, *Letters of Garrison* 3:208–9. In 1853 Clarke married Leander K. Lippincott.

p. 149 *"any particular whatever"*: William Lloyd Garrison to Helen Benson Garrison, Oct. 20, 1847, ibid., 532.

p. 149 *"decision in Boston"*: Ibid.

p. 149 *"my future home"*: Douglass to Amy Post, Oct. 28, 1847.

p. 150 *would be published*: See Quarles, *Frederick Douglass*, 80.

p. 150 *corresponding editor*: See Douglass to Sydney Howard Gay, Aug. 13, 1842.

p. 150 *"if you please"*: *Frederick Douglass' Paper*, June 26, 1851, quoted in Mary L. McMillan, "Mr. Editor, If You Please: Frederick Douglass in Rochester, 1847–1852" (Honors thesis, Mount Holyoke College, 1985), 1.

p. 150 *on Emerson*: See Henry James, *Partial Portraits* (London, 1888), 1–33.

p. 150 *"Gerrit Smith"*: Gerrit Smith to Douglass, Dec. 8, 1847.

p. 151 *of land each*: Octavius Brooks Frothingham, *Gerrit Smith: A Biography* (1878; reprint, New York, 1969), 103.

p. 151 *"and usefulness"*: Ibid.

p. 151 *crucial moments*: Ledger No. 1 for *North Star*, in Frederick Douglass Collection, Library of Congress, Reels 29–30.

p. 151 *"November 3rd, 1847"*: Ibid.

p. 151 *"blood as well"*: Nell Irvin Painter, "Martin R. Delany: Elitism and Black Nationalism," in Litwack and Meier, eds., *Black Leaders of the Nineteenth Century*, 150.

p. 152 *varied career*: See Ripley et al., eds., *Black Abolitionist Papers* 1:448n; and Dorothy Sterling, *The Making of an Afro-American* (Garden City, N.Y., 1971).

p. 153 *subscribed*: Subscription lists, *North Star*, in Frederick Douglass Collection, Library of Congress, Reels 29–30.

p. 154 *"looks better"*: Douglass to Abigail and Lydia Mott, Feb. 21, 1848.

p. 154 *"hard to spell"*: Jane Marsh Parker, "Reminiscences of Frederick Douglass," *The Outlook* 51 (April 6, 1895): 552. See also mortgage dated April 28, 1848, in Frederick Douglass Collection, Library of Congress, Reels 29–30.

p. 154 *were fruitless*: See Mrs. George D. Van Zandt to Anna M. Douglass, [March 1848], Rochester Ladies' Anti-Slavery Society Papers, University of Rochester library.

p. 155 *162 households*: See McMillan, "Mr. Editor," 14.

p. 155 *"behave himself"*: Stanton and Blatch, ets., *Stanton* 1:143.

p. 155 *"was represented"*: Ibid., 77.

p. 156 *"ridiculous"*: Lucretia Mott, quoted in ibid., 146.

p. 156 *"a small majority"*: Stanton and Blatch, eds., *Stanton* 1:147.

p. 156 *the North Star*: Flier with handwritten notes overleaf, Post Family Papers.

p. 156 *"claim for man"*: Douglass, "The Rights of Women," *North Star*, July 28, 1848, in Philip S. Foner, *The Life and Writings of Frederick Douglass*, 4 vols. (New York, 1950), 1:321.

p. 156 *with politicians*: David W. Blight, *Frederick Douglass' Civil War: Keeping Faith in Jubilee* (Baton Rouge, 1989), 30.

p. 158 *"so good"*: Douglass, "What Good Has the Free Soil Movement Done," *North Star*, March 25, 1849, in Foner, *Writings of Douglass* 1:368.

p. 158 *to end slavery*: See Blight, *Frederick Douglass' Civil War*, 50.

p. 158 *"is inevitable"*: Douglass in *North Star*, March 25, 1849, in Foner, *Writings of Douglass* 1:367.

p. 158 *American slavery*: A footnote in the original edition of *My Bondage and My Freedom* asserts that the letter "was written while in England" (Douglass, *Bondage*, 421).

p. 158 *"public manner"*: Douglass, *Bondage,* 421.
p. 158 *"regularly to school"*: Ibid., 426.
p. 159 *"in the market"*: Ibid.
p. 159 *"in the woods"*: Ibid., 427.
p. 159 *"blast her"*: Ibid., 427–28.
p. 160 *"a brute"*: Douglass, *Bondage,* 422.
p. 160 *"notoriety I could"*: Ibid., 425.
p. 160 *"system of slavery"*: Ibid., 428.
p. 160 *"not your slave"*: Ibid.
p. 160 *Seward Seminary:* See *Daily American Directory of the City of Rochester for 1849–50.*
p. 160 *" 'I am colored' "*: Douglass to H. G. Warner, March 30, 1849 (open letter, *North Star*), in Foner, *Writings of Douglass* 1:371.
p. 160 *the principal:* Ibid.
p. 161 *"unwomanly conduct"*: Ibid., 372.
p. 161 *carried home:* Ibid.
p. 161 *"and prejudice"*: Douglass to H. G. Warner, March 30, 1849 (open letter, *North Star*), in Foner, *Writings of Douglass* 1:373–74.
p. 162 *"nobody else can"*: Isaac Post to Amy Post, May 15, 1849, Post Family Papers.
p. 162 *"her explanations"*: Ibid.

CHAPTER 14

p. 163 *"people* Crazy*"*: Margaret Fox to Amy Post (no month or day), 185 [1], Post Family Papers.
p. 164 *and left:* Isaac Post to Amy Post, May 15, 1849, ibid.
p. 164 *prettiness:* Ibid.
p. 164 *"very talented"*: Ibid.
p. 164 *"as he did her"*: Isaac Post to Amy Post, May 19, 1849, Post Family Papers.
p. 164 *"glorious example"*: Amy Post to Douglass (draft) Sept. 11, 1849, ibid.
p. 164 *from Massachusetts:* Harriet Jacobs to Amy Post, [1850], ibid.
p. 165 *with money:* Douglass to Richard D. Webb, Sept. 12, 1850.
p. 165 *"more now"*: Gerrit Smith to Douglass, June 1, 1850.
p. 166 *"Lucky Fellow"*: William C. Nell to Amy Post, July 15, 1850, Post Family Papers.
p. 166 *James Russell Lowell:* Douglass to Richard D. Webb, Sept. 12, 1850.
p. 166 *the matter:* Lowell then resigned from the club, declaring he was "an unfit companion for people too good to associate with Douglass." The incident is described in Martin Duberman, *James Russell Lowell* (Boston, 1966), 185.
p. 166 *"circumstances"*: Fredrika Bremer to Marcus and Rebecca Buffum Spring, Sept. 22, 1850, Houghton Library, Harvard University.
p. 166 *"cotton fields"*: Harriet Beecher Stowe to Douglass, July 2, 1851.
p. 167 *"spirits blush?"*: B. M. Combs to Amy Post, Dec. 1, 1850, Post Family Papers.
p. 167 *"Campaignism"*: Parker, "Reminiscences of Frederick Douglass," 553.
p. 167 *a correspondence:* Douglass to William Henry Seward, [July] 31, 1850.
p. 167 *"party of freedom"*: Douglass to William Henry Seward, April 23, 1853.
p. 167 *"at this day"*: Douglass to Salmon P. Chase, May 30, 1850.
p. 168 *"of abolitionists"*: Douglass to Gerrit Smith, March 30, 1849, Gerrit Smith Papers, Syracuse University.
p. 169 *"(Laughter.)"*: Douglass, "The American Slave's Plea to Mankind," May 7, 1851, in Blassingame et al., eds., *Frederick Douglass Papers* 2:336.
p. 169 *abolitionist aims:* Samuel J. May, quoted in headnote to Douglass, "The American Slave's Plea to Mankind," in ibid., 331.
p. 169 *"of emancipation"*: Douglass, "Change of Opinion Announced," *North Star,* May 23, 1851, in Foner, *Writings of Douglass* 2:155–56.

p. 169 Frederick Douglass' Paper: As no complete run of Douglass's Rochester newspapers is known to exist, the precise dates of each are difficult to establish. Vol. 1, no. 1, of the *North Star* was published on Friday, Dec. 3, 1847. The paper's name was changed to *Frederick Douglass' Paper* in late May or June of 1851; it is believed to have continued publication until Feb. 17, 1860. *Douglass' Monthly,* which began as a supplement to *Frederick Douglass' Paper,* became a separate journal with vol. 1, no. 8, the issue of Jan. 1859, and continued to be published until Aug. 1863; there were no issues for January–March 1860, when Douglass was in England. See the reprint set, *Douglass' Monthly Magazines, Vols. 1–5,* 2 vols. (Westport, Conn., 1969).

p. 169 *"freedom in 1856":* Douglass to Gerrit Smith, Nov. 10, 1852.

p. 169 *antislavery family:* See Douglass, letter, *Syracuse Standard,* Nov. 3, 1851.

p. 170 *"ordinary looking":* Samuel J. May, Jr., to Anne Weston, June 4, 1849, Weston Sisters Letters.

p. 170 *"is capable of":* Isabel Jennings to Mary Estlin, May 24, [1851], ibid.

p. 171 *"a citizen":* Douglass to Samuel Porter, Jan. 12, 1852, Porter Family Papers, University of Rochester library.

p. 171 *"as to think so":* Ibid.

p. 171 *"and friendship":* Ibid.

p. 171 *teach her to read:* See Parker, "Reminiscences of Frederick Douglass," 552.

p. 171 *"close at once":* Douglass to Samuel Porter, Jan. 12, 1852, Porter Family Papers.

p. 172 *in 1865:* See Deeds and mortgages, 1821 forward, Monroe County Clerk's Office, Rochester, N.Y.

p. 172 *"to his door":* Parker, "Reminiscences of Frederick Douglass," 553.

p. 172 *"was twelve":* Amy Post, quoted in Howard Coles, *The Cradle of Freedom* (Rochester, N.Y., 1941), 161.

p. 172 *through Rochester:* See Kathleen Barry, *Susan B. Anthony—A Biography* (New York, 1988), 63.

p. 172 *would be "D.F.":* "D.F." to [Samuel Porter, Sept. 1851], Porter Family Papers.

p. 172 *Fifth of July Speech:* See Douglass, "What to the Slave Is the Fourth of July?" (Fifth of July Speech), July 5, 1852, in Blassingame et al., eds., *Frederick Douglass Papers* 2:359–88.

p. 172 *"to speak today?":* Ibid., 368.

p. 172 *"for Republicans?":* Ibid., 370.

p. 173 LIBERTY DOCUMENT*":* Ibid., 385.

p. 173 *"undeveloped destiny":* Ibid., 363.

p. 173 *"at midnight":* Ibid., 364.

p. 173 *"with nations":* Ibid., 361.

p. 174 *of "Liberty":* Douglass, "The Heroic Slave," in Julia Griffiths, ed., *Autographs for Freedom* (Boston, 1853), 176, 178.

p. 174 *"polished iron":* Ibid., 179.

p. 174 *wife behind:* Ibid., 181.

p. 174 *"and slave-traders":* Ibid., 205.

p. 174 *"admired":* Ibid., 221, 223.

p. 174 *"night's work":* Ibid., 234.

p. 174 *to Virginia:* Ibid., 238.

p. 174 *"MADISON WASHINGTON":* Ibid., 239.

p. 175 *"Mr. Garrison":* William C. Nell to Amy Post, Feb. 8, 1853, Post Family Papers.

p. 175 *"as formerly":* Ibid.

p. 175 *in Worcester:* See *Letters of Garrison* 4:228n.

p. 175 *"two Horses":* William C. Nell to Amy Post, April 24, 1853, Post Family Papers.

p. 176 *"recognize them":* Douglass to Gerrit Smith, June 1, 1853.

p. 176 *stayed away:* Mary Post Hallowell to Amy Post, May 13, 1853, Post Family Papers.

p. 176 *"the matter up":* William C. Nell to Amy Post, Aug. 12, 1853, ibid.

p. 177 *talking to":* Douglass to Gerrit Smith, Aug. 18, 1853.

p. 177 *"patent from them":* Ibid.

p. 178 *"friend of both":* Douglass to Gerrit Smith, Dec. 23, 1853.

p. 178 *"Battle axe state":* William C. Nell to Amy Post, Dec. 10, 1853, Post Family Papers.

p. 178 *an "apostate":* Garrison quoted in Harriet Beecher Stowe to William Lloyd Garrison, Dec. 19, 1853, in Annie Fields, *Life and Letters of Harriet Beecher Stowe* (Boston, 1897), 214.

p. 178 *"temporary purpose":* Ibid.

p. 178 *"will show":* Ibid., 215.

p. 179 *by the drama:* Griffiths quoted in Douglass to Gerrit Smith, March 13, 1854.

p. 179 *"of this nation":* Douglass to Gerrit Smith, May 6, 1854.

p. 179 *"will pass":* Douglass to Charles Sumner, Feb. 27, 1854.

p. 179 *"His own glory":* Douglass, "Slavery, Freedom, and the Kansas-Nebraska Act," Oct. 30, 1854, in Blassingame et al., eds., *Frederick Douglass Papers* 2:559.

p. 180 *"tender" flesh:* Douglass, *Bondage,* 88.

p. 181 *"but an infant":* Ibid., 52.

p. 182 *"Canada lately":* Julia Griffiths to Amy Post, Oct. 16, 1853, Post Family Papers.

p. 182 *"worker of iniquity":* William Lloyd Garrison to Samuel J. May, May 21, 1856, *Letters of Garrison* 4:137.

CHAPTER 15

p. 183 *man she met:* Ottilia Assing, preface to *Sklaverei und Freiheit* (Hamburg, 1860), her translation of *My Bondage and My Freedom,* quoted in Terry H. Pickett, "The Friendship of Frederick Douglass with the German, Ottilie Assing," *Georgia Historical Quarterly,* 73 (Spring 1989): 92. Assing signed her name "Ottilia" when writing in English, "Ottilie" when writing in German.

p. 183 *"highly cultivated":* Ibid.

p. 183 *to Lutheranism:* He changed his name from David Assur when he converted. The full names of his daughters were Ottilie Davide Assing and Rosa Ludmilla Assing. (See Lieselotte Blumenthal, "Assing, verehelichte Grimelli, Rosa Ludmilla," in *Neue Deutsche Biographie,* 15 vols. to date [Berlin, 1953–87], 1:419.)

p. 184 *"ennobled":* See Hannah Arendt, *Rahel Varnhagen: The Life of a Jewish Woman,* trans. Richard W. Winston and Clara Winston (New York, 1974), 186.

p. 184 *"Goethe cult":* Ibid., xv.

p. 184 *German American population:* See Kathleen Neils Conzen, "Germans," in Stephen Thernstrom et al., eds., *Harvard Encyclopedia of American Ethnic Groups* (Cambridge, Mass., 1980), 413.

p. 184 *reports from America:* Pickett reports 125 contributions by Assing to *Morgenblatt fuer gebildete Staende* between 1851 and 1865. (See Pickett, "Friendship," 101.)

p. 184 *"a matter of course":* Terry H. Pickett, Draft of article on Ottilia Assing (Typescript, in author's possession), 7.

p. 185 *"in Germany":* Ibid.

p. 185 *Ottilia's "spirit":* Helene von Racowitza, *Princess Helene von Racowitza: An Autobiography* (New York, 1911), 371.

p. 185 *"be grateful":* Douglass, quoted in Pickett, "Friendship," 90, 91.

p. 185 *"bonds of wedlock":* Helene von Racowitza, *Von Anderen und mir: Erinnerungen aller Art* (Berlin, 1909), 274.

p. 185 *"have loved":* Ottilia Assing to Ludmilla Assing, March 26, 1874, quoted in Pickett, "Friendship," 99.

p. 186 *from Boston:* Benjamin Quarles establishes the date as 1848, from a reference to the meeting in the *North Star;* Douglass's recollection in 1881 was that the meeting was in 1847. (See Quarles, *Frederick Douglass,* 170.)

p. 186 *"and fire":* Douglass, *Life and Times,* 272.

p. 186 *"times of trouble":* Ibid.

p. 186 *"right to live":* Ibid., 273.

p. 187   *"opposition to it":* Oswald Garrison Villard, *John Brown, 1800–1859: A Biography Fifty Years After* (1910; reprint, Gloucester, Mass., 1965), 334.

p. 187   *"of the negro":* Douglass to Susan B. Anthony, June 5, 1861.

p. 188   *for "freedom":* Douglass in interview in *Weekly Telegraph* (Kenosha, Wis.), Oct. 26, 1854, quoted in footnote to Douglass, "Slavery, Freedom, and the Kansas-Nebraska Act," Oct. 30, 1854, in Blassingame et al., eds., *Frederick Douglass Papers* 2:541.

p. 188   *"my own effigy":* Stephen Douglas, quoted in Robert W. Johannsen, *Stephen A. Douglas* (New York, 1973), 451.

p. 188   *"right to do so":* Edwin Erie Sparks, ed., *The Lincoln–Douglas Debates of 1858,* Collections of the Illinois State Historical Library, vol. 3, Lincoln Series, vol. 1 (Springfield, Ill., 1908), 166.

p. 189   *of Akron, Ohio:* Villard, *Brown,* 153.

p. 189   *"for murder":* Douglass, "Capital Punishment Is a Mockery of Justice," Oct. 7, 1858, in Blassingame et al., eds., *Frederick Douglass Papers* 3:244.

p. 189   *"action!!":* Douglass, article in *Frederick Douglass' Paper,* Sept. 12, 1856, in Foner, *Writings of Douglass* 2:404–5.

p. 189   *"could stand on":* Lewis Tappan to Douglass, Nov. 27, 1856.

p. 190   *"such sentiments":* Lewis Tappan to Douglass, Dec. 6, 1856.

p. 190   *true allies:* See David M. Potter, *The South and the Sectional Conflict* (Baton Rouge, 1968), 208.

p. 191   *"and the magnet":* Franklin Preston Stearns, quoted in Stephen A. Oates, *To Purge This Land with Blood: A Biography of John Brown* (Amherst, Mass., 1984), 189.

p. 192   *a quick visit:* See Oates, *To Purge This Land,* 224.

p. 192   *his roof:* See Parker, "Reminiscences of Frederick Douglass," 552.

p. 192   *"and devastation":* Douglass, speaking in June 1849, quoted in Foner, *Writings of Douglass* 2:50.

p. 192   *Harpers Ferry:* See Oates, *To Purge This Land,* 243; and Robin W. Winks, *The Blacks in Canada: A History* (New Haven, Conn., 1971), 243–47.

p. 193   *about the man:* Quarles, *Frederick Douglass,* 174.

p. 193   *"my prejudice":* Douglass, *Life and Times,* 317.

p. 193   *constant begging:* See Ottilia Assing, "The Insurrection at Harpers Ferry," *Morgenblatt fuer gebildete Staende,* trans. Barbara Schwepcke.

p. 194   *100,000 white people:* See Oates, *To Purge This Land,* 274.

p. 194   *an insurrection:* See James Redpath, quoted in ibid., 284.

p. 194   *a certain remoteness:* See Potter, *Impending Crisis,* 357.

p. 196   *"offered for me":* Douglass, *Life and Times,* 318.

p. 196   *"an hour":* Ibid., 319.

p. 197   *"help hive them":* Ibid., 320.

p. 197   *"to the mountains":* Ibid.

p. 197   *"his old plan":* Ibid., 319.

p. 197   *black men parted:* Ibid., 317.

p. 197   *"de ole man":* Shields Green, quoted in ibid., 321.

p. 197   *a slave insurrection:* Philadelphia *Evening Bulletin,* Oct. 17, 1859.

p. 197   *"below Thirteenth":* Ibid., Oct. 18, 1859.

p. 197   *"written note":* Douglass, *Life and Times,* 392.

p. 198   *"mouthful with me":* Douglass to John Brown, Dec. 7, 1857, quoted in *Rochester Union,* Oct. 22, 1859.

p. 198   *"servile insurrection":* Henry Wise to James Buchanan, Nov. 13, 1859, quoted in Douglass, *Life and Times,* 309.

p. 198   *knew of the insurrection:* See testimony of Lind F. Currie, Jan. 11, 1860, U.S. Senate, Mason Committee, *Report on the Invasion of Harper's Ferry,* 36th Cong., 1st sess., Senate Report 278 1860, II, (serial set 1040), 58.

p. 199   *"in my company":* Douglass, *Life and Times,* 307.

p. 199   *"northern latitude":* Ibid., 308.

p. 199 *"an* anxious *night":* Ibid.
p. 199 *"in my high desk":* Ibid.
p. 200 *"have done so":* William Still to Amy Post, Oct. 1859, Post Family Papers.
p. 200 *"Parker never did":* Potter, *Impending Crisis,* 375.

CHAPTER 16

p. 201 *"the whole south:* Assing, "The Insurrection," 8.
p. 202 *"Douglass fails":* C. W. Slack to Henry David Thoreau and Ralph Waldo Emerson, Oct. 31, 1859, *The Correspondence of Henry David Thoreau,* ed. Walter Harding and Carl Bode (New York, 1958), 564.
p. 202 *"for a moment":* Samuel May, Jr., to Richard D. Webb, Nov. 16, 1859, Weston Sisters Letters.
p. 202 *"inactive exile":* Douglass to Amy Post, Oct. 27, 1859, Post Family Papers.
p. 202 *before Brown's raid:* See headnote to Douglass, "Slavery and the Limits of Nonintervention," Dec. 7, 1859, in Blassingame et al., eds., *Frederick Douglass Papers* 3:276.
p. 203 *to her father:* Rosetta Douglass to Douglass, Dec. 6, 1859.
p. 203 *"was progress":* Douglass, "Slavery and the Limits of Nonintervention," Dec. 7, 1859, in Blassingame et al., eds., *Frederick Douglass Papers* 3:286, 287.
p. 204 *splitting in two:* Douglass, "John Brown and the Slaveholders' Insurrection," Jan. 30, 1860, in ibid., 315.
p. 204 *"too great length":* Douglass, "The American Constitution and the Slave," March 26, 1860, in ibid., 344.
p. 204 *"devilish":* Ibid., 345.
p. 205 *"not [pro-]slavery":* Ibid., 366.
p. 205 *at its center:* See Milner S. Ball, "Stories of Origin and Constitutional Possibilities," *Michigan Law Review* 87 (Aug. 1989): 2280–2319.
p. 205 *Constitution in 1851:* See Douglass, "Change of Opinion Announced," *North Star,* May 23, 1851, in Foner, *Writings of Douglass* 2:155–56. See also William M. Wiecek, *The Sources of Antislavery Constitutionalism in America, 1760–1848* (Ithaca, N.Y., 1977).
p. 205 *his argument:* See Anthony Lewis, *Gideon's Trumpet* (New York, 1964); and Sanford Levinson, *Constitutional Faith* (Princeton, N.J., 1988).
p. 206 *reopen the trade:* Douglass, "The American Constitution and the Slave," March 26, 1860, in Blassingame et al., eds., *Frederick Douglass Papers* 3:355.
p. 206 *"itself an insurrection":* Ibid.
p. 207 *"plundered rights":* Ibid., 364.
p. 207 *to come home:* Rosetta Douglass to "Aunt Harriet," April 20, 1860, Yale University Frederick Douglass Papers.
p. 207 *work in school:* See Annie Douglass to Douglass, Dec. 7, 1859.
p. 207 *"as the white":* Rosetta Douglass to "Aunt Harriet," April 20, 1860.
p. 208 *more martyrs:* See U.S. Senate, Mason Committee, *Report on the Invasion of Harper's Ferry,* 36th Cong., 1st sess., 1860, II, Senate Report 278 (Serial Set 1040).
p. 208 *"combined against it":* Douglass, "Slavery and the Irrepressible Conflict," Aug. 1, 1860, in Blassingame et al., eds., *Frederick Douglass Papers* 3:381.
p. 208 *in New York State:* See Blight, *Frederick Douglass's Civil War,* 60.
p. 209 *"trained pugilist": New York Tribune,* quoted in headnote to Douglass, "The Legacy of John Brown," in Blassingame et al., eds., *Frederick Douglass Papers* 3:388. This address, scheduled for Dec. 3, 1860, was not delivered.
p. 209 *"Sit down!": Boston Post,* quoted in headnote to Douglass, "The Legacy of John Brown," in ibid., 399.
p. 209 *"Go on nigger":* Ibid., 401.
p. 209 *"kill freedom":* Ibid.
p. 210 *pile of chairs:* Ibid., 403.

p. 210 *"Nigger Hayes":* Ibid., 404.

p. 210 *"the niggers!":* Ibid., 406.

p. 210 *"a Union man":* Ibid., 404.

p. 210 *"dinner time Fred":* Ibid., 405.

p. 211 *by the police:* Ibid., 406–7.

p. 211 *"masculines":* Ibid., 412.

p. 211 *he thundered:* Douglass, "John Brown's Contributions to the Abolition Movement," in Blassingame et al., eds., *Frederick Douglass Papers* 3:416.

p. 211 *"slave catchers":* Ibid., 419.

p. 211 *"war":* Ibid., 413.

p. 212 *"absolution":* Benjamin Percival, "Abolitionism in Lynn and Essex County" (Typescript, Lynn, Mass., Lynn Historical Society, Nov. 12, 1908), 14.

p. 212 *"rebel states":* Douglass, "The American Apocalypse," June 16, 1861, in Blassingame et al., eds., *Frederick Douglass Papers* 3:437, 445.

p. 213 *"hand of the black man":* Douglass, "Fighting the Rebels with One Hand," Jan. 14, 1862, in ibid., 478, 477, 483.

p. 213 *"and effect as he":* Christian Recorder, Jan. 18, 1862, quoted in headnote to Douglass, "Fighting the Rebels with One Hand," in ibid., 473.

p. 213 *"unutterable loathing":* Douglass, quoted in Ken Burns, *The Civil War* (New York: Florentine Films, 1990), Part 1, "1861," segment 15.

p. 214 *"all the money":* Douglass, "The War and How to End It," March 25, 1862, in Blassingame et al., eds., *Frederick Douglass Papers* 3:512.

p. 214 *"worthy of our hemp":* Ibid., 515.

p. 214 *"under Foote":* Ibid., 514.

p. 214 *"lesson of the Hour":* Ibid., 508.

p. 214 *"abolition of slavery":* Ibid., 519.

p. 214 *"of this rebellion":* Douglass, "The Slaveholders' Rebellion," July 4, 1862, in Blassingame et al., eds., *Frederick Douglass Papers* 3:531.

p. 215 *"in the air":* Douglass, "The Proclamation and a Negro Army," Feb. 6, 1863, in ibid., 568.

p. 216 *"all in place":* Ibid., 568–69.

CHAPTER 17

p. 218 *"strike the blow":* Douglass, "The Proclamation and a Negro Army," Feb. 6, 1863, in Blassingame et al., eds., *Frederick Douglass Papers* 3:566.

p. 218 *"easier for me":* Rosetta Douglass to Douglass, Oct. 9, 1862.

p. 218 *"without doubt":* Julia Griffiths Crofts to Douglass, Dec. 2, 1862.

p. 218 *"read a little":* Rosetta Douglass Sprague, "Anna Murray-Douglass," 100.

p. 219 *"sure counsel":* Rosetta Douglass to Douglass, Dec. 2, 1862.

p. 219 *later recalled:* Rosetta Douglass Sprague, "Anna Murray-Douglass," 99.

p. 219 *"towards my mother":* Rosetta Douglass to Douglass, Sept. 24, 1862.

p. 220 *recent acquaintance:* Rosetta Douglass to Douglass, April 4, 1862.

p. 220 *male teachers:* Ibid.

p. 220 *"in their house":* Rosetta Douglass to Douglass, Aug. 31, 1862.

p. 220 *in Washington:* See Julia Griffiths Crofts to Douglass, Dec. 2, 1862.

p. 221 *beginning Latin:* Oberlin College Catalogue, 1854–55, 20, 43; and Roland M. Bauman, archivist, Oberlin College, to the author, April 13, 1990.

p. 221 *Salem schools:* Rosetta Douglass to Douglass, Aug. 31, 1862.

p. 221 *"bought three towels":* Rosetta Douglass to Douglass, Sept. 24, 1862.

p. 221 *"his house":* Rosetta Douglass to Douglass, Aug. 31, 1862.

p. 221 *"has become low":* Ibid.

p. 221 *"to the whites":* Rosetta Douglass to Douglass, Sept. 24, 1862.

p. 222 *to board:* Ibid.

p. 222 *"family differences":* Rosetta Douglass to Douglass, Oct. 9, 1862.

p. 222 *"his manners":* Ibid.

p. 222 *Nathan Sprague:* See Julia Griffiths Crofts to Douglass, Dec. 10, 1863.

p. 223 "as a slave": Thomas Wentworth Higginson to "Dear Sir," Dec. 26, 1862, Brown Family Papers.

p. 223 *Douglass's help:* See Quarles, *Frederick Douglass,* 204.

p. 224 *son, Charles:* See Douglass to Gerrit Smith, May 6, 1863, quoted in ibid., 205; and Luis F. Emilio, *History of the Fifty-fourth Regiment of Massachusetts Volunteer Infantry, 1863–1865* (Boston, 1894), 12.

p. 224 *since February:* See Blassingame et al., eds., *Frederick Douglass Papers* 3:xxxv.

p. 224 *"Black hair":* Service records of Charles R. Douglass and Lewis H. Douglass, National Archives.

p. 225 *"Rebel States":* John A. Andrew, quoted in Emilio, *History of the Fifty-fourth,* 27.

p. 226 *"savage instincts":* Charles Russell Lowell, quoted in Dudley Cornish, *The Sable Arm: Black Troops in the Union Army, 1861–1865* (New York, 1966), 150.

p. 226 *frontal assault:* See ibid., 153.

p. 226 *"but I am here":* Lewis H. Douglass to Amelia Loguen, July 20, 1863, quoted in James M. McPherson, *The Negro's Civil War: How American Negroes Felt and Acted during the War for the Union* (New York, 1965), 190.

p. 226 *"to this war":* Ibid.

p. 226 *"splattered all about":* Shelby Foote, *The Civil War: A Narrative,* 3 vols. (New York, 1958–74), 2:697.

p. 227 *heart of the city: Life and Times,* 356.

p. 227 *"white soldiers":* U.S. Grant to Richard Taylor, July 4, 1863, *The Papers of Ulysses S. Grant,* ed. John Y. Simon, 16 vols. (Carbondale, Ill., 1967–85), 8:468.

p. 228 *at recruitment:* See Douglass to George Luther Stearns, Aug. 1, 1863 (open letter), *Douglass' Monthly,* Aug. 1863), in Foner, *Writings of Douglass* 3:367–69.

p. 228 *"be executed":* Abraham Lincoln, quoted in Cornish, *Sable Arm,* 168.

p. 228 *some not:* Douglass to George Luther Stearns, Aug. 12, 1863.

p. 229 *into officer ranks:* Ibid.

p. 229 *officer in the army:* Ibid.

p. 229 *"employing colored troops":* Ibid.

p. 229 *to hold to it:* Ibid.

p. 229 *visitor totally:* Ibid.

p. 230 *"with the Fifty-fourth":* John A. Andrew to Edwin M. Stanton, March 14, 1864, in service record of Charles R. Douglass, National Archives.

p. 230 *in St. Michaels:* See Lewis H. Douglass to Douglass, June 9, 1865.

p. 230 *"to be discharged":* Douglass to [Abraham Lincoln], undated, in service record of Charles R. Douglass, National Archives.

p. 230 *"A. Lincoln":* Abraham Lincoln, endorsement, Sept. 1, 1864, ibid.

p. 230 *recruitment rhetoric:* In Douglass, *Life and Times,* 350, but nowhere else, Douglass claimed that Frederick jr. had done recruiting in the Mississippi Valley; there is no other record of the third Douglass son having been involved in the war.

p. 231 *made a major:* See Quarles, *Frederick Douglass,* 213.

p. 231 *"of the people":* Douglass, "The Mission of the War," Feb. 13, 1864, in Foner, *Writings of Douglass* 3:386.

p. 231 *"shadow of death":* Ibid., 388.

p. 231 *"have the power":* Ibid., 393.

p. 231 *"National regeneration:* Ibid., 401.

p. 231 *for such change:* See George M. Fredrickson, *The Inner Civil War: Northern Intellectuals and the Crisis of the Union* (New York, 1965), 183–98.

p. 231 *"of this war":* Douglass, "The Mission of the War," Feb. 13, 1864, in Foner, *Writings of Douglass* 3:403.

p. 232 *"save it afterwards":* Abraham Lincoln, memorandum of Aug. 23, 1864, in Roy P. Basler et al., eds., *The Collected Works of Abraham Lincoln,* 8 vols. (New Brunswick, N.J., 1953), 7:514.

p. 232 *"I am Frederick Douglass":* Joseph T. Mills, Diary, quoted in Basler et al., eds. *Collected Works of Lincoln* 7:507–8.

p. 232 *"on the patent":* Ibid.

p. 233 *"their independence":* Ibid.

p. 233 *"without it":* Ibid.

p. 233 *"alarmed condition":* Douglass to Theodore Tilton, Oct. 15, 1864, in Foner, *Writings of Douglass* 3:422.

p. 233 *carry it out:* Douglass to Abraham Lincoln, Aug. 29, 1864.

p. 234 *"vocation unmolested":* Ibid.

p. 234 *"away at Sumter":* Lewis H. Douglass to Douglass, Aug. 22, 1864.

p. 234 *displaced-persons' camps:* See Patricia Ann Schechter, " 'The First Free Spot of Ground in Kentucky': The Story of Camp Nelson" (B.A. thesis, Mount Holyoke College, 1986).

p. 234 *"in Washington":* Douglass to Abraham Lincoln, Aug 29, 1864. Even LaWanda Cox, in her sympathetic account of Lincoln's growing concern for the black people he was helping set free, can point to no firm Lincoln plan for Reconstruction. (See LaWanda Cox, *Lincoln and Black Freedom* [Columbia, S.C., 1981].)

p. 234 *"when company comes":* Douglass to Theodore Tilton, Oct. 15, 1864, in Foner, *Writings of Douglass* 3:424.

p. 235 *"your excellency":* Douglass to Abraham Lincoln, Aug. 29, 1864.

p. 235 *did not ask:* See Douglass, *Life and Times,* 362–64, for his account of being spotted by President Lincoln and Vice-President Johnson at the inaugural, an account that has the ring of Douglass, after the fact, giving a prophetic reading to a momentary impression.

p. 235 *from Point Lookout:* Lewis H. Douglass to Douglass, June 9, 1865.

p. 236 *named "after you":* Ibid.

p. 236 *"to know you":* Ibid.

p. 236 *"to move away":* Ibid.

CHAPTER 18

p. 238 *"last five years":* Ottilia Assing to Ludmilla Assing, Feb. 3, 1865, Varnhagen Collection, Jagiellonian University library, Kraków, Poland. The translations of Assing's letters are by Terry H. Pickett.

p. 239 *at the hospital:* Charles R. Douglass to Douglass, Feb. 9, 1865.

p. 240 *cotton lands:* Charles R. Douglass to Douglass, Feb. 19, 1865.

p. 240 *"Julia G. Crofts":* Julia Griffiths Crofts to Douglass, April 28, 1865.

p. 242 *"may cease":* Douglass to J. Miller McKim, May 2, 1865.

p. 242 *"in the Church":* Ibid.

p. 242 *"of the South":* Ibid.

p. 242 *"hobble along with":* Ibid.

p. 243 *"a degraded relation":* Douglass, "The Douglass Institute," in Foner, *Writings of Douglass* 4:178. Foner gives the date as Oct. 1865, but contemporary newspaper accounts date the occasion as Sept. 29, 1865.

p. 243 *"of the community":* Baltimore Sun, Sept. 29, 1865.

p. 243 *rose to speak:* See *Baltimore Sun,* Sept. 30, 1865.

p. 244 *"have not failed":* Douglass, "The Douglass Institute," 175.

p. 244 *"they belong":* Ibid., 179.

p. 244 *"self-sustaining civilization":* Ibid.

p. 244 *"track of blood":* Ibid., 180.

p. 244 *"minds enlightened":* Ibid., 182.

p. 244 *"the coming fact":* Ibid., 176.

p. 245 *"who lave in its waters":* Ibid., 182.

p. 245 *"stopped work"*: Baltimore Sun, Sept. 30, 1865.

p. 245 *"mobbed and beaten"*: Christian Recorder, [Aug. 1866].

p. 245 *"Follow up the Work"*: Douglass to James Lynch, Aug. 13, 1866.

p. 245 *"to save themselves"*: Douglass, "The Douglass Institute," 177.

p. 246 *"emancipation without this"*: Douglass to Lydia Maria Child, July 30, 1865, in Foner, *Writings of Douglass* 4:16.

p. 246 *"whom they live"*: Douglass, quoted in New York Tribune, March 12, 1866, in ibid., 4:17.

p. 246 *Henry to Rochester*: See Charles R. Douglass to Douglass, Aug. 2, 1865.

p. 247 *war would ensue*: Article by "Observer," New York Tribune, Feb. 12, 1866, in Foner, *Writings of Douglass* 4:21–23.

p. 248 *nothing more*: Ibid.

p. 248 *"of little Annie"*: Rosetta Douglass Sprague to Douglass, Feb. 21, 1865.

p. 248 *"Maryland biscuit"*: Julia Griffiths Crofts to Douglass, May 19, 1865.

p. 248 *a college degree*: See Quarles, *Frederick Douglass*, 108.

p. 249 *"desirous of succeeding"*: Henry O. Waggoner to Douglass, Aug. 27, 1866.

p. 249 *"onward March"*: Ibid.

p. 249 *"for being a woman"*: Douglass to Elizabeth Cady Stanton, Feb. 16, 1866.

p. 250 *"the word male"*: Susan B. Anthony to Ottilia Assing, March 1, 1866, in Patricia G. Holland and Ann D. Gordon, eds., *Papers of Elizabeth Cady Stanton and Susan B. Anthony* (Wilmington, Del., Wilmington Scholarly Resources, 1989), microfilm.

p. 250 *including Charles Douglass*: See Charles R. Douglass to Douglass, Aug. 20, 1868.

p. 250 *that supported Johnson*: Douglass to John Van Voorhis, Aug. 30, 1866 (open letter, Rochester Union and Advertiser, Sept. 1, 1866).

p. 251 *excitement than either*: See Quarles, *Frederick Douglass*, 229.

p. 251 *"foolish bravado"*: Thaddeus Stevens, quoted in ibid., 231.

p. 251 *"of a statesman"*: Douglass to Elizabeth Cady Stanton, Feb. 6, 1882.

p. 251 *"Army of Equal Rights"*: Douglass to Anna Dickinson, Sept. 10, 1866.

p. 251 *it had really been*: Douglass, *Life and Times*, 391.

p. 252 *"were to be here"*: Ibid., 392.

CHAPTER 19

p. 254 *or the Senate*: May, *Some Recollections*, 296.

p. 254 *"North and West"*: Douglass to John Curtiss Underwood, Nov. 14, 1866.

p. 254 *were up to*: See Dorothy Sterling, *Captain of the Planter: The Story of Robert Smalls* (Garden City, N.Y., 1958); and Russell Duncan, *Freedom's Shore: Tunis Campbell and the Georgia Freedmen* (Athens, Ga., 1986).

p. 254 *"a press in Virginia"*: Douglass to John Curtiss Underwood, Nov. 14, 1866.

p. 254 *not "our," city*: Douglass, "The Douglass Institute," in Foner, *Writings of Douglass* 4:178.

p. 255 *"straight through"*: Ottilia Assing to Ludmilla Assing, July 16, 1868, Varnhagen Collection.

p. 255 *"enchanted" her*: Otillia Assing to Ludmilla Assing, Jan. 19, 1868, ibid.

p. 255 *"liberty, and equality"*: Douglass, "Reconstruction," Atlantic Monthly 18 (Dec. 1866): 761.

p. 255 *"to protect themselves"*: Ibid., 762.

p. 255 *"for his protection"*: Ibid.

p. 256 *for blacks nationwide*: Douglass to Anna Dickinson, May 21, 1867.

p. 256 *for the nineteenth*: Charles R. Douglass to Douglass, Dec. 14, 1866.

p. 256 *"send her love"*: Nathan Sprague to Douglass, March 26, 1867, with postscript by Rosetta Douglass Sprague.

p. 257 *air as well*: Rosetta Douglass Sprague to Douglass, April 11, 1867.

p. 257 *board with Rosetta*: See Charles R. Douglass to Douglass, April 19, 1867.

p. 257 *"side if possible"*: Charles R. Douglass to Douglass, May 9, 1867.

p. 257 *"with colored men"*: Charles R. Douglass to Douglass, July 11, 1867.

p. 257 *"one of these?"*: Charles R. Douglass to Douglass, May 9, 1867.

p. 258 *"a voter here"*: Ibid.

p. 258 *he proudly declared*: Charles R. Douglass to Douglass, April 30, 1867.

p. 258 *"his mining company"*: Charles R. Douglass to Douglass, May 25, 1867.

p. 258 *"over exert herself"*: Rosetta Douglass Sprague to Douglass, April 24, 1867.

p. 259 *to the audience*: Douglass to "Gentlemen," June 23, 1867. The letter to which Douglass was replying has been lost, and the identity of the senders is not known.

p. 259 *"of human greatness"*: Ibid.

p. 259 *"deepest pathos"*: Douglass to James J. Spelman, July 11, 1867.

p. 259 *at the job*: Charles R. Douglass to Douglass, July 18, 1867.

p. 260 *"given the boy"*: Charles R. Douglass to Douglass, July 24, 1867.

p. 260 *"lacks moral courage"*: William Slade to Douglass, July 29, 1867.

p. 260 *"by President Johnson"*: Douglass to William Slade, Aug. 12, 1867.

p. 260 *"of the Bureau"*: Ibid.

p. 260 *to Mrs. Slade*: Ibid.

p. 261 *"in all quarters"*: Charles R. Douglass to Douglass, Aug. 20, 1867.

p. 261 *to reconsider*: William Slade to Douglass, Aug. 14, 1867.

p. 261 *"look for more?"*: Douglass to Theodore Tilton, Sept. 2, 1867.

p. 261 *"to sustain Johnson"*: Charles R. Douglass to Douglass, Feb. 24, 1868.

p. 261 *prospect of a "coup"*: Ottilia Assing to Ludmilla Assing, Feb. 22, 1868, Varnhagen Collection.

p. 261 *"to meet them"*: Charles R. Douglass to Douglass, Feb. 24, 1868.

p. 262 *class at home*: See Ottilia Assing to Ludmilla Assing, July 16, 1868, Varnhagen Collection.

p. 262 *a "traitor"*: Ottilia Assing to Ludmilla Assing, May 29, 1868, ibid.

p. 262 *cause of equality*: Ottilia Assing to Ludmilla Assing, July 16, 1868, ibid.

p. 262 *to Mount Vernon*: Charles R. Douglass to Douglass, July 22, 1868.

p. 262 *their own songs*: Ottilia Assing to Ludmilla Assing, July 16, 1868, Varnhagen Collection.

p. 262 *in a huff*: Ibid.

p. 262 *"at all gone"*: Ibid.

p. 263 *"incomprehensible speed"*: Ottilia Assing to Ludmilla Assing, Aug. 24, 1868, Varnhagen Collection.

p. 263 *"of your heroism"*: Douglass to Harriet Tubman, Aug. 29, 1868.

p. 264 *"your native State"*: Charles R. Douglass to Douglass, Feb. 26, 1870.

CHAPTER 20

p. 265 *"but of citizens"*: Elizabeth Cady Stanton to Thomas Wentworth Higginson, July 13, 1868, in Stanton and Blatch, eds., *Stanton* 2:120.

p. 266 *"the Negro's hour"*: Theodore Tilton, quoted in Quarles, *Frederick Douglass,* 246.

p. 266 *"not for woman"*: Barry, *Susan B. Anthony,* 171.

p. 267 *"this bombshell"*: Susan B. Anthony to Douglass, Dec. 15, 1866.

p. 267 *women's suffrage*: See *Weekly Monitor* (Fort Scott, Kans.), Aug. 21 and Sept. 25, 1867.

p. 267 *"as a voter"*: Ibid., Oct. 9, 1867.

p. 267 *"probably forty"*: Ibid., Oct. 20, 1867.

p. 268 *"for several minutes"*: Ibid., Oct. 30, 1867.

p. 268 *more than 150 votes*: See ibid., Nov. 7, 1867.

p. 269 *"not seem generous"*: Douglass to Josephine Griffing, Sept. 27, 1868.

p. 269 *"has come of it"*: Amy Carpenter to Douglass, Jan. 26, 1868.

p. 270 *"the WHOLE PEOPLE"*: Broadside announcing the *New Era,* Feb. 1869.

p. 270 *"conduce to action"*: Henry O. Waggoner to Douglass, Sept. 17, 1870.

p. 270 *sought the post*: See Charles E. Wynes, "Ebenezer Don Carlos Bassett, America's First Black Diplomat," *Pennsylvania History* 51 (July 1984): 232–40; Douglass to Ebenezer D. Bassett, April 13, 1869; and Douglass to George T. Downing, April 25 and April 26, 1869.

p. 270 *"the United States"*: Foner, *Writings of Douglass* 4:39.

p. 270 *"moiling life":* Henry David Thoreau, *Walden; or, Life in the Woods* (1854; reprint, Boston, 1948), 186.
p. 271 *"the Printer's Union":* Douglass, "My Son, Lewis Douglass," in Foner, *Writings of Douglass* 4:218.
p. 271 *"from choice?":* Ibid., 219.
p. 271 *"color or race?":* Ibid., 220.
p. 272 *December 1869: New Era,* Jan. 13, 1870.
p. 272 *"for his family":* Resolution quoted in ibid.
p. 272 *of the country:* Resolution quoted in ibid.
p. 272 *"in this city":* Charles R. Douglass to Douglass, Jan. 5, 1870.
p. 273 *"are still awful":* Ottilia Assing to Ludmilla Assing, March 20, 1870, Varnhagen Collection.
p. 273 *sentimental occasion:* Ottilia Assing to Ludmilla Assing, April 15, 1870, ibid.

CHAPTER 21

p. 274 *"intensely beautiful":* Rochester Democrat and Chronicle, June 3, 1872.
p. 274 "were destroyed": *Rochester Union and Advertiser,* June 3, 1872.
p. 274 *badly scorched:* See ibid., June 17, 1872.
p. 274 *"an incendiary":* Ibid., June 3, 1872.
p. 275 *at a neighbor's:* Ibid., June 6, 1872.
p. 275 *"in bad temper":* Ibid., June 17, 1872.
p. 275 *"a white citizen": New National Era,* quoted in ibid.
p. 275 *"the guilty party": Rochester Union and Advertiser,* June 17, 1872.
p. 275 *on his insurance:* See W. A. Richardson to Douglass, Sept. 25, 1872.
p. 276 *"not be long": New National Era,* quoted in *Rochester Union and Advertiser,* June 17, 1872.
p. 276 *"Grant and Sumner":* David H. Donald, *Charles Sumner and the Rights of Man* (New York, 1970), 474.
p. 277 *"a tropical island":* Ottilia Assing to Ludmilla Assing, March 3, 1871, Varnhagen Collection.
p. 277 *thirty years earlier:* Douglass to Charles Jervis Langdon, undated, quoted and commented on in *Bangor* (Maine) *Daily Whig and Courier,* Aug. 23, 1872.
p. 279 *in the deliberations:* Douglass in *New National Era,* May 2, 1872.
p. 280 *"health and happiness":* Douglass to Orville E. Babcock, Nov. 13, 1873, Babcock Papers, Newberry Library, Chicago, Ill.
p. 280 *to be flourishing:* See photograph of New York City branch passbook in Carl R. Osthaus, *Freedmen, Philanthropy, and Fraud: A History of the Freedman's Savings Bank* (Urbana, Ill., 1976), 56.
p. 281 *maintain that fiction:* See photograph of Mobile, Alabama, branch passbook in ibid., 57.
p. 281 *among the freed people:* Ibid., 49.
p. 282 "friends of the Negro": John W. Alvord to Mahlon T. Hewitt, Dec. 27, 1866, quoted in ibid.
p. 282 *excellent sense:* See Michael R. Winston, "Charles Burleigh Purvis," in Logan and Winston, eds., *Dictionary of American Negro Biography,* 507.
p. 282 *of the loan:* See Osthaus, *Freedmen, Philanthropy, and Fraud,* 146–47.
p. 282 *"fabric of credit":* U.S. Congress, House of Representatives, *Freedman's Bank,* House Report 502, 44th Cong., 1st sess., 1876, quoted in ibid., 158.
p. 282 *"of the Freedmen":* John W. Alvord to Mahlon T. Hewitt, Dec. 26, 1866, quoted in Osthaus, *Freedmen, Philanthropy, and Fraud,* 140.
p. 282 *selling securities:* See Osthaus, *Freedmen, Philanthropy, and Fraud,* 165.
p. 282 *left the board:* See ibid., 155.
p. 283 *for the bank:* See ibid., 198.
p. 283 *were black:* See ibid., 184.
p. 283 *"affairs of the bank":* U.S. Congress, House of Representatives, *Report of the Commissioner*

of the Freedman's Savings and Trust Company, House Miscellaneous Document 16, 43d Cong., 2d sess., 1874, quoted in ibid., 183.

p. 284 *which was worthless:* See Osthaus, *Freedmen, Philanthropy, and Fraud,* 160.

p. 284 *to its depositors:* See ibid., 182.

p. 285 *the failed bank:* See ibid., 198.

p. 285 *"criminal proceedings":* U.S. Congress, House of Representatives, Committee on Banking and Currency, *Freedman's Savings and Trust Company,* House Report 58, 43d Cong., 2d sess., 1875.

p. 286 *"elected its president":* Douglass to Gerrit Smith, July 3, 1874.

p. 286 *George Washington Williams:* See John Hope Franklin, *George Washington Williams: A Biography* (Chicago, 1985).

p. 286 *"declined to answer":* J. R. Davis (Williams's secretary) to Douglass, March 28, 1888.

p. 286 *"an insolvent bank":* Ibid.

p. 286 *institution went under:* John Mercer Langston in *Herald* of May 5, 1884, quoted by Douglass in his response in *Cleveland Leader,* reprinted in *New York Times,* May 12, 1884.

p. 286 *"the reason why":* J. R. Davis to Douglass, March 28, 1888.

p. 287 *defended himself:* Charles R. Douglass to Douglass, May 13, 1873.

p. 287 *"in my life":* Rosetta Douglass Sprague to Douglass, Sept. 17, 1876.

p. 287 *"reason on nonsense":* Gustave Frauenstein to Douglass, May 4, 1873.

p. 287 *"women have loved":* Ottilia Assing to Ludmilla Assing, March 26, 1874, Varnhagen Collection.

p. 288 *"bewitched a person?"* Ibid.

p. 288 *"manages to earn":* Ottilia Assing to Ludmilla Assing, Dec. 23, 1875, Varnhagen Collection.

p. 288 *as a stableman:* It is unlikely that the two Sprague families were related. Nathan's family was from Maryland; Salmon P. Chase's daughter was married to Senator William Sprague of Rhode Island.

p. 288 *was on display:* See *Index to American Art Exhibit Catalogues from the Beginning through the 1876 Centennial Year,* ed. James L. Yarnall and William H. Gerdts (Boston, 1986), 4:2530.

p. 289 *"during the campaign":* Ottilia Assing to Ludmilla Assing, April 30, 1876, Varnhagen Collection.

p. 289 *"Capitol of the Nation":* Harriet Jacobs to Douglass, March 14, 1877.

p. 289 *"intellect and culture":* Mary G. Wright to Douglass, April 1, 1877.

p. 290 *"a beneficent influence":* Ottilia Assing to Ludmilla Assing, March 26, 1877, Varnhagen Collection.

CHAPTER 22

p. 292 *"the Executive Mansion":* Douglass, *Life and Times,* 425.

p. 292 *have been acceptable:* Grace Greenwood, *New York Times,* March 24, 1877.

p. 292 *took him to be:* Douglass to Grace Greenwood, May 20, 1877, in Joseph Borome, "Two Letters of Frederick Douglass," *Journal of Negro History* 36 (Jan. 1951): 81.

p. 292 *"know what will":* Grace Greenwood, *New York Times,* March 24, 1877. See also *Washington Evening Star,* May 12, 1877; *National Republican,* May 13, 1877; and Douglass to Grace Greenwood, May 20, 1877, in Borome "Two Letters," 81.

p. 292 *"regard to him":* "MKJ" to Douglass, June 3, 1877.

p. 293 *"of the President":* Douglass, *Life and Times,* 426.

p. 293 *wasn't happy:* Preston, *Young Frederick Douglass,* 182.

p. 293 *Baltimore Sun reporter: Baltimore Sun,* June 17, 1877.

p. 293 *"in grim disapproval":* Preston, *Young Frederick Douglass,* 182.

p. 293 *"gave me my muscle":* Ibid., 183.

p. 294 *"no progress": Baltimore Sun,* June 17, 1877.

p. 294 *until she died:* Douglass, *Life and Times,* 442–43

p. 294 *"in the woods":* Douglass, *Bondage,* 427.

p. 294 *"depart in peace"*: Douglass, *Life and Times,* 444.

p. 294 *quiet satisfaction:* Ibid., 442–44.

p. 295 *"defenseless animals"*: Ottilia Assing to Douglass, July 12, 1877.

p. 295 *"beware of Compromise"*: "Citizen" to Douglass, April 5, 1877.

p. 295 *"anytime since slavery"*: Ibid.

p. 295 *"the colored man"*: G. C. Jenks to Douglass, May 22, 1877.

p. 296 *"crime and violence"*: Ottilia Assing to Douglass, July 12, 1877.

p. 296 *was "lucrative"*: Ottilia Assing to Ludmilla Assing, March 26, 1877, Varnhagen Collection.

p. 297 *Washington than he:* See Louise Daniel Hutchinson, *The Anacostia Story, 1608–1930* (Washington, D.C., 1977), 51, 53, 70, 86.

p. 297 *mother had died:* John Sears to Douglass, Jan. 10, 1878; and Thomas Sears to Douglass, Feb. 1, 1878.

p. 297 *his skeletal legs:* Henry O. Waggoner to Douglass, March 23, 1878.

p. 297 *"shelter for him"*: Douglass to Amy Post, April 14, 1879.

p. 298 *to Cedar Hill:* See Preston, *Young Frederick Douglass,* 189–91.

p. 298 *the Morgenblatt:* See Eliza Werpop to Douglass, Aug. 28, 1881.

p. 298 *tried advertising:* See E. J. Loewenthal to Douglass, Dec. 17, 1882.

p. 298 *in closer days:* See Douglass to Henry Bergh, Nov. 7, 1884.

p. 298 *after a visit:* See E. J. Loewenthal to Douglass, Dec. 17, 1882.

p. 299 *"period since slavery"*: Richard T. Greener, "The Emigration of Colored Citizens from the Southern States," *Journal of Social Science* 11 (May 1880): 22–23.

p. 300 *"traveling camps"*: Douglass, quoted in "Frederick Douglass and the Exodus," *National Republican,* May 5, 1879.

p. 300 *cold comfort in 1879:* Ibid.

p. 301 *"spirit of controversy"*: Douglass to Franklin B. Sanborn, Sept. 9, 1879.

p. 302 *was perverse:* Douglass, "The Negro Exodus from the Gulf States," *Journal of Social Science* 11 (May 1880): 1–2.

p. 302 *"the sunlight unharmed"*: Ibid., 20.

p. 302 *"of her destiny"*: Ibid., 3–4.

p. 303 *"reason as well"*: Ibid., 5, 9, 12.

p. 303 *"indescribable and impossible"*: Ibid., 20, 18, 20.

p. 304 *would take action:* Nell Irvin Painter, *Exodusters: Black Migration to Kansas after Reconstruction* (New York, 1976), 249.

CHAPTER 23

p. 305 *"a heavy loss"*: Marshall Jewell to Douglass, Sept. 22, 1880.

p. 305 *"altogether too modest"*: Douglass, quoted in *New York Times,* Jan. 26, 1881.

p. 305 *"the American people"*: Ibid.

p. 305 *"feel them too"*: Samuel L. Clemens to James A. Garfield, Jan. 12, 188[1], James A. Garfield Papers, Library of Congress, Reel 84.

p. 306 *"is very important"*: Douglass to Samuel L. Clemens, Jan. 22, 1881, Mark Twain Papers, Bancroft Library, University of California, Berkeley.

p. 306 *"myself and family"*: John Sears to Douglass, Feb. 23, 1882.

p. 306 *"at the White House"*: Douglass to George T. Downing, March 13, 1882; and Douglass to Godlove Orth, Feb. 14, 1882.

p. 307 *"when a boy"*: Douglass, *Life and Times,* 445.

p. 307 *"my last look"*: Douglass, *Narrative,* 32.

p. 308 *"in all directions"*: Douglass, *Life and Times,* 447.

p. 308 *sweeping the air:* Ibid.

p. 310 *"once left home"*: Ibid., 449.

p. 310 *the great house:* Ibid., 448.

p. 310 *"a glorious future"*: Ibid., 450.

p. 311 *newspaper, the* Alpha*:* See *Washington Post,* Jan. 25, 1884.

p. 311 *"for thirty years":* Douglass to Grace Greenwood, March 24, 1877.

p. 311 *"would have objected":* Douglass to Elizabeth Buffum Chace, Jan. 23, 1881, quoted in Lillie Buffum Chace Wyman and Arthur Crawford Wyman, *Elizabeth Buffum Chace, 1806–1899* (Boston, 1914), 139. Many of the old antislavery comrades were gone. Later that year, when Stephen S. Foster died, Douglass wrote a warm letter to his wife. (See Douglass to Abby Kelley Foster, Oct. 13, 1881.)

p. 311 *general dissatisfaction:* See Douglass to Sylvester Betts, Oct. 30, 1881; Douglass to Park Publishing Co., Nov. 11 and Dec. 16, 1881; and Douglass to John Lobb, Feb. 20, 1882.

p. 312 *the Dominican Republic:* Ottilia Assing to Douglass, Jan. 6, 1879.

p. 312 *"dangerously ill":* Frederick Douglass, Jr., to Amy Post, July 8, 1882. The card was canceled at midnight in Washington and arrived in Rochester the next evening.

p. 312 *mother, he added:* Douglass to Amy Post, July 14, 1882.

p. 312 *"alive she is":* Douglass to Parker Pillsbury, July 18, 1882.

p. 312 *"of your youth":* Henry O. Waggoner to Douglass, Aug. 7, 1882; another of many letters of condolence came from Helen Pitts's mother. (See Jane Wills Pitts to Douglass, Aug. 20, 1882.)

p. 312 *"in your trouble":* Douglass to Amy Post, Aug. 21, 1882. He had had a similar invitation from Susan B. Anthony.

p. 312 *"become a wanderer":* Douglass to Grace Greenwood, Oct. 9, 1882.

p. 313 *"is abroad here":* Ibid.

p. 313 *to cheer him:* One of Rosetta's letters was in reply to one from her father "written by the friendly hand of Mrs. Greene" (Rosetta Douglass Sprague to Douglass, July 18, 1883).

p. 314 *of his name:* Douglass to Lewis H. Douglass, July 18, 1883.

p. 314 *scheduled for Washington:* See *Cleveland Gazette,* Sept. 22, 1883.

p. 314 *"great political revolution":* *Washington Bee,* May 5, 1883.

p. 314 *"Is Arthur a Negro?":* T. Thomas Fortune, quoted in draft of letter, Douglass to T. Thomas Fortune, May 26, 1883.

p. 314 *on the subject:* Draft of letter, Douglass to T. Thomas Fortune, May 26, 1883.

p. 315 *"each other's motive":* Ibid.

p. 315 *"deliberate falsehoods":* Douglass to George Washington Williams, open letter, *Washington Bee,* May 5, 1883.

p. 315 *"on the color line":* Douglass, "Address to the People of the United States," Sept. 24, 1883, in Foner, *Writings of Douglass* 4:373, 377–78, 379.

p. 316 *being "indolent":* Ibid., 382.

p. 316 *"Ohio or elsewhere":* Douglass, letter, *New York Times,* Oct. 6, 1883.

p. 317 *"state and nation":* Ibid.

p. 317 *"all is well":* Sarah O. Pettit to Douglass, Sept. 26, 1883.

p. 317 *nine hundred dollars:* See undated memorandum by Dickson J. Preston in the Yale University Frederick Douglass Papers; and Preston, *Young Frederick Douglass,* 177.

p. 317 *"of the Constitution":* Douglass, "The Return of the Democratic Party to Power," 1885 (no month or day), in Foner, *Writings of Douglass* 4:423.

p. 318 *"that emergency":* Slaughterhouse Cases, 16 Wallace: 81.

p. 318 *"might shrink":* Douglass, "Speech at the Civil Rights Mass-Meeting," Oct. 22, 1883, in Foner, *Writings of Douglass* 4:393–96.

p. 318 *"humbled the Nation":* Ibid., 397–98.

p. 319 *was surprised too: National Republican,* Jan. 25, 1884.

p. 319 *"residence of Miss Pitts":* Ibid.

p. 319 *to be the bride:* Ibid.

p. 320 *"elegant wedding supper":* Ibid.

p. 320 *"in the stables":* Letter, *Weekly News* (Pittsburgh), Feb. 14, 1884.

p. 321 *"to the union":* Elizabeth Cady Stanton to Douglass, Jan. 27, 1884.

p. 321 *"most sincere congratulations":* Julia Griffiths Crofts to Douglass, Feb. 11, 1884.

p. 322 *"lost in the past":* Martha Greene to Douglass, April 9, 1884.

p. 322 *in South Hadley:* Helen Pitts Douglass to Anna Edwards, April 29, 1884, Mount Holyoke College Archives, South Hadley, Mass.

p. 322 *"District of Columbia":* Helen Pitts Douglass to Anna Edwards, June 13, 1884, ibid.

p. 322 *swallowed its contents:* See Paris City Morgue Register No. 64, 1884, p. 111.

p. 322 *"will please him":* Ottilia Assing, Will, Codicil, and Inventory, 1885, 4425 "I," Hudson County, Department of State, Division of Archives and Records Management, Trenton, N.J. When Douglass died, the principal of the trust fund, the largest part of Assing's estate, was to go to the American Society for the Prevention of Cruelty to Animals.

p. 323 *"and good wishes":* Douglass to Amy Post, Aug. 27, 1884.

CHAPTER 24

p. 324 *"soft blue sky":* Douglass to Lewis H. Douglass, Feb. 20, 1887.

p. 324 *"off the steamer":* Helen Pitts Douglass, Diary, Sept. 14, 1886, Frederick Douglass Collection, Library of Congress, Reel 1.

p. 324 *"I slept all night":* Ibid.

p. 324 *"to a funeral":* Douglass, Diary, Sept. 15, 1886, Frederick Douglass Collection, Library of Congress, Reel 1.

p. 325 *"by our presence":* Ibid., Sept. 18 and Sept. 16, 1886.

p. 325 *"smell of mugwumpery":* Helen Pitts Douglass, Diary, Sept. 14, 1886.

p. 325 *"dark green plush":* Ibid.

p. 325 *for his tour:* Douglass, Diary, Sept. 19 and Sept. 20, 1886.

p. 325 *"forty-one years ago":* Helen Pitts Douglass, Diary, Sept. 22, 1886.

p. 325 *"tower on Nantucket":* Ibid., Sept. 24, 1886.

p. 325 *"heart breaking strains":* Douglass, Diary, Sept. 23, 1886.

p. 326 *"a struggle here":* Helen Pitts Douglass, Diary, Sept. 24, 1886.

p. 326 *"the working people":* Douglass, Diary, Sept. 22, 1886.

p. 326 *"appearance of interest":* Helen Pitts Douglass, Diary, Sept. 25, 1886.

p. 326 *"go to St. Neots":* Douglass, Diary, Sept. 24, 1886.

p. 326 *"real English home":* Helen Pitts Douglass, Diary, Oct. 1, 1886.

p. 326 *"Frederick (the trio)":* Ibid., Oct. 2, 1886.

p. 326 *"of popular prejudice":* Douglass to J. D. Husbands, Jan. 12, 1888.

p. 327 *"Wesleyan meeting":* Helen Pitts Douglass, Diary, Oct. 3, 1886.

p. 327 *"the vaulted roof":* Ibid., Oct. 4, 1886.

p. 327 *"and less drunkedness":* Douglass to Lewis H. Douglass, Nov. 7, 1886.

p. 327 *"the French Colonies":* Douglass to "Dear Friends Hayden and Watson," Nov. 19, 1887 [actually 1886], *Amistad* 3 (Aug. 1985).

p. 328 *"all our little circle":* Douglass to Lewis H. Douglass, Nov. 7, 1886.

p. 328 *"for his race":* Douglass to "Dear Friends Hayden and Watson," Nov. 19, 1887 [1886].

p. 328 *"save my boots":* Douglass to Theodore Stanton, Jan. 13, 1887, in *Independent,* May 23, 1895.

p. 328 *"by Alex. Dumas":* Douglass, Diary, Jan. 7, Jan. 10, Jan. 11, and Jan. 13, 1887.

p. 329 *"impaired her English":* Ibid., Jan. 25, 1887.

p. 329 *"and powerful slaveholders":* Ibid., Jan. 28, Jan. 31, and Feb. 4, 1887.

p. 330 *"permitted to visit":* Ibid., Feb. 11 and Feb. 13, 1887.

p. 330 *"ladies on board":* Ibid., Feb. 14, 1887.

p. 330 *"queer places":* Ibid., Feb. 16, 1887.

p. 330 *"not yet won":* Douglass to [?], in *Christian Recorder,* Feb. 10, 1887.

p. 330 *"to study ethnology":* Douglass, Diary, Feb. 16, 1887.

p. 330 *"or physical ability":* Ibid.

p. 330 *"kind of work":* Douglass to Lewis H. Douglass, Feb. 20, 1887.

p. 331 *"thousand years ago":* Douglass, Diary, Feb. 16, 1887.

p. 331 *"faith of the prophet":* Ibid., Feb. 17, 1887.

p. 331 *"no body was hurt":* Ibid., Feb. 18, 1887.

p. 332 *"to the white race":* Douglass to Lewis H. Douglass, Feb. 20, 1887.
p. 332 *"in the United States":* Ibid.
p. 332 *"to have it so":* Douglass, Diary, Feb. 18, 1887.
p. 332 *"Mountains of Sparta":* Ibid., March 19, 1887.
p. 333 *"with her call":* Ibid.
p. 333 *"by Othello":* Ibid.
p. 333 *"no snobbery about her":* Douglass to Amy Post, June 10, 1887.
p. 333 *"early training":* Laura Hayes, quoted in Jeanne Madeline Weimann, *The Fair Women* (Chicago, 1981), 108.
p. 333 *separation "bravely":* Douglass to Amy Post, June 10, 1887.

CHAPTER 25

p. 334 *"good ship Kearsarge":* Helen Pitts Douglass to "Dear Ones," Oct. 12, 1889, Yale University Frederick Douglass Papers.
p. 334 *was not seasick:* See Douglass to Lewis H. Douglass, Oct. 7, 1889.
p. 334 *into the harbor:* Helen Pitts Douglass to "Dear Ones," Oct. 12, 1889, Yale University Frederick Douglass Papers.
p. 334 *"at us the while":* Ibid.
p. 335 *a cabinet post:* See Willard B. Gatewood, Jr., "Frederick Douglass in Arkansas," *Arkansas Historical Quarterly* 41 (Winter 1982): 303–15; and Douglass to Helen Pitts Douglass, Feb. 4, 1889.
p. 335 *his old post back:* See Ebenezer D. Bassett to Douglass, March 6, 1889.
p. 335 *"than Black":* Jeremiah E. Rankin to Douglass, April 22, 1889.
p. 335 *"Excellency, the President":* See Douglass to James G. Blaine, June 25, 1889.
p. 335 *the minister's house:* See Nancy Gordon Heinl, "Ebenezer Don Carlos Bassett," in Logan and Winston, eds., *Dictionary of American Negro Biography,* 32.
p. 336 *could carry out:* Stephen Preston, quoted in Ebenezer D. Bassett to Douglass, July 11, 1889.
p. 336 *to accept it:* See Martha Greene to Douglass, July 8, 1889; Julia Griffiths Crofts to Douglass, July 17, 1889; and Ebenezer D. Bassett to Douglass, June 27, 1889.
p. 337 *the Légitime government:* See Rayford W. Logan, *The Diplomatic Relations of the United States with Haiti, 1776–1891* (1941; reprint, New York, 1969), 426.
p. 337 *into the country:* See ibid., 433–34.
p. 338 *in full command:* Ebenezer D. Bassett to Douglass, Aug. 27, 1889.
p. 338 *"vive Haiti!":* Ebenezer D. Bassett to Douglass, July 11, 1889.
p. 338 *to Haiti:* Stephen Preston, quoted in Ebenezer D. Bassett to Douglass, Sept. 2, 1889.
p. 339 *"of General Hypolite":* William P. Clyde to Douglass, Sept. 30, 1889.
p. 339 *Lucie Villa:* Helen Pitts Douglass to "Dear Ones," Oct. 12, 1889, Yale University Frederick Douglass Papers.
p. 340 *"where it belongs":* Amelia Loguen Douglass to Helen Pitts Douglass, Feb. 2, 1890, ibid.
p. 340 *from one another:* See David Nicholls, *From Dessalines to Duvalier: Race, Colour, and National Independence in Haiti* (Cambridge, Eng., 1979).
p. 341 *would prove able:* Douglass to James G. Blaine, Oct. 31, 1889, in Norma Brown, *A Black Diplomat in Haiti: The Diplomatic Correspondence of U.S. Minister Frederick Douglass from Haiti, 1889–1891,* 2 vols. (Salisbury, N.C., 1977), 1:24.
p. 341 *by Hannibal Price:* See Douglass to James G. Blaine, Nov. 9, 1889, in ibid., 26.
p. 341 *"not to be trifled with":* Douglass to James G. Blaine, Nov. 18, 1889, in ibid., 34, 35.
p. 341 *"in Haitien circles":* Douglass to James G. Blaine, Dec. 9, 1889, in ibid., 58.
p. 342 *on December 14:* See Douglass to James G. Blaine, Dec. 14, 1889, in ibid., 71–74.
p. 342 *nearby in Jamaica:* Douglass to James G. Blaine, Dec. 20, 1889, in ibid., 87.
p. 342 *"stability" and "peace":* Douglass to James G. Blaine, Jan. 17, 1890, in ibid., 131, 132.
p. 342 *"evidence of discontent":* Douglass to James G. Blaine, Feb. 20, 1890, in ibid., 141.
p. 342 *was dying:* Nathan Sprague to Douglass, Nov. 29, 1889.

p. 342 *"like a hospital":* Rosetta Douglass Sprague to Douglass, Feb. 6, 1890.
p. 342 *"Virginia was my all":* Frederick Douglass, Jr., to Helen Pitts Douglass, Jan. 31, 1890.
p. 343 *"of the Holy See":* Douglass to James G. Blaine, March 5, 1890, in Brown, *Black Diplomat* 1:146, 145, 147.
p. 343 *"favorable to peace":* Douglass to James G. Blaine, March 13, 1890, in ibid., 154, 155, 156.
p. 343 *had been picked up:* See Douglass to James G. Blaine, May 14, 1890, in ibid., 169–74.
p. 343 *Hyppolite's government:* See Douglass to James G. Blaine, July 16, 1890, in ibid., 2:25–28.
p. 344 *dictator on its hands:* Douglass to James G. Blaine, May 28, 1890, in ibid., 1:195, 196.
p. 344 *on July 20:* See Douglass to James G. Blaine, June 6, 1890, in ibid., 215–17.
p. 344 *recognized the Hyppolite government:* See Douglass to James G. Blaine, July 16, 1890, in ibid., 2:34–35.
p. 344 *"the next twenty days":* James G. Blaine to Douglass, Oct. 3, 1890.

CHAPTER 26

p. 347 *"ordinance of God":* Stephen Bleecker Luce, "The Benefits of War," *North American Review,* 153 (Dec. 1891): 672, 680, 683.
p. 347 *"escape being hit":* Helen Pitts Douglass, "Haiti," Frederick Douglass Collection, Library of Congress, Reel 1.
p. 348 *any European power:* Ebenezer D. Bassett to Douglass, Sept. 2, 1889.
p. 348 *"disturb my equanimity":* Douglass, "Haïti and the United States: Inside History of the Negotiations for the Môle St. Nicolas," Part I, *North American Review* 153 (Sept. 1891): 341.
p. 348 *to the* Philadelphia*:* See Douglass to James G. Blaine, Jan. 29, 1891, in Brown, *Black Diplomat* 2:57–65.
p. 348 *"in recognizing it":* Douglass, "Haïti and the United States," Part I, 341.
p. 348 *"me to expect":* Ibid., 342.
p. 349 *"the admiral's address":* Ibid., 343.
p. 349 *"autonomy of Haïti":* Ibid., 343–44.
p. 349 *"with courage":* Ibid., 344.
p. 349 *victory over Légitime:* Ibid.
p. 350 *"not ashamed":* Ibid., 344–45.
p. 350 *a naval station:* In his letter to the secretary of state three days after the meeting, Douglass said that he and Gherardi together would prepare the lease. (See Douglass to James G. Blaine, Jan. 29, 1891, in Brown, *Black Diplomat* 2:57–65.)
p. 350 *"my full approval":* Douglass, "Haïti and the United States," Part II, 450.
p. 350 *"a sudden halt":* Ibid., 450–51.
p. 350 *"amazingly inaccurate":* Douglass to James G. Blaine, April 20, 1891, in Brown, *Black Diplomat* 2:93–94.
p. 351 *"and without conditions":* Douglass, "Haïti and the United States," Part II, 452.
p. 351 *"lease of Môle":* Douglass to James G. Blaine, April 23, 1891, in Brown, *Black Diplomat* 2:106.
p. 352 *for the arsenal:* Douglass to James G. Blaine, May 30, 1891, in ibid., 149.
p. 352 *confronting the rebels:* New York Sun, July 10, 1891.
p. 352 *led the massacre:* Douglass, quoted in *New York Sun,* July 4, 1891.
p. 352 *"those they loved":* Helen Pitts Douglass, "Haiti."
p. 352 *"get out of here":* New York Sun, July 8, 1891.
p. 352 *"were not blamed":* Ibid.
p. 353 *head of state:* See *New York Sun,* July 7 and July 8, 1891; and Douglass to James G. Blaine, with enclosures, June 17, 1891, in Brown, *Black Diplomat* 2:155–203.
p. 353 *"fear of Hyppolite":* New York Sun, June 19, 1891.
p. 354 *"stranger never sees":* New York Herald, Sept. 18, 1891.
p. 354 *"forgotten his duties":* New York Sun, June 19, 1891.

p. 354 *"intelligent darkey"*: Helen Pitts Douglass, "Haiti."
p. 354 *"lead to peace"*: Ibid.
p. 355 *"to be taken"*: Logan, *Relations of the United States with Haiti,* 456–57.
p. 355 *"of the Gulf"*: New York Sun, June 30, 1891.
p. 356 *"up for Haiti"*: Ebenezer D. Bassett to Douglass, July 14, 1891.
p. 356 *" 'monster' Hyppolite"*: Anna Gardner to Douglass, July 18, 1891.
p. 356 *for office furniture*: See T. Thomas Fortune to Douglass, May 22, 1891.
p. 356 *as his replacement*: Ebenezer D. Bassett to Douglass, Aug. 1 1891.
p. 356 *"towards the President"*: Douglass to William F. Wharton, acting secretary of state, July 30, 1891, in Brown, *Black Diplomat* 2:237.
p. 356 *a "yellow man"*: New York Herald, Sept. 18, 1891.
p. 357 *and the United States*: Antenor Firmin to Douglass, Oct. 22, 1891.
p. 357 *"friend Charles Sumner"*: Douglass, "Haïti and the United States," Part I, 340.
p. 357 *who need defending*: Ibid., 337, 338.
p. 358 *"at defiance"*: Ibid., 338.

CHAPTER 27

p. 359 *discovery of America*: See Secretary of State (of the Republic of Haiti) to Douglass, Feb. 11, 1892.
p. 359 *granddaughter Estelle*: Douglass to Booker T. Washington, Nov. 20, 1891.
p. 360 *"its ancient moorings"*: Douglass to Marshall Pierce, Feb. 18, 1892.
p. 360 *"all around us"*: Ibid.
p. 360 *"and unattractive"*: Douglass to DeWolfe, Fisk, & Co., Nov. 18, 1892.
p. 361 *on the subject*: See W. B. Franklin to Douglass, May 12, 1892.
p. 361 *"without a trial"*: Douglass, "Lynch Law in the South," *North American Review* 155 (July 1892): 17.
p. 361 *"imputed to him"*: Ibid., 23.
p. 361 *"likely to commit"*: Ibid.
p. 361 *"and respectability"*: Ibid., 21, 23.
p. 361 *from the North*: Ibid., 23–24.
p. 362 *"rise to Heaven"*: Douglass to Ida B. Wells, Oct. 25, 1892, published as preface to Ida B. Wells, *Southern Horrors,* pamphlet (New York, 1892), 3.
p. 362 *"being so themselves"*: Douglass, quoted in Wells, *Crusade for Justice,* 69, 72.
p. 362 *"teeth for souvenirs"*: Wells, *Crusade for Justice,* 84.
p. 363 *"encounter opposition"*: Bulletin of Atlanta University, 38 (June 1892), 8.
p. 363 *"and your country"*: Ibid.
p. 363 *"a fair chance"*: E. W. Blake, "An Account of the Tuskegee Institute Commencement," *Southern Workman* 21 (July 1892), in Louis Harlan, ed., *The Booker T. Washington Papers,* 14 vols. (Urbana, Ill., 1972–89), 3:231.
p. 363 *"old man" undeniable*: Douglass to "Mrs. Walters" [Katie Knox Walters?], June 11, 1892.
p. 363 *"and for always"*: "Friends" from Terrebonne, La., to Douglass, [June 1892].
p. 364 *reelection in 1892*: See James D. Brady to Douglass, June 17, 1892.
p. 364 *in the years 1890–92*: See James Russell Duncan, Jr., "Rufus Brown Bullock, Reconstruction, and the 'New South,' 1834–1907: An Exploration into Race, Class, Party, and the Corruption of the American Creed" (Ph.D. diss., University of Georgia, 1988), 286.
p. 364 *"plan of campaign"*: Douglass to J. C. Dancy, open letter, in "Cleveland's Election and Its Effect upon the Future of the Negro," *A.M.E. Zion Quarterly Review* 3 (1892–93): 166–69.
p. 365 *"if she tried"*: Estelle Sprague to Douglass, April 3, 1893.
p. 365 *"than I can stand"*: Sam Small, address to Populist convention, quoted in unidentified newspaper (clipping lacks newspaper name and date but has been marked "July 20, 1892").
p. 365 *after a lingering illness*: See Henry O. Waggoner to Douglass, Aug. 9, 1892.
p. 365 *had been working*: See M. L. Robinson to Douglass, July 26, 1892.

p. 365 *at fourteen:* Strangely, the boy's full name appears to have been Frederick Aaron Douglass; no explanation has been found for the surprising middle name. See Frederick Douglass Collection, Library of Congress, Reel 27.

p. 365 *in his stead:* E. M. Hewlitt to Douglass, Feb. 22, 1893.

p. 366 *expense allowances:* See, for example, Douglass to Charles A. Preston, June 4, 1892.

p. 366 *the Haitian pavilion:* See A. M. Lewis to Douglass, Jan. 2, 1893.

p. 367 *"be duly obligated":* Fannie Barrier Williams to Albion W. Tourgée, Jan. 14, 1893, quoted in Rossiter Johnson, ed., *A History of the World's Columbian Exposition Held in Chicago in 1893,* 4 vols. (New York, 1897–98), 4:76.

p. 367 *government had put it:* Secretary of State (of the Republic of Haiti) to Douglass, Feb. 11, 1892.

p. 368 *"evolution of man":* Harlan Ingersoll Smith, quoted in Robert W. Rydell, *All the World's a Fair* (Chicago, 1984), 57.

p. 368 *"anthropological revelation":* Otis T. Mason, quoted in ibid., 55.

p. 368 *"Nubians and Sudanese":* Isaac Benyakar to Douglass, July 20, 1893.

p. 368 *"the Mayalo-Polynesian":* Otis T. Mason, quoted in Rydell, *World's a Fair,* 59.

p. 369 *"the Columbian Exposition":* *Cleveland Gazette* and *New York Age,* quoted in ibid., 52.

p. 369 *"there assembled":* Douglass and Ida B. Wells, "To the Friends of Equal Rights," open letter, *Baltimore Afro-American,* April 29, 1893.

p. 369 *the "whited sepulcher":* Douglass and Ida B. Wells, quoted in Rydell, *World's a Fair,* 52.

p. 369 *he had blown away:* See W. E. Curtis to Douglass, July 18, 1892; and Mrs. Epes Sargent to Douglass, May 9, 1892.

p. 369 *of curious tourists:* Wells, *Crusade for Justice,* 116.

p. 369 *"as a unity":* Henry Adams, *The Education of Henry Adams* (1918; reprint, Boston, 1973), 343.

p. 370 *"Fair ground gates":* Fredericka Sprague to Douglass, July 20, 1893.

p. 371 *"Apparently Not Interested":* Virginia Cunningham, *Paul Laurence Dunbar and His Song* (New York, 1969), 102.

p. 371 *"a penny whistle":* Ibid., 103.

p. 371 *"fought against it":* Douglass, quoted in ibid., 103, 104.

p. 371 *"during the fair":* Wells, *Crusade for Justice,* 119.

p. 372 *"stopping to rest":* Haley George Douglass to Douglass, Aug. 17, 1893.

p. 372 *"enough to go around":* Charles R. Douglass to Douglass, May 15, 1893.

p. 372 *terrible loneliness:* See Annie Sprague Morris to Douglass, April 3, 1893.

p. 372 *pregnant and ill.* See Fredericka Sprague to Douglass, July 5, 1893.

p. 373 *wife would recover:* Charles S. Morris to Douglass, Oct. 3, 1893.

p. 373 *"dazed and crushed":* Rosetta Douglass Sprague to Douglass, Nov. 11, 1893.

p. 373 *"she shouldn't travel":* Rosetta Douglass Sprague to Douglass, Nov. 27, 1893.

p. 373 *lecture tour ended:* Helen Pitts Douglass to Douglass, Nov. 27, 1893.

p. 373 *with russets:* See Charles R. Douglass to Douglass, Oct. 4, 1893.

p. 373 *"our younger days":* Douglass to Ruth Adams, March 9, 1894.

p. 373 *"hold out much longer":* Douglass to Ruth Adams, March 20, 1894.

p. 374 *"land of the living":* Ibid.

CHAPTER 28

p. 375 *"no such thing":* "Shun Tammany" to Douglass, Aug. 13, 1893.

p. 376 *"signature authorized":* "Petition to the World Congress at Chicago," received June 12, 1893, Yale University Frederick Douglass Papers.

p. 376 *looked forward to:* Wells, *Crusade for Justice,* 120.

p. 378 *"the whole country":* Frederick Douglass, *The Lessons of the Hour* (Baltimore, 1894), 3, 4.

p. 378 *white Southern shoulders:* See Douglass, "Lynch Law in the South."

p. 378 *"caused by terror":* Douglass, *Lessons,* 6.

p. 378 *many more burnings:* Atticus G. Haygood, quoted in ibid., 7.

p. 378 *"the infamous crime":* Daniel Henry Chamberlain, quoted in ibid., 7.

p. 379 *"own roof tree":* Douglass, *Lessons,* 7.

p. 379 *"mantle of odium":* Ibid., 7–8.

p. 379 *"charge against him":* Ibid., 9.

p. 379 *"Congresses at Chicago":* Ibid., 10.

p. 380 *"of Southern barbarism":* Ibid., 13–14.

p. 380 *"entire disfranchisement":* Ibid., 15.

p. 380 *"both wrong":* Ibid., 20.

p. 380 *"a party of morals":* Ibid., 23–24.

p. 380 *"Caucasian blood":* Ibid., 26.

p. 381 *"hooks of steel":* Ibid., 28.

p. 381 *false, pernicious:* Ibid., 29.

p. 381 *"of the war":* Ibid., 32.

p. 381 *"will be solved":* Ibid., 33.

p. 381 *"rule over another":* Ibid., 36.

p. 381 *"does not grow old":* Isabel Somerset, "Hail and Farewell to Frederick Douglas," *The Woman's Signal* (London), March 14, 1895.

p. 382 *"at the funeral":* John W. Hutchinson to Helen Pitts Douglass, Feb. 22, 1895, Yale University Frederick Douglass Papers.

p. 382 *"has fallen":* Robert Smalls to Helen Pitts Douglass, Feb. 21, 1895, ibid.

p. 382 *"takes four days":* Henry O. Waggoner to Helen Pitts Douglass, Feb. 21, 1895, ibid.

p. 382 *"go to heaven":* Hudson, Journal, Aug. 26, 1845.

p. 383 *"majestic in his wrath":* Stanton and Blatch, eds., *Stanton* 2:311.

CHAPTER 29

p. 385 *"fugitive slave":* Douglass to James Redpath, July 29, 1871.

p. 386 *quotation marks:* Douglass, *Narrative,* 66.

p. 386 *"the Chesapeake Bay!":* Julia Griffiths Crofts to Douglass, Nov. 25, 1865.

p. 386 *"I'll try it":* Douglass, *Narrative,* 66.

Bibliography

ARCHIVES

The chief source of Douglass material—letters, manuscripts of speeches, and the like—is the Frederick Douglass Collection in the Library of Congress, available on microfilm in fifty-two reels. In addition, photostatic copies of Douglass's correspondence have been generously supplied by archivists in the United States, the United Kingdom, and Ireland to the Yale University Frederick Douglass Papers, now being prepared for publication. The following archives and collections have also been useful.

AMHERST, MASSACHUSETTS
University of Massachusetts library
  Susan B. Anthony Papers
  Erasmus Darwin Hudson Manuscript Journal

ANNAPOLIS, MARYLAND
Maryland Hall of Records
  State and county records
  Records of the Sharp Street African Methodist Episcopal Church

BALTIMORE, MARYLAND
City records office
Maryland Historical Society

BOSTON, MASSACHUSETTS
Boston Public Library
  American Anti-Slavery Collection
  William Lloyd Garrison Papers
  Thomas Wentworth Higginson Papers
  Weston Sisters Letters

CAMBRIDGE, MASSACHUSETTS
Houghton Library, Harvard University

  Thomas Wentworth Higginson Papers
  Franklin B. Sanborn Papers
  Charles Sumner Papers
Schlesinger Library, Harvard University
  Harriet Beecher Stowe Papers

DUBLIN, IRELAND
Irish National Library
  City Directory Collection

KRAKÓW, POLAND
Jagiellonian University library
  Varnhagen Collection (Ottilie Assing Papers, photostatic copies)

LONDON, ENGLAND
Dr. Williams Library
  Bristol and Clifton Auxiliary Ladies Anti-Slavery Papers
Friends Historical Collection

NANTUCKET, MASSACHUSETTS
Foulger Library, Nantucket Historical Association

NEW BEDFORD, MASSACHUSETTS
New Bedford Public Library
Old Dartmouth Historical Society, Whaling Museum

ROCHESTER, NEW YORK
University of Rochester library
   Porter Family Papers
   Post Family Papers
   Rochester Ladies' Anti-Slavery Society Papers

SOUTH HADLEY, MASSACHUSETTS
Mount Holyoke College Archives

SYRACUSE, NEW YORK
Syracuse University
   Gerrit Smith Papers

WASHINGTON, D.C.
National Archives

WORCESTER, MASSACHUSETTS
American Antiquarian Society
   Brown Family Papers
   Abigail Kelley Foster Papers

NEWSPAPERS

The Alpha (Washington, D.C.)
Anti-Caste (Somersetshire, England)
The Awl (Lynn, Mass.)
Baltimore Afro-American
Baltimore Sun
Bangor (Maine) *Daily Whig and Courier*
Boston Daily Globe
Christian Recorder (Philadelphia)
Cleveland Gazette
Cleveland Leader
Essex County (Mass.) *Whig*
Independent
Inquirer and Mirror (Nantucket, Mass.)
The Liberator (Boston)
Morgenblatt fuer gebildete Staende (Frankfurt, Germany)

National Republican (Washington, D.C.)
New Era (Washington, D.C.)
New York Herald
New York Sun
New York Times
New York Tribune
Philadelphia Evening Bulletin
Rochester Courier
Rochester Democrat and Chronicle
Rochester Union and Advertiser
Seneca County Courier (Seneca Falls, N.Y.)
Syracuse Standard
Washington Bee
Washington Evening Star
Weekly Monitor (Fort Scott, Kans.)

SELECTED WRITINGS OF FREDERICK DOUGLASS

AUTOBIOGRAPHIES

Narrative of the Life of Frederick Douglass, an American Slave, Written by Himself. Boston: Anti-Slavery Office, 1845.

Narrative of the Life of Frederick Douglass, an American Slave. Dublin: Webb and Chapman, 1845.

Narrative of the Life of Frederick Douglass, an American Slave. Wortley, near Leeds, Engl.: J. Barker, 1846.

Narrative of the Life of Frederick Douglass, an American Slave. London: R. Yorke and Co., 1847.

Vie de Frédéric Douglass, esclave américain, écrite par lui-même. Translated by S. K. Parkes. Paris: Pagnerre, 1848.

My Bondage and My Freedom. New York and Auburn, N.Y.: Miller, Orton & Mulligan, 1855.

Sklaverei und Freiheit: Autobiographie von Frederick Douglass. Translated by Ottilie Assing. Hamburg: Hoffmann and Campe, 1860.

Life and Times of Frederick Douglass, Written by Himself. Hartford, Conn.: Park Publishing Co., 1881.

Life and Times of Frederick Douglass, Written by Himself: His early life as a slave, his escape from bondage, and his complete history to the present time. New rev. ed. Boston: DeWolfe, Fisk, & Co., [1892].

NOVELLA
"The Heroic Slave." In Julia Griffiths, ed. *Autographs for Freedom.* Boston, 1853.

JOURNALS
North Star (Rochester, N.Y.), 1847–51.
Frederick Douglass' Paper (Rochester, N.Y.), 1851–60.
Douglass' Monthly (Rochester, N.Y.), 1859–63; issues prior to January 1859 were supplements to *Frederick Douglass' Paper.*
New National Era (Washington, D.C.), 1870–74.

ARTICLES AND SPEECHES
Address by Frederick Douglass, Formerly a Slave to the People of the United States of America. [Edinburgh: H. Armour, 185?].
"The American Apocalypse," Rochester, N.Y., June 16, 1861. In Blassingame et al., eds., *Frederick Douglass Papers* 3:435–45.
"The American Constitution and the Slave," Glasgow, Scotland, March 26, 1860. In Blassingame et al., eds., *Frederick Douglass Papers* 3:340–66.
The Anti-Slavery Movement: A Lecture by Frederick Douglass before the Rochester Ladies' Anti-Slavery Society. Rochester, N.Y.: Lee, Mann & Co., 1855.
"Capital Punishment Is a Mockery of Justice," Rochester, N.Y., Oct. 7, 1858. In Blassingame et al., eds., *Frederick Douglass Papers* 3:242–48.
The Claims of the Negro Ethnologically Considered: an Address before the Literary Societies of Western Reserve College, at Commencement, July 12, 1854. Rochester, N.Y.: Lee, Mann & Co., 1854.
The Constitution of the United States: Is It Pro-Slavery or Anti-Slavery? [Halifax, England: T. and W. Birtwhistle, 1860?].
"The Douglass Institute," Baltimore, Sept. 29, 1865. In Foner, *Writings of Douglass* 4:174–82.
"The Equality of All Men before the Law Claimed and Defended." In *Speeches by Hon. William D. Kelley, Wendell Phillips, and Frederick Douglass, and Letters from Elizur Wright and Wm. Heighton.* Boston: Press of G. C. Rand & Avery, 1865.
"Fighting the Rebels with One Hand," Philadelphia, Jan. 14, 1862. In Blassingame et al., eds., *Frederick Douglass Papers* 3:473–88.
"Haïti and the United States: Inside History of the Negotiations for the Môle St. Nicolas," Parts I, II. *North American Review* 153 (Sept., Oct. 1891): 337–45, 450–59.
"Is the Plan of the American Union under the Constitution, Anti-Slavery or Not?" New York, May 20–21, 1857. In Blassingame et al., eds., *Frederick Douglass Papers* 3:151–162.
"John Brown and the Slaveholders' Insurrection," Edinburgh, Scotland, Jan. 30, 1860. In Blassingame et al., eds., *Frederick Douglass Papers* 3:312–22.
The Lessons of the Hour. Baltimore: Thomas & Evans, 1894.
"Letter to His Old Master." In Frederick Douglass, *My Bondage and My Freedom,* 421–28. New York, 1969.
"Lynch Law in the South." *North American Review* 155 (July 1892): 17–24.
"The Negro Exodus from the Gulf States." *Journal of Social Science* 11 (May 1880): 1–21.
"The Proclamation and a Negro Army," New York, Feb. 6, 1863. In Blassingame et al., eds., *Frederick Douglass Papers* 3:549–69.
"Reconstruction." *Atlantic Monthly* 18 (Dec. 1866): 761–65.
"The Revolution of 1848: Speech at West India Emancipation Celebration," Rochester, N.Y., Aug. 1, 1848. In Foner, *Writings of Douglass* 1:321–30.
"The Rights of Women," July 1848. In Foner, *Writings of Douglass* 1:320–21.
"The Slaveholders' Rebellion," New York, July 4, 1862. In Blassingame et al., eds., *Frederick Douglass Papers* 3:521–43.
"Slavery and the Irrepressible Conflict," Geneva, N.Y., Aug. 1, 1860. In Blassingame et al., eds., *Frederick Douglass Papers* 3:366–87.
"Slavery and the Limits of Nonintervention," Halifax, Eng., Dec. 7, 1859. In Blassingame et al., eds., *Frederick Douglass Papers* 3:276–88.

"Slavery, Freedom, and the Kansas-Nebraska Act," Chicago, Oct. 30, 1854. In Blassingame et al., eds., *Frederick Douglass Papers* 2:538–59.
"Speech at the Civil Rights Mass. Meeting," Washington, D.C., Oct. 22, 1883. In Foner, *Writings of Douglass* 4:392–403.
"Toussaint L'Ouverture: An Estimate by a Fellow African." *Independent* 55 (April 23, 1903): 945–49.
Two Speeches by Frederick Douglass; one on West India Emancipation, . . . ; the other on the Dred Scott Decision. . . . Rochester, N.Y.: C. P. Dewey, [1857].
"The War and How to End It," Rochester, N.Y., March 25, 1862. In Blassingame et al., eds., *Frederick Douglass Papers* 3:508–21.
"What I Found at the Northampton Association." In *The History of Florence, Massachusetts, including a Complete Account of the Northampton Association of Education and Industry,* edited by Charles A. Sheffeld. Florence, Mass., 1895.
"What to the Slave Is the Fourth of July?" (Fifth of July Speech). In Blassingame et al., eds., *Frederick Douglass Papers* 2:359–88. Separately published as *Oration, Delivered in Corinthian Hall, Rochester . . . July 5, 1852.* Rochester, N.Y.: Lee, Mann & Co., 1852.

BOOKS AND PAMPHLETS

Abels, Jules. *Man on Fire: John Brown and the Cause of Liberty.* New York, 1971.
Abzug, Robert H. *Passionate Liberator: Theodore Dwight Weld and the Dilemma of Reform.* New York, 1980.
Adams, Henry. *The Education of Henry Adams.* 1918. Reprint. Boston, 1973.
Aikin, Lucy. *Memoir of John Aikin, M.D.* Philadelphia, 1824.
Anacostia Neighborhood Museum, Smithsonian Institution. *The Frederick Douglass Years: A Cultural History Exhibition.* Washington, D.C., 1970.
Andersson, Charles John. *Lake Ngami; or, Explorations and Discoveries During Four Years' Wanderings in the Wilds of South Western Africa.* New York, 1857.
Andrews, Ethan Allen. *Slavery and the Domestic Slave Trade in the United States.* 1836. Facsimile ed., Freeport, N.Y., 1971.
Andrews, William L. *To Tell a Free Story: The First Century of Afro-American Autobiography, 1760–1865.* Urbana, Ill., 1986.
Arendt, Hannah. *Rahel Varnhagen: The Life of a Jewish Woman.* Translated by Richard Winston and Clara Winston. New York, 1974.
Armistead, Wilson. *A Tribute for the Negro.* Miami, 1969.
Atterbury, Anson P. *Islam in Africa.* 1899. Reprint. New York, 1969.
Ball, Milner S. *The Promise of American Law: A Theological, Humanistic View of Legal Process.* Athens, Ga., 1981.
––––––. *Lying Down Together: Law, Metaphor, and Theology.* Madison, Wis., 1985.
Ballou, Adin. *Autobiography of Adin Ballou.* Lowell, Mass., 1896.
Barnett, Ida B. Wells. (See Wells, Ida B.)
Barry, Kathleen. *Susan B. Anthony—A Biography: A Singular Feminist.* New York, 1988.
Bartlett, Irving H. *Wendell and Ann Phillips: The Community of Reform, 1840–1880.* New York, 1979.
––––––. *Wendell Phillips: Brahmin Radical.* Boston, 1961.
Basler, Roy P., et al., eds. *The Collected Works of Abraham Lincoln.* 8 vols. New Brunswick, N.J., 1953.
Bebler, Emil. *Gottfried Keller und Ludmilla Assing.* Zurich, 1952.
Berlin, Ira. *Slaves without Masters: The Free Negro in the Antebellum South.* New York, 1974.
Bingham, Caleb, comp. *The Columbian Orator: Containing a Variety of Original and Selected Pieces: Together with rules, calculated to improve youth and others in the ornamental and useful art of eloquence.* 18th ed. New York, 1816.
Blackett, R. J. M. *Building an Antislavery Wall: Black Americans in the Atlantic Abolitionist Movement, 1830–1860.* Baton Rouge, 1983.

Blaine, Harriet Bailey. *Letters of Mrs. James G. Blaine.* Edited by Harriet S. Blaine Beale. New York, 1908.

Blanchard, Paula. *Margaret Fuller: From Transcendentalism to Revolution.* New York, 1978.

Blassingame, John W. *The Clarion Voice.* Washington, D.C., 1976.

Blassingame, John W., et al., eds. *The Frederick Douglass Papers.* 3 vols. to date. New Haven, Conn., 1979–.

Blassingame, John W., and Mae G. Henderson, eds. *Antislavery Newspapers and Periodicals.* Boston, 1980.

Blight, David W. *Frederick Douglass' Civil War: Keeping Faith in Jubilee.* Baton Rouge, 1989.

Bontempts, Arna. *Free at Last: The Life of Frederick Douglass.* New York, 1971.

Bourne, George. *The Book and Slavery Irreconcilable.* Philadelphia, 1816.

Bowditch, Vincent Yardley. *Life and Correspondence of Henry Ingersoll Bowditch,* 2 vols. Boston, 1902.

Boyer, Richard O. *The Legend of John Brown: A Biography and a History.* New York, 1973.

Bragg, George Freeman. *History of the Afro-American Group of the Episcopal Church.* Baltimore, 1922.

Bragg, George Freeman. *Men of Maryland.* Baltimore, 1914.

Bremer, Fredrika. *The Homes of the New World: Impressions of America.* Translated by Mary Howitt. 2 vols. New York, 1853.

Brink, Carol. *Harps in the Wind: The Story of the Singing Hutchinsons.* New York, 1947.

Brown, Norma. *A Black Diplomat in Haiti: The Diplomatic Correspondence of U.S. Minister Frederick Douglass from Haiti, 1889–1891,* 2 vols. Salisbury, N.C., 1977.

Brown, Stewart J. *Thomas Chalmers and the Godly Commonwealth in Scotland.* New York, 1982.

Brown, William Wells. *The Negro in the American Rebellion: His Heroism and His Fidelity.* Boston, 1867.

Buchholz, Heinrich Ewald. *Governors of Maryland, from the Revolution to the Year 1908.* Baltimore, 1908.

Buckley, James M. *A History of Methodism in the United States.* 2 vols. New York, 1897.

Burchard, Peter. *One Gallant Rush: Robert Gould Shaw and his Brave Black Regiment.* New York, 1965.

Burton, Jean. *Lydia Pinkham Is Her Name.* New York, 1949.

Campbell, Stanley W. *The Slave Catchers: Enforcement of the Fugitive Slave Law, 1850–1860.* Chapel Hill, N.C., 1970.

Castel, Albert. *The Presidency of Andrew Johnson.* Lawrence, Kans., 1979.

Charnetzky, Jules, and Sidney Kaplan, eds. *Black and White in American Culture: An Anthology from* The Massachusetts Review. [Amherst, Mass.], 1969.

Chapman, John Jay. *Memories and Milestones.* New York, 1915.

———. *William Lloyd Garrison.* New York, 1913.

Chapelle, Howard I. *The Search for Speed under Sail, 1700–1855.* New York, 1967.

The Character of the Late Thomas Chalmers, D.D., LL.D., and the Lesson of His Life. Pamphlet. Charleston, S.C., 1848.

Chesnutt, Charles W. *Frederick Douglass.* Boston, 1899.

———. *The Wife of His Youth and Other Stories of the Color Line.* Ridgewood, N.J., 1967.

City of Lynn, Massachusetts, Semi-Centennial of Incorporation. Events and Exercises of the 50th Anniversary Celebration. Lynn, Mass., 1900.

Coles, Howard. *The Cradle of Freedom: A History of the Negro in Rochester, Western New York and Canada.* Rochester, N.Y., 1941.

Congdon, Charles. *Reminiscences of a Journalist.* Boston, 1880.

Cook, Charles. *A Brief Account of the African Christian Church, in New Bedford, Being the First of the Christian Denomination in the United States Formed by People of Colour.* New Bedford, Mass., 1834.

Cornish, Dudley. *The Sable Arm: Black Troops in the Union Army, 1861–1865.* New York, 1966.

Couser, G. Thomas. *American Autobiography: The Prophetic Mode.* Amherst, Mass., 1979.

Cover, Robert M. *Justice Accused: Antislavery and the Judicial Process.* New Haven, Conn., 1975.

Cox, LaWanda. *Lincoln and Black Freedom: A Study in Presidential Leadership.* Columbia, S.C., 1981.

Cromwell, Otelia. *Lucretia Mott.* Cambridge, Mass., 1958.

Cunningham, Virginia. *Paul Laurence Dunbar and His Song.* New York, 1969.

Daniels, William Haven. *The Illustrated History of Methodism in Great Britain and America, from the Days of the Wesleys to the Present Time.* New York, 1880.

Davis, Allison. *Leadership, Love, and Aggression.* San Diego, 1983.

Davis, Charles T., and Henry Louis Gates, Jr., eds. *The Slave's Narrative.* New York, 1985.

Davison, Kenneth E. *The Presidency of Rutherford B. Hayes.* Westport, CT, 1972.

Dawley, Alan. *Class and Community: The Industrial Revolution in Lynn.* Cambridge, Mass., 1976.

Dickens, Charles. *American Notes.* 1842. Reprint. New York, 1985.

Dillon, Merton L. *Benjamin Lundy and the Struggle for Negro Freedom.* Urbana, Ill., 1966.

Doenecke, Justus D. *The Presidencies of James A. Garfield and Chester A. Arthur.* Lawrence, Kans., 1981.

Donald, David H. *Charles Sumner and the Rights of Man.* New York, 1970.

Douglass, Helen Pitts, ed. *In Memoriam: Frederick Douglass.* 1897. Reprint. Freeport, N.Y., 1971.

Drago, Edmund. *Black Politicians and Reconstruction in Georgia: A Splendid Failure.* Baton Rouge, 1982.

Drake, Thomas E. *Quakers and Slavery in America.* Gloucester, Mass., 1965.

Drinkwater, John. *Abraham Lincoln, a Play.* London, 1918.

Duberman, Martin. *James Russell Lowell.* Boston, 1966.

DuBois, Ellen Carol. *Feminism and Suffrage: The Emergence of an Independent Women's Movement in America, 1848–1869.* Ithaca, N.Y., 1978.

Du Bois, W. E. B. *The Philadelphia Negro: A Social Study.* New York, 1967.

Duncan, Russell. *Freedom's Shore: Tunis Campbell and the Georgia Freedmen.* Athens, Ga., 1986.

Edelstein, Tilden G. *Strange Enthusiasm: A Life of Thomas Wentworth Higginson.* New Haven, Conn., 1968.

Elmes, James. *Thomas Clarkson: A Monograph, Being a Contribution towards the History of the Abolition of the Slave-Trade and Slavery.* London, 1854.

Emilio, Luis F. *History of the Fifty-fourth Regiment of Massachusetts Volunteer Infantry, 1863–1865.* Boston, 1891.

Faler, Paul G. *Mechanics and Manufacturers in the Early Industrial Revolution: Lynn, Massachusetts, 1780–1860.* Albany, N.Y., 1981.

Faulkner, William. *Absalom, Absalom!* New York, 1936.

Fehrenbacher, Don E. *Slavery, Law, and Politics: The Dred Scott Case in Historical Perspective.* New York, 1981.

Feuerbach, Ludwig. *The Essence of Christianity.* Translated from the 2d German edition by Marian Evans [George Eliot]. New York, 1855.

Fields, Annie. *Life and Letters of Harriet Beecher Stowe.* Boston, 1897.

Fields, Barbara Jeanne. *Slavery and Freedom on the Middle Ground: Maryland during the Nineteenth Century.* New Haven, Conn., 1985.

Finkelman, Paul. *An Imperfect Union: Slavery, Federalism, and Comity.* Chapel Hill, N.C., 1981.

———. *Slavery in the Courtroom: An Annotated Bibliography of American Cases.* Washington, D.C., 1985.

Fletcher, Robert S. *A History of Oberlin College from Its Foundation through the Civil War.* Oberlin, Ohio, 1943.

Foner, Eric. *Reconstruction: America's Unfinished Revolution, 1863–1877.* New York, 1988.

Foner, Philip S. *Frederick Douglass: A Biography.* New York, 1964.

———. *The Life and Writings of Frederick Douglass.* 4 vols. New York, 1950.

———, ed. *Frederick Douglass on Women's Rights.* Contributions in Afro-American and African Studies, No. 25. Westport, Conn., 1976.

Foote, Shelby. *The Civil War: A Narrative.* 3 vols. New York, 1958–74.

Forbes, Hugh. *Manual for the Patriotic Volunteer on Active Service in Regular and Irregular War. Being the art and science of obtaining and maintaining liberty and independence.* New York, 1855.

Forman, H. Chandlee. *Old Buildings, Gardens, and Furniture in Tidewater Maryland.* Cambridge, Md., 1967.

Forrest, Leon. *There Is a Tree More Ancient Than Eden.* New York, 1973.

Forten, Charlotte L. *The Journal of Charlotte Forten: A Free Negro in the Slave Era.* Edited by Ray Allen Billington. New York, 1981.

Fox, Early Lee. *The American Colonization Society, 1817–1840.* Baltimore, 1919.

Franklin, John Hope. *The Emancipation Proclamation.* Garden City, N.Y., 1963.

————. *George Washington Williams: A Biography.* Chicago, 1985.

Fredrickson, George M. *The Inner Civil War: Northern Intellectuals and the Crisis of the Union.* New York, 1965.

Frothingham, Octavius Brooks. *Gerrit Smith: A Biography.* 1878. Reprint. New York, 1969.

Garrison, Wendell Phillips, and Francis Jackson Garrison. *William Lloyd Garrison, 1805–1879: The Story of His Life Told by His Children.* 4 vols. New York, 1885–89.

Garrison, William Lloyd. *The Letters of William Lloyd Garrison.* Edited by Walter M. Merrill and Louis Ruchames. 6 vols. Cambridge, Mass., 1971–81.

Gates, Henry Louis. *The Signifying Monkey: A Theory of Afro-American Literary Criticism.* New York, 1988.

Gay, Peter. *The Bourgeois Experience: Victoria to Freud.* Vol. 1, *Education of the Senses.* New York, 1984. Vol. 2, *The Tender Passion.* New York, 1986.

Gerritt Smith and the Vigilant Association of the City of New York. Pamphlet, New York, 1860.

Gerteis, Louis. *Morality and Utility in American Antislavery Reform.* Chapel Hill, N.C. 1987.

Glatthaar, Joseph T. *Forged in Battle: The Civil War Alliance of Black Soldiers and White Officers.* New York, 1990.

Goodell, William. *Views of American Constitutional Law in Its Bearing upon American Slavery.* Utica, N.Y., 1844.

Graham, Leroy. *Baltimore: The Nineteenth Century Black Capital.* Washington, D.C., 1982.

Graham, Shirley. *There Was Once a Slave: The Heroic Story of Frederick Douglass.* New York, 1947.

Grant, Ulysses S. *The Papers of Ulysses S. Grant.* Edited by John Y. Simon. 16 vols. Carbondale, Ill., 1967–88.

Griffith, Elisabeth. *In Her Own Right: The Life of Elizabeth Cady Stanton.* New York, 1984.

Griffiths, Julia, ed. *Autographs for Freedom.* Boston, 1853.

Haight, Gordon, ed. *Selections from George Eliot's Letters.* New Haven, Conn., 1985.

Hall, Robert L., and Carol B. Stack, eds. *Holding on to the Land and the Lord: Kinship, Ritual, Land Tenure, and Social Policy in the Rural South.* Athens, Ga., 1982.

Hallowell, Anna Davis. *James and Lucretia Mott: Life and Letters.* Boston, 1884.

Harlan, Louis. *Booker T. Washington: The Making of a Black Leader, 1856–1901.* New York, 1972.

————. *Booker T. Washington: The Wizard of Tuskegee, 1901–1915.* New York, 1983.

————, ed. *The Booker T. Washington Papers.* 14 vols. Urbana, Ill. 1972–89.

Harlow, Ralph Volney. *Gerritt Smith: Philanthropist and Reformer.* New York, 1939.

Harrison, Benjamin. *The Correspondence between Benjamin Harrison and James G. Blaine, 1882–1893.* Edited by Albert T. Volwiler. Philadelphia, 1940.

Harrold, Stanley. *Gamaliel Bailey and Antislavery Union.* Kent, Ohio, 1986.

Hewitt, Nancy A. *Women's Activism and Social Change: Rochester, New York, 1822–1872.* Ithaca, N.Y., 1984.

Hill, Errol. *Shakespeare in Sable: A History of Black Shakespearean Actors.* Amherst, 1984.

Hill, Samuel S., ed. *Encyclopedia of Religion in the South.* Macon, Ga., 1984.

Hinton, John Howard. *The History and Topography of the United States.* London, 1830–32.

Hobbs, Clarence W. *Lynn and Surroundings.* Lynn, Mass., 1886.

Holland, Frederic May. *Frederick Douglass: The Colored Orator.* New York, 1891.

Holland, Patricia G., and Ann D. Gordon, eds., *Papers of Elizabeth Cady Stanton and Susan B. Anthony.* Wilmington, Del.: Wilmington Scholarly Resources, 1989.

Hood, James W. *One Hundred Years of the African Methodist Episcopal Church.* New York, 1895.

Howitt, Mary. *Mary Howitt: An Autobiography.* Edited by Margaret Howitt. London, 1889.

Huggins, Nathan Irvin. *Slave and Citizen: The Life of Frederick Douglass.* Boston, 1980.

Humanus [pseud.]. *An Appeal to the Members of the Free Church on the Subject of Fellowship with Slaveholders.* Aberdeen, Scotland, 1846.

Hutchinson, John Wallace. *Story of the Hutchinsons (Tribe of Jesse).* Edited by Charles E. Mann. 2 vols. 1896. Reprint. New York, 1977.

Hutchinson, Louis Daniel. *The Anacostia Story, 1608–1930.* Washington, D.C., 1977.

James, Henry. *Partial Portraits.* Introduction by Henry Nash Smith. London, 1888.

Johannsen, Robert W. *Stephen A. Douglas.* New York, 1973.

Johnson, David N. *Sketches of Lynn; or, The Changes of Fifty Years.* Lynn, Mass., 1880.

Johnson, Michael P., and James L. Roark. *Black Masters: A Free Family of Color in the Old South.* New York, 1984.

Johnson, Paul E. *A Shopkeeper's Millennium: Society and Revivals in Rochester, New York, 1815–1837.* New York, 1978.

Johnson, Rossiter, ed. *A History of the World's Columbian Exposition Held in Chicago in 1893.* 4 vols. New York, 1897–98.

Joyner, Charles. *Remember Me: Slave Life in Coastal Georgia.* Atlanta, 1989.

Kaplan, Sidney, and Emma Nogrady Kaplan. *The Black Presence in the Era of the American Revolution, 1770–1800.* Rev. ed. Amherst, Mass., 1989.

Keckley, Elizabeth. *Behind the Scenes: Thirty Years a Slave, and Four Years in the White House.* 1868. Reprint. New York, 1968.

Keegan, John. *The Mask of Command.* New York, 1987.

[Kelley, Jesse Fillmore]. *History of the New Bedford Churches.* New Bedford, Mass., 1854.

———. *History of the Churches of New Bedford: To Which Are Added Notices of Various Other Moral and Religious Organizations.* New Bedford, Mass., 1869.

Kent, James. *Commentaries on American Law.* 4 vols. New York, 1826–30.

Konvitz, Milton, and Stephen Whicher, eds. *Emerson: A Collection of Critical Essays.* Twentieth Century Views Series. Englewood Cliffs, N.J., 1962.

Kraditor, Aileen S. *Means and Ends in American Abolitionnism: Garrison and His Critics on Strategy and Tactics, 1834–1850.* New York, 1969.

Kraut, Alan M., ed. *Crusaders and Compromisers: Essays on the Relationship of the Antislavery Struggle to the Antebellum Party System.* Westport, Conn., 1983.

Laurie, Bruce. *Working People of Philadelphia, 1800–1850.* Philadelphia, 1980.

Leibowitz, Herbert. *Fabricating Lives: Explorations in American Autobiography.* New York, 1989.

Letter of the Rev. Dr. Chalmers on American Slave-Holding, with Remarks by the Belfast Anti-Slavery Committee. Pamphlet. Belfast, 1846.

Levine, Lawrence. *Black Culture and Black Consciousness: Afro-American Folk Thought from Slavery to Freedom.* New York, 1977.

Levinson, Sanford. *Constitutional Faith.* Princeton, N.J., 1988.

Lewis, Anthony. *Gideon's Trumpet.* New York, 1964.

Lincoln, Colm. *Steps and Steeples: Cork at the Turn of the Century.* Urban Heritage Series, Vol. 1. Dublin, 1980.

Lincoln, Victoria. *A Private Disgrace: Lizzie Borden by Daylight.* New York, 1967.

Litwack, Leon, and August Meier, eds. *Black Leaders of the Nineteenth Century.* Urbana, Ill., 1988.

Logan, Rayford W. *The Diplomatic Relations of the United States with Haiti, 1776–1891.* 1941. Reprint. New York, 1969.

———. *Haiti and the Dominican Republic.* London, 1968.

Logan, Rayford W., and Michael R. Winston, eds. *Dictionary of American Negro Biography.* New York, 1982.

Lovett, William. *Life and Struggles of William Lovett.* 1876. Reprint. London, 1967.

Lundy, Benjamin. *The Life, Travels and Opinions of Benjamin Lundy. Including his Journeys to Texas and Mexico with a sketch of contemporary events, and a notice of the revolution in Hayti. Compiled under the direction and on behalf of his children.* Edited by Thomas Earle. 1847. Reprint. New York, 1969.

McKivigan, John R. *The War against Proslavery Religion: Abolitionism and the Northern Churches, 1830–1865.* Ithaca, N.Y., 1984.

McPherson, James M. *The Negro's Civil War: How American Negroes Felt and Acted during the War for the Union.* New York, 1965.

Malin, James C. *John Brown and the Legend of Fifty-six.* Memoirs of the American Philosophical Society, Vol. 17. Philadelphia, 1942.

Martin, Waldo E. *The Mind of Frederick Douglass.* Chapel Hill, N.C., 1985.

Martineau, Harriet. *Harriet Martineau's Autobiography.* Edited by Maria Weston Chapman. Boston, 1877.

Mathews, Donald G. *Slavery and Methodism: A Chapter in American Morality, 1780–1845.* Princeton, N.J. 1965.

May, Samuel J. *Some Recollections of Our Antislavery Conflict.* Boston, 1869.

Meier, August. *Negro Thought in America, 1880–1915: Racial Ideologies in the Age of Booker T. Washington.* Ann Arbor, Mich., 1963.

Meier, August, and Elliott M. Rudwick. *From Plantation to Ghetto.* New York, 1976.

Merrill, Walter M. *Against Wind and Tide: A Biography of William Lloyd Garrison.* Cambridge, Mass., 1963.

Mohr, James C. *The Radical Republicans and Reform in New York during Reconstruction.* Ithaca, N.Y., 1973.

Mooney, Robert F., and André R. Sigourney. *The Nantucket Way: Untold Legend and Lore of America's Most Intriguing Island.* Garden City, N.Y., 1980.

Mott, A[bigail], comp. *Biographical Sketches and Interesting Anecdotes of Persons of Color, to Which Is Added, a Selection of Pieces And Poetry.* New York, 1837.

Neal, John. *True Womanhood: A Tale.* Boston, 1859.

Nelson, Truman, ed. *Documents of Upheaval: Selections from William Lloyd Garrison's* The Liberator, *1831–1865.* New York, 1966.

Newhall, James R. *History of Lynn, Essex County, Massachusetts, Including Lynnfield, Saugus, Swampscott, and Nahant, 1629–*[*1893*]. 2 vols. Lynn, Mass., [1890]–97.

Nicholls, David. *From Dessalines to Duvalier: Race, Colour, and National Independence in Haiti.* Cambridge, Eng., 1979.

Nott, Josiah C., and George Gliddon. *Types of Mankind; or, Ethnological Researches, based upon the Ancient Monuments, Paintings, Sculptures, and Crania of Races, and upon their Natural, Geographical, Philological, and Biblical History.* Philadelphia, 1855.

Oates, Stephen D. *To Purge This Land with Blood: A Biography of John Brown.* Amherst, Mass., 1984.

Osthaus, Carl R. *Freedmen, Philanthropy, and Fraud: A History of the Freedman's Savings Bank.* Urbana, Ill., 1976.

Painter, Nell Irvin. *Exodusters: Black Migration to Kansas after Reconstruction.* New York, 1976.

Paulson, Ross Evans. *Women's Suffrage and Prohibition: A Comparative Study of Equality and Social Contact.* Glenview, Ill., 1973.

Payne, Daniel A. *History of the African Methodist Episcopal Church.* 1891. Reprint. New York, 1969.

————. *Recollections of Seventy Years.* 1888. Reprint. New York, 1968.

Pease, Jane H., and William H. Pease. *Bound with Them in Chains: A Biographical History of the Antislavery Movement.* Westport, Conn., 1972.

————. *They Who Would Be Free: Blacks' Search for Freedom, 1830–1861.* New York, 1974.

Pennington, James W. C. *The Fugitive Blacksmith; or, Events in the History of James W. C. Pennington.* 1850. Reprint. Westport, Conn., 1971.

Perry, Lewis. *Childhood, Marriage, and Reform: Henry Clark Wright, 1797–1870.* Chicago, 1980.

Perry, Lewis. *Radical Abolitionism: Anarchy and the Government of God in Antislavery Thought.* Ithaca, N.Y., 1973.

Perry, Lewis, and Michael Fellman, eds. *Antislavery Reconsidered: New Perspectives on the Abolitionists.* Baton Rouge, 1979.

Pichanick, Valerie Kossew. *Harriet Martineau: The Woman and Her Work, 1802–76.* Ann Arbor, Mich., 1980.

Pickett, Terry H. *The Unseasonable Democrat: Karl August Varnhagen von Ense (1785–1858).* Bonn, 1985.

Pocock, J. G. A. *The Machiavellian Moment: Florentine Political Thought and the Atlantic Republican Tradition*. Princeton, N.J., 1975.

Potter, David M. *The Impending Crisis, 1848–1861*. New York, 1976.

———. *The South and the Sectional Conflict*. Baton Rouge, 1968.

Preston, Dickson J. *Talbot County: A History*. Centreville, Md, 1983.

———. *Young Frederick Douglass: The Maryland Years*. Baltimore, 1980.

Prichard, James Cowles. *The Natural History of Man*. 3d ed. London, 1848.

Proceedings in Lynn, Massachusetts, June 17, 1897, Being the Two Hundred and Fiftieth Anniversary of the Settlement. Lynn, Mass., 1897.

Quarles, Benjamin. *Frederick Douglass*. 1948. Reprint. New York, 1968.

———. *The Negro in the Civil War*. Boston, 1953.

———, ed. *Frederick Douglass*. Great Lives Observed Series. Englewood Cliffs, N.J., 1968.

Rachleff, Peter J. *Black Labor in the South: Richmond, Virginia, 1865–1890*. Philadelphia, 1984.

Racowitza, Helene von. *Princess Helene von Racowitza: An Autobiography*. Translated by Cecil Mar. New York, 1911.

———. *Von Anderen und mir: Erinnerungen aller Art*. Berlin, 1909.

Redpath, James. *The Public Life of Capt. John Brown: With an Autobiography of His Childhood and Youth*. Boston, 1860.

———. *The Roving Editor; or, Talks with Slaves in the Southern States*. New York, 1859.

———, ed. *A Guide to Hayti*. 1861. Reprint. Westport, Conn., 1970.

Reynolds, David S. *Beneath the American Renaissance: The Subversive Imagination in the Age of Emerson and Melville*. New York, 1988.

Rice, Allen Thorndike, ed. *Reminiscences of Abraham Lincoln by Distinguished Men of His Time*. New York, 1886.

Rice, C. Duncan. *The Scots Abolitionists, 1833–1861*. Baton Rouge, 1981.

Richards, Leonard L. *"Gentlemen of Property and Standing": Anti-Abolition Mobs in Jacksonian America*. New York, 1970.

———. *The Life and Times of Congressman John Quincy Adams*. New York, 1986.

Richardson, Robert D., Jr. *Henry Thoreau: A Life of the Mind*. Berkeley, Calif., 1986.

Ripley, C. Peter. *Slaves and Freedmen in Civil War Louisiana*. Baton Rouge, 1976.

Ripley, C. Peter, et al., eds. *The Black Abolitionist Papers*. Vol. 1, *The British Isles, 1830–1865*. Chapel Hill, N.C., 1985. Vol. 2. *Canada, 1830–1865*. Chapel Hill, N.C., 1986.

Rodman, Samuel. *The Diary of Samuel Rodman*. Edited by Zephaniah W. Pease. New Bedford, Mass., 1927.

Rossbach, Jeffrey. *The Ambivalent Conspirators: John Brown, the Secret Six, and a Theory of Black Political Violence*. Philadelphia, 1982.

Rydell, Robert W. *All the World's a Fair: Visions of Empire at American International Expositions, 1876–1916*. Chicago, 1984.

Schwartz, Harold. *Samuel Gridley Howe, Social Reformer*. Cambridge, Mass., 1956.

Scott, Otto J. *The Secret Six: John Brown and the Abolitionist Movement*. New York, 1979.

Sewall, Samuel. *The Selling of Joseph: A Memorial*. Edited by Sidney Kaplan. [Amherst, Mass.], 1969.

Sewell, Richard H. *Ballots for Freedom: Antislavery Politics in the United States, 1837–1860*. New York, 1976.

Shaw, Robert, comp. *The Seraph; or, Baltimore Collection of Church Music*. Baltimore, 1836.

Shepperson, George. *Abolitionism and African Political Thought*. Pamphlet. Edinburgh, 1963.

———. *Perspectives of Commonwealth and American History*. Pamphlet. Edinburgh, 1965.

Sherman, John. *Recollections of Forty Years in the House, Senate, and Cabinet: An Autobiography*. 2 vols. Chicago, 1895.

Siebert, Wilbur H. *The Underground Railroad from Slavery to Freedom*. New York, 1899.

Simpson, Craig M. *A Good Southerner: The Life of Henry A. Wise of Virginia*. Chapel Hill, N.C., 1985.

Simpson, Matthew, ed. *Cyclopaedia of Methodism*. Philadelphia, 1881.

Smedley, Robert C. *History of the Underground Railroad in Chester and the Neighboring Counties of Pennsylvania.* Lancaster, Pa., 1883.

Smith, Gerrit. *Sermons and Speeches of Gerrit Smith.* 1861. Reprint. New York, 1969.

Smith, William A. *Lectures on the Philosophy and Practice of Slavery, As Exhibited in the Institution of Domestic Slavery in the United States: With the Duties of Masters to Slaves.* Nashville, 1856.

Socolofsky, Homer E., and Allan B. Spetter. *The Presidency of Benjamin Harrison.* Lawrence, Kans., 1987.

Sorin, Gerald. *Abolitionism: A New Perspective.* New York, 1972.

Sparks, Edwin Erie, ed. *The Lincoln–Douglas Debates of 1858.* Collections of the Illinois State Historical Library, vol. 3, Lincoln Series, vol. 1. Springfield, Ill., 1908.

Spooner, Lysander. *The Unconstitutionality of Slavery.* Boston, 1845.

Stake, Virginia Ott. *John Brown in Chambersburg.* Chambersburg, Pa., 1977.

Stange, Douglas Charles. *British Unitarians against American Slavery, 1833–65.* Rutherford, N.J., 1984.

Stanton, Elizabeth Cady, Susan B. Anthony, et al. *The History of Woman Suffrage.* 6 vols. Rochester and New York, 1889–1922.

Stanton, Theodore, and Harriot Stanton Blatch, eds. *Elizabeth Cady Stanton, As Revealed in Her Letters, Diary and Reminiscences.* 2 vols. 1922. Reprint. New York, 1969.

Starbuck, Alexander. *History of the American Whale Fishery.* 1878. Reprint. New York, 1964.

Stepto, Robert B. *From behind the Veil: A Study of Afro-American Narrative.* Urbana, Ill., 1979.

Sterling, Dorothy. *Captain of the Planter: The Story of Robert Smalls.* Garden City, N.Y., 1958.

———. *The Making of an Afro-American: Martin Robison Delany, 1812–1885.* Garden City, N.Y., 1971.

———, ed. *We Are Your Sisters: Black Women in the Nineteenth Century.* New York, 1984.

Stewart, James Brewer. *Holy Warriors: The Abolitionists and American Slavery.* New York, 1976.

———. *Wendell Phillips: Liberty's Hero.* Baton Rouge, 1986.

Stowe, Harriet Beecher. *Men of Our Times; or, Leading Patriots of the Day.* Hartford, Conn., 1868.

Surrency, Erwin C. *History of the Federal Courts.* New York, 1987.

Taylor, Clare. *British and American Abolitionists: An Episode in Transatlantic Understanding.* Edinburgh, 1974.

Temperley, Howard. *British Antislavery, 1833–1870.* Columbia, S.C., 1972.

Thernstrom, Stephan, et al., eds. *Harvard Encyclopedia of American Ethnic Groups.* Cambridge, Mass., 1980.

Thomas, John L. *The Liberator: William Lloyd Garrison.* Boston, 1963.

Thomas, Lately [Robert V. P. Steele]. *The First President Johnson: The Three Lives of the Seventeenth President of the United States of America.* New York, 1968.

Thompson, Dorothy. *The Chartists: Popular Politics in the Industrial Revolution.* New York, 1984.

Thoreau, Henry David. *The Correspondence of Henry David Thoreau.* Edited by Walter Harding and Carl Bode. New York, 1958.

———. *Walden; or, Life in the Woods.* 1854. Reprint. Boston, 1948.

Tilghman, Oswald. *History of Talbot County, Maryland, 1661–1861.* Baltimore, 1915.

Tise, Larry E. *Proslavery: A History of the Defense of Slavery in America, 1701–1840.* Athens, Ga., 1987.

Townsend, George Alfred. *The Entailed Hat; or, Patty Cannon's Times: A Romance.* 1884. Reprint. Cambridge, Md. 1955.

Trefousse, Hans L. *Andrew Johnson: A Biography.* New York, 1989.

———, ed. *Toward a New View of America: Essays in Honor of Arthur C. Cole.* New York, 1977.

Tushnet, Mark V. *The American Law of Slavery, 1810–1860: Considerations of Humanity and Interest.* Princeton, N.J. 1981.

Villard, Oswald Garrison. *John Brown, 1800–1859: A Biography Fifty Years After.* 1910. Reprint. Gloucester, Mass., 1965.

Volwiler, Albert Tangeman, ed. *The Correspondence Between Benjamin Harrison and James G. Blaine, 1882–1893.* Philadelphia, 1940.

Walker, Peter F. *Moral Choices: Memory, Desire, and Imagination in Nineteenth-Century American Abolition.* Baton Rouge, 1978.

Walters, Ronald G. *The Antislavery Appeal: American Abolitionism after 1830.* Baltimore, 1976.

Washburn, Robert Collyer. *The Life and Times of Lydia E. Pinkham.* New York, 1931.

Washington, Booker T. *Frederick Douglass.* 1907. Reprint. New York, 1968.

Webb, Richard D. *The Life and Letters of Captain John Brown, Who was Executed at Charlestown, Virginia, Dec. 2, 1859, For an Armed Attack Upon American Slavery; With Notices of Some of His Confederates.* 1861. Reprint. Westport, Conn., 1972.

Weimann, Jeanne Madeline. *The Fair Women.* Chicago, 1981.

Weitenkampf, Frank. *Political Caricature in the United States in Separately Published Cartoons: An Annotated List.* New York, 1953.

Weld, Theodore Dwight. *American Slavery As It Is: Testimony of a Thousand Witnesses.* New York, 1839.

Welles, Sumner. *Naboth's Vineyard: The Dominican Republic 1844–1924.* 2 vols. Mamaroneck, N.Y., 1966.

Wells, Ida B. *Crusade for Justice: The Autobiography of Ida B. Wells.* Edited by Alfreda M. Duster. Chicago, 1970.

———. *The Reason Why the Colored American Is Not in the World's Columbian Exposition.* Chicago, 1893.

———. *Southern Horrors.* Pamphlet. New York, 1892.

White, Frank F., Jr. *The Governors of Maryland, 1777–1970.* Annapolis, Md., 1970.

Wiecek, William M. *The Sources of Antislavery Constitutionalism in America, 1760–1848.* Ithaca, N.Y., 1977.

Wiggins, William H., Jr. *O Freedom! Afro-American Emancipation Celebrations.* Knoxville, Tenn., 1987.

Wigham, Hannah Maria. *A Christian Philanthropist of Dublin: A Memoir of Richard Allen.* London, 1886.

Williams, George Washington. *History of the Negro Race in America from 1619 to 1880: Negroes as Slaves, as Soldiers, and as Citizens: Together With a Preliminary Consideration of the Unity of the Human Family, an Historical Sketch of Africa, and an Account of the Negro Governments of Sierra Leone and Liberia.* New York, 1883.

Wilson, Hill Peebles. *John Brown, Soldier of Fortune: A Critique.* Lawrence, Kans., 1913.

Winks, Robin W. *The Blacks in Canada: A History.* New Haven, Conn., 1971.

Winston, Robert. *Andrew Johnson: Plebeian and Patriot.* New York, 1928.

Wright, Gavin. *Old South, New South: Revolutions in the Southern Economy since the Civil War.* New York, 1986.

Wright, Henry C. *Marriage and Parentage; or, The Reproductive Element in Man, as Means to His Elevation and Happiness.* Boston, 1854.

Wright, James M. *The Free Negro in Maryland, 1634–1860.* Studies in History, Economics, and Public Law. New York, 1921.

Wright, John P. *An Historical Parallel between the Anti-Vivisection Movement in England and the Anti-Slavery Movement in America.* Pamphlet. No place, 1854.

Wyatt-Brown, Bertram. *Yankee Saints and Southern Sinners.* Baton Rouge, 1985.

Wyman, Lillie Buffum Chace, and Arthur Crawford Wyman. *Elizabeth Buffum Chace, 1806–1899: Her Life and Its Environment.* Boston, 1914.

ARTICLES, DISSERTATIONS, AND INTRODUCTORY ESSAYS

Andrews, William L. "Frederick Douglass, Preacher." *American Literature* 54 (Dec. 1982): 592–97.

———. Introduction to *My Bondage and My Freedom,* by Frederick Douglass. 1855. Reprint. Urbana, Ill., 1987.

Assing, Ottilia. "The Insurrection at Harpers Ferry." *Morgenblatt fuer gebildete Staende.*

Augar, Phillip John. "The Cotton Famine, 1861–5: A Study of the Principal Cotton Towns during the American Civil War." Ph.D. diss., Clare College, Cambridge University, 1979.

Axeen, David. "Heroes of the Engine Room: American 'Civilization' and the War with Spain." *American Quarterly* 36 (Fall 1984): 481–502.

Baker, Houston A., Jr. Introduction to *Narrative of the Life of Frederick Douglass, an American Slave,* by Frederick Douglass. 1845. Reprint. New York, 1982.

Ball, Milner S. "Stories of Origin and Constitutional Possibilities." *Michigan Law Review* 87 (Aug. 1989): 2280–2319.

Barnard, Ella K. "Elisha Tyson, Philanthropist and Emancipator." *Journal of the Friends' Historical Society* 9 (April 1912): 108–12.

Blumenthal, Lieselotte. "Assing, verehelichte Grimelli, Rosa Ludmilla." In vol. 1 of *Neue Deutsche Biographie.* 15 vols. to date. Berlin, 1953–87.

Bogin, Ruth. "Sarah Parker Remond: Black Abolitionist from Salem." *Essex Institute Historical Collections* 110 (April 1974): 120–50.

Borome, Joseph. "Two Letters of Frederick Douglass." *Journal of Negro History* 36 (Jan. 1951): 80–83.

Braithwaite, William. "I Saw Frederick Douglass." *Negro Digest* 6 (Jan. 1948): 36–39.

Cadbury, Henry J. "Negro Membership in the Society of Friends." *Journal of Negro History* 21 (April 1936): 151–213.

Calderhead, William. "The Role of the Professional Slave Trader in a Slave Economy: Austin Woolfolk, a Case Study." *Civil War History* 23 (Sept. 1977): 195–211.

Cary, Lorin Lee, and Francine C. Cary. "Absalom F. Boston, His Family, and Nantucket's Black Community." *Historic Nantucket* 25 (Summer 1977): 15–23.

Cooper, Frederick. "Elevating the Race: The Social Thought of Black Leaders, 1827–50." *American Quarterly* 24 (Dec. 1972): 604–25.

Dawley, Alan. "The Artisan Response to the Factory System: Lynn, Massachusetts, in the Nineteenth Century." Ph.D. diss., Harvard University, 1971.

De Pietro, Thomas. "Vision and Revision in the Autobiographies of Frederick Douglass." *CLA Journal* 26 (June 1983): 384–96.

Dublin, Thomas. "Rural-Urban Migrants in Industrial New England: The Case of Lynn, Massachusetts, in the Mid-nineteenth Century." *Journal of American History* 73 (Dec. 1986): 623–44.

Duncan, James Russell, Jr. "Rufus Brown Bullock, Reconstruction, and the 'New South' 1834–1907: An Exploration into Race, Class, Party, and the Corruption of the American Creed." Ph.D. diss., University of Georgia, 1988.

Faler, Paul G. "Workingmen, Mechanics and Social Change: Lynn, Massachusetts, 1800–1860." Ph.D. diss., University of Wisconsin, 1971.

Fields, Barbara Jeanne. "The Maryland Way from Slavery to Freedom." Ph.D. diss., Yale University, 1978.

Freeman, Rhoda Golden. "The Free Negro in New York City in the Era before the Civil War." Ph.D. diss., Columbia University, 1966.

Fulkerson, Raymond Gerald. "Frederick Douglass and the Anti-Slavery Crusade: His Career and Speeches, 1817–1861." Ph.D. diss., University of Illinois at Urbana-Champaign, 1971.

Gardner, Bettye J. "Ante-bellum Black Education in Baltimore." *Maryland Historical Magazine* 71 (Fall 1976): 360–66.

———. "Free Blacks in Baltimore, 1800–1860." Ph.D. diss., George Washington University, 1974.

———. "William Watkins: Antebellum Black Teacher and Anti-Slavery Writer." *Negro History Bulletin* 39 (Sept.–Oct. 1976): 623–25.

Garonzik, Joseph. "Urbanization and the Black Population of Baltimore, 1850–1870." Ph.D. diss., State University of New York at Stony Brook, 1974.

Gatewood, Willard B., Jr. "Frederick Douglass in Arkansas." *Arkansas Historical Quarterly* 41 (Winter 1982): 303–15.

Ginzberg, Lori D. " 'Moral Suasion Is Moral Balderdash': Women, Politics, and Social Activism in the 1850s." *Journal of American History* 73 (Dec. 1986): 601–22.

Grayson, John T. "Frederick Douglass' Intellectual Development: His Concept of God, Man, and Nature in the Light of American and European Influences." Ph.D. diss., Columbia University, 1981.

Greener, Richard T. "The Emigration of Colored Citizens from the Southern States." *Journal of Social Science* 11 (May 1880): 22–35.

Gregory, Clarence Kenneth. "The Education of Blacks in Maryland: An Historical Survey." Ed.D. diss., Teachers College of Columbia University, 1976.

Grimké, Archibald. "Frederick Douglass." *The Southern Workman and Hampton School Record* 29 (Jan. 1900): 31–6.

Hall, Robert L. "Tallahassee's Black Churches, 1865–1885." *Florida Historical Quarterly* 58 (Oct. 1979): 185–96.

———. " 'Yonder Come Day': Religious Dimensions of the Transition from Slavery to Freedom in Florida." *Florida Historical Quarterly* 65 (April 1987): 411–32.

Hanaford, Phebe A. Introduction to *Harvest Gleanings in Prose and Verse,* by Anna Gardner. New York, 1881.

Hanmer-Croughton, Amy. "Anti-slavery Days in Rochester." *Rochester Historical Society Publication Fund Series* 14 (1936): 113–55.

Harlow, Ralph Volney. "Gerrit Smith and the Free Church Movement." *New York History* 18 (July 1937): 269–87.

Hertz, Deborah. "The Varnhagen Collection Is in Krakow." *American Archivist* 44 (Summer 1981): 223–28.

Hewitt, Nancy A. "Amy Kirby Post." *University of Rochester Library Bulletin* 37 (1984): 4–21.

Hinshaw, George Asher. "A Rhetorical Analysis of the Speeches of Frederick Douglass during and after the Civil War." Ph.D. diss., University of Nebraska at Lincoln, 1972.

James, Thomas. "The Autobiography of Rev. Thomas James." Abridged. *Rochester History* 37 (Oct. 1975): 1–32.

Kaplan, Linda Joan. "The Concept of the Family Romance." *Psychoanalytic Review* 61 (Summer 1974): 169–202.

Kibbey, Ann. "Language in Slavery: Frederick Douglass's *Narrative.*" *Prospects: The Annual of American Cultural Studies* (Cambridge, Eng.) 8 (1983): 163–82.

Kinney, Lois Belton. "A Rhetorical Study of the Practice of Frederick Douglass on the Issue of Human Rights, 1840–1860." Ph.D. diss., Ohio State University, 1974.

Lawson, Ellen N., and Marlene Merrill, " 'The Antebellum Talented Thousandth': Black College Students at Oberlin before the Civil War." *Journal of Negro Education* 52 (Spring 1983): 142–55.

Luce, Stephen Bleecker. "The Benefits of War," *North American Review* 153 (Dec. 1891): 672–83.

McElroy, James Logan. "Social Reform in the Burned-Over District: Rochester, New York, as a Test Case, 1830–1854." Ph.D. diss., State University of New York at Binghamton, 1974.

McGuire, Horace. "Two Episodes of Anti-Slavery Days." *Rochester Historical Society Publication Fund Series.* 4 (1925): 213–22.

McKivigan, John R., and Madeline Leveille. "The 'Black Dream' of Gerrit Smith, New York Abolitionist." *Library Associates Courier* (Syracuse University) 20 (Fall-Winter 1985): 51–76.

McMillan, Mary L. "Mr. Editor, If You Please: Frederick Douglass in Rochester, 1847–1852." Honors thesis, Mount Holyoke College, 1985.

Massa, Ann. "Black Women in the 'White City.' " *Journal of American Studies* 8 (1974): 319–37.

Migliorino, Ellen Ginzburg, and Giorgio G. Campanaro. "Frederick Douglass's More Intimate Nature as Revealed in Some of His Unpublished Letters." *Southern Studies* 18 (Winter 1979): 480–87.

Nichols, William. "Individualism and Autobiographical Art: Frederick Douglass and Henry Thoreau." *CLA Journal* 16 (Dec. 1972): 145–58.

Palmer, Erwin. "A Partnership for the Abolition Movement." *University of Rochester Library Bulletin* 26 (Autumn-Winter 1970–71): 1–19.

Parker, Jane Marsh. "Reminiscences of Frederick Douglass." *The Outlook* 51 (April 6, 1895): 552–53.
Pease, Jane H., and William H. Pease. "Black Power: The Debate in 1840." *Phylon* 29 (Spring 1968): 19–26.
――――. "Confrontation and Abolition in the 1850's." *Journal of American History* 58 (March 1972): 923–37.
――――. "Ends, Means, and Attitudes: Black–White Conflict in the Antislavery Movement." *Civil War History* 18 (June 1972): 117–28.
――――. "Negro Conventions and the Problem of Black Leadership." *Journal of Black Studies* 2 (Sept. 1971): 29–44.
――――. "The Role of Women in the Antislavery Movement." *Canadian Historical Association Historical Papers* (1967): 167–83.
Pease, William H., and Jane H. Pease. "Boston Garrisonians and the Problem of Frederick Douglass." *Canadian Journal of History* 2 (Sept. 1967): 29–48.
――――. "Samuel J. May: Civil Libertarian." *Cornell Library Journal* 3 (Autumn 1967): 7–25.
――――. "Walker's *Appeal* Comes to Charleston: A Note and Documents." *Journal of Negro History* 59 (July 1974): 287–92.
Percival, Benjamin. "Abolitionism in Lynn and Essex County." Typescript. Lynn, Mass., Lynn Historical Society, Nov. 12, 1908.
Pickett, Terry H. "The Friendship of Frederick Douglass with the German, Ottilie Assing." *Georgia Historical Quarterly* 73 (Spring 1989): 88–105.
Pocock, J. G. A. "*The Machiavellian Moment* Revisited: A Study in History and Ideology." *Journal of Modern History* 53 (March 1981): 49–72.
Porter, Dorothy Burnett. "The Remonds of Salem, Massachusetts: A Nineteenth-Century Family Revisited." *Proceedings of the American Antiquarian Society*, 95, pt. 2 (Oct. 1985), 259–95.
Porter, Dorothy B. "Sarah Parker Remond, Abolitionist and Physician." *Journal of Negro History* 20 (July 1935): 287–93.
Rankin, David C. "The Impact of the Civil War on the Free Colored Community of New Orleans." *Perspectives in American History* 11 (1977–78): 379–416.
Riach, Douglas. "Ireland and the Campaign against American Slavery, 1830–1860." Ph.D. diss., University of Edinburgh, 1975.
Riegel, Robert E. "The Split of the Feminist Movement in 1869." *Mississippi Valley Historical Review* 49 (Dec. 1962): 485–96.
Ripley, C. Peter. "The Autobiographical Writings of Frederick Douglass." *Southern Studies* 24 (Spring 1985): 5–29.
Rosenbaum, Arthur S. "Songs of the Coastal South." Paper read at Conference on Race and the Law," Sapelo Island, Ga., March 3, 1989.
Ruchkin, Judith Polgar. "The Abolition of 'Colored Schools' in Rochester, New York: 1832–1856." *New York History* 51 (July 1970): 377–93.
Rudwick, Elliott M., and August Meier. "Black Man in the 'White City': Negroes and the Columbian Exposition, 1893." *Phylon* 26 (Winter 1965): 354–61.
Schechter, Patricia Ann. " 'The First Free Spot of Ground in Kentucky': The Story of Camp Nelson." B.A. thesis, Mount Holyoke College, 1986.
Shepperson, George. "Frederick Douglass and Scotland." *Journal of Negro History* 38 (July 1953): 307–21.
――――. "The Free Church and American Slavery." *Scottish Historical Review* 30 (Oct. 1951): 126–43.
――――, ed. "Thomas Chalmers, the Free Church of Scotland, and the South." *Journal of Southern History* 17 (Nov. 1951): 517–37.
Smith, Henry Nash. "Emerson's Problem of Vocation." In *Emerson: A Collection of Critical Essays*, edited by Milton R. Konvitz and Stephen E. Whicher, 60–71. Englewood Cliffs, N.J. 1962.
Sprague, Rosetta Douglass. "Anna Murray-Douglass—My Mother As I Recall Her." *Journal of Negro History* 8 (Jan. 1923): 93–101.
Stowe, Harriet Beecher. "Sojourner Truth, the Libyan Sibyl." *Atlantic Monthly* 11 (April 1863): 473–81.

Tawney, R. H. Preface to *Life and Struggles of William Lovett,* by William Lovett. 1876. Reprint. London, 1967.

Terrell, Mary Church. "I Remember Frederick Douglass." *Ebony* 8 (Oct. 1953): 72–80.

Thomas, Bettye Collier. "The Baltimore Black Community: 1865–1910." Ph.D. diss., George Washington University, 1974.

————. "History of the Sharp Street Methodist Episcopal Church, 1787–1920." In *Sharp Street Memorial United Methodist Church, 1802–1977.* Brochure. Baltimore, 1977.

Thomas, Herman Edward. "An Analysis of the Life and Work of James W. C. Pennington, a Black Churchman and Abolitionist." Ph.D. diss., The Hartford Seminary, 1978.

Thomas, Sarah W. "Lionesses or Sheep for the Slaughter? A Comparative Study of the Transatlantic Experiences of Two American Abolitionists." B.A. thesis, Amherst College, 1989.

Thompson, William D. "Anti-Slavery Days in Lynn." Typescript. Lynn, Mass., Lynn Historical Society, Oct. 11, 1906.

Thoreau, Henry David. "A Plea for Captain John Brown." In Henry David Thoreau, *Reform Papers,* edited by Wendell Glick, 111–38. Princeton, N.J., 1973.

Tilghman, J. Donnell. "Wye House." *Maryland Historical Magazine.* 48 (June 1953): 89–108.

Van Deburg, William L. "Frederick Douglass: Maryland Slave to Religious Liberal." *Maryland Historical Magazine* 69 (Spring 1974): 27–43.

Ward, William Edward. "Charles Lenox Remond: Black Abolitionist, 1838–1873." Ph.D. diss., Clark University, 1977.

Wesley, Charles H. "The Participation of Negroes in Anti-Slavery Political Parties." *Journal of Negro History* 29 (Jan. 1944): 32–74.

Wynes, Charles E. "Ebenezer Don Carlos Bassett, America's First Black Diplomat." *Pennsylvania History* 51 (July 1984): 232–40.

————. "John Stephens Durham, Black Philadelphian: At Home and Abroad." *Pennsylvania Magazine of History and Biography* 106 (Oct. 1982): 527–37.

Acknowledgments

The writing of this book ends where it began—with students. I first became curious about Frederick Douglass when, as a beginning instructor, I read *Narrative of the Life of Frederick Douglass* with members of an American studies seminar; now I read about him with my grandson. I am in debt to a great many students—and others as well—who have discussed Douglass with me and have helped me in many different ways over the years that I have been working on this book. And yet I must begin these acknowledgments with an apology; neither my memory nor my records are adequate to the job of thanking all the people who should be thanked. History, as it should be, is a noncompetitive, shared craft, and I hope all who have helped but are not named will know how deeply grateful I am.

Archivists and librarians have been consistently cooperative—in many cases, particularly so when I mentioned the subject of my research. Frederick Douglass has a good many admirers. John Blassingame, editor of the valuable *Frederick Douglass Papers,* and his associates past and present, always made me welcome on Hillhouse Avenue. Richard Carlson, Jason Silverman, and particularly, Jack McKivigan went out of their way to assist me as I was working with Yale's copies of Douglass's correspondence. I am grateful to the many archivists in the United States and Great Britain who supplied these and other documents to the Yale University Frederick Douglass Papers.

As always, Sara Dunlap Jackson of the Historical Publications and Records Commission was both a good friend and a matchless guide to documents in the National Archives. Staff members at the Library of Congress amiably brought their professional skills to bear. Will Stapp and his associates at the National Portrait Gallery were helpful. And Tom Ehr, Karen Hendricks, and Lynn Holmes were good guides while I was in Washington.

The incomparable antislavery collection in the Boston Public Library was essential to my research, and I am particularly appreciative of Giuseppe Bisaccia's help. Doris O'Keefe, Georgia Barnhill, and their associates saw to it that I made good use of the American Antiquarian Society's excellent holdings.

At Mount Holyoke College, all of the librarians were exceedingly helpful; two who gave me particular assistance were Marilyn Dunn and Irene Cronin. In New Bedford and later in South Hadley, Patricia Albright found archival materials. At Amherst College, Margaret Groesbeck and Floyd Merritt provided expert assistance. The librarians at Smith College made available *The Columbian Orator* and Emma Nogrady Kaplan's useful transcription of the Erasmus Darwin Hudson journal; at the University of Massachusetts library, Kenneth Fones-Wolf supplied the original. My thanks also go to Elaine McIlroy and her associates in the Wellfleet (Massachusetts) Public Library. The same spirit of cooperation has been at work too in the main library of the University of Georgia; I am particularly grateful to Barbara Rystrom and her colleagues in the interlibrary loan department, who obtained materials so promptly.

All of us who are interested in Douglass's crucial early years on the Eastern Shore of Maryland enthusiastically record our debt to Dickson Preston. His *Young Frederick Douglass* is both good psychological analysis and a model of local history; his reconstruction of the Bailey family over some ten generations is a remarkable and valuable contribution. And his eagerness to have us know Douglass's country, its brooks and cornfields, was great; my regret is that Dick was too ill to take me over the country himself. Our telephone friendship meant much to me, and I felt he was at my elbow as I made my own way to the Tuckahoe.

Eugenia Herbert and Joseph Walsh, two fine Africanists, abetted my speculations about the possible African source of the Baileys' name. Malcolm Bell, Jr., checked my thinking on the function of a tutor in a grand slaveholding house, and Clifton F. Giles, Jr., of the Greenfield (Massachusetts) Public Library supplied information on Joel Page. Stephen Ellenburg helped me ponder the message that Frederick Bailey would have taken from *The Columbian Orator,* while Joel White, of Brooklyn, Maine, told me how a boat is caulked, a not unimportant detail in the Douglass story. Jacqueline Van Voris supplied material on Douglass's ties to the Florence, Massachusetts, community; Mary Beth Norton provided information on the Pitts family. John Grayson's fine study of the influence of the German idealists on Douglass's thought was important to my consideration of his intellectual life, as was the work of William Andrews, David Blight, and Waldo Martin. As always, conversations with Sidney Kaplan, whose knowledge of black history is encyclopedic, were stimulating.

Roland M. Baumann, archivist of Oberlin College, documented Rosetta Douglass's student days, while Thomas Riis supplied interesting information on Joseph Douglass, whose career as a concert violinist would make an interesting study. Ric and Ken Burns, two admirers of Douglass, led me to the fine frontispiece portrait, but in this realm Douglass himself deserves the greatest thanks. He seems to have been incapable of being the subject of an uninteresting photograph. Sarah Lockmiller did a creative job in making the prints for several of the book's illustrations. James Ingram, the University of Georgia's excellent cartographer, drew the map of Talbot County.

The archival holdings of the Maryland Historical Society in Baltimore proved disappointing, particularly as they pertained to the black population of what was the largest slaveholding city in the country. Not so the Hall of Records in Annapolis, with its extensive materials on Douglass's Baltimore and on the Eastern Shore. Phebe Jacobsen and her colleagues there were knowledgeable about their state's most distinguished son. Professor Walter Fisher of Morgan State University, Baltimore, a good friend who died in the course of my work on this book, knew Baltimore's history intimately and his help was always given with wit and wisdom, as was that of Professor Robert L. Hall, then at the University of Maryland, Baltimore.

At the New Bedford Public Library, itself a historical treasure, Paul Cyr provided valuable documentation on that remarkable city in the years that Douglass lived there, though curiously few reminiscences by residents of their famous fellow townsman survive. Paul, a master of New Bedford's past who is committed to making all of his neighbors in that ethnically diverse city conscious of their heritages, offered more friendly advice than I deserved. Carl Cruz has done valuable research on the black community in the city, and he too was generous with his help. Closer to the harbor, Richard Kugler and his associates at the excellent Whaling Museum—its name belies the richness and diversity of its holdings pertaining to the social history of the port—always made the visiting scholar welcome. Philip Purrington of the Old Dartmouth Historical Society also provided useful information.

Two excellent historians of Nantucket, Edouard Stackpole of the Nantucket Historical Association and Robert Mooney, lawyer and author (and excellent host), taught me much not only about the port city's impressive antislavery days, but also about the rich past of the island's black community. Although Douglass's life in Lynn is not well documented, the people in the Lynn Historical Society, assisted me in locating as much as could be found on Douglass's second Massachusetts home.

The valuable papers of Amy Post and her husband, Isaac Post, a druggist, both fascinating reformers, are in the Special Collections of the University of Rochester library. Karl Sanford Kabelac went out of his way helping me try to make sense of Douglass's Rochester years. Kathleen Muzdakis in the Monroe County Courthouse dug into records that shed light on Douglass's real-estate investments in and around the city. Two historians of Rochester, Florence Burr and Mary McMillan, supplied important information on Douglass's years in that city; the latter's study of Douglass as editor of the *North Star* was particularly important to my understanding of that phase of his life.

Although it is not a repository for documents, I cannot overstate my enthusiasm for Cedar Hill, the Frederick Douglass National Historic Site. First Tyra Walker and then Douglas Stover were my hosts there; Bernice Thorpe and the other excellent people of the National Park Service preside over the house as if it were their own. Because they take so much personal pride in Cedar Hill, they make Douglass's place far more than a sterile historical shrine. You feel at home. I will never forget my first visit; as I climbed the steep steps I found myself joining a group of grammar-school children whose faces betrayed the usual mixture of awe and why-am-I-here. They soon got the answer; Carnell Poole, with exactly the right touch (and demonstrating that he knew his Quarles) introduced them to their own great man.

Dorothy Porter's encyclopedic knowledge of America's leading African American figures was helpful on the Douglass family; Joellen ElBashir, at the Moorland-Spingarn Research Center at Howard University, was particularly helpful on the army careers of Lewis and Charles Douglass. Patricia G. Holland supplied information on Susan B. Anthony and Elizabeth Cady Stanton. Patricia Schechter, at work on a study of Ida B. Wells, checked my thinking on that important friend of Douglass's. Eliza McFeely and Mary Drake McFeely aided my thinking about Douglass's relationships with women, as did Dorothy Sterling, who knows her sisters well. Her biography of Abby Kelley will soon be out, and her research produced wonderful bits of lore about Douglass and Kelley, one of the most compelling of the abolitionists with whom he lectured. Justin Kaplan recalled Douglass's interesting link to Samuel Clemens. Mary McHenry offered not only encouragement, but shrewd insights into the Washington world in which Douglass lived.

Christopher Clarke of St. John's College, Cambridge, tracked down Julia Griffiths Crofts in her later years for me, but information on her remains discouragingly sparse. I could locate no photographs of her or of Ottilia Assing. Terry H. Pickett, doing research on the Varnhagen family in the Jagiellonian University library, Kraków, Poland, came across Assing's letters to her sister Ludmilla, which enabled me to reconstruct one of Douglass's most important friendships. I greatly appreciate not only Pickett's generosity in sharing his remarkable find, but also his help in arranging for me to get copies of the correspondence and in translating and evaluating the letters. My colleague at the University of Georgia, Ludwig Uhlig, and I spent several enjoyable afternoons going over these letters as well. Barbara Schwepcke not only aided in ascertaining the precise meaning of Assing's appraisal of racial matters in her letters, but unearthed other of her writings in German archives.

Nathan I. Huggins, whose own fine book on Douglass was important in my consideration of the man, was a welcoming friend at the W. E. B. Du Bois Institute at Harvard, and it is sad to realize that he is no longer there. Randall Burkett was exceedingly helpful during the time I was working there, and I gained from the collegial brown-bag lunches and the comments of George Shepperson and other Fellows.

Jean Robertson, of the University of Glasgow library, provided valuable information on that city's remarkably active antislavery society and on Douglass's important visits. Fiona Spiers was also helpful on Douglass's experiences in Great Britain, and Muirna Gedge provided crucial information on her family, the Jenningses, with whom Douglass stayed when in Ireland.

Colleagues at Mount Holyoke College were always encouraging, and I appreciate the leave of absence that enabled me to do much of my research. I am deeply grateful to the John Simon Guggenheim Foundation, which honored me with a fellowship. The University of Georgia has been exceedingly generous in affording me the time to complete this book, and I am indebted Dean John Kozak, his predecessor Jack Payne, and Professor Lester Stephens, the head of the History Department, for their encouragement, as well as to all my colleagues in LeConte Hall, especially Professors Thomas Dyer, Jean Friedman, and John Haag.

In Athens, in addition to the indispensable sustenance at the Blue Bird Cafe, there has been help in various and crucial ways from George I. Bush III, Stephen Lucas, Ernest Taylor, Milner Ball, and Michael Lomax. Among the many students who have helped over the years were Scott Ball, Alexa Birdsong, Jonathan Bryant, Philip Cafaro, Susan Daggett, Glenn Eskew, Greg Field, Tara Fitzpatrick, Ruth Jones, Jennifer Lund, Daphne Moore, and Christopher Phillips, whose knowledge about the black community in Baltimore was particularly valuable.

In the final stages of finishing the book I was fortunate to have the assistance of two highly intelligent, diligent, and astonishingly good-humored graduate students, Robert Croft and Elizabeth Walsh. I can only hope the experience won't cure them of writing altogether.

Lawrence Powell and Peter Ripley shared their intimate knowledge of Douglass materials; similarly, Jane and William Pease shared their knowledge of the antislavery movement and criticized drafts of several early chapters, as did Robert Engs. Drake McFeely's keen reading of these chapters was also highly valuable, and Russell Duncan not only read with great care but—like such other good friends as Tracy Kidder, Vann Woodward, Emory Thomas, Jim Goodman, and Barry Werth—kept me going when the writing was difficult.

It was helpful to read and discuss chapters at Professor Aileen Ward's seminar in biography at New York University's Humanities Institute, at a branch of the New Bedford Public Library, at Mount Holyoke College, and at the Humanities Center of the University of Georgia. I was also able to check my thinking on Douglass as I gave the John J. McCloy Lectures at Amherst College.

My editor and friend Jim Mairs was constantly encouraging, and I have nothing but admiration for Donald Lamm and the brilliantly ordered chaos that is W. W. Norton. All of the people there associated with the book have been exceedingly helpful; I am particularly grateful to Cecil Lyon, and it was good news when I learned that Anne Eberle would do the index. I am in debt once more to Hugh O'Neill, who knows how to look a subject straight in the eye. Working with Esther Jacobson was, once again, a remarkable intellectual experience; the relationship between writer and editor is one which grows increasingly interesting to me. My daughter Jennifer supplied the image that best suggests it; when you are trying to swim all the way to the other side of Gull Pond, it is good to have a strong swimmer alongside.

Perhaps my greatest debt is owed to Benjamin Quarles. There was not a day that I worked that I did not read in his fine *Frederick Douglass*. That book, now almost fifty years old, is so excellent that I have often wondered why I was attempting my study. But Professor Quarles did not feel that way; with a generosity as rare as it is fine, he and his wife welcomed me to Baltimore, and he encouraged me to undertake the biography. When it came to a name for my book, I could think of none that was right other than the straightforward one he used, and he agreed; I hope he will find that the Frederick Douglasses that we have imagined are kinsmen.

W.S.M.

WELLFLEET, MASSACHUSETTS
July 5, 1990

Index

FD and, 96, 114, 156–58, 168, 185–86, 250–52,
    254–55, 380. *See also* political parties
Garrisonian ideology on, 95, 106, 151, 156, 158
role of, in antislavery movement, 95, 106–7,
    151, 168
Polk, James K., 157, 208
Pomeroy, Samuel C., 228
Pompeii, Italy, 329
Pompey, Edward J., 89
Pompey family (Nantucket), 90
Poole, Lizzie, 122
poor and working-class African Americans, FD's
    attitude toward, 59, 80, 140, 242, 245, 256,
    299–300, 315–16, 384
popular sovereignty, 179, 187
Populist movement, 315, 359, 362
Port-au-Prince, Haiti
    discord and disturbances in, 342, 352
    Douglasses arrive in (1889), 334, 339
Porter, Samuel, 165, 170–71, 172, 275, 277
Portland, Me., 207
Post, Amy
    on divisions in antislavery movement, 148
    and (Anna) Douglass, 154
    FD's letters to, 132, 149, 202, 312, 322, 333
    FD visits after wife's death (1882), 312
    and (Julia) Griffiths, 164, 171, 172, 182
    helps FD after Brown's raid, 199, 200, 202
    at Seneca Falls convention, 156
    and women's franchise, 269
Post, Amy and Isaac, 99, 105, 152, 275
    accept FD's and Julia Griffiths' friendship, 163,
        164, 182
    harbor fugitive slaves, 172
    and *North Star* solvency, 165
Post, Isaac
    and (Julia) Griffiths, 161–62, 163–64
    helps FD after Brown's raid, 200
Pottawatomie, Kans., 188–89
Potter, David, 190
    Impending Crisis, The, 400
prejudice, racial. *See* racism
prejudice, as "spirit of caste," 318
Preston, Charles A., 366
Preston, Dickson, 8, 19, 66, 293, 294
Preston, Stephen, 338
Price, Asa: shipyard, Baltimore, 63–64
Price, Hannibal, 341
Prichard, James Cowles: *Natural History of Man,* 6,
    331
Prinz Willem III (ship), 354
private property, and civil rights, 314, 317–18
    antiproperty movement, 105, 107
prose style and purpose of FD, 22
proslavery people
    increasing militancy of, 179, 185
    and violence in Kansas, 179, 188
    See also antislavery movement, critics and
        opponents of; slave owners and masters
Provincial Freeman (newspaper), 166
public notice and acclaim of FD (1847), 148
    his acknowledgment of, 263
    in England, 139
    resentment of, 148

in Scotland, 132–33, 136
for speech in Nantucket (1841), 89–90
for speech on colonization (1839), 83
at World's Columbian Exposition (1893), 369
public office. *See* high office (elective or
    appointed), FD and
public opinion of FD
    after Brown's raid, 201
    image as "brute" made human, 91
    after second marriage, 320
    at World's Columbian Exposition (1893), 369
    See also criticism of FD
Purvis, Charles Burleigh, 282, 283, 296
Purvis, Harriet Forten, 113–14
Purvis, Robert, Sr., 113–14, 360
Putnam, Caroline Remond, 328
Putnam, Edmund Quincy, 328
Putnam, Frederic Ward, 367–68

Quakers
    in antislavery movement, 31, 39, 76, 86, 87
    assist fugitive slaves, 71, 74
    British and Irish, 123, 140, 141, 142
    divided over slavery question, 114
    in New Bedford, 74, 76
    send petition to World Auxiliary Congress on
        Evolution, 375–76
Quarles, Benjamin, 120, 231
Quincy, Edmund, 84, 87, 94
    and FD, 94, 147–48, 168–69, 176
    and *North Star,* 149

"Race Problem in America" address (1893), 371
racial characteristics. *See* ethnology
racism
    in antislavery movement, 94, 108, 114, 169, 176,
        191
    in Baltimore shipyards, 60–63
    in Boston, 166
    in churches, 81, 92, 93, 102, 242
    in Civil War, 227
    as component of capitalist labor system, 62–63
    in government offices, 257
    Jim Crow practices, 92–94, 377
    in labor movement, 271, 315
    in military services, 377
    in North, 79–80, 84, 92–94, 104
    in privately owned public places, 314
    in Rochester, N.Y., 160–61
    in schools, 92, 314, 377
    on ships and boats, 92, 94, 120, 148
    on trains, 92–93, 279, 380
    See also civil rights
Racowitza, Princess Helene von, 185
Radical Abolitionist party, 158
    Gerrit Smith as its candidate (1860), 208
radical convention (Philadelphia, 1866), 250–52
railroads. *See* trains
Ram's Horn (newspaper), 150
Randall, Alexander, 232–33
Rankin, Jeremiah E., 335
rape of white women by black men, 361, 379–80
reading, FD and, 29–30, 32, 39, 113
Readville, Mass., 224–25, 230